# UNDERSTANDING INDUSTRIAL AND ORGANIZATIONAL PSYCHOLOGY

*An Integrated Approach*

# UNDERSTANDING INDUSTRIAL AND ORGANIZATIONAL PSYCHOLOGY

## An Integrated Approach

### ROBERT L. DIPBOYE
*Rice University*

### CARLLA S. SMITH
*Bowling Green State University*

### WILLIAM C. HOWELL
*American Psychological Association*

**HARCOURT COLLEGE PUBLISHERS**

Fort Worth  Philadelphia  San Diego  New York  Orlando  Austin  San Antonio
Toronto  Montreal  London  Sydney  Tokyo

| | |
|---|---|
| **Editor-in-chief** | Ted Buchholz |
| **Senior acquisitions editor** | Eve Howard |
| **Senior developmental editor** | Meera Dash |
| **Project editor** | Steve Norder |
| **Production manager** | Erin Gregg |
| **Senior art director** | Serena Manning |
| **Cover design** | Nick Welch |
| **Picture editor** | Annette Coolidge |
| **Illustrator** | Jim Van Heyningen |

Library of Congress Catalog Card Number: 93-79057

Requests for permission to make copies of any part of the work should be mailed to: Permissions Department, Harcourt, Inc., 6277 Sea Harbor Drive, Orlando, FL 32887-6777.

*Address for Editorial Correspondence*  Harcourt College Publishers, 301 Commerce Street, Suite 3700, Fort Worth, TX 76102

*Address for Orders:* Harcourt, Inc., 6277 Sea Harbor Drive, Orlando, FL 32887-6777. 1-800-782-4479, or 1-800-433-0001 (in Florida)

Literary and photo credits appear on p. C1, following references. Cover image by c REMO/Photonica.

ISBN: 0-03-051552-1

Printed in the United States of America

0 1 2 3 4 5 6 7 8 9   128   20 19 18 17 16 15 14 13 12 11 10

*To our parents*

*Dessa and Walter Dipboye*
*Aneta and Carl Smith*
*Elisabeth and William Howell*

# About the Authors

Robert L. Dipboye received his PhD in industrial and organizational psychology from Purdue University. He is currently a professor of psychology at Rice University and director of the PhD program in I/O psychology. Dr. Dipboye's research interests include selection, leadership, group behavior, and work motivation. He is on the editorial boards of *Journal of Applied Psychology* and *Academy of Management Review*, and is a consulting editor for *Journal of Organizational Behavior*. He is a fellow of the Society for Industrial and Organizational Psychology, the American Psychological Society, and the American Psychological Association.

Carlla S. Smith earned her PhD in industrial and organizational psychology from Rice University and is currently an associate professor of psychology at Bowling Green State University. Dr. Smith's areas of special interest are organizational stress and stress management, and the effects of shift work on health and work-related performance and attitudes. She is a member of the American Psychological Association, Society for Industrial and Organizational Psycholgogy, Academy of Management, and Human Factors Society. She is on the editorial board of *Human Factors*.

William C. Howell received his PhD in psychology from the University of Virginia. He served at Rice University where he was a Herbert S. Autrey Professor and chair of the psychology department. After serving as Chief Scientist for Human Resources for the U.S. Air Force, he moved to Washington, D.C., in 1992 to lead the Science Directorate of the American Psychological Association. Dr. Howell is editor of *Human Factors*. His research interests have spanned the fields of engineering psychology and industrial and organizational psychology, with particular emphasis on topics in human information processing and decision making.

# PREFACE

When we began planning this book, we confronted a dilemma. Our general objective was to provide an interesting, relevant, and comprehensive survey of research, theory, and application in I/O psychology. We also felt, however, that the changes occurring in society and the field of psychology demand an approach to the subject matter that is somewhat different than past approaches. In the end, we decided to review the traditional topics that constitute I/O psychology's knowledge base, but in a fashion designed to promote three overarching (and critical) learning objectives: *integration*—understanding how the topics relate to one another—*conceptualization*—understanding in some depth the basic concepts that underlie each topic—and *contextualization*—understanding how the topics and concepts relate to a changing environment.

The integrative theme reflects our departure from the implication that the topics included under the *I* and *O* of Industrial and Organizational Psychology are entirely separate. Topics in industrial (or personnel) psychology (e.g., employee selection, job analysis, and training) and those in organizational psychology (e.g., work motivation, leadership, social roles, and organizational culture) are interrelated, and a truly comprehensive understanding of one requires at least some attention to the other. We have emphasized this point in several ways. We have provided numerous connections and cross references throughout the text to point out interrelationships among topics. We also have included a short opener to each of the major sections not only to provide a preview but also to relate the subject matter in the section to other parts of the book. Perhaps the most distinctive aspect of our integrative approach is our coverage of the organizational topics before the personnel topics. This reversal of the typical order of presentation was not meant to diminish the significance of human resource management functions but was intended to emphasize that such functions exists within a larger organizational domain and are influenced by such factors as the culture, structure, and leadership of the organization. However, we have written the chapters so that instructors can easily adapt the material to fit their own preferences.

The theme of conceptualizaton emphasizes understanding and the scientific process that generates this understanding. We hope to convey our excitement about research while also showing the ambiguity and complexity of the researcher's task. In addition to discussing the ongoing controversies in research and theory, we use a case at the end of each chapter to provide an opportunity for the reader to apply the concepts they have learned. Rather than constructing fictitious cases having simple answers, our cases involve controversial issues and are drawn from current events in real organizations. Our intent is to stimulate discussion and give the reader a taste of the intellectual debate that characterizes I/O psychology as a science.

The theme of contextualization ensures that I/O psychology is understood in the context of societal events and developments in organization theory and psychology. Like the "open systems" model on which it is based, I/O psychology has been shaped by external influences. One source of influence derives from its being a part of psychology, thereby drawing from the research, theory, and application in other psychological disciplines. For instance, a major force in recent years comes from cognitive research. Consequently, this book shows the impact of the cognitive revolution on many I/O psychology topics. Another context is provided by organizational theory, starting with scientific management and human relations approaches and continuing to present emphasis on open systems and contingency views. Perhaps most importantly, we show how I/O psychology always has been a "child of the times." Progress in I/O psychology seems to occur in spurts of intense activity as psychologists have attempted to solve the problems presented by war, economic depression, demographic shifts, technological innovations, and laws. The cases in each chapter show the relation of I/O psychology to societal issues and events such as violence in the workplace, sex discrimination, educational reform, and declining productivity. We hope to dispel the illusion of I/O psychology as a dusty relic of factory life and to show that I/O psychology is a live and vibrant discipline directly relevant to the crises facing today's society.

I/O psychology has continually evolved in dealing with past events, and it must continue to evolve to meet the challenges of the future. Related to contextualization is an emphasis on how times are changing in the workplace. Major shifts are occurring in the work force and in the structure of organizations and careers that will dramatically affect the management of human resources, the way people approach their careers, and the problems that capture the attention of I/O psychologists. Some of these issues are the high-technology workplace, corporate culture, globalization, and diversity of the work force. In each chapter we consider current trends and speculate on the future directions that we believe that the field of I/O psychology will or should take in research, theory, and application.

## Learning and Teaching Aids

*Understanding Industrial and Organizational Psychology: An Integrated Approach* attempts to bridge the gap between students' daily experiences and the vast amount of research and application offered by I/O psychology. The writing makes the material more accessible. We also have created several features to clarify the organization of the chapters and sections. Within the chapters, visual and pedagogical aids help students apply the material learned. Most chapters end with a summation and discussion questions. A separate set of questions helps the student integrate material from the chapter with the case.

In addition to the textbook, instructors and students will benefit from the following items:

- **Study Guide,** prepared by Janet Turnage, University of Central Florida. The study guide includes learning objectives, a study outline, key terms, a practice quiz, discussion questions, and exercises.
- **Instructor's Manual/Test Bank,** prepared by Janet Barnes-Farrell, University of Connecticut. The manual includes a chapter outline, summary of key issues, teaching suggestions, multiple-choice and essay test items, and transparency masters from the textbook.

## Acknowledgments

This book could not have been written without the assistance of colleagues. We wish to acknowledge those who provided feedback on earlier versions of the manuscript including Raymond Baird, University of Texas at San Antonio; Janet Barnes-Farrell, University of Connecticut; John Binning, Illinois State University; Mary Beth DeGregorio, Michigan State University; George Diekhoff, Midwestern State University; Wayne Harrison, University of Nebraska at Omaha; Jacob Hautaluoma, Colorado State University; Kenneth Heilman, University of Wisconsin; Allan Jones, University of Houston; Karl Kuhnert, University of Georgia; Robert Lowder, Bradley University; Michael McBride, Gonzaga University; Michael McCall, Ithaca College; Clay Moore, Northern Arizona University; Nora Reilly, Washington State University; Cyril Sadowski, Auburn University at Montgomery; John Sawyer, University of Delaware; Janet Sniezek, Cornell University; James Thomas, University of Nebraska; Janet Turnage, University of Central Florida; Robert Vance, Pennsylvania State University; Victor Wekselburg, University of Southern Mississippi; and Sheldon Zedeck, University of California at Berkeley.

We especially appreciate Lisa Friedel and Michelle Haff, who helped in our research and in obtaining permissions; Laura Galarza, who assisted in the preparation of the indexes, as well as Steve Norder and Meera Dash, who in their roles as editors at Harcourt Brace provided invaluable assistance. Also involved in the book's creation were Serena Manning as designer, Erin Gregg as production manager, and Annette Coolidge as picture editor. We would not be so crass as to blame all of these folks for the shortcomings of this book, but they certainly deserve a lot of credit for the things we have done right. Our sincere thanks to them all.

One last comment. For those who may wonder about the pronunciation of the first author's name, it is pronounced De (as in *decide* or *define*)–boy (as in *boy*). We assume that no such problems exist for the other authors.

R.L.D.
C.S.S.
W.C.H.

BRIEF
TABLE
OF
CONTENTS

# TABLE OF CONTENTS

# UNDERSTANDING INDUSTRIAL AND ORGANIZATIONAL PSYCHOLOGY

## An Integrated Approach

# SECTION

## 1

## I/O PSYCHOLOGY IN CONTEXT

As its name implies, industrial and organizational (I/O) psychology is a specialized field within the larger discipline of psychology that focuses on the workplace. Its aim is to increase our understanding of how people relate to work settings for the ultimate purpose of bringing about improvements. It is part science, contributing to the general knowledge base of psychology, and part application, using that knowledge to solve work-related problems.

To even begin to appreciate what all this means, you must have some grasp of what psychology is about, what sorts of work-related problems it has been applied to, and what kinds of tools it uses. That is, you must understand the *context* within which the core material of I/O psychology takes on meaning. Thus we begin our journey into the field of I/O psychology through its context. The purpose of the two chapters in this section is to prepare you for what lies ahead, and to convince you that it is worth the trip.

The first chapter locates our subject within three important and related contexts: the broader discipline of *psychology,* the *work organization,* and the larger *society* of which both are a part. You will see that what I/O psychology concerns itself with at any particular time is strongly influenced by what is

happening in these environments. And, with varying success, it affects all three.

Consider, for example, an important societal event of the early 1990s: the economic recession. It forced companies to look for ways to cut costs, which in many cases resulted in streamlining operations, "downsizing," and massive layoffs. Included among the victims were many white-collar workers, executives, and long-term employes—people who had never faced unemployment before or even considered the possibility of being laid off. Suddenly thrown out of work in a declining job market, often with skills that were in little demand, these unfortunate individuals suffered far more than mere financial hardship. Many lost confidence in themselves and felt worthless, impotent, and ashamed of being out of work. Clearly this was a situation crying out for psychological help at both the individual and organizational levels.

Some I/O psychologists responded by becoming directly involved in "outplacement counseling," a newly created service designed to help those about to be displaced find ways to cope with their job loss and improve their chances of finding new employment. Others began doing research aimed at gaining a better understanding of both the organizational and human consequences of downsizing. Still others worked with organizations to make sure that the layoffs were administered fairly, and the reorganization was implemented as smoothly as possible. Thus a *societal* phenomenon (recession) produced an *organizational* problem (downsizing) with profound *psychological* implications at the individual, organizational, and societal levels. It sensitized psychologists of all kinds to recession-related problems and generated a new or renewed interest among I/O specialists in a range of associated issues (e.g., organizational commitment, employee turnover, skill obsolescence and retraining, outplacement counseling).

Our main goal in Chapter 1, then, is to give you a sense of what I/O psychology is *about* by considering what it is *for*. In so doing, we will be setting the stage for a recurrent theme that will play out as each new topic takes its place in the spotlight. The theme, very simply, is that I/O psychology exists to help solve human problems in the workplace, but the workplace and its problems are always changing—largely because society changes. And the pace of these changes is accelerating. What is most exciting about I/O psychology today is its potentiality for addressing the problems of tomorrow. Each chapter will consider the implications of its content for a rapidly changing world.

The second chapter deals with another important context, the domain of the behavioral and social scientist. Most of the knowledge generated and applied by I/O psychologists is based on a philosophy shared by all sciences as well as research methods adapted to the special problems inherent in studying human beings. Like physicists and chemists, I/O psychologists accept as explanation only those theories and principles supported by scientifically admissible evidence. Like sociologists and political scientists, they gather that evidence largely by questioning or observing people under carefully defined conditions and interpret it using a variety of statistical techniques. Unless you understand the rationale and conventions underlying the scientific approach and the research strategies favored by I/O psychologists, you can hardly judge the merit of the principles, evidence, and explanations presented in this text.

The importance of mastering the scientific perspective cannot be overstated. Laypersons in general and businesspersons in particular have difficulty accepting scientific explanations for human behavior that are inconsistent with their own intuitions. They are inclined to trust their "gut feelings" over scientific evidence and to react accordingly, often with unhappy results. They are likely to say or do the wrong thing to a subordinate; make a bad business decision; maybe even feel guilty about something that was unavoidable.

If you are to benefit from what I/O psychology has to offer, you must be open to the possibility that intuitions can be wrong. You must be willing to weigh evidence dispassionately in seeking explanations for and solutions to problems that arise in the workplace. You must, in short, understand the scientific approach. For this reason, Chapter 2 is probably the most critical chapter in the entire book.

# CHAPTER

**1**

# Psychology, Organizations, and Society

- The I/O Psychologist

- The Psychological Context

- The Organizational Context

- The Societal Context

- Conclusions

It is one thing to write a concise definition of I/O psychology and quite another to convey in concrete terms what those words actually mean. We have given you the definition (see p. 2); now we will try to make it come alive. A technical "field" such as I/O psychology really consists of several things. It is a core body of knowledge, a set of tools used to expand and apply that knowledge, a setting or context in which that expansion and application take place, a collection of people who identify with the field, and a variety of institutions that hold all these components together (e.g., professional organizations, journals, meetings, training programs, and jargon). In this chapter we will introduce you to the people, institutions, and major contexts that comprise I/O psychology. Chapter 2 will go into some of the basic tools, and the rest of the book will present the core body of knowledge.

We begin this chapter at the personal level—with an introduction to the professionals who identify themselves as I/O psychologists. Then we move on to the broader context of psychology, looking particularly at its institutions. Next we explore the organizational context: the one that, more than any other, makes I/O unique within psychology while relating it to other key disciplines. The most noticeable of these related disciplines, incidentally, are known as *organizational theory* and *organizational behavior,* and we shall visit each briefly. Finally, we close with a chronological look at the societal context. The idea here is to reiterate the point we made earlier about the reciprocal influence between I/O psychology and major events in society. We will show how societal trends have consistently pushed our field in one direction or another, and how it has responded—sometimes more appropriately than others. And most importantly, we will consider the opportunities and challenges that lie ahead.

## THE I/O PSYCHOLOGIST

If you were to follow some I/O psychologists around to learn what they do for a living, you would find them engaged in a wide variety of activities as illustrated in the sample of job titles shown in Table 1.1. Some would direct the personnel functions of large corporations: designing (and managing) procedures for recruiting, selecting, placing, and training employees; developing evaluation and compensation systems; analyzing, describing, and evaluating jobs; helping "line managers" manage and plan more effectively; conducting attitude surveys of the workforce; and maybe even helping individuals cope with stress.

Others would perform some of the same functions but as consultants to a variety of clients rather than as full-time employees of one organization. Moreover, their services might include diagnosing an organization's management problems and, when necessary, recommending and helping to bring about company-wide changes. Such consultants might be totally self-

**Table 1.1**

## SAMPLE OF JOB TITLES HELD BY I/O PSYCHOLOGISTS

MANAGER, Executive and Organizational Development; Pepsi-Cola Company
DIRECTOR, Management, Education, & Leader Development, Space and Defense Sector; TRW
ASSISTANT PROFESSOR, Department of Psychology; State University of New York-Albany
SENIOR RESEARCH SCIENTIST, Educational Testing Service
MANAGING PRINCIPAL, HRStrategies, Inc.
PROFESSOR, School of Organization and Management; Yale University
CONSULTANT, Self-employed
DIRECTOR, Corporate Quality Office; Ford Motor Company
CHAIR, Department of Psychology; University of Maryland, College Park
PERSONNEL RESEARCH PSYCHOLOGIST, U.S. Air Force Human Resource Laboratory
DIRECTOR, Planning and Marketing Strategy; American Heart Association
EXECUTIVE VICE PRESIDENT, Northwest Mutual Life Insurance Company
INDUSTRIAL PSYCHOLOGIST, Washington State Patrol
MANAGEMENT PSYCHOLOGIST, Bleke & Boyd, PC
ASSOCIATE PROFESSOR, School of Management; University of Michigan-Dearborn
VICE PRESIDENT, Human Resources; Capitol Records
SENIOR MANAGER, Professional Development; Ernst & Young
PROFESSOR, Department of Behavioral Science; Pennsylvania State College of Medicine
DIVISION MANAGER, Human Resources; AT&T
HUMAN RESOURCE SPECIALIST, Walt Disney Imagineering
PRESIDENT, Texas A&M University
PSYCHOLOGIST, Labor Relations/Employee Development; Metro Washington Airports Authority
QUALITY PERFORMANCE MANAGER, Dow Chemical USA
VICE PRESIDENT, Corporate Personnel; Manufacturers Hanover Trust
ASSISTANT PROFESSOR, Department of Psychology; Lafayette College
ENGINEERING PSYCHOLOGIST, Human Factors; U.S. Consumer Products Safety Commission
STAFF PSYCHOLOGIST, Organizational Effectiveness and Training; Shell Oil
SUPERVISOR OF EXAMINATIONS, Milwaukee Fire and Police Commission
RESEARCH PSYCHOLOGIST, U.S. Army Research Institute
DIRECTOR OF RESEARCH, Coldwell Banker Residential Group
PROPRIETOR, Serendipity Unlimited

*Source: Membership Directory.* (1991). Arlington Heights, IL: The Society for Industrial and Organizational Psychology.

employed, work for a consulting firm, or hold full-time academic appointments while consulting on the side.

Still other I/O psychologists would be found in university psychology laboratories, corporate research and development groups, advertising agencies, marketing departments, and government research organizations. Those so engaged would most likely work as *scientists* whose primary function, like that of biologists, physicists, or other social scientists, is generating knowledge. Some might try to answer simple "applied" questions such as how teenagers will respond to a particular toothpaste ad, while others might be concerned with "basic" issues such as what motivates people to work. Most would be trying to answer questions that lie somewhere between these extremes. Regardless of scope or focus, all of them would use scientific methods such as those presented in Chapter 2 to gather new information, rather than rely on what they already know to solve problems.

And finally, of course, some would teach—in a university psychology department or business school, a management training or executive development program, or some other education or training setting. Most academic I/O psychologists combine teaching, research, and consulting.

Having observed this wide variation in activities and job descriptions, you might well question whether it makes sense to lump all these professionals together under the title of "I/O psychologist." What, if anything, do they share that distinguishes them from other professionals who do many of the same things? The answer, very simply, is *psychology*. While it is true that psychological principles and methods are used widely by other specialists and that many I/O psychologists focus on particular organizational functions, I/O psychologists share an important bond with the larger discipline of psychology. By training, outlook, and professional affiliation, even the most specialized practitioner is first a psychologist. To understand why this connection is important, we must now take a closer look at the parent discipline.

# THE PSYCHOLOGICAL CONTEXT

As we said, there is a scientific component and a practice component to I/O psychology. The same is true of psychology as a discipline, and this is one of its most distinctive features. By contrast, other practice fields, such as engineering or medicine, are largely independent of the scientific disciplines (such as physics and biochemistry) on which they depend for basic knowledge. Psychology is concerned broadly with how people think, act, and feel—in more technical terms, with *cognition, behavior,* and *affect.* Its scientific component seeks to understand these functions; its practice component seeks to use what is learned to benefit individuals, groups, and society.

## Psychological Specialties

Psychology also is differentiated according to field of specialization. But because there is no universally accepted basis for defining and classifying specialities, psychology has a rather long and confusing list of such fields. Some, such as *child* psychology, are defined largely by a focal population; others, such as *developmental* psychology, by the emphasis on how people change over time; others, such as *experimental* psychology, by the scientific methods used; and still others, such as *school* psychology, by the setting in which the field is practiced. Like school psychology, I/O psychology is identified primarily by its setting (the workplace).

The largest and most widely recognized specialities are clinical and counseling psychology. They provide similar mental health services to individuals and groups for somewhat different populations ("deviant" vs. "normal") and in somewhat different settings (e.g., mental hospitals vs. counseling centers). By tradition, four psychology specialities are currently recognized by most professional and legal bodies as official practice fields: clinical, counseling, school, and I/O. Collectively, they account for over 90% of the psychologists who offer services to the public. Of these, I/O is by far the smallest (approximately 3,000 practitioners) and most distinct from the others (Rosenfeld, Shimberg, & Thornton, 1983). Some have argued that psychologists should be classified into two main groups: those who provide direct health-care services (health-care providers or HCPs) and those who do not (Howard & Lowman, 1985). By this definition, I/O psychologists are not HCPs; clinical, counseling, and many school psychologists are. We shall have more to say about this in a moment.

## The Scientist–Practitioner Model

Psychology, then, consists of a scientific component and a practice component together with a variety of specialty fields. These specialties differ in setting, population served, methods, health-care orientation, and most important, the relative emphasis attached to the scientific and practice components. In sheer numbers, the HCP specialties are dominated by practitioners. Other specialty fields, such as experimental, developmental, or social psychology, are dominated by scientists (Howard, Pion, et al., 1986). The I/O specialty has always prided itself on maintaining a balance between the two orientations, both in its scope of activities and in the training of its professionals. It prepares the I/O psychologist to assume either role, and promotes the point of view that a mix of the two is vastly superior to either for even the most practical of purposes.

This philosophy, which requires that I/O professionals be trained both as scientists and practitioners, is known as the *scientist–practitioner model*. To enter the field, most I/O psychologists earn the PhD—a research degree—and accumulate supervised experience in one of the nonacademic work settings described earlier. For years the scientist–practitioner model was the unchallenged philosophy behind all professional training in psychology, for the health-care practitioner as well as for the other applied specialties. Today, however, the health-care practitioner community is badly split between those who favor the traditional model and a growing constituency who prefer a more practice-oriented "scholar–practitioner" or pure "practitioner" model culminating in a professional doctorate—the PsyD degree (Stricker, 1975). Trivial as arguments over training models and degree labels appear on the surface, they reflect profound philosophical differences that threaten to reshape the whole discipline of psychology (*American Psychologist,* 1987; Schover, 1980). Even the I/O field may eventually be affected, but for the foreseeable future, it stands among the psychological specialities firmly committed to combining science and practice.

## I/O's Role in Psychological Science

What does I/O psychology contribute to psychology's larger mission of understanding human cognition, behavior, and affect? Almost 90% of the adults in the industrialized nations of the world work for organizations (Perrow, 1986). We spend nearly half our waking hours at work, and what happens there directly affects the rest of our time. Thus, as we saw earlier in the case of "downsizing," organizational conditions play a major role in how we think, act, and feel (London & Moses, 1990).

If understanding human behavior and experience is its goal, the science of psychology must concern itself with such work-related phenomena. Questions arising from the workplace are many and fundamental. What does work mean to people? How important are the loss of a job or opportunities for advancement to their self-esteem? Are attitudes changing on the relative importance of security, pay, personal growth opportunities, the social atmosphere at work, and other job features? What constitutes good management? How do multiple roles affect women employees? What is the effect of dual breadwinners on the family? How do corporate mergers and acquisitions affect the stress level of employees? The list is virtually endless.

In their role as scientists, many I/O psychologists carry out research on these basic issues. In addition, by exposing and highlighting such problems, they encourage the interest of other branches of psychology. Unfortunately, however, the trend in psychology, like most scientific disciplines, has been toward increasingly narrow specialization, a condition that has limited this sort of healthy interaction (Altman, 1987). Most of what I/O researchers discover is published in journals such as the *Journal of Applied Psychology, Personnel Psychology, Administrative Sciences Quarterly, Academy of Management Review, Academy of Management Journal, Organizational Behavior and Human Decision Processes, International Review of Applied Psychology, Journal of Organizational Behavior,* and *Journal of Occupational Psychology.* Other specialities have their own professional journals.

## I/O's Role in the Practice of Psychology

Although I/O practitioners sort themselves into five major activity categories—individual evaluation, training, organizational behavior, organizational development, and employee development (Howard, 1990)—most fall within one of two overlapping domains known as human resource management (HRM) and organizational development (OD). Both HRM and OD are populated by a variety of professionals besides psychologists, although psychological knowledge plays a major role in each. They differ chiefly in the kinds of psychological content and techniques they use as well as in their general approach to organizational problems. The HRM approach emphasizes *measurement,* the idea being to help organizations make the best use of their people by getting precise measures of both human and work characteristics and then applying those measures in personnel management. In contrast, the OD approach relies on broad psychological theories in diagnosing and trying to correct organizational problems. Theories of social behavior and human motivation figure prominently in this strategy. For example, a common theme in OD practice, and one that came directly from such theory, is that nonmanagement employees ought to have some influence in decisions that affect them because people will work harder and stay more committed to goals that they understand and help set.

Table 1.2 lists the competencies that I/O psychologists should have as recommended by the Society for Industrial and Organizational Psychology (SIOP), the field's chief professional organization. As you can see, the list runs the gamut from HRM functions (e.g., staffing, compensation) to OD functions (e.g., attitude surveys, conflict resolution). HRM and OD approaches originated in different philosophies, but they have moved closer together in

**Table 1.2**

## COURSE TOPICS COVERED IN DOCTORAL I/O PSYCHOLOGY PROGRAMS

1. History and Systems of Psychology
2. Fields of Psychology
3. Work Motivation Theory
4. Organization Theory
5. Organizational Development Theory
6. Attitude Theory
7. Career Development Theory
8. Decision Theory
9. Human Performance/Human Factors
10. Consumer Behavior
11. Measurement of Individual Differences
12. Small Group Theory and Process
13. Performance Appraisal and Feedback
14. Criterion Theory and Development
15. Personnel Selection, Placement, and Classification
16. Research Methods
17. Statistical Methods and Data Analysis
18. Ethical, Legal, and Professional Contexts of I/O Psychology
19. Job and Task Analysis
20. Individual Assessment
21. Training Theory: Program Design and Evaluation

*Source:* Education and training committee, SIOP (1982). *Guidelines for Education and Training at the Doctoral Level in Industrial/Organizational Psychology.* College Park, MD: Society for Industrial and Organizational Psychology.

practice. A competent practitioner might prefer one set of techniques over another, but it is unlikely that he or she would fail to consider the possibilities afforded by the alternative set.

It should also be recognized that there is no standard way of packaging either set of functions within the formal structure of work organizations. Some firms have personnel departments that perform both OD and HRM functions; some house HRM activities in one office (e.g., personnel) and OD functions in another (e.g., management development); some maintain only one set of functions; some maintain neither and rely heavily on outside consultants or inside nonprofessionals.

## Ethics and Competence

Not everyone who offers psychological services to the public is trustworthy. Fully aware that most potential clients, including large organizations, lack the sophistication in psychology necessary to be wise consumers, unscrupulous practitioners—primarily nonpsychologists, we are happy to say—have opportunistically promoted questionable products and services. Managers faced with chronic problems in morale, production, or turnover find the promise of a quick and affordable cure to be as irresistible as it is unrealistic. Consequently, charlatans have prospered, usually at the expense of the organization, society at large, and the reputation of legitimate psychology. A good case in point is the growth industry known as "honesty," or "integrity" testing (*Science Agenda,* 1991). As we shall see later, the claims made for tests that purport to identify dishonest employees are frequently exaggerated, and many decent people have suffered personal indignities and financial loss as a result of their misuse.

Is there a defense against incompetent or irresponsible practitioners? The best protection is knowing something about the techniques used by legitimate practitioners, including their limitations. One aim of this book is to arm you with some of that knowledge as it pertains to I/O psychology. Another defense lies in knowing where to go for additional information. The practice of psychology is subject to both legal and professional regulation, like medicine or law. State laws require that psychologists meet certain educational and competency standards to practice, and special licensing boards set and enforce these standards. Additionally, a professional ethics code (see Table 1.3) mandates that practitioners function within their specialized areas of competence. Thus, at least some assurance of competence is available merely by determining whether a practitioner is licensed or certified as a psychologist by the state. Since states differ in their policies regarding licensure for non-health care-practitioner specialities, only about a third of the I/O psychologists in the U.S. are licensed (Howard, 1990). From the consumer's standpoint, a simple call to the ethics committee of the state psychological association or the American Psychological Association (APA) can often establish the legitimacy of services or credentials being offered by a practitioner.

**Table 1.3**

# ETHICAL PRINCIPLES OF PSYCHOLOGISTS

## Preamble

Psychologists work to develop a valid and reliable body of scientific knowledge based on research. They may apply that knowledge to human behavior in a variety of contexts. In doing so, they perform many roles, such as researcher, educator, diagnostician, therapist, supervisor, consultant, administrator, social interventionist, and expert witness. Their goal is to broaden knowledge of behavior and, where appropriate, to apply it pragmatically to improve the condition of both the individual and society. Psychologists respect the central importance of freedom of inquiry and expression in research, teaching, and publication. They also strive to help the public in developing informed judgments and choices concerning human behavior. This Ethics Code provides a common set of values upon which psychologists build their professional and scientific work.

This Code is intended to provide both the general principles and the decision rules to cover most situations encountered by psychologists. It has as its primary goal the welfare and protection of the individuals and groups with whom psychologists work. It is the individual responsibility of each psychologist to aspire to the highest possible standards of conduct. Psychologists respect and protect human and civil rights, and do not knowingly participate in or condone unfair discriminatory practices.

The development of a dynamic set of ethical standards for a psychologist's work-related conduct requires a personal commitment to a lifelong effort to act ethically; to encourage ethical behavior by students, supervisees, employees, and colleagues, as appropriate; and to consult with others, as needed, concerning ethical problems. Each psychologist supplements, but does not violate, the Ethics Code's values and rules on the basis of guidance drawn from personal values, culture, and experience.

## Principle A: Competence

Psychologists strive to maintain high standards of competence in their work. They recognize the boundaries of their particular competencies and the limitations of their expertise. They provide only those services and use only those techniques for which they are qualified by education, training, or experience. Psychologists are cognizant of the fact that the competencies required in serving, teaching, and/or studying groups of people vary with the distinctive characteristics of those groups. In those areas in which recognized professional standards do not yet exist, psychologists exercise careful judgment and take appropriate precautions to protect the welfare of those with whom they work. They maintain knowledge of relevant scientific and professional information related to the services they render, and they recognize the need for ongoing education. Psychologists make appropriate use of scientific, professional, technical, and administrative resources.

## Principle B: Integrity

Psychologists seek to promote integrity in the science, teaching, and practice of psychology. In these activities psychologists are honest, fair, and respectful of others. In describing or reporting their qualifications, services, products, fees, research, or teaching, they do not make statements that are false, misleading, or deceptive. Psychologists strive to be aware of their own belief systems, values, needs, and limitations and the effects of these on their work. To the extent feasible, they attempt to clarify for relevant parties the roles they are performing and to function appropriately in accordance with those roles. Psychologists avoid improper and potentially harmful dual relationships.

## Principle C: Professional and Scientific Responsibility

Psychologists uphold professional standards of conduct, clarify their professional roles and obligations, accept appropriate responsibility for their behavior, and adapt their methods to the needs of different populations. Psychologists consult with, refer to, or cooperate with other professionals and institutions to the extent needed to serve the best interests of their patients, clients, or

**Table 1.3 (continued)**

<u>**Principle C: Professional and Scientific Responsibility (continued)**</u>
other recipients of their services. Psychologists' moral standards and conduct are personal matters to the same degree as is true for any other person, except as psychologists' conduct may compromise their professional responsibilities or reduce the public's trust in psychology and psychologists. Psychologists are concerned about the ethical compliance of their colleagues' scientific and professional conduct. When appropriate, they consult with colleagues in order to prevent or avoid unethical conduct.

<u>**Principle D: Respect for People's Rights and Dignity**</u>
Psychologists accord appropriate respect to the fundamental rights, dignity, and worth of all people. They respect the rights of individuals to privacy, confidentiality, self-determination, and autonomy, mindful that legal and other obligations may lead to inconsistency and conflict with the exercise of these rights. Psychologists are aware of cultural, individual, and role differences, including those due to age, gender, race, ethnicity, national origin, religion, sexual orientation, disability, language, and socioeconomic status. Psychologists try to eliminate the effect on their work of biases based on those factors, and they do not knowingly participate in or condone unfair discriminatory practices.

<u>**Principle E: Concern for Others' Welfare**</u>
Psychologists seek to contribute to the welfare of those with whom they interact professionally. In their professional actions, psychologists weigh the welfare and rights of their patients or clients, students, supervisees, human research participants, and other affected persons, and the welfare of animal subjects of research. When conflicts occur among psychologists' obligations or concerns, they attempt to resolve these conflicts and to perform their roles in a responsible fashion that avoids or minimizes harm. Psychologists are sensitive to real and ascribed differences in power between themselves and others, and they do not exploit or mislead other people during or after professional relationships.

<u>**Principle F: Social Responsibility**</u>
Psychologists are aware of their professional and scientific responsibilities to the community and the society in which they work and live. They apply and make public their knowledge of psychology in order to contribute to human welfare. Psychologists are concerned about and work to mitigate the causes of human suffering. When undertaking research, they strive to advance human welfare and the science of psychology. Psychologists comply with the law and encourage the development of law and social policy that serve the interests of their patients and clients and the public. They are encouraged to contribute a portion of their professional time for little or no personal advantage.

*Source:* Ethical principles of psychologists. (1992). *American Psychologist, 47,* 1599–1600.

## An Historical Overview

How did the field develop as it did within psychology? The story is short because psychology itself is only a little over 100 years old, and we will only present a brief synopsis here.

For centuries, philosophers and other scholars have argued over the nature of mind and how it functions—the phenomena of *mental life.* But the relatively recent idea of using scientific methods to resolve such issues was what distinguished modern psychology. In 1879 Wilhelm Wundt, a professor at the University of Leipzig in Germany, opened the first laboratory devoted exclusively to the study of psychology. Experiments were carried out under carefully controlled conditions to answer basic questions about the human mind.

Because most of the important first-generation psychologists studied under Wundt, the new discipline began as a basic science concerned mainly with laws of conscious experience. However, Hugo Munsterberg and Walter Dill Scott, two of Wundt's students who established themselves in the United States, began to explore the applications of psychological principles to industrial problems. Both wrote important books on these applications. Munsterberg's (1913) was concerned primarily with industrial efficiency and Scott's (1908) with advertising. Between them they touched on many of the topics that have occupied I/O psychologists ever since.

At about the same time that Wundt was trying to describe the general laws that govern mental life, a British scholar and cousin of Charles Darwin, Sir Francis Galton, was studying how people come to differ from one another mentally. He devised the mental test as a means of indexing individual differences in mental ability. Coupled with the work of Charles Binet, the pioneer in intelligence testing who gave us the concept of IQ (intelligence quotient), Galton's approach spawned a tradition in psychology that developed largely in parallel with Wundt's mental science (Hothersall, 1984). It has often been called the "mental testing movement."

Testing for *individual differences* and doing experiments to discover *general mental principles* have remained fairly distinct approaches in psychology despite periodic efforts to draw them together (Cronbach, 1957). Wundt's mental science approach dominated early psychology in the United States, but the practical possibilities of testing are what captured industry's interest. Hence the individual differences approach became dominant in early industrial psychology and remained so for the next several decades.

During this period, Sigmund Freud's theories on the nature and treatment of mental disorders (and the role of *unconscious* events in mind and behavior) were also beginning to attract a great deal of attention, eventually helping to establish the health-care branch of psychology (Hothersall, 1984). Still, until nearly midcentury, psychology remained chiefly an academic discipline rooted in laboratory research. The industrial and clinical branches were considered peripheral, trivial, and rather suspect offshoots, often lumped together as "applied psychology."

The evolution of I/O psychology from a minor offshoot to a recognized specialty within the field can be traced to a number of influences, but none more important than the two world wars. We shall have more to say about these influences in our discussion of the societal context later in the chapter. The demands of two massive war efforts, each representing dramatic changes in the doctrine and technology of warfare, called for radical changes in the management of human resources. Psychologists of all kinds were summoned to help, and in the course of doing so they discovered a great deal about the potential applications of their specialized knowledge and techniques. All branches of psychology made huge advances under the exigencies of war—an ironic twist for a discipline pledged to the promotion of human welfare.

Both wars provided massive evidence of the value of testing for selection and assignment of people according to job requirements. Naturally, industry recognized the potential applications of these techniques, and the use of testing increased dramatically after both wars. In addition, World War II produced important advances in techniques used to train people, many of which found peacetime application. Educational, experimental, and industrial psychologists all contributed significantly to the design of these training programs. One notable example was *simulation training,* a technique in which the basic operations required in a job (e.g., flying an airplane) could be practiced on a replica of that job's environment (i.e., a *simulator*) without the risks and costs associated with learning in the actual situation. Today, the simulation approach has spread to the training of managers, professionals, and skilled technicians, and it remains a cornerstone of pilot training, both military and commercial. It was a critical factor in the successful allied operations in the Persian Gulf War.

In addition to selection, classification, and training developments, World War II fostered the creation of a whole new field based upon an entirely different strategy for improving human effectiveness. The essential idea behind it was that "human error" or poor performance is not always a matter of incapable or poorly trained personnel, but often reflects insufficient consideration of human characteristics in the design of the machines that people must operate. The field survived the war, and today constitutes a formally recognized discipline known in the United States as *human factors* (see Chapter 13 for a definition) and in the rest of the world as *ergonomics.* It encompasses a variety of human-oriented and design-oriented specialities, the psychological component of which is often called *engineering psychology.* Its connection to I/O psychology is distant, but, as we shall argue in Chapter 12, probably should be a lot closer (Howell, 1991).

In the three decades following World War II, all areas of professional psychology experienced tremendous growth, and the industrial field was transformed from a narrow applied specialty with a distinct emphasis on personnel functions (e.g., selection and training) to the multifaceted discipline that it is today. The official name was changed from *industrial* to *industrial/organizational* psychology in 1973 to reflect the growing influence of social psychology and other organizationally relevant social sciences.

One final trend in psychology has shaped the I/O field. Since the early 1900s, psychology has tended to be dominated by one or another theoretical perspective or kind of explanation (often called a "paradigm") during any given era. Early on, as we saw, the emphasis was on describing the general laws that govern conscious experience. Using introspection as a research tool, psychologists such as Wundt attempted to analyze and describe the contents of conscious experience (e.g., sensations, images, feelings) similar to the way a chemist might analyze the elements of matter. This paradigm was often referred to as *structuralism* because of its focus on the structure of mental content. Freud's work on the unconscious, however, coupled with a growing realization that much of what happens consciously occurs for a purpose, shifted attention to the more dynamic *functional* properties of mind. From the late 1920s until the 1940s, therefore, the emphasis was on the mental and biological underpinnings of functions such as motivation, emotion, learning, and perception. The primary concern of functionalists was how humans and other living organisms adjust to their environment.

This school of thought, which constituted America's first unique paradigm, became known as *American functionalism* (Hothersall, 1984). It was a much less restrictive school of thought than structuralism, a feature that enabled both the individual differences approach and applied psychology to develop within it. William James, a Harvard professor who has often been called America's most influential psychologist, was among the founders of American functionalism and, interestingly, the man who brought Hugo Munsterberg to this country.

Functionalism gave way to another paradigm, *behaviorism,* under the leadership first of John B. Watson, and later, B.F. Skinner (Hothersall, 1984). Behaviorism held that both the content and functions of mind are unsuitable subjects for scientific study because neither is open to public view. All that can be studied objectively are the behaviors (responses) that organisms exhibit and the environmental conditions (stimuli) that control them. In its most radical form, behaviorism denied the very existence of mind and maintained that all behavior could eventually be explained in terms of simple stimulus–response (S-R) laws.

From an applications standpoint, behaviorism focused on ways to shape or control behavior by manipulating stimulus conditions and consequences of behavior. Behavior modification ("B-mod") techniques became popular in clinical, counseling, developmental, school, and even I/O applications, and in various forms, remain so today. However, as a general philosophy, behaviorism never dominated the I/O specialty as it did the broader field of psychology during the 1950s and 1960s. That undoubtedly was attributable to I/O psychology's lack of *any* theoretical orientation during much of this period and its heritage in measurement and individual differences.

By the 1970s, the study of mental events, which behaviorism had all but eliminated from psychology, began making a dramatic comeback thanks largely to the evolution of the computer. Here at last was a convenient model for how the human mind might work. To function effectively, the mind must perform many of the same operations as a computer, such as sensing and interpreting input information, storing it in various ways, performing logic tests, and selecting responses. Mental functions could be inferred by analogy and cast into the form of hypotheses that could be tested rigorously in the laboratory. One could thus study mental processes without having to gain direct access to mental content.

This latest "paradigm shift" is still in full swing (Kendler, 1987). It emphasizes *cognitive* processes (thinking) and has touched virtually every corner of modern psychology, from clinical practice to the basic science of conscious experience—Wundt's domain. It has become a dominant paradigm in I/O psychology as well, although again, not to the extent that it has in some of the other specialities.

Industrial/organizational psychology, as we said at the outset, is above all an integral part of modern psychology. The purpose of this part of the chapter has been to show what this means and why it is important. We have now seen how the ebb and flow of events in psychology—the political controversies, the intellectual climate, the dominant paradigms, the growth in professionalism—have all affected our field despite its sustained effort to preserve its uniqueness and vitality. Though still relatively small, its impact on psychology is growing and has immense possibilities. An arena in which its contribution is already well established, and from which it has also gained new perspectives, is the organizational context, to which we now turn.

# THE ORGANIZATIONAL CONTEXT

Although work organizations have existed throughout recorded history, they were not subjected to serious study until the twentieth century. And even then, the primary effort was directed toward giving practical advice on how to manage rather than on gaining deeper insight into what organizations are and how they work. Managers wrote from experience, and their observations became the commandments for the next generation of managers. The few social scientists interested in the subject had little impact on either their respective disciplines or the practice of management until much later. Psychologists, as we saw earlier, were minimally involved, primarily in helping managers select and place people in existing jobs. They did not question either the nature of the work assignments nor the organizations that defined and controlled those jobs.

By the middle of the century, the situation had changed dramatically. All the social sciences, including psychology, had become interested in studying work organizations, and a whole new, multidisciplinary field called *organizational theory* (OT) had begun to emerge. Instead of a single set of management principles, managers now were faced with a confusing array of theories and data on topics such as leadership, work motivation, group dynamics, and organizational design. Not only was it hard to boil all this knowledge down to practical terms, the new theories often gave managers conflicting advice. The reason, of course, is that organizations are very complex entities. Thus, the better we understand them, the more there is to explain, and the harder it becomes to give simple answers to management questions. In the next part of the chapter we look at some of the dominant ideas on organization and management as they evolved over the century's first 70 years.

## Major Perspectives

The existing knowledge about work organizations derives from a variety of sources, both scientific and experiential. First came the attempts by practicing managers to capture their insights in the form of universal management principles. Probably the most influential of these was a book first published in 1916 by a French manager, Henri Fayol, *Administration industrielle et generale,* in which he spelled out 14 principles that he saw as key to successful management (Fayol, 1930). Included were such basic notions as division of labor (specialization), a clear chain of command, and subordination of individual interests to those of the organization.

Fayol's book was followed by a number of others carrying much the same message, a philosophy that became known as *classical organization* (or *administrative* or *management*) *theory* (Bedeian, 1980; Dessler, 1980). Collectively these works formed the basis of academic training in management from its beginnings in the 1920s through the 1950s. The classical philosophy focused on the formal *structure* of organizations: clear and efficient division of labor, lines of authority, and communication. The idea was to divide work up into clearly defined jobs, put them together in the most efficient way, and make sure workers performed according to plan by imposing a military-like system of authority over them. People were seen as mere instruments of production that required clear direction and tight control for the organization to be productive (productivity being the only legitimate goal an organization has).

As early management theorists formed these ideas, classical theory received an important boost from a most unlikely source: a mechanical engineer named Frederick Taylor who sought to extend engineering principles to the design and management of work (Taylor, 1911). His notion was to determine through precise measurement ("time and motion studies") the most efficient way to carry out work operations, to standardize them through clearly specified procedures, and to enforce them through the exercise of explicit management functions. The approach, which became known as *scientific management,* provided concrete techniques for implementing the classical philosophy. Needless to say, it became as popular among managers as it was despised by workers, who saw scientific management as just another attempt by management to exploit them (Gies, 1991).

Value judgments aside, it should be noted that Taylor's approach was anything but scientific except in the narrow sense of measuring things and using data in place of opinion. True science, as we will show in Chapter 2, is much more than that: its aim is to understand natural events. "Scientific management," on the other hand, was concerned with putting into practice a specific theory of management that its proponents accepted as valid. Like classical theory, it had nothing whatsoever to do with a search for knowledge, and in fact represented the antithesis of scientific inquiry.

In contrast to the prescriptions of classical theory and scientific management, the true scientific approach made a tentative entry into the field as early as the 1920s in what came to be known as the "Hawthorne Studies" (Roethlisberger & Dickson, 1934). Initiated at the Hawthorne plant of the Western Electric Company, these experiments, which studied how scheduling, environmental conditions, and other structural factors affect productivity, produced a new perspective on work organizations (Dessler, 1980). The results suggested that social factors, such as peer pressure, informal group dynamics and recognition, and personal feelings of freedom and self-worth, are more important than impersonal "structural" features, such as work methods and management control, for both productivity and worker morale.

The major conclusion from this decade of studies was that the whole classical approach is wrong. What really matters in organizations is not how well the work is packaged or the lines of authority are drawn, but rather, how well the organization recognizes and responds to the needs of its people. An efficient formal structure is of little value if people choose to ignore it as, indeed, they often seem inclined to do. Informal groups inevitably develop in the workplace, and these have a much greater impact on how people function than anything imposed by management.

In short, it was suggested that classical theory misses the point by emphasizing the structural or mechanistic rather than the psychological and social aspects of the organization. This proposition evolved into a directly competing philosophy of organization and management, the *human relations movement,* that eventually brought social psychologists, sociologists, political scientists, and a variety of other scholarly disciplines into the discussion. Increasingly, the debate over how to organize and manage shifted from the realm of experience to that of science. Social scientists framed questions drawn from their respective disciplines into organizational research issues and set about trying to answer them. Psychologists, for example, sought to find out what human needs must be satisfied in the workplace. Sociologists attempted to learn more about how work groups function and how leadership is exercised. Political scientists, recognizing the importance of influence processes within the organization, focused on how power is acquired and exercised.

Gradually, an understanding of the true complexity of work organizations began to emerge, and the insufficiency of simplistic prescriptions such as those offered by either classical management theory or the human relations movement became apparent. One cannot ensure effective management by making workers happy and capitalizing on informal group processes any more than one can by planning and directing their every move. How an organization should be designed and run for best results depends on a host of considerations at the individual, group, and macro-organizational levels. This general philosophy, often referred to as *contingency theory,* evolved directly from the knowledge accumulated from scientific research and remains dominant to this day (Scott, 1987).

With this growth in knowledge came a realization that no one discipline had the complete answer either to the question of what an organization is or to how it should be designed and managed. The next logical step was to regard the various perspectives on organization collectively, as an independent discipline, and with the 1950s the field of *organizational theory* (OT) began to take shape. It was dominated at first by macro theories from management science and sociology that focused on the organization as a whole rather than the individuals and groups which compose the organization. But by the late 1960s, the emphasis had shifted to a more micro level as psychological theories of personality, motivation, perception, attitude formation, leadership, and group behavior took over. Increasingly, the focus was on micro issues involving the behavior of individuals and groups rather than entire organizations (Perrow, 1973). Eventually the micro perspective assumed an identity of its own under the label of *organizational behavior* (OB), and OT reverted to its original preoccupation with macro issues of structure and design (Ford, Armandi, & Heaton, 1988; Jackson & Morgan, 1982).

The OB perspective requires no further explanation since it deals with topics in organizational psychology that you will encounter in future chapters: employee motivation and attitudes, leadership, social processes, and stress. It makes liberal use of psychological theories and relies heavily on research for answers. It focuses on individual and group behavior as they affect and are affected by organizational variables. The OT perspective is more central to management science and other social science disciplines than it is to psychology. Although OT includes some fundamental notions about the workplace that have influenced psychology's role in organizational affairs throughout its history, it has received relatively little attention from I/O psychology. This neglect is unfortunate because it deprives the student (or researcher, or practitioner) of a "big picture" view of the work organization through which to appreciate psychology's actual and potential roles. Thus, we must pause briefly to consider some of the major positions in OT, lest we be guilty of the same omission.

## Organizational Theory

The ideas that comprise the body of OT are many and varied. Furthermore, there is no universally accepted way of classifying them. Every writer presents a somewhat different picture; some include OB theories and some do not (Jackson & Morgan, 1982). For our purposes, a table from Scott (1987) is useful in that it organizes the theories according to three main distinguishing features and shows roughly when each category made its appearance. Note, for example, the location of the theories we have already encountered: scientific management and administrative theories (the classical ones) are followed by human relations, contingency theory, and finally, socio-technical systems—an elaboration of the contingency view. Since our intent is merely to give you a sense of how different theorists have viewed the organization and to highlight a few of particular relevance to I/O psychology, our discussion will focus on the main category distinctions represented in Table 1.4.

### CLOSED- AND OPEN-SYSTEM VIEWS

The distinction between *closed-* and *open-system models* refers to the relative emphasis placed on the internal affairs of the organization versus its interaction with its environment. (For our purposes, we can think of "model"

**Table 1.4**

## MAJOR TYPES OF ORGANIZATION THEORIES CLASSIFIED BY LEVEL OF ANALYSIS AND CHRONOLOGY WITH EXAMPLES

| LEVELS OF ANALYSIS | CLOSED-SYSTEM MODELS | | OPEN-SYSTEM MODELS | |
| --- | --- | --- | --- | --- |
| | 1900–1930 Rational Models Type I | 1930–1960 Natural Models Type II | 1960–1970 Rational Models Type III | 1970– Natural Models Type IV |
| **SOCIAL PSYCHOLOGICAL** | Scientific Management Taylor (1911)<br><br>Decision Making Simon (1945) | Human Relations Roy (1952) Whyte (1959) | Bounded Rationality March & Simon (1958) | Organizing Weick (1969)<br><br>Negotiated Order Strauss et al (1963)<br><br>Ambiguity and Choice March & Olsen (1976) |
| **STRUCTURAL** | Bureaucratic Theory Weber (1904–5)<br><br>Administrative Theory Fayol (1919) | Cooperative Systems Barnard (1938)<br><br>Human Relations Mayo (1945) Dalton (1959) | Contingency Theory Lawrence & Lorsch (1967)<br><br>Comparative Structure Udy (1959) Blau (1970) Pugh et al. (1969) | Sociotechnical Systems Miller & Rice (1967)<br><br>Strategic Contingencies Hickson et al. (1971) Pfeffer (1978) |
| **ECOLOGICAL** | | | Transactions Costs Williamson (1975) Ouchi (1980) | Population Ecology Hannan & Freeman (1977) Aldrich (1979)<br><br>Resource Dependence Pfeffer & Salancik (1978)<br><br>Marxist Theory Braverman (1974) Edwards (1979)<br><br>Institutionalist Theory Selznick (1949) Meyer & Rowan (1977) DiMaggio & Powell (1983) |

*Source:* Scott, W.R. (1987). *Organizations: Rational, Natural, and Open Systems.* 2nd ed., Englewood Cliffs, NJ: Prentice-Hall.

as a theory or way of conceptualizing the organization.) This is an extremely important distinction. Early theorists held the closed view. They tended to think in terms of what one might do to the organization itself—its structure, its people, its decision process—to make it successful, paying little attention to how well it adapted to markets, suppliers, competition, government, and other critical outside forces. Later theorists favored an open view, recognizing that such forces must at the very least be reckoned with, and might even dictate how best to manage internal affairs.

## RATIONAL AND NATURAL THEORIES

The distinction between rational and natural theories is also fundamental. Theories based on a *rational* perspective see the organization as an entity deliberately constructed to achieve specific goals (e.g., profitability). Hence the focus is prescriptive, meaning that efforts are made to find the most efficient means to that end, and to advise managers to manage that way. By contrast, the *natural* view sees the organization as a social collective, operating according to many of the same principles as other social systems, not necessarily in pursuit of a clear set of goals. The theoretical emphasis is descriptive, meaning that the emphasis is on understanding these social principles rather than telling managers what they should do to maximize efficiency. Ultimately, of course, even natural theorists have tended to get into the business of prescribing how organizations should be run, for understanding in and of itself has limited practical value. The difference is that prescriptions based on natural theories derive from ideas about how people *actually* function rather than how they *ought* to function as rational entities. It is this subtle distinction, incidentally, that has often separated economists and psychologists. The dominant economic perspective has always been a rational one, whereas psychology has consistently followed a descriptive (natural) path.

## LEVELS OF ANALYSIS

Levels of analysis refers to the unit of the organization on which the theorist focuses primary attention. The *social psychological* level, essentially the same as what we have been calling the micro perspective, regards the individual or work group as the proper unit of analysis, and in doing so includes material that some would reserve for OB. Scientific management is located here because of its focus on the individual. Obviously it did not really represent social psychology, but it did have a micro perspective.

At the *structural* level, the focus shifts to the whole organization, and at the *ecological* level, to the larger social systems of which the organization is a part. Together they encompass the macro perspective. The ecological theories cited are mainly economic and political philosophies that have little direct relevance for I/O psychology. They do, of course, have indirect relevance in that they try to explain key features of the societal environment, but this is beyond the scope of our present discussion.

## SELECTED THEORIES

Applying these distinctions to the now familiar classical (administrative), scientific management, and human relations theories, you can easily see how they were alike as closed-system views but very different in their rational versus naturalistic orientation. Moreover, you can appreciate the significant way in which they all differed from the open system contingency perspective.

Here are several other theories from Table 1.4 that were particularly important in shaping a context for I/O psychology.

**Weber's Bureaucracy**  Max Weber was a noted German sociologist whose ideas, though consistent with the other classical theories and published about the same time, developed independently. Because they were published in German and represented a more academic than practical orientation, Weber's notions had little impact on the management literature until they were translated into English after World War II. Undoubtedly the strained relations between the U.S. and Germany through two world wars had something to do with this delay, a rather vivid illustration of how societal events have influenced both the theory and practice of management.

The essence of Weber's position was that the most defensible way to design and manage an organization is through a rational-legal authority system, or *bureaucracy*. The key requirements include division of labor, clear specification of roles, a hierarchical (military-like) authority structure, explicit rules and regulations, and assignment of people to positions based on *merit* rather than social position, charisma, nepotism, or political clout (the chief ways in which people landed good jobs at the time).

Though very similar to the prescriptions set forth by Fayol, Taylor, and the others, Weber's views were based on scholarly philosophical argument and historical analysis rather than sheer practical experience (Weber, 1946). Thus, when social science became embroiled in issues of organization and management, Weber's arguments gave scholarly credibility to the classical philosophy.

Weber saw in the bureaucratic form a number of advantages, such as fairness and efficiency, that alternative organizing schemes lacked. It is ironic that these are the very criteria for which modern bureaucracies are most vigorously criticized. To most of us, the very word "bureaucracy" has come to mean red tape, waste, and mediocrity, the direct opposite of the efficiency and fairness Weber had in mind. Thus it is important to distinguish the concept, as envisioned by Weber, from the way the concept has often been implemented. Perrow (1986) reminds us that despite its imperfections, and the prediction by its midcentury critics that its days were numbered (Bennis, 1966), bureaucracy has not only survived, it has outlived all the competition. It stands today as the dominant form in both capitalistic and socialistic industrialized societies.

**Barnard's Cooperative Systems View**  Chester Barnard was an executive with extensive experience in both public and private sector management. Yet unlike the early classicists, his views were shaped as much by the emerging work of social scientists (e.g., see p. 142 for a discussion of the Hawthorne studies and human relations theorists) as by personal experience. In fact, his principal contribution was the attempt to reconcile the contradictory classical and human relations views through his concept of *natural cooperation*. For Barnard (1938), the essence of organization is the existence of a shared goal or *purpose*. Every member of the organization, whatever his or her role or position, owes allegiance to that goal, for unless they put it above sheer personal goals, the organization is unlikely to survive. And a defunct organization has little to offer society or its members. A basketball team exists primarily to win games; a business, to make a profit; a government, to serve its public. If the members are preoccupied with scoring points, amassing personal wealth, or achieving political power to the detriment of the shared objective, no one wins. While this is consistent with the classical position, an organization cannot survive if it fails to recognize the needs of its members— goals that are often in direct conflict with the shared purpose. Moreover, formal authority is of little value unless those to whom it is applied choose to accept it. Disgruntled workers can restrict production, engage in sabotage, or simply quit. It is the organization's responsibility, therefore, to give individuals a fair return on their personal investment in terms that matter to them. In so doing, it ensures their compliance. It is management's responsibility to "sell" subordinates on the collective purpose and to help them see their stake in it. The college coach must convince her recruits, all of whom were star point scorers in high school, that they must pass off more often and concentrate on defense if they are to be winners at the college level.

Recognizing that employees must be willing participants in the joint enterprise rather than mere pawns in management's grand scheme, and that management's job is to see that it happens, is consistent with the human relations view. Barnard did not, however, discount the importance of formal structure as did many human relations theorists. In fact, he saw structure as essential to the achievement of collective goals. The college coach cannot win solely by getting her players to adopt a team orientation and by treating them as human beings: She must also have rules, the power to enforce them, and an overall concept of how individuals can work together. The key point in Barnard's theory, therefore, is that all facets of an organization (individual and social, formal and informal) must be directed toward *cooperation* in pursuit of a common goal. In essence, both workers and managers take their orders from the requirements of the situation. It is easy to see how such thinking would lead eventually to an open-system perspective.

**Contingency Theory**   Simply stated, the contingency concept holds that how one should organize and manage depends on the circumstances. No single strategy will work under all sets of internal and external conditions. This clearly implies an open-system perspective in that it recognizes the importance of the organizational *environment* (broadly or narrowly defined). It also suggests that putting theory into practice requires identifying what the alternative organizing strategies are, what the determining conditions are, and how the two should be matched.

A number of models following this logic have appeared, at the OB as well as the OT level of analysis. For instance, the Lawrence and Lorsch version cited in Table 1.4 is a rational model that prescribes different structural solutions for specified internal and external demands. The primary consideration in both cases is the *uncertainty* facing the organization (Galbraith, 1977). If external conditions (e.g., labor costs, foreign competition, market preferences, or government regulation) are relatively stable and predictable (low in uncertainty), the efficiencies inherent in rational planning and formal structure have a good chance to pay off. When the environment is "turbulent," however, and such critical conditions are unpredictable (high in uncertainty), the built-in rigidity of a classic bureaucracy becomes a severe handicap. What is needed instead is the ability to react quickly to transient opportunities and shifting demands, an ability that calls for a more fluid structure and less centralized (i.e., less "top-down") control of decision making.

Important contingencies are not limited, however, to the external environment. Uncertainty can also arise from *internal* conditions, and the organization must find ways to cope with these as well. Consider the basic concepts of division of labor and specialization that exist in virtually all modern organizations. Whenever you divide up work among people, you create uncertainty: Each person knows less about the total process and what the others are doing than if he or she performed the entire job alone. Add to that the condition that each person must be a specialist, and the level of mutual understanding declines even further. Lawrence and Lorsch (1969) used the term *differentiation* to denote this conceptual separation. Galbraith (1977) included it among his sources of uncertainty. By clearly differentiating roles and functions within the organization and reinforcing these differences with a formal authority system, classical bureaucracy tends to promote differentiation. Managers and workers occupy different worlds; accountants and engineers speak different languages. Hence, to operate smoothly as a unit, the organization must use what Lawrence and Lorsch call *integrating* mechanisms to pull everyone together. The more differentiation you have, the more integration you need.

Classical bureaucracy relied primarily on formal communication and structured authority, plus the common language of rules and procedures, for integration. But these have their limitations. Human relationists, on the other hand, saw informal social relations, meaningful work units, and participative management as the way to integrate. But these, too, have their limitations. Contingency theory suggests that a whole host of integrating mechanisms can be used, from pure structural to pure human relations techniques. Which and how much of each are needed depend on the amount and kind of differentiation. The classical mechanisms may suffice if the workforce is largely uneducated and plentiful, the work is routine, and nothing much changes (e.g., under the low uncertainty conditions of yesterday's workplace). As the work and the workers become more complicated—as with today's higher technologies and education requirements—classical mechanisms quickly become overwhelmed, and more powerful mechanisms such as participative management must be brought into play.

Virtually all modern organization theories have a contingency as well as an open-system perspective. The ones classified in Table 1.4 in the rational-structural category (e.g., Lawrence and Lorsch) are there because of their emphasis on design: the assumption that even though *one* structure does not fit all, *some* structure is right for each set of conditions. Those classified in the natural category differ chiefly in their emphasis on description versus prescription.

**Decision Theories**   One set of ideas that merits special attention is the partly economic, partly psychological view of organizations as *decision-making* entities. Classical economic theory assumes that both individuals and organizations are rational economic entities that make informed choices aimed at maximizing the benefit to them. They act consistently in accordance with their preferences which, in the long run, yield them more of what they want (profit, salary, power) than would any other choices they might have made. In short, people and organizations act to *optimize* personal gain: They are rational, goal-oriented decision makers.

In contrast to this traditional view, a school of thought championed by Herbert Simon, a Nobel-prize–winning psychologist–economist, and James March, an organization theorist, argued that neither people nor organizations make strictly rational decisions (Cyert & March, 1963; March & Simon, 1958). For one thing, they have limited information-handling capability; for another, they have only a vague sense of what they really want. Hence, our decision behavior is guided more by the *adequacy of the option before us* than by whether it is the *best of all available options*. We "satisfice" rather than "optimize," to use Simon's (1957) terms. Moreover, when we operate within an organization our options are shaped by subtle social forces so we are offered even less opportunity to make choices strictly in our own best interests. We act, at best, with what Simon (1957) called "bounded rationality."

For its part, the organization behaves even less like a rational, goal-directed entity than individuals do. Composed of a host of individual and collective goals, many in direct conflict with each other, it functions as a loose, shifting coalition that makes do in the present rather than following a charted course to some future goal. When it succeeds, it does so by incremental improvements over its present condition, not by systematic pursuit of a well-defined objective.

March and Simon's (1958) view suggests, among other things, that a person must understand human cognition, motivation, and influence mechanisms to manage effectively. Moreover, designing organizations to function optimally in a rational sense, though perhaps a useful exercise for other reasons, cannot begin to achieve the hoped-for results. Decision theory appears in Table 1.4 under the social-psychological level of analysis. It is included in three of the model categories because it evolved over time from the classical economic view (*Decision Making* in the table) into the *Bounded Rationality* position we have just described, and eventually into an even more open *Ambiguity and Choice* position. We will encounter decision theory in its different forms in the rest of this book.

**Sociotechnical Systems**    In essence, this type of theory is simply an elaboration on the contingency notion, the idea being that organizations are complex entities operating in an environment. They are sociotechnical because they involve people interacting with each other and with machines (technologies). Systems theories belong in the *open* category in Table 1.4 because they recognize the importance of the interactions with the environment. In fact, this general philosophy is often referred to as *open-system theory.* It is classified as structural in the table because it attempts to account for the behavior of the entire organization, not because it focuses on structural features alone.

In fact, by taking a big picture view of organizations and including the contingency notion (that everything depends on everything else), open-system theory makes a place for individuals, groups, technologies, and environments as well as structure. Thus it serves as a useful perspective from which to view other I/O topics. Its essential features are illustrated in Figure 1.1 for an industrial concern, but the general ideas apply to any organization. As this diagram shows, the central mission of the organization is transforming some inputs, such as labor, materials, and capital, into outputs, such as products or services, for distribution to its customers. The resources it gains from this transaction (e.g., revenues) are applied to outside agencies to replenish the input required for the next cycle. In addition, resources may be needed to protect the organization from outside disturbances such as unwanted government controls (lobbying), loss of customers to the competition (consumer research, advertising), or a striking labor union (legal expertise, arbitration).

If you imagine a boundary drawn around the three boxes representing input, processing, and output in Figure 1.1, you can appreciate the *open-closed* distinction. Closed systems ignore everything outside the boundary; open systems not only recognize what is out there, they adapt to it internally. If the customer base, or labor market, or prime interest rate changes, or the government introduces a new environmental regulation, the system knows about it and responds. In fact, it attempts to anticipate the changes so as to respond early enough to cushion or avert the blow. For example, an auto manufacturer might conduct market surveys to determine how potential buyers (customers) would like a proposed change in the design of its automobiles. If the results indicated a strong negative reaction, the company might think twice before implementing it, thereby avoiding a costly mistake.

It is important to recognize that the boundary separating the system from its environment is more than just the physical limits within which it operates. A boundary can have symbolic, cultural, and psychological features as well. For instance, political action groups such as Mothers Against Drunk Driving (MADD) or anti-abortionists (right-to-life movement) are *primarily* distinguished by these conceptual boundaries, which they work constantly to expand.

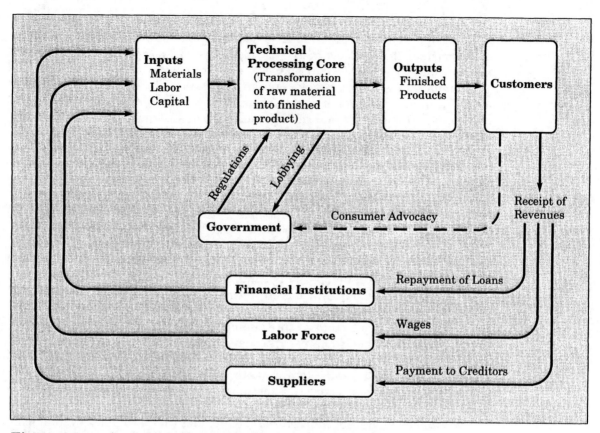

**Figure 1.1**    *An industrial organization as an open system*

*Source:* Robbins, S.P. (1990). *Organization Theory: The Structure and Design of Organizations.* 3rd ed., Englewood Cliffs, NJ: Prentice-Hall.

Open systems have a number of key characteristics besides the transformation of inputs into outputs and the spanning of boundaries. One characteristic that is similar to the contingency notion is *interdependency;* everything depends on and affects everything else. The environment affects and is affected by the system; internal components affect one another. If a firm changes its technology in response to foreign competition, for example, it may need to change the size and composition of its workforce, its job descriptions, its compensation schedules, its management structure, and a host of other internal characteristics to continue functioning effectively. Moreover, its relations with outside entities such as labor unions may be affected.

Another set of features characteristic of open systems involves stability. A *completely* closed system would run down over time because it would eventually use up its supply of energy and other resources imported from the outside. According to open-system theory, a system must actually import *more* of these critical resources than it outputs to have the wherewithal to repair itself, gather critical information, and exploit opportunities when they present themselves. In other words, the natural tendency for any system is to decline and die; active effort is necessary to maintain a steady state or even consider the prospect of growth. Your car will not go far without gas or last indefinitely without maintenance.

An organization that seeks only to maintain a steady state (i.e., avoid a slow death) also has dim prospects because it can only protect against what it can control (mainly, its internal elements). Thus, it may survive when the environment is calm, but not when things become turbulent—the point made by Lawrence and Lorsch (1969). It must, therefore, continually balance two sets of forces that are often in conflict: external pressures to change and internal pressures to maintain stability. Classical theory focused on the latter objective; other types of theories, including some which we will not discuss, such as *environmental* and *developmental* theories, focused on the need to keep changing. Open-system theory incorporates both sets of concerns by recognizing the full complexity of these forces and the importance of trying to balance them. It emphasizes the importance of keeping both internal and external forces within limits—satisficing, if not optimizing, the balance.

To make this point in concrete terms, a company cannot squander its resources on reorganization every time there is a shift in some outside condition: This would produce total internal chaos. On the other hand, it cannot afford to dig in its heels against internal change in the face of major outside trends such as the U.S. auto industry faced in the growth of competition from Japan. It may be *necessary* to automate some jobs, lay some employees off, change the management structure, or adopt a new marketing strategy to keep from being overwhelmed by events.

A final open-system characteristic is the fact that a complex system usually has many routes to any stated objective. The principle is called *equifinality,* a fancy name for the simple idea that there are many ways to skin a cat. But in practice it is a powerful idea because it dictates against the all-too-common tendency on the part of theorists, consultants, and managers to frame problems in very narrow terms. Classicists considered only structural options; human relationists, only humanistic options; economic theorists, only rationally based options; leadership theorists, only interpersonal influence options; many managers, only intuitively appealing options. Open-system theory suggests that *all* the perspectives—micro and macro, rational and descriptive, internally and externally focused—hold potential solutions.

## THE SOCIETAL CONTEXT

The most important feature of the open-system model is the recognition that no organization is an island. No matter how big, rich, or well designed it is, or how well it treats its people and manages its internal affairs, it will not survive long unless it is closely attuned to what is going on outside.

Failure to appreciate this fact was a principal weakness of both classical and humanistic theories of organization, and it remains a leading cause of death among failed organizations. W.T. Grant Company, a once-flourishing national retail store chain, is a classic case in point (Higgins, 1983). In the early 1970s it was among the top 20 U.S. retailers and still growing, yet by 1975 it had filed for bankruptcy. There were probably many reasons for its rapid demise, but among those often cited was the failure to read two key aspects of its environment properly: its customers and its competitors. Some competitors, such as Sears, cultivated a full-service image, while others, such as K-Mart, grew rapidly as discounters. W.T. Grant failed to establish either image, confused its customers, and lost business to both kinds of competitors. Rather than developing a marketing strategy to cope with these trends, it simply chose to get bigger and eventually died of its own weight.

The plight of the thrift industry (savings and loan institutions) in the late 1980s is another dramatic illustration. Aggressive lending practices based on the assumption that real estate values and income-producing interest rates would never seriously decline, coupled with the government's failure to police these practices adequately, led to huge profits, corruption, and eventually a national disaster. The economic environment changed, and virtually the entire industry was caught unprepared—in some cases, with a hand in the till.

Clearly, therefore, the societal context must be considered to understand or manage any organization. Societal events—economic, political, attitudinal—affect the organization's people directly as well as indirectly through what happens to the employer. Each of us is paying dearly for the thrift fiasco: The cost to American taxpayers will exceed $325 billion (*San Antonio Light,* 1990). But the human costs in terms of career uncertainty, lost jobs, and general anxiety borne by the thrift employees and the public is incalculable.

Thus I/O psychology has plenty of reason to concern itself with societal events, whether they are as broad as world geopolitics or as narrow as an organization's local economy. The field has contributed in a few important areas such as advancing the cause of fair employment practices and softening the blow of organizational upheaval from mergers, hostile takeovers, downsizing, and labor disputes (Moses, 1990; Stagner, 1982). But on the whole, I/O psychology has been slow to recognize the implications of societal change for its own agenda. It has generally waited until organizational problems have actually surfaced before getting involved rather than anticipating them and trying to minimize their impact (Offerman & Gowing, 1990). For example, I/O psychology had little to do with organized labor during its period of ascendancy and has had little to do with it in its current period of decline, despite the fact that labor unions critically affect millions of workers in their day-to-day lives. Certainly the opportunity has existed for the field to make more of a contribution to labor relations than it has (Nord, 1980).

This part of the chapter, therefore, is about the *potential* as much as the *actual* impact of the societal context on I/O psychology. It begins with a look at some critical events that shaped the field, then explores a sampling of current issues that bear watching.

### The Early Years (1900–1929)

During this period, American industry was enjoying the combined benefits of a host of positive business conditions. Technological innovations such as mass production, seemingly unlimited natural resources, a plentiful supply of cheap labor immigrating from Europe, strong government support, expanding markets, and a social climate that lionized material success: All the ingredients for rapid growth and prosperity were in place. The great American experiment was working! Evolving business organizations, like the country itself, saw themselves as virtually invulnerable to outside forces. If a firm, or an individual for that matter, did not succeed, only it (or he) was to blame. Initiative and growth could overcome virtually any obstacle that might arise.

Against this kind of background, it is easy to see why efficiency-oriented, inward-looking philosophies such as the classical management principles and

Classical management theory and scientific management took hold early in the twentieth century when industry enjoyed the benefits of mass production and a plentiful supply of cheap labor.

scientific management took hold. It is also easy to understand why industrial psychology began as it did, and why the World War I demonstration of mental testing attracted industry's attention. Labor, after all, was just a commodity necessary for doing business, like capital and raw materials. But in the labor-intensive factories of the era, it was a primary cost factor and the most uncertain component in the production process. Anything one could do to improve human reliability, interchangeability, and work output, therefore, would have a profound impact on profitability. The principles of work standardization and simplification coupled with tight management control obviously made sense. And the prospect of being able to weed out the most incompetent or unreliable workers in advance through simple paper-and-pencil testing, particularly in the more highly paid skilled jobs, was equally attractive. Management theory, scientific management, and industrial psychology provided tools for lowering unit production costs just as surely as new machinery did.

What managers failed to realize at the time, of course, was that the success of these tools in controlling labor costs was heavily dependent on the existing conditions, such as the labor supply, low skill requirements, government support, and public confidence. More importantly, no one expected the situation to change—except for the better. Our industrial growth was simply too big and too strong, they thought, to be significantly affected by *anything*. Even the evolving threat of organized labor seemed manageable. Where necessary, private armies could be hired to prevent unions from forming, and if that failed, union members could be brought into line by threat of dismissal. If a strike still occurred, striking workers could simply be replaced. Were some do-gooding politician or newspaper editor to take issue with these methods, as some did, that too could be handled by the proper application of money or pressure in the right places—notably to the politician's sources of funding or the newspaper's ownership. In short, there was little apparent reason to worry about societal change, and the only real issue in managing people was ensuring that their humanness interfered as little as possible with their output.

The financial crash of 1929 followed by the depression of the 1930s shattered both of these myths together with the national spirit of rugged individualism and self-confidence. The suspicion arose and spread that perhaps unfettered capitalism is not the answer to all organizational and social problems. Clearly there must be forces at work in society powerful enough to bring down even the biggest and strongest. Our society began to recognize that neither individuals nor organizations are the complete masters of their fate.

## The Depression Years (1930–1939)

The Great Depression of the 1930s was a worldwide economic phenomenon that led to a host of societal changes, most of which are beyond the scope of this book. For example, it undoubtedly contributed to conditions in Germany that culminated in the next epoch-making event, World War II. Further, it reinforced the growing recognition that for all its success, the U.S. is not immune from foreign influence. This, unfortunately, has remained a difficult lesson for Americans to learn even as we approach the twenty-first century.

For present purposes, it is sufficient to mention some direct consequences of the depression for corporate America in the 1930s. First, government influence became much stronger, becoming a force to be reckoned with in business decision making, including union-management relations and internal personnel management policy. President Franklin D. Roosevelt's sweeping reform programs (the National Recovery Act, his reshaping of the Supreme Court, the New Deal, etc.), put serious restrictions on the free enterprise system and created a favorable climate for organized labor. During the 1930s union membership grew to nearly 30% of the nonagricultural workforce (Kochan & Barocci, 1985). No longer could management dominate labor-management relations as it had in the past.

Second, public support for these government programs signaled a dramatic shift in society's attitudes. For the first time the public could identify with the plight of the downtrodden worker. Because misfortune had touched everyone, it was no longer limited to what society perceived as the ignorant, the lazy, and the largely "foreign element" that dominated the working class (who in society's view probably *deserved* mistreatment). Certainly not everyone was to blame for their current state of poverty and joblessness. Corporate greed and abuses became an alternative explanation, and sentiment shifted from supreme confidence in big business to distrust and a plea for government intervention.

Finally, while massive unemployment did nothing to hurt their favorable labor market, organizations began to feel pressure from a variety of sources to shoulder more responsibility for employee welfare. In addition to the social and government pressures that we just discussed, social science began to receive some attention. For example, the Hawthorne studies, which began in the euphoric 1920s as a search for ways to increase worker output, concluded in the depressed 1930s that management should recognize workers as human and treat them accordingly. Scholars of organization and management such as Chester Barnard began to look upon the worker-employer relationship as a bargain between equally valid self-interests, both subsumed under the larger purpose of the organization.

Corporate America, of course, was largely oblivious to such intellectual discussion. What it did for workers it did largely because the new labor laws and the growing muscle of unionism forced it to, not because of the egg-headed human relations argument that it was somehow a good idea (and maybe, in some larger sense, the *right* thing to do). As for industrial psychology, it was, if anywhere, in management's camp.

## World War II and the Postwar Years (1940–1959)

We have already discussed the effect of World War II on psychology and how psychology proved itself in new applied arenas. The postwar period ushered in a sustained economic boom that was to extend, with minor fluctuations, over most of the next three decades. The birth rate, which had been depressed during the 1930s, rebounded dramatically (the so-called baby boom). Labor unions continued to grow in membership and influence and the nation's standard of living became the envy of the world (Kochan & Barocci, 1985).

Buoyed by our military success, yet conscious of the devastation that the war had wrought on friend and foe alike, the old spirit of self-confidence returned, together with a healthy sense of compassion. Our society at long last was forced to accept the fact that the United States is indeed a major player on the stage of world events. Isolationism, the idea that America could do nicely without the rest of the world and should not meddle in its affairs, was prevalent before the war but was overwhelmed by subsequent events. Comprehensive economic aid plans for war-torn Asia and Europe were implemented by our government and supported enthusiastically by the public. Undoubtedly, forward-looking business leaders also realized that such restoration represented an initial step toward opening vast new markets for their wares, although this was of little immediate consequence given the pent-up demand for goods and services at home. What even the most enlightened failed to anticipate was that the restoration of Japan and Western Europe would also bring serious *competition,* not just in foreign markets, but right in our own back yard.

Among the most significant of all the consequences of the war was the economic and political division of the world along capitalistic-communistic lines, the emergence of the Soviet Union as a superpower, and the threat of nuclear war. For the next 45 years the cold war isolated Eastern from Western societies and created on both sides a sustained atmosphere of fear, political competition, and military escalation. Military spending became a dominant force in the economies of both the U.S. and U.S.S.R., as President Dwight Eisenhower foresaw when he warned in his farewell address against uncontrolled "growth in the military-industrial complex." Psychological research was a beneficiary of this spending as the military services sought behavioral means to improve the effectiveness of fighting forces.

During this postwar era, formal education in business management also experienced rapid growth. Undergraduate and graduate degree programs became an increasingly common route to management careers, replacing the prewar model of rising through the ranks. While business school curricula did not typically feature them, the radical new ideas on management arising out of the human relations movement were included in some courses. Thus, many formally educated managers were at least aware of them, and in a few notable cases, companies were persuaded to change their entire approach to management as a result.

Rensis Likert, a University of Michigan professor and social psychologist, was among the most influential change agents of the era. An essential component of his theory was that better performance will result if the whole organization moves toward a more open, participative system in which employees are allowed to become involved in important decisions (see Chapter the management style of a failing textile manufacturer, the Weldon Company. Although various explanations have been offered for what happened at Weldon, its profitability did improve and the increased supportiveness and participation of management were widely cited as reasons (Likert, 1961; Marrow, Bowers, & Seashore, 1967). Consequently, both Likert and his theory received a lot of attention. In fact, a play based on this case, *The Pajama Game,* became a major Broadway hit!

We see in this era, then, the beginnings of serious research on the social psychology of organizations and some isolated applications in the management of Western-block firms. The groundwork was laid for what was to become organizational psychology and the field of OB.

## The Chaotic Period (1960–1979)

During these two decades change was the norm in our society. Large numbers of baby boomers entered early adulthood, society finally was forced to come to grips with its discriminatory treatment of minorities and women, the nation became embroiled in a prolonged military conflict in Viet Nam from which we have yet to completely recover, and foreign competition began to make significant inroads into our unchallenged leadership as supplier of the world's manufactured goods. In general, it was a period of sustained prosperity in the United States, yet the contrast between the "haves" and "have nots" was never more visible. Furthermore, the economic foundation that was supporting our relative affluence was beginning to erode. By the late 1970s, inflation rates had reached nearly 14% and the growth in productivity that we had come to take for granted had declined to zero (Kochan & Barocci, 1985).

And most disturbingly of all, a society that prided itself on its orderly, civilized institutions of governance and justice suddenly found itself replacing leaders through assassination and forcing change through violent protest. The whole fabric of our society seemed to be coming apart at the seams. Violent disagreement over the Viet Nam War, civil rights, economic policy, environmental policy, consumer affairs, and many other issues split our society into polarized factions. Among the most vocal were the baby boomers, who forced the nation to take a good, hard look at its collective values.

The implications of all this for organizations and I/O psychology were profound. The prevailing attitude among young people about to enter the workforce was that our institutions in general, and profit-making organizations in particular, were suspect—even immoral. They saw them as part of the establishment that gave us war, poverty, discrimination, and pollution purely to satisfy its own selfish motives. Many of these young people dropped out of school, the workforce, and modern society. Companies found recruiting very difficult, and the young people they were able to attract were difficult to assimilate into the traditional corporate culture. This new breed of employees had its own ideas about personal appearance, lifestyle, and corporate values. They tended to question authority. It was not an easy time for managers raised in the classical tradition.

Other longstanding traditions were challenged as well, such as the organization's prerogative to hire, promote, and fire whomever it wished. Out of the turmoil came a mass of legislation and case law on civil rights, and a federal agency, the Equal Employment Opportunity Commission (EEOC), to implement it. Companies were forced to break old patterns of discrimination against women and minorities, although in most cases not without considerable resistance.

As the end of the era approached, new problems began to surface. An embargo in the Middle East shocked our society into the realization that the United States had become dependent on foreign governments, many of them unstable at best, for its most vital source of energy: oil. Gasoline shortages, dramatic increases in the price of everything related to energy (gasoline, electricity, heating oil, manufactured products, etc.), and the search for alternative sources of energy became issues of the highest national priority. Moreover, the energy crisis exacerbated a worsening economic trend that saw our inflation growing, our productivity declining, our national debt soaring, and our balance of payments (value of exports over imports) becoming negative. We were about to relinquish our position as the world's largest lender nation to become the world's largest debtor nation. The era of prosperity was clearly headed for trouble.

Not surprisingly, the management philosophies and personnel management techniques that had earlier been dismissed as impractical resurfaced under these chaotic circumstances. The climate was right for organizations to consider new ways of managing their affairs. In many instances they had no choice. The new generation of employees, civil rights laws, declining productivity, and foreign competition were the new realities; something had to be done.

Frequently, that something turned out to be a contribution from disciplines like OT, OB, or I/O psychology. Thus, we saw industrial psychology broaden its base to include the organizational component. In addition, its longstanding interest in individual differences, selection, and other HRM tools turned out to be extremely valuable for implementing the new fair employment laws. Psychologists began to more precisely define the difficult concepts involved in "fairness" (see Chapter 12). The core idea was that tools such as tests used in making personnel decisions (hiring, promoting, firing) should be proven valid for their intended purpose. People should be selected on the basis of their aptitude for doing the job rather than for spurious reasons such as race, sex, or age. Describing job requirements and validating selection procedures had always been the industrial psychologist's stock in trade, so I/O psychology quickly became relevant. It has remained a major contributor to fair employment practices ever since.

### The Reagan/Bush Years (1980–1992)

In response to the growing socio-economic problems of the late 1970s, a national shift toward political conservatism ushered in the 1980s. Its symbol,

Ronald Reagan, rode into the office of president on a popular mandate to reduce inflation, strengthen our military posture, and eliminate the federal budget deficit (the national debt), all while reducing taxes. The man who was to become his vice president and succeed him in office, George Bush, initially labeled this approach "voodoo economics." Others called it "Reaganomics."

The plan to accomplish this feat was based on the premise that federal spending for nonmilitary purposes (primarily social programs) and government bureaucracy had gotten out of hand. Get government off the backs of industry, the argument ran, and you will stimulate investment, productivity, and a reversal in the entire cycle that was strangling our economic growth. The relative merits of this supply-side or trickle-down philosophy and its role in subsequent events will probably be debated for years to come. But some of the events that happened during this period unquestionably affected I/O psychology. Many social programs *were* cut, and military spending *did* increase along with military strength. Corporations *did* receive some tax relief, and there *was* some improvement in the productivity statistics. Inflation dropped from nearly 14% in 1979 to a low 3.9% in 1982. The size of government did not shrink, however, and the size of the budget deficit continued to grow. Moreover, national unemployment rose from 5.8% in 1979 to 9.7% by 1982 (Kochan & Barocci, 1985).

Most important of all, a systematic effort was initiated to undo or weaken many of the federal regulations and controls that had been put in place during the previous era to promote and enforce civil rights, fair employment practices, energy conservation, pollution control, and other organizational abuses. Federal court appointments were made in support of this conservative philosophy just as they had been made in support of FDR's liberal policies a half-century earlier.

The full implications of these developments are still being sorted out (Offerman & Gowing, 1990; Skrycki, 1989). One development, the stimulation of a frenzy of corporate mergers, takeovers, and buy-outs, primarily benefited the financial middle-people and attorneys. For the organizations involved and the individuals comprising them, the outcome was generally severe trauma. For the public, this development meant what it always means: higher prices and taxes. In any case, the need for OD consultants grew substantially (see Chapter 5 for a discussion of OD), and with it, the market for this kind of I/O psychologist. In addition, downsizing created a need for greater attention to all aspects of *human resource planning,* and this too has become a growth area (Greenhalgh, Lawrence, & Sutton, 1988; Jackson & Schuler, 1990).

Another outcome was a general decline in the I/O activities associated with fair employment practices legislation, a trend that is still apparent. The boom industry in test validation and compensation fairness seems to have waned during these years as the result of less aggressive enforcement by the federal government of civil rights laws and the appointment of more conservative judges to federal courts. Rising concerns over what appeared to be lack of progress in civil rights led to the passage of the Civil Rights Act of 1991 and the Americans With Disability Act of 1990. Whether these new acts lead to

Increasing computerization and greater diversity of the work force are among the changes occurring in the workplace that will challenge both scientists and practitioners in I/O psychology.

increased activity by I/O psychologists in the area of fair employment practices remains to be seen.

One final development during the era was the coming of age of computer technology in the workplace. Almost overnight, the computerized check-out counter became a standard retail store fixture and the computer workstation replaced the typewriter on every secretary's desk. The full impact of this trend is yet to be realized (Moses, 1990; Turnage, 1990).

## Transition to the 21st Century

The 1992 election reflected another dramatic shift in America's political mood. Bill Clinton, the first "baby boomer" to hold the office, was elected president chiefly because the voters were convinced that the government was not coping effectively with the nation's deepening economic and social problems. They demanded change in a loud voice, nearly 20 million of them voting for a candidate, Ross Perot, who had never held public office and represented neither political party. Sensing the mood, a record number of congressional incumbents chose not even to run for reelection.

It remains to be seen what direction the new government will take in trying to overcome the myriad problems. A massive national debt, deteriorating public education and health-care systems, the ever-increasing blight of crime and drug abuse and poverty, the continuing difficulty of competing in a world economy, the proliferating military and economic and humanitarian demands of developing third-world and former Eastern-block nations, the

AIDS epidemic, rapid technological change and its implications for the work-place: the list is virtually endless.

Psychology in general, and I/O psychology in particular, have important contributions to make in each of these problem areas. How much of this potential will be realized, however, remains unclear because neither government nor the public have tended to view such problems in behavioral or psychological terms. For example, the deficit is partly a productivity problem. Much of this text is devoted to techniques that affect *productivity,* yet few see the deficit in anything but *economic* terms. The most effective approach to combatting AIDS is prevention, which requires behavioral and psychological interventions, yet few see it as anything but a *medical* problem. As with other health problems, the research dollars spent in search of biomedical "cures" dwarfs those invested in behavioral and psychological (preventative) studies.

Lack of public awareness of and support for psychology's potential contributions in these areas is a chronic problem arising from a general misperception of the field (which most people equate with psychotherapy). This is due, at least in part, to a reluctance by research psychologists to promote the practical relevance of their work. By all indications, however, the field is waking up to the fact that it is not only in its best interest, but also its social *responsibility,* to be more proactive.

To this end, a conference of some 70 behavioral science organizations was convened in 1990 to develop a national research agenda focused on behavioral science applications to specific social problems. The upshot of this conference, a research planning and advocacy project dubbed the *Human Capital Initiative,* targets six broad problem areas for special attention: worker productivity, schooling and literacy, the aging society, drug and alcohol abuse, mental and physical health, and violence. Obviously, I/O psychology has an important role to play in this initiative. Equally as important, it may well provide the impetus for I/O psychology to expand its horizons beyond its traditional management-oriented perspective.

## CONCLUSIONS

We have covered a lot of ground in our search for the meaning of I/O psychology. We started by looking at its practitioners and found them to be a diverse lot—educators, researchers, consultants, and technical specialists who perform a variety of OD and HRM functions for management in virtually every kind of organization. What binds them together and distinguishes them from others who fill similar roles is their grounding in the specialized knowledge, methods, institutions, and culture of psychology. Because methods and knowledge come later in the book, we zeroed in on I/O's cultural and institutional background to discover how psychology grew from a handful of academic scientists into a huge, multifaceted profession in less than a century. We explored the stresses and strains that have accompanied this growth, notably science versus practice and health-care versus nonhealth-care issues, and saw how I/O's commitment to a scientist–practitioner philosophy has helped define its niche in the overall picture of modern psychology.

To other kinds of psychologists the most unique thing about I/O psychology is its workplace connection, so we were obliged to retrace our steps to find out what is so special about this context. We discovered that psychology has collaborated with other social scientists and management specialists for nearly a half century to understand how organizations work and how to run them better. The I/O psychologists have played a leading role in one new discipline, OB, which focuses on individual and group processes, and a significant but diminishing role in OT, which takes a more macro view. Through these disciplines and the perspective of the practicing manager, which is often at variance with either scientific perspective, the I/O psychologist comes to understand the issues that require attention. He or she also has the opportunity to help define and address future issues, although I/O psychologists have been slow to accept this challenge. To understand the scope of these issues and the three main perspectives on them (OB, OT, and practicing manager), we traced the development of a few influential philosophies as represented in the classical, human relations, bureaucracy, cooperative systems, contingency, decision, and open-systems theories.

Modern thinking, we discovered, is dominated by the open-systems view, which recognizes the critical importance of the social-political-cultural-economic-technical environment in which the organization operates. This discovery sent us on a chronological tour in search of societal conditions that helped to shape (and be shaped by) the evolution of work organizations in the twentieth century. Signs of I/O psychology were found mainly in the latter half of the century as environmental turbulence forced employers to cope with an alarming array of new problems. As we approach the present and look to the future, we will see that the role of I/O psychologist is in transition from technician/analyst to change agent/strategist (London & Moses, 1990).

## DISCUSSION QUESTIONS

1. What do we mean when we say that I/O psychology attempts to adhere to a scientist–practitioner model?
2. Which of the topics in the table of contents of this book would be most relevant to HRM practitioners? Which would be most relevant to OD practitioners?
3. How would you go about evaluating the competence of an I/O psychologist who is attempting to sell his or her consulting services?
4. Describe the key attributes on which the various organizational theories can be compared and contrasted.
5. Organizational theory has evolved in the direction of open-system perspectives. What societal changes have influenced this shift?
6. How have societal events over this century shaped the field of I/O psychology?

# CHAPTER

2

# I/O Psychology as a Science

- Distinguishing Science from Nonscience

- The Scientific Method

- Ethics of I/O Research

- The Academic Model versus Practical Realities

- Case: In Search of Excellence

In Chapter 1, I/O psychology was described as a discipline concerned with the behavior of people in work settings, and the scientific method was described as the means of acquiring knowledge of behavior at work. This chapter examines the essential aspects of scientific research as it is conducted in I/O psychology. But why should you be concerned about this topic? Although you may never conduct a study, one day you will be a consumer of research on human psychology in the workplace. You will read articles and watch TV shows that offer advice on how to choose a job, interview, deal with your boss, and survive in the world of work. You may even encounter one of the growing number of consultants who use the old "science has found" routine to peddle their wares. In this chapter we hope to help you distinguish between truth and the many half-truths and shams by examining the differences between scientific and nonscientific research and the standards against which scientific research should be judged.

# DISTINGUISHING SCIENCE FROM NONSCIENCE

A basic message of this text is that scientific research should be used when attempting to understand and predict human behavior in organizations. It is important to realize, however, that there are many alternative sources of knowledge, such as personal experience, observations of others, authority, logic, intuition, and analogy. So that you will have some understanding of what the scientific approach to understanding organizations entails, let us first devote some attention to what it is *not*.

## Nonscientific Sources of Knowing

Perhaps the most common source of knowledge and the most influential is *personal experience*. Managers acquire a sense of what works and does not work from participating in the real world. There is a long history of corporate leaders who have offered advice on how to best run an organization. Several of these were mentioned in the last chapter (e.g., Henri Fayol, Chester Barnard). More contemporary examples of this genre of executives include Lee Iacocca, Ross Perot, Robert Townsend, Steven Jobs, and Sam Walton, all of whom have confidently drawn from their experiences to proclaim the right ways to manage.

Reliance on the personal experience of others presents us with another source of knowledge—*authority*. An individual may be relied upon because of fear, love, or respect, because of tradition, or because of that individual's past successes. Knowledge of how organizations should be run can also be derived from or dictated by religious authorities. Some managers may take the Christian dictim "Do unto others as you would have them do unto you" as a principle that guides their daily activities. Others might rely on the teachings of Buddha, Mohammed, Tao, or the Talmud for knowledge of organizations.

Closely related to authority is *intuition*. Managers often take a course of action because it feels right to them. Intuition also can come in the form of mysticism, altered states (drug or naturally induced), religious experiences, or inspiration. In all cases, the person arrives at some "truth" through "gut feelings" rather than through logic or factual information.

Very different from intuition is knowledge that is *logically deduced* from basic assumptions. Similar to a mathematician who starts with certain axioms and through rules of logic deduces mathematical statements, people may start with stated or unstated assumptions about organizations from which they logically derive what they consider to be true. For example, a manager may start with a universal belief that workers desire only money and are lazy. It would logically follow from this assumption that workers need to be closely supervised, that they should be offered only monetary incentives, and that no attempts should be made to seek their opinions or ideas.

Knowledge can be based on *analogy,* such as "A good manager is to an organization as a quarterback is to a football team." Books on organizations and management reveal a plethora of other analogies, including the manager as a Samurai warrior and as a Mafia boss.

Finally, there is the knowledge that comes from the values and norms that members of a society share and that constitute their *culture*. Members of an organization may come to see those beliefs that they hold in common as fact rather than mere preference. Take, for example, norms for how one should dress. There is no logical reason that an accountant should wear a suit to work as opposed to overalls, but social norms dictate that the former is more acceptable (see Chapter 5 for a further discussion of norms). Similarly, what are accepted as self-evident truths about organizations reflect to a significant degree what we are accustomed to doing. Differences in norms are particularly important if you compare different countries. In Japan, for example, the individual is considered more subordinate to the collective effort of the organization than in the United States, where there is a strong belief in individualism. Consequently, the wisdom of using groups and consensus decision making is more apparent in Japan than in the United States, where distrust in groups and reliance on the lone manager as hero prevails.

## Scientific Knowledge

All of the above are common ways in which people seek and acquire knowledge, but what are the defining characteristics of scientific knowledge? Unlike the above sources of knowledge, science is empirical, objective, concerned with understanding general principles, precise, probabilistic, and logical.

### SCIENCE IS EMPIRICAL

Perhaps the most important attribute of science is that it relies on observation of events rather than relying solely on logic, authority, or intuition. For instance, you might be curious about what workers want the most in a job. Rather than assuming or deducing some answer to this question, you could use the scientific approach to survey, observe, or in some other way gather data on employees' needs (see Chapter 3).

### SCIENCE IS OBJECTIVE

Science does not rely on personal experience or intuition but generates objective knowledge. Objective here means that different scientists can arrive at the same conclusions using the same methods. This requires that terms be carefully defined along with procedures used in gathering data. What if you observed that higher performance results from supervisory styles that are supportive and participative? While you are free to state observations and opinion, you cannot wear the mantle of science unless you state procedural details that will allow other I/O psychologists to repeat your study. This could include describing how supervisory style and performance were measured, the type of employees used, sampling procedures, and the statistical techniques that were used. In comparison, intuition and personal experience are often intensely personal and incapable of replication. For instance, Lee Iacocca and other executives may have profound insights, but their knowledge derives from their unique experiences.

### SCIENCE IS CONCERNED WITH UNDERSTANDING GENERAL PRINCIPLES

Industrial and organizational psychologists often attempt to understand what accounts for organizational events. Their ultimate concern, however, is not with what caused a specific event at a specific time (e.g., why did Wal-Mart perform so well last year or why did Fred, a manager at High Tech, Inc., fail in motivating his employees?) but with general principles that can be used to understand a wide variety of events (e.g., what are the factors that distinguish consistently successful firms from unsuccessful firms and successful managers from unsuccessful managers?).

### SCIENCE IS PRECISE

Industrial and organizational psychologists attempt to define their terms and collect their data in as *precise* a manner as possible. Consequently, measurement is a particularly important activity performed by I/O psychologists. It is not enough to distinguish satisfied from dissatisfied employees, or good performers from bad, for example, but measures must be developed that distinguish among *degrees* of satisfaction and performance.

### SCIENCE IS PROBABILISTIC

A hallmark of science is that it never states a truth with total confidence. In testing hypotheses, scientists never prove, but only fail to disprove. This is perhaps the aspect of science that is most frustrating to the layperson and to managers in particular. Managers often want unequivocal answers, and they want them fast. The scientist is prone to state conclusions in terms of probabilities, conditions, and hypotheses. Scientists of all types, including I/O psychologists, can sound like Tevye in the play *Fiddler on the Roof* who is forever agonizing over decisions as he recites "On the one hand . . . but on the other hand . . . ." Of course, I/O psychologists are no different than most good scientists who realize that science is a neverending process and that today's wisdom may be open to question tomorrow. In this sense, science is much different from other sources of knowledge that too often are marked by dogma, rigidity, and a complete unwillingness to revise in the face of facts.

### SCIENCE IS LOGICAL

Scientists are logical in at least two senses. First, they derive hypotheses from general principles using deductive logic. They then test these hypotheses through research and draw inferences using inductive logic. They rely on the tools of mathematics and logic, but unlike pure rationalists, scientists always test the products of their logic through observation.

# THE SCIENTIFIC METHOD

In acquiring knowledge about behavior in the workplace, I/O psychologists attempt to fulfill the criteria for what constitutes science. But a variety of approaches qualify as good science. We next describe how I/O psychologists conduct scientific research on behavior at work and the issues involved in this research.

## The Goals of Scientific Research

The three basic goals of science are description, prediction, and explanation (Kaplan, 1964). In the following sections we consider how I/O psychologists attempt to achieve each of these goals. First, however, we need to define several important terms that are central to scientific research and then describe some of the statistical tools that are used in the practice of science in I/O psychology.

## Some Basic Terms

I/O psychologists, like all scientists, operate at different levels of abstraction (Kerlinger, 1973). At the most concrete level they observe and record the events of organizational life. They seldom are content to deal with only observable data, however, and invariably use more abstract notions such as variables, constructs, and theories in their attempt to describe, predict, and explain human behavior in organizations.

A *variable* is an attribute or property that can assume different numerical values. In some cases the variables are inherently quantiative in that we can assign numbers to represent different levels or magnitudes. For instance, scores on a vocabulary test could be used to distinguish among different levels of verbal ability performance or scores on a job satisfaction scale could be used to measure degrees of satisfaction. Other variables such as gender, race, or social class are inherently qualitative in that there is no meaningful way to distinguish among different magnitudes or levels of the variable. Even these variables could be assigned numerical values for the purposes of research(e.g., male = 1, female = 2), although the values in these cases reflect the presence or absence of a property rather than "low" or "high."

A *construct* is a particular type of variable that is crucial to the explanation of human behavior in organizations and is inferred from observations of related events. According to Binning and Barrett (1989, p. 479), "Psychological constructs are labels for clusters of covarying behaviors. In this way, a virtually infinite number of behaviors is reduced to a system of fewer labels, which simplifies and economizes the exchange of information and facilitates the process of discovering behavioral regularities." We will encounter a variety of psychological constructs in future chapters, and in each case the construct is associated with a domain of behaviors that are believed to be interrelated. Thus, quantitative ability is used to summarize and explain the interrelationships among tests of addition, subtraction, multiplication, and division. Verbal ability is used to summarize and explain interrelationships among tests of reading, spelling, and vocabulary. Job performance is used to summarize and explain interrelationships among individual aspects of employee performance (e.g., quantity, quality, creativity). Job satisfaction is used to summarize and explain the interrelationships among expressed attitudes toward supervision, compensation, the work itself, coworkers, and other facets of the work.

A *theory* is a set of constructs and the interrelationships assumed to exist among those constructs (Selltiz, Wrightsman, & Cook, 1976, p. 16). Thus, we might have a theory that employees with high levels of verbal and quantitative ability perform at higher levels on the job than employees with low levels of these abilities. The theory in this case is defined by the set of constructs (verbal ability, quantitative ability, job performance) and their interrelationships (positive relationships between the abilities and performance). In subsequent chapters we describe many of the theories that have been set forth by I/O psychologists to describe behavior in organizations. Theory is often the source of the questions that guide research. In the so-called *deductive* approach, the researcher starts with a theory, deduces from this theory a specific statement of how variables related to the constructs will be related, and then gathers data to test the hypothesized relationships. Whether the theory is seen as accurate depends on whether the statements deduced from the theory are supported by the data. An opposite strategy of research is the so-called *inductive* approach. The researcher starts by gathering data and then derives a theory from the observed relationships. Even in the inductive approach the researcher is likely to have some prior notion of what constructs are important and their possible relationships. Whichever strategy is adopted, the ultimate objective of research in I/O psychology is to arrive at a theory that can be used in the description, explanation, and prediction of behavior in organizations.

## Statistics

Although description, prediction, and explanation are goals that differ in important respects, all three involve gathering data on relationships among variables. Statistics is a vital tool used in summarizing these relationships and in estimating the odds that they reflect something more than mere chance. We obviously will not cover all of statistics in this short chapter. Nevertheless, it is important that we mention some basic statistical methods that researchers use.

Scientists usually begin their research with an interest in a specific population of persons and situations. For instance, a study might arise from an interest in whether women employees are less satisfied with their jobs than men employees. One approach to studying this relationship would be to measure satisfaction for *all men and women* employees. Given the size of the population, however, this is unrealistic. Instead, samples of people are drawn from the two populations and differences between the samples are examined. *Descriptive statistics* are used to describe these samples. *Inferential statistics* are used to infer whether differences observed between the samples are likely to occur among members of the populations from which the samples were drawn.

### DISTRIBUTIONS

To understand inferential and descriptive statistics you need to consider the manner in which the values obtained for a variable are distributed. In the world around you there is an amazing symmetry in almost everything. For example, the seasons change predictably, and the right side of your body looks very similar to your left side. Statistical principles are based on the assumption that this regularity holds for many different variables. Take, for instance, weight and height. We all know people who weigh very little, such as a little baby, and people who weigh a lot, such as your fat Uncle Henry. Likewise, dwarfs are very short and professional basketball players are very tall. Most people, however, fall somewhere between these two extremes in height and weight. If you graphed the weights of a large number of people you would produce a frequency distribution much like the *normal distribution* in Figure 2.1. As the figure illustrates, most people fall in the large hump in the middle of

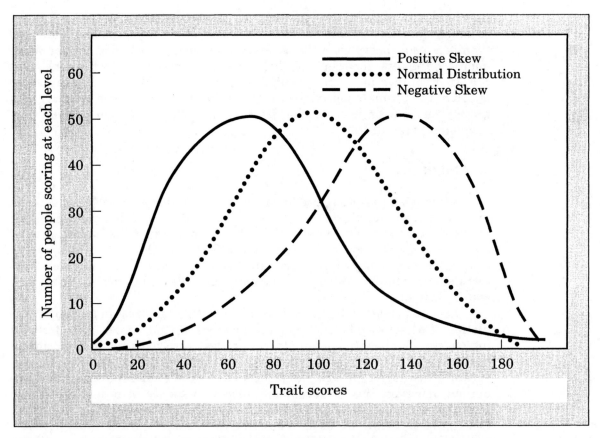

**Figure 2.1** *Normal, negatively skewed, and positively skewed distributions*

the distribution with relatively few people found in the tails. Many of the variables that are the focus of research in I/O psychology (e.g., intelligence test scores) are distributed in this manner, but it is not uncommon for distributions of variables to deviate from normality. For instance, the salaries of employees, the rate at which employees in different organizations leave the firm (turnover), and the number of thefts committed by each employee are more likely to take the form of *positively skewed* distributions in which there are few high values of the variable and many low values. On the other hand, the distribution of supervisor ratings of employee performance is often *negatively skewed* in that supervisors give relatively few very low ratings and many more moderate-to-high ratings.

## DESCRIPTIVE STATISTICS

Several numerical indices have been developed to *describe* frequency distributions in terms of their central tendency and variability. These include the mean, median, mode, variance, and standard deviation. Other statistics describe the correlations among variables.

**Measures of Central Tendency**  The mean is the arithmetic average of all scores in a frequency distribution. The median is the middle score (value) in a range of measured values; 50% of the values fall below the middle value and 50% are above that value. The mode is simply the most frequently occurring score. The mean, median, and mode are collectively referred to as measures of *central tendency.* In a normal distribution, the mean, median and mode have the same value. In skewed distributions, the extreme scores pull the mean away from the center of the distribution, and the mean is no longer a good measure of central tendency (see Figure 2.1). Consequently, the median is a better measure of central tendency for skewed distributions. The mode is much less frequently used than the median and mean but is a more meaningful description of central tendency in cases in which the variable is qualitative in nature (e.g., religious preference, race, gender).

**Measures of Variability**  Among the numerical indices that can be used to describe the spread of values in a distribution are the range, variance, and standard deviation. The simplest of these, the *range,* is computed by taking the difference between the smallest value and the largest value in the distribution. More informative is the *variance,* which measures the extent that values deviate from the mean of the distribution and is calculated using the following formula:

$$S^2 = \frac{\Sigma(X - M)^2}{N}$$

where $S^2$ is sample variance, $\Sigma$ indicates summation, X stands for the values found for the variable, N is the number of Xs observed in the sample, and M is the sample mean of the Xs. As shown in Figure 2.2, some distributions have large variances, with scores spread out from the mean, whereas others have small variances, with scores clustered around the mean.

The variance is a squared term. The square root of the variance is the standard deviation and is a more useful measure of variability. There are several reasons for this. The standard deviation is in the same unit of the original measurements, whereas the variance is in squared units. Also, if the distribution is normal, you can, on the basis of knowing the standard deviation of an individual's score, estimate how many persons in the population have lower or higher scores. We know that 68% of the cases in a normal distribution are within $+1$ and $-1$ standard deviation of the mean, whereas 95% are within $+2$ and $-2$ standard deviations, and 99% are within $+3$ and $-3$ standard deviations. By converting scores into standard deviation units, you also can make comparisons between individuals that might be impossible with raw scores. For instance, if one supervisor is very lenient and gives primarily ratings that are above 3 on a five point scale whereas another supervisor is very severe and gives ratings that are below 3, it would be hard to compare the subordinates of the two supervisors on these ratings. You could, however, compute the standard deviation of each supervisor's ratings and then convert each subordinate's rating into a *standard score.* One type of standard score is the *z score* and is computed by taking the raw score minus

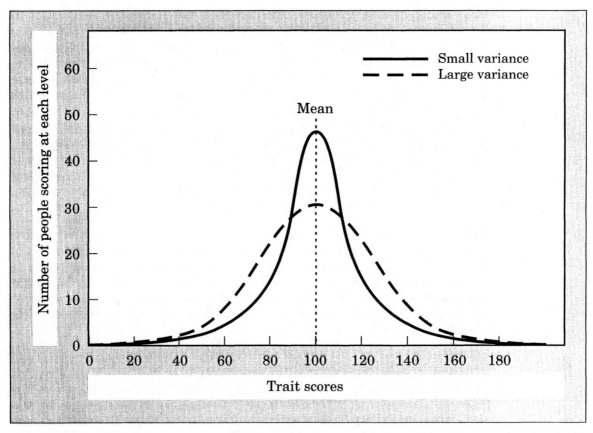

**Figure 2.2**  *A distribution with a large variance compared with a distribution with a small variance*

the mean and dividing by the standard deviation. Thus, we could take each subordinate's performance appraisal, subtract the mean of that supervisor's ratings from this appraisal, and then divide by the standard deviation of the supervisor's ratings. Each z score would tell you the relative status of the subordinate's rating in the supervisor's distribution of ratings.

**Correlation**    Researchers are usually interested in describing and drawing inferences for the relationships among two or more variables. First, let us consider bivariate correlations as described in the *bivariate frequency distributions* shown in Figure 2.3. The most frequently used statistic in describing relationships such as those presented in Figure 2.3 is the *bivariate correlation coefficient*. As seen in the figure, several potential relationships can exist between two variables. Some variables are positively related in that as values for one increase, the values for the other variable also increase. An example would be the relationship between cognitive ability and job performance. As ability increases, performance tends to increase. Other sets of measurements are negatively related to each other. That is, as one set of measurements

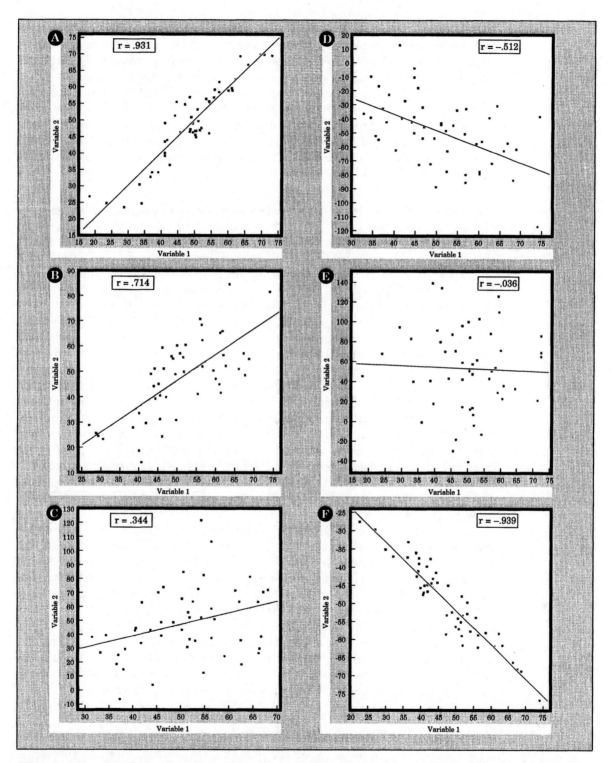

**Figure 2.3** *Bivariate frequency distributions showing positive and negative relationships*

increases, the other set decreases. For example, ratings of job-related stress and job satisfaction are usually negatively related. As people report higher stress ratings, they also report lower satisfaction ratings; conversely, as people report lower stress ratings, they also report higher satisfaction ratings.

It is useful to summarize the strength and direction of relationships such as those depicted in Figure 2.3 with single numbers. The Pearson product-moment correlation coefficient (denoted with $r$) is such a number and provides both the direction (positive or negative) and magnitude (weak, moderate, or strong) of the relationship between two sets of measurements. The formula for computing this coefficient is as follows:

$$r_{xy} = \frac{N\Sigma XY - (\Sigma X)(\Sigma Y)}{\sqrt{[N\Sigma X^2 - (\Sigma X)^2][N\Sigma Y^2 - (\Sigma Y)^2]}}$$

where $r_{xy}$ is the correlation coefficient, $\Sigma$ indicates summation, the X and Y stand for the values found for two variables, and N is the number of paired X and Y values. The purpose of a correlation is to determine the direction and strength of the association of two sets of measurements or variables. The coefficient ranges from $-1$ to $+1$; these extreme values indicate perfect (very high) negative and positive relationships, respectively. As the value of the coefficient converges toward zero from either direction, the coefficient becomes weaker in magnitude. For example, $r_{xy} = -.30$ or $+.40$ are both weaker in magnitude than $r_{xy} = -1.0$ or $+1.0$. A correlation of zero indicates a complete absence of a relationship. For the variables of interest to I/O psychologists, perfect correlations are rarely found, whereas correlations between $+.3$ and $-.3$ are frequently reported. The Pearson product-moment correlation coefficient can only tell us about linear relationships. In contrast, a non-linear relationship occurs, for example, when the Y variable increases with increases in the X variable up to moderate levels of X and then decreases at the higher values of the X variable. In such cases, other computational techniques (e.g., eta) are used to calculate the degree of nonlinear relationship between the two variables.

In cases in which I/O psychologists want to describe the relationship between more than two variables they use *multivariate* statistical methods. The most common situation occurs when there is interest in the relationship between two or more predictor variables and a criterion variable. For instance, you might want to know the relationship of a battery of two tests with a criterion measure of performance on the job. A *multiple correlation* could be computed that would indicate the combined relationship of the predictors with the criterion. If the two tests were totally unrelated (i.e., the bivariate correlation of the two was 0), then the multiple correlation with the criterion would be the square root of the sum of the squared correlations of the tests with the criterion. This is expressed in the equation below:

$$R_{p.12} = \sqrt{r^2_{1p} + r^2_{2p}}$$

where $R_{p.12}$ is the multiple correlation coefficient predicting performance from tests 1 and 2; $r^2_{1p}$ is the squared correlation between test 1 and performance; and $r^2_{2p}$ is the squared correlation between test 2 and performance. In almost all cases, however, the predictors are interrelated to some extent. The multiple correlation in this case is computed with the following equation:

$$R_{p.12} = \sqrt{\frac{r^2_{1p} + r^2_{2p} - 2r_{12}r_{1p}r_{2p}}{1 - r^2_{12}}}$$

Even more complicated multivariate statistical procedures could be used such as *canonical correlation*, in which the relationship between a set of two or more predictors and a set of two or more criteria is computed.

## INFERENTIAL STATISTICS

Researchers do not stop at descriptions of samples, but also draw conclusions for the populations from which the samples were drawn. Inferential statistics are used in performing this second task.

Let us assume that a researcher hypothesizes that older workers are more productive than younger workers. The researcher draws a sample of workers 30 years or older and another sample of younger workers under 30 years in age. A mean performance of 4.8 is found for the older sample and a mean of 3.0 is found for the younger workers. Can the researcher now conclude that the hypothesis is correct and older workers are indeed better performers? To answer this question we would need to conduct a statistical test of the significance of the difference in the means to allow a determination of whether this difference is statistically significant or attributable to chance. Inferential statistics always involves comparing a hypothesis to some *alternative hypothesis.* In this case the alternative hypothesis would be that no difference exists in the mean performances of younger and older employees. This alternative is called the *null hypothesis,* and the statistical test tells you the likelihood that the observed difference between the samples would be obtained if the null hypothesis were true and the means of the populations from which the samples were drawn were actually the same.

In concluding whether a difference is large enough to be considered statistically significant, it has become common practice to expect that the probability of a significant difference is less than 5 in 100 or even lower (less than 1 in 100). Assume that the mean performance of older employees is found to be greater than the mean performance of younger employees at a probability of less than .05 ($p < .05$). This would be equivalent to saying that the chance is less than 5 in 100 of drawing samples that differ this much if older employees and younger employees actually did not differ in performance. Such a difference would be referred to as a *statistically significant difference.* There is nothing absolute about requiring a probability level of .05 or lower. We could decide to require another probability level, say, .10 or .25. Nevertheless, requiring a .05 or lower level reflects the general reluctance of scientists to accept differences as real unless the possibility of the difference's being a chance event is low.

In addition to testing the significance of differences in means, inferential statistics also can be used to test the statistical significance of correlations. For example, you might measure age and performance in a sample and compute the correlation between these two variables. If you found a correlation of

.714, as indicated in Figure 2.3, you would want to estimate the likelihood of obtaining this level of correlation given that the relationship in the population from which we drew the sample was some other value. For instance, you could estimate the likelihood that the correlation obtained in the sample is larger than an assumed population correlation of 0. You could also compute the statistical significance of differences in correlations computed for different samples. As in the case of testing the significance of the difference between means, the statistical test would tell you the likelihood of obtaining a difference between correlations of the magnitude found if the difference between correlations in the respective populations was actually 0.

## Measurement of Variables

Now that we have discussed some statistical concepts, we need to return to the basic objectives of scientific research: to describe the variables that are the focus of the research as precisely as possible and in a way that others can repeat the research. The rules by which a person, object, or event are assigned a value on a variable is referred to as *measurement*. The specific instruments or devices used to assign the values are referred to as *scales* or *measures*.

### ALTERNATIVE TYPES OF SCALES

The scales used by I/O psychologists can be distinguished according to the source (observations by others, self-reports), whether the measure is based on current or retrospective observations (current, retrospective), and the extent to which inference is required (behavior observation, inference of underlying dispositions). In performance appraisals, for example, supervisors often *infer* employee traits (dependability, energy, initiative, etc.) from *recollections* of the employee's past behavior (retrospective observation). In measuring how employees go about coping with stressful aspects of their jobs, some researchers use retrospective, self-reports by the employee of specific behavioral strategies taken to cope with stress (e.g., do you use time management? do you exercise?). Although I/O psychologists usually have advocated observing behavior rather than relying on the memory of the observer, self-reports and retrospective accounts are frequently used out of necessity. Moreover, for some variables self-reports make more sense. For example, given that job satisfaction is a construct involving personal feelings about various facets of the job, self-reports seem preferable to behavioral observation.

### ERRORS OF MEASUREMENT

In evaluating a measure we are primarily concerned with the issue of why people vary or differ in their scores on that measure. In the ideal situation all variation can be attributed to true differences among individuals on the measured variable. We live in an imperfect world, however, and some of the perceived differences invariably reflect *errors in measurement* as well as true differences. Some errors are *constant* in that they reflect systematic, stable influences. If you used several rulers to measure length, you might find that one ruler always yields a reading that is somewhat more than the other rulers. In the case of performance evaluations you might find that some supervisors of the employees are more lenient and assign higher ratings. Thus, some of our ten employees have higher performance because of a constant tendency of their supervisors to give better ratings. Errors resulting from random events are called *random errors*. A ruler might yield somewhat different readings, for example, because of variations in temperature or momentary fatigue of the person reading the ruler. In the case of performance appraisal, variations can result from transient events such as machines that break down, supervisors that have a bad day, or inattention by the people recording the performance data.

## RELIABILITY

The concept of reliability refers to the extent that a measure is relatively free of random error and is consistent in the numbers assigned to objects or events. There are four approaches to estimating the reliability of a measure. The *test–retest* method focuses on the measure's stability over time. For instance, you could estimate the reliability of a job satisfaction scale by giving the scale to a group of employees and checking whether the employees maintain the same relative order on satisfaction at each testing. If on retest, the most satisfied employees are among the least satisfied while the least satisfied are among the most satisfied, then the measure is likely to be unreliable. A second approach to assessing reliability is to examine the *internal consistency* of the measure. Often a single psychological scale consists of several components (items, trials, samples, observations, etc.), and these components are combined on the assumption that the values yielded across components are consistent. Job satisfaction might be measured by taking the mean response to each of ten questions about satisfaction with such issues as pay and supervision. If there are large inconsistencies across items in which high satisfaction with one facet is accompanied by dissatisfaction with another facet, then combining the separate items would yield an unreliable measure. Related to internal consistency, but less commonly used, is the third method, *parallel forms*. In this case the researcher constructs equivalent forms of a measure and examines the correlation of scores on the two forms. To the extent that the scores on the two forms are highly related, the measures are reliable. It is crucial in using this method that the two forms are actually equivalent in that they have equal means, variances, and the same correlations with other measures. The fourth approach to assessing reliability is *inter-rater reliability*. For instance, researchers might measure the performance of employees by asking three supervisors to each rate the performance of the employees and then averaging the three supervisory judgments. To be reliable, the rank order of employees on this performance measure should be similar across the three supervisors. It is important to note that while a reliable measure is relatively free of random error, it could still be subject to considerable *constant* error. Thus, each of several supervisors might consistently err in a lenient or severe direction in their ratings of the performance of employees, but their ratings could still be reliable in that the ordering of the employees is consistent across the three supervisors. Similarly, in a test–retest situation, it is not uncommon to find that test scores of employees improve as the result of practice. A high degree of reliability could still be found, however, if the employees all improve together and maintain a similar rank ordering of scores across the two testings.

## VALIDITY

The second major basis for evaluating a measure is *validity*. The validity of a measurement refers to whether the number obtained truly reflects what the user intended to measure. If I intend to measure job satisfaction with a series of questions, do these questions in fact reflect job satisfaction? If I intend a battery of tests to measure competence to perform the job, do my tests really tap competence? Reliability and validity are related, but it is crucial to understand the differences between the two concepts. A reliable measure provides consistent readings but is not necessarily valid. A palm reader might provide very reliable readings of future job success but the measure in this case would be totally lacking in validity as a measure of performance potential. On the other hand, measurement is unlikely to be valid unless it is also reliable. A measure that yields wildly discrepant readings from one time to the next is unlikely to provide what it is intended to provide. In general, reliability is a necessary but not sufficient condition for validity, with reliability setting the upper bound to the level of validity that one can expect to find in a measure.

Validity is not a property of the measure but instead refers to the truthfulness of the inferences that we draw from the measure. Take, for example, tests of achievement motivation, a common form of personality test discussed in Chapter 3. It is inaccurate to call a test of achievement motivation valid or invalid in any absolute sense. Rather, we must evaluate validity in reference to the use we make of the test. An achievement motivation test might be quite valid in the sense that scores on this test relate to behaviors and attitudes in ways that our theories of achievement motivation would hypothesize. On the other hand, it might be quite invalid as a predictor of future job success. Thus, a measure may be valid for some inferences but invalid for others.

Past descriptions of validation have caused confusion. The traditional approach has been to present three strategies of conducting validation, as if there were three distinct types of validity (the trinitarian model of validity). In recent years, I/O psychologists have brought attention to the fact that validity is a unitary concept and should be treated as such (Schmitt & Landy, 1993). We will first describe the trinitarian conception of validity, followed by the more appropriate unitarian approach.

Traditionally three types of validity have been presented. *Criterion-related validity* refers to whether the measures allow correct predictions of a criterion variable. For instance, a common concern in I/O psychology (discussed in Chapter 10) is whether tests of abilities predict performance on the job. One way of computing criterion-related validity is to use a predictive design in which the ability tests are given to job applicants. The correlation coefficient is later computed to show the relationship of ability scores on the tests of those who are hired and the later job performance of these same employees (often measured by supervisor ratings). Another approach is to use a concurrent design in which we give the ability tests to a sample of current employees and examine the correlation of their scores with their performance. In both cases, the tests are said to have criterion-related validity to the extent that they allow the prediction of job performance. The correlation coefficient of predictor and criterion is known as the validity coefficient of the test.

A second approach to validating a measure is to examine its *content validity*. A measure is content valid insofar as it provides a good sample of the domain of behaviors that it is intended to measure. Take, for instance, a typical exam in a course. The test is content valid to the extent that it provides a good sample of material from the lectures, classroom discussions, text, and other materials that students are expected to know. If all the questions were taken from one chapter to the neglect of other chapters, then the test would obviously be low in content validity. Likewise, a test of achievement motivation might be content valid to the extent that it provides a representative sample of achievement-related behaviors. Unlike criterion-related validation, there is no single quantitative index of content validity, although there is some work on developing such an index (Lawshe, 1975). The evaluation of content validity requires that the sampled domain is carefully specified and rests largely on the judgment of experts that the sampling from this domain is unbiased.

*Construct validity* is the most general of the various approaches to validity and refers to whether scores on a measure reflect the construct that it is purported to measure. Whereas the primary question in criterion-related validity is "Does the measure predict?" and the primary question in content validity is "What does the measure contain?", the essential question in construct validity is "What does the measure really measure?" Construct validation goes hand-in-hand with theory development and testing (Binning & Barrett, 1989). According to Nunnally (1978), the construct validation of a measure requires three steps:

1. *Specify the domain of observables related to the construct.*
   This is similar to what was discussed under content validity. If the researcher intends to measure a construct, then he or she needs to define the construct and outline the various observable behaviors that might constitute the domain of the construct. For instance, in developing a measure of employee performance, the researcher would want to carefully consider the various behaviors that should be included in the performance domain. While we might exclude behaviors such as being ingratiating to the boss, we might include other

behaviors such as providing good customer service. If a researcher were developing a job satisfaction measure, that researcher might define the domain to include attitudes about pay, fellow employees, the work itself, company policies, and the work environment. In developing a measure of anxiety, the domain might be specified as including such responses as fear of the dark, worrying about what might happen, anxiety about catching diseases, panic attacks, or freezing on tests.

2. *Examine the relations among observables that are specified as part of the construct.* The next step is to determine whether the many observables specified in the first step coalesce. For instance, the researcher might have persons rate the extent to which they experience the various fears and anxieties specified in step one. He or she would then examine the extent to which these responses were positively correlated. In other words, if people who state that they frequently have panic attacks and freeze on tests also have anxieties about catching diseases and fear the dark, then the total score on this test is more likely to reflect a single construct of anxiety. Note that this is essentially the same as evaluating the reliability of a measure by using the internal consistency approach. If responses to the various items are not highly related, then this not only suggests that the measure is not reliable but that it lacks validity as a measure of the construct.

3. *Examine the relationships with different constructs.* Our theories should dictate how the construct underlying our measure relates to other constructs. Validating the measure becomes a process of empirically verifying that our measure of the construct is related to measures of the other constructs in a manner that is consistent with the theory. Thus, from a theory of anxiety we might hypothesize that highly anxious people experience more job stress when faced with high job demands. We might then examine the correlation of the measure of anxiety with measures of job stress under low and high levels of job demands. If the hypothesis is supported by the data, then not only is the theory supported, but the construct validity of the measure is also supported. A basic assumption behind construct validation efforts is that we have good theories and valid measures of the other constructs. For instance, if we find support for the above hypothesis, we cannot conclude support for construct validity of the anxiety measure unless we are confident in the theory and the validity of the measures of job demands and stress. From the discussion so far it should be apparent that construct val-

idation is a continuing process rather than a one-shot affair. As more hypotheses are tested and a measure is shown to relate to other valid measures in a manner that is consistent with theory, our confidence may increase that the scale indeed measures the construct that it purports to measure. But given that there are an infinite number of hypotheses that we might pose regarding other constructs, we can never really complete this process.

Attempting to show construct validity through examining the relationships of measures of various constructs that use the same method of measurement can result in artificially high levels of correlation. "Common method bias" refers to the fact that some degree of correlation is likely among similar methods of measurement even if the measures are intended to tap different constructs that should be unrelated. This is particularly a problem with self-report methods of measurement. Imagine that you are asked in a questionnaire to report on your own job performance, job satisfaction, and your relationship with your supervisor. As you answer the various questions, you might well tend to use the same part of the response scales. Also, the feelings expressed on one part of the questionnaire (e.g., self-perceived high levels of performance) might spill over into answers given to other parts of the questionnaire (e.g., expressions of job satisfaction and descriptions of good relations with the supervisor). A likely consequence would be a high level of correlation among the three measures.

An important strategy of construct validation that attempts to counter common method bias is the *multitrait-multimethod* approach (Campell & Fiske, 1959). In this approach data are gathered with the measure of primary interest and correlations are computed between this measure and the scores obtained with other measures of the same construct that use different approaches, scores obtained with measures of different constructs that use the same approach, and scores obtained with measures of different constructs that use different approaches. Assume you are interested in determining the construct validity of a self-report measure of achievement motivation. You gather data from a group using not only this instrument but also a measure of achievement motivation that relies on peer evaluations. At the same time, you gather data from the same group on another trait, self-esteem, using both self-reports and peer evaluations to measure this trait. Convergent validity for the measure would be shown if you found that your measure was highly related to different, well-established measures of the same trait. For instance, you would want to show that the self-report measure of achievement motivation was highly related to a peer evaluation of achievement motivation that you know to be valid. Moreover, you want to show that the level of correlation achieved between different methods of measuring the same construct is (1) higher than the correlation obtained between different methods of measuring different constructs (e.g., the correlation of self-report of achievement motivation and peer evaluation of self-esteem) and (2) higher than the correlation obtained between the same methods of measuring different constructs (e.g., the correlation of self-report of achievement motivation and self-report of self-esteem). If you find that the correlation between self-reported achievement motivation and self-reported self-esteem is as high or higher as the correlation of self-reported achievement motivation and peer-rated achievement motivation, then it is possible that the relationships found between this measure and the other measures are due to "common method bias."

Although criterion-related, content, and construct validity often have been discussed as if they were three distinct types of validity, in recent years I/O psychologists have stressed that validity is a unitary concept that should not be subdivided (Binning & Barrett, 1989; Guion, 1980; Landy, 1986). One of the three validation approaches may seem most relevant in the attempt to support the validity of the measure, but all three approaches should be used in the process of validating the measure. For instance, consider the typical personnel selection situation in which there is interest in inferring from a predictor measure the position of employees on the construct of performance in the job. We choose a measure (e.g., a test of cognitive ability) on the basis of an assumption that the construct underlying the measure (i.e., cognitive ability) is related to the performance domain. To validate the predictor measure we collect data on how employees score on the predictor and how they score on a measure of a criterion of job performance. This criterion-related approach yields a validity coefficient that we can use to justify the use of the predictor. While the criterion-related approach seems to be the most important approach in this context, the hypothesis that scores on the predictor are related to the construct of performance could also be supported with content- and construct-validity approaches as well. Using the construct-validity approach, we could assess whether the predictor measure is a good measure of the underlying criterion domain. The construct-validity approach could also be used to assess whether the accumulated evidence on the criterion construct and the predictor construct suggests a positive relationship. For example, we could review the research literature that discusses the relationships of cognitive ability tests to constructs similar to the performance domain in which we are interested. Finally, we could use a content-validity approach to determine whether the predictor measure provides a representative sample of the performance domain. While we cannot conclude from evidence gathered with these other approaches that the predictor measure will predict performance on the criterion measure, all of this evidence is relevant for justifying the validity of the inference that the predictor measure is related to the performance domain.

## Designing Research for Explanation

While developing good measures is a crucial objective in scientific research, it is often only a means to the ultimate ends of explanation and prediction. Especially important in applying the scientific method to research on human behavior is the explanation of the relationships that are found among variables. The process of applying the scientific method in this case is a process of considering alternative explanations and then conducting research that eliminates as many alternatives as possible.

For any single relationship between a variable X and a variable Y many alternative explanations can usually be proposed. For example, you might hypothesize a causal relationship between leader participativeness (variable X) and the job performance of workers (variable Y) in which participation actually causes higher performance (i.e., a worker who is allowed to participate in decisions is a more productive worker). In support of this relationship, you might find positive correlations between measures of these two variables. However, a simple correlation does not in most cases allow you to rule out alternatives to the causal assertion that X causes Y. Let us consider some of these alternative explanations:

1. *Reverse causation.* It might be that job performance causes the leader to be participative rather than *vice versa.*
2. *Reciprocal causation.* Causation might be a two-way street in which leader participation not only causes worker performance but performance also causes leader participation. Thus, the good performances of a worker might result in the leader allowing more participation, and this participation might, in turn, induce even higher levels of performance.
3. *A third variable is causing both X and Y.* Leader participativeness and worker performance might be causally unrelated, and the observed correlation might only reflect a third unmeasured variable that causes both variables. For instance, it is possible that worker intelligence is such a third variable. Workers who are more intelligent might be allowed to participate by their leaders because of their intelligence. Likewise, more intelligent workers might perform better because of their ability. However, there might not be a direct causal relationship between participation and performance. The correlation between the two variables would be spurious in that it results from the causal effects of intelligence rather than the causal relationship of participation and performance. These third variables are often called *confounding variables.*
4. *The relationship of X and Y is mediated by a third variable.* The relationship between leader participativeness and worker performance might be mediated by an intervening variable that is caused by one of the two variables. The intervening variable then serves as the direct cause of the other variable. For instance, leader participativeness might cause higher levels of worker knowledge of their tasks, and this knowledge might then cause higher levels of performance.

Many times finding a mediating variable does not prove that the relationship between X and Y is spurious but may only help interpret this relationship.

5. *The relationship of X and Y is moderated by a third variable.* A *moderator variable* influences the relationship between two other variables without directly causing either variable. For instance, leader participativeness might be positively related to worker performance only when the task is highly ambiguous. When the task is highly routine and unambiguous, the relationship between participativeness and performance might be much weaker. In this case, task ambiguity serves as a moderator variable and is said to *moderate* the relationship between participativeness and performance. As in the case of mediators, finding a moderator may only establish the boundaries of an effect and help interpret the observed relationship.

We can never eliminate all of the possibilities, but through properly conducted research, the number of alternatives can at least be reduced. A *research design* is a plan for how to treat variables that can influence results so as to rule out alternative interpretations. In the design of a study, researchers can *hold constant, eliminate, manipulate, measure, randomize,* or *match* variables. Those variables that cannot be treated in one of the above ways serve as potential sources of error. In conducting research on a phenomenon there are probably an infinite number of variables and interrelationships that can be examined. The art of designing research is a matter of deciding how to treat the variables that can potentially influence the phenomenon under study so as to rule out alternative interpretations of a relationship.

## HOLD CONSTANT OR ELIMINATE VARIABLES

Some variables can be controlled by either holding their values constant or eliminating them. In studying leader participation and employee satisfaction you might hold constant the task on which the employees are working or the sex and age of the employees so as to obtain a clearer look at the relationship of primary concern. Similarly, in studying the effects of noise on performance you would want to conduct the experiment in a setting where street noise can be eliminated and the experimenter can have total control over noise levels.

## MANIPULATE THE VARIABLE

Other variables are manipulated so that they assume certain values. In research on leadership and employee satisfaction, the researcher might arrange things so that some employees are assigned a participatory leader and others are assigned a nonparticipatory leader. The variable that is manipulated in a study to determine its effect on some other variable is called an *independent variable* (IV) because it is assumed to be independent of all other potential influences in the situation. The variable that is presumed to be caused by the independent variable and consequently dependent on this variable is referred to as the *dependent variable* (DV). The best way to determine what is causing what is to directly manipulate the variables believed to be the causes. Of course, some variables may not be amenable to manipulation, a topic that will be discussed later.

### MEASURE THE VARIABLE AS IT NATURALLY OCCURS

Other variables can be measured as they occur without any attempt to directly manipulate them. For example, if you were conducting research on leadership, you might wish to observe leaders and measure the type of leadership they exhibit as it naturally occurs. If one variable is manipulated (the independent variable) and other variables are measured to assess the influence of the manipulated variable, the value of the measured variable depends on the values of the independent variable. You might also measure potential mediators, moderators, and confounding variables to explore their influence on the relationship between the IV and DV.

### RANDOM ASSIGNMENT

Random is sometimes associated with something bad or arbitrary, but in research it is the most powerful means of dealing with all the unmeasurable, unmanipulated, and uncontrollable variables that are potential sources of error. *Random* means that various events have an equal chance of occurring. If you were interested in comparing employees under participative and nonparticipative leaders, you could allow each employee to pick the leader he or she preferred and then compare the performance of those who picked a participative leader with those who picked a nonparticipative leader. This would be *nonrandom* in that there is an unequal chance of each employee working with one or the other leader. The employees who strongly prefer making their own decisions or who have prior experience on the task might prefer and choose, for instance, the participative leader, whereas those with low need to make their own decisions or who have no prior experience might prefer and choose the nonparticipative leader. To ensure that each employee has an equal chance of working with each type of leader, you would want to use a randomization procedure such as flipping an unbiased coin for each employee (heads you work for the autocratic leader, tails you work for the democratic leader). An even more sophisticated approach would be to use a table of random numbers to assign employees to each of the conditions.

Randomization will help protect against systematic errors confounding the comparison of two or more groups, but random error will still exist within each of the groups compared. For example, the employees assigned to participatory leaders may not be older or more experienced than those assigned to nonparticipatory leaders, but employees within each group may differ considerably among themselves on both age and experience.

### MATCH ON THE VARIABLE

A possible means of reducing the within-group variation mentioned above is to measure the variable and then make sure that matching sets of people are selected as subjects. In an experiment in which subjects are exposed to either a participatory or nonparticipatory leader, pairs of subjects could be formed who are matched on a set of variables (e.g., experience and age). For each pair, one of the employees would then be assigned on a random basis to either a participative or nonparticipative leader.

## Different Types of Research

Several varieties of research can be distinguished based on how the investigator treats variables in the research design. We will categorize research as experimental versus nonexperimental, laboratory versus field, and obtrusive versus unobtrusive.

### EXPERIMENTAL VERSUS NONEXPERIMENTAL

The essential attribute of an experiment is that participants are assigned at random to various levels of the independent variables. In some cases, an experiment involves an independent variable that is under the control of the experimenter. In other cases, the independent variable is a naturally occurring event rather than a manipulated variable; we will call these *natural experiments*. A researcher who knows that an organization plans to change over to a new technology, for example, might persuade the organization to compare the effects on morale and productivity of those given the new technology and those who are not given the technology. As long as there is random assignment of employees to the new technology and the old technology groups, this would qualify as an experiment. Natural experiments in I/O psychology are relatively rare. In most of the experiments we will discuss, the experimenter not only randomly assigned participants to various conditions of the experiment but also manipulated the independent variable.

In nonexperimental research the people studied are assigned on a nonrandom basis to conditions. One variety of nonexperimental research is the *correlational* study. Here all the variables are measured as they naturally occur, and the researchers have no direct control over what happens. For example, a researcher might simply measure the participativeness of a leader and then see how it relates to the productivity of employees without any direct intervention to change the leader's behavior.

A *quasi-experiment* lies between a correlational study and a true experiment and could involve an independent variable that is either manipulated or naturally occurring (Cook & Campbell, 1979). The one important difference between a quasi-experiment and a true experiment is that the assignment of participants is nonrandom in the former and random in the latter. For instance, evaluations of training programs often must rely on nonrandom assignment procedures. Employees participating in a program may volunteer for this program whereas those in the no-training control are chosen from among those who do not volunteer. This type of quasi-experiment is called a *nonequivalent control group study,* and despite the lack of random assignment, can still provide valuable information on the trained and nontrained groups. Procedures exist that allow the investigator to statistically control for differences between the two groups. Also, through measuring the dependent variable (e.g., measure of training effectiveness) many times and examining the trends before and after the training intervention, some of the alternative interpretations of results can be eliminated.

## Laboratory versus Field Research

Research must be conducted somewhere and the research setting is another important basis for distinguishing among varieties of research. *Laboratory research* is conducted in settings created for the purpose of research. Laboratories are usually designed for the explicit purpose of controlling and

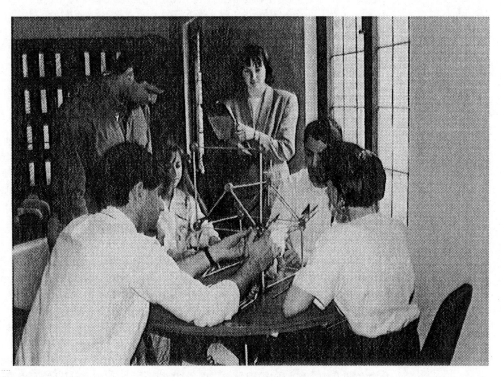

I/O psychologists conduct research not only in organizations but also in laboratory settings such as the leadership experiment shown here.

eliminating extraneous variables and allowing an uncontaminated manipulation of the independent variables. In *field research* the settings are for some nonresearch purpose such as work or education. Thus, if we enter an organization and have employees complete a survey in their work places on their attitudes toward their supervisors, this would qualify as a field study. On the other hand, if we had workers come to a special room set aside for the purpose of research outside the work setting and respond to the same questionnaire, this would be a laboratory study.

## OBTRUSIVE VERSUS UNOBTRUSIVE

Some research is done in a manner that makes it obvious to participants that they are the objects of study. Research in which participants' awareness is high is called *obtrusive,* whereas research in which awareness is low is *unobtrusive.* The setting of the research largely determines its obtrusiveness. Almost all laboratory research is obtrusive, but obtrusiveness in field research varies considerably. The manner in which variables are measured is another important factor. Self-reports in which participants are asked to provide introspective accounts of their satisfaction would be highly obtrusive, whereas using hidden observers who record signs of satisfaction and dissatisfaction among the rank-and-file would be relatively unobtrusive. Finally, the method by which variables are manipulated is still another source of obtrusiveness. Typically, laboratory experimenters try to create as much impact as possible in as covert a way as possible to avoid the suspicion associated with a highly obvious manipulation.

## Factors Influencing the Validity of Explanations

The discussion so far should clearly indicate that a variety of approaches can be taken in conducting research. Although all are scientific, each has its strengths and drawbacks. How do you evaluate the merits of an investigation? Cook and Campbell (1979) set forth three primary means of evaluating research design: internal validity, construct validity, and external validity.

## THREATS TO INTERNAL VALIDITY

Research in I/O often is concerned with whether one variable causes another. A study is internally valid if it can be concluded from a relationship between an independent variable X and a dependent variable Y that X causes Y. Nonexperimental research can be a good starting point, but if substantial knowledge about causal relationships is desired it is necessary to conduct experiments. Let us describe some of the major threats to the internal validity of nonexperimental research and then show how various experimental designs can help eliminate these threats as alternative explanations.

Correlational findings are usually subject to multiple interpretations. For instance, a fairly strong correlation exists between the act of getting married and the occurrence of pregnancy. Obviously, it would be incorrect to conclude that the marriage ceremony itself caused pregnancy. The causal factor is a third variable—sexual intercourse. Although correlational research is probably the least powerful approach to explanation, a correlational study can set the stage for more rigorous explorations of causality. Also, even though a correlational finding cannot be used to show definitive proof that a causal relationship exists between two variables, common sense can allow the elimination of some alternatives. Finding that age of employees is positively correlated with performance on the job does not justify concluding that age actually caused performance. It is safe to conclude, however, that performance did not cause age.

Another nonexperiment that is frequently found in organizations is the simple *pretest–posttest* design. The dependent variable is measured prior to the manipulation of the independent variable and again after the manipulation. The effects of the manipulation are then evaluated in terms of changes in the dependent measure. Suppose, for example, you evaluated the effects of a new incentive program in which each employee is rewarded individually based on his or her productivity. In a pretest–posttest design, you would measure the productivity of the employees prior to the changeover to the new incentive program and then again afterward. What if you found an increase in productivity following the introduction of the incentives? Should you conclude that increases in productivity were the result of the incentives? This type of simple design, although quite common, is vulnerable to all sorts of threats to internal validity. Here are some of the more common ones.

**History**   How do you know that posttest improvements were not caused by something that happened to employees between the pretest and posttest? For example, employees might have heard a rumor of an impending layoff if the company did not improve its profit position. As a consequence of fear of losing their jobs, employees might have improved their productivity. It is often the case that many things are going on at the same time as major interventions in organizations, and these other things can lessen the researcher's confidence in concluding that the independent variable caused the dependent measure.

**Maturation**   Other factors that can create problems are the growth and learning that can occur between the pretest and posttest. For example, if the incentive program was imposed on workers who were in the process of learning a new job then you could expect gains regardless of the incentives.

**Testing**   When persons are pretested in an obtrusive manner, changes observed at the posttest could reflect the pretest more than the manipulation of the independent variable.

**Instrumentation**   Still another threat to internal validity results from changes in the measurement process. What if, for instance, productivity was tracked more carefully after the intervention than before? Increases in productivity might reflect the careful attention now being given to productivity rather than the implementation of the incentive program. Other examples of changes resulting from instrumentation are observers becoming fatigued and mechanical instruments losing calibration.

The above threats to internal validity could be dealt with by providing a *control group* that does not receive the manipulation of the independent variable. In other words, you could use a *pretest–posttest control group* design. In the above example, this might mean that the experimental group receives the incentive program while a control group does not. The crucial issue is how to determine who is assigned to the experimental and control groups. If the assignment is nonrandom then the following factors could still threaten internal validity.

**Selection Bias**    Perhaps the major threat when participants are assigned to the control group on a nonrandom basis is selection bias. If employees were allowed to volunteer for the new incentive program, for instance, any differences between the experimental and control groups on the dependent measure could reflect the fact that the employees who volunteered differed from those who did not. Employees who were committed to the organization and involved in their jobs may have been more likely to volunteer, whereas employees who were low in commitment and involvement would be less likely to do so. Thus, improvements in productivity observed after the incentive program could result from the greater motivation of the employees who volunteered, rather than from the specific manipulation.

**Mortality**    The term *mortality* as a threat to internal validity was taken from animal research in which subjects died between the pretest and posttest. In most organizational research, it is unlikely that employees die at a fast enough rate to influence the results, but it is not uncommon for employees to show differential dropout rates during the course of an experiment. Consequently, differences observed in the dependent measure could reflect who is left more than they reflect the effects of the independent variable.

**Awareness of Being a Research Subject**    In a complex organization experiments are difficult to conduct because participants are often aware that some employees are receiving something and others are not. The control group may feel neglected and consequently show a decline in productivity. Differences can also result from groups feeling some degree of rivalry. A control group may see itself as inferior because it is treated differently and may compensate for this stigma by increasing performance.

The surest way to protect against most of the threats to internal validity is to randomly assign people to the experimental and control groups. Even more confidence can be gained if, in addition to random assignment, pretests and posttests are taken at multiple points in time. The problems that arise when participants know they are the object of research, however, are not easily avoided through random assignment or multiple measurement. Indeed, some critics of traditional research methods (e.g., Argyris, 1980) have argued that subject awareness is a fatal flaw that invalidates much of the psychological research in the field and the lab. Argyris' solution is to allow subjects to participate fully rather than keeping them ignorant of the research design. I/O psychologists have been reluctant to discard rigorous research, however, and have seen the alternatives to randomization and control as introducing even more serious problems.

## CONSTRUCT VALIDITY

Internal validity is concerned with whether the action of the independent variable is actually the cause of the changes observed in the dependent variable. The construct validity of the independent variable in an experiment, on the other hand, refers to whether the manipulation of the independent variable actually reflects the underlying construct that it is intended to reflect. Thus, an investigator may intend to examine the effects of anxiety on motivation by manipulating anxiety through a supervisor's verbal abuse. Motivation might be measured by examining the quality of the subject's performance on a task. Legitimate questions could be raised as to the construct validity of both the independent and dependent variables in this example (not to mention the ethics of the research). Does the act of verbally abusing subjects arouse anxiety or other emotions such as hostility or frustration? Likewise, do differences in quality of performance reflect differences in motivation or differences in skill, knowledge, or ability?

Randomization and control groups cannot protect against threats to the construct validity of the independent variable. The only recourse may be to repeat the experiment with other manipulations of the independent variable to see if the same results are found. For example, if you intend to manipulate anxiety, you might conduct one experiment in which subjects are threatened with physical pain in the form of electric shocks, another experiment in which stressful movies are shown, and still another in which subjects are threatened with failure on a task. If the same results were obtained from all three experiments, then you would have more confidence that the manipulations were actually tapping the anxiety construct.

## EXTERNAL VALIDITY

If a relationship is found between two variables in a study then an additional issue is whether the finding is capable of being repeated with different settings, subjects, and procedures. A continuing debate has been whether findings in the laboratory with college students can be generalized to work settings (Dipboye, 1990).

Critics of laboratory research claim that the artificial nature of the laboratory setting makes participants acutely aware of their status as subjects. This awareness, in turn, can cause them to behave in ways that are limited to the laboratory. For instance, subjects in laboratory experiments often try hard to do what they think the experimenter wants them to do. The power of the laboratory was made clear to one of the authors in an experiment in which he participated as an undergraduate. The experiment required that he swallow a sensing device on a string so that the acidity level in his stomach could be measured. Electric shocks were administered to his arms and legs when he failed to respond quickly enough to a randomly occurring signal. In addition to all this, he had to drink a glass of bicarbonate soda every 30 minutes and was not allowed to go to the bathroom. The author submitted for over eight hours. Some critics would argue that the passive acceptance of experimental demands shown by the author, and frequently observed among subjects in laboratory experiments, is unrepresentative of how people behave in nonlaboratory settings.

Another criticism of laboratory research is that it provides an unrepresentative sampling of stimuli, settings, and subjects. Whereas the manipulated variables in a lab experiment may be the only stimuli presented, events in the outside world usually must compete for our attention. One consequence of this can be that the effects observed in the laboratory are greater than what would typically be found in the external world. For example, some researchers have tested the hypothesis that performance appraisals are biased against women by giving subjects an essay that is described as being written by either a man or a woman. Some of this research has shown that the same essay is rated lower if the author is believed to be a woman than if the author is believed to be a man. Is bias against women in a lab situation likely to generalize to performance appraisals in organizations? Critics of this type of laboratory research have argued that in the messy world of the organization, those evaluating performance are presented with many other factors in addition to the sex of the ratee. In a lab experiment such as the one described here, the manipulation of sex is so obvious that it is hard to miss. In a similar vein, Murphy, Gannett, Herr, and Chen (1986) have speculated that effects found in laboratory experiments are stronger than those found in an organization because raters in the lab do not have as much difficulty distinguishing the signal (e.g., the sex of the ratee) from the noise as they do in the workplace.

The biggest complaint against the external validity of laboratory research is that its subjects are usually college students. You may be a college undergraduate and may agree that students like yourself are representative of "normal" humans. Some critics have expressed their doubts, however. Sears (1986) claims that the typical American undergraduate is less likely than the general public to have a fully formulated sense of self and more likely to show large shifts in self-esteem, to have feelings of insecurity and depression, to be egocentric, and to strive for peer approval. College students, according to Sears, are not even representative of other young people in that they have higher cognitive abilities, yet are more compliant to authority and have more unstable peer relationships. The result of using students as subjects, according to Sears, has resulted in a view of human beings as "lone, bland, compliant wimps who specialize in paper-and-pencil tests" (p. 527). Consistent with this claim, Gordon, Slade, and Schmitt (1986) found 12 studies that postulated major differences between students and nonstudents and concluded that research with college students should not be conducted if the intention is to draw conclusions about behavior in work organizations.

With all these complaints about the validity of the laboratory as a setting for research you would think that laboratory research would cease. Nevertheless, the laboratory is often needed for the simple reason that some phenomena cannot be studied in the field. It is infrequent, for example, that investigators can go into an organization and manipulate the leadership styles of supervisors. Consequently, laboratory experiments are needed to provide controlled investigations of leadership dynamics.

Despite the need for laboratory research, can we conclude anything substantial about "the real world of work" from using college sophomores in highly contrived settings? The laboratory has had its defenders. One argument is that being representative of the outside world is not an important consideration when examining basic psychological processes. Indeed, in many laboratory experiments the investigator is more interested in determining whether something can occur, not the frequency or strength with which it typically occurs in the external world. Other defenders of the laboratory have argued that the lab does not have to *look* like the outside world to yield results that can be generalized. The more important issue for Berkowitz and Donnerstein (1982) is that lab subjects interpret their situation in the same manner they would interpret the field setting to which the research will be generalized. Others have argued that *essential similarities* or *boundary variables* determine whether lab findings can be generalized, not general similarity. Assume, for example, that the essential variable influencing whether subjects act as they would in the field is whether they are held accountable for their behavior. If our reasoning is correct, the laboratory need not be similar in all respects to the field but only with regard to this essential variable. By making subjects accountable for their actions, we should improve the external validity of our research.

Another defense of the laboratory is that research in these settings is usually focused on general processes and theory. A novel or even ridiculous situation may be required to flush out the phenomenon under investigation. Through such research, it might be possible to validate a theory or model of the phenomenon that can then be generalized across a variety of situations. The findings of an individual, specific experiment may not be generalizable, but the theory that is tested and developed through experimentation is generalizable.

The above arguments are only a few of the pros and cons of lab research. The best approach is to use more than one method, realizing that each is limited in some respects and that all research involves tradeoffs. In field research the researcher attains more realism but at the cost of precision and control. In lab research the researcher has control but at the cost of realism. By testing hypotheses in both the lab and the field and determining empirically whether findings from one setting are transportable to the other, we can empirically evaluate the extent to which laboratory research suffers from low external validity. There are a few areas of research in which enough work has been done in both settings to allow such comparisons. Edwin Locke (1986) reviewed findings in the laboratory and field from several areas of research and provided an optimistic view of the generalizability of laboratory research, in that the most reliable effects uncovered in the lab appeared generalizable to field settings.

## Prediction in I/O Psychology

Another legitimate goal of scientific research and a major focus of some I/O psychologists is prediction of future events. For example, Chapter 10, which is concerned with personnel selection, focuses on the use of tests, interviews, and other procedures to forecast future performance. Highly predictive techniques can be used to select employees.

Statistics is a critical element to achieving accurate prediction. The statistical procedure used in prediction is *regression* and, while it is similar to the concept of correlation, there are some important differences. Take the bivariate frequency distributions in Figure 2.3. In these scatterplots, each dot represents the position of an individual on variable 1 and variable 2. The correlation coefficients describing these bivariate frequency distributions can give us a general sense of how accurately we can predict from variable 1 to variable 2, but it cannot give us an equation we can use to actually make these predictions. Regression techniques, however, yield a specific equation that we can use for this purpose. Using regression procedures we would determine the equation for the line that best fits the bivariate distribution. This is the *regression line;* one is drawn through each of the plots in Figure 2.3. The equation that represents this line (the regression equation) can be used for prediction. Thus, in the case of scatterplot B in Figure 2.3, knowing that an individual has a score of 45 on variable 1, we could predict that the score for this individual on variable 2 would be about 41. Of course, unless there is a perfect relationship, there will be some error in predicting variable 2 from variable 1. The spread around the regression line represents the amount of error, with more error associated with wider spreads.

As Chapter 10 suggests, regression techniques are useful in selecting applicants for scarce positions. We know, for example, that there is a moderately large positive correlation between Scholastic Aptitude Test (SAT) scores and grades in the freshman year of college. The real value of this relationship, however, lies in the ability to predict how successful the student will be in college based on his or her performance on the SAT. In fact, that is how cutoff scores are frequently determined for acceptance into colleges or universities, and why prestigious schools have high cutoff scores. The mass of predictive data concerning SAT scores and college grades indicates that if a student does not perform at a certain level on the SAT, then the likelihood of success in college course work drops.

Regression can be extended to include more than one predictor. For example, in predicting first year college grade point averages, universities often consider the high school grade point average, letters of recommendation, and SAT scores. The use of multiple predictors to enhance our ability to predict the outcome (in this case, college grades) is referred to as *multiple regression.* Chapter 10 discusses how multiple regression is used in determining how to optimally combine a battery of tests in predicting future job performance.

It is important to recognize that achieving good prediction does not necessarily require an explanation of why variables are related. Why students with higher SATs achieve higher grades is still open to debate, but this has not stopped the use of SATs in college admissions. On the other hand, a relationship between two variables may have a good explanation, but it may not be possible to predict one variable from the other.

# ETHICS OF I/O RESEARCH

In discussing how best to conduct research it is easy to lose sight of the fact that human beings are the focus of the research. I/O psychologists, along with all other psychologists, must adhere to an ethical code in conducting their research (see Table 1.3). We now summarize some of the guidelines associated with this code.

The I/O psychologist carefully considers prior to the research the possible risks involved and takes safeguards to protect the rights of human participants. Perhaps the most important safeguard is that "Prior to conducting research . . . psychologists enter into an agreement with participants that clarifies the nature of the research and the responsibilities of each party" (Standard 6.10, "Ethical principles of psychologists," 1992). Although there are exceptions, such as in archival research, naturalistic observations, and anonymous surveys, in many cases the investigator must inform the participants prior to the research of those aspects of the research that might influence their decision to participate. Moreover, the investigator should be available to answer the questions of participants. Sometimes research requires that subjects be kept in the dark on various aspects of the methodology. Investigators are under no ethical obligation to divulge everything to everyone prior to the research, but they must take care to protect subjects from physical or psychological harm. Most importantly, the *informed consent* of subjects must be obtained, in which subjects are told about potential risks and are given the opportunity to decline to participate or to withdraw during their participation. After the research is completed, the investigators are obligated to make a full disclosure of what was done and why. Any information collected on individual participants is considered confidential and is not to be shared with others without the permission of the participant.

When research is conducted in a field setting with actual employees the ethical responsibilities become more complex. Not only is the investigator held to the above responsibilities, but there are also responsibilities to the organization and the management of that organization. An I/O psychologist is obligated to inform the organization of what he or she is doing and must ask its permission to undertake the research. A particularly difficult issue can arise when the I/O psychologist is a consultant to the organization. If an employer wishes to disclose the results of research, the psychologist must tell participants prior to the research who will receive the results. Moreover, a prior agreement must be struck with management that participation is voluntary and that each employee has the right to decline to participate or to withdraw at any time without being punished. Each participating employee must agree to the disclosure of his or her data. If the organization does not agree to these procedures, then the I/O psychologist should look for an organization that will. Those psychologists who violate the ethical standards can be reported to ethics committees at the state and national level.

## THE ACADEMIC MODEL VERSUS PRACTICAL REALITIES

Some I/O psychologists work in industry, some in consulting firms, and some in universities. The demands placed on them differ, and as a consequence, their views of how to best conduct research can differ considerably. Psychologists in industry are under pressure to come up with answers to problems. The psychologist in academia is expected to conduct careful, programmatic research and to avoid rash conclusions. The former may view the latter as ivory tower eggheads with little conception of the outside world. The latter may view the former as flimflam artists willing to sell any method that can make a buck regardless of the scientific evidence.

Such stereotypes are unfortunate, and while they do occur, they are not widespread. Indeed, one of the major strengths of I/O psychology is the diverse mixture of practitioners and academics who contribute to the storehouse of knowledge. Nevertheless, there are differences between the ideal scientific model and the way research often must be conducted in organizations. Virginia Boehm (1980) provided a thoughtful comparison of the two approaches. The academic model of research is presented in Figure 2.4 and starts with a topic chosen by the investigator. After a careful scrutiny of past work, a hypothesis is formed and a study designed to test this hypothesis. A correlational field study, lab experiment, field experiment, or some other type of research is conducted, the data analyzed, and a decision made as to whether the original hypothesis is supported by the data. If the hypothesis is not supported, then the investigator goes back to the drawing board, perhaps reanalyzing the data or forming alternative explanations to test in subsequent research. Once the investigator feels comfortable with the validity or invalidity of the original hypotheses, then the results are written in the form of a report for a professional meeting, a journal, or a book.

In contrast to the academic model of research, research conducted within an organization can follow a much different course (see Figure 2.5). The topic often is not chosen by the investigator but is prompted by an organizational problem that the investigator is asked (or told) to solve. After some analysis, a

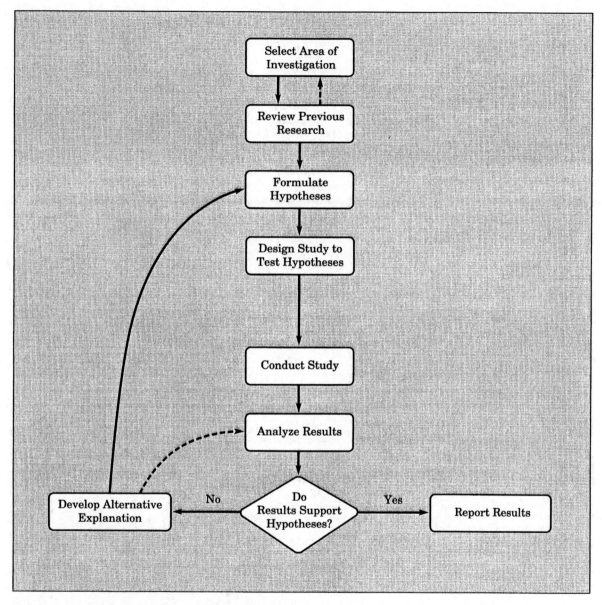

**Figure 2.4**  *The academic model of research*

*Source:* Boehm, V.R. (1980). Research in the "real-world"—a conceptual model. *Personnel Psychology, 33,* 495–504.

solution is proposed (a training program, a new performance appraisal system, etc.) and a study is designed to evaluate the solution. The investigator often has to persuade the organization that the research is worthwhile and even after conducting the study must sell the organization on the benefits of the proposal. Investigators must often go to Herculean efforts to maintain

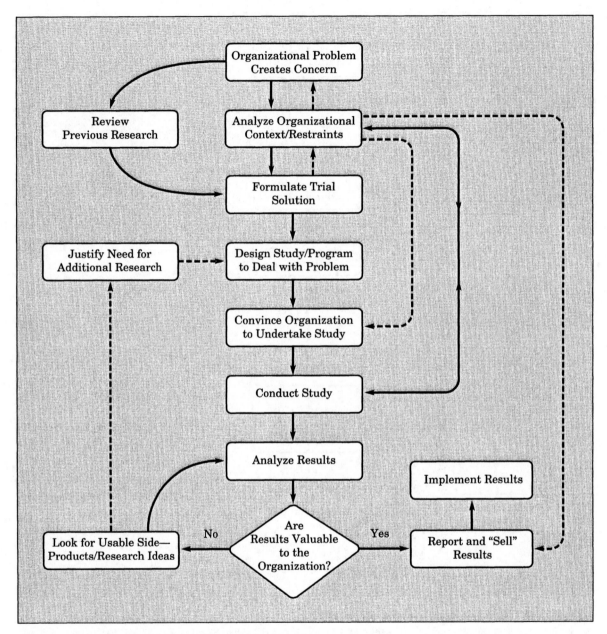

**Figure 2.5** *The practitioner model of research*

*Source:* Boehm, V.R. (1980). Research in the "real world"—a conceptual model. *Personnel Psychology, 33,* 495–504.

rigorous experimental control when conducting research in an organization and frequently their efforts are frustrated by management's desire to rush a solution. The answer is not to give up on the standards of scientific research discussed in this chapter but to open the method to creative solutions. Well worth remembering is P. W. Bridgman's dictum that "the scientist has no other method than doing his damnedest" (Kaplan, 1964, p. 27).

## DISCUSSION QUESTIONS

1. What contribution, if any, can nonscientific sources of knowledge make in I/O research?
2. Describe the basic differences between descriptive and inferential statistics.
3. What are the characteristics of a good psychological measure?
4. It has been observed that all forms of validity are basically types of construct validity. Why is this the case?
5. What do we mean when we say that an experimental design is only as good as the number of alternative interpretations it can eliminate?
6. Is laboratory research with college students ever justified in attempting to understand behavior in organizations? Why? Why not?
7. Why is it often easier to maintain scientific standards in laboratory research than in field research?
8. Is it ever ethical to conceal findings from research participants? Explain.

## IN SEARCH OF EXCELLENCE

A type of book that has appeared with increasing frequency over the last ten years is one in which the authors take a sample of successful managers or companies and then set forth the attributes that supposedly account for their effectiveness. As popular as these books have been, are they based on scientific research?

A case in point is Peters and Waterman's (1982) best selling book of managerial advice, *In Search of Excellence*. The authors took a sample of 62 companies that they believed represented a diverse collection of U.S. industries. The companies, in their words, were "considered to be innovative and excellent by an informed group of observers of the business scene—businessmen, consultants, members of the business press, and business academics" (p. 19). An additional criterion imposed on the selection of the sample was that the companies be in the top half of their industry in four of six measures of financial performance during 1961–1980. Finally, the list was narrowed to 43 companies rated by industry experts as consistently innovative throughout the 20-year period. On the basis of interviews with company representatives as well as examination of documents and records, the authors arrived at a profile of eight attributes that they believed were responsible for the success of these excellent companies. Rather than conducting statistical analyses, the authors drew their conclusions on the basis of their subjective assessments of the individual organizations. These attributes were:

1. *An action bias.* The excellent companies do not endlessly study a problem but find answers and then move quickly to implement the solutions.
2. *A customer orientation.* They tend to closely monitor and respond to customer preferences.
3. *Autonomy.* They allow units of the organization to work independently without close supervision.
4. *Productivity through people.* The management of the firms trust and respect their employees and attempt to develop their aptitudes.
5. *Value focus.* These organizations make explicit a set of values that represents what the organization stands for and is the guiding factor of organizational strategy.
6. *Do what they know best.* The excellent organizations stay close to the business that they know and in which they have succeeded rather than diversifying into business activities that are far removed from their expertise.
7. *Both centralized and decentralized.* The excellent companies demand strict adherence to the core values of the firm, but they allow autonomy of action by employees at all levels of the organization.
8. *A simple organizational form with few staff.* The excellent companies tend to use straightforward, clear structural arrangements and avoid the proliferation of staff.

The companies that Peters and Waterman included among the excellent organizations were IBM, Texas Instruments, Hewlett-Packard, Xerox, Johnson & Johnson, Proctor & Gamble, Dana Corporation, 3M Corporation, McDonald's, Delta Airlines, Wal-Mart, Exxon, Disney Corporation, Maytag, Levi Strauss, Xerox, Tupperware, and Dow Chemical.

## CASE QUESTIONS

1.   How would you evaluate the validity of the research that served as the foundation for the conclusions of Peters and Waterman?
2.   In what respects did this research meet or fail to meet the standards of scientific research discussed in this chapter?
3.   In what ways would you improve on the research of Peters and Waterman?

# SECTION

# ORGANIZATIONAL PSYCHOLOGY:
## THE SOCIAL PSYCHOLOGY OF WORK BEHAVIOR

The first half of this text covers topics in *organizational psychology* (the O in the I/O), including work motivation, attitudes, groups, leadership, and stress. Much of this literature comes from the research of social scientists who view organizations as complex social systems. By starting with organizational psychology, we hope to convey the big picture of how organizations function prior to moving on, in the second half of the text, to the more applied issues that are the focus of *personnel* or *industrial psychology* (the I in I/O). For instance, our discussion of work motivation (Chapter 3) and communication processes (Chapter 5) will set the stage for our later discussion of performance appraisal and feedback (Chapter 9).

The basic component of the organization is the individual employee. It is appropriate then to begin this section with a consideration of work motivation (Chapter 3) and attitudes (Chapter 4). Much of the interest in these topics has come from the potential role that unmotivated and dissatisfied employees may play in the deteriorating economic competitiveness of U.S. firms. Could the declines in productivity observed over the last two decades reflect the declining motivation of the work force? Do employees feel that their

important needs are being met in their work? What are effects of the frustration and satisfaction of needs on work behavior? Do employees expect that they will be rewarded for working hard and making other contributions to the organization? How do these expectations influence motivation? Do employees feel that they have been fairly treated? How do feelings of equity or inequity translate into job performance? The present chapter explores each of these questions and the process by which needs, expectations, and equity influence the effort that employees invest in their work.

The answers to these questions have important implications for how organizations manage their employees. Traditional management practices often assume that employees are passive and lack the ability to contribute creative ideas. The human relations approach has promoted the opposite view that all employees want challenging work and the opportunity to develop their skills. Research on motivation, which has empirically examined these assumptions, has provided a more realistic and complex view than provided by either the traditional or human relations approaches. Much of this research has focused on content issues such as what employees want, whereas other studies have addressed the process of motivation. We discuss recent attempts to coordinate the various theories of motivation and the practical implications of these efforts.

Motivation leads directly to the topic of attitudes toward work and the organization. Some critics of modern management practices have claimed that today's workforce has become increasingly alienated by dehumanizing aspects of their jobs. Chapter 4 examines the research on changes in work-related attitudes such as job satisfaction, organizational commitment, and job involvement. We examine some of the methods that have been developed to tap these work-related attitudes, and the research findings using these methods. Research has not supported some widely held beliefs, such as the assumption that job satisfaction leads directly to good performance. Nevertheless, worker attitudes are crucial to understanding and predicting other important behaviors in the job, such as turnover.

In contrast to the chapters on attitudes and motivation, which are concerned with behavior of individual employees, Chapter 6 is concerned with social behavior in the workplace. The importance of this topic becomes apparent when you consider that an organization is essentially a group of groups. Much of the activity in an organization consists of people communicating, influencing, competing, fighting, and helping. Social structures, such as roles and norms, emerge to add predictability to these processes. Much of the social behavior that can be observed in an organization comes as the result of the formal departments and other subunits that management forms to get the work done. Just as important, however, are the informal relationships that emerge and sometimes conflict with formal social arrangements. Whether formal or informal in nature, groups often fail to achieve their potential success. We conclude this chapter by examining some of the interventions used to improve group effectiveness in organizations.

The social behavior chapter leads naturally to our next topic—leadership. This is perhaps the most controversial of the social-psychological aspects of organizations. Although those who hold formal positions of leadership are usually held responsible for the success of the organization, some organizational theorists have questioned whether leaders are really as important as most people believe. Is leadership mainly in the mind of the beholder, so that anyone who manages the right impressions can become a leader? Is leadership an outdated concept reflecting mainly the needs of followers to believe that someone is in charge? If leadership is important to the success of the organization, what can be done to improve the effectiveness of leaders? Is it primarily a matter of selecting the people with the right traits? Can we train people to show the right behaviors regardless of their traits? Do great leaders transform rather than simply manage their followers? In exploring the research that has addressed these questions, we show how simplistic views of what makes an effective leader have been replaced by more complex contingency models. Essentially, these models state that the effectiveness of leadership depends on whether the traits and behaviors of the leader are appropriate to the situation. Different situations call for radically different types of leaders.

A hallmark of organizational psychology has been the concern with the well-being of the employee in addition to the performance of the organization. It is appropriate that this section ends with a consideration of employee stress. Work stress is considered epidemic among employees in many occupations, but is it really as bad as the popular press suggests? Chapter 8 examines the personal and situational factors that can determine the physiological and psychological reactions of employees to unusual demands (sometimes called stressors). In addition to examining the antecedents and consequences of stress, this chapter also evaluates research on coping strategies and the applications of this work to helping employees manage stress in the workplace.

# CHAPTER

3

# Work Motivation

- Work Motivation and Personal Characteristics: Need Theory

- Work Motivation and Environmental Characteristics: Behaviorism and Behavior Modification

- Work Motivation: Personal and Environmental Characteristics

- Integrative Approaches to Work Motivation Theory

- A Final Summation and a Look at the Future

- Case: The American Worker: Lazy or Overworked?

You have undoubtedly been asked why you wanted to attend college. Without much hesitation, you probably answered that you wanted to prepare for a career that required college-level training, or that college would help you obtain a more skilled and higher paying job. Consider other scenarios. Why did Lisa pass up theater dates, dances, and trips to the beach to study for the bar exam? Why did Ken work 12-hour days and weekends on an important project at work, thus neglecting his wife and young son? Why did Marie willingly accept a job offer in New York City, which is 2,000 miles from her family and friends?

Each of these seemingly different scenarios has a common theme. Each deals with goal-directed behavior. When you ask why someone behaves in a certain way, you are inquiring about the reasons underlying his or her goal-directed behavior. When you observe Lisa's, Ken's, or Marie's behavior, you typically infer or guess at the underlying reasons for their behavior. Motivation theorists generally attempt to answer three questions relating to goal-directed behavior: 1) What energizes goal-directed behavior; 2) what focuses goal-directed behavior; and 3) how is goal-directed behavior sustained over time? Goal-directed behavior is usually energized by forces within the person. For example, a personal need, such as a need to achieve or gain power, may prompt a person to work overtime. Goal-directed behavior is often focused or channeled toward something in the environment, such as a promotion or college degree. Goal-directed behavior is sustained by considering how forces in the person and in the environment interact to reinforce or redirect that goal-directed behavior. For example, a person who has a need to achieve may reevaluate his goals to go to medical school after receiving poor grades in biology and chemistry. This viewpoint embodies a systems orientation because it considers the interaction of both personal and environmental factors (Steers & Porter, 1991).

Our exploration of human motivation in the workplace involves those perspectives of work motivation that have targeted personal characteristics, such as achievement needs; environmental characteristics, such as incentives provided by the organization; and combinations of both personal and environmental characteristics, such as how people with different achievement needs are affected by organizational incentive systems. First, those perspectives dealing primarily with personal characteristics, such as need theories, are presented, followed by those perspectives dealing with environmental characteristics, such as reinforcement theory. The third topic covers motivational theories, such as equity theory and expectancy theory, that consider both factors in the person and the environment. In all three sections, the theoretical framework for each perspective is presented as well as the empirical research which has tested the theory. The implications of both theory and research for application in organizations are also discussed. The last topic covers recent efforts to combine the various motivation theories into larger, integrative theoretical frameworks, or meta-theories.

# WORK MOTIVATION AND PERSONAL CHARACTERISTICS: NEED THEORY

When you describe a friend, you may use words like "aggressive, domineering, competitive, nurturing, and sociable." If so, you are using personal descriptors or characteristics that many psychological theorists have identified as basic human needs that are present in everyone. Need theorists believe that people are motivated to satisfy these needs to a greater or lesser degree. For example, if you have a greater need to socialize than your friend Bob, then you will probably seek out the company of others more frequently than Bob will. We will shortly discuss the relevance of these personal characteristics to motivation at work and the strong impact need theorists' ideas have had on organizational practices.

The pioneering work on need theory was accomplished by a personality psychologist, Henry Murray, in the 1930s (Murray, 1938). Murray proposed more than 20 human needs. Viscerogenic needs are associated with physiological functioning and included food, water, sex, urination, defecation, and lactation. Psychogenic needs are mostly learned and included the needs for achievement, affiliation, dominance, autonomy, and aggression. Murray differed from earlier theorists in that he believed that psychogenic needs are learned, not inherited. Furthermore, he believed that psychogenic needs are only activated by environmental cues. For example, people with a need for affiliation would only seek companionship when other people are available. Murray also believed that all people possess the same basic needs, although in different amounts. For example, you and your friend Sally both have a need to achieve, but your need to achieve might be greater than Sally's. Therefore, every person has the same needs, but every person is unique in the relative importance of each of these needs.

Unfortunately, Murray said little about needs within the context of work motivation. His ideas and measurement techniques, however, did influence work motivation theories. In particular, his conception of human needs and development of a projective test, the Thematic Apperception Test (TAT), to measure these needs had a tremendous impact on Abraham Maslow and David McClelland, whose theories of work motivation are discussed next.

## Maslow's Need Hierarchy

In the 1950s, Abraham Maslow proposed a theory of human motivation that grew out of the humanistic movement in psychology. By observing clients in his clinical practice, Maslow determined that people are motivated by five types of needs: physiological needs, safety needs, social needs, ego needs, and self-actualization needs. The physiological needs are those needs fundamental to survival, such as the need for food, water, sleep, and reproduction (sex). The safety needs include the needs for law and order and for protection from physical harm. The social needs deal with the desire to obtain emotional attachments, such as friendship and love. The ego needs involve the need to gain self-esteem and respect; the ego needs can be focused inwardly, such as the desire for mastery, or outwardly, such as the desire for recognition. The self-actualization needs involve needs associated with personal growth and development; more specifically, self-actualization refers to realizing one's potential and becoming the best one can be.

According to Maslow, these needs are arranged in a hierarchy of importance: Higher order needs are not important until lower order needs are satisfied. For example, if you are hungry or thirsty, you will not be concerned with fulfilling your needs for friendship and protection from harm until your hunger or thirst is satiated. Maslow thought that, for most people, the lower order needs are more satisfied than the higher order needs; that is, the needs for food and sex are more often satisfied than the need for relationships with other people. However, he did not believe that all lower order needs must be satisfied to trigger higher order needs: The one exception to the hierarchical notion of needs is self-actualization. Maslow said that self-actualization, or the need to realize one's potential in life, can never be fulfilled. In essence, Maslow conceived of self-actualization as a lifelong growth process. An artist who strives for self-actualization, according to Maslow, does not need to be a Picasso or Rembrandt, but only the best artist he can be. This self-improvement process continues throughout a person's lifetime (Maslow, 1943; 1954).

In spite of its intuitive appeal, Maslow's need hierarchy has not been supported empirically. As you recall, the need hierarchy requires that, as a need is satisfied, it becomes less important and the next higher need assumes more importance. The most appropriate way to test this process is to examine how need satisfaction varies over time. Hall and Nougaim (1968) conducted a longitudinal study to test this aspect of the need hierarchy. Over a five-year period, they found that satisfied needs became more, not less, important to the workers in their study. Lawler and Suttle (1972) also found no support for Maslow's need hierarchy theory in a study involving a six-month period. Rauschenberger, Schmitt, and Hunter (1980) reported that increases in the importance of one need were accompanied by increases in the importance of other needs as well. In addition, factor analyses of the five proposed dimensions of the need hierarchy have not shown these dimensions to be independent or even separable (Payne, 1970). Wahba and Bridwell's (1976) review of organizational need hierarchy research reported that existing data only supported the presence of two categories of needs, a lower order category, composed of physiological, safety, and social needs, and a higher order category, composed of ego and self-actualization needs. They further maintained that even these two categories did not fall into a rigid hierarchy. In answer to the deficiencies of Maslow's theory, Alderfer (1969) proposed a modified version of the need hierarchy, called ERG theory, which we will discuss shortly.

Although Maslow never envisioned it as a theory of work motivation, the need hierarchy has been broadly applied in many organizations. One implication of the need hierarchy for work settings is that management must determine where workers are located on the hierarchy. If workers are primarily concerned with their safety needs at work (for example, job security), they will not respond to attempts to satisfy their esteem needs (for example, recognition or status). Because people may be at any place in the hierarchy, Maslow's theory also implies that each worker may require something different to satisfy his or her needs. Another implication of the need hierarchy is that, if organizations can manage to fulfill workers' basic needs, then organizations should address the higher order needs, ego and self-actualization. As a consequence, the need hierarchy has been cited as the impetus for diverse organizational change efforts, from the creation of pleasant work environments and employee-oriented supervision to participative management programs and job enrichment.

Much of the organizational fervor can be attributed to popular management theorists, such as McGregor (1960). McGregor introduced the concepts of Theory X and Theory Y management philosophies. Theory X describes a task-oriented, directive management style. Theory Y describes an employee-oriented, unstructured management style. A Theory Y manager would attempt to determine the unsatisfied needs of his or her subordinates (in Maslow's terms, their location on the need hierarchy). The Theory Y manager would then attempt to satisfy those needs, whether the employees required more social interaction at work or enriched jobs. According to McGregor, only by satisfying the needs of their workers can organizations expect to obtain maximum productivity from them.

## ERG Theory

The most popular modification of Maslow's need hierarchy is Alderfer's (1969) existence–relatedness–growth or ERG theory. Alderfer altered the need hierarchy by adopting a three-level classification system and abolishing the concept of a rigid hierarchy. The three categories are: 1) existence needs, which subsume Maslow's physiological and safety needs; 2) relatedness needs, which include Maslow's social needs; and 3) growth needs, which subsume Maslow's ego needs and self-actualization.

Unlike Maslow, Alderfer believed that people could move up and down this hierarchy and be motivated by more than one need simultaneously. For example, if you failed to obtain a coveted job promotion by taking on extra assignments at work, you may decide to spend more time on your social life while still striving for a future promotion or you may decide to spend all your time on your social life. Alderfer would label this latter option frustration/regression because, as a consequence of your thwarted attempts to achieve, you decided to regress down the hierarchy to satisfy lower needs. Table 3.1 compares ERG Theory with other need theories. Few empirical tests of ERG theory

**Table 3.1**

| COMPARISON OF THREE NEED THEORIES: MURRAY'S, MASLOW'S, (NEED THEORY), AND ALDERFER'S (ERG) THEORIES | | |
|---|---|---|
| **MURRAY** | **MASLOW** | **ALDERFER** |
| Psychogenic: Abasement Achievement Affiliation Aggression Autonomy Deference Dominance | Self-actualization | Growth |
| | Esteem | |
| | Social | Relatedness |
| Viscerogenic: Food Water Sex Urination Defecation Lactation | Safety | Existence |
| | Physiological | |
| Divided into two categories but not arranged according to level or importance | Arranged in a hierarchical level of prepotency | Arranged in a hierarchy, but all can be simultaneously active |

*Source*: Adapted from Cherrington, D.J. (1983). *Personnel Management*. Dubuque, IA: Wm. C. Brown, p. 255.

exist, and what do exist provide mixed support (Alderfer, 1972; Scherf, 1974; Wanous & Zwany, 1977). Undoubtedly, the failure of Maslow's theory to hold up under empirical scrutiny has discouraged research on any type of needs hierarchy. This is particularly unfortunate, given that Alderfer addressed many of the deficiencies of Maslow's hierarchy.

## Need for Achievement

Although we have discussed need theory in detail, we have not examined any specific needs, such as aggression, dominance, or nurturance, because theorists such as Murray and Maslow did not specify any particular needs as being more important than others. However, David McClelland and his colleagues have identified a single need, the need for achievement (nAch), as being especially important from personal, social, and organizational perspectives (Atkinson, 1964; McClelland, 1965). According to McClelland, our competitive and success-oriented society values and reinforces the need to achieve; friends, supervisors, and the media constantly encourage us to excel, to be "on top." Unlike some of the earlier theorists who viewed needs as innate and unchanging characteristics, McClelland believes that the achievement motive is a learned need that we acquire from our parents. At first glance, the implications of the achievement motive for personal and organizational functioning are very impressive: The need to achieve would logically seem to have an impact on the type of job or career you desire, the level of job or career performance you attain, and the attitudes you hold about that job or career.

McClelland and his colleagues have defined the need to achieve as behavior oriented toward competition with a standard of excellence. The method of measuring the achievement motive has relied primarily on a projective test, the Thematic Apperception Test, or TAT. If you were to take the TAT, you would be shown a variety of pictures and asked to tell a story about these pictures. Your achievement score would be calculated by determining the number of times competition with a standard of excellence is mentioned.

Cards like this are used in the Thematic Apperception Test (TAT) to assess needs.

The TAT has been used to assess the achievement motive so extensively that McClelland has even developed norms against which to evaluate individual scores.

✳ Three salient characteristics define high-need achievers. First, they are task–performance-oriented. People high in the achievement motive take personal responsibility for solving a problem or performing a task. Second, they require feedback about their performance. Only with performance feedback can the high-need achiever improve poor performance or bask in the glow of successful performance. Third, they set moderately difficult goals rather than very difficult or easy goals. The rationale here is that moderately difficult goals are challenging but still attainable.

How has need achievement fared under the scrutiny of systematic investigation? Like other types of need theories, the achievement motive, although intuitively appealing, has been roundly criticized by researchers. Empirical evidence for the theory's propositions is mixed (Brockhaus, 1980; Klinger, 1966; McClelland, 1976). The TAT, like most projective tests, has also been criticized for its weak measurement properties (Entvisle, 1972), although some recent research using sophisticated quantitative analyses is more supportive (Spangler, 1992).

Despite these criticisms, McClelland and his associates have developed a training program to enhance the achievement motive. They claim to have increased the need to achieve in many groups of people who participated in these programs. The training program consists of four major components: 1) obtain information on the achievement motive and its importance for success; 2) set high performance goals and maintain a record of performance accomplishments; 3) try to think of yourself as a high achiever and a winner; and 4) seek out group support from other people who are (or who are trying to become) high achievers.

Probably the training program's most well-known success story involved 52 business managers in India (McClelland, 1962). According to McClelland, several months after experiencing the training program, these managers doubled the amount of their performance-oriented, and, therefore success-oriented, activities. These results concur with McClelland's contention that the achievement motive can be increased through training, and that groups of people or whole cultures can become more achievement oriented. A moment's thought, however, reveals that the achievement motive training program contained elements other than need achievement, specifically goal-setting and social support. Any one or a combination of other factors may have produced the desired outcome. Consequently, if or when the training program works, we cannot determine what made it successful.

## Need for Power

Another need with implications for work motivation is the need for power (nPow), defined as the need to control other people. Characteristics associated with the need for power include a desire to control other people, maintain leader-follower relations, and influence and direct others (Cherrington, 1989). McClelland (1970) describes two faces of power: personal power, or striving for power for its own sake, and social or institutional power, or striving for power for the attainment of organizational goals. Social or institutional power facilitates organizational effectiveness more than personal power because those individuals with a high need for social power will work toward organizational objectives rather than personal, ego-satisfying objectives (McClelland, 1970). In fact, McClelland and Burnham (1976) have stated that the need for power, particularly social power, is a far more important managerial attribute than the need for achievement (see Chapter 6 for further discussion of this). A limited amount of empirical research supports McClelland's assertions. For example, McClelland and Boyatzis (1982) reported that a high need for power and low need for affiliation (the desire to be with and show concern for other people) predicted managerial success over a sixteen-year period at AT&T. The need for achievement did not predict managerial success as well, particularly at the higher organizational levels. At this time, however, no direct applications of the need for power have been developed for use in organizations.

*Summary*

The need theories have not proven to be particularly useful in explaining motivation in the work context, possibly because they were mostly formulated from clinical observations of human behavior, rather than from well-grounded theory or data. One exception is ERG theory, which Aldefer (1969) developed in response to empirical research on the need hierarchy. Probably because of the disenchantment among researchers over need theory in general, few empirical tests of ERG theory have been conducted. Another conceptually well-developed need theory, the need for achievement, has generated considerable criticism. However, recent tests of specific hypotheses derived from a refinement of McClelland's original propositions are more supportive (Spangler, 1992). A need with important organizational implications is the need for power. Although limited data exist, researchers believe the need for power may be more important than need achievement in influencing managerial effectiveness (McClelland & Burnham, 1976).

There are other criticisms of ERG theory and the needs for achievement and power. Such theories have been considered to have limited value because they are difficult to adequately test (e.g., they require longitudinal designs: Hall & Nougaim, 1968; Lawler & Suttle, 1972), and they rely on measures ( e.g., the TAT) that are suspect (Entvisle, 1972). These very practical impediments bode poorly for the future of need theories in organizational research, even ERG and need achievement theory. This situation is unfortunate, given the obvious and fundamental importance of needs in understanding human behavior.

# WORK MOTIVATION AND ENVIRONMENTAL CHARACTERISTICS: BEHAVIORISM AND BEHAVIOR MODIFICATION

You would undoubtedly agree that your environment affects your behavior. For example, if the skies are dark and cloudy tomorrow, you will probably decide to take an umbrella or raincoat when you depart for work or school. If your company's policies discourage tardiness, you will surely attempt to be punctual, particularly if you are working toward a promotion. The discipline of behaviorism systematically studies how aspects of the environment influence human behavior. The behaviorist believes that psychologists should study only observable behavior, not feelings or affect, and that behavior is shaped solely by environmental factors. Before we discuss behaviorally oriented motivation research, however, some learning principles must be briefly reviewed.

## Theoretical Assumptions

The behavioral psychologist recognizes two basic learning processes: classical conditioning and operant conditioning. Classical conditioning (Michael & Meyerson, 1962; Pavlov, 1902) is concerned with involuntary or reflexive behavior and is not directly applicable to our discussion about work motivation. Operant or voluntary conditioning (Michael & Meyerson, 1962; Skinner, 1969), however, has been broadly applied in work motivation research. In *operant conditioning,* rewards (and punishments) are contingent upon the subject's response or failure to respond.

If your door bell rings, you will probably answer the door. The reason for your action is that you have been operantly conditioned to answer a ringing door bell; from many prior experiences, you know that someone is on the other side of the door. The stimulus is the ringing door bell; the response is answering the door; and the (positive) consequences are greeting and visiting with a friend or acquaintance. Your decision to answer the door, however, is always totally voluntary and under your control. A common example of operant conditioning in a work setting would be the administration of praise by a supervisor for a task well performed. The worker completes a report in a timely and thorough manner and is therefore praised by his supervisor. This sequence of events increases the probability that the worker will decide to respond similarly when preparing future reports.

All of the principles advocated by behaviorists involve *positive reinforcement,* which means that a positive consequence, such as praise, follows the desired response and increases the frequency of the response. *Negative reinforcement* refers to the removal of a negative consequence, such as criticism, which follows the desired response and also increases the frequency of that response. *Punishment,* on the other hand, involves an undesirable or noxious consequence (or withholding a positive consequence), which follows from an undesired behavior. An example of punishment would be if the supervisor reprimanded the worker (or withheld a pay raise) because the worker did not produce a timely and thorough report. Although punishment is commonly used in all phases of life, including organizations (see Arvey & Ivancevich, 1980), behaviorists do not generally advocate its use (Skinner, 1969; Whyte, 1956). Punishment is generally perceived to be cruel and ineffective compared with positive reinforcement. One reason for punishment's ineffectiveness is that it demonstrates what should not be done, but does not demonstrate what should be done. Therefore, the reprimanded employee knows what he or she did wrong, but may not know how to correct the behavior.

Behaviorists are concerned with different types of *schedules of reinforcement.* For example, to produce optimal performance, should the supervisor praise the employee for every good performance, or should the praise be given only occasionally? Surprisingly, partial reinforcement, in which reinforcement occurs only some of the time, was thought to produce more permanent learning (Ferster & Skinner, 1957). These partial reinforcement schedules vary either according to specified intervals of time *(interval schedules),* such as receiving a bonus every six months, or according to a specified number of responses *(ratio schedules),* such as receiving a bonus after producing 1,000 widgets. Both interval and ratio schedules can also be fixed or variable. Under fixed schedules, the reward is received after a fixed time, such as every hour, or after a fixed number of correct responses, such as five. Under variable schedules, the reinforcement schedule is not obvious to the recipient because it varies around some average time interval or number of responses. For example, if the reward is administered after an overall average of one hour or five responses, any one instance of reinforcement may vary considerably from this average.

According to Hamner (1991), the potential utility of the different types of schedules in organizations has largely been ignored. Promotions and praise should achieve their optimal effects if administered on a variable interval schedule, which means that reinforcement (e.g., praise) is dispensed irregularly. Variable schedules keep people on their toes because they never know when to expect the reinforcement. However, promotions in many organization occur very predictably every six months to a few years. Under this type of system, which is formally called a *fixed interval schedule,* workers increase their effort immediately prior to the time of the expected promotion and decrease their effort at other times.

Supplementary bonuses, such as Christmas bonuses, are often dispensed on a routine basis. A more fruitful approach would be to administer these bonuses irregularly throughout the year according to productivity level. This is a variable ratio schedule because reinforcement is given irregularly after a desired number of responses. Under this type of reward system, employees can see a direct link between their performance and organizational bonuses, which should be a tremendous incentive builder.

## Research and Application

Organizational research on the effectiveness of different types of reinforcement schedules has been inconclusive. Saari and Latham (1982) reported that a variable ratio schedule was associated with higher performance than continuous reinforcement schedules. In studies that attempted to modify the behavior of tree planters (Yukl & Latham, 1975; Yukl, Latham, & Pursell, 1976), workers who were paid on a ratio schedule (according to the number of trees they planted) planted more trees than workers paid on an interval schedule (hourly wage). Pritchard and his colleagues (Pritchard, Hollenbeck, & DeLeo, 1980; Pritchard, Leonard, Von Bergen, & Kirk, 1976) investigated the effects of different reinforcement schedules on workers' performance on self-paced tests of job-related knowledge. Results indicated that employees who were contingently reinforced, or paid according to the number of tests they passed, performed better than those who received an hourly wage. Whether they were paid on a fixed or variable ratio schedule, however, made no difference.

Now that we have reviewed some simple tenets of behaviorism, we can examine how behavioral principles have been applied in organizations. According to Komaki, Coombs, and Schepman (1991), a reinforcement program typically follows four steps: specify desired behavior; measure desired performance; provide frequent, contingent, positive consequences; and evaluate effectiveness on the job. The exact behavior or behaviors that the program is attempting to motivate the workers to achieve should be specified, along with an accompanying time line.

If, for example, the organization would like to motivate its salespersons to increase their sales volume by 20% within six months, then that goal should be clearly stated. Sales volume should be carefully measured and recorded to provide documentation for the performance changes. It is very important that performance changes (in this case, sales volume) be publicly posted often so these changes are salient to all involved workers. This step provides frequent direct feedback on their stated performance goal(s). Finally, to assess the effectiveness of the program, the performance changes must be evaluated quantitatively. In the sales example, such an evaluation should be straightforward. However, statistics often are needed to determine if the performance changes are meaningful.

A good example of behavioral research in an organization was reported by Luthans, Paul, and Baker (1981). Their goal was to motivate employees in a large retail department store to improve work performance. Some of the specified behaviors were assisting a customer within 5 seconds after he or she arrived in the sales area and keeping the shelves stocked within 70% of capacity. The experimenters observed and recorded employee behavior on the sales floor. The rewards were various amounts of time off, depending on how well the performance goals were met. Because the most common motivational technique prior to the behavioral intervention had been threats by management, the absence of punishment (the threats) and customer responsiveness

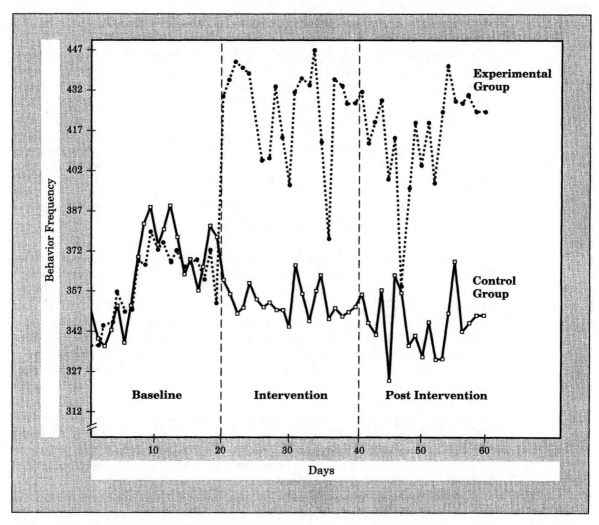

**Figure 3.1** *Aggregate retailing behavior as a consequence of providing contingent reinforcement (experimental group)*
*Source:* Luthans, F., Paul, R., & Baker, D. (1981). An experimental analysis of the impact of contingent reinforcement on sales persons' performance behavior. *Journal of Applied Psychology, 66,* 319.

served as positive, frequent reinforcement. The evaluation of the experiment over a 60-day interval is illustrated in Figure 3.1. The baseline period refers to a period of time during which the experimenters observed the employees prior to the intervention; the purpose of these observations was to provide information on typical work performance. After the intervention was initiated, performance increased dramatically in the experimental group and remained high even after the reward program was discontinued (the postintervention phase). (High postintervention performance does not always occur.

Sometimes performance even decreases below baseline after the intervention is discontinued.)

Probably the most well-known and resounding success story using a behaviorally based motivation program was the Emery Air Freight Corporation program. A focus of this program was to motivate workers to use containers properly in packaging items for shipment. The employees were shown how to properly package items, performance goals for packaging were stated, verbal praise was used as a reinforcer or reward, and performance progress was charted. Although the program has been discontinued, it apparently achieved some success at the time it was implemented. According to Emery, the program saved the organization $2 million in 1975 alone.

## Implications and Current Trends

From both the empirical research and applications in industry, it seems obvious that behavioral principles do work. Contingent reinforcement schedules, particularly ratio schedules, are often quite effective in motivating workers to alter their behavior (although the distinction between variable and fixed schedules does not appear to be important). Despite their effectiveness, behavioral programs have not been widely applied in organizations. One reason is practicality. The record keeping and paper work required to implement and maintain these types of programs are prodigious. Moreover, such programs can have a boomerang effect: If they are discontinued, performance may fall below baseline. Strict behaviorism has also been criticized for its "black box" approach to human behavior; that is, it ignores the obvious influence of cognitive and unconscious factors (Bandura, 1982, 1986). An additional concern expressed by many psychologists is that behavioral programs can be unethical because they attempt to blatantly manipulate workers' behaviors (Rogers & Skinner, 1956).

An interesting extension of behavioral theory is the application of *social learning theory* (Bandura, 1982; 1986) to organizational research. One of the tenets of social learning theory is that most learning results not from rewarding or punishing behavior, but from observing the behaviors of other people; this is called *observational learning*. For example, children learn many behaviors, such as how to cross the street, by observing older children and adults. O'Reilly and Puffer (1989) nicely demonstrated an application of social learning theory to organizational research. In both laboratory and field studies, they found that the observation of rewards and punishments affected observers' job attitudes. For example, when they witnessed an inappropriate reward or sanction toward a fellow subject or worker, such as receiving punishment that was not deserved, the observers' perceived motivation, satisfaction, and equity decreased. More cognitively oriented approaches to behaviorism, as illustrated by the O'Reilly and Puffer (1989) study, address one of the major criticisms of behavioral research and application, namely, the neglect of cognitive factors. The future of behaviorism in organizations clearly lies in the marriage of behavioral and cognitive principles.

# WORK MOTIVATION: PERSONAL AND ENVIRONMENTAL CHARACTERISTICS

So far, we have discussed the effects of personal characteristics, particularly in the form of various need theories, and environmental characteristics, in the form of environmental contingencies, on worker motivation. Although both of these perspectives, particularly need theories, have significantly influenced research and application, most motivation perspectives emphasize the *interactions* between various personal and environmental factors. Such interactive theories attempt to explain how, for example, needs and rewards are translated into motivated behavior; these more complex theories are often referred to as *process* theories because they attempt to understand the forces guiding motivation. One pervading theme across all process theories is an emphasis on purposeful, conscious thought, typically in the form of specific types of cognitive processes. In contrast, the need and environmental theories discussed earlier are *content* theories because they focus only on what motivates workers; content theories make no attempt to understand the process by which motivation occurs. Applications of process theories also have provided the framework for the worker-oriented motivational programs found in contemporary organizations (e.g., participative management).

The major process theories of work motivation covered in this chapter include equity theory, goal setting theory, expectancy theory, cognitive evaluation theory, and the job characteristics model.

## Equity Theory

### THEORETICAL ASSUMPTIONS

Have you ever discovered that a coworker you considered your equal in terms of such factors as job type, tenure, and training made a much higher salary than you? If so, how did you initally respond? You were probably surprised and angry. You may have even said, "Well, because I am doing the same work as Joe but making less money, I will simply not work as hard." Because you perceived that you and Joe put the same amount of work into your jobs (inputs) but received quite different salaries (outcomes), you labeled the situation as unfair. Your response to this inequity would be to reduce your inputs; that is, because you received less, you should produce less. If you felt the inequity was really extreme or could not be resolved, you might eventually quit your job and seek more equitable employment elsewhere.

More formally, this process is labeled a *social exchange* process (Adams, 1965; Homans, 1961). The foundation for this process is that people make investments (inputs; typically work of some sort) for which they expect specific rewards (outcomes; often money). People typically have predetermined expectations about how much and what type of inputs are required for certain outcomes. They evaluate the fairness or equity of their inputs and outcomes through interactions with relevant others in which direct comparisons between self and relevant others determine whether the exchange is favorable.

The social exchange theory presented here is Adams' (1963; 1965) equity theory. Adams' equity theory is the most widely used social exchange theory in organizational research, and has focused mostly on the effects of workers' reactions to organizational compensation decisions.

The two major components of equity theory are *inputs* and *outcomes*. Inputs are those tangible and intangible commodities a person brings to the exchange relationship. Examples of inputs are effort at work, training, education, and experience. Outcomes are the products of the exchange. Examples of outcomes include pay, bonuses, promotions, and recognition. According to Adams, people weigh the importance of their different inputs and outcomes and sum across them. The total inputs and total outcomes between a person (p) and a relevant other person or comparison other (o) are compared in the form of a ratio:

$$\text{Equity:} \ \frac{O_p}{I_p} = \frac{O_o}{I_o} \quad \text{Inequity:} \ \frac{O_p}{I_p} < \frac{O_p}{I_o} \ \text{or} \ \frac{O_p}{I_p} > \frac{O_o}{I_o}$$

A state of equity exists when the ratio of the person's inputs and outputs is equal to the other's ratio of inputs and outcomes. Inequity exists when the person's ratio is less or greater than the other's ratio.

Several characteristics of the equity formulas must be explained. The equity formulas do not imply that the amounts of input and outcome for the person and the other are equal, but that the relative amounts are equal. For example, Sally may not work as hard as Don, but if she also receives a lower salary than Don, then a state of equity exists. The formulas also do not imply that "true" equity exists. Both the person and the other may receive very little output for a great amount of input, but if they serve as each other's basis of comparison, equity will still prevail. In addition, the equity or inequity expressed by the formulas does not imply that equity or inequity exists in any objective sense. Sally may perceive that she does not work as hard as Don, although her supervisor or other coworkers may disagree. Equity (or inequity) is totally perceptual and highly subjective.

Although we have only discussed inequity perceptions in terms of pay differentials, Adams (1965) described six different methods of equity resolution:

1. Alter inputs. Example: Change the quantity or quality of work.
2. Alter outcomes. Example: Change the amount of compensation for work.
3. Leave the field. Example: Turnover is an extreme reaction to perceived inequity; absenteeism would be a less extreme reaction.
4. Cognitively distort inputs or outcomes. Example: Reevaluate work so that inputs seem less or greater than previously.

5. Try to change the inputs or outcomes of the comparison other. Example: Convince the comparison other to change the quantity or quality of his or her work.
6. Change the comparison other. Example: Pick a comparison other more similar in terms of experience, training, and job duties.

## RESEARCH AND APPLICATION

The empirical research on Adams' equity theory has focused almost exclusively on the first option, alter inputs. One of the possible reasons for this myopic focus is that equity research has followed a rather narrow, well-defined path. Most studies have been laboratory studies in which undergraduates were hired to perform very simple tasks such as the proofreading of manuscripts. (With simple tasks, differences in performance should result from motivational, not ability, differences.) Two different perceived inequity manipulations have been used: *qualifications* and *circumstances*. In the qualifications manipulation, subjects are told that they are either under-qualified or overqualified for the job, and therefore the payment they receive will not reflect their qualifications. In the circumstances manipulation, subjects are told that because of budgetary factors they will be paid either more or less than promised. Regardless of the type of equity manipulation, subjects are supposed to attempt to restore equity by either decreasing or increasing the quality or quantity of their inputs. These conditions have been studied under two types of compensation systems: piece-rate and hourly payment. Piece-rate refers to payment according to the number of products produced, and hourly refers to payment according to the number of hours worked. Table 3.2 illustrates the specific equity predictions according to the type of equity manipulation and compensation system.

In general, the reviews of empirical research support equity theory predictions, particularly in the underpayment conditions (both piece-rate and hourly compensation) (Campbell & Pritchard, 1976; Goodman & Friedman, 1971). Because of the counterintuitive nature of the overpayment condition, however, much more research has focused on the overpayment than the underpayment manipulation. Two explanations for the inconsistent results in the overpayment condition have been offered by researchers (Campbell & Pritchard, 1976; Goodman & Friedman, 1971). First, the qualifications manipulation, which has been frequently used, undoubtedly threatens many subjects' self-esteem. Therefore, it is logical that they would work harder to prove their capabilities (Andrews & Valenzi, 1970; Weiner, 1970). Indeed, studies that have used the circumstances manipulation have reported less support for equity theory predictions in the overpayment condition (Pritchard, Dunnette, & Jorgenson, 1972; Valenzi & Andrews, 1971). Second, people in general seem to be able to rationalize overpayment. Workers in real organizations are rarely told they are overpaid. A more likely outcome is that they adjust their perceived inputs to match their outputs and therefore believe they are receiving what they deserve (Locke, 1976).

**Table 3.2**

| EQUITY THEORY PREDICTIONS OF WORKER REACTIONS TO INEQUITABLE PAYMENT | | |
|---|---|---|
| | **OVERPAYMENT** | **UNDERPAYMENT** |
| **Piece-Rate** | Workers overpaid by piece-rate will provide fewer units of higher quality than equitably paid employees. | Workers underpaid by piece-rate will provide a large number of low-quality units in comparison with equitably paid employees. |
| **Hourly** | Workers overpaid by the hour produce more or higher quality output than equitably paid employees. | Workers underpaid by the hour produce less or poorer quality output than equitably paid employees. |

*Source:* Adapted from Mowday, R.T. (1991). Equity theory predictions of behavior in organizations. In R.M. Steers & L.W. Porter (eds). *Motivation and Work Behavior.* New York: McGraw-Hill.

Research has demonstrated fairly conclusively that equity theory predictions, particularly for underpayment, work. Overall, equity theory holds promise as a viable theory of work motivation. However, because the richness of Adams' theory has not been adequately explored by researchers, many facets remain to be tested. Because almost all equity research has been conducted in the laboratory, we also have little data on equity resolution in work settings. The recent research of Greenberg (1988; 1989; 1990; see below) is a notable exception, and his results generally support extensions of equity theory to organizations.

## IMPLICATIONS AND CURRENT TRENDS

Mowday (1991) has discussed four basic conceptual weaknesses of Adams' equity theory that point to directions for future theory refinement and research. They include the need for a broader conceptualization of equity, alternative methods of resolving equity other than changes in input, ambiguities about the choice of a comparison other, and individual differences in equity resolution.

The "equity norm" is deeply rooted in our early socialization; we believe that people should be compensated according to their merit. However, other norms, such as equality and responsiveness to needs, also exist (Leventhal, 1976). If bonuses are distributed equally to employees in an organization (a common occurrence), then the distribution of rewards follows an equality norm. If bonuses are distributed according to need, then the employee with six children would receive the largest bonus. Although use of a needs norm may seem rather unusual, one of the authors has observed an organization that used need to justify larger bonuses to male employees with dependents. It is obvious that the blanket assumption that only the equity norm guides workers and organizations is naive.

It is ludicrous to assume that people are so simplistic that they resolve perceived inequity only by altering their inputs. In fact, Adams' (1965) original conceptualization included six different methods of equity resolution. Unfortunately, researchers have failed to capture the complexity of equity resolution because they have concentrated solely on behavioral measures, such as quality and quantity of input. Lawler, Koplin, Young, and Fadem (1968) found that their subjects initially resolved overpayment inequity by increasing the quality of their work. However, in later sessions, subjects cognitively distorted their perceived qualifications. Cognitively distorting inputs to match outputs is undoubtedly commonplace in organizations. More recently, Greenberg (1989) reported that clerical workers cognitively reevaluated their outcomes in response to underpayment inequity. After a pay cut, these workers increased the perceived importance of their work environment in contributing to their payment equity. Clearly, equity theory will be only a partially developed theory until researchers have explored other methods of equity resolution.

In most of the laboratory studies that have tested equity theory predictions, subjects were provided with a comparison other. However, in the outside world these referents are not so obvious. Goodman (1974) classified "comparison others" according to similar others, self-standards, and system referents. Self-standards refer to standards people set for themselves, such as comparisons of past and present work inputs. System referents refer to implicit or explicit expectations between the worker and his or her organization, which typically begin when the worker is hired. Goodman's (1974) sample of managers used multiple referents; he found that those managers with more education tended to use external referents, or comparison others outside their organization. It seems obvious that testing equity theory only with "other" referents does not capture the essence of the equity resolution process.

Personal qualities of the referent other may even affect feelings of equity. Griffeth, Vecchio, and Logan (1989) conducted a study in which they manipulated the perceived attractiveness of the referent other. The interpersonal attractiveness manipulation involved presenting information about the referent other to the subject that indicated the referent other's attitudes were similar to or dissimilar to the subject's attitudes. Because we tend to like people better if they possess attitudes similar to our own, we should prefer the referent other with similar attitudes. Consistent with predictions, subjects in the overcompensation condition perceived inequity and attempted to compensate by producing more products if they had an attractive referent; little inequity seemed to be perceived for the unattractive referent other (Figure 3.2). According to the researchers, this study illustrates a potential problem in generalizing equity research conducted in the laboratory to the outside world. Specifically, if we do not know someone, we usually assume they possess attitudes similar to our own; this situation has occurred in virtually all

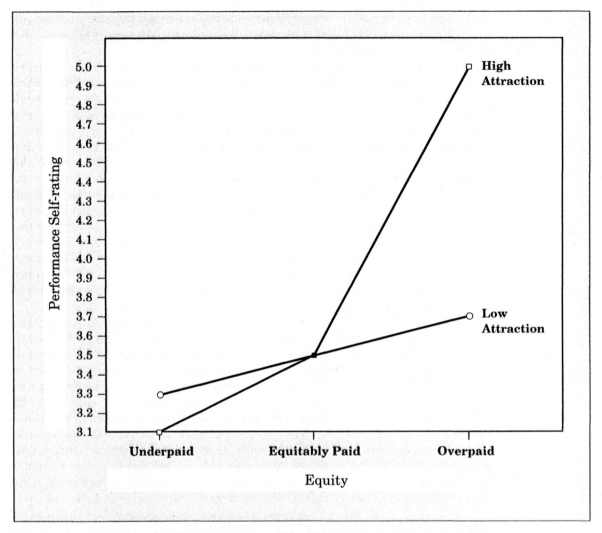

**Figure 3.2**  *Self-rated performance: Plot of the equity X attraction interaction*
*Source:* Griffeth, R., Vecchio, R., & Logan, J., Jr. (1989). Equity theory and interpersonal attraction. *Journal of Applied Psychology, 74*, 394–401.

laboratory research in which a subject has been paired with a referent other. However, in organizations people come to know the attitudes of their coworkers, which may directly influence the choice and perceptions of the comparison other.

Given the complex judgments people must engage in to resolve inequity, equity theory is indeed a theory of the individual. It is therefore surprising that little research has examined individual differences in reactions to inequity. According to Mowday (1991), a person's locus of control (Rotter, 1966) may influence equity judgments. Individuals with an internal locus of

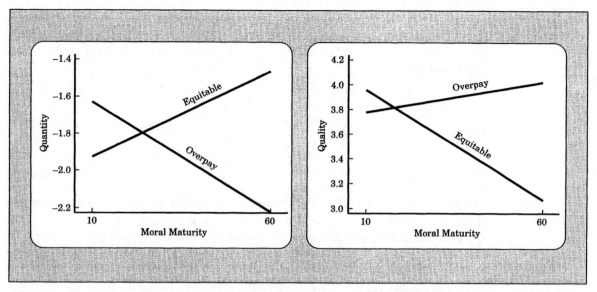

**Figure 3.3**  *Interaction of moral maturity X equity conditions on quantity and quality of performance*
Source: Vecchio, R. (1981). An individual-differences interpretation of the conflicting predictions generated by equity theory and expectancy theory. *Journal of Applied Psychology, 66,* 470–481.

control, who generally perceive events in the world as being under their control, might be more inclined to actively try to reduce inequity. Probably one of the most interesting studies on individual differences in equity perceptions was reported by Vecchio (1981). He examined the role of moral maturity on the resolution of piece-rate overpayment in an interviewing task. People who score high on a measure of moral maturity should be more sensitive to the inequity of being overpaid relative to other people. Those individuals low on moral maturity, on the other hand, should seek to maximize their outcomes and therefore not be so concerned with equity resolution (see also Kohlberg, 1968). Consistent with his predictions, Vecchio (1981) found that subjects high in moral maturity behaved according to equity theory predictions; they produced less with higher quality than equitably paid subjects. Subjects low in moral maturity did not conform to overpayment predictions (Figure 3.3). This rather provocative experiment underscores the potential importance of individual differences in understanding the process of equity resolution.

A more process-oriented approach to equity theory concepts is embodied in recent research on *procedural justice,* or the perceived fairness of the means or methods used to distribute compensation. Folger and his colleagues have determined that the perceived equity of the outcomes may be less important, particularly in terms of work-related attitudes, than the perceived fairness of the procedures used to determine the allocation of outcomes (Folger, 1984; Folger & Konovsky, 1989). Although the basic assumptions underlying equity theory are cognitive (for example, equity perceptions), equity researchers have largely assumed, but not examined, the cognitive processes associated with equity perceptions and resolution. Procedural justice research may provide new insight into the cognitive processes Adams hypothesized almost 30 years ago.

## Goal-Setting Theory

### THEORETICAL ASSUMPTIONS

Do you know what Weight Watchers and time management experts have in common? They both advocate setting specific, attainable goals to achieve some desired outcome. The Weight Watchers program recommends that its members set weekly goals (for example, a two-pound weight loss) that are attainable, instead of simply attempting to lose weight. These weekly goals are also much less psychologically distressing than the thought of having to lose 40 pounds to achieve your long-term goal. Time management experts recommend that specific, attainable goals should be set for each project. If a project is large or long-term, it should be divided into smaller projects, each with its own goals.

Suppose you must write a term paper for your psychology class. Because many students consider writing a term paper a difficult task, they often postpone starting the paper until only a few days before it is due. The consequences are frequently a poorly conceived and written paper that receives a low grade. Perhaps you also have been in this unfortunate circumstance of misusing and wasting valuable time. If so, time management experts would suggest that you divide the task of writing the paper into discrete, manageable portions and set specific goals for their attainment. First, early in the semester, plan to go to the library to research your topic; set specific time limits for this first phase. Then, draw up an outline that describes the various sections of the paper. Again, allow yourself only a certain amount of time. Finally, following your outline, write one section of the paper at a time, reviewing and editing the "old" sections when you write the new or later ones. This last phase probably consumes the most time. (A helpful secondary goal would be, for example, to work on the paper at least one hour every two days.) If you write your term paper in the manner just described, you will produce a carefully conceived and written product that has introduced little, if any, stress into your life. Specifically, you will not need to pull any all-nighters or hand in a late paper.

The goal-setting process just described really works. Many successful dieters from Weight Watchers programs and time management devotees would definitely agree about the effectiveness of setting goals. Not surprisingly, the potential usefulness of goal-setting techniques also attracted the attention of industrial organizational psychologists such as Edwin Locke. Locke (1968) proposed goal setting as a theory of work motivation. In goal-setting theory, conscious intentions precipitate behavior, an idea also advocated by Ryan (1970). The theory is simple and elegant: People plan what they are going to do and act according to their plans. Events in the external environment, such as the successful completion of a college course or a potential promotion for superior work performance, trigger a cognitive process in which the person evaluates the events against his or her values. Values in this context refer to what the individual wants to attain. If the person's values are not satisfied by the external event, he or she will experience a negative emotion, such as dissatisfaction with the event. The outcome of this emotional experience will be conscious intentions directed toward the completion of a goal. For example, suppose Meredith is criticized by her supervisor for poor job performance. Because Meredith places a high value on work, she is very unhappy with her negative evaluation. Consequently, she sets a goal to improve her job performance before her next six-month review.

### RESEARCH AND APPLICATION

The simple elegance of goal-setting theory has captured the attention of many organizational researchers over the past twenty years, so much, in fact, that goal setting is currently our most widely researched theory of work motivation. Not only does the simplicity of the theory's assumptions distinguish it from other motivational theories, but research on goal setting has generally been very supportive of two major propositions of the theory (Locke, Shaw, Saari, & Latham, 1981). The most fundamental proposition of goal-setting theory is that specific hard goals (e.g., lose 2 lbs per week) produce higher task performance than easy or ambiguous goals (e.g., do your best) as long as the hard goal is accepted (Locke, 1968; Latham, Mitchell, & Dossett, 1978; Latham & Steele, 1983). Approximately 90% of all laboratory and field studies have confirmed this prediction. For the goal to achieve optimal results, a person must not only develop conscious intentions of achieving the goal and translate those intentions into behavior, but he or she must also set difficult and specific goals. Without these concrete guideposts, people do not have enough structure to perform optimally.

Other elements of Locke's goal-setting theory of work motivation have received less empirical support. Locke stated that knowledge of results, or feedback, should not improve performance unless the feedback results in setting higher performance goals. Similarly, he argued that worker participation in decision making (i.e., participation in setting the goals) and monetary incentives improve task performance only if they enable higher and more acceptable goals to be set. However, many empirical studies have found that feedback is a necessary condition for goal setting; that is, goal setting does not work without the feedback that enables a person to improve performance (Erez & Kanfer, 1983). Contrary to predictions, participation in decision making does not seem to be necessary to improve performance. Research has shown that people who set their own goals individually or with another person perform no better than people who are assigned goals (Dossett, Latham, & Mitchell, 1979; Latham, Steele, & Saari, 1982). Monetary incentives appear to improve task performance whether or not goal setting occurs (Tolchinsky &

King, 1980). Not surprisingly, money seems to be a strong motivator regardless of the circumstances.

Similar to equity research, goal-setting research has mostly been conducted in the laboratory with student subjects. Therefore, like equity theory, direct applications of goal-setting theory to organizations have not been numerous. Exceptions include studies of goal-setting programs for applications in logging work and loading trucks (Latham & Yukl, 1975). However, goal setting is the major focus of a widely used management tool, *management by objectives (MBO)*. Although MBO seems to have developed independently of goal-setting theory, it uses mutual goal setting between the supervisor and the subordinate (McConkie, 1979). MBO programs typically stress clear, specific, and attainable goals, with frequent performance feedback. If possible, the goals should be assessed in terms of measurable outcomes, such as product quality or number of units sold. The research that exists, although often subject to alternative interpretations, appears to support the effectivness of MBO. Rodgers and Hunter (1991) found that 68 of 70 studies showed productivity gains; only two showed losses. Interestingly, when top management supported the programs, the average productivity gain was 56%. When commitment was low, the gain was only 6%. Unfortunately, even though MBO appears successful, we do not know what produces these effects because MBO embodies not only goal setting, but also other management techniques, such as participative management. Like McClelland's need achievement training program, it seems to work, but we do not know why.

The basic assumptions of goal-setting theory have been supported for more than twenty years through hundreds of empirical studies. The basic theoretical framework of goal setting seems robust: Specific, difficult goals lead to higher performance than no goals, easy or moderate goals, or "do your best" goals. In fact, one of the most fundamental criticisms of goal-setting theory reflects on this simplicity. The theoretical foundation for goal setting has not been highly developed compared with other motivational theories. Over the last twenty years, goal-setting theory has been largely amended through empirical, not theoretical, considerations. Consequently, some researchers have referred to goal setting not as a theory, but a general motivational approach (McCormick & Ilgen, 1985). This perspective seems reasonable given that goal-setting theory is compatible with other motivational theories, a topic we will discuss in a later section.

## IMPLICATIONS AND CURRENT TRENDS

Recent research has questioned some of the earlier, widely accepted goal-setting propositions, or at least demonstrated that the goal-setting–performance relationship is not as straightforward as originally believed. In fact, much contemporary goal-setting research has redefined the boundary conditions under which goal setting will be effective. These studies have demonstrated that the original assumptions of goal setting are not necessarily simplistic, just underdeveloped. For example, Wright (1990) conducted a

quantitative review (or meta-analysis) of the effects of different operationalizations of goal difficulty on the goal difficulty–performance relationship.
(Remember, difficult goals produce the highest performance.) He examined
several operationalizations, such as assigned goal levels and self-set goal levels, and found that the type of operationalization used affected the goal
difficulty–performance relationship.

A recent study questions the finding that participation does not affect
goal performance. Earley and Kanfer (1985) found that when subjects were
given total participation (self-set goals and goal strategy), their performance
was higher. A meta-analysis (Mento, Steel, & Karren, 1987) also found positive effects for participation, although the conclusions were based on only six
studies.

Some recent research challenges the finding that monetary rewards
increase performance regardless of goal setting. Using computerized letter
typing and digit classification laboratory tasks, Erez, Gopher, and Arzi (1990)
reported that self-set goals without monetary rewards led to the highest performance, whereas self-set goals with monetary rewards were detrimental to
performance (Table 3.3). The researchers called for future research on goal
setting and monetary incentives to resolve these intriguing results. They also
questioned whether the simultaneous performance of two different tasks,
which is considered to constitute a complex task, may have influenced the
results.

Tubbs' (1986) meta-analysis of goal-setting research showed that the
goal-setting–performance effects were stronger in laboratory than in field
studies. He suggested that the reason might be that subjects are willing to
accept and work toward harder goals in short-term situations, such as laboratory experiments. Like equity theory research, goal-setting research has been

**Table 3.3**

| THE EFFECTS OF ORIGIN OF GOAL AND MONETARY REWARDS ON TASK PERFORMANCE (HIGH GOAL CONDITION) | | | | | |
|---|---|---|---|---|---|
| **ORIGIN OF GOAL:** **MONETARY REWARD:** | | **ASSIGN ABSENT** | **SELF ABSENT** | **ASSIGN PRESENT** | **SELF PRESENT** |
| A. Letter typing | | | | | |
| Mean performance | *Mean* | .567 | .717 | .556 | .607 |
| rate | *Standard Deviation* | .089 | .125 | .111 | .099 |
| B. Digit Classification | | | | | |
| Mean performance | *Mean* | .885 | .975 | .932 | .789 |
| rate | *Standard Deviation* | .220 | .152 | .221 | .087 |

*Source:* Adapted from Erez, M., Gopher, D., & Arzi, N. (1990). Effects of goal difficulty, self-set goals, and monetary rewards on dual task performance. *Organizational Behavior and Human Decision Processes, 47,* 247–269.

conducted mostly in laboratory settings with student subjects performing simple tasks, such as listing novel uses for familiar objects (for example, a coat hanger or paper clip). Subjects in these experiments are typically asked to perform the task over several trials of minutes in duration after being assigned or participatively setting their goals. However, in field settings, goals are frequently set for much longer time intervals, such as weeks or months.

In another meta-analysis of goal-setting research, Wood, Mento, and Locke (1987) assessed the moderating effects of task complexity on goal effects by examining whether the type of task affected the goal-setting–performance relationship. They found that goal-setting effects were strongest for easy tasks (reaction time, brainstorming) and weakest for the most complex tasks (business game simulations, scientific and engineering work). Therefore, it seems obvious that stronger goal effects are demonstrated with simple tasks in the laboratory. (Recall that in the Erez et al., 1990, study on monetary rewards standard goal effects were not found for the dual or complex task.) Locke (1986) argued strongly that the effects of goal setting generalize across settings and situations. This is undoubtedly true, but the strength of the goal-setting–performance relationship definitely seems to be affected by contextual factors (e.g., the type of task performed).

Other factors, such as personality characteristics, probably also influence goal setting. However, no consistent effects for personality variables, such as self-esteem or locus of control, have been found (Locke et al., 1981). The one exception to this statement is individual ability. High task-ability people reliably outperform low task-ability people in response to increases in goal difficulty. Some recent research (Hollenbeck, Williams, & Klein, 1989) has examined the influence of personality characteristics on commitment to difficult goals. Not only must individuals initially accept the goal, they must also be committed to its completion. Commitment gives them the determination and persistence to achieve the goal. In a study of college students with academic goals, Hollenbeck and his colleagues discovered that commitment to difficult goals was higher for those individuals who had an internal locus of control (or thought they personally exercised control over their environment) and were high in need achievement. These findings were particularly strong for self-set goals (Figure 3.4). As this study suggests, personality variables may exert their influence indirectly, through goal acceptance or goal commitment. If so, researchers have been looking in the wrong place by examining only the direct influence of personality variables on goal performance. Future research is needed to clarify these possibilities.

Like many other contemporary theories of work motivation, goal setting is a cognitive theory that views people as active and rational processors of information with the purpose of developing conscious intentions toward goal-directed behavior. It therefore is logical that goal-setting researchers would investigate the efficacy of various types of cognitive strategies on goal performance. Earley, Connolly, and Ekegren (1989) hypothesized that the assumption that specific, difficult goals enhance performance would not apply to

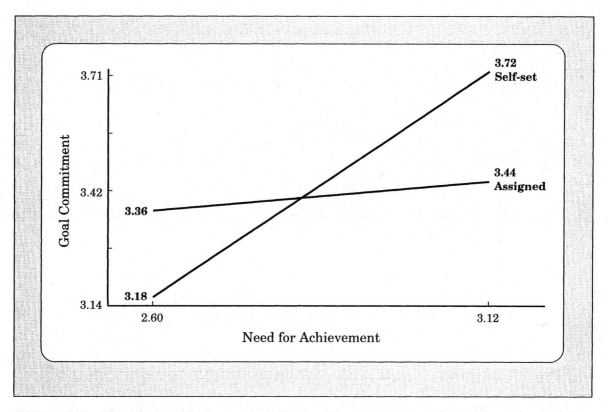

**Figure 3.4**  *The relationship between need for achievement and goal commitment scores for self-set and assigned goal conditions*
Source: Hollenbeck, J., Williams, C., & Klein, H. (1989). An empirical examination of the antecedents of commitment to difficult goals. *Journal of Applied Psychology, 74,* 18–23.

novel tasks that allow multiple, alternative strategies. They used a stock prediction task to test their hypothesis on 34 undergraduates. Consistent with the prediction, they found that, compared with more general goals (e.g., "do your best"), subjects assigned specific, difficult goals engaged in much more strategy search. This additional search time did not improve performance (Figure 3.5). The researchers stated that the results of this experiment may define a boundary condition for the most basic assumption of goal-setting theory.

Another study (Mitchell & Silver, 1990) found that people who used individual goals on a task that required cooperation performed more poorly than those who used group goals. Individual task strategies tended to be more competitive and less cooperative than group strategies. As we will discuss in Chapter 5, lack of cooperation in the performance of an interdependent task can be disastrous because such tasks require cooperation among group members. Smith, Locke, and Barry (1990) also investigated the effects of cognitive strategy in the form of planning time and quality. Using 16 simulated organizations (i.e., organizational games), they examined the actual time spent

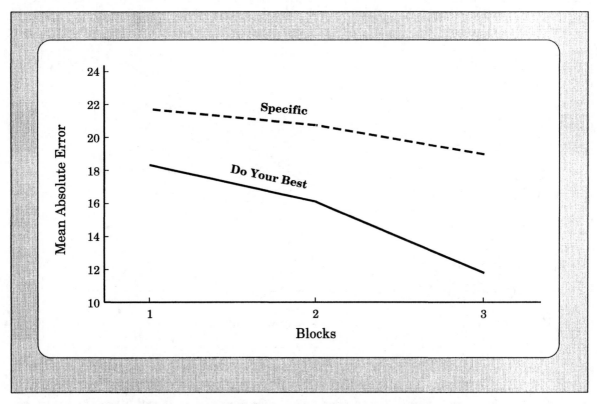

**Figure 3.5** *Mean absolute error (MAE) across goal-setting conditions*
*Source:* Earley, P.C., Connolly, T., & Ekegren, G. (1989). Goals, strategy development, and task performance: Some limits on the efficacy of goal setting. *Journal of Applied Psychology, 74,* 24–33.

planning and the quality of the planning process. (Planning quality was measured by the presence of such factors as the development and communication of action plans.) The researchers found that more time spent planning was associated with high performance only if the planning quality was high. These studies indicate the importance of considering the type of task performed and the type of task strategy used in goal-directed performance.

Recall that one of the earliest empirical findings of goal-setting research was that feedback is necessary to improve performance. Contemporary researchers have attempted to examine the role of feedback in some detail, particularly the efficacy of different types of feedback. Podsakoff and Farh (1989) investigated the influence of positive and negative feedback on goal performance. They reported that subjects who received (bogus) negative feedback outperformed those who received (bogus) positive feedback, particularly when the feedback was credible to the subjects. Another study (Vance & Colella, 1990) explored the differential effects of two types of feedback, goal discrepancy and past-performance discrepancy; goal discrepancy feedback refers to how subjects performed relative to the assigned goal and past-performance discrepancy refers to how much subjects' performance changed from trial to trial. The results indicated that many subjects shifted from goal to past-performance feedback over trials as they experienced negative goal discrepancy feedback. These two studies illustrate an exciting trend in goal-setting research that may enhance its usefulness in organizations.

Research studies such as these have broadened and enriched the theoretical assumptions of goal setting to the extent that it may now more precisely be considered a motivational theory, not simply a motivational approach, as critics have alleged. This more comprehensive picture of the goal-setting process is needed before its principles can be widely (and successfully) applied in work settings.

## Valence–Instrumentality–Expectancy (VIE) Theory

### THEORETICAL ASSUMPTIONS

Imagine the following situation. You have just signed up for an industrial psychology class that you have been wanting to take for two semesters. You are excited because the topic is one you find really interesting, and the instructor has been recommended by your friends. You are even considering graduate study in industrial psychology. After attending the first class session, you are bubbling over with excitement. You savor every word the instructor utters and read the textbook chapters with care. You study many hours for the first exam because it is extremely important for you to excel in this course. Your dismay is indescribable when your grade on the first exam is a C−. Disappointed but determined, you then try harder: You listen even more closely to the instructor and study even more than before. Imagine your shock when, on exam 2, you receive another C! As exam 3 and the end of the term approach, your enthusiasm wanes. You invent excuses not to attend class and have difficulty concentrating on your reading assignments.

What has happened? You began with a great expectancy of success; you believed that the appropriate effort (in the form of attending class and studying hard) would pay off in superior test performance and an A in the class. You also believed that a good grade would increase the probability of your being accepted into graduate school. As the term progressed, however, the expectancy that your effort would result in high performance decreased, and, consequently, the probability that the course grade would enhance your chances for admission to graduate school decreased. You would probably agree that your motivation to expend effort on the course decreased during the term. Motivation researchers also would agree with the preceding statement. In fact, the components just discussed, the expectancy that effort will lead to some level of performance and the probability that this level of performance will lead to some valued outcome or outcomes, have been incorporated into one of the leading theories of work motivation, valence–instrumentality–expectancy, or VIE, theory.

Although many versions of VIE theory exist, the most well-known version was proposed by Vroom (1964), which originated from an earlier theory of work motivation called path-goal theory (Georgopolos, Mahoney, & Jones, 1957). VIE theory is fairly complex; however, the fundamental idea behind it is simple. The theory is based on the notion that, before expending any effort to achieve some outcome, people ask themselves, "What is in this for me?" If, as illustrated in the example, they cannot see the association between their effort and the attainment of desired outcomes, they simply will not be motivated to exert effort.

Unlike goal-setting theory, VIE theory has a well-developed and quantified theoretical framework. The major components of the theory are called valence, instrumentality, and expectancy. *Valence* refers to the desirability or undesirability of some outcome. In the previous example, the valent or desired outcomes were an A in the course and admission to graduate school. Although we did not consider negative outcomes here, VIE theory does account for negatively valued outcomes, such as being fired or flunking out of school. Valence ratings of outcomes are often made on a scale from +10 (very positively valent) to −10 (very negatively valent); a rating of 0 indicates no valence or preference.

*Instrumentality* refers to the perceived association between outcomes. The perceived association between a high grade in the course and admission to graduate school is an example of an instrumentality. Although many motivation researchers have treated instrumentalities as perceived or subjective probabilities ranging from 0 to +1, Vroom originally conceived of instrumentalities as ranging from +1 to −1. Vroom's metric therefore treats instrumentalities as perceived correlations between outcomes. A value of 0 indicates no relationship, a value of +1 indicated a high positive relationship, and a value of −1 indicates a high negative relationship between outcomes. The instrumentalities expressed in the preceding example are positive. An example of a negative instrumentality would be that an outcome of a high grade in the course is a limited social life. Most researchers subsequent to Vroom have not acknowledged negative instrumentalities.

*Expectancy* refers to the perceived likelihood that the effort expended will result in some desired level of performance. The expectancy discussed in the example is the perceived likelihood that attending class diligently and studying hard will result in superior test performance. Expectancy is expressed in terms of a subjective or perceived probability ranging from 1 (no doubt performance can be achieved) to 0 (under no circumstances can performance be achieved).

According to Vroom's formulation of VIE theory, these components interact in a multiplicative fashion such that the instrumentality for each outcome is multiplied by its valence. All of these products are added together to produce a total valence score. The expectancy is then multiplied by this total valence score to obtain a value called F, which is the *motivational force* to strive for a certain level of performance. An example of two people is provided in Table 3.4. Susan and Joe are two salespeople deciding if they want to devote their time and energy to selling insurance policy A or the new insur-

**Table 3.4**

## ILLUSTRATION OF VIE THEORY

**PROBLEM:** Joe and Susan are two salespeople in an insurance company who, up until now, have sold more of policy A than of any other type. However, the company would prefer that in the future they devote more of their efforts to selling policy B, a more profitable type of insurance that was recently developed. How could you use VIE theory to predict which policy Joe and Susan will be more motivated to sell? Assume that through interviews you have determined that they both anticipate several positive outcomes to result from selling the policies — a cash bonus, pride in achievement and supervisory recognition — as well as a negative outcome in the form of a loss of leisure time. You also have found that Joe and Susan anticipate different levels of satisfaction from achieving each of these outcomes (i.e., the valences of the outcomes differ). To use VIE theory you would now need to ask the following additional questions.

1. What is the expected satisfaction or valence (V) of selling policy A?

| | Susan | | | Joe | | |
|---|---|---|---|---|---|---|
| Outcome | v | i | v × i | v | i | v × i |
| Salary bonus | 9 × | .3 | = 2.7 | 7 × | 1.0 | = 7.0 |
| Pride in achievement | 9 × | .4 | = 3.6 | 6 × | .5 | = 3.0 |
| Supervisor recognition | 5 × | .1 | = .5 | 4 × | 1.0 | = 4.0 |
| Loss of leisure time | −1 × | .9 | = −.9 | −7 × | .3 | = −2.1 |

Valence (V) of selling policy A = Sum of products of v's and i's

$$\text{Valence for Susan} = 2.7 + 3.6 + .5 - .9 = 5.9$$

$$\text{Valence for Joe} = 7.0 + 3.0 + 4.0 - 2.1 = 11.9$$

2. What is the expected satisfaction or valence (V) of selling policy B?

| | Susan | | | Joe | | |
|---|---|---|---|---|---|---|
| Outcome | v | i | v × i | v | i | v × i |
| Salary bonus | 9 × | 1.0 | = 9.0 | 7 × | 1.0 | = 7.0 |
| Pride in achievement | 9 × | .5 | = 4.5 | 6 × | .4 | = 2.4 |
| Supervisor recognition | 5 × | .6 | = 3.0 | 4 × | .7 | = 2.8 |
| Loss of leisure time | −1 × | .9 | = −.9 | −7 × | .6 | = −4.2 |

Valence (V) of selling policy B = Sum of products of v's and i's

$$\text{Valence for Susan} = 9.0 + 4.5 + 3.0 - .9 = 15.6$$

$$\text{Valence for Joe} = 7.0 + 2.4 + 2.8 - 4.2 = 8.0$$

**Table 3.4** *Continued*

3. What is the expectancy (E) of each employee that he or she can sell each policy?

**Expectancy of Selling Each Policy?**

| Policy | Susan | Joe |
|--------|-------|-----|
| A | .4 | 1.0 |
| B | .3 | .8 |

4. What is the motivational force (E × V) to sell each policy?

| Policy | Susan | Joe |
|--------|-------|------|
| A | 2.36 | 11.90 |
| B | 4.68 | 6.40 |

5. What would the within-subjects version of VIE theory (Vroom, 1964) predict that each employee is most likely to do?

Susan will work harder to sell policy B than policy A.

Joe will work harder to sell policy A than policy B.

v = valence of individual outcomes, measured on a − 10 (very undesirable) to + 10 (very desirable) scale.

i = instrumentality of selling policy for obtaining an outcome, measured on a −1.0 (negatively related) to +1.0 (positively related) scale.

E = expectancy of selling the policy, measured on a 0 (no chance at all) to 1.0 (absolutely sure) scale.

ance policy B. Both employees consider the same outcomes in making their decisions, and both consider the same behavioral options (i.e., work to sell policy A or try to sell policy B). If we apply the within-person model as originally conceived by Vroom (1964) and perform the arithmetic operations, it is obvious that, considering valences, instrumentalities, and expectancy, Susan will choose to exert more effort to sell the new policy B, and Joe will be content to push policy A.

Other motivation theorists have elaborated on Vroom's version of VIE theory. Probably the most well known of these refinements is the VIE theory proposed by Porter and Lawler (1968) (Figure 3.6). In addition to the three basic components of valence, instrumentality, and expectancy, this model incorporates abilities and traits, role perceptions, intrinsic and extrinsic rewards, and the perceived equity of the rewards. The model assumes that, for effort to translate into a desired level of performance, the person must have the ability to perform well (abilities and traits), and he must understand

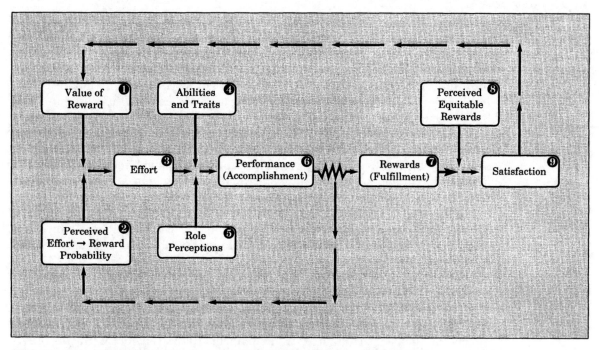

**Figure 3.6**  *The Porter-Lawler (1968) refinement of the VIE model*
Source: Porter, L., & Lawler, E. (1968). *Managerial Attitudes and Performance.* Homewood, IL: Dorsey.

the demands of his job (role clarity). The model acknowledges that people work for both extrinsic rewards, such as money and promotions, and intrinsic rewards, such as pride in one's work and a sense of accomplishment. The model also assumes that the level of performance a person attains will affect the level of rewards he perceives to be equitable. Specifically, if a person expends a great amount of effort that culminates in high performance levels, he will perceive that he deserves a substantial reward. Because Porter and Lawler's model is also a theory of job satisfaction, it is discussed in greater detail in Chapter 4.

### RESEARCH AND APPLICATION

How has VIE theory held up under empirical investigation? Since Vroom published his book in 1964, considerable research on VIE theory has been published. This research has been conducted in the laboratory and in the field using both student and employee samples. Most of the early studies only weakly supported the theory's major assumptions. The result was that, by the early to mid 1970s, researchers had grown somewhat disenchanted with VIE theory (Campbell & Pritchard, 1976; Mitchell, 1974). However, the empirical research was flawed by the use of between-subject designs. Vroom (1964) originally conceived of the theory as a within-subjects approach to individual choice. That is, he thought the VIE theory would most accurately measure the alternative choices considered by one person. For example, in Table 3.4, Joe and Susan individually consider which of two alternative actions to pursue. Should they continue to sell policy A or should they work harder to sell policy B? Ignoring Vroom's emphasis, researchers mostly attempted to predict how different employees compare in their behavior with regard to single behavioral options. This between-subjects version of VIE can be illustrated in Table 3.4 by focusing solely on sales of the new policy (policy B) and questions about expectancies, valences, and instrumentalities for that particular behavioral option. Because Joe has more motivational force (higher $E \times V$) than Susan to sell policy B ($6.40 > 4.68$), he would be predicted to show more motivation in attempting to sell policy B than Susan. Research using a between-subjects approach has yielded results that are much weaker than the results of research using a within-subjects approach (Pinder, 1984). The within-subjects approach is a more appropriate test of Vroom's (1964) VIE theory, which was originally presented as a process of individuals choosing among different behavioral options.

A second criticism was that the multiplicative function proposed by Vroom is unnecessarily complex and does not reflect true decision processes (Stahl & Harrell, 1981). Other researchers claim that either instrumentalities, valences, or expectancies alone account for the observed motivational effects (Jorgenson, Dunnette, & Pritchard, 1973; Lawler & Suttle, 1973; Schmitt & Son, 1981). A related issue is that, contrary to what psychologists know about human nature, VIE theory assumes people are rational decision makers. A more realistic assumption is that people have limited cognitive capabilities and often are guided by unconscious motivations (Locke, 1975; Pinder, 1984; Staw, 1977).

Another major criticism of VIE theory was that researchers typically presented their subjects with a list of standard outcomes (money, promotions, etc.) and asked them to rate the desirability (valence) of each outcome. However, standard lists do not necessarily capture the important outcomes for each person. For instance, Joe (in Table 3.4) may value none of the outcomes that he is given to rate. Subsequent research showed that when subjects were allowed to generate their own lists of outcomes, the theory received more support (Matsui & Ikeda, 1976). Using only desirable outcomes also seems to be more effective than using both desirable and undesirable outcomes (Leon, 1981).

Unlike such programs as MBO and need achievement training, no motivational programs specifically use the VIE framework. However, the implications of valence, expectancy, and instrumentalities for management are obvious. Several recommendations to management were offered by Pinder (1991). First, managers should make sure that their employees can perform their jobs, both in terms of ability and training (expectancy). The work environment should be conducive to good performance by providing adequate supplies and facilities. Second, managers should offer rewards that their employees value (valence). Promotions and job transfers, for example, although perceived by management as suitable rewards for superior performance, may not be desired by some employees. Third, managers should forge the link between performance and positively valent rewards (instrumentalities). Employees must also perceive this linkage. Management assumes that employees see the association between their performance and valued rewards, which is often an unfounded assumption. Instrumentality-related factors should always be clearly defined for the employee.

Current research on VIE theory has corrected many of the faults of earlier studies and subsequently demonstrated more support for VIE theory predictions (Pinder, 1984). Despite suffering early theoretical and measurement setbacks, VIE theory is currently a motivational perspective of choice for many organizational researchers. People do make personal behavioral choices after weighing their expectancies, valences, and instrumentalities. The assumptions of VIE theory also seem to be compatible with many other motivational theories; this compatibility has been supported by integrative motivational research, such as the studies of Matsui, Okada, and Mizuguchi (1981) and Harder (1991), which are discussed next.

## IMPLICATIONS AND CURRENT TRENDS

Much of the recent VIE research, and work motivation research in general, has focused on an integrative approach. Rather than testing the theoretical predictions of any one theory, integrative approaches pit competing theories to determine which theory obtains more support from the data. This type of research also defines boundary or limiting conditions for theories and provides researchers with a gestalt, or overview, of motivational processes. Integrative studies are discussed here and in the next sections.

The predictions of VIE theory and goal-setting theory seem to contradict one another. VIE theory assumes that difficult goals produce little effort because expectancy (the effort-performance association) is low. Goal-setting theory, however, predicts that difficult goals lead to higher performance. Matsui, Okada, and Mizuguchi (1981) investigated these competing assumptions. They assumed that difficult goals would be associated with a lower expectancy of successful performance. However, they also assumed that difficult goals would have a higher positive valence because people value success on difficult tasks. For goal-setting predictions to be valid, therefore, the valence of the goal must overcome the low expectancy of performance.

The researchers had student subjects perform a clerical accuracy task (number comparison) in either an easy- or difficult-goal condition. Not surprisingly, they found a difficult-goal effect: subjects in the difficult-goal condition outperformed subjects in the easy-goal condition. Subjects in the difficult-goal condition also had a lower expectancy of success than those in the easy-goal condition. In addition, they found that the valence of the outcomes from goal attainment (such as a sense of achievement, clerical ability, and persistence) was rated higher by subjects with difficult goals than by subjects with easy goals (Table 3.5). These results confirmed the researchers' predictions that the higher valence of difficult goals, if they are accepted,

**Table 3.5**

| | | Goal condition | | |
| Variable | | Easy | Hard | *t* |
|---|---|---|---|---|
| **Performance** | | | | |
| *Mean* | | 6.90 | 12.70 | 6.64* |
| *Standard Deviation* | | 4.46 | 5.23 | |
| **Valence of goal attainment** | | | | |
| *Mean* | | 84.50 | 140.30 | 10.06* |
| *Standard Deviation* | | 29.16 | 32.49 | |
| **Expectancy of reaching goal** | | | | |
| *Mean* | | 5.40 | 3.90 | 7.22* |
| *Standard Deviation* | | 1.08 | 1.23 | |

**MEANS AND STANDARD DEVIATIONS FOR PERFORMANCE, VALENCE, AND EXPECTANCY IN EASY- AND HARD-GOAL CONDITIONS.**

Means are based on performance scores for easy (or hard) goal minus performance scores for practice trials. $N = 63$.
* $p < .01$.

*Source:* Adapted from Matsui, T., Okada, A., & Mizuguchi, R. (1981). Expectancy theory prediction of the goal theory postulate, "The harder the goals, the higher the performance." *Journal of Applied Psychology, 66,* 54–58.

overcomes the low expectancy of success. Mento, Cartledge, and Locke (1980) also proposed a similar hypothesis. Expectancies and valences influence whether a goal is accepted. However, after a goal is accepted, goal-setting propositions govern performance.

More recently, Kernan and Lord (1990) found that valences and expectancies functioned differently in single- versus multiple-goal situations. Using students who performed either a single clerical task or multiple clerical tasks, they found that VIE variables were more influential in the multiple-task (goal) condition. The researchers reasoned that the cognitive VIE variables were more useful when subjects had to choose which task to focus on (multiple goal), not how to perform a specific task (single goal).

Using a rather unusual sample, free-agent nonpitchers in the 1977–1980 baseball seasons, Harder (1991) examined the competing predictions of VIE theory and equity theory under conditions of perceived underreward and strong expectancy and instrumentalities. Recall that under conditions of underpayment or reward, performance should decline, whereas strong expectancies and instrumentalities should be associated with high performance. He proposed a synthesis of the two theories: specifically, equity effects depend on the strength of the VIE variables expectancy and instrumentality. Free agents probably felt underrewarded before entering the free agent market but had expectations of higher salaries later. Consistent with predictions, batting average declined prior to free agency, whereas home run ratio, which has a stronger relation to salary than batting average, did not decline. Harder's research is a good example of an attempt to define the boundary conditions of the two theories.

Although Miller and Grush (1988) did not examine competing theories of work motivation, they did examine Fishbein and Ajzen's (1975) hypothesis that some individuals will be more affected by internal factors, such as expectancies, and others by environmental factors, such as social norms (influence from friends, family, and teachers). As predicted, those persons who were dispositionally attuned to social norms were much less affected by personal expectancies. Conversely, those persons who were unattuned to social norms were more greatly influenced by personal expectancies. These findings illustrate the importance of individual differences in understanding motivated behavior.

The future of VIE theory undoubtedly lies in the integrative approach, in which the boundary conditions of the theory are specified and relations to other perspectives clarified, and in the consideration of a broader range of variables than the theory's components (valence, instrumentality, and expectancy), such as individual differences. The embrace of a broader and richer framework should enable VIE theory to remain the most comprehensive motivational theory.

## Cognitive Evaluation Theory

### THEORETICAL ASSUMPTIONS

Suppose your supervisor lavished you with praise, saying that your work was excellent and that you were a model employee. You would probably start to envision the new stereo and clothes you would purchase with your hard-earned raise. Imagine your surprise when she told you that, because you were such an excellent worker, she was not recommending you for a raise. Her response to your incredulous *"Why?"* was that money destroys drive and incentive, so she is only going to reward you with praise.

Does this little scenario seem ridiculous to you? Probably, but some motivation theorists would definitely agree with the supervisor. According to Deci (1975) and his colleagues, the conditions promoting intrinsic motivation are at odds with the current practice of rewarding motivated behavior with money or similar extrinsic rewards. Drawing on the work of deCharms (1968), Deci hypothesized that people have a need to feel they are competent and in control of their lives. He assumed that they will be intrinsically or internally motivated to perform a task if it fulfills these two needs; under such conditions, people will perform a task solely for the personal pleasure that the task itself provides. If, however, people are offered external inducements, such as money, to perform an intrinsically motivating task, they will lose their sense of competence and control because they will perceive that external forces guide their behavior.

## RESEARCH AND APPLICATION

To test his hypotheses, Deci (1971; 1972) conducted a series of laboratory experiments in which he manipulated intrinsic motivation by giving subjects puzzles to solve; such tasks are generally perceived to be challenging and inherently interesting. Subjects were typically paid either hourly, contingently (according to the number of puzzles they completed), or not at all. After the experimental session, subjects were given free time to use as they wished. Those subjects who were originally paid, particularly contingently paid, spent less time working on the puzzles in their free time than the unpaid subjects. Deci concluded that, when people perceive they are extrinsically motivated to perform a task through external sources such as money, their intrinsic motivation to perform the task decreases.

Not surprisingly, researchers attempted to replicate Deci's counterintuitive results. Although some studies (Calder & Staw, 1975; Hamner & Foster, 1975) failed to clearly replicate Deci's results, others (Pritchard, Campbell, & Campbell, 1977) supported his results, even after controlling for some methodological weaknesses in the original research.

Although Deci's results have not technically been refuted, the generalizability of his results to work settings is suspect. First, the differences between reward conditions in the time spent working on the puzzles were typically minutes or seconds. Although these differences were statistically significant, the practical significance of whether a person works five or seven minutes on an intrinsically motivating task is probably trivial. A related issue is the short time interval (the experimental session) subjects spent working on the puzzles. Although for short periods of time such tasks may be intrinsically interesting, they may not be so appealing after hours or days. Workers in organizations often must perform the same tasks daily for years. Second, Deci's findings seem to apply to those situations in which people do not expect to be paid, such as a laboratory experiment, not to situations in which they do expect to be paid, such as a job (Staw, 1977). Third, in most work environments, management tries to motivate people who are unmotivated or extrinsically motivated. Deci's theory primarily concerns the effects of extrinsic factors on the performance of someone who is already intrinsically motivated.

To date, few direct applications of cognitive evaluation theory exist. The obvious implication of this research, according to Deci, is that workers should be paid noncontingently, or not contingent on their performance. Their performance should be rewarded with, for example, praise and more satisfying work. However, neither researchers nor managers have applied Deci's suggestions to work environments.

## IMPLICATIONS AND CURRENT TRENDS

The future of intrinsic motivation research may lie in how the theoretical assumptions of intrinsic motivation can be integrated with other motivation theories. This integrative approach is nicely illustrated in a study by Shapira (1989). Shapira examined the role of intrinsic motivation in goal set-

# Table 3.6

## GOAL EFFECTS ON PERFORMANCE

| Goal condition | Difficult tasks[a] | Easy tasks[a] |
|---|---|---|
| **Chosen task** | | |
| Standard goal | 4/9 | 5/7 |
| Moderate goal | 2/7 | 7/8 |
| Hard goal | 1/8 | 7/9 |
| **Assigned task** | | |
| Standard goal | 5/9 | 5/7 |
| Moderate goal | 5/7 | 5/8 |
| Hard goal | 6/8 | 3/9 |

*Note.* Entries represent the ratio of successful subjects by total number of subjects in the specific condition.
[a] Difficult and easy tasks relate to the subjects' chosen tasks.

*Source:* Adapted from Shapira, Z. (1989). Task choice and assigned goals as determinants of task motivation and performance. *Organizational Behavior and Human Decision Processes, 44,* 141–165.

ting. He hypothesized that hard goals can be detrimental to performance for intrinsically motivated subjects, but helpful to subjects who are not intrinsically motivated. (Remember, the major assumption of goal-setting theory is that hard or difficult goals lead to the highest performance.) Intrinsic motivation was operationalized as the condition in which subjects were able to choose their preferred level of task difficulty. In the nonmotivated condition, subjects were assigned their level of task difficulty. Across three experiments, Shapira found support for his hypothesis that hard goals decrease task performance in situations in which persons are intrinsically motivated (Table 3.6). This research underscores our earlier contention that the individual contribution of any one theory of motivation may not be substantial. However, the determination of situations in which different theories of motivation interactively predict some facet of motivated behavior may indeed be a powerful research tool.

## The Job Characteristics Model

### THEORETICAL ASSUMPTIONS

Perhaps more than any of the other motivation perspectives, the job characteristics model is an amalgam of both environmental and personal characteristics and was developed for direct application in organizations. This perspective drew its roots from the work of Turner and Lawrence (1965) on the association between specific attributes of jobs, such as the number of work tasks that must be performed and the requisite skill to perform those tasks, and organizational outcomes, such as performance and satisfaction. The most famous spin-off of Turner and Lawrence's research was the job characteristics model proposed by Hackman and Oldham (1976). This perspective has a straightforward assumption: Well-designed work tasks fulfill the psychological needs of workers, and the fulfillment of those needs motivates them.

Hackman and Oldham (1976) proposed that five fundamental task or job dimensions were important in determining worker behavior. These dimensions are skill variety, task significance, task identity, autonomy, and task feedback. *Skill variety* refers to the degree to which one's job requires the use of several skills. For example, a manager's job would be high in skill variety because it requires many skills, such as supervision, planning, delegating, negotiation, and decision making. *Task significance* indicates the importance of the work task to other people. A nurse's work tasks, for example, would be high on task significance because of their relevance to other people's welfare. The third dimension, *task identity,* refers to those characteristics of work tasks that enable a worker to identify with a complete product or service. For example, a factory worker who performs only one component of the manufacturing process may fail to see the relevance of his or her individual job to the manufacture of the completed product, such as a car. A job is high in *autonomy* if workers have freedom or discretion in deciding how to perform the job. The typical manager's job is often fairly high and the factory worker's job fairly low on autonomy. *Task feedback* indicates whether the performance of job tasks gives the worker feedback about his or her work effectiveness. A teacher, for example, may not get much task feedback in the process of teaching her students. She may only be aware that the students did not learn the material after grading their exams.

Hackman and Oldham hypothesized that each of the core job dimensions would contribute to the development of three critical psychological states. Specifically, they hypothesized that task variety, task identity, and task significance would lead to the experienced meaningfulness of work; task autonomy would contribute to the development of the experienced responsibility for outcomes of work; and task feedback would lead to the knowledge of the actual results of work. In turn, these psychological states are hypothesized to be associated with positive work and personal outcomes, such as high work motivation, performance, satisfaction with work, and low absenteeism and turnover. In addition, they proposed that workers who are high in growth need strength will react more positively to a job that is high in the five job dimensions than a worker who is low in growth need strength. Similar to Maslow's need hierarchy, therefore, Hackman and Oldham proposed that workers who were concerned with higher-order or growth needs would be best described by the model. The relationships in the job characteristics model are presented in Figure 3.7.

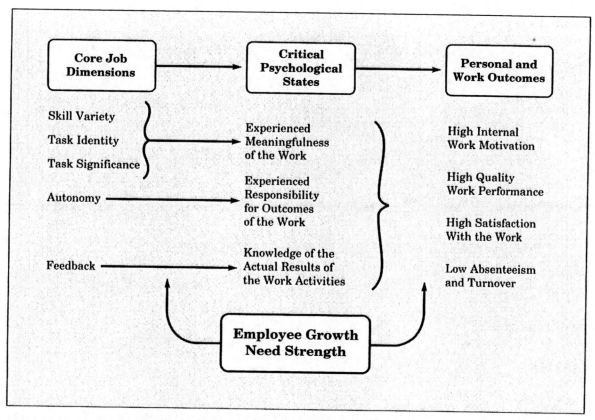

**Figure 3.7**  *The job characteristics model of work motivation*
Source: Hackman, J., & Oldham, G. (1976). Motivation through the design of work: Test of a theory. *Organizational Behavior and Human Performance, 16,* 250–279.

Hackman and Oldham further proposed that the motivating potential of any job is not simply an additive function of the five job dimensions, but rather a multiplicative function:

$$\text{MPS} = \left( \frac{\text{skill variety} + \text{task identity} + \text{task significance}}{3} \right) \times \text{autonomy} \times \text{feedback}$$

A job with a high MPS score should have more motivating potential than a job with a lower score. From inspecting the formula, you can see that autonomy and feedback are the most important factors in the MPS because, if either is zero, the MPS is zero. However, skill variety, task identity, and/or task significance can be zero or low and the MPS could still be reasonably high if autonomy or feedback is high.

Hackman and Oldham (1975) developed the job diagnostic survey (JDS) to measure the components of the model (the task dimensions, psychological states, and outcomes). The JDS is a rather unusual instrument because the items for each component are typically scattered across different sections of the survey, and more than one item format is used to measure

**Table 3.7**

### EXAMPLES OF JOB DIAGNOSTIC SURVEY (JDS) ITEMS

DIRECTIONS:
Listed below are a number of statements that could be used to describe your job. You are to indicate whether each statement is an *accurate* or *inaccurate* description of your job. Write a number in the blank beside each statement, based on the following scale.

How accurate is the statement in describing your job?

| 1 | 2 | 3 | 4 | 5 | 6 | 7 |
|---|---|---|---|---|---|---|
| Very Inaccurate | Mostly Inaccurate | Slightly Inaccurate | Uncertain | Slightly Accurate | Mostly Accurate | Very Accurate |

Skill Variety
_____ The job requires me to use a number of complex or high level skills.

Feedback for the Job Itself
_____ Just doing the work required by the job provides many chances for me to figure out how well I am doing.

Task Significance
_____ This job is one where a lot of people can be affected by how well the work gets done.

Task Identity
_____ The job provides me the chance to completely finish the work I begin.

Autonomy
_____ The job gives me considerable opportunity for independence and freedom in how I do the work.

*Source:* Hackman, R.J., & Oldham, G.R. (1980). *Work Redesign.* Reading, MA: Addison-Wesley, appendix A: The Job Diagnostic Survey, sec. 2, items 1, 4, 8, 11, 13, pp. 280-281.

each component (see Table 3.7). The original purpose of this variability in item location and format was to reduce response bias by forcing the respondents to carefully read each item.

### RESEARCH AND APPLICATION

Similar to the history of expectancy theory research, early work on the job characteristics model was not very supportive. Critics charged that the five task dimensions as assessed were not independent dimensions (Brief & Aldag, 1975; Dunham, 1976) and that growth need strength did not operate as predicted by the model (Brief & Aldag, 1975). Wall, Clegg, and Jackson (1978) reported that the hypothesized psychological states were not even associated with the task dimensions in their sample. Other researchers found that perceptions of the task characteristics of any particular job depend on such individual differences as the age and job level of the respondent; studies have reported that younger and supervisory-level workers perceived jobs to be more complex than older and nonsupervisory workers (Birnbaum, Farh, & Wong, 1986; Fried & Ferris, 1986).

Much of the criticism has focused on methodological issues, such as the measures used to assess the components in the model (JDS). The research has been quite mixed in its support of the five dimensions, with some studies replicating the 5-factors of Hackman and Oldham in specific samples (Dunham, Aldag, & Brief, 1977) but other studies failing to replicate the 5-factor structure (Dunham, 1976; Lee & Klein, 1982; Pokorney, Gilmore, & Beehr, 1980). Recently, a study by Harvey, Billings and Nilan (1985) shed some light on this confusion. They used a type of statistical analysis called confirmatory factor analysis to examine dimensions of the JDS. Confirmatory factor analysis can test different hypotheses about the number and type of dimensions in any scale and was therefore helpful in determining whether a one- or five- (or in-between) dimension model best described their data. The results of this study showed support for Hackman and Oldham's original five dimensions if the differences in scale format were controlled. Another study (Idaszak & Drasgow, 1987) reported that the negative wording of some of the JDS items masked the interpretation of the task dimensions. Hackman and Oldham originally added variability to the item format to reduce response bias. Paradoxically, however, it seems that their attempts to reduce bias actually increased it, presumably by confusing respondents.

Other measurement problems with the job characteristics model have also been acknowledged. One concerns the motivating potential score (MPS) developed by Hackman and Oldham. According to Ferris and Gilmore (1985), the multiplicative function is inferior to simpler, weighted average scores (that is, scores on all dimensions are simply added together, although some are treated as more important than others) in predicting job satisfaction. Other criticisms have focused on the exclusive use of self-report measures, such as the JDS, and cross-sectional designs in collecting job characteristics data (Aldag, Barr, & Brief, 1981; Roberts & Glick, 1981). In these studies, the components of the model were assessed by simply administering the JDS to workers at a single point in time; typically, these data have not been collected with alternative procedures, such as interviews, or at different time intervals to assess changes in perceptions.

A quantitative review or meta-analysis was performed on the job characteristics model for 28 studies that had used the JDS (Loher, Noe, Moeller, & Fitzgerald, 1985). The results of the meta-analysis supported relations implied by the model. Specifically, the meta-analysts found that the average correlation between job characteristics and job satisfaction is .39. For workers high in growth need strength, this correlation is .68 and for workers low in growth need strength, .38; these correlations are consistent with the model because the relation between job characteristics and satisfaction is higher for workers high in growth need strength.

It indeed seems strange that a model of worker behavior and attitudes that has so much generalizability to work settings has seen few applications.

The most obvious application of the job characteristics approach would be a controlled field study in which the components of the model are assessed for certain jobs, and then the jobs are changed in the ways prescribed by the model. The jobs would then be reassessed after the changes had been implemented. If the model is valid, worker behaviors and attitudes should change, particularly for those workers who are high in growth need strength. However, very few field interventions of this type have been conducted; Loher et al. (1985) found only three such studies to include in their review.

## IMPLICATIONS AND CURRENT TRENDS

Some recent research on the job characteristics model has focused on both methodological and theoretical refinements and extensions of the model. The Harvey et al. (1985) study sensitized researchers to the measurement problems of the JDS. Both Glick, Jenkins, and Gupta (1986) and Spangler (1989) warned that the problem of response bias in the JDS scales may be even worse than previously suspected. Spangler (1989) pointed out that the JDS instructions given to workers may prime them to answer in certain ways. For example, phrases such as "task variety" and "experienced meaningfulness" are included in the instructions. Also, survey items are arranged in the same order as the variables occur in the model (Table 3.7). Both of these circumstances may elicit responses that would not have been obtained otherwise. In sum, there seems to be unanimous agreement that the JDS needs a complete overhaul, although this has not yet been attempted.

A theoretical argument about the sequence of events in the job characteristics model has also arisen. A basic assumption of the original model is that certain environmental characteristics of jobs directly influence worker perceptions of the characteristics; these perceptions form the basis for the processes implied by the model. One school of thought says that, because workers are satisfied with their jobs, they may, in turn, report that their jobs have more of the desired job characteristics, such as task variety or significance (Adler, Skov, & Salvemini, 1985; James & Tetrick, 1986). A recent laboratory study by Kraiger, Billings, and Isen (1989) even found that subjects' mood (i.e., whether they were in a positive state of mind) affected both reports of their task (job) characteristics and their task satisfaction. Another viewpoint assumes that the social cues workers get from their coworkers and job environment may be more important in determining reported task characteristics than objective job characteristics. This perspective, which has been labeled social information processing theory (Salancik & Pfeffer, 1978; Griffin, 1983), is discussed in Chapter 5.

Because of the methodological and theoretical problems with Hackman and Oldham's job characteristics model, several other approaches to task design have been proposed (Schwab & Cummings, 1976; Umstot, Mitchell, & Bell, 1978), although none appears to have gained widespread popularity. Campion and Thayer (1985) advocated expanding Hackman and Oldham's original model rather than abandoning it. They proposed that Hackman and

Oldham's model is only one of many perspectives of job or task design. They labeled the job characteristics model a motivational model and proposed three other models drawn from other disciplines. For example, the biological approach draws from human physiology and biomechanics to emphasize physical strength and endurance in task design. The end product in this type of model would be jobs or tasks that are physically easier and safer to perform. These researchers demonstrated that the different approaches function independently because they were related to different criteria. (The items measuring the biological model, for example, were negatively related to the need for medical care, whereas the items measuring the motivational model were positively related to job satisfaction.) Campion and Thayer's (1985) broad conceptualization of job characteristics and task design implies that any one perspective, such as Hackman and Oldham's original model, represents only part of the total picture. Although some subsequent research (Campion, 1988) has been supportive, this more eclectic perspective is still too new to critically evaluate.

# INTEGRATIVE APPROACHES TO WORK MOTIVATION THEORY

At this point, you are probably asking yourself which theory of work motivation is the best. Which theory should you recommend to managers to improve the motivation of their workers? Given our discussion of several theories, it seems that each possesses certain strengths and weaknesses; each theory does an admirable job of describing motivation under certain conditions for some people. This is indeed the conclusion many motivation theorists have reached. For that reason, one of the major focuses in contemporary work motivation research has been the integration of different theories.

In the last few sections we discussed the integration of different motivation theories in single studies for the purpose of pitting different theoretical perspectives against each other or refining existing theories. Other integrative approaches have also appeared. According to Kanfer (1991), the integrative approaches in work motivation research include the new paradigm approach, the converging operations approach, and the amalgamation approach.

The *new paradigm* approach involves the development of new theoretical perspectives using constructs and themes from different areas of psychology, such as social, cognitive, or clinical psychology. We alluded to such approaches in discussing the impact of social learning theory in social justice research and social norms in VIE research; the interested reader is referred to Kanfer (1991).

The *converging operations* approach compares the competing predictions of different theoretical approaches, usually with the aim of clarifying the boundary conditions for each theory. We will attempt to give a broader overview of this aspect of integrative research.

The third approach, the *amalgamation approach,* uses constructs from existing work motivation theories in combination to improve the validity obtained from using only one or a few theories. The product of this effort could be called a meta-theory because it subsumes several major theoretical perspectives. We will discuss one amalgamation approach, Katzell and Thompson's (1988, 1990) integrative model of work attitudes, motivation, and performance, although we acknowledge the existence of other comprehensive models (such as Naylor, Pritchard, and Ilgen's, 1980, and Locke's, 1991, models).

## Converging Operations Approach

The converging operations approach (Kanfer, 1991) is used when predictions from one theory are inconsistent with those from another theory. For example, goal-setting theory predicts that difficult goals lead to higher performance than easy goals. VIE theory assumes that people are motivated only as long as they can determine an association between their effort and performance; in such circumstances, you would expect that people prefer easy goals because they are more easily attainable. VIE theory, therefore, would predict that people exert the most effort (and perform best) in an easy-goal condition. Need achievement theory provides yet a third perspective. Recall that one of the assumptions of need achievement theory is that people with a high need for achievement prefer moderately difficult tasks because they are challenging but attainable. Consequently, need achievement theory would predict that people perform best when given moderate goals.

Which theory is correct? This issue has been debated for some time, and theorists have proposed a few answers. Mento, Cartledge, and Locke (1980) maintained that expectancy, valence, and goal difficulty all affect performance. Specifically, a person's expectancy of performance success and the valence of outcomes influence whether a goal is accepted; once accepted, however, the difficulty of the goal is the primary determinant of performance. Matsui, Okada, and Mizuguchi (1981) explored these possibilities in detail. They found that, compared with the easy-goal condition, subjects in the difficult-goal condition had lower expectancies of success but higher valences for the outcomes. The researchers reasoned that people find difficult goals attractive because they value successful performance on difficult tasks. However, the valence of these performance outcomes must overpower the lower expectancies of task success, or there will be no motivation to perform.

Shapira (1989) provided some insight into why need achievement predictions are not inconsistent with other theoretical perspectives. Goal-setting theory predicts only that difficult goals enhance performance, but says nothing about *task* difficulty. Need achievement theory states that high-need achievers prefer moderately difficult tasks. Need achievement theory, therefore, is a theory of task choice, not goal choice. Once the task is accepted, people who are high in the need to achieve will work diligently toward their goals. VIE theory states that people will be motivated to perform only as long as they can see the association between their effort and performance. Given moderately difficult *tasks,* the effort-performance link should be obvious.

Motivation theorists have also debated the relation between equity theory and expectancy theory. In the overpayment piece-rate condition, equity theory predicts that workers will increase the quality but decrease the quantity of their product. VIE theory predicts that the motivation to perform should be high whenever attractive (valent) outcomes are contingent upon performance. (In the hourly condition, the two theories agree because, under hourly payment, pay is tied directly to outcomes.) Lawler (1968) suggested that these two perspectives may not be contradictory in the piece-rate condition. From the results of his study, Lawler concluded that as payment increases and therefore perceived inequity increases, workers decrease the attractiveness or valence of payment. Under these circumstances, both equity and VIE theories would predict a reduction in output.

In summary, it seems that a person's level of need achievement affects the type of preferred task; perceived equity affects the valence of outcomes; the expectancy of successful performance and the valence of outcomes both influence whether a performance goal is accepted; and the difficulty of the goal directly influences goal performance. All of this adds up to a much broader perspective of work motivation than has been offered by any one theory. For that reason, some motivation researchers have suggested what Kanfer (1991) termed the amalgamation approach, or the construction of meta-theories.

## Amalgamation Approach

The amalgamation approach involves the use of work motivation theories in combination to improve the validity obtained from using only one or a few theories. Katzell and Thompson (1988; 1990) proposed one such meta-theory of work motivation and attitudes. They started with the premise that the existing theories are not wrong, but incomplete (Katzell, 1983). Katzell and Thompson reviewed the empirical research to determine the relations among the most important motivation constructs. Based on this review, they constructed an integrative model of attitudes, motivation, and performance that identifies equity theory, need theory (personal dispositions), VIE theory (instrumentality and expectancy), goal-setting theory, and behavioral theory (reinforcement) (Figure 3.8). Katzell and Thompson's model is broader than our review of the major motivation theories because it contains such constructs as norms (Chapter 5), attitudes (Chapter 4), and the work environment (Chapter 12).

The constructs in the model are read roughly from left to right. The solid lines between constructs in the model indicate a causal relationship between them. For example, the work environment in the form of organizational policies and practices determines incentives and rewards, such as pay

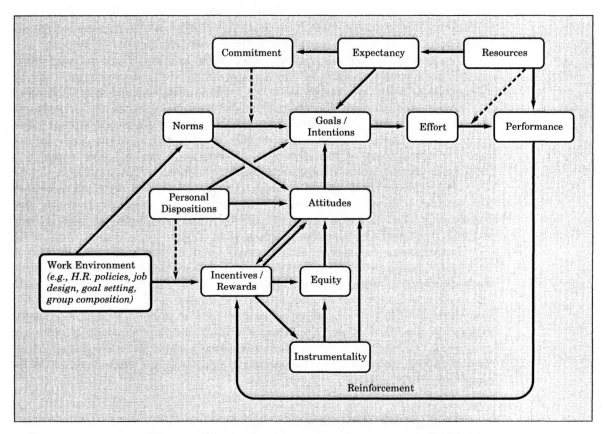

**Figure 3.8** *Integrative model of work attitudes, motivation, and performance*
*Source:* Katzell, R., & Thompson, D. (1990). An integrative model of work attitudes, motivation, and performance. *Human Performance, 3,* 63–85.

and promotions. A dotted line indicates a moderating relationship. For example, the relation between the work environment and incentives and rewards is affected by workers' personal dispositions, such as the need for achievement. Incentives and rewards also influence perceived equity and instrumentality, or the link between performance and outcomes. In addition, incentives and rewards have a reciprocal association with job attitudes in that incentives and rewards in the organization affect job attitudes, such as job satisfaction, while job attitudes, in turn, affect perceptions of incentives and rewards. After accounting for the causal and moderating effects of many other constructs, the model assumes that performance feeds back to incentives and rewards, which serve as reinforcement for future performance.

Katzell (1986) empirically tested the integrative model using data from 350 workers in three organizations and generally found support for the relations hypothesized by the model. Not only does this model nicely integrate the different motivation theories and clarify their interrelations, it also provides a framework for organizational development interventions (Chapter 5) (Katzell & Thompson, 1988). For example, according to the model, if the incentives and rewards system in an organization is improved, employee attitudes, perceived equity, and instrumentalities should first show the effects of the change. Specifically, if the intervention is effective, employee attitudes should improve, and perceived equity and instrumentalities should increase. Based on the work of Katzell and other theorists (Locke & Latham, 1990), the future of work motivation research seems to lie in global perspectives of motivation that can be directly applied to solving real organizational problems. Considering the historical emphasis on abstract theory and laboratory research in work motivation, we believe this new trend is a very positive one.

# A FINAL SUMMATION AND A LOOK AT THE FUTURE

As we have seen in this chapter the research and theory on work motivation offers some answers to the often asked question: "How do I motivate employees to work harder?" The early work of the need theorists, especially Murray, set the stage for one of the first theories of work motivation, the need hierarchy. According to Maslow, people are motivated by five types of needs (physiological, safety, social, esteem, and actualization) that are arranged in a hierarchy of importance. The concepts of Maslow's theory have been widely applied in organizations. Alderfer proposed existence–relatedness–growth (ERG) theory to address some of the deficiencies in the need hierarchy. Other organizational research on human needs has concentrated on a single need to explain motivated behavior, such as need for achievement or need for power. Whereas need theory considers the personal characteristics of workers, another approach, behaviorism, focuses on the environment as the source of motivated behavior. An interesting extension of behavioral theory is social learning theory.

Other theories of work motivation, often referred to as process theories, include both personal and environmental characteristics. They include equity theory, goal-setting theory, expectancy theory, and cognitive evaluation theory. Goal-setting theory is based on the simple premise that conscious intentions guide behavior. Two of its major propositions are that harder goals produce higher performance as long as the goal is accepted, and specific goals produce higher performance than no goals or "do your best." Unlike the simple predictions of goal setting, valence–instrumentality–expectancy (VIE) theory has a more complex framework. The basic components include valence, the desirability of some outcome; instrumentality, the perceived association between one outcome and another outcome; and expectancy, the perceived likelihood that the effort expended will result in some desired level of performance. Perhaps the most obvious practical implication of VIE theory is that employees can be motivated to work harder if their performance is tied to valued outcomes. Somewhat at odds with VIE theory, Deci's cognitive evaluation theory assumes that if people perceive they are performing a task for external inducements, such as money, they will lose their sense of competence and control because they will perceive that external forces guide their behavior. The primary focus of Hackman and Oldham's job characteristics model is, as its name implies, the task itself. They propose that well-designed work tasks fulfill the psychological needs of workers, and the fulfillment of those needs motivates them. Specifically, they predict that five core job dimensions contribute to the development of critical psychological states, and that these psychological states are linked to positive work and personal outcomes. They also propose that these relations are stronger for workers high in growth needs.

All of the motivational theories provide useful insights into various facets of work motivation. The research, however, has provided much more support for some theories than others. Probably the least support has been found for the need theories. The behavioristic principles of reinforcement work, but behavioral modification programs are often difficult to implement and maintain in industry. Research has fairly conclusively demonstrated that equity theory predictions work, especially for underpayment, with most of the evidence coming from laboratory experiments. Goal-setting theory is currently our most widely researched and best-supported theory of work motivation and has clear practical implications. VIE predictions received only modest support in early research but more recent studies have corrected some methodological flaws and seem to have yielded much more consistent support for the theory. Similarly, support for the job characteristics model and the JDS have been mixed, but stronger support has been found in recent research using sophisticated statistical analyses. Deci's cognitive evaluation theory also has some support, but most of the research has been conducted in rather artificial laboratory situations and seems to possess little external validity.

The focus of most contemporary work motivation theory and research has been the development of integrative approaches. According to Kanfer, there are three major integrative approaches. The new paradigm approach involves the development of new theoretical perspectives using constructs and themes from different areas of psychology. The converging operations approach compares the competing predictions of different theoretical approaches of work motivation theory, such as goal-setting and VIE theories. Research using the converging operations approach has demonstrated that the different theories all contribute uniquely to knowledge about work motivations. The amalgamation approach uses constructs from existing work motivation theories in combination to improve the validity obtained from using only one approach. The future of work motivation research and application seems to lie in these more global perspectives.

There has always been a strong interest in work motivation among psychologists, but changes in American society suggest that this interest will become even stronger. One challenge is presented by the increasing diversity of the American work force. With the influx of more women, minorities, and the disabled into the work force, it will become important for managers to take into account the differences among these subgroups in their values and needs. The old simplistic views that all workers want the same thing, whether money or self-fulfillment, are unlikely to prove useful as sources of ideas. Motivation theorists and researchers will need to address ways of individualizing reward systems in organizations to address these differences.

Changes occurring in organizations present other challenges. Kanter (1989) has observed a move away from careers in which an individual proceeds through "almost-automatic promotions to bigger and better jobs inside a company." According to Kanter, people will have to contend with less job security and will be expected to engage in entrepreneurial activities. Organizations are also involving workers in decisions that previously would have been left to management and expecting them to take personal responsibility and show initiative. The increasing use of teams will require that people value and work well with others. In this new corporate world, what do we do with people who have needs and values that are out of synch with these trends? Should we attempt to change their needs and values to match the organization? Should we instead change the work situation to accommodate different types of people? Or do we select people whose needs and values match the organization? These are only a few of the questions that will need to be addressed in future research on motivation.

## DISCUSSION QUESTIONS

1.  Why have the need theories largely failed to live up to their early promise as theories of work motivation? Why are they still popular among many managers today?
2.  Why have behavioral principles not been widely applied in industry to increase work motivation? Would you expect that behavioral principles could be applied as easily to, for example, an assembly line worker's job as to a manager's job?
3.  Why are some theories of work motivation referred to as content and some as process theories? Why is that distinction important?
4.  How do equity theory, goal-setting theory, VIE theory, and cognitive evaluation theory differ in terms of: a) their theoretical assumptions? b) how the research to test the theory was conducted? c) their current status as work motivation theories?
5.  What is meant by integrative approaches to the study of work motivation? Give three examples of single studies that have used this approach. What other integrative approaches have been suggested?

# The American Worker: Lazy or Overworked?

While the United States has the highest productivity of the major industrial powers, Japan has shown a much higher rate of increase in productivity and threatens to surpass the United States. Some believe that a major culprit is the American worker, who is not as motivated to work as hard as the typical Japanese worker. In February 1992, during a meeting of the Japanese parliament, Prime Minister Klichi Miyazawa commented, "I have felt that the ethic of working by the sweat of one's brow has seemed to be lacking" among American workers in recent years. Miyazawa later amended this statement, adding that "I did not intend to criticize U.S. workers at all." His retraction, however, fell on the deaf ears of enraged American workers, who, a few weeks prior, had been called lazy and illiterate by another member of the Japanese parliament. Is this proclamation correct? Is the American work ethic fading? Are American workers really unmotivated to labor for an honest day's wages?

There is some evidence to support Prime Minister Miyazawa's assertions. Sengoku (1985) believes that the Japanese attitude toward work fundamentally differs from the American attitude. Japanese workers have what he calls *yaruki* or "willingness to work" in which the worker "looks for the reason of his being or identity in hard work and even tries to improve himself by it. . . . Workers say that they are tired and want to go home, yet they stay on the job until they find a solution for problems they may have had that day." Robert Eisenberger (1989) argues in *Blue Monday: The Loss of the Work Ethic in America* that in contrast to Japan, there has been a steady decline in the work ethic in the United States. "As America became affluent, a preoccupation with leisure and sensual pleasure began to replace traditional work values, making managers, workers, and students less willing to undergo the self-denial required to achieve long-term goals. . . . More than ever before, Americans view school and work as an unpleasant interlude in their relaxation and entertainment, to be gotten out of the way with a minimum of effort" (p. ix).

In addition to this anecdotal evidence, several facts seem to support the contention that the Japanese work harder than Americans. Japan has the lowest absence rate among industrialized countries, around 2% compared with 3.5% in the United States. Only about 40% of employees in Japan use their paid vacation. On the average, the Japanese worker was entitled to 15.5 days of vacation in 1990 but took only 53% or 8.2 days of the time they were allowed. In 1980 the Japanese took 61% of the time allowed, suggesting that the trend has been toward more time at work. The average Japanese employee works some 200 hours more a year than the average American employee, and recent attempts by the Japanese government to reduce working hours have been largely unsuccessful.

Additional evidence comes from surveys of the attitudes and values of American workers. A 1990 Roper survey found for the first time in 15 years that Americans rated leisure as more important in their lives than work. David Cherrington (1980) surveyed 3,000 individuals in 53 companies employed as production workers, supervisors, clerks, and middle-level managers. Among his conclusions was that hard work and pride in craftsmanship were not as important to younger workers as to older workers. A survey of managers found that 79% believed that American productivity has suffered because of an eroding work ethic (Lipset, 1992).

There is also evidence that Japanese students work harder than American students. The typical American school year lasts 178 days compared with 240 days in Japan. The typical Japanese seventh grader is assigned an average of 4.7 hours of math homework every week compared with only 2.9 hours in the United States. On the other hand, students in the United States are far ahead of the rest of the world in hours of television watching. According to one study, most American children have spent more hours watching television by the time they are 16 than they have going to school (Eisenberger, 1989). The number of college students majoring in the sciences has declined and Eisenberger (1989) attributes this to laziness. College students, according to his observations, are increasingly avoiding majors that require hard work. To see firsthand the work motivation of younger employees, one human resource manager worked for two weeks in a fast food restaurant (Sheehy, 1990). He observed that "The basic work ethic of the teenagers and college students was dominated by a type of gamesmanship that revolved around 'taking the system' or 'milking the place dry.'"

If we assume that Japanese workers have a stronger work ethic, what are the possible reasons? Some would argue that American workers today, more than in previous decades, see personal fulfillment from their work as a fundamental right (Ludeman, 1989). Others would point to management practices in the United States as the primary cause of a decline in work ethic. Declining value on work may reflect the frustration of workers faced with authoritarian management, outdated equipment, and poor training. Moreover, top management has not set a good example in many organizations. For instance, the gap between the salaries of top management and the lowest level workers is much larger than the gap in

Japan, and despite the economic problems of U.S. firms in recent years, the gap is growing. Another reason for the purported decline in the work ethic could be due to the fact that Americans are having to work longer hours out of necessity, often in dead-end jobs. According to several recent newspaper and magazine articles American workers are being asked to do more for less merely to retain their jobs (Davis & Milbank, 1992; Verity, Peterson, Depke, & Schwartz, 1991). The pressured workers see their wages dwindling in an inflationary economy, while simultaneously perceiving few options in a tight job market. One steel worker provides an example of the unfortunate plight of many American workers. Bob Burak was laid off from a job that he had held for 34 years; after becoming reemployed at another steel mill, he lost his job within five years. Burak complained, "You really don't trust the company because you don't know what it's going to do." He also said that many steelworkers are complaining more and turning down overtime, regardless of the pay.

While much has been written about the laziness of the American workers, there are opposing views. With regard to generational differences, some have argued that young people today are just as motivated to work hard in their jobs as previous generations, but want more balance in their lives (Nelson-Horchler, 1991). Juliet Schor (1991) in her book *The Overworked American* states that Americans are spending more and more time at work when they should be spending more time in leisure! Support for this is presented in a recent *Fortune* magazine article, appropriately titled "Welcome to the age of overwork" (Fisher, 1992). The article notes that with continuing layoffs and downsizing in major corporations, the work load of surviving managers and other professionals is steadily increasing and approaching the 12-hour days and work-filled evenings so typical of Japanese managers. Schor strongly advises against imitating Japan and argues that shortening the work week even further and increasing vacation time could actually lead to improved productivity. For instance, when firms in the United States switched to shorter workdays during the Great Depression, there was evidence that productivity increased. A more recent example was Medtronic Corporation in Minneapolis, which gave employees 40 hours' pay for 36 hours of work. Although no additional employees were hired, work output increased. According to Schor, "When hours are shorter, workers can physically and mentally sustain more intense effort" (p. 156).

## CASE QUESTIONS

1. Would you agree or disagree with Prime Minister Miyazawa that American workers no longer value working hard by the "sweat of their brow." Why?
2. There is clear evidence that the productivity of Japanese workers is increasing at a faster rate than that of American workers. Nevertheless, asking whether American workers are as "motivated" as Japanese workers could be considered a meaningless question. Why, and what questions might make more sense to ask?
3. What motivation theory or theories would best explain why Japanese workers and students put in more working hours, and less leisure time, than American workers and students?
4. What remedies might increase the motivation of the average American worker?
5. How would you evaluate Schor's assertion that Americans are currently overworked and should be given more leisure time?

# CHAPTER

4

# Job Attitudes

- A Brief History of Job Attitudes

- Theories of Job Satisfaction

- The Measurement of Job Satisfaction

- Correlates of Job Satisfaction

- Other Job Attitudes: Job Involvement and Organizational Commitment

- The Three Job Attitudes: An Integrated Perspective

- A Final Summation and a Look at the Future

- Case: A Question of Job Attitudes: The Case of the "New" Big Blue

Consider Grace Clements' description of her job making the molded inner lining of suitcases in a plant that manufactures luggage:

> All day long is the same thing over and over. That's about ten steps every forty seconds about 800 times a day. . . . I daydream while I'm working. Your mind gets so it automatically picks out the flaws [in the luggage]. . . . You get to be automatic in what you're doing and your mind is doing something else. . . . I hope I don't work many more years. I'm tired. I'd like to stay home and keep house.

Contrast Grace's description of her job to that of Kay Stepkin, the director of a small nonprofit bakery that produces and sells bread:

> We try to have a compromise between doing things efficiently and doing things in a human way. Our bread has to taste the same way every day, but you don't have to be machines. On a good day it's beautiful to be here. We have a good time and work hard and we're laughing. . . . I think a person can work as hard as he's capable, not only for others but for his own satisfaction. . . . I am doing exactly what I want to do. . . . Work is an essential part of being alive. Your work is your identity. It tells you who you are. . . . There's such a joy in doing work well. (Excerpted from *Working: People talk about what they do all day and how they feel about what they do* by Studs Terkel, 1974.)

We are sure you would agree that Grace's feelings about her job are quite different from Kay's: Grace views each work day as a wearisome burden, whereas Kay anticipates each work day with eagerness and challenge. Consequently, you would probably say that Kay is much more satisfied with her job than Grace. If you thought about Grace and Kay for awhile, you might also predict that Kay is probably absent less from work, performs better at her job, and is generally healthier (mentally and physically) than Grace. If you made these predictions, you followed a similar line of reasoning to the behavioral scientists who have researched job satisfaction.

Job satisfaction has been a major interest of behavioral scientists for many years. Locke (1976) estimated that over 3,000 studies had been published on job satisfaction by 1972, and there is no indication the trend has changed in the last 20 years. Why, you may ask, has job satisfaction generated so much interest among researchers? As illustrated with the stories of Grace and Kay, the implicit assumption has been that if workers are satisfied with their jobs, they will perform better, have fewer absences, be less likely to quit, and generally feel better about themselves. You will soon discover that these assumptions are often not warranted.

When you ask people about their attitudes concerning their jobs, you ask for some highly personal, individualistic information. As we will discuss shortly, I/O psychologists typically collect job attitude data from individual responses to job attitude questionnaires. Such information reflects what is called a micro orientation (Chapter 1). At first glance, it is difficult to see how such an orientation fits into a systems model that encompasses the worker, the organization, and the larger environment. However, job attitudes can affect personal and organizational functioning, which can further affect job attitudes, and so on. When viewed from this perspective, job attitudes play a major role in the human-organizational system.

Our explorations into job attitudes will cover a short history of job attitudes research, a discussion of major theoretical perspectives on job satisfaction, and how job satisfaction is measured and its relationships with a number of personal (e.g., age and occupation) and organizational (e.g., performance and absenteeism) variables. Because this chapter is about job attitudes, not just job satisfaction, we will also discuss two other widely researched attitudes, organizational commitment and job involvement.

# A BRIEF HISTORY OF JOB ATTITUDES

## Scientific Management

Most of the data-based or empirical job satisfaction research has been published since the late 1930s and early 1940s. The impetus for this research emanated from the results of a series of innovative studies conducted in Chicago in the 1920s and 1930s called the Hawthorne studies. However, before we examine the Hawthorne studies, we need to step even further back in time to appreciate why the Hawthorne studies were so revolutionary that they forever changed the way we think about work.

Our current thinking about job satisfaction contrasts sharply with the scientific management philosophy of Frederick Taylor, an engineer who lived in the late nineteenth and early twentieth centuries. Taylor is associated with the well-known concept of time-and-motion studies, which attempted to streamline jobs by identifying unnecessary or ineffective work behaviors. This type of information was collected by observing people as they actually performed work (Chapter 1).

Taylor's scientific management was founded upon four premises (Dessler, 1980):

1. Finding the "one best way" to perform the job. This typically meant simplifying the job so it could be more easily and quickly accomplished.
2. Systematic personnel selection and placement to match the best worker to each job. Well-developed selection and training programs that consider workers' strengths and limitations were emphasized.
3. Strict division of labor between management and workers. Managers were supposed to manage and plan while the

workers accomplished the work; boundaries between labor and management were rigidly guarded.

4. Monetary incentives to attract and motivate workers to perform optimally. Systematic selection and simplification of jobs served as only a baseline for efficiency. The profit motive provided the balance.

Unlike the typical, despotic management practices of the nineteenth century, Taylor's ideas were grounded in an ethic of worker-management cooperation and increased worker benefits. Even if his motives were irreproachable, his assumptions about human motivation and attitudes were not. Taylor assumed that if workers were provided with a decent job and wages linked to productivity, they would strive for peak performance. As the researchers in the Hawthorne studies discovered, however, this simplistic notion was grossly inaccurate. Increased productivity could not be achieved merely by lining workers' pockets with money.

## The Hawthorne Studies

The experiments conducted at the Chicago Hawthorne works of the General Electric Company in the late 1920s and 1930s remain the most influential organizational research of all time. The results of these studies made behavioral scientists aware, for the first time, that worker behavior could be influenced by factors other than monetary incentives and the physical work environment. Although these studies were not flawlessly designed or executed, they provide a fascinating example of how the scientific method can be applied to organizational questions (Dessler, 1980).

The Hawthorne research encompassed several separate studies and spanned more than a decade. However, we only briefly discuss three studies here: the illumination studies, the relay assembly test room studies, and the bank wiring room studies. The *illumination studies,* which began in 1924, are the earliest studies, and not formally considered to be part of the Hawthorne studies. Rather, the results of these initial studies provided the stimulus for later research. The illumination studies began as a typical industrial engineering question about the relationship between worker productivity and the level of illumination in the work environment. The researchers were guided by the prevailing organizational philosophy of that era, scientific management, which assumed that workers are motivated solely by tangible factors, such as money and working conditions (illumination).

In the initial experiment, workers in three departments were exposed to varying lighting levels. To their surprise, the researchers discovered that productivity did not always decline when they lowered illumination. Intrigued, the researchers conducted two more illumination studies, each with tighter experimental controls than the first. However, even with the systematic manipulations of lighting levels, worker productivity did not decline relative to the amount of illumination present. In one group, productivity continued to increase with decreasing illumination, even to the point that the workers complained that "they were hardly able to see what they were doing."

These results provoked the researchers to implement the second set of experiments, the *relay assembly test room studies.* In these studies, the goal was to isolate and investigate the work behavior of small groups of workers. The researchers feared that the results of the illumination experiments may have been biased by such organizational influences as personnel changes and departmental policies.

The job the researchers chose to study was the assembly of telephone relays. Putting together the assembly fixture required considerable motor skill and, because completing a relay required only about one minute, was highly repetitive. Each operator could assemble about 500 relays each day. All operators were women.

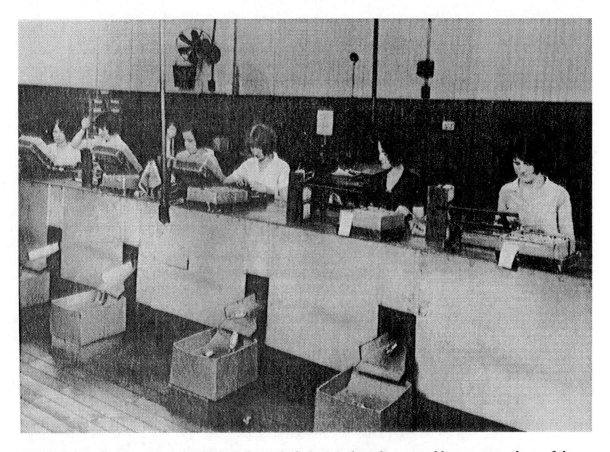

A small group of women was observed while at work during the relay assembly test room phase of the Hawthorne studies in the late 1920s.

The relay assembly test room studies have also been labeled the *rest-pause experiments* because the formal purpose of these studies was to explore the effects of work pauses on employee fatigue and productivity. During the course of these experiments, the researchers tested the effects of many different types of work-rest cycles. For example, manipulations included 5-minute breaks in the morning and afternoon, 10-minute breaks in the morning and afternoon, a series of six 5-minute breaks, and a 15-minute break in the morning and a 10-minute break in the afternoon. In all cases, productivity increased over baseline.

In the next phase of the relay assembly test room studies, the researchers investigated how worker productivity was influenced by shortening the work day. The manipulations included shortening the work day by 30 minutes (with rest pauses) and the work week by one-half day (with rest pauses). In both cases productivity did not decrease. The overall findings across all of the relay assembly test room studies were that productivity rose regardless of the length of the work day.

The total failure of the manipulations of the physical work environment to affect productivity in the previous experiments convinced the researchers that social processes had exerted a tremendous influence on work output. They therefore decided specifically to study social influences in work groups, and the *bank wiring room studies* were born. From the 14 men who were intensively studied as they worked, the researchers surmised that the work group had a powerful influence on individual worker productivity. For example, the workers had developed a concept of a "proper day's work" and exerted pressure on any worker who did not comply with the group's standard. This social pressure was particularly evident for those workers who attempted to exceed the group's output quota. These findings were quite surprising to the researchers and management because the organization's incentive system was based on higher pay for higher output.

Across the series of experiments, the Hawthorne researchers concluded that employee attitudes and morale and the influence of the informal work group were major determinants of productivity. From these conclusions, they conceptualized the organization as a sociotechnical system (Chapter 5) in which "the technical organization and the human organization . . . are interrelated and interdependent" (Roethlisberger & Dickson, 1939).

The Hawthorne studies have been roundly criticized for several flaws, both philosophical and methodological (Dessler, 1980). Critics have charged that the researchers gave a one-sided interpretation to their data, which was heavily influenced by the human relations movement and its emphasis on worker-management harmony. More well-known condemnations, however, have targeted the flaws in the design and execution of the experiments. The researchers in these studies deviated in several respects from what we now know to be good research design (Chapter 2). Perhaps the most glaring error was that there was never an attempt to randomly assign workers to experimental and control groups. In fact, workers were often chosen because they were congenial and productive. In the course of the experiments, these already superior workers were given preferential treatment by both the researchers and management. At no time was the output of workers in the experiments compared with the output of other, comparable workers in the organization. Also, the number of workers actually studied was so small that sample size precluded any generalizations to the larger organization.

In spite of these well-warranted criticisms, however, the Hawthorne studies had a profound and enduring influence on the study of worker behavior. Their significance lies not so much in the specific results or conclusions, but in the way they shaped future research. In fact, this chapter on job attitudes would probably not exist—at least not in its present form—if the Hawthorne studies had not convinced behavioral scientists of the pervasive effects of job attitudes on both organizational and personal functioning.

## The Hoppock Study

This last bit of historical information is an early study of job satisfaction in one community. Unlike the Hawthorne studies, the goals and interpretation of the Hoppock research were entirely empirical (data-based). Robert Hoppock was a graduate student who was interested in applying newly developed scaling (measurement) techniques to the study of job satisfaction. He devised questions that people answered by referring to a scale ranging from 100 (extreme dissatisfaction) to 700 (extreme satisfaction). Although this seems like a common and simple task, collecting such data was a novel concept in the 1930s. With the aid of his father-in-law, he collected data from most working adults in New Hope, Pennsylvania. Hoppock discovered that approximately 88% of those sampled were satisfied with their jobs. He also found that the most satisfied workers were in the professional, managerial, and executive occupations (Hoppock, 1935).

Hoppock's research is significant for two reasons. First, he developed one of the first contemporary job attitude surveys, and, therefore, provided a template for the data collection method that would be used in most subsequent job attitude research. Second, Hoppock's results have been replicated repeatedly for over 55 years. In Table 4.1, the job satisfaction of the five categories of occupations Hoppock sampled is provided, together with the rank order of responses in each category and the average or mean response in each category. (Remember that the scale ranges from 100 to 700, with higher scores indicating greater satisfaction.) Compare Hoppock's results with data reported by Kahn (1981; excerpted from Quinn & Shepard, 1974) in Table 4.1; here workers in seven occupational categories responded to a job satisfaction survey in which the scale values ranged from 1 (very dissatisfied) to 5 (very satisfied). The pattern of results is very consistent across these two samples collected approximately 40 years apart.

If we take into account the scaling differences in the two job satisfaction studies (that is, 100–700 vs. 1–5), another point becomes obvious.

**Table 4.1**

## COMPARATIVE DATA ON JOB SATISFACTION BY OCCUPATIONAL CATEGORIES IN THE 1930s AND 1970s

| Occupation | Mean Score | Rank |
|---|---|---|
| Hoppock (1935) Study[1] | | |
| • Professionals, managers, executives | 560 | 1 |
| • Subprofessionals, business and lower level supervisors | 548 | 2 |
| • Skilled manual and white collar workers | 510 | 3 |
| • Semiskilled workers | 483 | 4 |
| • Unskilled/manual workers | 401 | 5 |
| Quinn & Shepard (1974) Study[2] | | |
| • Professionals and technical workers | 4.11 | 1 |
| • Managers and administrators | 4.00 | 2 |
| • Craft workers | 3.89 | 3 |
| • Salespersons | 3.82 | 4 |
| • Clerical workers | 3.67 | 5 |
| • Machine operators (except transport) | 3.39 | 6 |
| • Laborers (nonfarm) | 3.28 | 7 |

*Source:* [1] Adapted from Hoppock, R. (1935). *Job Satisfaction.* New York: Harper, p. 255.
[2] Adapted from Quinn, R.P., & Shepard, L.J. (1974). *The 1972–1973 Quality of Employment Survey.* Ann Arbor, MI: Survey Research Center, University of Michigan.

Considerable overlap exists among categories, with many laborers having reported as much job satisfaction as many professionals. Also, across all occupations, the average satisfaction score is skewed or distorted toward the high (satisfied) end of the scale. The high job satisfaction reported by most workers across all occupations is also an enduring finding of job satisfaction research. The existing data on relative levels of job satisfaction totally dispute the anecdotal perception that people are unhappy (or have ever been unhappy) with their jobs. Of course, these conclusions are based on mean or average responses; any one worker may report extreme dissatisfaction with his or her job.

This short survey of the history of job satisfaction research demonstrates how the Hawthorne and Hoppock studies influenced the way industrial/organizational psychologists and managers currently perceive job satisfaction: as a relatively enduring attitude shaped largely by social and interpersonal processes in the work environment. We next examine how this thinking about the nature of job satisfaction developed into several different theoretical perspectives.

# THEORIES OF JOB SATISFACTION

If you are like most people, by early adulthood you have worked at a full or part-time for at least a few months. By the end of a few months, you undoubtedly had formed some attitudes about your job: You probably felt either satisfied, dissatisfied, or neutral about your job. Did you ever stop to think about the factors in your employing organization and in yourself that may have contributed to your attitudes? For example, if you were dissatisfied, perhaps your organization was bound by rules and procedures although you desired autonomy and freedom in your work. Behavioral scientists have advanced various theories of job satisfaction that attempt to explain the guiding forces behind worker attitudes.

Our review of job satisfaction theory covers three broad topics: two-factor theory, comparison theories, and cognitive/dispositional theories. Two-factor theory, which was the first major job satisfaction theory, attempts to explain how job satisfaction is affected by the presence of extrinsic job factors, such as salary and working conditions, and intrinsic job factors, such as responsibility and achievement. Comparison theories of job satisfaction draw upon the concepts of needs and values. According to these theories, we examine what we obtain from our jobs and then determine if that matches what we need or value. Other theories of satisfaction focus on the cognitive processes and personality characteristics of workers.

## Two-Factor Theory

Two important reviews of the research literature on job satisfaction were published in the 1950s, one by Brayfield and Crockett (1955) and the other by Herzberg, Mausner, Peterson, and Capwell (1957). Both reviews focused on the relationship between job satisfaction and job performance. Brayfield and Crockett concluded that no relationship existed between satisfaction and performance; Herzberg et al. concluded that there was a significant relationship between job satisfaction and performance. How could these two groups of researchers reach such different conclusions? Brayfield and Crockett considered only studies of job performance; they excluded studies of performance-related behaviors (e.g., absenteeism, accidents) that Herzberg et al. included. Brayfield and Crockett were also more conservative in their evaluation of the studies in their review than were Herzberg and his colleagues. Consequently, the two sets of researchers considered different studies and used different decision criteria in their reviews. The ensuing years have produced few changes in this regard: Reviewers still frequently disagree because they focus on different research and standards of evaluation.

Although from a scientific perspective Brayfield and Crockett were more rigorous, Herzberg et al. had a much greater impact on job satisfaction research because they reached some rather revolutionary conclusions. Specifically, they maintained that satisfaction and dissatisfaction were actually different concepts, at least in their relationships with other variables. Herzberg, Mausner, and Snyderman (1959) conducted an empirical study to test this hypothesis. The researchers interviewed over 200 engineers and accountants about their jobs; these workers were asked to recall job-related incidents that were associated with especially good and bad feelings. These data indicated that good feelings were associated with such job-related factors as achievement, responsibility, advancement, recognition, and work (task) activities. Bad feelings were frequently associated with working (environmental) conditions, supervision, salary, job security, organizational rules and practices, and interpersonal relationships at work.

From his data, Herzberg proposed the *motivator-hygiene theory,* or as it is more commonly known, *two-factor theory.* Two-factor theory assumes that everyone has two types of needs, hygiene needs and motivator needs. Hygiene needs include factors extrinsic to the work itself, such as the work environment, supervision, and pay. Motivator needs include intrinsic factors, such as achievement, recognition, and work activities.

According to Herzberg, when hygiene needs are not fulfilled, the worker is dissatisfied. When hygiene needs are fulfilled, the worker is not dissatisfied. The fulfillment of the hygiene needs does *not* produce a state of satisfaction, but rather a state of neutrality. For example, if your garbage is not collected, you will undoubtedly become dissatisfied. However, the fact that your garbage is collected will not make you happy. Your attitude toward garbage collection is probably best described as a neutral state that is disrupted only by the absence of garbage collection.

When motivator needs are fulfilled, the worker is satisfied; when they are not fulfilled, the worker is not satisfied. However, the state of being "not satisfied" is not equivalent to being dissatisfied (similar to hygiene needs). For example, when workers obtain a sense of achievement and responsibility from their jobs, they are satisfied. However, if they do not obtain achievement and responsibility at work, they do not feel satisfied, which is different from being dissatisfied. Two-factor theory even implies that a worker can be simultaneously satisfied and dissatisfied because satisfaction and dissatisfaction are separate states.

Although Herzberg's two-factor theory has generated much enthusiasm over the years, empirical research has not been very supportive of the major tenets of the theory. The motivator and hygiene factors are related to both satisfying and dissatisfying situations (Dunnette, Campbell, & Hakel, 1967; House & Wigdor, 1967). A major criticism of the theory concerns the manner in which the data were gathered. Herzberg used a data collection procedure called *critical incidents;* that is, he asked workers to recall especially good and bad job-related incidents. Because people prefer to present themselves in a favorable light, they might attribute good incidents to themselves or their efforts (recognition, achievement) and bad incidents to other factors in the work environment (supervision, working conditions). This type of defensive bias would produce data in which motivators are associated with satisfaction and hygiene factors with dissatisfaction (Ondrack, 1974).

Given its lack of empirical support, you may question whether two-factor theory has had any real impact on organizational research and practice. Two-factor theory's lasting value lies in the fact that it focused attention on the influence of motivators, such as achievement and responsibility, on worker attitudes. Prior to Herzberg's work, organizational interventions had focused entirely on hygiene factors, for example, pay and the work environment. Therefore, like the Hawthorne studies that preceded it, two-factor theory made a lasting contribution despite its apparent flaws.

## Comparison Theories

Two-factor theory is primarily a descriptive theory. That is, it attempts only to describe the conditions under which workers are influenced to feel satisfied or dissatisfied. Other theories have attempted to explain the cognitive processes workers use to determine if they are satisfied or dissatisfied. Comparison theories are one such class of cognitive, process-oriented theories of job satisfaction. Comparison theories ask workers to consider how much of some characteristic they have in their present jobs and how much of this characteristic they would like to have in their present jobs. The characteristic in question is typically framed in terms of different types of comparisons, such as need, value, or social comparisons. For example, you might be asked to consider how much opportunity for social interaction you have in your present job and how much you would prefer to have. The larger the discrepancy between the amount present and the amount desired, the lower your reported job satisfaction (Porter, 1962).

Lawler (1973) incorporated the concept of attained versus desired needs in his model of facet satisfaction (Figure 4.1). This model is an extension of the Porter-Lawler model of motivation discussed in Chapter 3. It is a facet satisfaction model because satisfaction with various components or facets of the job, such as supervision, pay, or the work itself, is considered. Lawler's model specifies that workers compare what their jobs should provide in terms of job facets, such as promotions and pay, to what they currently receive from their jobs. However, simple need comparison theory is extended by also weighing the influence of certain worker characteristics (such as skill, training, and age) and job characteristics (such as degree of responsibility and difficulty). In addition, the model draws concepts from the equity theory of motivation by assuming that workers ultimately determine their job satisfaction by comparing their relevant job inputs and outputs to referent (comparison) others (see Chapter 3).

An example will clarify the relationship implied by Lawler's model. In determining her level of job satisfaction, a worker might consider that she brings an MBA and ten years of business experience to a responsible managerial job. A coworker, her referent other, has only a bachelor's degree and eight years of experience. The coworker's job is also a managerial position, but with less responsibility and a slightly higher salary. Consequently, the worker,

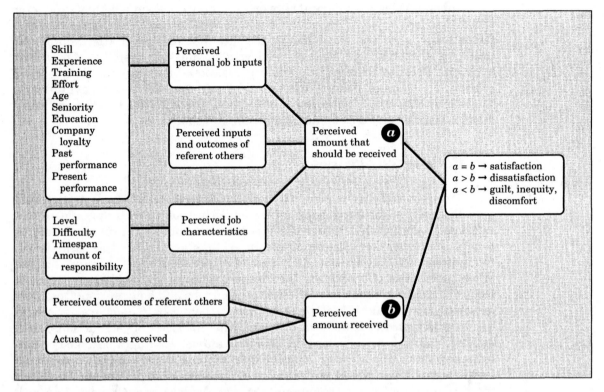

**Figure 4.1** *Lawler's (1973) model of facet satisfaction*
*Source:* Lawler, E.E. (1973). *Motivation in Work Organizations.* Monterey, CA: Brooks/Cole.

after weighing the various inputs, outcomes, and amounts received, feels dissatisfied with her pay.

The need comparison theories have been criticized both conceptually and statistically. Need comparison theory assumes that people make logical and rational comparisons among what they have, what relevant others have, and what they need. Psychologists have accumulated considerable evidence over the years that demonstrates that people are typically not rational decision makers engaging in methodical comparison processes (Slovic, Fischoff, & Lichtenstein, 1977). Critics also have expressed concern about how need comparison data are collected. Specifically, the comparisons have been evaluated by subtracting what the subject has (or what relevant others have) from what he or she desires or needs. This type of difference score has been criticized because what subjects have frequently predicts their attitudes better than the difference between what they have and what they need (Wall & Payne, 1973). However, Rice, McFarlin, and Bennett (1989) recently reported support for some comparison theory predictions that were tested using carefully constructed measures and sophisticated statistical analyses.

Locke (1976) proposed a somewhat different type of comparison theory. Locke's value theory of job satisfaction is based upon the premise that people will be satisfied with their jobs if their jobs provide them with what they desire or value. He distinguishes between the concept of needs as imperative for survival versus values as highly subjective desires. Locke has emphasized the value or importance of certain aspects of the job in determining job satisfaction. However, according to Locke, values affect the range of responses more than the actual level of satisfaction. For example, if you value autonomy, or the freedom to make decisions relevant to your job, any attempt to increase or decrease your level of autonomy will be reflected in wide variations in job satisfaction. However, if you do not value autonomy, then you will probably be indifferent to changes in the level of job autonomy. The concept of values can potentially be very useful in understanding worker attitudes. Although workers may need a certain amount of autonomy or pay, their attitudes toward their jobs may differ if their values differ. Specifically, because people work for valued outcomes, values should predict job satisfaction beyond the influence of needs. Few empirical tests of value theory exist, although the limited data are supportive (Mobley & Locke, 1970; Rice, Gentile, & McFarlin, 1991).

All of these comparison theories assume that workers focus on their own needs or values to assess job satisfaction. However, Salancik and Pfeffer (1977) proposed that people form job attitudes by observing the attitudes of relevant others or by attending to available contextual information; they labeled this perspective *social information processing theory*. Although this assumption may seem far-fetched, some research does support it. White and Mitchell (1979) devised a laboratory experiment in which subjects were given either an interesting or a dull task to complete. Subjects also heard coworkers (accomplices of the researchers) exclaim either how interesting or dull the task was. Consistent with Salancik and Pfeffer's predictions, subjects who heard the task was interesting were more satisfied with the task than subjects who heard the task was dull, regardless of the objective characteristics of the task they performed. In a similar vein, Caldwell and O'Reilly (1982) told subjects to imagine they were either satisfied or dissatisfied with their jobs. Both groups were given the same job description and then asked to rate how enriched their jobs were. Those subjects who imagined they were satisfied rated their jobs as more enriched (e.g., having more skill variety and task feedback) than those who imagined they were dissatisfied (Table 4.2). According to the researchers, these data demonstrated that job attitudes can influence workers' perceptions of the objective characteristics of their jobs.

One obvious and disturbing implication of Salancik and Pfeffer's theory is that the simple act of answering job attitude surveys may elicit certain types of responses. For example, if an attitude survey asks workers to report how interesting their work is, that question may prime them to think of their work as more interesting than they usually perceive it to be. Responses will reflect this mindset more than their true attitudes toward the job. In addition, if the job satisfaction items on a survey precede the items assessing job characteristics, the workers' responses to the job characteristics items may be contaminated by the mindset developed in answering the job satisfaction items. Although a few field tests have supported social information processing theory (e.g., Griffin, 1983), most of the tests of the theory have used college

**Table 4.2**

### TASK PERCEPTIONS OF SATISFIED- AND DISSATISFIED-ROLE GROUPS

| Variable | Role Means | | t |
| --- | --- | --- | --- |
| | Satisfied | Dissatisfied | |
| Skill variety | 3.71 | 2.52 | 7.05** |
| Task feedback | 3.55 | 2.32 | 6.67** |

** $p < .01$.

*Source:* Adapted from Caldwell, D.F., & O'Reilly, C.A. (1982). Task perceptions and job satisfaction: A question of causality. *Journal of Applied Psychology, 67,* 361– 369.

students who performed artificial tasks in the laboratory for short periods of time. In organizational settings, so many factors affect job attitudes that the priming effects of specific items on a survey are probably less than the laboratory results have suggested. Even if we choose to ignore the artificiality of most of the past research, the experiments conducted so far have provided only weak support for the hypothesis that social cues influence perceptions of the task and job satisfaction (Zalesny & Ford, 1990). Social information processing has stimulated much debate and research but has yet to prove its value in understanding the formation of job attitudes.

## Opponent Process Theory

Landy (1978) proposed a unique theory of job satisfaction that he called *opponent process theory.* In contrast to the cognitive processes emphasized in comparative theories, opponent process theory hypothesizes that job attitudes emanate from a person's physiological state. Such a perspective is consistent with Schachter and Singer's (1962) theory of emotions, which assumes that certain events in the environment produce general physiological arousal. The arousal is identical regardless of the stimulus provoking it. However, depending on the nature of the environmental event, the person will label this arousal as, for example, either anger or elation. Opponent process theory assumes that when you experience an extreme emotional state, central nervous system mechanisms attempt to bring you back to a state of emotional equilibrium or neutrality. In returning to neutrality, the emotional state may even surpass equilibrium and progress to the opposite emotional state.

An example might clarify opponent process theory. After obtaining your first salary increase or a coveted promotion, you probably feel happy, even elated. This positive emotional state decreases over time to a neutral state or perhaps to a slightly depressed or unhappy state. According to the theory, the magnitude of the opponent process changes over time, increasing each time it is activated. Consequently, upon receiving future salary increases or promotions, your eventual opponent process reaction will be considerably more negative than prior reactions.

Opponent process theory presents an intriguing explanation of why job attitudes change over time and why workers may become bored with jobs they once found satisfying. It does not explain, however, why some workers are continually either very satisfied or dissatisfied with their jobs. Landy's theory has not been tested empirically, so we cannot judge whether it is a viable theory of job satisfaction.

## Locke and Latham's High Performance Cycle

Another contemporary trend is the integration of work motivation (Chapter 3) and job attitude theories. Locke and Latham (1990) recently proposed an integrated model of work motivation and satisfaction they call the high performance cycle (Figure 4.2). This model uses the motivational framework of goal-setting theory (Chapter 3) and predicts that high goals and high success expectations lead to high performance. High performance, in turn,

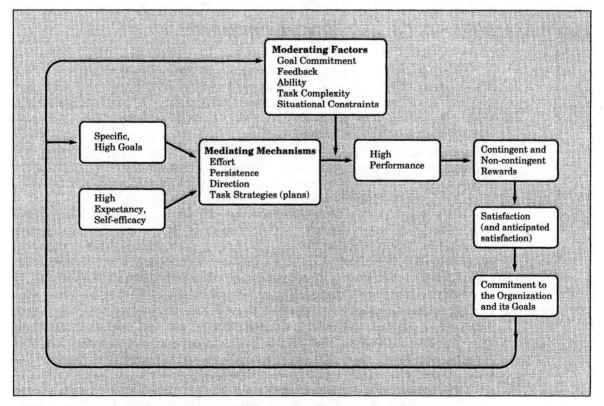

**Figure 4.2**   *Locke and Latham's (1990) high performance cycle*
*Source:* Locke, E.A., & Latham, G.P. (1990). Work motivation and satisfaction: Light at the end of the tunnel. *Psychological Science, 1,* 240–246.

produces rewards, satisfaction, and commitment to future goals. The model also considers the influence of personal and situational factors, such as ability and task complexity. Such integrative perspectives hold considerable promise for enhancing our understanding, not only of motivation and satisfaction, but of other organizational behaviors as well.

### Summary

We have reviewed several of the major theoretical perspectives of job satisfaction. Some of these perspectives are now primarily of historical interest (two-factor theory); some have not been well supported by empirical research (need comparison theory); some have had mixed support (social information processing); some have not generated much (or any) research (opponent process theory); and some show promise of becoming major theories (high performance cycle and value theory). Relatively little work has been done to develop comprehensive theories of job satisfaction or to test the theories that have been proposed. Regardless of which perspective you choose, however, if it is to be studied, job satisfaction must be measured. We next examine the most common measures of job satisfaction.

## THE MEASUREMENT OF JOB SATISFACTION

Early job satisfaction researchers typically developed their own satisfaction questionnaires. One undesirable consequence of this practice was that the content of each researcher's questionnaire often differed substantially from the content of another researcher's questionnaire. For example, researcher A's satisfaction questionnaire contained mostly items that measured satisfaction with supervision and coworkers, whereas researcher B's questionnaire measured satisfaction with the work itself. The varying content of the different job satisfaction measures was particularly problematic when the researchers attempted to compare results across studies.

Fortunately, numerous standardized job satisfaction measures have been developed and refined within the last 30 years. Contemporary researchers have relied increasingly on these standardized scales to measure job satisfaction. Virtually all of these modern scales measure job satisfaction as an attitude and use a self-report format. An attitude can be defined simply as a belief, feeling, or action tendency toward an object (in this case, the job), although some theorists have defined attitudes as complex systems of several interlocking variables (Zanna & Rempel, 1988). Job satisfaction scales typically measure only the belief and/or feeling components of an attitude. For example, you may report that your work allows you to be creative (a belief) or that you find your work to be exciting (a feeling).

The self-report nature of the items in the satisfaction questionnaire requires respondents to report their attitudes toward their jobs. The actual format of the responses can take a bewildering array of forms, from the semantic differential, in which workers indicate their attitudes by a mark between two bipolar (extreme) adjectives, to the Likert-type scale, in which workers indicate their attitudes by agreeing with one of several response alternatives.

Researchers have typically measured job satisfaction as an overall attitude toward the job. In the more contemporary job satisfaction measures, however, facet job satisfaction is also frequently assessed. *Facet satisfaction* refers to satisfaction with different components of the job, such as supervision, coworkers, or pay. The measurement of facet satisfaction is preferable to global satisfaction if the interest lies in which components of the job workers find most or least satisfying. Indeed, facet satisfaction may be preferred over global satisfaction if the researcher is interested in specific types of job satisfaction (e.g., Lawler's model of facet satisfaction) or if a manager is interested in assessing his or her subordinates' dissatisfaction with different components of work.

We next discuss three of the most widely used standardized job satisfaction scales.

### Faces Scales

The oldest of the three scales discussed here is a single-item scale called the Faces Scale (Kunin, 1955). As Figure 4.3 demonstrates, this scale requires

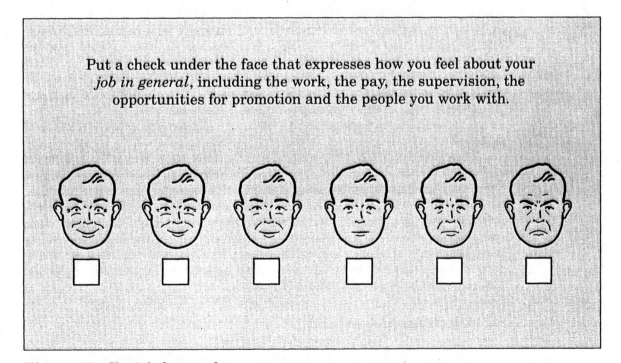

**Figure 4.3**  *Kunin's faces scale*
*Source:* Smith, P.C., Kendall, L.M., & Hulin, C.L. (1969). *The Measurement of Satisfaction in Work and Retirement.* Chicago: Rand McNally. Adapted from T. Kunin. (1955). The construction of a new type of attitude measure. *Personnel Psychology, 8,* 65–77.

respondents to indicate their degree of job satisfaction by checking the drawing of the human face that most closely approximates their feelings about their job. Both a male and a female (Dunham & Herman, 1975) version of the Faces Scale exist, and either form seems to be appropriate for both male and female workers. Although the scale looks simple, Kunin (1955) actually used a complex scale construction procedure to develop a set of expressions that spans extremes in attitude and also captures equal intervals between the extremes.

The Faces Scale is acceptable as a global measure of job satisfaction. It may even be preferable to more typical job satisfaction questionnaires because it is very quick and easy to answer. If workers have little time to fill out attitude surveys and/or minimal reading or language skills, the Faces Scales may be the job satisfaction questionnaire of choice.

## Minnesota Satisfaction Questionnaire (MSQ)

Weiss, Dawis, England, and Lofquist (1967) devised this 100-item job satisfaction scale with five items, each composing 20 facet scales. The facets include such dimensions as satisfaction with advancement, compensation, coworkers, responsibility, and working conditions. The scale can be scored both as a global measure by summing across the 100 items or as a facet measure by summing across the five items in any facet scale. Because of its length, most researchers have used a 20-item short form of the MSQ (Table 4.3). Typically, this 20-item version has been used to assess global satisfaction. Factor analyses of the short form revealed two dimensions or facets within the 20 items, labeled intrinsic and extrinsic satisfaction. The intrinsic items refer to aspects of the work or job itself ("The chance to do different things from time to time"), and the extrinsic items refer to conditions or situations external to the job or work ("The way company policies are put into practice").

The authors of the MSQ systematically drew upon previously published scales and organizational theory to develop their scale. Their goal was to produce a job satisfaction instrument with superior measurement properties (i.e., good reliability and validity). As a global measure of job satisfaction, the MSQ achieves this goal admirably. However, researchers have expressed some reservations about the adequacy of the intrinsic and extrinsic dimensions as separate facets of global job satisfaction (Cook, Hepworth, Wall, & Warr, 1981). Most users of the MSQ have scored only items for global satisfaction and therefore have escaped this criticism.

## Job Descriptive Index (JDI)

The Job Descriptive Index is unlike the previously discussed job satisfaction measures in that it was developed specifically to measure satisfaction with different job components or facets. Smith, Kendall, and Hulin (1969) cre-

**Table 4.3**

## EXAMPLES OF ITEMS FROM THE MINNESOTA SATISFACTION QUESTIONNAIRE

Ask yourself: How satisfied am I with this aspect of my job?

VS means I am very satisfied with this aspect of my job.

S means I am satisfied with this aspect of my job.

N means I can't decide whether I am satisfied or not with this aspect of my job.

DS means I am dissatisfied with this aspect of my job.

VDS means I am very dissatisfied with this aspect of my job.

| On my present job, this is how I feel about: | VDS | DS | N | S | VS |
|---|---|---|---|---|---|
| My pay and the amount of work I do | [ ] | [ ] | [ ] | [ ] | [ ] |
| The freedom to use my own judgment | [ ] | [ ] | [ ] | [ ] | [ ] |
| The working conditions | [ ] | [ ] | [ ] | [ ] | [ ] |
| The feeling of accomplishment I get from the job | [ ] | [ ] | [ ] | [ ] | [ ] |

*Source:* Weiss, D.J., Dawis, R.V., England, G.W., & Lofquist, L.H. (1967). *Manual for Minnesota Satisfaction Questionnaire: Minnesota Studies in Vocational Rehabilitation.* University of Minnesota: Vocational Psychology Research, Items 13, 15, 17, 20.

ated the JDI by systematically developing and testing over 100 potential items. The authors sought to create a scale that is easy to read and answer. That goal appears to have been attained: Respondents are required only to check off the adjectives or phrases describing their jobs (Table 4.4). The five facet satisfaction scales are the work itself, pay, promotion opportunities, supervision, and coworkers.

Some researchers have summed across the five facet scales to obtain an acceptable measure of global job satisfaction (Hulin, Drasgow, & Komocar, 1982). However, because the facets are only moderately intercorrelated, the authors do not recommend summing the facets to obtain an overall score. A global job satisfaction instrument, the Job In General (JIG), which is very similar to the JDI in format and scoring, has recently been developed (Ironson, Smith, Brannick, Gibson, & Paul, 1989).

The JDI is the most widely used measure of job satisfaction. Research on the measurement properties of the JDI has shown that it provides reliable and valid job facet satisfaction scales. One possible weakness of the JDI is that the five job facets are not comprehensive by today's standards. Four of the facets measure extrinsic satisfaction, or satisfaction with work conditions, and only one measures intrinsic satisfaction (i.e., the work itself). However, if interest does not extend beyond the five facet scales, the JDI is definitely the preferred measure of job facet satisfaction.

**Table 4.4**

## EXAMPLES OF ITEMS FROM THE REVISED JOB DESCRIPTIVE INDEX (Revised JDI)

Each of the five scales was presented on a separate page.
The instructions for each scale asked the subject to put Y beside an item if the item described the particular aspect of his job (work, pay, etc.), N if the item did not describe that aspect, or ? if he could not decide.

| WORK | PAY | SUPERVISION |
|---|---|---|
| _____ Boring | _____ Income adequate for normal expenses | _____ Asks my advice |
| _____ Creative | _____ Less than I deserve | _____ Hard to please |

| | PROMOTIONS | COWORKERS |
|---|---|---|
| | _____ Good opportunity for promotion | _____ Helpful |
| | _____ Opportunity somewhat limited | _____ Stupid |

*Source:* Balzer, W.K., Smith, P.C., Kravitz, D.E., Lovell, S.E., Paul, K.B., Reilly, B.A., & Reilly, C.E. (1990). *User's Manual for the Job Descriptive Index (JDI) and the Job in General (JIG) Scales.* Bowling Green, OH: Bowling Green State University.

*Summary*

Job satisfaction researchers currently have some valid and reliable measures at their disposal. The typical job satisfaction scale is self-report, and we discussed three of the most common of these: the Faces Scale, the Minnesota Satisfaction Questionnaire, and the Job Descriptive Index. These measures have been used in hundreds (and probably thousands) of studies across many different types of settings and samples in the past few decades. We next examine some of the findings of the research using these and other scales.

## CORRELATES OF JOB SATISFACTION

Have you ever thought that women or members of racial minority groups are less satisfied overall with their jobs than other people? If a coworker received a poor performance rating or has been absent from work frequently, did you automatically assume that he was also not satisfied with his job? Have you ever observed that a friend who complains continually about her job also frequently expresses dissatisfaction with other phases of her life, such as her college and social activities? If you answered "yes" to any of these questions, then you have been an "implicit" job satisfaction researcher and have thought about many of the questions researchers have pondered over the years.

Many of the studies on job satisfaction have investigated relationships between job satisfaction and personal characteristics (e.g., age and sex), job-related behaviors (e.g., performance and absenteeism), and nonwork factors (e.g., life satisfaction). We next discuss each of these three areas of job satisfaction research.

## Personal Characteristics

A popular notion has been that job satisfaction varies as a function of personal characteristics such as age, sex, race, and perhaps even personality. For example, the media has frequently reported that women, blacks, and older people are more or less satisfied than the typical young, white, male worker. Historically, research on differences in job satisfaction as a function of personal characteristics often has not found large differences among these groups.

When large differences have been found among demographic subgroups, they are often surrogates for other variables, such as occupational level, education, and tenure. For example, workers in high-status jobs are consistently more satisfied than workers in lower status jobs. Women, minorities, and younger workers are often overrepresented in lower status jobs. Therefore, it is not surprising that these groups often report lower job satisfaction than older, white, male workers.

As you will soon discover, however, several studies have found significant individual differences in job satisfaction. This is particularly true for some recent research on the association between personality types and job attitudes.

### GENDER

Two recent reviews of research on gender-related differences in global job satisfaction (Brush, Moch, & Pooyan, 1987; Smith, Olsen, & Falgout, 1991) reported no difference between the job satisfaction of men and women. In fact, the calculated correlations between global job satisfaction and sex in both reviews were near zero.

Studies that have investigated sex effects in facet satisfaction also discovered few meaningful differences. Both men and women have reported satisfaction with intrinsic (e.g., job autonomy) and extrinsic (e.g., pay) job characteristics (Andrisani & Shapiro, 1978; Weaver, 1978). Almost thirty years ago, Hulin and Smith (1964) claimed that no sex differences in job satisfaction exist. They maintained that any sex differences are really surrogates for differences in pay, education, tenure, and job level. Subsequent research seems to support their contention.

### RACE

Most of the research on racial differences in job satisfaction has focused on black and white differences. The data have shown fairly consistently that black workers are not as satisfied as white workers (Forgionne & Peeters, 1982; Slocum & Strawser, 1982; Weaver, 1977), although the differences are usually not large.

Moch (1980) attempted to disentangle the relationships between race and job satisfaction in white, black, and Hispanic samples by examining two potential reasons for racial differences in satisfaction: cultural and structural. Structural reasons refer to organizational factors that may contribute to racial differences; for example, relative to whites, blacks may not have ready access to mentoring relationships with (white) senior managers. Cultural reasons refer to cultural differences in values or expectations; for example, blacks may value interpersonal relations at work more than white because they have a cultural norm for affiliation. Moch's data indicated that both factors were related to job satisfaction: Workers of different races differed in reported job satisfaction both because of differences in how they were treated at work and in their own personal value systems.

## AGE

Data suggest that global job satisfaction does increase with age for all demographic groups, including women and minorities (Bourne, 1982; Rhodes, 1983). However, the only facet satisfaction measure that has consistently increased with age across studies is satisfaction with work itself (Hunt & Saul, 1975; Rhodes, 1983). One explanation for these findings is that workers may be initially dissatisfied with their jobs but eventually seek work they find more satisfying. Another explanation is that people actually become more satisfied with (or perhaps more realistic about) their lives, including their work lives, over time. Because older workers often perceive they have fewer job options or alternatives (Pond & Geyer, 1987) and may become resigned to their job situations, some evidence supports this latter possibility. Attempts to explore theoretical explanations for the relation between age and job satisfaction have been inconclusive (Janson & Martin, 1982).

## PERSONALITY

The associations between a few personality variables and job satisfaction have been explored. Some research has found that people with a high internal locus of control (or the belief that they are responsible for their own successes and failures) (King, Murray, & Atkinson, 1982) and high self-esteem and a sense of competence (Sekaran, 1986) report higher job satisfaction.

Researchers also recently have investigated the association between Type A behavior and job satisfaction. As originally conceived, Type A behavior is a constellation of personality characteristics that predisposes a person to develop coronary heart disease (Chapter 7). These characteristics include such diverse dimensions as high achievement orientation, impatience, and general irritability. Bluen, Barling, and Burns (1990) reported a negative relationship between impatience and irritability and job satisfaction and a positive relationship between achievement striving and job satisfaction in a sample of 117 life insurance salespeople. Specifically, those salespeople who reported higher levels of achievement striving and lower levels of impatience and irritability also reported higher job satisfaction. In other words, the happiest employees were the most mild-tempered and the highest achievers!

Another study (Howard, Cunningham, & Rechnitzer, 1986) investigated the link between Type A and coronary risk factors, such as high blood pressure and increased fat deposits in the blood. The researchers tracked approximately 200 managerial and professional men over a two-year period. They found that individuals who reported lower job satisfaction at the beginning of the study also showed increased coronary risk factors at the end of two years and that these relationships were stronger for Type As. The Howard et al. (1986) study demonstrates the important roles job satisfaction and personality type potentially play in the development of chronic health problems.

However, perhaps the personality correlate that has generated the most recent interest is *negative affectivity,* or the disposition to experience aversive emotional states, such as distress, agitation, pessimism, and dissatisfaction. Levin and Stokes (1989) conducted both laboratory and field studies and found that people who were high in negative affectivity expressed lower task or job satisfaction than those low in negative affectivity. The relationship between negative affectivity and job satisfaction was even stronger in the field (organizational) than in the laboratory study, presumably because situational constraints in the laboratory dampened the influence of personal characteristics. In other words, the artificial control used in this laboratory study stifled individual differences in behavior.

## IS JOB SATISFACTION A STABLE TRAIT?

Perhaps the most controversial of the contemporary approaches to job satisfaction is the research treating job attitudes as enduring traits or personal dispositions. This perspective assumes that, because of their personalities, some people are more satisfied with life (including their work life) than other people. Some studies have presented compelling evidence for treating job satisfaction as a disposition rather than a response to a particular work environment. Staw and Ross (1985) investigated the job satisfaction of a national sample of 5,000 male workers over a five-year interval. Regardless of whether the workers changed jobs or occupations, the researchers found that reported job satisfaction was very stable over time.

Arvey and his colleagues (Arvey, Bouchard, Segal, & Abraham, 1989) completed an unusual study of job satisfaction in 34 pairs of identical twins who were reared apart. If researchers assume that job attitudes are at least partially determined by personal characteristics, then there is probably a genetic component to job satisfaction. This proposition can only be tested with identical twins reared apart because identical twins possess the same genetic makeup and any differences between them would necessarily result from environmental factors. The researchers discovered that approximately 30% of the variance in job satisfaction was due to genetic factors. Many of the twin pairs also had similar lifestyles and jobs. From these data, Arvey surmised that people may be genetically programmed to seek out certain occupations or jobs and to respond to them in particular ways.

The potential (if not extreme) implications of the research on job satisfaction as a disposition are both provocative and disturbing. If people are predisposed to be more or less satisfied, employers may benefit from selecting only satisfied people. Because organizations may have less influence over employee attitudes than commonly believed, job enrichment and other changes in the work environment may not be especially worthwhile. The ethical dilemmas posed by these possibilities for employee selection and development programs are obvious. On the brighter side, all studies have found that environmental factors are still more important than personal factors. (Recall that, in the twin study, genetic factors accounted for only 30% of the total variance.) In addition, Arvey et al. (1989) stated, "Job enrichment efforts may, however, have the intended effect of raising mean levels of job satisfaction for the individuals involved, even though rank ordering of individuals is preserved" (p. 191). This means that changing the job to enhance intrinsic satisfaction will make everyone more satisfied, but that some workers will always remain relatively more satisfied (or dissatisfied) than others.

## Job-Related Behaviors

In talking to managers (and college students), it has been our experience that they frequently assume that an employee who is satisfied with his or her job will perform well, rarely be absent, and not seek alternate employment. However, as you will soon discover, the link between job satisfaction and job-related behaviors is often indirect or nonexistent. Nevertheless, the implicit association between satisfaction and behavior is so natural to most people that these beliefs often persist despite overwhelming data to the contrary.

### Performance

One of the most enduring myths about worker behavior is the supposed causal link between job satisfaction and performance; more specifically, satisfied workers outperform unsatisfied workers. In their early review of job satisfaction research, Brayfield and Crockett (1955) determined that no relation existed between job satisfaction and performance. Years later, Vroom (1964) corroborated Brayfield and Crockett's conclusion. Iaffaldano and Muchinsky (1985) conducted a quantitative review or meta-analysis of research that had examined the job satisfaction–performance relationship. Similar to their predecessors, they found only a weak link between satisfaction and performance; the average correlation was .14.

Today, there is little doubt that job satisfaction does not cause job performance, and researchers have turned their attention to the investigation of other types of relationships between satisfaction and performance. Locke and his colleagues (Locke, 1970; Locke & Latham, 1990) have even suggested the opposite relationship: High performance causes high satisfaction. Locke's goal-setting research demonstrated rather conclusively that people derive satisfaction from attaining difficult, performance-related goals.

Many contemporary researchers, however, assume that the link between satisfaction and performance is much less direct than hypothesized. Specifically, the relationship may be moderated by other variables. This simply means that the relationship between satisfaction and performance varies depending on certain conditions, such as different types of workers, research settings, and organizations. In their review, however, Iaffaldano and Muchinsky (1985) investigated some of these possible moderators of the satisfaction-performance link and found little evidence of any moderating effects.

Despite the discouraging results of the Iaffaldano and Muchinsky (1985) review, one variable that has shown promise as a moderator of the relationship between satisfaction and performance is the administration of rewards. If high-performing workers receive higher rewards, such as praise, promotions, or money, than poor-performing workers, then the correlation between satisfaction and performance should be positive. If rewards are not administered contingent upon performance, then the correlation between satisfaction and performance should be negative. Because, in reality, rewards may or may not be contingent upon performance, the positive and negative relationships should sum up to a total not far from zero, such as Iaffaldano and Muchinsky's (1985) correlation of .14 between satisfaction and performance.

Cherrington, Reitz, and Scott (1971) demonstrated the influence of rewards on the satisfaction-performance link in a laboratory experiment. Two groups of subjects were given a task to perform; one group received rewards based on performance and the other group did not (Table 4.5). For the group that was appropriately rewarded, the correlation between satisfaction and performance was positive, for the group that was not appropriately rewarded, the correlation between satisfaction and performance was negative. However, when the satisfaction-performance correlation was computed for both groups combined, the correlation was near zero.

Fisher (1980) voiced an interesting perspective on this issue. She maintained that the low relationship between satisfaction and performance is partially a function of how researchers typically measure satisfaction and performance. That is, the relationship between global satisfaction and some type of specific task performance is usually measured. Some years ago, social psychologists Fishbein and Ajzen (1975) discussed this level of specificity problem: General attitudes more appropriately predict general behaviors and specific attitudes, specific behaviors. If Fisher is correct, researchers would be well advised to collect some type of comparable facet satisfaction measure (e.g., satisfaction with coworkers) when a specific type of job performance (e.g., group or team performance) is assessed.

**Table 4.5**

## DATA ON THE SATISFACTION-PERFORMANCE RELATIONSHIPS FROM CHERRINGTON, REITZ, AND SCOTT (1971)

| Satisfaction indexes | All Ss[a] | Appropriately reinforced Ss[b] | Inappropriately reinforced Ss[b] |
|---|---|---|---|
| General affective tone | −.03 | .55*** | −.51*** |
| General arousal | .02 | .42** | −.26 |
| Personal competence | .13 | .48** | −.16 |
| General satisfaction with pay | .03 | .67*** | −.56*** |
| Equity of pay | −.09 | .45** | −.51*** |
| Adequacy of pay | −.03 | .59*** | −.57*** |
| Attractiveness of fellow workers | .20 | .44** | .04 |
| Attractiveness of task | −.06 | .32* | −.16 |

[a]$n = 90$    [b]$n = 42$    *$p < .05$    **$p < .01$    ***$p < .001$

Source: Cherrington, D.J., Reitz, H.J., & Scott, W.E., Jr. (1971). Effects of contingent and noncontingent reward on the relationship between satisfaction and task performance. Journal of Applied Psychology, 55, 531–536.

## WITHDRAWAL BEHAVIORS: ABSENTEEISM AND TURNOVER

Withdrawal behavior is defined as any type of behavior that removes the worker from the work setting regardless of the circumstance provoking the behavior. For example, workers may be absent because they desire a day of leisure or because they are too ill to work. According to Steers and Rhodes (1978), worker absenteeism is extremely costly to organizations, with estimates running into many billions of dollars annually. Estimates for the 1990s would be even higher.

Steers and Rhodes (1978) proposed a process model of attendance (Figure 4.4). According to the model, work attendance depends on both satisfaction with the job (as determined by various job characteristics) and motivation to attend. Various factors, such as personal values and ability to attend, affect or moderate the relations in the model. For example, a worker who has a stressful job with little variety and autonomy may be dissatisfied with her job, which may reduce her motivation to attend. She may also have a weak work ethic, many family obligations, and extremely marketable job skills. According to the model, such a worker has a high probability of being absent from her job.

As intuitively obvious as Steers and Rhodes' model seems to be, empirical research has not supported a strong link between satisfaction and employee attendance (absenteeism) (Breaugh, 1981; Nicholson, Brown, & Chadwick-Jones, 1976; Watson, 1981). Researchers have found that nonatti-

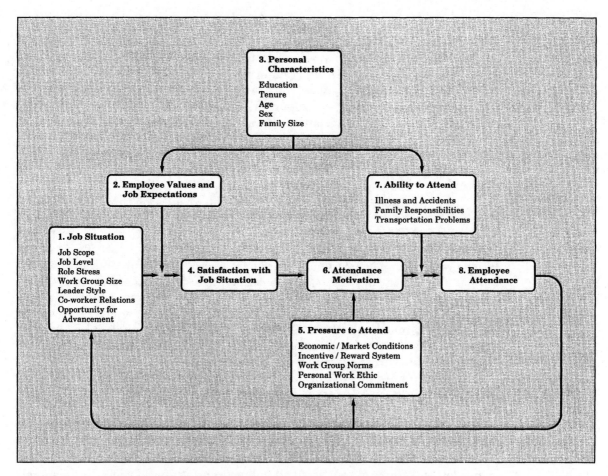

**Figure 4.4** *Steers and Rhodes' (1978) process model of attendance*
Source: Steers, R.M., & Rhodes, S.R. (1978). Major influences on employee attendance: A process model. *Journal of Applied Psychology, 63*, 391–407.

tudinal variables, for example, a worker's previous history of absenteeism (Ivancevich, 1985), are better predictors of absenteeism than satisfaction. However, a quantitative review of the relation between job satisfaction and absenteeism (Scott & Taylor, 1985) suggests that methodological and statistical problems, such as variability in the types of satisfaction and absenteeism measures across studies and insufficient sample sizes, account for the weak results of empirical research. Zaccaro, Craig, and Quinn (1991) also maintained that prior researchers had not tested hypotheses that were directly derived from the attendance models and had used inappropriate statistical tests. Zaccaro and colleagues tested some complex hypotheses that were directly derived from Steers and Rhodes' (1978) process model. Using sophisticated analytical techniques, they found support for these hypotheses in a sample of chemical manufacturing workers.

An alternative model of employee attendance was proposed by Chadwick-Jones, Nicholson, and Brown (1982). Unlike the Steers and Rhodes model, which is based on worker satisfaction and motivation, they hypothesized that absenteeism is a function of social exchange processes. The Chadwick-Jones et al. model assumes that an exchange relationship exists between the organization (employer or supervisor) and the employee. This social exchange is influenced by group norms and expectations. In any organization, the employee soon discovers how much absenteeism is tolerated and the price that must be paid for absenteeism. For example, an employee may learn that one or two unexcused absences per month are tolerated if he is willing to work overtime and weekends when needed.

Hackett (1989) recently summarized the results of three job satisfaction–absenteeism reviews. He determined that some of the strongest relations were between absence frequency and work facet satisfaction ($r = -.21$) and between absence duration and global job satisfaction ($r = -.23$). These correlations were stronger for women than men. Hackett interpreted these sex differences as indicating that, because women are still frequently "secondary" wage earners with heavy domestic responsibilities, "their 'threshold' at which dissatisfaction is manifested in absenteeism may be lower on the average than it is for males" (p. 245). Hackett's results suggest that some types of absence measures have small to moderate relationships with some types of satisfaction measures, especially for women.

Considerable research on job satisfaction and turnover has found that dissatisfied workers frequently quit their jobs, but this relationship is both indirect and complex. Mobley (Mobley, 1977; Mobley, Horner, & Hollingsworth, 1978) developed a model of the turnover process that attempts to explain the indirect and complex link between satisfaction and turnover (Figure 4.5). According to the model, an employee who is dissatisfied with his or her job will think of quitting and will search for another job. If the search process reveals favorable and available alternatives, the employee will develop an intention to quit, which directly predicts quitting (a type of turnover). However, if the search process reveals unfavorable and/or no available alternatives, the employee will probably develop instead an intention to stay on the job, which directly predicts staying.

Mobley, Horner, and Hollingsworth (1978) tested the models' validity on approximately 200 hospital employees, from whom they collected job satisfaction, thinking of quitting, intention to search and intention to quit/stay data and, after 47 weeks, turnover data. The results were supportive of the model: Job satisfaction was more highly related to thinking of quitting and intention to search than to actual turnover. However, intention to quit or stay was significantly related to actual turnover.

Although, like absenteeism, turnover is costly to organizations, sometimes turnover can be quite functional. Hollenbeck and Williams (1986) studied retail sales employees and found that over half of the department store turnover was functional; that is, supervisors had rated these salespeople as marginal or unsatisfactory. The organization presumably benefits from func-

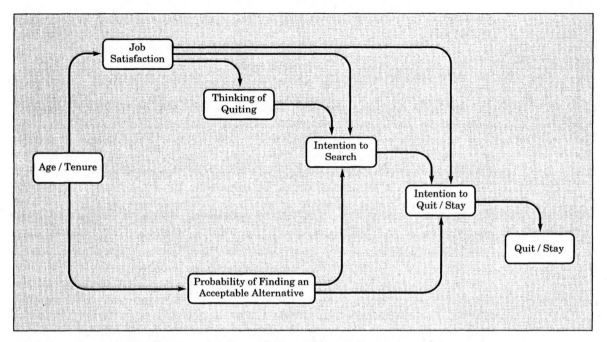

**Figure 4.5**   *Mobley, Horner, and Hollingsworth's (1978) model of job satisfaction and turnover*
*Source:* Mobley, W.H., Horner, S.O., & Hollingsworth, A.T. (1978). An evaluation of precursors of hospital employee turnover. *Journal of Applied Psychology, 63,* 408–414.

tional turnover because these positions potentially can be filled by more successful employees.

Because of the personal risks involved in quitting one's job (such as not being able to meet financial obligations), turnover, more than absenteeism, is affected by external market conditions. Carsten and Spector (1987) reported that turnover is much higher in good economic times, when many jobs are available, than in poorer economic times, when fewer jobs are available. The researchers also found that the correlation between job satisfaction and turnover was much stronger during economic prosperity than during economic adversity. Because workers cannot freely leave the organization during periods of economic adversity, the turnover rate is not a good indicator of workers' true feelings about whether they would prefer to leave or stay. As a consequence, organizations may incorrectly infer employee attitudes from turnover rates.

In one of the authors' experiences, this incorrect assumption almost cost a public sector organization its most valued employees. Management assumed, because the agency's turnover rate had dropped considerably, that pending employee development programs were unnecessary. Fortunately, data about current market conditions and current employee attitude statistics in the agency convinced management that employees were still disgruntled and would leave as soon as jobs outside the agency became available. The employee development programs then proceeded as originally scheduled.

## Life Satisfaction

Perhaps you have observed that people who express negative attitudes toward their jobs also express negative attitudes toward other aspects of their lives. If so, you are in the company of many behavioral scientists. Psychologists have long been intrigued by the relation between job and life (nonwork) satisfaction (Weitz, 1952; Dubin, 1956). Although Dubin (1956) classified people's central life interests as either job-oriented, non–job-oriented, or flexible focus (neither), more recent theorists have attempted to specify the exact nature of the relationship between job and life satisfaction. Kabanoff (1980) proposed three potential models of job and life satisfaction: a *spillover model,* in which satisfaction in one area influences the other; a *compensatory model,* in which a lack of satisfaction in one area is compensated by the other; and a *segmentation model,* in which satisfaction in one area is independent of the other. For example, if a person is dissatisfied with her job, she may also express dissatisfaction with other facets of her life (e.g., family, friends) (spillover model); she may turn to other areas of life for fulfillment (compensatory model); or she may or may not express dissatisfaction with other facets of her life (segmentation model).

Tests of the three models proposed by Kabanoff have not clearly supported one model over the other (Kabanoff & O'Brien, 1980; Pond & Green, 1983). Rice, Near, and Hunt (1980) suggested the *disaggregation model* as a refinement of the spillover model. Specifically, they maintained that work and life satisfaction would influence each other only for those who place a high value on work, such as Dubin's job-oriented individuals. However, neither Rice et al. (1980) nor subsequent researchers (Steiner & Truxillo, 1989; Steiner, 1990) have found consistent support for the disaggregation hypothesis.

The unclear (and confusing) relationship between job and life satisfaction has led researchers to question whether there is any real association between these two factors (Rice et al., 1980). A survey of the research on the relation between job and life satisfaction (Tait, Padgett, & Baldwin, 1989) reported a moderate association (0.44) between the two. Interestingly, the relation between life and work satisfaction was stronger for men before 1974. Since 1974, the job-life correlation increased sharply for women, so that few male-female differences currently exist. The authors interpreted these findings to suggest that both job and life opportunities (and attitudes) for women are now more similar to those of men.

An intriguing research study related to sex differences in job and life satisfaction was reported by Staines, Pottick, and Fudge (1986). Previous research has well established the positive association of wives' employment with their own mental health, but a negative association with the mental health of their husbands. In other words, married women's mental health benefits from working, whereas their husbands' mental health suffers. Staines et al.'s data indicated that husbands of working wives perceived themselves to be less adequate providers than did husbands of housewives, which accounted for the husbands' lower levels of both job and life satisfaction.

Another line of research has assumed that job and life satisfaction are related (spillover model), but has investigated whether life satisfaction precedes job satisfaction or vice versa (Orpen, 1978; Schmitt & Mellon, 1980). Specifically, does your level of life satisfaction influence your level of job satisfaction, or does your level of job satisfaction influence your level of life satisfaction? Studies suggest spillover effects in both directions, in, for example, a large sample of civil service employees (Schmitt & Bedeian, 1982) and a survey of over 1,500 workers (Near, Smith, Rice, & Hunt, 1984).

# OTHER JOB ATTITUDES: JOB INVOLVEMENT AND ORGANIZATIONAL COMMITMENT

After reading about the myriad theories and empirical studies on job satisfaction, you may be convinced that job satisfaction is the only job-related attitude that has captured the attention of researchers. Although job satisfaction is the oldest and most widely researched job attitude, it is definitely not the only one. For example, the concepts of personal involvement in work and commitment to the employing organization cannot be assessed by measuring job satisfaction. Next, we examine these other job attitudes, job involvement and organizational commitment.

## Job Involvement

Job involvement is defined as the extent to which a person psychologically identifies with his or her job (Kanungo, 1982; Lodahl & Kejner, 1965; Rabinowitz & Hall, 1977). Jobs occupy a central role in job-involved people's lives. Any change in their employment conditions or status can seriously affect their psychological well-being or self-esteem. You can identify highly job-involved workers as the people who work overtime to finish a project and take pride in their job-related accomplishments or products. When these people are unable to perform their jobs, for example, because of illness, layoffs, or retirement, they may become discontented or depressed. Job involvement is also perceived to be a relatively stable personal characteristic based in personal value orientations. For that reason, job involvement is thought to be less yoked to contextual or environmental factors and thus conceptually distinct from job satisfaction.

The most widely used measure of job involvement is a 20-item scale developed by Lodahl and Kejner (1965) (Table 4.6). They administered the 20 items to 137 nurses and 70 engineers. Lodahl and Kejner and subsequent

**Table 4.6**

## EXAMPLES OF ITEMS FROM THE JOB INVOLVEMENT SCALE

DIRECTIONS:

1. Read each item carefully

2. Respond to each item according to the way you feel about your job

3. Refer to the choices below when making these judgments

    1 = strongly agree

    2 = agree

    3 = disagree

    4 = strongly disagree

4. Mark your answer (number) in the blank to the right of the item.

| | |
|---|---|
| The major satisfaction in my life comes from my job. | _____ |
| The most important things that happen to me involve my work. | _____ |
| I feel depressed when I fail at something connected with my job. | _____ |
| Sometimes I'd like to kick myself for the mistakes I make in my work. | _____ |

*Source:* Lodahl, T.M., & Kejner, M. (1965). The definition and measurement of job involvement. *Journal of Applied Psychology,* 49, 24–33.

researchers (Cook et al., 1981) reported that the scale (both the full 20 items and shorter versions) possesses acceptable reliability and validity. Researchers also found that the involvement scale is multidimensional, although they have not systematically attempted to investigate the different dimensions. Probably because the overall measurement qualities of the total involvement scale are adequate, little interest has been generated to explore these different dimensions conceptually.

As a result, more than 25 years later researchers are still not certain exactly what Lodahl and Kejner's 20-item scale measures. Although the scale developers conceived of job involvement as a fairly stable personal value or orientation toward work in general (the first two items in Table 4.6), they also included items that measure the extent to which a worker desires to perform well in a particular job (the third and fourth items in Table 4.6). In their review of the job involvement literature, Rabinowitz and Hall (1977) concluded that some of the scale items measure a stable value orientation and some measure situational or specific job factors.

The failure to investigate the dimensionality of the job involvement scale has contributed to some confusion in interpreting subsequent research (Blau

& Boal, 1987). For example, the value orientation items may be more or less important than the situational items in defining job involvement. The different types of items may also show different types of relationships with other variables (e.g., job-related stress or motivation); if researchers use a composite of all items, these differences may be masked.

The implied differences between the value orientation items and the situational items in the job involvement scale also present problems in providing feedback to organizations about the job involvement of their employees. If the value orientation items are more important in defining job involvement, then organizations could do little to change employee job involvement. The most practical approach, in this case, would be to select workers who initially express high levels of job involvement. If, however, job involvement is defined more by the situational items, organizations may be able to increase employee involvement through various organizational change strategies.

Some empirical research supports both the value orientation and situational perspectives. For example, Noe and Schmitt (1986) reported that job involvement directly influenced training effectiveness. In a sample of educators who experienced administrative and interpersonal skills training, highly job-involved trainees acquired more knowledge from the training program than trainees who reported less involvement. Noe and Steffy (1987) found that assessment center evaluations for secondary school principals were associated with job involvement. Specifically, assessment center evaluations influenced job involvement such that individuals who received less favorable recommendations reported less job involvement.

The correlates of job involvement are generally similar in direction and magnitude to those of job satisfaction (Cook et al., 1981; Brooke, Russell, & Price, 1988). The personal correlate age is strongly related to job involvement across many types of workers and cultures; specifically, older workers report higher levels of job involvement than younger workers (Morrow & McElroy, 1987; Rhodes, 1983). No sex differences are apparent in job involvement: Women report similar levels of job involvement to men (Chusmir, 1982; Rabinowitz & Hall, 1977). The behavioral correlates of absenteeism and turnover are also associated with job involvement; highly job-involved workers are less apt to be absent from work or quit their jobs (Brooke, 1986).

## Organizational Commitment

Organizational commitment is defined as a workers' identification with and involvement in a particular organization. Organizational commitment embodies three concepts: readiness to exert effort on behalf of the organization, acceptance of organizational goals and values, and desire to remain with the organization (Cook et al., 1981). Although, like job satisfaction, organizational commitment refers to one's affect toward his or her employing organization, organizational commitment is thought to be more global and enduring than job satisfaction. Specifically, organizational commitment refers to employee attitudes about the whole organization and therefore is probably less influenced by daily events (e.g., a disagreement with the supervisor).

Like the highly job-involved individual, the highly committed worker takes his or her work seriously. However, the allegiances of the highly committed worker reside with the organization, not the job or work. Over 30 years ago, Whyte (1956) warned about the personal dangers of overcommitment to the organization in *The Organization Man.* Whyte claimed that the "organization man" identified so totally with his work group or organization that he substituted the organization's goals and beliefs for his own. In essence, according to Whyte, the overcommitted worker submerged his own identity for the good of the organization. Subsequently, researchers have echoed Whyte's concerns (Mowday, Porter, & Steers, 1982; Randall, 1987), although some researchers have maintained that overcommitment is desirable, particularly for the organization (e.g., Lawrence, 1958; Ouchi & Wilkins, 1985). Romzek (1989) suggested that overcommitment may not be a zero-sum game (either all good or all bad). In a sample of public sector employees, Romzek found that those individuals who reported higher levels of organizational commitment also reported higher nonwork and career satisfaction two years later.

The most commonly used organizational commitment scale is the 15-item scale developed by Porter and Smith (1970; published in Mowday, Steers, & Porter, 1979) (Table 4.7). Researchers have reported adequate reliability and validity data for the organizational commitment scale across numerous settings and samples (Cook et al., 1981).

Unlike job involvement, researchers have proposed and investigated different dimensions of organizational commitment. The most commonly measured dimension (from the Porter and Smith scales) is *affective* or attitudinal, that is, an emotional attachment to and involvement and identification with the organization. The other dimension is behavioral. This second dimension, often labeled *continuance commitment,* refers to the perceived costs associated with leaving the organization, such as giving up pension plans and profit sharing (Becker, 1960; Hrebiniak & Alutto, 1972).

Recent research has empirically supported theoretical distinctions between the two types of commitment (Allen & Meyer, 1990; McGee & Ford, 1987; Meyer, Paunonen, Gellatly, Goffin, & Jackson, 1989). In the Meyer et al. (1989) study, affective commitment correlated positively with job performance and continuance commitment correlated negatively with job performance in a sample of first-level managers in a food service company. Specifically, high emotional attachment to the organization was associated with high performance, whereas high behavioral attachment (attachment only for extrinsic benefits) was associated with low performance.

Similar to the job involvement scale, the correlates of organizational commitment are generally similar in direction and magnitude to those of job satisfaction (Brooke et al., 1988; Cook et al., 1981). (Almost all research has used only the affective commitment dimension.) The associations between employee absence and turnover variables and organizational commitment are

**Table 4.7**

## EXAMPLES OF ITEMS FROM MOWDAY, STEERS, AND PORTER'S (1979) ORGANIZATIONAL COMMITMENT SCALE

### Instructions

Listed below are a series of statements that represent possible feelings that individuals might have about the company or organization for which they work. With respect to your own feelings about the particular organization for which you are now working (company name) please indicate the degree of your agreement or disagreement with each statement by checking one of the seven alternatives below each statement.

I am willing to put in a great deal of effort beyond that normally expected in order to help this organization be successful.

I am proud to tell others that I am part of this organization.

This organization really inspires the very best in me in the way of job performance.

I really care about the fate of this organization.

Responses to each item are measured on a 7-point scale with scale point anchors labeled: (1) strongly disagree; (2) moderately disagree; (3) slightly disagree; (4) neither disagree nor agree; (5) slightly agree; (6) moderately agree; (7) strongly agree.

Source: Mowday, R.T., Steers, R.M., & Porter, L.W. (1979). The measurement of organizational commitment. *Journal of Vocational Behavior, 14*, 224-247.

particularly noteworthy: Organizationally committed individuals are less likely to be absent from or quit their jobs compared with their less committed coworkers (Williams & Hazer, 1986; Farkas & Tetrick, 1989).

Some researchers have also explored the causal ordering of organizational commitment and job satisfaction. The assumption here is that organizational committment is a determinant of (precedes) job satisfaction or vice versa. In other words, do more committed workers become more satisfied, or do more satisfied workers become more committed? Although many researchers have assumed that satisfaction is a determinant of commitment (Koch & Steers, 1978; Reichers, 1985), at least one study found that commitment precedes satisfaction (Bateman & Strasser, 1984). Using more sophisticated statistical analyses than previous researchers, Curry, Wakefield, Price, and Mueller (1986) investigated these issues in a sample of over 500 hospital nursing employees. Their results did not support either perspective: Their data indicated that satisfaction and commitment were causally independent; neither influenced the other. If these results are correct, different characteristics in the person and the organization contribute to the development of job satisfaction and organizational commitment. More recently, a study by Mathieu (1991) showed that satisfaction and commitment were reciprocally related in a sample of 588 ROTC cadets. For example, increased satisfaction caused increased commitment and, in turn, increased commitment caused further increases in satisfaction. However, the influence of satisfaction on commitment was stronger. Further research is needed to clarify the nature of these relationships.

Another interesting theoretical view of organizational commitment, like the Chadwick-Jones approach to absenteeism, treats commitment as a social exchange process. Specifically, workers become more committed to their employing organization if they perceive that the organization values their contributions and cares about their well-being. Eisenberger, Huntington, Hutchison, and Sowa (1986) presented data to support this exchange program, stating that "employees' commitment to the organization is strongly influenced by their perception of the organization's commitment to them" (p. 500).

# THE THREE JOB ATTITUDES: AN INTEGRATED PERSPECTIVE

After reading about job satisfaction, job involvement, and organizational commitment, you are probably convinced that they are, both conceptually and empirically, more similar than dissimilar. If so, you are questioning an important aspect of the construct validity of these measures (see Chapter 2 for a further discussion of construct validity). Moreover, your sentiments have been voiced by researchers who have been concerned about the relative independence of these job attitudes, or their *discriminant validity*. The correlations among job satisfaction, job involvement, and organizational commitment reported in numerous studies average approximately 0.50 (Brooke et al., 1988) The patterns of relations between these three job attitudes and other job-related variables, such as absenteeism and turnover, are highly similar. Unfortunately, until recently, most researchers did not collect data on all three attitudes simultaneously to permit comparisons. The distinction between job satisfaction and organizational commitment is particularly problematic because both refer to workers' affective responses to their employing organizations. Brooke, Russell, and Price (1988) examined the discriminant validity of the three variables in a sample of 577 medical facility employees. These employees could distinguish among their liking for their jobs (job satisfaction), their emotional attachment to their jobs (job involvement), and their loyalty to their employing organization (organizational commitment). A second study (Mathieu & Farr, 1991) replicated these results in a sample of bus drivers and a sample of engineers.

Another variable related to but distinct from job satisfaction, job involvement, and organizational commitment is professional or *career commitment*. Career commitment is a form of work commitment defined as identification with and involvement in one's profession, such as teaching, nursing, or engineering (Morrow & Wirth, 1989). Several studies have demonstrated that professional commitment is empirically independent of both job involvement and organizational commitment (Blau, 1985, 1988, 1989; Morrow & Goetz, 1988). In addition, professional commitment has shown significant relations with turnover in a sample of bank tellers (Blau, 1989) and with several other job-related behaviors in a sample of accountants (Morrow & Goetz, 1988).

Although research on job involvement and organizational commitment has generally been atheoretical, researchers have recently proposed some integrative theories of job attitudes. Blau and Boal (1987) presented a theoretical integration of job involvement and organizational commitment to explain worker turnover and absenteeism. For example, Blau and Boal predicted that workers high on job involvement and low on organizational commitment ("lone wolves") do not identify with the organization, although work is important to them. These individuals never really integrate themselves into the organization and may quit their jobs with little provocation if better opportunities arise. Absenteeism for the lone wolves may reflect their career-enhancing behaviors, such as looking for a better job. In contrast, "corporate citizens" are those individuals who are low on job involvement and high on organizational commitment. They identify strongly with the organization, although the work itself is not especially important to them. To the extent that some absence is tolerated by the organization, they will take advantage of sanctioned absences because they are not very involved in their work. However, corporate citizens, being very organizationally committed, will probably not voluntarily quit their jobs. Empirical support for this theory has been reported in the prediction of turnover (Blau & Boal, 1987) and absenteeism (Blau, 1986; Mathieu & Kohler, 1990), although a study (Huselid & Day, 1991) using improved measures and statistical tests found no support for the presence of a commitment-involvement interaction in predicting turnover.

Hopefully, theoretical models such as Blau and Boal's will enhance our understanding of the associations among job attitudes and job-related behaviors. Complex multiattitude models probably predict employee behaviors such as absenteeism and turnover better than single attitudes. However, to date, little direct evidence exists to support these assertions.

In summary, the three job attitudes, job satisfaction, job involvement, and organizational commitment, are distinct, independent constructs that have associations with a variety of job-related criteria, such as absenteeism and turnover. Although job satisfaction has generated the most theoretical and empirical research, interest in job involvement and organizational commitment has increased markedly in recent years. Theoretical models that integrate multiple attitudes hold great promise for the future of job attitude research.

# A FINAL SUMMATION AND A LOOK AT THE FUTURE

The historical roots of job satisfaction research began with the experiments conducted at the Hawthorne works of General Electric and Hoppock's early research on the measurement of job satisfaction. We discussed four contemporary job satisfaction theories: two-factor theory, comparison theories, opponent process theory, and the high performance cycle.

Satisfaction is measured as either a general or a specific attitude about different facets of the job, such as supervision or pay. Both overall and facet satisfaction have been measured with a number of widely used self-report job satisfaction scales, such as the Faces Scale, the Minnesota Satisfaction Questionnaire, and the Job Descriptive Index.

Over the years, researchers have studied the correlates of job satisfaction. Personal characteristics, such as sex and race, have not shown consistent associations with job satisfaction. However, job satisfaction does seem to increase with age for all types of workers. Researchers have investigated the influence of a few personality characteristics on job satisfaction; Type A behavior and negative affectivity both show promise as personality correlates of job attitudes.

Researchers generally agree that job satisfaction is not causally linked to job performance. However, there is some evidence that rewards contingent upon performance moderate the satisfaction-performance relationship. Withdrawal behaviors, absenteeism and turnover, have demonstrated stronger associations with job satisfaction than job performance. Results of empirical research have indicated that a moderate positive correlation exists between job and life satisfaction. Various theoretical models have been developed to explain the association between job and life satisfaction. The model with the most support is a reciprocal version of the spillover model, which assumes that satisfaction with work influences satisfaction with life and vice versa.

Although job satisfaction is the most widely known job attitude, it is not the only one. Job involvement is the extent a person psychologically identifies with his or her job. Organizational commitment is the extent to which a person identifies with and is involved in a particular organization. Even though job satisfaction, job involvement, and organizational commitment are positively related (the typical r is about .50), empirical research has confirmed the discriminant validity, or relative independence of these three job attitudes. Another variable related to the three job attitudes but distinct from them is career commitment, which is the identification with and involvement in one's profession.

Some integrative theories of job attitudes have recently been proposed. Blau and Boal developed an integrative theory of commitment and involvement to explain worker absenteeism and turnover. Although the empirical research on this theory has been inconsistent, such integrative theories hold promise for the future of job attitude research.

Trends occurring in the work place present new challenges for research on job-related attitudes. One of the strategies that corporations in the United States use in an attempt to compete is downsizing through layoffs and forced retirements of employees. Another strategy is the use of outsourcing, in which outside consultants and temporary employees perform work that permanent employees did previously. The trend toward downsizing and outsourcing has ended the notion that an employee can devote himself or herself to a firm in exchange for job security. Even high performing employees cannot be confident that they can stay with a company and steadily move upward in the hierarchy to jobs with more pay and responsibility. Progression in a career increasingly means moving from one company to another and from one project to another, rather than upward progression in the hierarchy of a single corporation. Moreover, rapidly changing technologies have required an increasing number of people to change careers in midlife, and this trend seems to be escalating.

What are the implications of these changes for job satisfaction, job involvement, and organizational commitment? If organizations can no longer depend on a committed workforce, can they achieve the productivity and innovation that will be required in the workplace of the future? As Kanter (1989) notes, "If people are encouraged to rely on themselves, then how can the corporation rely on them? A response is urgently required. The 'contract' between corporations and their people must be rewritten to provide new forms of security that, in turn, engender a new, more powerful kind of loyalty" (p. 321). Future research on job-related attitudes will perhaps provide the answers to these and other questions.

## DISCUSSION QUESTIONS

1. How did the early job satisfaction research (the Hawthorne studies and two-factor theory) influence later thinking and research on job satisfaction?
2. How do the opponent process and dispositional theories of job satisfaction differ from other theories of job satisfaction? What are the practical implications of these theories?
3. How has job satisfaction usually been measured? Which scale would be more appropriate for workers with limited education? Which scale would tell a manager if his or her employees are dissatisfied with their pay?
4. Which correlates of job satisfaction have been the strongest? How is life satisfaction related to job satisfaction?
5. What job attitudes have been studied apart from job satisfaction? How are they alike and different from job satisfaction? How have they been used in integrative theories of job attitudes?

## A Question of Job Attitudes: The Case of the "New" Big Blue

According to many media sources in the spring of 1991, the Chairman and Chief Executive Officer (CEO) of IBM, John Akers, was mad. Although IBM (commonly known as Big Blue) had previously blamed the sluggish economy for its recent problems, Akers placed a large measure of the blame on IBM employees themselves. He contended that IBM's recent overall market share slump from 37% to 23% worldwide had resulted from too many missed deadlines and inferior quality products.

Akers stated: "The fact that we're losing market share makes me ——— mad. I used to think my job as a [sales] rep was at risk if I lost a sale. Tell them theirs is at risk if they lose one." Moreover, Akers claims "The tension level is not high enough in the business—everyone is too damn comfortable at a time when the business is in crisis" (Carroll, 1991, B1).

IBM issued a news release on November 26, 1991, that described a new corporate structure. This new structure would streamline the computer giant to make it more efficient. The plan was to create individual, autonomous businesses from the parent corporation. In this process, 20,000 of IBM's 325,000 workers would be eliminated both through voluntary programs, such as retirement, and termination of marginal employees. In December 1992, an additional cut of 25,000 jobs was announced, and even more layoffs seem likely to follow. These may not seem so unusual until you consider that IBM had a 71-year tradition of no layoffs and was one of the last major American companies with such a policy. In the past, many IBM employees considered the implicit job security of IBM positions as one of the real perks of working for the computer corporation; a job at IBM traditionally was considered tanta-

mount to lifetime employment. The situation has definitely changed. From the highest to the lowest levels of the organization, IBM employees now know that their jobs are at risk if they do not produce. IBM's CEO, John Akers, has said "If the people in labs and plants miss deadlines . . . tell them their job is on the line, too" (Carroll, 1991, B1). Marginal employees are being terminated, and no job is beyond scrutiny. On January 25, 1993 Akers stepped down as CEO and chairman after IBM suffered a record loss of $4.97 billion. The layoffs are likely to continue despite Akers' departure.

Interestingly, the word "layoff" is not used when the new policy is described. Managers have been told to identify those employees within their units that are unessential. These so-called surplus employees are given a month to find another job within IBM. If employees refuse a job that is offered to them, they are terminated with no benefits.

Defenders of IBM's actions argue that increasing competition in the computer industry has made a no-layoff policy impractical. Moreover, IBM had become far too large and bureaucratic to react quickly to marketplace demands and had to downsize to survive. Another argument in favor of the new policy is that employees will be motivated to higher levels of productivity if they believe their jobs depend on it. Akers has been quoted as saying: "Our people have to be competitive, and if they can't change fast enough, as fast as our industry . . . goodbye" (Carroll, 1991, B2).

Not surprisingly, the end of the no-layoff tradition has had its critics. One IBMer said that he thought it was time for top management at IBM to take some of the blame for the corporation's woes and not simply pass the buck on to the employees. Another lamented that, "I feel betrayed. If IBM isn't growing, is it the fault of the employees or of the senior management?" From coast to coast, IBM workers who agreed to talk to the media anonymously said that they were panicked. According to one programmer at an Austin, Texas, IBM facility, "Everyone thinks they're going to be out of a job." One engineer, who took a voluntary retirement after 26 years, wrote "IBM, like many other American enterprises under competitive siege in recent years, has turned from a challenging and caring employer to one ruled by fear and intimidation. Benevolence has become malevolence. People once praised for their excellence now fear for their jobs" ("Point counterpoint on IBM," *The New York Times*, April 12, 1992, p. F16).

An IBM engineer in California said that he was not waiting to be fired. Rather, like many of his coworkers, he was seriously considering another job offer to escape even the possible threat of termination. He claimed that IBM had mishandled the staff reduction problem by announcing that anyone who received a performance ranking of 4 or 5 (on a scale from 1 to 5) was likely to be terminated. This is indeed a surprising practice for an organization that has been widely known for its promotion of individual development and corporate loyalty.

## CASE QUESTIONS

1.  What are some of the advantages and disadvantages of the downsizing that IBM and many other large corporations have used to reduce costs and improve productivity?
2.  For IBM employees, which of the three job attitudes (job satisfaction, job involvement, and organizational commitment) do you think would be most affected by the current situation at IBM? Why?
3.  Some researchers (e.g., Eisenberger, Huntington, Hutchinson and Sowa, 1986) have treated job attitudes as a social exchange process. Why might that perspective be particularly applicable in the case of IBM?
4.  How can a large company such as IBM maintain organizational commitment, job involvement, and job satisfaction while downsizing?

# CHAPTER

**5**

# Social Behavior in Organizations

- Social Processes

- Social Structures in the Organization

- The Maturation and Decline of Social Systems

- Improving Group Effectiveness

- A Final Summation and a Look at the Future

- Case: The Bell Atlantic Way

On January 13, 1982, Air Florida flight 90 departed from the National Airport in Washington, DC, in the midst of a winter storm. A heavy accumulation of ice on the wings of the aircraft led to loss of lift. The plane hit the 14th Street bridge and crashed into the Potomac river with the loss of 78 lives. Social behavior in the cockpit appears to have been an important factor in this tragedy. Subsequent analysis of flight recordings revealed that the first officer advised the captain several times that there were problems, but these warnings either were not heard or were ignored ("Air Florida 737 voice recorder transcribed," *Aviation Week & Space Technology,* January, 1982, p. 81). The failure of the captain to listen to the first officer's warnings and the lack of assertiveness with which the first officer communicated these warnings have been attributed to a social norm common among cockpit crews that the captain's decisions should not be questioned (Gersick & Hackman, 1990).

Flying traditionally has been viewed as the heroic effort of single individuals rather than as a team effort. Nevertheless, how well people work together is a crucial factor in the success of any organization or group. This inattention to teamwork has not been restricted to cockpit management but has been a common oversight in organizations in the United States. Employers have traditionally viewed their employees as collections of individuals held together through self-interest, rules, procedures, and the exercise of authority. When groups are acknowledged, they are often seen as barriers rather than vehicles for achieving organizational goals. This individualistic orientation was particularly true of scientific management proponents such as Frederick Taylor (Chapter 1) and continues to influence the way organizations in the United States are run.

There are signs, however, that employers are finally coming to grips with the inherently social nature of organizations. For instance, in response to tragedies such as the Air Florida crash, airlines have implemented Cockpit Resource Management (CRM) training to help crews work together as a team. Another sign is the increasing number of firms that are using group management approaches such as quality circles, self-managing teams, liaisons, task forces, and ad hoc committees. Some large corporations have even gone so far as to replace the chief executive officer with an executive team. For instance, AT&T in 1991 instituted a five-member executive committee in which the chairmanship rotates every six months (Lublin, 1991b).

As organizations rely increasingly on groups, it will become even more important to understand the dynamics of interpersonal relations in the workplace. The model in Figure 5.1 provides a framework for our discussion of this topic. To illustrate, imagine that you are an observer of a newly formed project team that has been appointed by the president of a major company to find solutions to an important problem. Your task is to follow this group over time to see how well they work as a team. As you watch, the first thing that becomes apparent are people in the group communicating. A closer look reveals that members of the group attempt to influence each other and that some are much more successful than others. Members sometimes seem to cooperate with one another, but at other times appear to be competing. On occasion conflicts break out as members attempt to win arguments and in

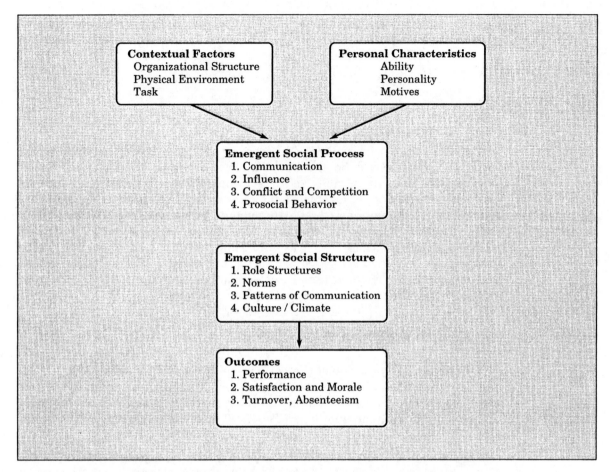

**Figure 5.1**  *A model of social process and structure in the organization*

other ways wield influence. These and other interactions that you observe at a single point in time are called *social processes.* In the first few meetings of the group you may find that it is hard to predict the behavior of the group, but with each successive meeting relations become more predictable. Some members begin to interact with each other more than they do with others. Expectations form for how people are to behave in the group. You may find that members eventually become positively attracted to each other, as the group becomes a strong, cohesive unit. These stable relations that emerge and add predictability and stability to relationships are called *social structures.* Whether the social processes and structures allow group members to deal with crucial task issues will determine whether the group succeeds or fails in achieving its goals.

In this chapter we examine the effects of social process and structure on the effectiveness with which individuals perform their organizational tasks. Much of this discussion applies to all types of *social systems,* from entire organizations to small groups. Consequently, we will refer at times to organizations and at others to groups, but the discussion is meant to apply to both. In the last section of the chapter, however, we focus primarily on how to improve the effectiveness of groups.

# SOCIAL PROCESSES

If you were to observe a project team or any other type of group at work, social processes would be the raw material for your observations. Social process consists of the various acts that people perform at a point in time as they interact, and includes such behaviors as talking, influencing, fighting, and helping. The emphasis in all this should be on the "ing." Weick (1979) aptly described the dynamic character of social processes when he described groups and organizations as continually being built up, torn down, and reconstructed. We will give special attention to four categories of social processes that are particularly important in organizations: communication, influence, conflict/competition/cooperation, and prosocial behavior.

## Communication in Organizations

Communication is one of the basic social processes (Argyle, 1991, p. 173) and can be defined as the exchange of information and meaning by two or more people. Many of the attempts to understand organizational communication have used Shannon and Weaver's (1949) model of communication (Figure 5.2).

**Feelings and Ideas**   As indicated in the model, communication begins with the feelings and ideas of the sender, with the intent often being to focus on the ideas and suppress the feelings. Contrary to the intent, feelings frequently leak into communications, so that the relationship between the sender and the recipient is conveyed as well as the content of the message. Thus, the content of your message to a fellow employee might be to hand you a tool. Depending on your facial expressions, tone of voice, and posture, however, "hand me that tool" could mean what it appears (i.e., "I need a tool") or could communicate something much different (e.g., "I think you are stupid").

**Encoding**   At the second step in the process, the thoughts and feelings of the sender are encoded, which means that they are transformed into some form that can be transmitted. Putting thoughts or feelings into words is one example of encoding. An obvious example of breakdowns at this point would be if the sender and recipient spoke different languages. More subtle encoding problems can occur as the result of differences in the backgrounds of the sender and receiver. For instance, employees in the same organization often come to share a similar jargon that is understandable to members of the organization but is uninterpretable to those outside the organization.

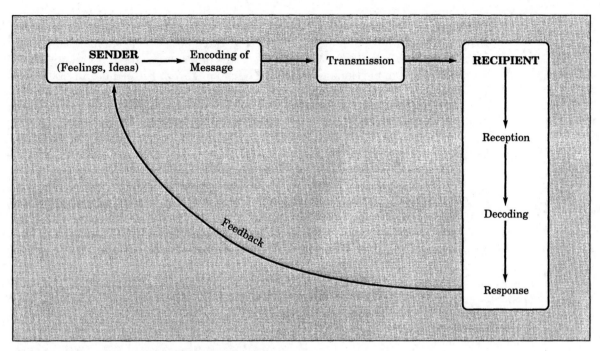

**Figure 5.2**  *The communication process*

**Transmission**  Once encoded, the message is transmitted through a medium. Breakdowns in transmission are likely to occur in the form of distortion and filtering. *Filtering* refers to the omission of parts of the message as it is transmitted. In *distortion* the various parts of the message may be retained but the transmitted message still deviates from the message originally intended by the sender as the result of phrasing of the message or the nonverbal behavior of the communicator. Take as an example, Fred, a first-line supervisor in a manufacturing plant, who sees mechanical problems that will require expensive repairs. This is bad news because the plant is in the middle of a recession and cannot really afford such maintenance expenses. Although Fred conveys the problem to his immediate supervisor, the urgency of the needed repairs is deemphasized as the message passes through each level of management. By the time the message reaches the higher levels of management, the original statement by Fred that "We need repairs before next Tuesday or we will suffer a shutdown" may become "We *may* need a *few minor* repairs before next Tuesday to keep things going smoothly." In addition to distortion, filtering occurs as important parts of the message fail to be passed along (e.g., the fact that the repairs are needed next Tuesday may be omitted). As you have probably observed yourself, negative news is less likely to be transmitted than positive news (Tesser & Rosen, 1975).

As implied in this example, the likelihood of filtering and distortion increases if a message must pass through several levels of the hierarchy in an organization (Nichols, 1962; Davis, 1968; Read, 1962; O'Reilly & Roberts, 1974). For example, one study found that only 20% of the information originating with a board of directors made it through five levels of management to the lower-level operations employees (Nichols, 1962). Filtering and distortion also appear to increase as the size of a group or organization increases. With large groups, communications can fail not only because there are more people through whom the message must pass, but also because there is less overall participation and more dominance by a few members (O'Reilly & Roberts, 1977).

Physical distances and barriers are additional hindrances to transmission. In an attempt to eliminate these factors, architects in the 1950s and 1960s introduced the open office plan, which consists of eliminating the fixed walls that separate employees in the traditional workplace (Chapter 12). Typical office design consists of either cellular or open office arrangements. *Cellular offices* are small private rooms for use by one or a few people. *Open offices*

Open offices make it easier for employees to communicate informally with one another, but noise and a lack of privacy are potential problems with this type of workspace.

imply a common working area for several employees, although office space is usually not totally open, but rather subdivided with temporary partitions. In most open offices, employees who work together are also located together. Although the intent was to enhance communication by making employees more accessible to each other, evaluations of the open office plan have provided mixed results (Sundstrom, 1986). The open office plan appears to encourage informal conversations, but it does not appear to improve formal communication and may violate personal privacy by making it difficult to engage in confidential conversations. A nationwide survey (Steelcase, 1978) revealed that workers in open offices found concentration and confidentiality difficult, if not impossible. Not surprisingly, workers in open offices also reported twice as many headaches as those workers in other office arrangements (Hedge, 1984).

This discussion may lead you to assume that open office plans should be abandoned. However, from an organizational perspective, open offices conserve space and easily permit reorganizations of work groups. In choosing office arrangements, organizations need to consider the type of worker. Zalesny and Farace (1987) asked employees for their perceptions of their work environment both before and after moving from a traditional closed office to an open office setting. They found that managerial and professional workers perceived open office environments less favorably than clerical employees. The researchers speculated that the higher level employees disliked their new office setting because loss of defined (private) office space implied a loss of status. Organizations should also consider the type of activity or task workers are performing. Employees who require confidentiality or privacy (e.g., counselors or therapists) would probably not be well served by an open office plan. Those employees who must interact and communicate freely (e.g., a marketing team) undoubtedly would benefit from an open office plan. In addition, research has shown that people who work on complex or difficult tasks prefer very private (closed) environments, which facilitate concentration (Block & Stokes, 1989).

**Reception**   An especially important step in the communication process is the reception of the message. Serious misunderstandings can arise when the message does not catch the recipient's attention. Written messages often fail at this point. Thus, a supervisor's memo to "stop using the phone for personal calls" may be buried among all the other memoranda received that day or may end up in the trash with the junk mail. Failures in reception also occur because the amount of information exceeds the processing capacity of the recipient. In coping with an overload of information, both individuals and organizations have been shown to filter and distort (Miller, 1960).

The psychological state of the recipient is another source of breakdowns in reception. A message can be clearly transmitted but the recipient's expectations might prevent receiving the message as it was intended. If a person is expecting to be criticized, for instance, he or she may only hear a supervisor's negative comments and may fail to hear the positive comments. Incomplete reception seems most likely when people are under stress. For instance, research has shown that intense emotions can lead people to focus their attention on a much smaller range of stimuli (Easterbrook, 1959).

**Decoding**   Even if the words of your message are received, the communication will only succeed if the recipient decodes or interprets the message as you intended. In decoding, the recipient interprets the message with his or her personal codebook, similar to the way a message sent by Morse code might be translated by a telegrapher. Differences in the codes of superiors and their subordinates are seen as one of the most consistent and important determinants of breakdowns in communication (Jablin, 1979). Take, for example, the problems that occur if a supervisor's conception of a "personal phone call" differs from that of a subordinate's. In an empirical demonstration of the effects of cognitive codes on communication, Triandis (1959) measured the similarity with which supervisors and their subordinates conceived of the concepts art, friend, God, power, science, church, money, literature, sex, and theory. He found that supervisors and subordinates communicated more effectively the more similar their interpretations of these concepts.

**Response**   How the recipient behaves in response to the message is the next step in the process. The failure to respond as intended may or may not reflect a problem of communication. Instead, a lack of ability, knowledge, or motivation could be the causes. Rather than improving communication, the solution to the problem may require implementing incentives, task redesign, training, or other solutions that directly address the sources of the unintended response.

**Feedback**   The final step is crucial to improving communications and avoiding future breakdowns. This involves a feedback loop in which the sender receives information on the consequences of the message. This might come in the form of acknowledgment on the part of the recipient that the message was heard and understood as well as evidence that the recipient has behaved as desired. One of the most effective ways of building a feedback loop into the communication process is to make sure that the recipient feels free to ask questions and give comments. Without feedback a sender can imagine how things are going but can never be entirely sure if the message is being received or decoded as intended.

The model presented in Figure 5.2 can help in the diagnosis of communication breakdowns. Think back to some instance when you attempted but failed to communicate with another individual. You may have done what is only natural and blamed the breakdown on the other person's lack of motivation or ability. The model suggests that you should instead consider each step in this process as a potential source of the miscommunication. Could your communication have failed at the initial encoding of the message? Perhaps you did not convey all that you intended to convey, or perhaps your feelings unintentionally leaked into the message. Did your communication fail in transmission because of noise or other people who were competing for the receiver's attention? Did the message fail to be received because of the emotional state or expectations of the recipient? Could decoding be a problem in that the recipient heard the words correctly but gave them a different interpretation? Finally, could the breakdown reflect a failure of the recipient to respond as intended to the message? In this case the ability, knowledge, or motivation of the recipient may be the source of the problem rather than encoding, transmission, reception, or decoding. The final and perhaps most important question to ask is did you receive feedback on the impact of your communication. This may mean asking recipients to repeat what you have communicated and to state what they plan to do in response to the messages you have transmitted.

## MATCHING THE MEDIUM TO THE MESSAGE

Let us examine in more detail one of the decision points in the model presented in Figure 5.2, the decision as to what type of medium or channel to use in transmitting the message. In attempting to understand social processes in an organization, it is especially important to examine the media that people choose and the effectiveness with which they use them in communicating. Different situations call for different media. A model presented by Lengel and Daft (1988) suggests that the decision should be based on the "richness" of the medium. A rich medium has the ability simultaneously to convey multiple information cues and to provide rapid feedback and a personal focus. Face-to-face conversation is the richest, and possibly accounts for the fact that it is also the favorite medium of people in organizations (Brenner & Sigband, 1973; Burns, 1954; Carlson, 1951; Conrath, 1973; Hinrichs, 1964; Housel & Davis, 1977; Klemmer, 1971; Mintzberg, 1973). Telephone conversations are also a rich medium but lack the personal impact and diversity of the nonverbal cues present in face-to-face interaction. Even lower on the richness hierarchy are "personal static media" such as memos and letters. These have a personal focus but contain limited cues and provide little feedback. Finally, impersonal static media are the leanest media and include flyers circulated among large groups of employees and bulletin boards.

Daft and Lengel (1984) proposed that a communication medium should be chosen whose richness is appropriate to the routineness of the problem. For highly routine problems, a lean medium is most effective, but a rich medium is needed when the problem is nonroutine. For example, if an executive needed to discuss the personal problems an employee was having with his or her peers, a face-to-face conversation would be better than a memo. If the intent was to communicate a simple, uncontroversial policy concerning use of the photocopier, a memo would be better than calling a face-to-face meeting.

## COMPUTER-MEDIATED COMMUNICATION

Special issues pertaining to communication media have emerged as the result of advances in computer technology. Not only can employees communicate face-to-face, but they also can use electronic mail, computer conferences, electronic bulletin boards, and electronic blackboards. These new tools allow large amounts of information to be transmitted instantly across

In computer-mediated meetings group members appear to participate more equally in the discussion than in traditional meetings where one or a few members often dominate.

great distances to large numbers of people. In the case of computerized conferences, a group of employees sits at individual computers and provides input to the meeting by means of keyboards. Companies using computer-mediated meetings have claimed that the computer has allowed tremendous increases in the productivity of meetings (Bulkeley, 1992).

With these advantages, it is tempting to use the newer forms of media and forgo the more traditional face-to-face vehicles. This would be a mistake, however. Daft and Lengel's (1984) discussion of media richness makes clear that some problems require a richer medium than provided by computers. Inappropriate use of computer communication has been implicated, for example, in the Challenger space shuttle disaster (Weick, 1987). In this case, the concern of some engineers regarding the launching of the shuttle in cold weather may not have been adequately expressed in the messages exchanged through NASA's electronic communication network.

Because research on the relative effectiveness of various media has only begun, many of the propositions of Daft and Lengel remain speculative. Initial research findings, however, have yielded some interesting insights into the advantages and disadvantages of communicating by means of computers. A positive benefit of computer-mediated communication is that participants differ less in the amount they participate in the exchange, possibly as the result of status distinctions being less noticeable. By contrast, in face-to-face meetings a few individuals (e.g., the boss, the older members, outgoing individuals) are likely to dominate the process.

The lessening of status distinctions and the equalization of participation could be a tremendous boon to the creativity of a group, but the anonymity responsible for these same factors also can create problems. The lack of non-verbal cues makes it more difficult for participants to determine how others feel about the issues under discussion. Consequently, individuals in computer-mediated meetings, as opposed to face-to-face meetings, take longer to reach agreement on issues and are less satisfied with the process. Some of the inefficiencies of computer-mediated meetings have been demonstrated in an interesting research program conducted by Siegel, Dubrovsky, Kiesler, and McGuire (1986). In one experiment, students were given a series of tasks to perform as a group and either had to communicate face-to-face or by means of linked computer terminals. The computer-mediated communications were marked by a higher frequency of uninhibited behavior (or flaming) as reflected in instances of swearing, insults, and name-calling. Indeed, 34 instances were found in the computer-mediated discussion but none were found in the face-to-face discussions. A possible explanation, according to the authors, was that the anonymity and absence of feedback associated with the technology led to feelings of loss of identity and a subsequent release of restraints.

The free exchange of information that would result from a full implementation of computer-mediated communication might well prove a strain for organizations that operate as traditional hierarchical bureaucracies. One example comes from a recent incident at a large corporation. The chairman sharply criticized management and employees as feeling too secure and comfortable at a time when the company's performance was in decline (Carroll, 1991). The comments were made in a small, private meeting, and supposedly were not intended for widespread dissemination. Through electronic mail, however, the comments were immediately circulated throughout the company and eventually published in the newspapers. Computer technology in this case allowed immediate distribution across a large audience but also led to loss of control of the message.

Despite the problems, the increased use of computer-mediated communication in organizations appears inevitable (Kirkpatrick, 1992). Before the full potential of this medium is realized, however, much more research and development is needed. Computer-mediated communication systems will require that computer specialists collaborate with social scientists in designing software (sometimes called groupware) that is sensitive to the realities of social process in organizations.

## Influence and Power

Have you ever been in a group meeting in which there was a struggle between two members who both wanted to lead the group? Have you ever seen a group in which one member had such clout that all others went along even though they privately disagreed with his or her views? Have you ever found yourself conforming with the majority view in a group to avoid their criticisms? If your answer to any of these questions is yes, you have observed two additional basic social processes: influence and power. Communication is closely interwoven with these two processes in that communications not only serve as the primary vehicle for exerting influence and power, but the power that individuals possess in a relationship can, in turn, shape the nature of communications (Ferris & Mitchell, 1987). We define *influence* as the actual change of one person's perceptions, attitudes, or behavior by another person or persons. The amount of influence that is achieved depends on *social power*, which we define as the ability to influence others. French and Raven (1959) proposed that there are five bases of power, each originating from a different type of relationship between the agent of power and the recipient of the influence attempts.

1.  Reward Power

    The amount of reward power that person A has over person B is a function of how much B can be rewarded and the perception that A controls these rewards. For instance, a supervisor might have a large amount of reward power if the organization made available monetary incentives that could be administered at the discretion of the supervisor.

2.  Coercive Power

    The extent of coercive power is a function of the amount of punishment that can be administered and the perceptions of the person that compliance will lead to an avoidance of these punishments. Coercive power also occurs as a consequence of believing that rewards can be withheld. An example of coercive power would be the ability of a group to get individual members to go along with work practices through threats of isolation and rejection.

3.  Legitimate Power

    Individuals have this type of power to the extent that others perceive them as having the lawful authority to influence them. Who is granted this authority depends on the values of the organization. Thus, older people might have little problem telling others what to do, whereas younger people might have difficulty doing this because they are not seen as having the right to issue directives. Legitimate power also can derive from the pyramidal structure of the typical hierarchical organization. Thus, a vice president has the right to direct department heads; department heads have the right to direct first-line supervisors; first-line supervisors have the right to direct workers.

4. Referent Power

   Referent power is the ability to influence that stems from the person's attraction to the agent of influence. An example would be a group member who concedes to the demands of peers because he or she wants to be accepted by them. The motivational source of referent power is the ability of the leader to affect the followers' feelings of personal acceptance, approval, and self-esteem.

5. Expert Power

   Expert power is the ability to influence others as the result of being perceived as having special knowledge and expertise. An employee in an organization might have access to information that others do not have because of that individual's special training, native intelligence, or location in the organization. The range of influence is likely to be restricted to topics on which the person is considered knowledgeable. Agreeing with a person because he or she is an expert on engineering problems, for instance, does not mean that you will agree with the person on a marketing or human resource management problem.

Two important aspects of the French and Raven model need to be emphasized. The bases of power discussed by French and Raven (1959) are the consequence of how others *perceive* that individual, regardless of whether these perceptions have any basis in reality. For example, a person may have no actual expertise but still may be seen as an expert. Power is the end result of a combination of forces, including the past attempts of the person to influence, the characteristics of the person, and the situational context. A second point is that these bases of power are interrelated. Thus, individuals may acquire referent power as the result of rewarding others. Similarly, individuals who possess expertise may acquire legitimate power as the result of others' seeing them as having the right to issue directives.

Whereas power is defined by the *potential* to influence others, *influence tactics* are what an individual actually does to influence others. As in the case of power, questionnaires have been constructed to measure these alternative influence tactics. Perhaps the best known was developed by Kipnis, Schmidt, and Wilkinson (1980) on the basis of a study in which they asked working students to describe incidents in which they had succeeded in influencing others. A second sample of subjects then used these items to describe the tactics with which they attempted to change the mind of a boss, a coworker, or a subordinate. Later replications and extensions of this research led to the development of a measure having the nine dimensions defined in Table 5.1 (Yukl & Tracey, 1992). Research with this measure revealed that the most frequently used tactics were consultation, rational persuasion, inspirational appeals, and ingratiation, and the least frequently used were exchange tactics (Yukl &

**Table 5.1**

## INFLUENCE TACTICS

1. Pressure tactics: The person uses demands, threats, or intimidation to convince you to comply with a request or to support a proposal.

2. Legitimating: The person seeks to establish the legitimacy of a request by claiming the authority or right to make it or by verifying that it is consistent with organizational policies, rules, practices, or traditions.

3. Exchange tactics: The person makes an explicit or implicit promise that you will receive rewards or tangible benefits if you comply with a request or support a proposal, or reminds you of a prior favor to be reciprocated.

4. Coalition tactics: The person seeks the aid of others to persuade you to do something or uses the support of others as an argument for you to agree also.

5. Ingratiating tactics: The person seeks to get you in a good mood or to think favorably of him or her before asking you to do something.

6. Rational persuasion: The person uses logical arguments and factual evidence to persuade you that a proposal or request is viable and likely to result in the attainment of task objectives.

7. Inspirational appeals: The person makes an emotional request or proposal that arouses enthusiasm by appealing to your values and ideals, or by increasing your confidence that you can do it.

8. Consultation tactics: The person seeks your participation in making a decision or planning how to implement a proposed policy, strategy, or change.

9. Personal appeals: The person appeals to your feelings of loyalty and friendship toward him or her before asking you to do something.

*Source:* Adapted from Yukl, G., & Tracey, J. Bruce. (1992). Consequences of influence tactics used with subordinates, peers, and the boss. *Journal of Applied Psychology, 77,* 525-535.

Tracey, 1992). Although a similar rank was found in the reported use of the tactics for downward, lateral, and upward influence, slight differences were found in the reported frequency in the use of these influence tactics as a function of the direction of influence attempted. Rational persuasion was more likely to be used to influence superiors (upward influence) than peers (lateral influence) or subordinates (downward). Inspirational appeals and ingratiation were more likely to be used to influence subordinates than either peers or superiors.

## Competiton, Conflict, and Cooperation

In observing any group or organization at work, you will become aware of a third basic category of social process. Some people in the group will work together to achieve their goals, whereas others will work against each other. Some may even appear to be at war as they ridicule, demean, and in other ways block the activities of other people in the group. This third category of social process involves competition, conflict, and cooperation, three different but interrelated social behaviors.

There is disagreement among organizational scholars on how best to define these processes, but we will follow the distinctions made by Tjosvold (1986). *Conflict* is defined as activities that are incompatible in that one activity obstructs, interferes, impairs, or in some other way lessens the effectiveness of another activity. *Competition* and *cooperation* refer to the interdependence of goals as perceived by two or more people. Competition arises when the achievement of one person's goal is seen as negatively related to the achievement of another person's goal, as in a footrace, in which one person's win necessitates another person's loss. Cooperation occurs when the achievement of one person's goal is seen as positively related to the achievement of another person's goal. Crucial to building an effective team is developing an attitude that "we are all in this together and we will only win if we all win." It is possible that people can conflict but still maintain an overall cooperative relationship. For instance, to reach a creative solution group members may play the devil's advocate and argue heatedly against each other's solutions while defending their own positions. Yet, this conflict can occur in an atmosphere of cooperation in which group members see arguing as beneficial to achieving the group's goals.

The wielding of influence and power inevitably leads to some competition that can be beneficial in energizing individuals, shaking them loose from their habitual routines, and pushing them toward achieving their potential. The danger is that what was intended to be a healthy contest can turn into a destructive fight that hurts the performance of the organization and prevents future cooperation. Indeed, some of the failures of the U.S. economy in recent years have been blamed on self-defeating conflicts in organizations and the apparent inability to cooperate (Kanter, 1989). While competition is still revered in American culture, there seems to be a trend among some of the largest firms to encourage collaborative efforts between as well as within firms ("This is what the U.S. must do to stay competitive," *Business Week*, December 16, 1991; "Take this job and love it," *The New York Times*, January 26, 1992). Crucial to the effectiveness of organizations is being able to manage competition so that people can disagree and still work together to achieve their common objectives.

In observing social process, then, we need to look for possible conflicts, the causes of these conflicts, and methods that are used to resolve them. As in the case of the other social processes, conflict and conflict resolution are a function of contextual factors, such as scarcity of resources, as well the personalities of the individuals involved.

## CONTEXTUAL CAUSES OF CONFLICT

Conflict can emerge because of the organizational context. Walton and Dutton (1969) and Robbins (1974) have discussed several such factors, including task interdependence, goal and reward structure, competition for scarce resources, communication obstacles, and various jurisdictional anbiguities.

**Task Interdependence**     Perhaps the most fundamental antecedent of conflict is the extent to which the successful performance of one person or unit depends on the performance of another. When people depend on each other, breakdowns in cooperation can easily escalate into conflict (Dutton & Walton, 1972). On the other hand, when task interdependence is low, conflict is much less likely.

**Goal and Reward Structures**     Whether conflict occurs in a group or organization depends to a large extent on the formal goals defining task achievement and the rewards given to people for their performances. A *cooperative goal structure* positively links the goals of group members so that one person's goal achievements are beneficial to the achievement of other members' goals. In an *individualistic goal structure,* there is no such correlation; the achievement of one person's goals is unrelated to the goal achievement of others in the group. A third type of goal structure is a *competitive goal structure* in which the goal attainment of one member is negatively related to other members' goal attainments. In other words, individual members cannot attain their goals unless other members fail in theirs. Similar to goal structures, people can be rewarded for their collective efforts (cooperative rewards), their individual performance independent of others' performance (individualistic rewards), or on a winner-take-all basis (competitive rewards).

The individualistic orientation of organizations in the United States has led to an emphasis on individualistic and competitive structures. Many a manager has felt that the surest way to improve productivity in the work force is to pit employees against each other and see who comes out the winner. The unfortunate consequence of this competition is that too often everyone comes out a loser. Research suggests that competition is not the best approach if the parties involved must cooperate to get the job done. A clear example of the dysfunctional consequences of competitive rewards was provided by Blau (1954) in a public employment service. The employment counselors in this agency were to keep track of job openings and then match those clients who best fit the available openings. A decision was made by management to evaluate each counselor on the basis of the number of clients that he or she placed in jobs. The result was conflict in which counselors hoarded information on job openings rather than sharing with other counselors.

Experiments have further demonstrated the harmful effects that competitive reward systems can have on the performance of a group's tasks. In one of the first studies addressing this issue, Deutsch (1949) had students in a class work on a project under one of two conditions designed to induce cooperation or competition. In the *cooperative groups,* individuals within groups were graded on the basis of how well their group performed on class projects by rank ordering the groups according to their performance. Moreover, the students' course grades were based on the rankings of their groups on these projects. In the *competitive groups,* group members were ranked on their contribution to the group product and then graded according to their individual contributions. The course grade of each student was based on how they individually ranked in their performance on the projects in the course. The cooperative groups were found to work together more effectively in several respects: They were more likely to to coordinate their activities and to show higher quantity and quality of performance on course projects than students who were rewarded competitively.

Subsequent research has supported Deutsch's (1949) contention that cooperative reward systems achieve better results than rewarding people competitively (Johnson, Maruyama, Johnson, Nelson, & Skon, 1981). Moreover the research tends to show that imposing cooperative goal structures is more effective than imposing individualistic goal structures. However, in explaining the effects of goal structures we need to distinguish both the effect of reward systems and *task interdependence,* that is, whether people must cooperate to perform the task. In a situation in which cooperation is important to performance of the task, as was the case with the class projects in Deutsch's study, rewarding performance on a competitive or individualistic basis may encourage competition that detracts from effective performance. On the other hand, if the task does not require cooperation, competitive and individualistic rewards might even serve as a boost to performance.

**Scarce Resources**    Closely related to the effects of reward and goal structures is the conflict that can emerge when different units within an organization must use limited or scarce resources. These resources may be concrete, such as money, supplies, personnel, or space. An all-too-common example in universities is the "space war" that can occur among academic departments for rooms and other physical accommodations. Competition can occur over more abstract resources as well, such as prestige, popularity, or power. When resources become leaner as the result of budget cuts, employees are more inclined to compete for resources and this competition can degenerate into conflict.

**Barriers to Communication**    By necessity, the organization must restrain communication to some extent through physical separation and organizational arrangements. Different functional units (e.g., marketing, production, research and development, finance) are usually located in different places. Also, employees seldom have direct access to employees in other functional units but must usually go through channels. The inability of those involved to openly communicate their intentions can lower trust and can serve as another source of conflict.

**Status Incongruence**    *Status* refers to the rank or worth attributed to an employee by other employees. Status is *achieved* when it results from the efforts of the employee, as in the case of status afforded by the education and training of the individual. Status is *ascribed* when it is inherited or in some other way acquired as the result of factors that are outside the employee's control. Depending on what members of the group or organization value, ascribed status could result from such factors as race, sex, religion, or color. When persons of higher status are dependent on those of lower status, the resulting status incongruency can easily stimulate conflict. A particularly common source of conflict is when a low status employee initiates work for a higher status employee. For example, Whyte (1949) found that conflict between waitresses and cooks in restaurants often occurred because of the incongruency of lower status waitresses giving customer orders to the higher status cooks.

**Ambiguity in Work Responsibilities**   Another common source of conflict is uncertainty over who should do what, how they should perform their tasks, and the relative responsibilities of employees. When there is a lack of accountability for the performance of units in an organization, disagreements can arise over who has responsibility for successes and failures.

**Organizational Differentiation**   Perhaps the most common antecedent of conflict in organizations is the organizational differentiation that occurs as the result of division and specialization of labor. Lawrence and Lorsch (1967) observed that the various departments within an organization can differ greatly on the formality of their structures (low vs. high), the extent to which they are task oriented versus relationships oriented, and their orientation to time (short term vs. long term). For example, the sales department is characterized by a shorter term orientation to time, more formality in structure, and a greater focus on interpersonal relations than a research department. As the result of these organizational differences, people can develop very different views of the way things should be done, and these differences in orientation can lead to conflict.

## PERSONAL CAUSES OF CONFLICT

Despite the importance of contextual factors, conflict is most often blamed on the characteristics of the individuals involved in the fight. This commonsense notion is overly simplistic, but has some merit. Some people *do* seem more predisposed to aggressive, noncooperative behavior than others. Both Stagner (1962) and Bass and Dunteman (1963) found that plant managers and union stewards with high needs for power and dominance were more likely to engage in conflict, whereas those with high needs for affiliation were more likely to cooperate. The combination of personalities in a situation may be more important than the personality of single individuals, however. For instance, if two domineering people are assigned to a group and both attempt to control the meeting, conflict seems more likely than if a domineering individual is paired with a submissive individual.

## THE DEVELOPMENT OF CONFLICT

For whatever reasons a conflict begins, once started it can have a life of its own. Each party comes to believe that the other is out to win and consequently acts in a manner that is consistent with these perceptions. The result is that perceptions of the situation can become self-fulfilling as competitive, conflictive behavior evokes similar behavior from the other. Often conflict can take the form of a *vicious circle* in which each action and reaction raises the stakes and takes the conflicting people farther and farther from a desirable state of affairs (Masuch, 1985). In the worst situations, conflict can spiral out of control and lead to tragic consequences. The following scenario, for example, unfortunately is all too common. A decline in productivity leads management to issue threats and warnings that if employees do not work harder they will be punished. These threats lead to resentment on the part of workers and further declines in productivity, which, in turn, trigger more punitive actions on the part of management.

According to Masuch (1985), vicious circles are self-sealing and "build up like malignant tumors in the body" (p. 26). Partly this is because of the cognitive biases that accompany such conflicts. Each person tends to attribute the other's actions to personal traits (e.g., an evil personality or selfish intentions). Even more damaging is the tendency to accept the situation and view fighting as a normal way of life that does not need to change. Another factor that can cause a conflict to become self-sealing is that the groups or individuals involved are likely to reduce their communications with each other. By not communicating, irrational beliefs can continue unabated and become even more distorted.

## MANAGING CONFLICT

It is important to recognize that too much harmony in an organization can be as harmful as too little. Conflict can be a source of energy and creativity and can keep individual persons or units from becoming too powerful. While conflict cannot and *should not* be done away with entirely, it must be managed. Miles (1980) distinguished among four general strategies for managing conflict. These included changes in (1) the organizational structure or context, (2) the issues, (3) the relationships of those in conflict, and (4) the individuals involved in the conflict.

1. *Altering the structure or context.* In cases in which conflict results from poor job design or lack of clarity of responsibilities, the obvious approach to conflict resolution is to remedy these problems. For example, we know that conflict is particularly likely when one person of higher status is dependent on the work of someone lower in status. It may be possible to "decouple" such people. If employees who pack a product into boxes must wait for another unit to provide the boxes, conflict between the units might be resolved through providing a *buffer* stock of boxes so that the packing unit is not as dependent on the other group. Another approach is to use an *integrator* or *coordinator* whose special job is to see that the

supply of boxes is maintained. Increasingly, organizations are also making use of mediation to resolve conflicts that in the past would have been settled through lawsuits (Carlson, 1991). A *mediator* helps the conflicting parties negotiate a mutually acceptable solution.

Structural means of resolving a conflict involve organizational entities or procedures that channel conflict in constructive directions. Where workers are represented by a union, the structural form for resolving disputes is the *grievance procedure*. It can serve as an avenue of resolving conflicts that arise between workers and supervisors as well as a means of clarifying ambiguous or incomplete aspects of the contract. The first step is to take the grievance to the shop steward or the employee representing the union. The steward may tell the employee to abandon the grievance or attempt to directly resolve the issue with the supervisor. If attempts to resolve the issue fail, the next step is to pass the grievance over to a grievance committee. This committee usually consists of employees elected by the union membership who meet with management representatives to present the case of the grievant. If a resolution cannot be achieved, then the final step may be to take the case for outside arbitration. A neutral person such as a judge, lawyer, or professional arbitrator hears both sides of the grievance and renders a binding decision.

*Cross-functional project teams* are another structural approach that organizations can use to avoid the conflict that is so often observed among different functional groups (e.g., engineering vs. production vs. research and development). An example is Motorola, which uses teams of people from a variety of disciplines to design new products (Therrien, 1989). Simply forming such a team, however, may not be enough to avoid the conflicts that occur as the result of turf battles among the departments that team members represent. GM's Cadillac did not sell well in the early 1980s partly as the result of a design that too closely resembled cheaper models (White, Patterson, & Ingrassia, 1992). This cheap-looking design apparently was the result of the cost-conscious project members from the finance department wielding the most influence on the project teams. In contrast, when Japanese firms such as Toyota form a team to develop a new car, members of the team all work in the same place and report to a team leader who has total charge of the project (Taylor, 1990; White, Patterson, & Ingrassia, 1992).

2. *Changing the issues.* Employees who are at odds with each other frequently have difficulty resolving their conflict because they state the issues in diffuse and all-encompassing

terms. Labor unions may claim that management is out to exploit them; management claims that the union is trying to financially ruin the company. As long as the issues stay at this level, it is impossible to move toward resolution. In *issue control* the issues are subdivided into smaller, more manageable components and these specific issues are then tackled one at a time. For instance, in a labor-management negotiation, disputes could be subdivided into relevant issues (benefits, pay, work rules) and each of these negotiated separately.

3.  *Changing the relationship.* Conflict can also be handled by acting directly on the relationship between the conflicting parties. The various relational approaches can be distinguished according to whether they are aimed at changing the behavior of those involved in the conflict or attempt to achieve some fundamental change in attitudes as well. Behavioral change might be achieved by separating the conflicting parties. Thus, if two employees constantly bicker, a manager in the situation might tell them to stay away from each other. To change attitudes she may need to use a more drastic approach called *superordinate goals.* In using this strategy, she would present the conflicting parties with an objective that is highly important to both parties but requires close cooperation to achieve (Sherif, Harvey, White, Hood, & Sherif, 1961). A possible example is the goal of overcoming foreign competition, which has become a major threat to the survival of U.S. firms. The need to successfully compete against foreign firms has led unions and management in some firms to put aside their differences and cooperate in recent years.

4.  *Changing individuals.* In some cases changing one or more of the conflicting parties is necessary to resolve a conflict. Moving a recalcitrant individual out of a unit or even dismissing an employee could be a solution. Racial conflict in an organization that results from stereotypes and the inability to communicate may call for efforts to eliminate stereotypes and improve communication skills. Another example is training in which employees are sensitized to discriminatory behavior in their interactions with persons of different gender or race. For instance, it is estimated that current concerns over sexual harassment will lead more than 90% of the top 500 companies to eventually offer special training to eliminate this problem (Lublin, 1991a).

Which approach is best? Conflict management depends on the diagnosis of the cause of the conflict. If a diagnosis points to structural arrangements as the primary cause, then structural interventions may suffice. If attitudes or personalities are at the root of the conflict, then deeper interventions are needed. Resolving conflicts is not a matter of the *one best* approach but how to effectively combine a variety of techniques. A manager might want to begin by separating the conflicting parties, and after a cooling-off period, follow up with attempts to improve the relationships and attitudes of those involved. Neilson (1972) further suggests that managers should consider the costs associated with a tactic, their ability to successfully implement the tactic, and the compatibility of the tactic with their personal values. Whatever approach is used, however, people who must work together in an organization must ultimately perceive themselves to share common goals that require cooperation to attain.

*Summary*

When people are dependent on one another for achieving their goals, the inevitable competition and conflict generated can either help or hinder achieving the organization's goals. Conflict and competition can emerge both from personalities of the individuals involved and the organizational situation in which they find themselves. A variety of methods can potentially be used to resolve conflict; the specific mode used should be dictated by the diagnosis of the situation as well as a self-appraisal by the manger of her own strengths, weaknesses, and values.

## Prosocial Behavior

In any organization or group you will find that while some people are cooperative, they do little more than they have to in their dealings with others. These employees stand in stark contrast with others you observe who not only cooperate but generally go out of their way to contribute to the group and the organization. The latter type of behavior has gone by a variety of labels, including *organizational citizenship* (Organ, 1988), *prosocial behavior* (Brief & Motowidlo, 1986), and *extrarole behavior* (Katz & Kahn, 1978). There are small differences in the definitions of these concepts, but they are all concerned with individuals attempting to assist others, even though there is no requirement to do so and no personal gains are expected. We will use the term "prosocial behavior," defined by Brief and Motowidlo (1986) as behavior "performed with the intention of promoting the welfare of the individual, group, or organization toward which it is directed" (p. 711). Among the behaviors that Brief and Motowidlo (1986) used to illustrate prosocial behaviors were assisting coworkers with job-related and personal matters, helping customers, and representing the organization favorably to outsiders.

Given that organizations are only likely to be effective to the extent that employees are willing to collaborate, how can an organization cultivate prosocial behavior? As in the case of conflict and cooperation, both contextual and personal factors are involved. Some employees appear to approach life with a generally positive outlook and are more likely to be prosocial than others. A variety of situational factors may influence prosocial behavior as well. The reward system in an organization can encourage or discourage cooperation. Prosocial behaviors appear less likely to emerge in a high-stress environment than in a low-stress environment. Leaders who are considerate and employee oriented are more likely to encourage prosocial behavior among subordinates than inconsiderate task masters. Also, the warm and friendly atmosphere that exists in some organizations encourages prosocial behavior, whereas the cold, punitive atmosphere of other organizations discourages such behavior. Evidence of this was provided by Puffer (1987, p. 617) who found that prosocial behavior among salespersons was more likely when they felt secure in their work situation and trusted management.

# SOCIAL STRUCTURES IN THE ORGANIZATION

Much of the social behavior you observe in a group or organization will appear fleeting or even random in nature. As you continue to watch the same set of people interact, however, you will find that stable patterns of behavior begin to emerge. This stability is essential to the survival and success of a group or organization. Just as life would quickly become intolerable if you suddenly lacked the ability to predict how others would respond to everyday events, life in an organization would become chaotic if people had no idea of how others in the organization would probably behave in various situations. Fortunately, as people interact, they learn what to expect of each other. Also, groups emerge as some individuals interact more frequently and come to see themselves as possessing common goals. Social structure refers to behavioral and attitudinal patterns that add stability to relationships and that define how one social system differs from another. Social systems lack the fixed physical structures of biological systems and are instead structured around the *meanings* that organizational members attach to organizational events (Katz & Kahn, 1978; Rentsch, 1990). Five particularly important structural concepts are interaction patterns, norms, roles, cohesiveness, and climate/culture.

## Interaction Patterns

"Who interacts with whom?" is an obvious question to ask when analyzing a social structure. Individuals in any group or organization come to interact more with some people than with others. Let us assume that you observe a group of design engineers who have been assigned to a project team. You note that some of these engineers interact on a frequent basis for the obvious reason that they have been assigned to work together on the same task and to report to the same boss. Many of the most interesting relationships you observe, however, are those that are not intended by the organization but instead emerge from daily interactions. You might, for instance, find that two of the design engineers are loners who work by themselves, whereas three others work together closely. Two employees from another unit are frequently observed in the offices of these three to chat about work and nonwork related matters. Moreover, one of the isolated design engineers has a personal relationship with a manager in another department. These types of relationships define the "hidden organization" and can be as important as the formal relationships identified in the organizational chart.

A common method of studying interaction patterns is to observe and tally who actually interacts with whom. In one such study, 29 clerical employees in a large office were observed over a two-week period (Gullahorn, 1955), with observations made every 15 minutes of interactions. From 1,558 recorded interactions, three clusters of secretaries were identified that seemed to constitute informal relationships. Data such as these can be subjected to *network analysis,* a quantitative technique that can identify clusters of interactions and measure the characteristics of these clusters. Using this technique, for instance, a network's *openness* could be measured by examining how many interactions people inside the network have with those outside the network. Networks are open to the extent that there are numerous interactions with outsiders. Another important structural characteristic is *connectedness,* or the number of direct interactions among members of the network relative to the total possible interactions. The network with the highest degree of connectedness would be one in which every member interacts with every other member.

An important characteristic of any social network is the degree to which the network is centralized. In a highly *centralized* network, information must pass through a person in a central position, whereas in a *decentralized* network information passes more freely among members. In the 1950s and 1960s social psychologists conducted many experiments in which they manipulated the nature of the communication network and examined the effects on group functioning (Shaw, 1964). Group members were placed in cubicles and different paths were arranged through which they could send messages. Figure 5.3 presents several of the four-person networks that were examined. The most centralized of these were the kite and wheel (in which there was a central person), whereas the more decentralized networks were the comcon (in which everyone could communicate with everyone else) and the circle (in which each member could communicate with the adjacent members).

A consistent finding was that members of decentralized networks were more satisfied than members of centralized networks. The most satisfied members of the centralized networks were those in the central positions. The effects of the network on performance depended on the nature of the task. With simple tasks, for which the answers were obvious and the group only needed to pull together all the available information, the centralized networks performed better than the decentralized networks. In complex tasks, however, the central person tended to become overloaded with data and performance deteriorated. Consequently, decentralized networks tended to per-

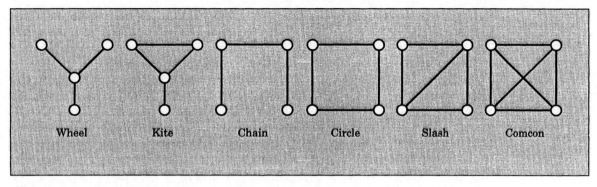

**Figure 5.3**  *Four-person communication networks*

form better than centralized networks on complex tasks. Although the research conducted with these configurations is quite artificial, the findings appear to support a general principle that holds across a variety of social and biological systems. The so-called *Ashby's Law of Requisite Variety* states that as the information in the environment becomes increasingly complex, the social system must also increase in complexity to process the information.

Network analysis can help identify a social entity that is crucial to accomplishing the objectives of an organization: the *group*. Although there are differences among scholars on how to best define a group, we will define it as a collection of individuals who not only interact frequently, but also perceive themselves to be a group. *Formal groups* consist of those collections that are created by the organization to achieve work objectives. *Informal groups* are those that emerge from the daily interactions of people in the organization and are not officially recognized by the organization. How well an organization functions and the satisfaction of its members are influenced by whether the informal groups are congruent with the formal groups.

How do groups form? For a group to emerge there must first be an *opportunity* and then a *reason* for interaction. People who are physically close, and who consequently have an opportunity to interact, are more likely to form a group than those who are farther apart. For instance, in the observation of the 29 secretaries described earlier, 78% of the interactions occurred in the row in which the employee sat. The three groups that emerged consisted of employees who sat in the same row. In addition to an opportunity, employees must also have a reason to interact. This is most likely to occur when individuals are interdependent and must cooperate to achieve their individual and collective goals. People are also likely to interact when interaction fulfills personal needs. The needs for affiliation and esteem are perhaps most obviously related to why individuals might form a group, but groups can form to fulfill other needs such as hunger, security, and self-actualization. An additional reason that groups emerge is to define reality. People attempt to validate their personal beliefs (e.g., opposition to abortion, belief in God, advocacy of gun control) by joining with others who share similar beliefs. *Social information processing theory,* which was discussed in the last chapter, proposes that an employee's feelings about his or her job are influenced more by the views of fellow group members than by objective reality (Salancik & Pfeffer, 1978).

Different types of groups form within an organization, depending on the needs that they fulfill. Some groups serve to fulfill primary task goals, as when two employees decide to collaborate and bypass the formal chain of command. This collaboration may not be insubordination as much as a desire to get the job done. Similarly, the information that flows through the grapevine in an organization can provide valuable information that assists in performing tasks. Other groups form on the basis of purely personal attraction. Not surprisingly, people are more likely to form groups if they are similar in their attitudes, gender, personalities, race, economic status, education, and age than if they differ on these and other personal characteristics (Lincoln & Miller, 1979). It seems unlikely that you could clearly separate where friendship ends and work begins in the informal networks that emerge within organizations. An unfortunate consequence of groups based on gender is that men may form an organizational network that effectively limits the career opportunities of women (Brass, 1985).

## Social Norms

The beliefs that people hold in common and that govern their behavior and attitudes are a second type of social structure you would look for in observing an organization or group. In observing a group, for instance, you might notice that all members wear a coat and tie when attending meetings, that they address the team leader and each other by formal titles (e.g., Dr., Mr., Ms.), and that members never openly criticize the organization. You have undoubtedly experienced norms first hand, although you may not have been fully aware of them at the time. Consider those situations in which you were the newcomer and found that your behavior did not match the behavior of others. If you were lucky, someone took you aside and warned you that "we don't do *that* around here." If your weren't so lucky, you may have suffered embarrassment or public ridicule. An interesting aspect of this type of situation is that people in an organization may be quite shocked that you did not act as they do. In other words, individuals often take the norms that dictate their behavior for granted, seldom thinking about them until a deviant violates them.

Norms are essentially *expectations* for how persons in a group or organization should behave, what attitudes they should express, and how they should appear. Norms can come from the demands of the task, the formal rules set down by the organization's management, or from people's past experiences in dealing with particular situations. Norms exist only for issues that are of particular significance for the group (Feldman, 1984, p. 47). Feldman (1984) describes four conditions under which norms emerge and are enforced:

1.  When they facilitate group survival, as in the case of norms against discussing salaries or discussing internal problems of a group with outsiders.
2.  When they help members perform tasks by making behaviors expected by group or organizational members more predictable.
3.  When they help the group avoid embarrassing or disruptive situations, as in the case of norms against coworkers openly discussing romantic relationships.
4.  When they express some central value or clarify what is unique about the organization or group. For example, the conservative dress that is expected in an accounting firm may exist in part to convey stability, whereas the flashy clothes that are the norm in an advertising agency could convey creativity.

There are several ways of measuring norms. Observing the behavior of group members and looking for patterns is one approach. A more direct method is to ask group members what types of behaviors and attitudes are approved and disapproved. Researchers using Jackson's (1965) *return potential model* (RPM) to measure norms have each person in a group rate how others would react if he or she behaved in a certain way. If you used the RPM to measure the norms of a work group for productivity, you would first ask each employee to indicate for several levels of productivity the extent to which other employees would approve or disapprove. The expected approval or disapproval for each level of performance would define the norm. The shape and other characteristics of this relationship would indicate important attributes of the norm. For instance, a particularly important feature of the RPM is the levels of productivity believed to evoke the greatest approval and the greatest disapproval.

Assume that you ask members of two different work groups how much other group members would disapprove or approve if they were to show various levels of productivity (highly approve, indifferent, highly disapprove). On the basis of the members' combined responses you could draw a *return potential curve* for each of these work groups showing the distribution of approval-disapproval among members. You might note that the return potential curves look something like those in Figure 5.4. Group A is management's dream team in that members expect that more productivity will lead to higher peer approval and low productivity will lead to strong disapproval. Group B is perhaps more representative of past research on productivity norms (Roethlisberger & Dickson, 1939; Roy, 1952; Hickson, 1961). In this group, members expect some disapproval if their productivity is too low, but they also expect that if they rise above a certain level of productivity their peers will react with strong disapproval. There are several possible reasons that members might have norms that restrict productivity (Rambo, 1982). Such norms may represent an agreement to cooperate rather than compete, thereby

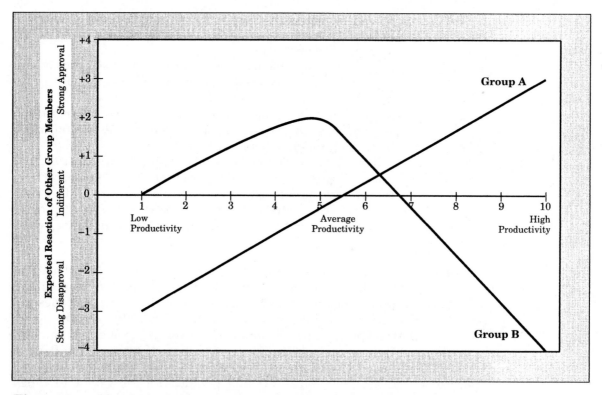

**Figure 5.4** *The application of Jackson's RPM to describe two norms*

maintaining congenial relations. The most frequently cited reason for restriction in productivity is the anticipation of group members that management will adjust work standards upward in response to increased productivity. These norms also may emerge as the result of attempts to maintain equity (see Chapter 3 for a discussion of equity theory). Restricting productivity can allow for free time in which employees release tension and enjoy themselves (Roy, 1960; Johnson, 1974). Finally, restricting productivity can be a form of aggression against management. One of the authors of this text observed this firsthand in a steel mill where employees slowed production to a level far below standards as a way of retaliating against a dictatorial plant manager.

Several characteristics of the norms can be measured by the RPM. The *point of maximum return* is defined as the level of behavior that receives the highest approval. In group A the most approval is given to the highest level of performance, whereas in group B it is the moderate level of performance that receives the most approval. The *range of tolerable behavior* refers to the range of behaviors that is approved by group members. In group A the range of productivity that is approved is narrower than in group B. The *potential return difference* is computed by taking the highest level of approval and subtracting from this value the highest level of disapproval. Group B's negative potential return difference (−2) suggests that this group relies more on punishment in enforcing productivity norms, whereas the zero value for group A suggests that it relies as much on positive as negative reinforcement. Finally, the *crystallization of the norms* is computed by assessing how much members agree on what they expect to result from each level of a behavior. In the examples in Figure 5.4, the more group members agree on the extent to which each productivity level is approved or disapproved, the stronger the norms.

When a norm is widely accepted by the group, members who deviate from this norm can find themselves under severe pressures to conform. Observations of work groups have clearly demonstrated that such groups are quick to pressure their members. One of the important findings of the Hawthorne studies (Chapter 4) was that members of work groups exerted pressure on their fellow employees to enforce norms for productivity. When an employee violated a productivity norm, other members would give that employee a playful whack on the arm (a "bing") as a reminder to slow down. The types of power that groups use in attempting to achieve conformity to norms include all the power bases that we discussed earlier (i.e., rewards, coercions, reference to legitimate authority, friendship, expertise). Although there are individual differences in susceptibility to group pressure (Miller & Grush, 1988; Chapter 3), group members generally show a remarkable willingness to comply even when the pressures are subtle.

## Social Roles

Another pattern of behavior you will observe in groups and organizations is how people divide up their duties. Not everyone does exactly the same thing. Some of the division of labor is the result of a formal process whereby people are hired into formal positions with specific responsibilities. Some of the division of labor is more informal, however, and emerges from interactions of individuals with each other. A *social role* can be defined as a type of norm dictating how a person in a particular position should act or feel. Figure 5.5 contains Katz and Kahn's (1978) model of the process by which a role emerges. According to their model, each person in the organization occupies an *office* and is engaged in a network of relationships with other people inside and outside the organization. Katz and Kahn (1978, p. 189) use the following analogy: "Imagine the organization spread out like a vast fish net, with each knot in this net representing an office and each string a functional relationship between offices. If we pick up the net by seizing any office, the offices to which it is directly attached are immediately seen." The other knots to which the office is directly attached constitute the *role set,* which consists of those who participate in defining the role of the focal person. Supervisors and coworkers are likely to be the most obvious members of the role set. Other persons are not as obvious, but just as important, such as the spouse who

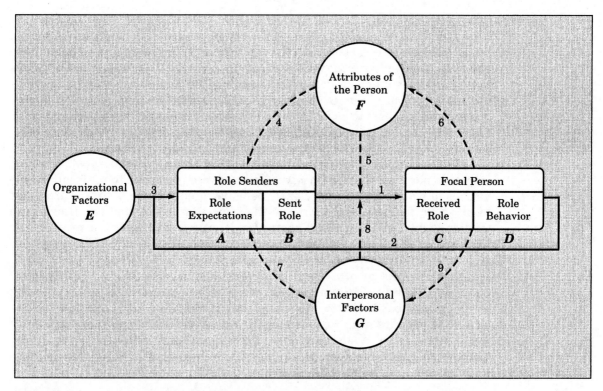

**Figure 5.5**  *Katz and Kahn's (1978) model of role taking*
*Source:* Katz, D., & Kahn, R.L. (1978). *The Social Psychology of Organizations.* New York: John Wiley.

expects more time at home or the members of the bowling team who expect Wednesday nights to be spent practicing.

In Katz and Kahn's role-taking model, roles emerge from communication and influence processes. People adopt a particular role through repeated episodes in which members of the role set communicate what they expect and then act to bring the focal person in line with these expectations. A problem with the Katz and Kahn approach is that they view the sending and taking of roles as a one-way process. In reality, a role emerges as the result of a two-way process in which the focal person not only takes a role but to some extent *makes* a role (Graen, 1976). Employees seldom give in entirely to demands of others but often engage in subtle negotiations with the members of the role set in defining what is appropriate role behavior.

An almost endless number of social roles can be identified in a group or organization. However, two general categories of roles within groups have repeatedly emerged (Benne & Sheats, 1948). Some roles focus on socioemotional issues, such as resolving conflicts among people, meeting individual member needs, and ensuring that everyone has a chance to participate in group tasks. Other roles focus more on task issues, such as clarifying responsibilities, planning, organizing, and keeping the group on track. These roles seem to reflect two fundamental requirements of any social system: to maintain the system by making sure that people do not leave the system (maintenance function) and to fulfill the goals of the system (task functions). In the next chapter, we discuss how leadership styles can be distinguished along these same basic functions.

## Social Cohesion

Have you ever been in a group whose members were very close to one another and believed deeply in the group's mission? Have you ever been in a group whose members generally disliked each other and seemed on the verge of disbanding with every meeting? This structural aspect of groups, *social cohesiveness,* has been defined as the *resultant* of forces acting on members to keep them in the group and forces acting on members to leave the group (Cartwright & Zander, 1968). In other words, consider all the forces pushing members to stay with the group and then subtract all the forces that encourage their leaving the group. The difference (the resultant) would be group cohesiveness. Cohesiveness has been criticized for a lack of clarity in its conceptualization (Drescher, Burlingame, & Fuhriman, 1985; Mudrack, 1989). Nevertheless, psychologists continue to use it as a construct because of its strong heuristic value in understanding groups in organizations.

The attractiveness of the group for its members seems to be the primary force keeping members together, and can result from such factors as similarity in the personal characteristics of members, their success in achieving goals together, external threats, and the satisfaction of their individual needs (e.g., their affiliation needs) (Lott & Lott, 1965). The attractiveness of alternative group memberships serves as a primary force on members to leave the group. Thus, if members have other groups to join that can fulfill their needs or achieve important goals, then the group is less likely to stick together than if there are few or no alternatives.

Cohesiveness has several important effects. The most direct effect is to maintain the membership of the group. Thus, the members of a highly cohesive group should show less turnover than a group that is low in cohesion. Another important effect of cohesion is to increase the power of the group over its members. As a consequence, individual differences among group members in their compliance to norms should decrease as the cohesiveness of the group increases (Seashore, 1954). Members of a cohesive group seem more likely to accept attempts of other members to influence them, less likely to blame the group for failures, and more likely to accept personal responsibility for the group's failures (Seashore, 1954; Schlenker & Miller, 1977). Finally, members of cohesive groups also appear more satisfied with the group, more likely to interact in a friendly and congenial fashion with each other, and less likely to experience anxiety and stress (Shaw, 1976).

With all these positive effects you might expect that a cohesive group is also a productive group. Contrary to expectations, however, the relationship with performance is complex, with past research showing cohesion to lead to low performance about as often as high performance (Stogdill, 1972). The task and the norms of the group are crucial contingency variables. If the task is adversely affected by high levels of stress, then cohesion may indeed enhance performance. For example, soldiers in cohesive groups appear to perform better in combat than soldiers in less cohesive units (Greenbaum, 1979; Shirom, 1976). Cohesion appears more likely to enhance performance on tasks that require cooperation than on tasks requiring mainly individual effort (Shaw, 1976). Finally, increased cohesion is likely to improve performance when the group has a strong norm for high performance, but it will lower performance if the group has a norm for low performance (Seashore, 1954).

## Climate and Culture

In describing a group or an organization the various structural characteristics often appear to hang together in a profile that defines the uniqueness of that organization or group. Imagine that you are an observer at Mystic Software. As you stroll through the corridors you find informally dressed employees (jeans, no neckties), and small groups engaged in lively conversations of a social nature. Offices are without doors and are decorated with posters and cartoons. Everyone shares the same cafeteria and parking spaces, and managers and nonmanagers are on a first-name basis. Across town in the corridors of Mystic's competitor, High Tech Incorporated, you find a much different organization. Employees dressed formally in dark business suits are busily at work. The conversation is more subdued than at Mystic Software and focused primarily on work matters. Managers have their own parking spaces and cafeteria. Managers tend to use first names in talking to their subordinates, whereas subordinates use Mr. or Ms. in referring to their managers. Managers have doors on their offices, whereas nonmanagerial employees do not. The hallways have a few paintings, but the walls of employee offices are mostly undecorated. What you have observed could be described as part of the *culture or climate* of these organizations. Culture and climate encompass all the structural forms we have covered and are analogous to the personality of an individual.

There is considerable disagreement as to whether culture and climate should be treated as separate concepts. Schein (1990) believes that climate is only the "surface manifestation of culture" and that measurement of culture requires more qualitative research, using in-depth interviews and observation to probe the values and norms of the organization. Schneider (1987) sees climate as that "which focuses on how the organization functions (what it rewards, supports, and expects), while culture addresses the assumptions and values attributed to why particular activities and behaviors are rewarded, supported, and expected. Culture focuses then on why things happen as they do, on the meaning or reason for what happens" (p. 448). We tend to agree with an alternative position that differences in these two concepts are superficial and that the similarities outweigh the differences (Glick, 1985). Nevertheless, given the differences in the intellectual roots of each approach, we will devote separate attention to the issues surrounding each concept.

## ORGANIZATIONAL CLIMATE

The concept of organizational climate emerged from Kurt Lewin's (1951) field theory. According to Lewin, an individual's behavior results from the characteristics of the person (i.e., that individual's personality traits, abilities, experience, etc.) and the psychological environment of the person (i.e., the way that individual perceives the surrounding environment). Organizational climate questionnaires attempt to measure the individual's perceptions of the total organizational environment. For example, the *Profile of Organizational Characteristics,* based on the work of Likert (1961), distinguishes among four basic types of organizations. *System 1* (exploitative authoritarian) organizations are characterized by little confidence and trust in subordinates, use of fear and threats, a lack of teamwork, downward flow of communication, and centralized decision making. At the other extreme are *System 4* organizations (participative), which are characterized by confidence and trust in subordinates, employee involvement, free-flowing communication, teamwork, and participative decision making. In between these two extremes are *System 2* (benevolent authoritarian) and *System 3* (consultative).

The 25 years of research on organizational climate have been marked by debates that are still largely unresolved (Glick, 1985). Critics of the concept have noted that organizational climate measures look suspiciously like measures of other constructs and may add little information. For instance, doubts have been raised as to whether organizational climate is conceptually distinct from job satisfaction (Guion, 1973). Other criticisms have been aimed at the failure to distinguish between objective organizational characteristics and the perceptions of these characteristics. Some have argued that *organizational climate* should be used for the former, whereas *psychological climate* should be used in referring to the latter (James & Jones, 1974).

## ORGANIZATIONAL CULTURE

Unlike organizational climate, which is the product of psychological research, the concept of organizational culture comes from anthropology and sociology. Perhaps the most common element in the many different definitions of culture is a *shared pattern of thought and action* that distinguishes the organization or group from other organizations or groups. Culture can be described in terms of both direction (e.g., whether the leadership is authoritarian or democratic) and intensity (e.g., whether people agree in their descriptions of leadership). Thus, organizations not only differ in cultural content, but also in the extent to which the values and other contents of the culture are shared by those in the organization. A *weak culture* is hard to describe because there is no widely shared set of values and assumptions. A *strong culture* is easier to describe because members are influenced by a common set of values and assumptions. In a strong culture each subsequent wave of new members is taught the correct assumptions, values, and beliefs of the organization by old members. Culture is maintained in part through the stories that people tell about heroic feats of members of the organization. The company's founder may be frequently discussed as a model that employees should attempt to imitate.

### FUNCTIONAL AND DYSFUNCTIONAL CULTURES

Some writers claim that highly successful firms almost always have strong cultures (Peters & Waterman, 1982). An example is Dillard's department stores, which have succeeded despite the failure of many other moderately priced department stores (Hymowitz & O'Boyle, 1991). Still run by its founder, Dillard's has no central personnel department and relatives of present employees are often given preference in hiring. According to one store manager, "There's real direction here because there's one vision and little management turnover. When I worked for another retailer, I had three different bosses in four years. One was into volume sales, another into cutting operational expenses, the third into image. At Dillard's you know the strategy: We carry lots of good, name-brand merchandise and deliver good service" (Hymowitz & O'Boyle, 1991, p. A9).

Strong cultures also can be dysfunctional. A possible example is a large defense contractor that has been accused of numerous legal violations in its dealings with the Pentagon (Wartzman, 1992). The violations of the law in this company seem to reflect a deep-rooted set of norms and values that the chairman of this corporation is attempting to change. He has set forth six values for the company: "delivering customer satisfaction, treating colleagues with respect, regarding suppliers as 'team members,' taking responsibility for quality, demonstrating integrity, and providing leadership" (Wartzman, 1992, p. A4). Among the steps taken to make sure that these values take root are personal visits by the company chairman with groups of employees and ethics classes for managers.

A dysfunctional organizational culture also has been implicated as a possible cause of sexual harassment. In recent years the public has become much more aware of the existence of sexual harassment in organizations, possibly as the result of the controversy surrounding the charges of Anita Hill against Supreme Court nominee Clarence Thomas. Although the personal characteristics of the individuals involved are important causes of these types of incidents, a study conducted by Gutek (1985) suggests that the organizational culture is also important. In her research she conducted telephone interviews with 827 working women and 405 working men in southern California. She found that sexual harassment was much more common in organizations where flirting and swearing were commonplace, and on the basis of this evidence suggested that sexual harassment is a "part of a cluster of unprofessional behavior and attitudes—an unprofessional ambience—that characterizes some work places" (p. 124). Scandals such as the assaults on

Anita Hill's charges against then Supreme Court nominee Clarence Thomas have focused attention on sexual harassment in the workplace. The culture of the organization can be an important factor in encouraging or discouraging harassing behavior.

women in the U.S. Navy's Tailhook association have spawned attempts by the military services to change those aspects of the culture that support the demeaning of women. These attempts have included training sessions to sensitize military personnel to the issues as well as integrating basic training to include both men and women recruits.

Changing norms, roles, and values that are deeply entrenched in an organizational culture is a difficult and in many cases impossible venture. Popular management books have led some managers and human resource practitioners into culture-building interventions that are terribly naive. One of the authors knows of a large organization in which a top level executive read some of the popular literature and directed his human resource management department to move quickly to develop a new culture for his organization. The response was to circulate a videotape that showed a series of employees stating the values of the company. Needless to say, there was no evidence that a strong culture suddenly took root. A culture must evolve over time and is difficult to manipulate or shape.

Not only is it difficult to quickly install a strong culture, but there are potential downsides in addition to those already discussed. It might lead an organization down the path to ruin by fostering resistance to change or insensitivity to the environment. Another potential problem is the stifling of diversity and creativity. Also, questions can be raised as to the ethics of demanding the conformity of all employees to a dominant set of values and norms.

### SHARED MEANING

A more recent trend is to focus on culture and climate as the *meaning* that employees attribute to organizational events. James and James (1989) found that employees follow the model presented in Figure 5.6 in making sense of their organizational environments. They propose that employees perceive their organizations in terms of four general factors: leader support and

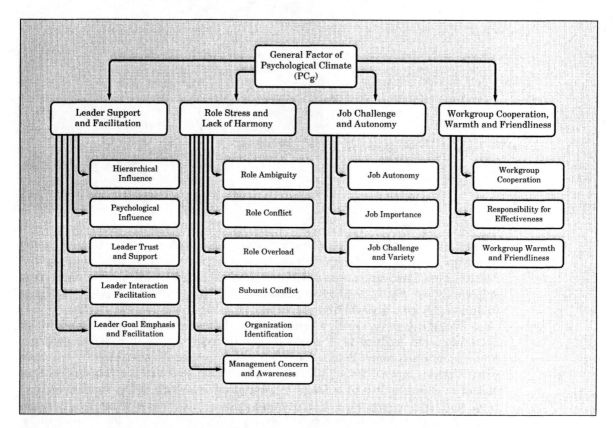

**Figure 5.6** *A hierarchical model of organizational climate*
*Source:* James, L.A., & James, L.R. (1989). Integrating work environment perceptions: Explorations in the measurement of meaning. *Journal of Applied Psychology, 74,* 739–751.

facilitation; role stress and lack of harmony; job challenge and autonomy; and work group cooperation, warmth, and friendliness. Each of these factors, in turn, can be reduced to more specific subfactors. Underlying all descriptions of the organization, however, is a factor they label *general psychological climate* ($PC_g$). This general factor reflects the tendency of employees to judge all aspects of the organization on the basis of whether it personally benefits them. The unresolved issue in this study is whether $PC_g$ differs to an important extent from job satisfaction.

### Summary

People in a group or organization develop stable patterns of relations that make life more predictable. The specific social structures that emerge are determined by the context, the personal characteristics of the people involved, and the functions that these structures serve. As the result of task and personal needs, individuals form stable work and social relationships within the organization. Norms and roles emerge that dictate how group participants should behave. Mutual attractions also form between individuals, and the extent to which there are many mutual attractions relative to the total possible attractions determines the cohesiveness of a group. Over time a culture or climate can emerge that encompasses all the other structural forms and reflects the meaning attached to events in the organization by employees.

# THE MATURATION AND DECLINE OF SOCIAL SYSTEMS

Have you ever been part of a group that struggled to achieve its objectives at the beginning but in which things "clicked" and fell into place at some critical juncture as people learned to work together? Have you ever been part of a group that worked together beautifully for a time, but then eventually became so fixed in its ways that it declined in effectiveness? These experiences reflect the fact that social systems, like individuals, mature, grow old, and die. Groups and organizations appear to move through phases as their members interact over time; the phases that emerge are likely to depend on the nature of the social entity.

Tuckman (1965) concluded from a review of research on discussion and therapy groups that groups go through four phases. First, there is the *forming* phase, in which members get to know each other. Second, there is the *storming* phase, in which differences in orientation and struggles for leadership emerge. Third, the group enters a *norming* stage, in which people's roles, norms, and other structural arrangements emerge and members have a clearer idea of what to expect of each other. Norming sets the stage for the *performing* phase, in which members get down to the task at hand.

The problem with the Tuckman model is that it is based mostly on observations of therapy groups in which people do not know each other in the beginning and the agenda is unstructured. Groups that are formed to accomplish specific tasks within a defined time may show a much different pattern of development. Gersick (1988) examined eight diverse work groups and found a pattern she called *punctuated equilibrium*. She observed that in the first meeting of the group, assumptions and orientations emerged in the discussion that served as a framework for the group's work for about the first half of its existence. Groups would typically show little visible progress until about half way through the allotted calendar time. At that point, a crisis would often occur in the life of the group in which members would become acutely aware of the urgency to get on with the task. According to Gersick, a group goes through a transition in its midlife that provides an opportunity for the group to alter its course of action and its plans.

Another developmental trend is the tendency for mature groups to become more inflexible and to lose some of their creative edge. Katz (1982) found that the productivity of project groups increased up to 3–5 years and declined thereafter. These downturns in performance were paralleled by downturns in communication among members within project groups, within organizations, and with external professionals (Figure 5.7). According to the researchers, working together over a long period leads to increasing homogeneity in task strategies and increasing isolation from outside information sources.

Schneider (1987) suggested that whole organizations may decline in the manner observed by Katz and proposed the *attraction–selection–attrition (ASA)* framework as a possible explanation. According to the ASA model, an organization becomes increasingly homogeneous in the characteristics of its employees as the result of three forces. First, people are initially attracted to organizations that appear to fit their personalities. For instance, people with strong needs for competition and achievement are more attracted to an organization whose climate stresses competition and achievement than people with strong needs for affiliation. Second, organizations tend to select those people whose personalities fit the characteristics of those currently employed. Third, those who join the organization who do not fit the characteristics of current employees will tend to leave. Over time, organizations become ingrown and "severely restricted in the range of types of people in them" (p. 444). This spells trouble if the organization must deal with a changing environment. An interesting aspect of the ASA model is that people are believed to make the place. In other words, norms, roles, and other structural forms emerge from the types of people drawn to a group or organization. According to Schneider, if an organization wishes to change, it should attract and retain different types of people rather than working exclusively on changing the structure of the organization.

Most of what has been written about the development of groups and organizations is speculative and many questions remain. Will a punctuated equilibrium model apply to groups that meet continuously without any specific, definable life? Is the decline of group performance observed by Katz

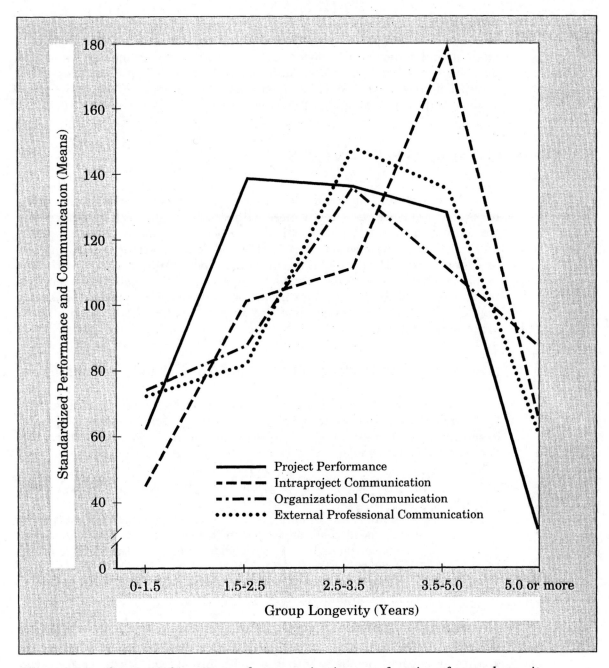

**Figure 5.7** *Group performance and communication as a function of group longevity*
*Source:* Katz, R. (1982). The effects of group longevity on project communication and performance. *Administrative Science Quarterly, 27,* 81–104.

more likely to occur in research and development groups than in other types of groups? Do groups and organizations that operate in a stable, predictable environment suffer from homogeneity to the extent that Schneider would lead us to believe in his ASA model? More research is needed on these fascinating issues before we can conclude much about how organizations and groups develop and the impact of this development on performance.

# IMPROVING GROUP EFFECTIVENESS

We have been concerned with describing the social processes and structures that influence the effectiveness with which people work together. Next we address the question of how this information can improve social processes and structures. The discussion so far has included a variety of social behaviors ranging from the dyadic interactions of individuals to the culture of whole organizations; we now focus on ways to improve the effectiveness of a particular type of social entity: the work group. We first consider some of the factors crucial to group effectiveness and the reasons that a group might fail to achieve its potential.

## Hackman and Morris's (1975) Model of Group Effectiveness

Hackman and Morris (1975) presented a model (Figure 5.8) that is helpful in understanding the factors that influence the effectiveness of groups. According to their reasoning, an effective group must deal with three key issues (summary variables):

1. The members of the group must invest *effort* in the task and *coordinate* their efforts.
2. Members must employ *task performance strategies* appropriate to the task. Strategies in this case refer to the "collective choices made by group members about how they will go about performing the task" (p. 65).
3. The group must use the *knowledge and skill* of its members in an optimal manner.

The input variables influence how well a group performs on these three summary variables. Group composition refers to such factors as whether the group has enough members with the right mix of abilities to perform the work. Group norms are the expectations of members for how they are to work together. Group task design includes whether the task is high in what Hackman and Oldham (1976) call motivating potential (Chapter 3) and whether the task encourages cooperation and the sharing of responsibility. These input variables can directly influence how the group performs on the three

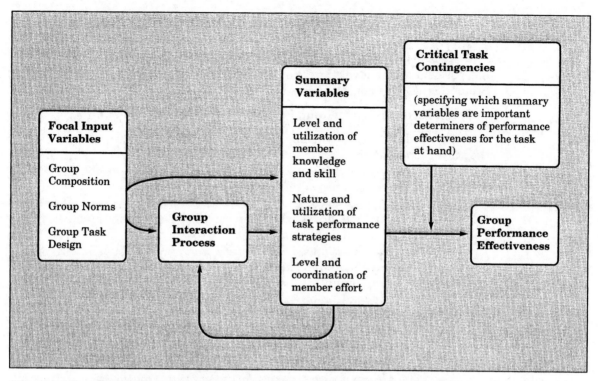

**Figure 5.8**   *The Hackman and Morris (1975) model of group effectiveness*
*Source:* Hackman, J.R., & Morris, C.G. (1975). Group tasks, group interaction process, and group performance effectiveness: A review and proposed integration. In L. Berkowitz (Ed.) *Advances in Experimental Social Psychology.* (Vol. 8) New York: Academic Press, p. 47–95.

summary variables as well as indirectly influence the summary variables through shaping interaction processes. Thus, a characteristic of group composition such as heterogeneity of member characteristics can directly influence the level of knowledge and skill brought to bear on the task. Heterogeneity of members also could influence the level of conflict in a group, thus indirectly shaping utilization of member knowledge, level of effort and coordination, and task strategies. This is not a one-way street. As shown in Figure 5.8, the group's interaction process not only influences how the group performs on the summary variables, but, in turn, how the group performs on these variables influences interaction processes. A final link in the model is the influence of the summary variables on the group's performance effectiveness. Although it is necessary to do well in relation to the three summary variables, whether achieving a high level of each of these factors translates into effective performance depends on the nature of the task. As stated in the model, the critical task contingencies determine which of the summary variables are most important. For instance, brute exertion of effort would probably be more important for a task that requires mostly effort than on a complex problem-solving task in which task strategies and member knowledge are crucial.

# Why Do Groups So Often Fail to Achieve Their Potential?

Decades of research on group effectiveness suggest that groups often do not perform at the level that they are capable of performing. Borrowing from Steiner (1972) one could express this as

Group Productivity = Group Potential − Process Losses + Process Gains

In other words, groups invariably lose in some ways and gain in others when they meet to tackle problems, but the losses often outweigh the gains. Indeed, the process gains often remain potential rather than being realized. Some of the potential process gains commonly observed in groups are:

1. *Social facilitation.* The mere presence of other members can have an energizing effect.
2. *Increased knowledge, ability, and effort.* Groups invariably have more information they can bring to a task than any one individual. Also, as the saying goes, "many hands make light the load." More energy can be devoted to a task by a group than by any single individual.
3. *Diversity of views.* The diversity of opinions and approaches can serve as a valuable resource for a group. One member's deficiencies are often balanced by others' strengths.
4. *Group pressures to conform to norms.* Once a group arrives at a decision, the pressures of the group on individuals can be a powerful force in implementing solutions.

Unfortunately, each of the above potential advantages can serve as a source of process loss:

1. *Social interference and loafing.* The mere presence of others can lead to anxiety and thus detract from performance, particularly on complex tasks. Also, group members tend to exert less effort when their individual products are not identifiable. So-called "social loafing" has been observed across a wide variety of tasks.
2. *Failure to use available knowledge and abilities.* Groups often assign weights to individual contributions within the group on the basis of perceived expertise rather than actual expertise. Some research, for example, has revealed that the amount of time that members spent talking was a stronger predictor of how much they influenced final group decisions than actual expertise.
3. *Diversity of views can lead to conflict.* Groups can fall into win-lose competition in which members fight to win arguments rather than work to achieve group goals.
4. *Groupthink.* Groups can tend to pressure their members into an unthinking conformity. Janis (1982, 1972) found that

high-level decision making groups in the government and military could fall prey to *groupthink*. He defined this phenomenon as "a mode of thinking that people engage in when they are deeply involved in a cohesive in-group, when the members' striving for unanimity overrides their motivation to realistically appraise alternative courses of action" (Janis, 1972, p. 9).

## Strategies for Improving Group Performance

The question now arises as to how to maximize the process gains and minimize the process losses. One approach is to use selection and recruitment to ensure that the right mix of skills are represented in the organization (Chapter 10). Here we focus on changing structure and process. The change strategies often are included in the general category of *organizational development* (OD), which has been defined as "a process of planned change . . . of an organization's culture from one which avoids an examination of social processes . . . to one which institutionalizes and legitimizes this examination" (Burke & Hornstein, 1972, p. xi). Among the strategies used to improve group performance are team building and process consultation, problem-solving techniques, autonomous work groups, feedback, goal setting, and rewards.

### TEAM BUILDING AND PROCESS CONSULTATION

These are the most comprehensive of all the interventions to improve group performance and are similar in many respects. In *team building,* attempts are made to improve group functioning through helping members learn to work together and through changing structural factors (e.g., norms, patterns of interactions, roles) (Porter, Lawler, & Hackman, 1975). As noted by Dyer (1987), team building is not a single action but an entire process. This process should begin with a diagnosis in which the consultant works with group members to collect information through interviews, observation, and questionnaires about how well the group works as a team. Next, the data are summarized and priorities set as to what the group should attempt to change. A problem-solving process ensues in which the group arrives at possible solutions to the identified problems. As they engage in this problem solving, the consultant provides feedback and coaching on how members of the group relate to one another. Finally, the group implements and later evaluates the effectiveness of the solutions.

Kaplan (1977) defined *process consultation* as "a method for diagnosing and acting upon the human processes of work groups. It is a mechanism by which the parties in a relationship, usually with the assistance of a consultant, attempt to discover and solve problems in their work together" (p. 347). Schein (1969) identifies several types of process interventions. With *agenda setting,* the attention of group members is focused on internal processes that are critical to task success but that are usually ignored by the group. A consultant might meet with a group after each of their meetings and review with them observations of events that occurred: How did the leader handle the discussion? How did members deal with conflict? Were there hidden agendas? What task strategies did the members use? *Survey feedback* involves the use of a questionnaire or series of interviews to gather data on how members see their process. The results of the survey are then presented to the group for discussion in a survey feedback meeting. Through the discussion of the results, members may identify problems that have blocked successful performance and generate solutions to these problems. The consultant usually guides them through this process. Finally, *coaching* of the group or members by the consultant is a third type of process intervention. The consultant might take a problem member aside, for instance, and attempt to counsel the member concerning his or her relations with the group.

The jury is still out on whether process consultation and team building can improve the performance of a group. Team building has been shown to improve members' satisfaction and their perceptions of how well the group is performing (Woodman & Sherwood, 1980; Neuman, Edwards, & Raju, 1989). However, the few well-controlled studies that have tracked the effects of team building on objective measures of performance are inconclusive (Buller & Bell, 1986). Similarly, few studies have evaluated the effects of process consultation on organizational tasks, and the evidence gathered so far does not appear encouraging (Kaplan, 1977).

There are severe problems in evaluating all types of OD interventions, including process consultation and team building. Because the content of these interventions can vary dramatically from one case to another, it is difficult to evaluate what is responsible for their success or failure. Findings with one team-building or process consultation intervention may not apply to another intervention.

Another potential problem in OD research is the reliance on self-report questionnaires in measuring social process. Staw (1975) and Gladstein (1984) suggested that self-reports of process may reflect members' personal theories of how effective groups behave rather than what actually happened in their group. For instance, Staw (1975) conducted an experiment in which groups worked on a task and then were given false feedback that they were in the upper or lower 20% on the task. Those receiving success feedback described their groups as more cohesive, more egalitarian, more open in communications, and less prone to conflict than those told they had failed. Similar findings were reported by Gladstein (1984) in a field setting. Social process cannot be ignored, but these findings clearly show that research using objective process measures is needed to evaluate process consultation and team building.

Golembiewski, Billingsley, and Yeager (1976) pointed out a second problem in using self-report measures to evaluate OD interventions. They proposed that changes in numerical ratings on the questionnaires typically used in evaluating OD interventions confound three types of change: alpha, beta, and gamma change. *Alpha change* is a shift in the numerical rating that reflects real change in the target of the intervention. *Beta change* is a recalibration of the scale. *Gamma change* is the redefinition of the construct under-lying the scale. As an illustration, assume that you participated in a team-building program intended to increase the openness of group members in communicating with each other. To evaluate the effectiveness of the program, members of your group are asked to rate on a scale of 1 to 7 how open the group is in its communications, with 1 labeled as "very closed" and 7 "very open." Assume that before the team-building intervention the average response was 6. After the intervention, the average response is 4. Should we conclude that the team-building intervention failed and actually led to more closed communications within the group? Golembiewski and his colleagues would answer "not necessarily."

Although we hope in using a measure that the difference in rating we observe is an alpha change, the extent of real change is often masked by two other types of changes (Golembiewski et al. 1976). The shift from 6 to 4 could reflect beta change in the form of a redefinition of the scale on which your group evaluated openness. You and your fellow members might, after going through the team-building intervention, decide that the 6 you gave to open-ness of communication prior to the training was actually a 2. This might reflect the fact that before the team building members perceived the group to be moderately high on open communications, but now that they have seen the extent to which people can achieve open communication, the previous state of the group's communications seems pretty dismal. A third type of change, gamma change, reflects a shift due to redefinition of the construct underlying the scale. Thus, before the team-building intervention, your group may have conceived of openness in communications as simply providing information when asked. The group was seen as open (a 6 on the scale) in terms of this definition of the construct. However, the team-building intervention leads you to redefine open communications as including actively giving feedback, expressing emotions, confronting the boss, and taking emotional risks. In reference to this redefined construct, group communications after the intervention are now seen as more open than before the intervention.

The implication of beta and gamma change is that our estimation of the real effects of OD interventions may be inaccurate. In our example, the intervention actually succeeded in increasing openness, but the numerical changes in the rating scales suggested a decline in openness. Although a variety of methodologies have been proposed to identify the various changes, as yet there is no consensus among researchers on the best manner of dealing with the problem of recalibration (beta change) and concept redefinition (gamma change). Perhaps the best advice is that those evaluating OD intervention should rely less on self-reports and make more use of unobtrusive and behavioral observation measures.

In addition to the methodological difficulties of evaluating OD interventions such as process consultation and team building, questions have also been raised as to whether the values underlying these interventions fit the realities of organizational life. A pervasive assumption underlying OD is that relationships among employees should be open and authentic. It is important to recognize, however, that openness is not always consistent with the inherent political nature of organizations (Eisenberg & Witten, 1987). For instance, leaders in the midst of a crisis are unlikely to inspire confidence and might well create panic if they were totally open in expressing their doubts and fears to followers. Another potential problem with clear and unequivocal communication is that it can leave few alternatives for future action and can breed conflict. Ambiguity, on the other hand, can allow the recipients some freedom and discretion as they attempt to achieve organizational goals and can allow disputing parties to simultaneously claim victory. Despite the problems with being completely open in all situations, we would tend to agree with the underlying assumptions of OD insofar as most organizations would benefit from more open communications. The best rule, perhaps, is "nothing in extreme."

## GROUP PROBLEM-SOLVING TECHNIQUES

An increasingly common use of groups in organizations is the problem-solving group. Group problem solving is often a crucial component of *total quality management* (TQM) programs in which organizations strive for continuous improvement in work processes. Another variety of group problem solving is the *quality circle (QC),* which is sometimes part of a larger TQM effort and consists of a small group of employees that meets on a regular basis to come up with better ways of doing things in the workplace. Similar to QCs, General Electric uses what it calls work-out groups to solve problems (Stewart, 1991b). Typically 40 to 100 employees chosen from various ranks and functions by management attend a meeting held at a hotel or conference center. The manager of the participants begins the discussion by presenting an agenda, and then the participants break into smaller groups that focus on a single aspect of the agenda. After about three days the teams present their proposals to their manager, who can agree with the proposal, reject it, or request more information. Still another example comes from the Mellon Bank in Pittsburgh (Main, 1992). A team of eight employees from different departments was assigned the problem of improving procedures for dealing with credit card billing disputes. The team found that when customers called with a complaint, the employees often did not have all the documents needed to deal with the dispute. As the result of the team's problem-solving efforts, an improved process was implemented that cut outstanding complaints in half and reduced days taken to resolve them from 45 days to 25 days.

When problem solving is an important activity of the group, as is the case in QCs, the quality improvements at Mellon Bank, and GE's work-outs, several techniques of group problem solving can have considerable value in improving group effectiveness. These problem-solving techniques include:

1. *Consensus decision making.* As described by Hall and Watson (1971), members are given a set of guidelines for discussion that include the following prescriptions: (1) Avoid arguing

just to win the argument. (2) Avoid agreeing just to avoid conflict. (3) Discuss the problem until all members can at least accept the rationale of the majority decision, even if they are not in total agreement. (4) Avoid use of conflict resolution techniques such as majority vote, averaging, or doing things because this is the way they have always been done.

2.  *Brainstorming.* This procedure is intended to loosen inhibitions of group members and to encourage the flow of ideas. Members are instructed to generate as many ideas as possible, no matter how ridiculous. A basic guideline during the free-floating discussion is that members are not to evaluate ideas. Many of the ideas generated in such a session are likely to be farfetched. Take, for example, the ideas for possible food products produced in a session held for the product managers in a major food company (Swasy, 1991). These included such gems as dog biscuits for humans with coffee breath and hot dogs made from fish (sea dogs). The hope in brainstorming is that the same release of inhibition that leads to such notions will also produce a few useful ideas.

    Despite the frequent use of group brainstorming, it does not entirely succeed in relaxing the restraints against generating new ideas. Research has shown that in attempting to state their own ideas, members may block or interfere with the ideas of other members (Diehl & Stroebe, 1987). More unique ideas are produced if members first generate their ideas silently under brainstorming instructions and these individual contributions are pooled than if the group members interact using traditional brainstorming instructions (Bouchard & Hare, 1970; Campbell, 1968).

3.  *Nominal group technique.* This technique resulted from the findings that pooling of individual contributions was more effective than group brainstorming. In the nominal group technique members first generate ideas silently without discussing them. The ideas are then listed in round-robin fashion. Members can then ask for clarification, but they are not allowed to evaluate. In the final stages, the group votes on what they consider the best three to five alternatives. After tallying the votes, additional rounds of clarification and voting may follow before the group arrives at a final decision. When compared with more interactive techniques, such as brainstorming and consensus decision making, the nominal group technique appears to yield better solutions (Delbecq, Van De Ven, & Gustafson, 1976) and more effective implementation of solutions (White, Dittrich, & Lang, 1980).

4.  *Preliminary planning.* Many groups tend to rush to reach a solution without adequate planning. In an interesting

experiment conducted by Hackman, Brousseau, and Weiss (1976), groups of students were given one of three sets of instructions: (1) spend a few minutes discussing and planning strategy; (2) avoid any preliminary discussion but jump right to solutions; or (3) no instructions. When members did not share the same task information, a preliminary planning discussion led to more effective task performance. If members all possessed the same information, however, preliminary planning actually detracted from the group's performance.

5.  *Dialectical inquiry and devil's advocacy approaches.* Both of these approaches attempt to improve creativity by forcing the group to consider alternative solutions. In dialectical inquiry one subgroup develops a recommendation and a second subgroup presents the opposite recommendation and attempts to negate the assumptions of the first subgroup. In the devil's advocacy approach one subgroup presents a recommendation and the second attacks this recommendation without presenting an alternative. In both approaches, the subgroups are expected to eventually agree on mutually acceptable solutions. In a recent review of the research evaluating these two techniques, Schwenk (1990) concluded that devil's advocacy achieved better results than dialectical inquiry. However, there is some evidence that members of groups using either approach are less satisfied with the group and less accepting of the final decision than members of groups using consensus decision making (Schweiger et al, 1986).

6.  *Stepladder technique.* In this procedure, a few members form a subgroup (the core) and the other members join them one at a time. As each new member joins the core, he or she presents a solution to the problem and discusses it with the other core members. After all members have joined the core, the group arrives at a final solution. Rogelberg, Barnes-Farrell, and Lowe (1992) found that stepladder groups produced higher quality solutions than groups taking a more conventional approach. Moreover, the group decision using the stepladder procedure was better than the solution of the best individual in the group 56% of the time. In conventional groups, the final group solution was better than the solution of the best individual only 13% of the time.

## AUTONOMOUS WORK GROUPS

In an autonomous work group, members control their own activities with minimal or no supervision. An increasing number of organizations have delegated to teams of workers the decision-making responsibility and authority previously reserved for managers. According to one estimate, 20% of U.S.

firms are using autonomous work groups today compared with only 5% a decade ago (Lublin, 1992a).

Autonomous work groups were introduced as part of the *sociotechnical approach* to job design and organizational development at the Tavistock Institute in England in the early 1950s. The sociotechnical approach attempts to integrate the technological, structural, and social components of the organization. The first major intervention of this type was conducted by Trist and Bamforth (1951) with a coal mine in England. In the traditional short-wall method, each of three shifts worked a small portion of the "face" in teams of two workers. When a shift ended, the two miners on the next shift took up where the previous shift stopped. The team was paid for its total productivity. After World War II, a new, more mechanized method of mining was introduced called the long-wall method. In this approach, each shift specialized in an aspect of the total task, with one digging the coal, another shoveling it onto the conveyor, and the third moving the mining equipment farther into the mine. The men were more specialized in their duties and were paid different pay rates. In addition, they worked at greater physical distances from each other.

Many problems arose as the result of the change to long-wall mining, including low productivity, high absenteeism, and high turnover. Trist and Bamforth attributed these problems to the incompatibility of the new technology with the social system. Working in small intimate groups helped reduce the anxiety associated with mining, but the long-wall method isolated the miners and left them vulnerable to stress. Another consequence of the new technology was that older workers felt status incongruence as the result of being assigned lower pay rates than new hires. Finally, intergroup conflict emerged as each shift blamed the other for coordination problems.

The solution was to redesign the work so that the social system fit the technological system. Each shift of workers was organized into an *autonomous work group* and was given the responsibility for all phases of the mining process: digging, extraction, and equipment setup. Group members were cross-trained so that they possessed all the skills necessary. The group decided which members would be assigned to which tasks. Moreover, members of a shift team were paid the same and were provided incentives based on the production of the entire team. This new arrangement appeared to decrease absenteeism and to increase production dramatically. Whether the sociotechnical intervention can account for these differences in outcomes cannot be determined, however, given the nonrandom assignment of employees to the groups and the absence of appropriate control groups.

Pasmore, Francis, Halderman, and Shani (1982) reviewed 134 experiments involving sociotechnical interventions and concluded that the most successful were those that incorporated some form of autonomous work group in the design. The reasons that an autonomous work group might be successful are still being debated. Wall, Kemp, Jackson, and Clegg (1986) found that the primary benefit of autonomous work groups came from the reduction in costs associated with the elimination of supervisory positions. Goodman, Devadas, and Hughson (1988) suggested that sociotechnical interventions succeed in improving performance only to the extent that they focus on "critical levers." They cite the Rushton Mining Company in Pennsylvania, where it was found that the amount of time equipment was out of action because of maintenance and repair was a crucial factor in how the mining crews performed. Consequently, autonomous work teams were designed with improvements of this critical lever in mind.

## PERFORMANCE FEEDBACK

Research has clearly shown that feedback can be beneficial to individual performance both by increasing the motivation of the recipient and by providing information on how to perform the task most effectively. Feedback also appears capable of improving group performance. The benefits of feedback were demonstrated in a study in which the productivity of five units at an Air Force base was measured before and after implementing a feedback/goal setting/reward system (Pritchard, Jones, Roth, Stuebing, & Ekeberg, 1988). After five months of monitoring the performance of the units, feedback was provided in the form of computer-generated reports. As indicated in Figure 5.9, the introduction of group-level feedback increased productivity by over 50%. Goal setting further increased productivity to 76% over baseline productivity.

The focus of the feedback in this Air Force study was productivity. Another type of feedback central to process consultation and team building is feedback to members on how well they are working together (i.e., process feedback). There is some evidence that combining performance and process feedback is the most effective approach to improving group performance (Nadler, 1979).

## GOAL SETTING

Just as setting specific, difficult goals can improve the performance of individuals (Chapter 3), setting goals for the performance of the entire group can also enhance group performance (Matsui, Kakuyama, & Onglatco, 1987). The effects of group versus individual goals depend on the nature of the task. In Mitchell and Silver's (1990) laboratory experiment, groups of three subjects were given the task of building a tower with wooden blocks. In the individual goal condition, subjects were told that their individual performance would be evaluated on their individual contributions to building the tower. In the group goal condition they were told that the group as a whole would be evaluated. In a third condition, goals were set for both the team and the individual group members. Finally, in a fourth condition no goals were set. Performance was equally high when goals were set for only the group, for both the individual and group, and when no goal was set. The poorest performance occurred when only individual goals were set. The results are not surprising given that the task employed in the experiment required subjects to cooperate. The most

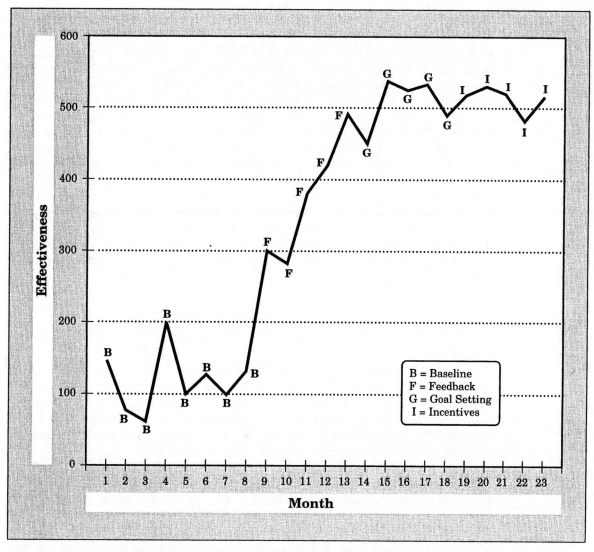

**Figure 5.9**  *The effects of a feedback / goal-setting intervention on group performance*
*Source:* Pritchard, R.D., Jones, S.D., Roth, P.L., Stuebing, K.K., & Ekeberg, S.E. (1988). Effects of group feed-back, goal setting, and incentives on organizational productivity. *Journal of Applied Psychology, 73,* 337–358.

important lesson of this experiment, however, is that imposing individual goals can harm group performance when the task requires cooperation.

## GROUP REWARDS

Improvements in group performance can also come from providing employees with incentives for working together as a group on their tasks. Indeed, Shea and Guzzo (1987) propose that "outcome interdependence" is one of the primary determinants of the group's effectiveness. The research on group rewards suggests that when the task requires members to cooperate, rewarding all members for the successful performance of the task can improve performance above the level of performance found with rewarding members individually (Miller & Hamblin, 1963; Johnson, Maruyama, Johnson, Nelson, & Skon, 1981). A type of group reward that has received considerable attention over the years is *gainsharing,* in which employees in an organization or a unit within an organization are paid a bonus for improving results on a variety of dimensions (e.g., quality, efficiency, customer satisfaction). The best known form of gainsharing is the *Scanlon plan.* In this program, employees in an entire plan are paid for reducing labor costs relative to productivity. A key aspect of this plan is that employees meet on a regular basis to consider possible improvements in productivity or reductions in cost. There are individual reward systems that can foster cooperation within groups. Most notable of these are *pay-for-skill* reward systems, in which individual employees are rewarded for the number of different tasks they have mastered.

## A FINAL SUMMATION AND A LOOK AT THE FUTURE

The reality of organizational life is that people must work together to get things done. Although some situations require more cooperation than others, organizations and groups are *social systems* that would not survive for long if employees were off following their own individual paths. The concern of this chapter was with how people relate to one another in the workplace. The continuing and ever changing ways in which individuals interact with one another are called *social processes.* The stable patterns of relationships that emerge from these processes are called *social structures.* In thinking about social structure and process it may be helpful to conceive of what you would observe in a collection of people brought together to perform a task. Your first observations would be of people communicating with one another verbally and nonverbally. Other processes that would soon become apparent are influence, competition, conflict, and cooperation. To make social life more bearable, people invariably evolve social structures, or stable modes of relating to one another. Patterns of interaction emerge as some individuals interact more with some people than they do with others. Roles form in which members of the organization come to expect that certain people will engage in specific activities. Norms define the behaviors expected of all members of a group or organization. The whole profile of norms, roles, and values constitutes the culture or climate.

Of the various social entities in an organization, perhaps the most important are the groups in which employees work together to achieve work goals. Groups seldom perform up to their potential, but because they are a fact of life they cannot be discarded in favor of individuals. Instead, attention must be focused on understanding the process losses that keep group members from effectively working together and devising interventions to minimize the losses and maximize process gains. We discussed several interventions, including team building, process consultation, and sociotechnical systems, as well as more focused interventions such as group problem-solving techniques, efforts to increase group cohesion, feedback, goal setting, and group rewards.

Changes currently underway in organizations show that it will become increasingly important to understand group dynamics and how to improve group functioning. Organizations appear to be moving away from the highly individualistic, authoritarian systems typical of the past toward structures that delegate important decisions to teams of workers. There are several potential reasons for the growing emphasis on groups in organizations. More than a half century of behavioral research demonstrating the importance of groups has encouraged this trend. Another factor is the growing awareness of managers that single individuals cannot effectively cope with the technological, political, and cultural changes confronting organizations today (Galbraith, 1977). Still another factor is the elimination of managerial positions, a strategy that many large corporations are using to reduce costs in recent years and that is necessitating a greater reliance on self-governing teams (Milbank, 1991). A fourth contributing factor is the successful use of groups by some foreign competitors, especially Japan (Ouchi, 1981). Whatever the reason, the move toward collaborative work arrangements is reshaping organizational life and will require that I/O psychologists devote more attention to social behavior in their research.

This chapter has treated social behavior in organizations and groups as if they simply emerged and ran on their own. Contrary to this view, however, the leaders of the organization have responsibility for the way things work. The next chapter is devoted to the factors that determine the effectiveness of leaders in the organization.

## DISCUSSION QUESTIONS

1. Think of a time when you experienced a miscommunication. Analyze the situation using the process described in Figure 5.1. Where do you think communication failed, and what could have been done to prevent the breakdown?
2. Why could all the social processes discussed in this chapter be considered communication?
3. Can power and influence be shared or do they inevitably lead to conflict? Explain.
4. What do we mean when we say that once started, conflict can have a life of its own?
5. What are the problems associated with too little conflict in an organization? What could be done to increase the level of conflict without having dysfunctional consequences?

6. Think of a group in which you currently participate. What are the norms of this group? What functions do they serve? What are the maintenance and task roles that members occupy?

7. Under what conditions does group cohesiveness increase performance, and under what conditions does it hinder performance? Why?

8. The attraction–selection–attrition (ASA) framework proposes that groups and organizations tend to become more homogeneous and suffer decline. Describe the process by which this occurs. Do you believe this model is an accurate description of what happens in organizations? Why?

9. What are the factors that can account for why groups so often perform at a level below their capabilities?

10. Many OD strategies are based on the belief that organizations and groups are more effective if they have open communications than if they have closed communications. Critics would argue that organizations are inherently political and being completely open may even be harmful. What do you believe and why?

## THE BELL ATLANTIC WAY

Earlier we raised the issue of how to change the whole culture of an organization. An interesting example of a large organization that is attempting to transform itself is the Bell Atlantic Corporation. Bell Atlantic was formed in 1983 after the court-ordered breakup of the AT&T system into seven regional telecommunications companies (the "Baby Bells"). The challenge facing Bell Atlantic and the other Baby Bells is that they no longer have a monopoly over telecommunications and now must compete in a deregulated marketplace. Old ways are hard to change, however. A common saying among employees is that so-and-so has "Bell-shaped hands," meaning that the individual is resistant to change and bureaucratic in orientation. To survive, each of the Bells is attempting to move away from the bureaucratic values characteristic of the old AT&T and to adopt a more entrepreneurial culture.

The primary architect of the changes in the corporate culture of Bell Atlantic is the chief executive officer, Raymond Smith, who has developed a program called the "Bell Atlantic Way." The hope is that employees within the company will take individual responsibility, attend less to defending their own individual turfs, and will be more collegial and collaborative. At the heart of the Bell Atlantic Way are two fundamental values (R.W. Smith, 1989). First, employees should accept greater individual responsibility rather than passing responsibility off on those above or below them in the hierarchy. The second fundamental tenet is that everyone in the company must see themselves as a member of the Bell Atlantic *team* rather than as a member of a narrowly defined function in the organization. An important aspect of the team orientation is coaching. Employees wear buttons saying "Coach me!" to encourage them to offer advice and help to each other. The hope is that subordinates will feel free to give feedback as well as accept it. According to Smith, Bell Atlantic's values mean "Expanding the scope of your jobs beyond the walls of your cubicle. Taking the initiative to learn about aspects of our business you never felt you had to know about. Finding a better way, rather than going by the book. Breaking the old habit of looking to others for leadership by becoming one yourself" (1989, p. 8).

To instill these values, 20,000 managers have attended two 1/2-day training sessions during 1990–1991 in which they are introduced to the Bell Atlantic Way. In 1992, 60,000 more employees were sent to the same workshops. Rather than being lectured about the system, the workshops require participants to engage in exercises that convey the central values that are part of the Bell Atlantic Way. In perhaps the most important of these exercises, six participants are given puzzle parts and told to assemble the parts to make six squares. Each team member is to put together one complete square, but the group is only able to assemble six squares if the team members share their puzzle pieces. The tendency is for those who have enough parts to complete a puzzle to go ahead and put them together and forget the others. Smith describes the impact of this experience in the following way: "As corny as it may seem, managers will now open sessions saying, 'We've got to break the squares today,' . . . meaning we've got to compromise here, break out of thinking about only our own territories. . . . In the old culture, if I contributed resources for the good of the corporation, I'd lose the support of my own group. Now it is no longer acceptable for someone to say, 'I've done my bit. I've met my goal. I'll sit back until you meet yours' " (Kanter, 1991, p. 123).

In another exercise, two teams compete in picking up poker chips on a table. The white chips are close to the participants, whereas the red and blue chips are farther away. A representative of each group is given one minute to pick up chips. Although the teams are unaware of the relative weights, white chips are worth 1, red chips 10, and blue chips 1,000. Since white chips are the easiest to pick up, teams invariably have more white chips than blue or red chips at the end of the minute. Although teams initially feel that they were tricked, the lesson is that it is the responsibility of team members to ask about relative values and to set priorities. Each participant is given a blue chip printed with "Bell Atlantic Way" and is encouraged to wear blue chips or keep one in a pocket to remind him or her of this lesson. Moreover, blue, red, and white are used to indicate the importance of tasks. The exercise demonstrates that, rather than adhering to habitual routines, employees must put "first things first."

In addition to the workshops, the corporation has been restructured in several respects to support the new culture. The compensation system was changed so that rewards now depend not only on individual performance, but also on how well the corporation and team performs. Downsizing has been another vehicle of change. A large number of employees were fired, with employees themselves providing input on where to cut. Another structural change has been the creation of small profit centers called client service groups or CSGs. These service groups are charged not only with providing services internally but also externally. For instance, the accounting department provides accounting services internally and is also responsible for finding external clients. When a project comes up internally, the CSGs must compete with external clients in bidding for the work. Another program, the Champion program, provides "money, guidance, and training to potential entrepreneurs who propose new products or services" (Kanter, 1991, p. 126). To further foster an egalitarian climate, Smith made the executive dining room into an employee cafeteria and moved the offices of the top executives to the areas of the employees they supervise.

Smith believes these efforts have worked. "The language is changing. The decision process is changing. People are becoming more accountable, more team-oriented, and more effective" (Kanter, 1991, p. 126). According to Smith, employee surveys show that employees now feel that Bell Atlantic is a better place to work because the "disaffected, cynical people have left" (p. 126). Moreover, now that fewer people are left to do the work load, "there is much less time for bureaucracy" (Kanter, 1991, p. 126). The result, according to Smith, is that employees within Bell Atlantic are developing entrepreneurial skills. More new technology-based services have been introduced by Bell Atlantic than by any of the other Baby Bells.

The reaction to these types of sessions is not uniformly positive, however. A recent article describing the Bell Atlantic Way provided the following observations: "One network manager, who spoke on conditions of anonymity, says he's considering early retirement to avoid wasting time on 'silly programs.' As for unionized workers, who won't experience the Bell Atlantic Way until next year, one 11-year veteran says he doubts he'll ever be allowed to 'coach' his own boss, calling the program 'another attempt to brainwash employees.' That kind of attitude exasperates Smith. 'Some people don't want to change under any circumstances, but this isn't going to go away,' he vows." (Lopez, 1991, p. 135).

## CASE QUESTIONS

1.  What social norms and values is Bell Atlantic attempting to modify in the activities described in this case?
2.  Do you believe that the attempts to change Bell Atlantic's culture will work? Why?
3.  Should a company attempt to change the values of employees? Do you agree with the comment of the employee that this is "another attempt to brainwash employees"? Justify your answer.

# Leadership in the Organization

- Leader Traits

- Leader Behavior

- Situational Influences in Leadership

- Cognitive Approaches

- Contingency Theories

- Charismatic, Inspirational, and Transformational Leadership

- A Final Summation and a Look at the Future

- Case: Leadership at Nucor

In the last chapter we discussed a variety of social behaviors that can influence the functioning of groups and organizations. In this chapter we focus on one type of social behavior: leadership. Not surprisingly, people attach great significance to the role of the leader in determining the success or failure of organizations. Consider, for example, the attention given in the United States to the top-level executives of large corporations. Most are richly rewarded with huge salaries; some even write best-selling autobiographies, become guests on talk shows, and in other ways attain celebrity status. Chief executives are heroes when things are going well, but they are the villains in the eyes of followers and the public when their organizations fail, as seen in the widespread criticisms of top executives in U.S. corporations during the recent recession. Some critics have gone so far as to blame most of our current social and economic problems on the self-absorbed leaders of today who have taken the place of the visionary leaders of times past (Bennis, 1989). Whether leaders today are less effective than leaders of yesteryear can be debated. That the future changes confronting our institutions will require leaders who can inspire commitment and creativity seems indisputable.

The special attention given to leadership reflects the prevalent view that leaders possess special powers and are the driving force of the organization (Meindl, Ehrlich, & Dukerich, 1985). According to the popular view, leaders tend to be seen as the primary cause of the good and bad things that happen to an organization. In contrast, I/O psychologists and other organizational scientists tend to adopt a broader perspective and to be more skeptical, with some even arguing that leadership is mostly in the minds of followers (Calder, 1977; Pfeffer, 1977).

As is usually the case, the truth lies somewhere between these extreme positions. In examining what behavioral research and theory say about effective leadership, we attempt to strike a balance between an overly romanticized view and the complete rejection of the concept. Let us first offer working definitions for some concepts that everyday thinking often confuses. *Leadership* is defined as the process by which an individual influences the behavior and attitudes of others. A leadership *role* is a position in an organization or group that is expected to have special influence in the organization. Most research has focused on leadership roles such as supervisory, managerial, and executive positions. We will also emphasize these types of leadership roles, but you should keep in mind that managers are not the only people in an organization who exercise leadership. Another important distinction can be made between becoming a leader and becoming an *effective leader*. In the former case, the person merely exercises influence, but in the latter he or she also achieves the goals of the group or organization. A quick review of history reveals numerous leaders who became highly influential but then led their followers to disastrous results.

In attempting to understand the origins of effective leadership, researchers have taken very different and often conflicting approaches. The *trait approach* emphasizes the personality, abilities, and other personal dispositions of the leader as the primary determinants of effectiveness. The *behav-*

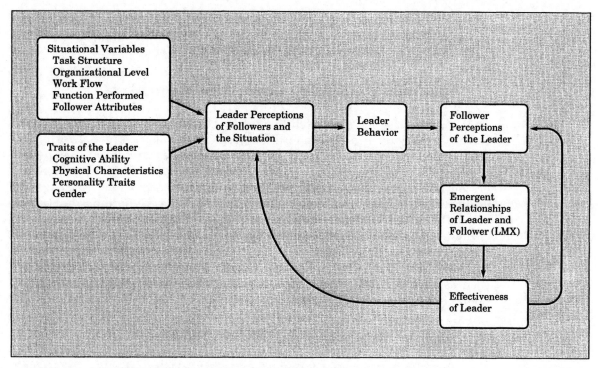

**Figure 6.1**   *A working model of the leadership process*

*ioral approach* hypothesizes that effective leaders differ as a function of what the leader does in performing his or her role. The *situational approach* stresses the organization, task, role, and other factors outside the leader as the crucial determinants. Finally, *cognitive approaches* emphasize the beliefs and perceptions of the leader and follower. We describe the extreme versions of these positions, but remember that no single approach can provide the whole story. Each contributes a piece of the puzzle by providing insight into a critical aspect of effective leadership. The model presented in Figure 6.1 can help conceptualize the leadership process and the part played in this process by traits, situations, behaviors, and cognitions. Toward the end of this chapter we consider several *contingency theories* that fit the various components of the process into one framework.

# LEADER TRAITS

At some time you have probably wondered whether you have "the right stuff" to be an effective leader. Part of the mystique of leadership is the belief that effective leaders possess special attributes that set them apart from most others and enable them to overcome seemingly impossible obstacles. The most extreme version of the trait theory would propose that leaders are born with innate characteristics that allow them to wield influence over others. People who lack these basic traits cannot be made into leaders regardless of how much they might want to lead. Do research findings support this view?

## What Traits Distinguish Leaders From Nonleaders?

Much of the trait research has focused on whether people who are perceived as leaders in a situation differ from those who are not. In a typical study, members of a work group identify those coworkers whom they believe are the leaders of the group. Perceived leaders are then compared to nonleaders on their personality traits, abilities, and other attributes. Although the early reviews of this research concluded that traits were unimportant as correlates of perceived leadership (Mann, 1959; Stogdill, 1948), more recent reviews suggest that traits are much more important than previously believed (House, 1988; Lord, DeVader, & Alliger, 1986). In a very thorough review of this literature, Lord, De Vader, and Alliger (1986) concluded that people are seen as leaders to the extent that they are *masculine* in their personalities, *highly intelligent,* and *dominant.*

## What Are the Traits of the Effective Manager?

Although personality traits are related to whether people are seen as leaders, this leaves unanswered the question of whether specific traits are related to effectiveness in performing leadership roles. Research on predictors of managerial effectiveness shows that the trait most clearly related to managerial effectiveness is *intelligence.* Intelligent managers are more likely to succeed than those who are less intelligent.

In addition to intelligence, *personality traits* also predict managerial effectiveness. Support for this contention is found in two surveys, both of which examined the relationship of personality to performance in management and several other occupational groups (Barrick & Mount, 1991; Tett, Jackson, & Rothstein, 1991). Five broad dimensions of personality traits (the big five) were examined in these studies: (1) extraversion, (2) emotional stability, (3) agreeableness, (4) conscientiousness (i.e., extent to which the individual is careful, thorough, responsible, achievement oriented, and persevering), and (5) openness (i.e., extent to which the individual is imaginative, cultured, curious, original, broad-minded, and artistically sensitive). Barrick and Mount (1991) found that extraversion and conscientiousness were the two traits most strongly related to management effectiveness. Somewhat at variance with this study, Tett et al. (1991) found that all of the big five traits were positively related to managerial performance. This study also found large variation across studies in the strength of the relationships between personality traits and managerial effectiveness, suggesting that personality traits may be much more valid in some situations than in others.

Although the research on the big five personality traits is promising, more specific traits than these broad categories are needed in actually selecting leaders. David McClelland and his colleagues at Harvard (McClelland & Boyatzis, 1982) have conducted extensive research on three traits: need for achievement (nAch), need for power (nPow), and need for affiliation (nAff). As mentioned in Chapter 3, the research on these dimensions has been fairly consistent in showing that effective managers have higher needs for power and lower needs for affiliation than ineffective managers. Similar findings were reported by Stahl (1986). McClelland (1985) speculated that the successful manager has both a *high need for power* and *high power inhibition*. Power inhibition refers to psychological constraints against exercising power in a coercive or bullying manner. Those who are high on both variables exercise power in a socialized manner, whereas those who are high on need for power but low on power inhibition tend to fail because of their personalized use of power. According to McClelland, need for achievement is also related to managerial success, especially in small business or sales positions in which the manager has considerable control over the task. In a large organization in which bureaucratic procedures and politics set severe limits on the manager, achievement motivation is not as likely to lead to managerial effectiveness (McClelland & Boyatzis, 1982). The results of House, Spangler, and Woycke (1991) suggest that the findings with managers also extend to U.S. presidents. They rated the nAch, nPow, nAff, and power inhibition of all U.S. presidents through Ronald Reagan on the basis of historical records such as letters, speeches, and biographies. Presidential performance in international relations and in domestic affairs was positively related to nPow and power inhibition but negatively related to nAch and nAff.

Other studies have provided similar conclusions regarding power/dominance and the achievement striving of the manager. Over 25 years ago Standard Oil of New Jersey (now Exxon Corporation) tested the personality of 443 managers and found a relationship to dominance. According to Campbell, Dunnette, Lawler, and Weick's (1970) description of the results of this study:

> Successful executives in the SONJ organization have shown a total life pattern of successful endeavors. They were good in college, are active in taking advantage of leadership opportunities, and see themselves as forceful, dominant, assertive, and confident (p. 169).

John Miner (1978) reported similar results with his Sentence Completion Test, which purportedly measures the "motivation to manage." The characteristics of the person with a high level of motivation to manage are a favorable attitude toward authority and desires to compete against others, use power, stand out from the group, and attract the attention of others. Moreover, motivation to manage is characterized by a positive view of routine administrative chores. Several studies with the Sentence Completion Test have shown that managerial success in large bureaucratic organizations is related to higher

John F. Kennedy

Lyndon B. Johnson

Richard M. Nixon

Jimmy Carter

Ronald Reagan

Robert House and his colleagues rated the needs for achievement, power, and affiliation of these and other U.S. presidents. See the appendix at the end of this chapter for their results.

levels of the motivation to manage. Interestingly, Miner has observed that college students' motivation to manage has declined by 35% since the early 1960s and continued to decline by about 3% per year in the 1970s.

In summary, although traits appear to predict managerial effectiveness, their relationships tend to vary across different managerial positions and organizations (Tett et al., 1991). Future research needs to explore the effects of situation on trait requirements. An example of one such attempt is *cognitive resource theory,* which presents some possible moderators of the relationship between intelligence and leader effectiveness (Fiedler & Garcia, 1987). Specifically, this theory predicts that leader intelligence is more likely to predict success of the group when the leader is directive in his or her approach to leading the group, the group is supportive of the leader, and the group's task is intellectually demanding. Intelligence can also predict success of the group when the leader is nondirective, but only if the group supports the leader. The leader's intelligence is predicted to become less important, and experience more important, as situational stress increases. In one of the few tests of this theory, support could be found only for the prediction that intellectual abilities were more strongly related to group performance for directive leaders (Vecchio, 1990). Cognitive resource theory has been hotly disputed, however (Fiedler, Murphy, & Gibson, 1992; Vecchio, 1992). While it is too early to conclude that it is valid or invalid, there is considerable merit in the general strategy of searching for situational moderators of trait and effectiveness relationships (see Chapter 2 for a discussion of moderators).

## Is Gender Related to Managerial Effectiveness?

You may have wondered about the findings we reported earlier that perceived leaders have "masculine" personalities (Lord et al., 1986). These findings, as well as evidence that there is a much smaller proportion of women in management than men (Morrison & Von Glinow, 1990), bring attention to a controversial question: Do women lack the basic traits required of leaders? Some research has shown a tendency to perceive even successful women managers as lacking leadership (Heilman, Block, Martell, & Simon, 1989). Are these stereotypes warranted?

Research that has compared "women in general" with "men in general" shows that women do differ from men in their personality traits. In a recent review of sex differences, Eagly and Johnson (1990, p. 235) concluded that "Women as a group, when compared with men as a group, can be described as friendly, pleasant, interested in other people, expressive, and socially sensitive." Other researchers claim that women may tend to have lower self-confidence (White, et al, 1981) and are less aggressive (Jacklin & Maccoby, 1975). Women do not appear to show any less need for power (Stewart & Winter, 1976), but there is some indication that they are more likely to show socialized power as opposed to personalized power (Chusmir & Parker, 1984).

Despite these differences between men in general and women in general, comparisons between the subsets of men and women who aspire to or occupy management roles reveal much smaller differences (Dipboye, 1987). More importantly, there is no consistent support for the position that women are deficient in the traits needed to succeed in management positions. The most reasonable conclusion so far is that women have as much potential to perform effectively in management as men. Although they cannot be used as proof, plenty of specific examples can be found in the successful performance of women military officers in the recent Persian Gulf War. We agree with others who have studied this issue and concluded that the relative lack of women in management is best explained in terms of situational barriers and cultural norms, not in terms of innate deficiencies (Ragins & Sundstrom, 1989).

*Summary*

The most extreme trait approach would state that leaders are born, not made. In other words, leaders are people whose success is the consequence of their innate personalities, cognitive abilities, and physical traits. Research has found that some traits are indeed related to perceived leadership and success in leadership roles, although such traits explain only a small part of the variance.

An interesting possibility is that as the nature of leadership roles changes, the traits required for becoming an effective leader in organizations may also change. The evidence that masculinity was related to being perceived as a leader (Lord et al., 1986) could reflect the stereotypes of leadership as a male activity that were dominant at the time the research was conducted. As women managers become a more familiar sight in organizations, so-called "masculine" traits may cease to be an important factor in the evaluation of managerial success. The increasing use of teams and the emphasis on participatory management suggest that in the future dominance and the need for power may become less important and need for affiliation more important. This conjecture on our part will need to be tested through continuing research on personality traits and management effectiveness.

# LEADER BEHAVIOR

If you want to be a leader but do not believe you possess a high degree of the traits that have been found related to leadership, the behavioral approach offers a different perspective. According to this conception of leadership, success as a leader depends mainly on adopting the right behaviors, and these behaviors can be learned. If you go beyond stereotypes and take a close look at how leaders behave, you will find remarkable diversity in the actions taken by people in leadership roles. Consider the following two examples.

The first is Roger Penske, the former race car driver, who in 1987 purchased from General Motors the controlling interest in Detroit Diesel, a manufacturer of diesel engines (White, 1991). During 1982–1987 Detroit Diesel had lost 600 million dollars, with a loss of market share from 7.7% to 3.2%. After Penske took the reins he met regularly in mass meetings with workers to answer their questions and to deal with their anxieties over loss of jobs. He continues to meet regularly in small groups with a wide variety of workers at Detroit Diesel. At the same time that Penske attempted to involve the hourly workers, he eliminated many salaried jobs that were old holdovers from the GM days.

Compare Penske's style to that of John Murphy, who was school superintendent of Prince George's County schools in Maryland (Putka, 1991). Soon after taking charge, he convened the principals and confronted them with evidence of declining scores on achievement tests, announcing that the schools would be run on the basis of a philosophy he called "applied anxiety." Principals and teachers would be held accountable for student achievement. As a consequence of failure to improve scores, teachers and principals could be transferred or demoted and could have their salaries frozen. During his years as Superintendent, Prince George schools rose from 21st out of 24 districts in the state to 10th.

Are there general dimensions that we can use to compare the behavior of such different leaders as Roger Penske and John Murphy, and do effective leaders differ from ineffective leaders on these dimensions? These two questions have been central concerns of behavioral research on leadership.

## The Search for Fundamental Dimensions of Leadership

Early work presented a one-dimensional model in which the leader was seen as having to choose between a democratic/employee orientation, a more autocratic/task orientation, or some point in between. This one-dimensional view can be seen in the research conducted at the University of Michigan (Katz, Maccoby, & Morse, 1950).

A one-dimensional model of leadership gave way to a more complex two-dimensional model as the result of an important program of research that began at Ohio State University in the late 1940s (Stogdill & Coons, 1957). Unlike the researchers at Michigan, who assumed a one-dimensional model, the Ohio State investigators started by having people in many different types of jobs generate a list of attributes to describe the behaviors of their leaders. These descriptions were then subjected to a statistical procedure called *factor analysis.* The results revealed that descriptions of leaders could be reduced to two fundamental dimensions: initiating structure and consideration. Initiation of structure was defined as behavior "in which the supervisor organizes and defines group activities and his relation to the group." Examples of items that reflect initiating structure are:

1.   Makes his or her attitudes clear to the group;
2.   Emphasizes the meeting of deadlines;
3.   Lets group members know what is expected of them.

Consideration was defined as behavior "indicating mutual trust, respect, and a certain warmth, and rapport between a supervisor and his group." Items reflecting this dimension include:

1.   Is friendly and approachable;
2.   Puts suggestions made by the group into operation;
3.   Treats all group members as equals.

These two dimensions were similar to the employee-oriented versus production-oriented distinction in the University of Michigan studies and an earlier distinction between authoritarian and democratic leadership by Lewin, Lippitt, and White (1939). Contrary to these earlier studies, however, the

Ohio State findings revealed that these were *independent* dimensions. In other words, people could be high on both, low on both, or high on one and low on the other. Several measures resulted from this research. The Leader Behavior Description Questionnaire (LBDQ) is used by subordinates to describe the leader. The Leader Opinion Questionnaire (LOQ) is used by the leaders themselves to describe their own behavior. A later modification of the LBDQ that makes it more suitable for industrial settings is called the Supervisor Behavior Description Questionnaire (SBDQ). In all cases, a leader receives a score on consideration and a score on initiating structure.

The evidence for two fundamental dimensions of leadership is impressive and is consistent with the ideas discussed in Chapter 5 that all social systems, from small groups to whole societies, must fulfill both task and internal/maintenance functions. Given these findings, it seemed logical to some theorists to propose that the most effective leaders are high on both dimensions. Blake and Mouton (1964) did exactly this when they set forth a two-dimensional view of leadership similar to that found in the Ohio State research. In their grid theory of leadership, they describe leaders along two nine-point dimensions: employee-oriented and task-oriented. Although 81 combinations are possible, the five most typical styles are the 9,1 (high task, low people: authoritarian); 1,9 (low task, high people: country club); 5,5 (medium task, medium people); 1,1 (low task, low people); and 9,9 (high task, high people). The ideal style, according to Blake and Mouton, is the 9,9 style.

One of the early studies in the Ohio State leadership research (Halpin, 1957) appeared to support the contention that high initiation of structure and high consideration are the best combination. Subsequent research with these scales, however, presents a considerably more complex picture (Schriesheim, House, & Kerr, 1976). When satisfaction of employees is examined, a consistent finding is that employees are more satisfied the more considerate their supervisor. This is not surprising and in fact provides at least partial support for the human relations school. The relationship of leader consideration to employee performance is also positive, but much weaker. Findings for initiation of structure vary considerably across studies, however, with high initiation of structure sometimes associated with high performance and satisfaction and other times associated with low levels of performance or satisfaction. Contrary to Blake and Mouton's contention that high consideration/high structuring leadership is best, the evidence fails to show that the 9,9 style is always superior to other leadership styles (Larson, Hunt, & Osburn, 1976; Nystrom, 1978).

Research in the United States has shown that each of the various combinations of initiating structure and consideration could be an effective style depending on the situation. Further evidence of this comes from research in Japan on a two-dimensional model of leadership called the *PM theory of leadership* (Misumi & Peterson, 1985). Similar to the two dimensions identified in the Ohio State leadership studies, these investigators proposed that two functions are served by the leadership of a group. The performance function (P) consists of leader behaviors aimed at fulfilling group goals; the maintenance function (M) consists of leader behavior that fosters group survival and well-being. Leaders can exhibit a high level of both functions (PM), a high level of one and a low level of the other (Pm, Mp), or a low level of both (pm). Unlike Blake and Mouton's (1964) grid theory, the findings of this research program have shown that the effectiveness of each style is contingent on the situation. Although a PM-type leadership seems generally preferable to the other styles, situations involving high anxiety may require an M-type leadership, whereas situations involving a short-term task, low-achieving group members, and time pressures may require P-type leadership.

The view that effective leaders *always* show a high degree of both structure and consideration is incorrect, but it is reasonable to recommend that groups and organizations fulfill both their maintenance and task functions. A situation in which only task concerns are met can achieve high levels of productivity in the short term, but at the long-term cost of the social and emotional well-being of the people involved. Likewise, a leader who fulfills social and emotional needs but neglects tasks may engender satisfaction but is unlikely to produce much in the way of results. It does not appear that the leader alone must fulfill maintenance and task functions, however. For instance, a leader who is low on fulfilling members' social and emotional needs could rely on other group members to fulfill these needs.

The Ohio State leadership studies made a valuable contribution in showing the two basic dimensions of leader behavior. Yet the LBDQ, SBDQ, and other measures produced by this research have not done well in predicting employee performance. Also, subsequent research shows that the two dimensions measured with these scales are usually positively related (sometimes as large as $r = .70$ or higher) and thus less independent than originally believed (Weissenberg & Kavanagh, 1972). These disappointing results are probably due to problems in the scales (Schriesheim & Kerr, 1974). Another basic issue is whether descriptions of leadership at this very general level are useful in making the fine distinctions in behavior that are necessary to predict leader effectiveness. There are many ways that a leader might express consideration or initiate structure in a work setting. For example, a leader who is high on initiating structure might set goals, give feedback, establish rules, provide clear communications, discipline troublemakers, or push for higher productivity, to name just a few. Several theorists have expanded the list of leadership dimensions beyond the two identified in the Ohio State studies. Stogdill (1974) suggested expanding the description of leadership to include ten other dimensions of leader behavior in addition to initiating structure and consideration. Bowers and Seashore (1966) of the University of Michigan proposed a more complex four-factor model that included giving support, facilitating interaction among group members, motivating employees to achieve goals, and work facilitation. Alternative behavioral dimensions have also been proposed by Bass and Valenzi (1974), House and Mitchell (1975), Yukl (1981), and others (see Bass, 1990). These models are not necessarily inconsistent with the two-dimensional model. In most cases the various distinctions could be viewed as elaborations on initiating structure or consideration. At the present time, these alternatives exist mainly as interesting possibilities that have received little attention in the empirical research.

## Influence and Power

Initiation of structure, consideration, and other such general behavioral dimensions provide an insufficient basis for recommending specific actions that managers can take to improve their leadership. To do this we need to go beyond abstract styles and delve into the specific behaviors that are involved in leading. Particularly important are influence and power, behaviors that we defined earlier as the essential components of leadership.

In Chapter 5 we discussed French and Raven's (1959) theory of social power in which five basic sources of influence were set forth: *reward, coercive, expert, legitimate,* and *referent.* A distinction can be made between those sources of social power that the organization can provide (*position power*) and those that come from the unique characteristics of the person (*personal power*). An organization can give an individual the means of rewarding and punishing through incentives, fines, and the authority to fire and discipline. An organization also can provide legitimate authority through clearly spelling out the rights and privileges of a position. The organization is likely to have difficulty, however, in bestowing expert and referent power. Managers must find their own friends in attempting to increase their referent power, and although training and education can enhance expertise, there is little assurance that others in the organization will recognize this expertise.

French and Raven's theory is intriguing, but attempts to use these power bases to predict employee performance and satisfaction have yielded trends but few consistent results (Podsakoff & Schriesheim, 1985). Expert and referent power tend to be positively related to subordinate performance, satisfaction with the supervisor, and job satisfaction, but the relationships vary considerably from study to study. Reward, coercive, and legitimate power are negatively related to the same variables, but the findings again vary from study to study. Much of the inconsistency in findings may reflect deficiencies in the instruments used to measure these power bases. Fortunately, the measure described in Table 6.1 seems to improve on previous scales and may lead to more consistent findings in future research.

As indicated in Chapter 5, power refers to whether a person *can* wield influence, whereas influence tactics refer to what the individual actually *does* to change others. An example of the latter is the typology proposed by Yukl and his associates (Yukl & Tracey, 1992) (see Table 5.1). In attempting to influence others, people in leadership roles may exert pressure, appeal to those above them, promise benefits in exchange for compliance, form coalitions, ingratiate, use rational arguments, inspire through appealing to values and ideas, allow others to participate in decisions, and use legitimate authority. The findings suggest that people in leadership roles are more likely to use consultation, rational persuasion, and inspirational appeals than any other

**Table 6.1**

## QUESTIONNAIRE TO MEASURE FRENCH AND RAVEN'S (1959) BASES OF POWER

Instructions: Below is a list of statements which may be used in describing behaviors that supervisors in work organizations can direct toward their subordinates. First carefully read each descriptive statement, thinking in terms of your supervisor. Then decide to what extent you agree that your supervisor could do this to you. Mark the number which most closely represents how you feel. Use the following numbers for your answers.

    (5) = strongly agree
    (4) = agree
    (3) = neither agree nor disagree
    (2) = disagree
    (1) = strongly disagree

*My supervisor can . . .*

(Reward Power)
02. increase my pay level.
27. influence my getting a pay raise.
33. provide me with special benefits.
38. influence my getting a promotion.

(Coercive Power)
04. give me undesirable job assignments.
18. make my work difficult for me.
21. make things unpleasant here.
22. make being at work distasteful.

(Legitimate Power)
07. make me feel that I have commitments to meet.
30. make me feel like I should satisfy my job requirements.
39. give me the feeling I have responsibilities to fulfill.
42. make me recognize that I have tasks to accomplish.

(Expert Power)
16. give me good technical suggestions.
19. share with me his/her considerable experience and/or training.
31. provide me with sound job-related advice.
40. provide me with needed technical knowledge.

(Referent Power)
03. make me feel valued.
06. make me feel like he/she approves of me.
08. make me feel personally accepted.
12. make me feel important.

The numbers next to each item refer to the order in which the item appears in the questionnaire.

*Source:* Hinkin, T.R., & Schriesheim, C.A. (1989). Development and application of new scales to measure the French and Raven (1959) bases of social power. *Journal of Applied Psychology, 74*, 561–567.

tactic. Moreover, these same three tactics appear to be more effective than the use of pressure, coalition, and legitimating (Yukl & Tracey, 1992).

The evidence that effective leaders use participation, rational persuasion, and inspiration is consistent with several theories of leadership and power. Katz and Kahn (1978) suggested limiting the term *leadership* to influence that comes from an *increment in compliance,* over and above the compliance the leader would achieve from routine directives. A manager who orders a group of workers already at work on an assembly line to "get to work" can hardly be seen as exerting leadership. If the same manager was able to get these workers to go beyond their normal rate of productivity, this could qualify as leadership. Jacobs (1971) elaborated on this notion by distinguishing among three types of influence. He defined *power* as the influence that results from being able to deprive another of rewards or to inflict costs (note the broader use of this term we use here and in Chapter 5). A second type of influence is *authority,* which results from the exercise of legitimate power. *Leadership,* the third type, is described as resulting from a two-way interaction in which the subordinates comply because they have personal respect for the manager (again note that Jacobs' use of the term differs from our much broader use of leadership). The implication of both Katz and Kahn (1978) and Jacobs (1971) is that managers who wield leadership, as they define it, are more effective than those who wield power, authority, or obtain compliance through routine directives. Moreover, some have argued that an individual who simply uses the rewards and punishments available to get others to do things or who is mainly involved in the day-to-day administration of a position is a manager but not really a leader (Zaleznik, 1977). The leader, according to this approach, is someone who is proactive, who goes beyond power and authority to inspire, to motivate, and to creatively solve problems. Similar reasoning underlies recent work on the transformational, inspirational, and charismatic approaches to leadership discussed later in this chapter.

Not only does the use of personal power (referent power or expert power) appear to achieve more positive outcomes than the use of position power (reward, coercive, and legitimate power), but overreliance on position power can have negative consequences. Kipnis (1976) conducted a series of studies demonstrating that *position power can corrupt.* First, he showed that when supervisors are given position power, such as the power to give pay raises, to deduct pay, to transfer and to fire, they use these influence tactics more frequently than personal persuasion. A second effect of position power is that supervisors with a high degree of reward and coercive power see compliance as resulting from their power rather than the followers' efforts or abilities. A third effect is that supervisors with a high degree of position power develop negative perceptions of their followers as well as an exalted view of their own abilities.

While power can corrupt, a lack of position power also can create problems. One study found that subordinates perceived their supervisors as *more* coercive after the ability of the supervisors to administer bonus rewards was withdrawn than before the withdrawal of this power (Greene & Podsakoff,

1981). The most reasonable conclusion is that supervisors need enough position power to carry out their responsibilities, but they also need to know how to use personal sources of power. We would suggest that position power in combination with a lack of personal power is the most dangerous combination.

## Communication

Communication is among the most basic of all leader behaviors; verbal communication constitutes over half of the typical manager's daily activities (Burns, 1954; Mintzberg, 1973; Stewart, 1976). Popular accounts of why leaders succeed or fail place considerable weight on the communication skills of the leader (Rice, 1991). Indeed, we could reduce all the leader behavioral styles discussed so far to specific communicative acts (Penley & Hawkins, 1985).

The success of influence tactics is likely to depend, for instance, on what the leader says in carrying out the tactics (Drake & Moberg, 1986). A leader can use language to sedate followers into not thinking about the attempts to influence them. Rather than using a direct order such as "take care of that customer complaint," a manager might say "that customer is very unhappy with service he received." In the latter case, the follower is less likely to think that he or she is the target of influence and is more likely to take care of the customer complaint.

Compliance with requests is also more likely if the person uses *powerful language* consisting of a rich vocabulary, expression of certainty, intense language, and verbal immediacy (Drake & Moberg, 1986). High immediacy in language places the communicator closer to the topic whereas low immediacy places distance between the communicator and the topic (*this* is my wife vs. *that* is my wife). According to Drake and Moberg, stating that "This is what we must do now" is more powerful than "That is what we may want to do." In contrast to powerful language, "powerless" language is characterized by negative politeness strategies in which the speaker tries to avoid making the recipient feel controlled and includes stating one's debt to the target, apologizing for imposing, and indirect questions. Compare "Do this project for me, please" with "I am sorry to bother you but would you mind doing this project for me?" *Powerless language* is also expressed in hedges (you know, kinda, I guess), question intonation in declarative contexts (the report will be ready at six?), and hypercorrect grammar (whom do you mean?).

Klauss and Bass (1982) studied whether managers who are effective in their communications tend to use styles of communicating that differ from less effective managers. They found that effective communicators were: (1) "careful transmitters" in their choice of words; (2) "open and two-way" with regard to other points of view; (3) "frank" in saying what they think; (4) "careful listeners" in the attention given to the recipient of the message; and (5) "informal" in that they were natural and relaxed when communicating. According to the model presented in Figure 6.2, the manager's style

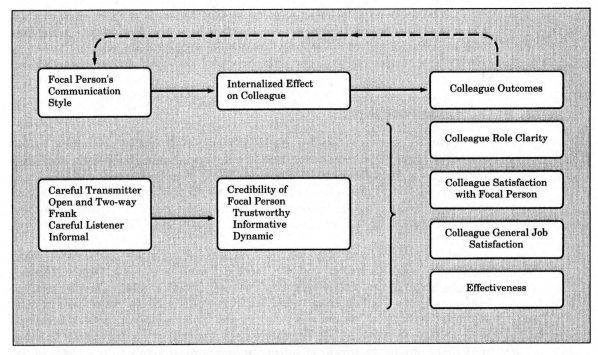

**Figure 6.2** *Model representing impact of focal person's communication style on colleagues*
Source: Klauss, R., & Bass, B. (1982). *Interpersonal Communication in Organizations.* New York: Academic Press.

influences his or her credibility, as indicated by the perceptions of others that the manager is trustworthy, informed, and dynamic. The perceived credibility of the communicator, in turn, influences the role clarity, satisfaction, and effectiveness of the recipients. A few additional comments are needed with regard to the "carefulness" of the leader's communication. The greater the power of people in leadership roles, the more carefully they need to choose their words. When a powerful person speaks, people listen to the point that they may read more into the message than was intended. An example is an offhand comment that President George Bush made in the fall of 1991 about wishing that credit card interest rates were lower (Holland, 1991). Soon after the comment, a bill was introduced in Congress and the stock market experienced its fifth worst day in its history. Apparently the president did not intend to launch a specific program, but his comments were interpreted by some in Congress as a call for action.

## Styles of Conflict Management

Leadership in an organization involves getting followers to work together in a coordinated effort to achieve the same goals. As was discussed in

Chapter 5, conflict is an inevitable part of organizational life. Whether leaders can resolve these conflicts among followers is an important determinant of whether they can achieve a unified effort. Blake and Mouton (1964) distinguished styles of conflict management along the two dimensions of their grid theory: concern for people and concern for task. *Withdrawal* is a style characterized by low concern for task and low concern for people in which individuals psychologically and physically remove themselves from the situation. *Smoothing* is a style characterized by great concern for people but little concern for task in which individuals attempt to minimize differences and accentuate communalities. *Forcing* occurs when leaders emphasize the task over people. Here the leader comes up with a solution and pressures others in the situation to accept this solution. In *compromise* the leader tries to balance concerns for task and people without maximally satisfying either. The leader attempts to get the conflicting parties to split the difference with one giving up something in return for a concession from the other. Finally, there is *problem solving*, which Blake and Mouton espouse as the best approach. Here there is high concern for task and people, as individuals openly exchange information and seek a solution to the basic sources of the conflict.

The questionnaires measuring styles of conflict resolution are typically based on the Blake and Mouton model. These questionnaire measures include Thomas and Kilmann's (1974) *Management of Differences Exercise* (MODE), Rahim's (1983) *Organizational Conflict Inventory* (ROCI), and Hall's *Conflict Management Survey* (Shockley-Zalabak, 1988). Research evaluating the most frequently used of these measures, the MODE questionnaire, found moderate support for the underlying theory (Van de Vliert & Kabanoff, 1990; Kabanoff, 1987). Nevertheless, this and the other measures patterned on the Blake and Mouton approach fall short of the measurement standards that are expected of psychological instruments. The reliance on self-reports is also a problem. Kabanoff (1987) found that self-descriptions of individuals on the MODE were largely unrelated to how their peers rated them on the five styles. The chief weakness, however, is the continued reliance on the grid approach of Blake and Mouton. The lack of support for the universal superiority of the 9,9 style suggests that theorists should seek a more solid conceptual foundation on which to base their investigations of conflict resolution.

## The Leader-Member Exchange (LMX) Model

An implicit assumption in much of the work on leader behavior is that leaders act the same toward all their subordinates. For instance, in measuring consideration and initiation of structure using the Ohio State leadership scales, subordinates' ratings are averaged to form a single measure of their leader's position on each dimension. Likewise, when managers describe their own styles, they typically are asked how they deal with subordinates as a group rather than how they deal with individual subordinates. Thus, leaders who are high on level of structuring are assumed to be structuring toward all those that they lead. Similarly, if the average description of a leader is high on consideration, that leader is assumed to be this way for all subordinates.

Graen and his associates (Graen, 1976; Graen & Scandura, 1987) question the assumption that the leader's behavior is uniform and present an alternative model of leadership called the *LMX* (leader-member exchange) model. They start with the assumption that the immediate supervisor is the primary influence in defining the social role of organizational members. The LMX model proposes that the supervisor will develop a close relationship with some subordinates and serve as a leader for these in-group people. The quality of the exchange will be higher for this in-group as the leader relies on referent and expert power. Most subordinates, however, are in the out-group. The quality of exchange is lower for this group as the leader relies mainly on formal authority, rules, and policies. Although the LMX approach is not without its critics (Dienesch & Liden, 1986), the essential point of the LMX model is well taken: We should examine the relationships that emerge between the leader and individual followers rather than assuming the leader treats all followers the same.

### Summary

The basic idea behind the behavioral approach is that *what* a person does in the leadership role is the crucial determinant of his or her effectiveness as a leader. The Ohio State leadership studies identified two dimensions underlying leader behavior: consideration and initiation of structure. These two dimensions appeared to be relatively independent, such that a leader could be high on both, low on both, or high on one and low on the other. In general, research has supported the idea of two basic dimensions, but the two dimensions do not appear to be as independent as originally believed (Weissenberg & Kavanagh, 1972) and attempts to predict performance of followers from these scales have been disappointing. Recent research has attempted to expand the basic dimensions. Other researchers have examined more specific leader behaviors, including communication styles, influence tactics, and styles of conflict resolution.

## SITUATIONAL INFLUENCES IN LEADERSHIP

The situational approach suggests that whether you are a leader or not is mainly a matter of external events. While the behavior approach emphasizes *what you do* and the trait approach emphasizes *who you are,* the situational approach stresses external factors over which you may have no control. These situational factors could include your followers (e.g., ability, motivation, cohesiveness of group), the task (i.e., the extent of variety, structure, autonomy), your position in the organizational hierarchy (lower, middle, higher level management), pressures on your unit to perform (e.g., severe deadlines), the organizational structure (e.g., degree of centralization of authority), and the environment of the organization (e.g., extent of competition with other organizations). These situational factors can determine how you behave as well as your effectiveness in performing the leadership role.

## The Effects of the Situation on Leader Behavior

The hypothesis that leaders are influenced by the situation is well documented. The following conclusions were reached by Yukl from research examining the effects of situational variables on leader behavior (1981, pp. 180–186).

1. The lower managers are in the hierarchy, the less likely they are to use participative leadership and the more likely they are to focus on technical matters and to monitor subordinate performance.

2. Managers of production functions will be more autocratic and less participative than sales or staff managers. The most participative are likely to be managers of staff specialists such as lawyers, human resource management personnel, and industrial engineers.

3. Leaders are more directive and less participative as the task becomes more structured. According to Yukl, this occurs because directive and autocratic behavior is easier to exercise on tasks for which one knows the answers. On more complex and less structured tasks, leaders will need to depend more on subordinates to determine the best way to perform the work.

4. Leaders are less participative and more autocratic as the number of followers they supervise increases. With increased size of the group, leaders are also less likely to show consideration or support of followers.

5. As the stress of the situation increases (severe time constraints, hostile environment) the leader becomes more directive and task oriented and less considerate.

6. As subordinate performance and competence decline, leaders are more likely to react with increasingly close, directive, punishing, and structuring behavior and less consideration and participation.

Questions remain to be answered about the above effects. We cannot determine from field research whether the differences observed are the result of the situation or the particular types of leaders attracted to the situation. A second complication is that we cannot in many cases separate the effects of the various situational factors. Type of task, for example, is often confounded with the type of worker performing the task. Laboratory research on many of the above variables has provided unconfounded estimates of the influence of various situational factors. The findings generally support the situational view that leader behavior can change markedly in response to changes in the situation (Zaccaro, Foti, & Kenny, 1991).

## The Effects of the Situation on Effectiveness

A second prediction of situational theory is that the performance of the group or organization is determined more by external forces than by the leader. Research supporting this hypothesis has come largely from studies on the effects of replacing top-level managers. A common practice when things go wrong is for heads to roll at the top of the corporate hierarchy. According to one analysis, the open rebuke and humiliation of fired managers is an increasingly frequent response to bad times as top executives attempt to convince employees and shareholders that something is being done to correct the firm's problems (Stern, Carroll, & McQueen, 1991).

If leadership is important in determining success, then a correlation should exist between success of the organization and changes in leadership. Contrary to popular conceptions, however, changeovers in top-level managers often appear less important than external factors as correlates of organizational performance (Allen, Panian, & Lotz, 1979; Lieberson & O'Connor, 1972; Rosen, 1969). For instance, one study looked at the performance of all major league baseball teams over a 53-year period (Allen, Panian, & Lotz, 1979). Contrary to the belief that firing the manager can turn the team around, there was little relationship between team performance and whether the team replaced the manager. The performance of the team was largely correlated with how well the team performed in the previous season.

While findings such as these debunk the overly romanticized view of the leader as the primary source of a group or organization's success, more recent studies cast doubt on the extreme view that leadership makes no difference. One study found that the chief executive officer was a major determinant of the profitability of corporations (Weiner & Mahoney, 1981). Another study, conducted with churches, found that bringing in a new minister who had been successful in the past improved the performance of the church (Smith, Carson, & Alexander, 1984). The best conclusion from the research on managerial success is that both the situation and the leader are potentially important determinants of how well the group or organization performs. Both can affect outcomes, with the circumstances dictating their relative importance.

## Implications of Situational Theory for Leader Effectiveness

What practical implications can be derived from the situational approach to effective leadership? The strongest situational views provide little help in this regard and perhaps should not be called leadership theories.

In placing primary emphasis on the situation, they deny that leaders can do much to change the forces acting on them and their followers. The focus instead should be on the organizational structure, the task, the competence of employees, and other situational factors.

In contrast to such a radical version of the situational perspective, the *substitutes of leadership* model (Kerr & Jermier, 1978) is a more moderate situational position. According to this approach, leaders must carefully assess the situation and determine what they can contribute, if anything, to external forces already at work. Two types of situational factors are distinguished. *Neutralizers* are factors that prevent a leader from having either a positive or negative effect on followers. For example, if subordinates were indifferent to the rewards offered by the organization or if the leader lacked control over organizational rewards, then attempts to exert leadership via a person-oriented or task-oriented behavior may have no effect.

The other situational factor is the *substitute*. Here the situation does not prevent the leader from exercising influence, but it makes leadership attempts redundant. Subordinates who are highly professional, intrinsically motivated, and belong to a highly cohesive work group can take the place of a person-oriented or task-oriented leader. Unlike neutralizers, when substitutes are present, exerting leadership is redundant and might do harm. For example, in attempting to structure and clarify a highly routine task, the leader may only add structure to an already structured situation and may make a boring situation even more boring. A structured task in this situation is a substitute for structuring leadership. Research testing Kerr and Jermier's substitutes model has yielded mixed results (Howell & Dorfman, 1981; Sheridan, Vredenburgh, & Abelson, 1984; Podsakoff, Todor, Grover, & Huber, 1984), but findings are positive enough to suggest that this is a promising approach that deserves more attention. The essential message is that effective leadership requires knowing when leadership is not needed. This may be quite difficult given the common belief that a leader should take charge and do *something*.

## Summary

A variety of situational forces can influence how people attempt to lead and whether they succeed or fail in these attempts. The implications of situational influences for effective leadership are most clearly stated in the recommendation of the *substitutes for leadership* model that leaders should avoid actions that are redundant with the situation. People can acquire power and influence as the result of fortuitous events, but it seems overly simplistic to conclude that leadership is only situational. Effective leadership is more likely a matter of the right person, in the right place, at the right time, doing the right things. In other words, leadership is a complex interaction of the person with the situation.

# COGNITIVE APPROACHES

The research on the traits, behaviors, and situations of leaders has identified some of the factors associated with leader effectiveness. The findings show, however, that even if leaders exhibit the right behavior, possess the requisite traits, and are in situations that make it easy to lead, they still may not influence followers or achieve their objectives. The basic assumption behind the cognitive approach is that leadership is the result of people's attempts to make sense of the world around them. If you believe you are a leader and others share this belief, then you are a leader. In some cases, perceptions may even be more important than reality. For instance, one study found that supervisors are more effective the more they monitor their subordinates (Komaki, 1986), supposedly because monitoring allows the supervisor to provide performance-contingent rewards and punishments. Contrary to this behavioral interpretation, however, another experiment suggested that the message that the monitoring conveys to followers (e.g., "I am greatly concerned about productivity and expect you to do well") is as important as the rewards and punishments that follow from the monitoring (Larson & Callahan, 1990).

## Cognitive Categorization in Leadership

The process by which persons are perceived as leaders follows the same basic social cognitive processes as occur in other contexts. In the attempt to make sense of the physical and social world, we use cognitive structures in the form of schemas and categories. These are essentially beliefs that help us to deal with the huge amount of information that we must process in our day-to-day interactions with others. *Cognitive categories* allow us to group together objects, individuals, events, and social roles that we consider equivalent. We carry around vivid instances of these categories (called prototypes) that we use in deciding what belongs and what does not belong in the category. When a critical level of similarity with the prototype is surpassed, we then assign the object, person, event, or role to the category with which the prototype is associated. Another cognitive structure that can enter into this process is the *schema,* which is a network of perceived relationships among beliefs or ideas. For instance, we might believe that introverted people are also unfriendly, cold, and aloof. The schema in this case is the belief we hold about how these traits are interrelated. This type of schema is also known as an *implicit personality theory* (IPT). Schemas and cognitive categories are similar in many respects and appear to work together in the perception of others. For instance, you might see a quiet person, who is thin, pale, and reads a lot. All of these acts are consistent with what you consider to be the prototypic intelligent person. On the basis of these behaviors you categorize him as intelligent. Once categorized you may come to believe that the person has other attributes (e.g., unfriendly, clumsy) on the basis of the schema you hold for intelligence.

Lord, Foti, and Phillips (1982) have explained the process by which people perceive others as leaders in terms of these basic cognitive processes. According to their cognitive categorization model, people develop cognitive structures that organize the way they think about leadership. The categories that are used in identifying leaders appear to be organized into a vertical hierarchy with a general leader category at the top and eleven basic-level categories associated with various contexts located lower in the hierarchy: national political, military, educational, business, religious, sports, world political, financial, minority, media, and labor leaders (Lord et al., 1982). Each of the subtypes can, in turn, be broken down into such subcategories as the successful versus the unsuccessful political leader or the evangelical versus the traditional religious leader. In some of their research Lord and his colleagues (Lord, Foti, & DeVader, 1984) attempted to describe the cognitive prototypes that are associated with these leadership categories. Students were asked to list the attributes of leaders in each of the eleven basic-level categories. These characteristics were then assembled to determine those that were most likely to be used in describing subcategories. Among the attributes that were most frequently used in describing leaders across all situations, in declining order of frequency with which they were used, were intelligent, honest, outgoing, understanding, verbally skilled, aggressive, determined, caring, decisive, dedicated, educated, and well-dressed.

Perceiving someone as a leader involves a categorization of the person into leader/nonleader or leader/follower categories and the use of schemas to infer other characteristics of the categorized person (Lord, 1985; Lord et al., 1982, p. 104). The categorization may be effortless if several behaviors of the leader clearly fit the person's conception of the good leader. Take, for example, an individual who is well-dressed, eloquent, and forceful. When such clear and vivid behaviors are exhibited, the person may be quickly labeled a leader without the observer's carefully thinking about whether the label is deserved. Shaw (1990, p. 627) compared the categorization process to "pigeonholes into which mail is sorted at a nonautomated post office. Each hole might be labeled with the last three digits of a zip code. As letters are sorted, the post office worker does not have to read the name or street address on the letter, or even look at the city or state of the address. The sorter need only glance at the last three digits of the zip code and—zip!—the letter is sorted into an appropriate pigeonhole."

Once a person is labeled as a leader, other behaviors and traits are attributed to the person that are consistent with the observer's conception of a leader. In some cases, these other behaviors and traits may never have been demonstrated by the person. For example, a person who is labeled as a leader may be seen by followers as intelligent and self-confident, despite the lack of direct evidence to support these perceptions. Evidence of this type of process has come from experiments demonstrating the effects of group performance on perceptions of leadership. In one study (Mitchell, Larson, & Green, 1977), students watched a tape of the same leader, who was described as having either a highly successful or unsuccessful group. Those who believed the group succeeded perceived the leader to initiate more structure and to show more consideration than subjects who believed the group had performed poorly. These differences were found even though the behavior of the leader was identical for both groups of subjects. Similar experiments conducted by Rush, Thomas, and Lord (1977) and Lord, Binning, Rush, and Thomas (1978) attributed the findings to the observers' leadership schemas (or implicit leadership theories). These are essentially preconceptions of what makes a leader effective or ineffective. The results of these studies suggest that most people have a leadership schema in which leaders who display a high degree of initiating structure and consideration are seen as more effective than those who are low on these dimensions. Rather than paying close attention to what the leader actually does, observers may rely on this preconception in their initial observation and recall of how the leader acted. The result is that as much as 40% of the variance in leadership ratings can be attributed to these preconceptions (Lord, Binning, Rush, & Thomas, 1978).

The lesson of these research findings is that in addition to acting like a leader, one must also be seen as a leader. Not only do the labeling and the categorization of a person as a particular type of leader appear to be crucial to the successful acquisition of power and influence (Cronshaw & Lord, 1987), but the same cognitive processes may underlie failures of leadership. Once labeled as a nonleader, even a highly qualified individual may find it extremely difficult to overcome this bias.

## Self-Fulfilling Prophecies of the Leader

We can turn this process around to consider leaders' perceptions of their followers and the influence of these perceptions on the way they lead and the outcomes of their leadership. Several management theorists have proposed that the expectations of managers toward their followers have a self-fulfilling effect. The best known of these theorists, Douglas McGregor (1960) (Chapter 3), distinguished between theory X leaders, who have little confidence in the ability or motivation of employees, and theory Y leaders, who believe that employees are hard working and decent. McGregor (1960) proposed that in response to a theory X manager, "People, deprived of opportunities to satisfy at work the needs which are now important to them, behave exactly as we might predict—with indolence, passivity, resistance to change, lack of responsibility, willingness to follow the demagogue, unreasonable demands for economic benefits. It would seem that we are caught in a web of our own weaving" (p. 71). On the other hand, McGregor theorizes, if management takes a Theory Y approach and provides the opportunity for subordinates to fulfill their self-actualization and esteem needs in the work place, then they will fulfill the expectations of management with highly responsible, creative, and productive behavior.

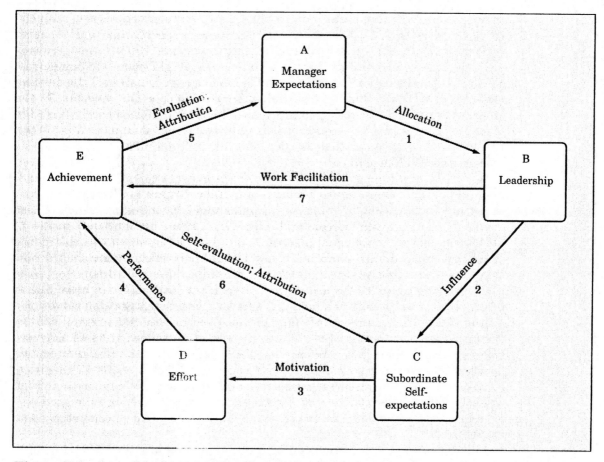

**Figure 6.3**  *A model of self-fulfilling prophecy at work*

Source: Eden, D. (1990). *Pygmalion in Management: Productivity as a Self-Fulfilling Prophecy.* Lexington, MA: Lexington Books.

Eden (1984) attempted to clarify the processes by which self-fulfilling prophecies can occur in leader-follower relationships (Figure 6.3). In linkage 1, leader expectations influence how leaders attempt to lead followers. Leaders who have high expectations are likely to behave in ways that convey their high expectations, such as allowing participation. Leaders with low expectations behave in ways that convey these low expectations, such as criticizing, punishing, and allowing minimal input into decisions.

As the result of these leader behaviors, followers develop self-expectations, that is, a belief in their own competence and motivation (linkage 2). The higher the expectation of followers that they can succeed, the more effort and time they devote to organizational tasks (linkage 3) and the better they perform (linkages 4 and 7). Higher performance then confirms and strengthens self-expectations. Those who perform well continue to have high expectations for future performance, whereas those who perform poorly have low expectations for future performance (linkage 6). These processes come full circle as leaders conclude that follower performance supports their initial expectations. If the leader starts with high expectations and the follower performs well, then the leader thinks that this person is a bright, motivated employee. This confirms the high expectations and leads to a continuation of the positive leadership behavior that was partially responsible for the outcome. If the leader starts with low expectations and the follower performs poorly, then the leader concludes that the follower lacks competence or is unmotivated. What the leader may fail to consider is how the leadership influenced the follower's performance (linkage 5).

Particularly important in all this are the causal explanations of the leaders and followers themselves. Leaders and followers are not always mindless in responding to what is going on around them but often ask "why" these events have occurred. Green and Mitchell's (1979) attributional model of leader-member interactions proposed that leaders attempt to explain the causes of subordinate performance and that their explanation shapes how they lead the subordinate. If factors external to the subordinate (e.g., the task, working conditions) are seen as important, the leader is more apt to focus on the situation by changing the task or improving working conditions. To the extent that leaders attribute follower performance to internal causes, corrective actions aimed at the follower are likely to follow. Leaders are more likely to be punitive when followers fail if they attribute the failure to factors internal to and under control of the employee (e.g., lack of effort). Likewise, leaders are more likely to be participative and considerate in response to high levels of follower performance to the extent that they attribute the good performance to internal factors under the follower's control (e.g., competence and motivation).

The followers' attributions enter into the process in Figure 6.3 by mediating the effects of the leader's actions. Thus, a leader's distrust of followers might lead to very close supervision that prevents the followers from developing the skills necessary to perform the job. Rather than attributing their failures to the leader, however, the followers may attribute failure to their own lack of ability and consequently continue to fail in the future. Similarly, if the leader has high expectations, then followers see their own effort and competence as responsible for the success and continue their successful performance.

## Impression Management

Cognitive process theories imply that people in leadership roles need to do more than adopt the right behaviors or manage the situation. They also need to manage what others *believe about their leadership*. Effective leadership becomes creating the right image and shaping the belief in superiors, subordinates, peers, and clients that the leader deserves credit for the successes of the group but not the blame for the failures (Pfeffer, 1977). An interesting example of this can be found in the letters written to shareholders by chief executive officers (CEOs). Several studies (Salancik & Meindl, 1984; Bettman & Barton, 1983; Staw, McKeachnie, & Puffer, 1983) have shown that the CEOs in these letters tended to credit themselves (e.g., their past decisions, their creativity, etc.) when the firm has done well, but to attribute poor performance to external factors (e.g., the economy, excessive government regulation). We do not wish to suggest that effective leaders should always engage in impression management. Obviously, such activities can be unethical. It is important to recognize, however, that in the highly political environment that characterizes many organizations, most people engage in some degree of impression management, even if it consists of no more than dressing for success. Moreover, impression management can be used to achieve good as well as bad ends. Leaders might attempt to take all the credit for successes and magnify their own importance at the expense of followers. On the other hand, impression management could be a means of enhancing the self-respect and confidence of followers.

### Summary

Cognitive approaches focus on perceptions as a crucial mediator of leadership. A factor to consider is whether individuals are categorized as leaders. Followers are hypothesized to compare a person's behavior with reference to a leader prototype. Once the person is labeled as a leader, other attributes are assigned that are consistent with the prototype. On the other hand, a person who is not labeled as a leader is unable to wield influence because others do not recognize or interpret his or her actions as those of a leader.

Labeling on the part of the leader and follower can result in self-fulfilling prophecies. Leaders' expectations and attitudes toward followers can bias their treatment of followers in ways that evoke the behaviors they expect. The self-fulfilling prophecy reaches full cycle when leaders fail to see the influence of their own leadership and conclude that followers' actions confirm their original expectations. The clear implication is that leaders need self-insight into their own expectations and the potential influence of these expectations on leader-follower relationships. A second implication is that doing the right thing is not always enough: Leaders need to manage impressions so that they are given credit for doing the right thing.

# CONTINGENCY THEORIES

If you are still wondering whether you are a leader, the answer of the contingency approach is "It all depends." Each of the theories we have discussed has provided valuable insight into a piece of the leadership puzzle, but no one theory is sufficient to account for the complexity of leadership in an organization. Contingency theorists attempt to predict the type of leadership needed in specific situations. The three contingency models that have generated the most research are Fiedler's *contingency theory,* House's *path-goal theory,* and Vroom/Yetton/Jago's *decision model of participative leadership.* An approach that has received more attention from practicing managers than from researchers is the Hersey and Blanchard *situational theory of leadership.* None of these has incorporated all the factors we have discussed here, but they have taken some promising steps in the right direction.

## Fiedler's Contingency Theory

Fred Fiedler (1978) proposes in his contingency theory of leadership that the most effective type of leadership depends on the leader's traits and the favorability of the situation. Situation favorability affects the ease with which leaders can manage and results from task structure, leader-member relations, and position power. It is easier to be a leader, Fiedler argues, when there is a high degree of task structure, followers have great respect for the leader, and the leader has considerable amounts of reward, coercive, and legitimate powers (position power) than when there is a lack of these conditions. By classifying situations as either high or low on each of these three dimensions of favorability, eight situational categories can be identified, ranging from the most favorable to the least favorable. Octant 1 represents the most favorable set of conditions; octant 8 represents the worst. The specific ordering of octants is based on the assumption that leader-member relations is the most important factor, whereas position power is the least important.

How the leader behaves and the effectiveness of these actions depend on the combination of leader personality and the situation's favorability. The personality trait of concern to Fiedler is measured using the least preferred coworker (LPC) scale. If you took the LPC you would be asked to rate on several attributes the person with whom you have the most difficulty working (e.g., pleasant-unpleasant, friendly-unfriendly, cooperative-uncooperative, efficient-inefficient). If you rated this least preferred coworker negatively, you would be a low LPC leader. If you rated the least preferred coworker positively, you would be a high LPC leader. But what does the LPC score really mean? In earlier interpretations, Fiedler claimed that the LPC was a straightforward measure of leader behavior or style. Thus, a low LPC leader is task-oriented and a high LPC leader is relationships-oriented in interactions with followers. After finding low correlations between the LPC and other measures of leadership style, however, Fiedler shifted to a more complex interpretation. Now, the LPC scale is believed to be a motivational construct reflecting the leader's hierarchy of needs. The low LPC leader seeks satisfaction through task accomplishment first but if the task needs are fulfilled, this leader shifts the emphasis to relationships. The high LPC leader shows the opposite. The first priority for the high LPC leader is maintaining good interpersonal relations, but once these relationships are assured, this leader emphasizes task accomplishment.

**Table 6.2**

| RESULTS OF FIELD RESEARCH TESTING FIEDLER'S CONTINGENCY THEORY | | | | | |
|---|---|---|---|---|---|
| Situational Favorability | Octant | Leader-Member Relationships | Task Structure | Power | Correlation of LPC and Performance |
| High | 1 | Good | High | Strong | −.42[+] |
| | 2 | Good | High | Weak | −.42[+] |
| | 3 | Good | Low | Strong | −.33[+] |
| | 4 | Good | Low | Weak | .28[+] |
| | 5 | Poor | High | Strong | .45[+] |
| | 6 | Poor | High | Weak | −.01 |
| | 7 | Poor | Low | Strong | .13[+] |
| Low | 8 | Poor | Low | Weak | −.50[+] |

[+]Direction of the correlation supports predictions of the Fiedler contingency model.

*Source:* Peters, L.H., Hartke, D.D., & Pohlmann, J.T. (1985). Fiedler's contingency theory of leadership: An application of the meta-analysis procedures of Schmidt and Hunter. *Psychological Bulletin, 97,* 274–285.

According to contingency theory, the low LPC leader is most effective in highly favorable and highly unfavorable situations (Table 6.2). In the most recent version of the theory, followers in a highly unfavorable situation need strong direction, and it is in this type of situation that the low LPC leader is most likely to be directing. Task success seems assured at the other end of the continuum where there is task structure, good group relationships, and high position power. Consequently, the low LPC leader focuses less on the task and more on relationships among followers. Again, this is exactly what the group needs, according to the theory. While the low LPC leader acts in a way that is appropriate to what is needed in the situation in the two extremes, the high LPC leader is likely to act in a way that conflicts with what is needed in these same situations. Thus, a high LPC leader in the unfavorable situation is most concerned with relationships when the primary focus should be on the task. In the favorable situation the same leader is most concerned with the task when the group does not need the structure. Where the high LPC leader is predicted to be most effective is in the moderately favorable situations.

Contingency theory has been tested in numerous studies conducted all over the world. Recent surveys of the correlations between the LPC measure and performance in each of the eight conditions tend to support the predictions of the model (Strube & Garcia, 1981; Vecchio, 1983; Peters, Hartke, & Pohlmann, 1985). Consistent with Fiedler's predictions, a positive correlation between LPC and performance is found in the middle octants (Table 6.2). A positive correlation indicates that high-LPC leaders are more effective in these situations. Also consistent with the model, a negative correlation is found between LPC and performance in the extremely favorable and unfavorable octants, indicating that a low-LPC leader is effective in these situations. The pattern of results found in the research generally supports the model's predictions, but the level of correlations reported is small and leaves much unexplained.

Fiedler's contingency theory has some interesting implications for practice. As a first step, he suggests measuring each manager's leadership orientation (using the LPC index) and the favorability of the situation (on position power, leader-member relations, and task structure). Leaders should be assigned to situations that match their LPCs. If the situation is moderately favorable, a high-LPC leader would provide the best fit. If the situation were highly unfavorable or highly favorable, a low-LPC leader would provide the best fit. If the leader's LPC does not match the situation, then change the situation to provide a better fit. Thus, if a high-LPC leader found himself or herself in a highly unfavorable situation, then one alternative is to move situational favorability toward the moderate position on the continuum by adding to the leader's position power, improving relations with the group, or structuring the task. Because Fiedler defines LPC as a trait, he believes that changing the leader is much more difficult than engineering the situation to suit the leader. Fiedler, Chemers, and Mahar (1976) have developed a training program called LEADER MATCH in which they instruct leaders in how to assess their own style and then modify the situation to fit this style.

Despite empirical support, numerous critics have pointed out weaknesses in the logic and the research underlying Fiedler's theory (Ashour, 1973; Evans & Dermer, 1974; Graen, Alvares, Orris, & Martella, 1970). Perhaps the most damning criticisms are aimed at the construct validity of the LPC measure. As we have shown, Fiedler has changed his views several times on what the LPC is, viewing it at one time as a measure of leader style and more recently as a measure of leader priorities. Another problem is the tendency in some of the research to categorize situational favorability after the data are collected rather than starting with a priori classifications of the situation. Despite its shortcomings, Fiedler's theory is intuitively appealing and is more comprehensive than most other leadership models.

## Path-Goal Theory of Leadership

This model of leadership proposes that the most important function of the leader is to motivate followers to invest effort in achieving organizational goals (House, 1971; House & Mitchell, 1975). The leader's behavior is predicted to influence followers as a consequence of the same factors stated in the VIE model of motivation (Chapter 3): (1) the subjective probability that effort will result in effective performance, (2) the instrumentality of effective performance for valued outcomes, and (3) the positive valence of these outcomes. According to the path-goal theory of leadership, the leader should carefully examine the situation, including the needs and expectations of the employees, and act in ways that will increase the employees' expectations that effort will lead to positively valued outcomes. Predictions have been derived from these basic propositions for four dimensions of leader behavior: (1) directiveness (structuring), (2) supportiveness (consideration), (3) participativeness, and (4) achievement orientation.

## LEADER DIRECTIVENESS

This dimension of behavior is essentially the same as initiating structure. The effects of leader directiveness are predicted to depend largely on the degree of structure that exists in the tasks that subordinates perform and on how much subordinates need clarity and structure. If the task is structured or if subordinates have a low need for clarity, then directive leadership could lessen employee satisfaction and performance. A directive approach is needed, however, when the task is unstructured and subordinates have a high need for structure. Research has supported these predictions, in that while more directive leaders tend to have more satisfied subordinates on unstructured tasks, they tend to have dissatisfied subordinates on more structured tasks. The predictions of path-goal theory for directiveness have held more for satisfaction than for performance (Schreisheim & DeNisi, 1981). There is also some indication that leader initiation of structure is more positively related to satisfaction for employees who have a personal need for clarity than for those who are more tolerant of ambiguity (Keller, 1989).

## LEADER SUPPORTIVENESS

This dimension of behavior is very similar to leader consideration. Path-goal theory predicts that supportive leadership will be associated with higher job satisfaction when the job is dissatisfying than when it is intrinsically satisfying. A similar prediction is that supportive or considerate leadership will have a more positive relationship to job satisfaction when the task is stressful than when it is nonstressful. In the case of a dissatisfying or stressful task, supportiveness *complements* the situation by providing rewards (praise, emotional support, etc.) where there are few intrinsic rewards. Again, the research generally has supported the predictions. In one study, police dispatchers were observed throughout an eight-hour shift, and the degree of quantifiable work load was measured by taking the hourly rate of incoming telephone calls, radio transmissions, and communications from supervisors and peers (Kirmeyer & Lin, 1987). Under high work load, the dispatchers who received more support from the supervisor engaged in more coping behavior and reported less tension and anxiety. The degree of support made little difference, however, when the work load was low.

## LEADER PARTICIPATIVENESS

A third prediction involves the degree to which the leader allows subordinates to get involved in making decisions. The job satisfaction resulting from participative leadership should depend on both the structure of the task and the authoritarianism of the subordinates. Authoritarianism is a personality trait that purportedly measures the extent to which people submit to authority figures. High-authoritarian subordinates prefer a high degree of control in their environment, whereas low-authoritarian subordinates value their independence. According to House, low-authoritarian subordinates are more satisfied with a job when the supervisor allows them to participate in decisions regarding the job than when the supervisor is nonparticipative. Moreover, the low-authoritarian subordinate values participation for its own sake, not for its effect on goal achievement. On the other hand, the job satisfaction of a high-authoritarian subordinate is enhanced by participation only in unstructured tasks. Supposedly participation enhances satisfaction among these subordinates because their expectations that their efforts will result in task success are increased. Schuler (1976) found support for these predictions in research with employees in a manufacturing plant.

## ACHIEVEMENT-ORIENTED LEADERSHIP

An achievement-oriented leader, according to House and Mitchell (1975):

> sets challenging goals, expects subordinates to perform at their highest level, continuously seeks improvement in performance, and shows a high degree of confidence that the subordinates will assume responsibility, put forth effort, and accomplish challenging goals (p. 455).

The path-goal theory prediction is that achievement-oriented leadership will cause subordinates to have more confidence in their own ability and that this will cause them to increase their efforts to succeed. Again, however, this expectation holds only for unstructured tasks in which subordinate expectations are likely to be low. There is insufficient research evaluating path-goal predictions for achievement-oriented leadership to allow any conclusions.

The research on these four dimensions of leadership has generally supported several path-goal theory predictions regarding job satisfaction. The relationships reported between leadership style and job satisfaction are not particularly strong, however, and are subject to other interpretations. Also, because most of the evidence is correlational, there is uncertainty as to which factors are causal.

## Vroom/Yetton/Jago's Decision Model of Leadership

More organizations are attempting to involve employees in decision making in order to improve productivity and quality. Take, for example, the letter to shareholders in General Electric's 1992 annual report ("GE is not a place for autocrats, Welch decrees," *The Wall Street Journal*, March 3, 1992, p. B1). In this letter, GE's chief executive officer announced that autocratic leaders would no longer be tolerated, even if they performed well: "Too often all of us have looked the other way—tolerated these . . . managers because 'they always deliver'—at least in the short term . . . but in an environment where we must have every good idea from every man and woman in the organization, we cannot afford management styles that suppress and intimidate" (p. 5). Although these views are gaining in popularity in U.S. companies, the research on leadership suggests that participative leadership is not always effective and that autocratic leadership has its place. The Vroom/Yetton/Jago model was developed explicitly to help managers decide when they should involve followers in decisions and the level of this involvement (Vroom & Yetton, 1973; Vroom & Jago, 1988). As in the case of all contingency models, these theorists do not promote universal leadership styles but instead suggest that the degree of follower participation should vary with the situation. A unique aspect of this model is that it views leadership as a choice among various degrees of participation.

Vroom and associates present five levels of participative decision making that range from the most autocratic (AI) to the most participative (GII) in the case of groups. These five alternative decision methods are presented in Table 6.3 and are self-explanatory. In deciding among these alternative leadership

**Table 6.3**

### ALTERNATIVE GROUP DECISION-MAKING METHODS IN THE VROOM/YETTON/JAGO MODEL

| SYMBOL | DEFINITION |
|---|---|
| AI | You solve the problem or make the decision yourself using the information available to you at the present time. |
| AII | You obtain any necessary information from subordinates, then decide on a solution to the problem yourself. You may or may not tell subordinates the purpose of your questions or give information about the problem or decision on which you are working. The input provided by them is clearly in response to your request for specific information. They do not play a role in the definition of the problem or in generating or evaluating alternative solutions. |
| CI | You share the problem with the relevant subordinates individually, getting their ideas and suggestions without bringing them together as a group. Then you make the decision. This decision may or may not reflect your subordinates' influence. |
| CII | You share the problem with your subordinates in a group meeting. In this meeting you obtain their ideas and suggestions. Then you make the decision, which may or may not reflect your subordinates' influence. |
| GII | You share the problem with your subordinates as a group. Together you generate and evaluate alternatives and attempt to reach agreement (consensus) on a solution. Your role is much like that of chairperson, coordinating the discussion, keeping it focused on the problem, and making sure that the critical issues are discussed. You can provide the group with information or ideas that you have, but you do not try to "press" them to adopt "your" solution, and you are willing to accept and implement any solution that has the support of the entire group. |

*Source:* Vroom, V.H., & Yetton, P.W. (1973). *Leadership and Decision-making.* Pittsburgh: Univesity of Pittsburgh Press.

approaches, Vroom and associates state that the leader should carefully diagnose the situation in terms of the basic attributes that are shown in Table 6.4. Using the rules in Table 6.5, the leader then computes the overall effectiveness of different decision strategies and chooses that alternative that is likely to have the highest overall effectiveness. Overall effectiveness is calculated in the following manner:

$$\text{Overall effectiveness} = \text{Decision effectiveness} - \text{Cost} + \text{Development}$$

*Decision effectiveness* in the above equation is a function of (1) the importance of the technical quality of the decision, (2) the degree to which followers must be committed to the solution, and (3) the extent to which the time involved

**Table 6.4**

---

### PROBLEM ATTRIBUTES USED IN DECIDING AMONG ALTERNATIVE DECISION-MAKING METHODS IN THE VROOM/YETTON/JAGO MODEL

QR: **Quality requirement**
How important is the technical quality of this decision?

CR: **Commitment requirement**
How important is subordinate commitment to the decision?

LI: **Leader information**
Do you have sufficient information to make a high-quality decision?

ST: **Problem structure**
Is the problem well structured?

CP: **Commitment probability**
If you were to make the decision by yourself, is it reasonably certain that your subordinate(s) would be committed to the decision?

GC: **Goal congruence**
Do subordinates share the organizational goals to be attained in solving this problem?

CO: **Subordinate conflict**
Is conflict among subordinates over preferred solutions likely? (Group problems only).
Is conflict between you and your subordinates over a preferred solution likely? (Individual problems only)

SI: **Subordinate information**
Do subordinates have sufficient information to make a high-quality decision?

TC: **Time constraint**
Does a critically severe time constraint limit your ability to involve subordinates?

GD: **Geographical dispersion**
Are the costs involved in bringing together geographically dispersed subordinates prohibitive? (Group problems only)

MT: **Motivation-time**
How important is it to you to minimize the time it takes to make the decision?

MD: **Motivation-development**
How important is it to you to maximize the opportunities for subordinate development?

*Source:* Adapted from Vroom, V.H., & Jago, A.G. (1988). *The New Leadership: Managing Participation in Organizations.* Englewood Cliffs, NJ: Prentice-Hall.

**Table 6.5**

---

## DECISION RULES FOR CHOOSING AMONG ALTERNATIVE GROUP DECISION-MAKING METHODS IN THE VROOM/YETTON/JAGO MODEL

**I. FOR GROUP PROBLEMS, TO IMPROVE DECISION QUALITY:**
1. AVOID the use of AI when:
   a. the leader lacks the necessary information.
2. AVOID the use of GII when:
   a. subordinates do not share the organizational goals, and/or
   b. subordinates do not have the necessary information.
3. AVOID the use of AII and CI when:
   a. the leader lacks the necessary information, and
   b. the problem is unstructured.
4. MOVE toward GII when:
   a. the leader lacks the necessary information, and
   b. subordinates share the organizational goals, and
   c. there is conflict among subordinates over preferred solutions.

**II. FOR GROUP PROBLEMS, TO IMPROVE DECISION COMMITMENT:**
1. MOVE toward GII when:
   a. subordinates are not likely to become committed to the leader's decision.
2. MOVE toward GII when:
   a. subordinates are not likely to become committed to the leader's decision, and
   b. there is conflict among subordinates over preferred solutions.

**III. FOR GROUP PROBLEMS, TO REDUCE DECISION COSTS (TIME):**
1. MOVE toward AI, especially if:
   a. a severe time constraint exists, and/or
   b. the problem is unstructured.
2. AVOID use of CII and GII if:
   a. subordinates are geographically dispersed, or
   b. there is conflict among subordinates over preferred solutions.

The considerations under III would be irrelevant if time were of no importance and if there were no severe time constraint on the making of the decision. They should play an increasing role in one's thinking and one's choices as the importance of time increases.

**IV. FOR GROUP PROBLEMS, TO INCREASE SUBORDINATE DEVELOPMENT:**
1. MOVE toward GII when:
   a. the problem possesses a quality requirement.
2. MOVE toward CII and GII when:
   a. subordinates share organizational goals, and
   b. there is conflict among subordinates over preferred solutions.
3. MOVE away from CII and GII when:
   a. subordinates do not share organizational goals, and
   b. there is conflict among subordinates over preferred solutions.

The considerations under IV would be irrelevant if development of subordinates is of no importance. They should play an increasing role in one's thinking and one's choices as the importance of development increases.

*Source:* Adapted from Vroom, V.H., & Jago, A.G. (1988). *The New Leadership: Managing Participation in Organizations.* Englewood Cliffs, NJ: Prentice-Hall.

incurs a penalty. In some cases, the quality dimension is unimportant, whereas the degree of commitment to the solution is important. In these situations there is no rational basis for declaring that one solution to the problem is superior to another, and all that matters is whether the followers accept the solution. In other cases, degree of commitment makes little difference and only quality is a concern. Many of the important problems facing management, however, require both quality and commitment. If time is not a relevant consideration, the time penalty is zero and decision effectiveness is determined solely by the quality and commitment requirements. To the extent that the decision must be made quickly, participative decision alternatives are less effective.

In addition to the decision effectiveness, a manager must also consider a second factor in the above equation, the *costs of the participation itself.* Cost is a function of the time and effort required to implement the decision alternative. Generally, the more managers attempt to involve followers in a decision, the more cost is incurred as time is taken away from other activities. GII involves more cost than CII, which in turn is more costly than the CI, AII, or AI alternatives. Managers are well aware of the costs associated with participation, but they frequently do not recognize the third factor in the equation: *development.* This refers to the *value* added from employee participation as the result of increased understanding of the problem, possible payoffs for teamwork, and increased identification with the organization. Generally, the more participation, the greater the developmental gains of the decision process.

Figure 6.4 illustrates the use of the model for group decisions where developing employee skills has high priority. (Note that some of the situational attributes in Table 6.4 are not included in the decision tree.) For example, if the technical quality of the decision was unimportant (low branch on the QR attribute) but subordinate commitment to the decision was important (high branch on the CR attribute), then you would skip the leader information (LI) and problem structure (ST) attributes and ask whether subordinates would be committed to the decision if you made the decision yourself (CP). If the answer was yes, then you would arrive at AI, meaning that you would want to make the decision yourself without involving the group. If the answer was no, then you would want to use GII, meaning that you would fully involve the group in the decision.

Training managers in the use of the model involves calculating the decision rules that they actually use in choosing among levels of participation and then giving them feedback on how their rules deviate from the rules recommended in the Vroom/Yetton/Jago model. To do this, numerous hypothetical cases are presented that vary along the eight situational attributes. A manager reads each case and then chooses the alternative decision styles that he or she would use in that situation. A computer analysis shows where the manager conforms to the model and where he or she deviates from it.

The model has an important advantage over many of the other approaches that we have discussed in that it sets forth specific hypotheses.

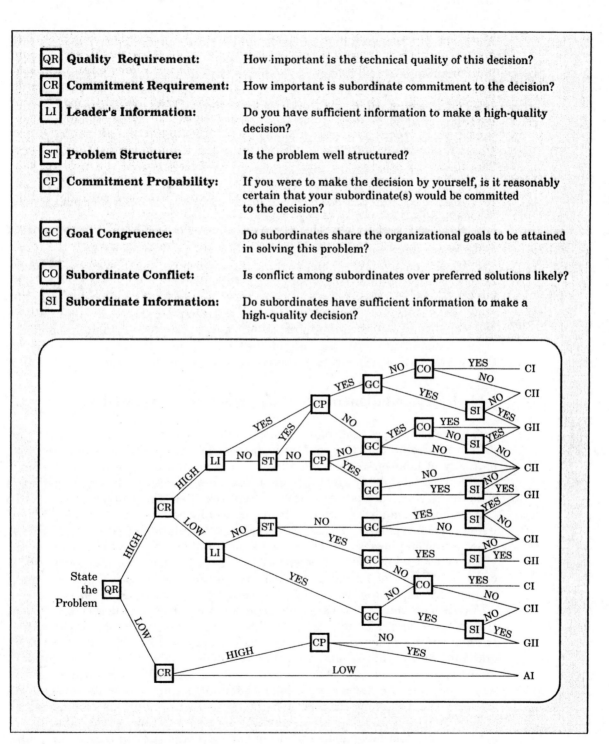

**Figure 6.4**  *Development driven decision tree—Group problems*
*Source:* Vroom, V.H., & Jago, A.G. (1988). *The New Leadership: Managing Participation in Organizations.* Englewood Cliffs, NJ: Prentice-Hall.

Moreover, the research has generally supported its predictions. The most frequent approach in testing the model has been to ask managers to recall some of their successful and unsuccessful decisions. Findings indicate that decision-making styles used in successful decisions are more likely to fit the model's recommendations than are the decision-making styles used in unsuccessful decisions (Vroom & Jago, 1988). In another study providing support for the model, Field (1982) gave five problems that varied along the attributes in the Vroom/Yetton/Jago model to small groups to solve in a laboratory experiment. The leader of each group was instructed to follow one of the five decision styles across all five problems. Generally, leaders were more effective when they used a decision process that the model defined as effective for a situation than when they used a style that was defined as ineffective.

Potential problems in the model have been identified. In several studies researchers have shown that the model is more valid in describing the managerial perspective on problems than the subordinate perspective (Field & House, 1990; Heilman, Hornstein, Cage, & Herschlag, 1984). Specifically, the predictions of the Vroom/Yetton/Jago model were better supported when the data were collected through managers' self-reported decisions than when the data were collected through subordinates' reports of what happened. When respondents took the role of the subordinate, they tended to report that participative styles were effective regardless of the situation.

## Hersey and Blanchard's Situational Leadership Model

A contingency that many practicing managers would endorse as an important factor, but that has been largely ignored in the research, is the *maturity* of followers. A common view is that immature workers need more directive leadership. For instance, in a *New York Times* article a management consultant claimed that workers in their twenties and thirties need to be treated in the same way that a teenager would be treated by a parent. By using what he called a "re-parenting strategy," he claimed that the productivity of young employees could be raised to acceptable levels within two or three years (Shechtman, 1991). Not surprisingly, these views were sharply criticized in a series of letters published in a subsequent issue ("Re-parent the young workers? Not on your life," *New York Times*, December 1, 1991).

Whether younger workers are generally immature and deserving of this type of treatment is doubtful, but the idea of adjusting leadership style to the *maturity* of the followers is consistent with Hersey and Blanchard's (1982) *situational theory*. Hersey and Blanchard describe leadership in terms of two dimensions that they call task orientation and relationship orientation. These are essentially the same dimensions as found in the Ohio State leadership studies. The particular combination of these two dimensions that is most effective depends on followers' maturity, which they define as "the capacity to set high but attainable goals (achievement-motivation), willingness and ability to take responsibility, and education and/or experience of an individual or a group" (p. 161). They recommend that less task orientation and more relationship orientation are needed as the maturity of followers increases, up to the point that the group reaches a moderate level of maturity. Past this point, leaders should de-emphasize *both* tasks and relationships in their leadership. A highly mature group is most effective with a leader who has a low-relationship/low-task orientation. A moderately mature group is more effective with a high-relationship/low-task orientation leader. A group with a somewhat less than moderate level of maturity needs a high-task/high-relationship orientation leader. Finally, a highly immature group is most effective with a leader who is high in task orientation and low in relationship orientation. The rationale of this last prediction is that a highly immature group needs a taskmaster and a relationship orientation may send them the wrong signals.

Criticisms of Hersey and Blanchard's model have focused on several conceptual weaknesses, most notably the ambiguity of the maturity dimension (Graeff, 1983). There is also little evidence to support a nonlinear relationship between follower effectiveness and either leader task orientation or leader relationship orientation (Graeff, 1983). In one of the few empirical tests of the Hersey and Blanchard model, high school teachers were surveyed concerning the supervision they received from their principals (Vecchio, 1987). In support of the theory, teachers tended to have higher performance and satisfaction if their principal's leadership style fit the recommendations of the Hersey and Blanchard model. The strongest support was for the low-maturity condition. As predicted, principals who were low in consideration and high in structuring were most effective when their teachers were low in maturity. Mixed support was found for the other predictions, however.

# CHARISMATIC, INSPIRATIONAL, AND TRANSFORMATIONAL LEADERSHIP

You may have some doubts at this point as to whether the various approaches we have discussed have really captured the essence of leadership. Perhaps you share the popular view of leadership as something special, unique, and almost mystical in nature. Psychologists have attempted to subject leadership to dispassionate scientific analysis and, in the process, they have stripped away much of the romance associated with the concept. While this research has led to insights into factors associated with leader effectiveness, some theorists have come to believe that there is something to the romantic view that research and theory need to recapture. Specifically, leaders such as Martin Luther King, Jr., Winston Churchill, and Adolph Hitler did not simply wield influence but profoundly changed the lives of many of their followers. Bass (1990) distinguished among three concepts of leadership that incorporate this aspect of leadership and that are receiving increasing attention from theorists and researchers: charismatic, inspirational, and transformational leadership. All of these bear some resemblance to the personal sources of power (referent and expert) in the French and Raven model discussed earlier.

The concept of the *charismatic leader* can be traced to the writings of Max Weber (1924/1947, pp. 358–359), who described the charismatic leader as "set apart from ordinary men and treated as endowed with supernatural, superhuman, or at least . . . exceptional powers and qualities . . . (which) are not accessible to the ordinary person but are regarded as of divine origin or as exemplary, and on the basis of them the individual concerned is treated as a leader." There is a certain amount of craziness involved in Weber's depiction of charisma in that the leader so motivates followers that they will go to almost any extreme to fulfill the leader's mission. Although the charismatic leader is believed to possess extraordinary characteristics by followers, it is important to recognize that charisma as Weber and others have described it derives not only from the leader but also from the characteristics of the followers, the situation, and the relationship of the leader and followers. Trice and Beyer (1986) described charismatic leadership as a process in which an individual with extraordinary personal attributes successfully implements a radical solution in a crisis. Repeated successes of the leader cause followers to identify with the leader and imbue him or her with almost superhuman powers. House (1977) presented a theory of charismatic leadership that builds on Weber's writings. He proposed that charismatic leaders are more likely in their communications to refer to basic values, the collective identity of the group or organization, long-term goals, and followers' worth and efficacy as individuals. Moreover, charismatic leaders are likely to convey confidence in their own abilities as well as those of their followers. As a consequence of these actions, followers are motivated to strive to achieve high levels of performance as a consequence of linking their self-esteem to task successes. House (1977) further proposed that charismatic leaders emerge and are effective when the means of achieving goals are unclear, when extrinsic rewards cannot be clearly linked to individual performance, and when the organizational and environmental conditions are unstable. House, Spangler, and Woycke (1991) tested some of these notions in an interesting study in which they rated the charisma of all the U.S. presidents from George Washington to Ronald Reagan on the basis of historical documents. (As an exercise, go back to the photos of the presidents on p. 244 and try to estimate their relative charisma. See the appendix for the answers.) The charisma shown by a president appeared to be shaped both by the personality of the president and by the situation over which he presided. The extent of charisma was positively related to the president's need for power, power inhibition, and the magnitude of the crises he faced during his administration, but negatively related to his need for achievement. In turn, the more charismatic the president, the more effective he was in dealing with the economy and domestic affairs.

Followers are personally attracted to the personal attributes of the charismatic leader, but followers of an *inspirational leader* are more influenced by the goals of the leader rather than his or her personal attributes. According to Bass (1990), an inspirational leader is likely to state uplifting goals and then instill in followers confidence in their ability to achieve these goals. *Envisioning* is a crucial skill in inspirational leadership and involves "creating of an image of a desired future organizational state that can serve as a guide for interim strategies, decisions, and behavior" (Bass, 1990, p. 214). At the same time that they can envision, inspirational leaders know how to *enable* and *empower* followers by obtaining resources they need, removing constraints, and showing them how to accomplish their objectives. This may involve giving employees autonomy and discretionary opportunities, getting support from higher level authorities for their efforts, and providing frequent encouragement. Furthermore, "Leaders can promote enabling by stressing that everyone can be a winner through constant learning and improvement. Risks can be taken, and mistakes can be tolerated" (p. 213). Additionally, an inspirational leader *intellectually stimulates* followers by engaging them in a creative process of problem solving, encouraging them to get out of their habitual routines, and stimulating innovative solutions. According to Bass (1990), impression management is another important aspect of inspirational leadership. Such leaders frequently attempt to project an attractive image that inspires confidence and reinforces the values and goals of the leader.

The concept of *transformational leadership* was first introduced by Burns (1978), who contrasted it with transactional leadership. A *transactional* leader is one who influences followers through an implicit or explicit exchange. In other words, the leader and follower strike a bargain in which followers devote energy and time to pursuing goals set forth by the leader and, in return, the leader provides them with material rewards and security. In contrast to this type of leader, the transformational leader changes the values, needs, beliefs, and attitudes of followers. A somewhat different approach was taken by Bass (1990) who viewed transformational leaders as using and expanding upon transactional leadership tactics. Moreover, Bass conceived of transformational leadership as containing elements of both the charismatic and inspirational styles. A variety of behaviors has been associated with transformational leadership, but they appear to fall into the following six categories (Podsakoff, MacKenzie, Moorman, & Fetter, 1990):

1. *Identifying and articulating a vision.* Behavior on the part of the leader aimed at identifying new opportunities for his or her unit/division/company, and developing, articulating, and inspiring others with his or her vision of the future.
2. *Providing an appropriate model.* Behavior on the part of the leader that sets an example for employees to follow that is consistent with the values the leader espouses.
3. *Fostering the acceptance of group goals.* Behavior on the part of the leader aimed at promoting cooperation among employees and getting them to work together toward a common goal.
4. *High performance expectations.* Behavior that demonstrates

the leader's expectations for excellence, quality, and/or high performance on the part of followers.

5. *Providing individualized support.* Behavior on the part of the leader that indicates that he/she respects followers and is concerned about their personal feelings and needs.

6. *Intellectual stimulation.* Behavior on the part of the leader that challenges followers to re-examine some of their assumptions about their work and rethink how it can be performed (p. 112).

The work on charismatic, inspirational, and transformational leadership represents an important step in the direction of taking these concepts out of the realm of the mystical and into a form that can be used to improve organizational leadership. A recent experiment suggests that charisma can be manipulated in the laboratory (Howell & Frost, 1989). A training program to teach charismatic skills has been introduced that includes instruction in "modeling (the use of exemplary behavior), appearance, body language, and verbal skills (with an emphasis on rhetoric [word choice]), metaphors, analogies, and paralanguage (word intent)" (Conger & Kanungo, 1988, p. 317). Leaders also are taught how to express confidence in subordinates, the use of participative leadership, ways of providing autonomy from bureaucratic restraints, and goal-setting techniques. Bass (1990, pp. 215–216) suggested that to teach managers how to envision and to be more inspirational, exercises should be used in which "executives are asked to talk about how they expect to spend their day at some future date, say five years hence, or what they expect their organization to look like at some future date. Or they may be asked to write a business article about their organization's future." Whether training can actually allow an organization to develop its own charismatic, inspirational, or transformational leaders is open to question. Perhaps some people, because of their individual characteristics, simply cannot effectively adopt these styles. There is also the danger of manufacturing actors who lack values, vision, and ideas but can manipulate followers. Still, the needs for leadership to cope with present and future crises in organizations and in society are so great that any attempt to develop skills in inspiring and transforming followers is worth a try.

# A FINAL SUMMATION AND A LOOK AT THE FUTURE

In this chapter we have examined the various theories of leadership that psychologists and other behavioral scientists have subjected to empirical analysis. We contrasted the trait, behavioral, situational, and cognitive approaches, and noted that, while none of these has provided the complete answer, each has provided insights into a different aspect of the leadership process.

The empirical work has demonstrated that traits are related to perceptions of leadership and managerial effectiveness. Findings that successful leaders tend to be extraverted, assertive, self-confident, and dominant seem to confirm the stereotype of the business leader as power hungry and ambitious. Just as interesting, however, are the findings that successful leaders appear remarkably diverse on other trait dimensions.

The hope of the behavioral approach has been that by identifying what successful leaders do, organizations will be able to instruct managers in how to become effective leaders. Behavioral research has shown that leaders can be distinguished along two general dimensions: initiation of structure and consideration. Although these and other behavioral measures relate to important leadership effectiveness criteria, the results are generally weak and indicate a need to investigate more specific leader behaviors.

Situation also plays an important role in leadership. How leaders behave and their effectiveness can be shaped largely by external factors over which they have little control. Still, leadership is more than being in the right situation at the right time. Successful leadership requires knowing when to go with situational forces rather than attempting to take charge. Leaders must know what to do once they are in a situation, even if this means doing nothing.

Finally, the cognitive elements involved in leadership must be taken into account. Even if an individual possesses the right traits, exhibits the appropriate behaviors, and is fortunate enough to be in a favorable situation, attempts at leadership may fail unless others perceive that the individual is a leader. Leaders' perceptions of their followers can influence how they behave toward subordinates. For instance, followers who are seen as competent and motivated are more likely to be allowed to participate in important decisions, whereas those labeled incompetent or unmotivated are more likely to experience close and authoritarian supervision. The perceptions that leaders have of followers and the perceptions that followers have of leaders can lead to self-fulfilling prophecies. One implication of the cognitive approach is that leaders need to manage the impressions that others have of them and need to be sensitive to the effects that their beliefs can have on the way they treat followers. A more disturbing implication is that leaders can gain influence and power through projecting images that have little substance.

The first attempts to synthesize these various determinants of leadership have come from the contingency theorists. Their basic prediction is that different situations require different types of leadership. The implication for practice is that the leader should carefully diagnose the situation and then lead in a manner that fits the situational requirements. This requires flexibility as the leader shifts his or her behavior to meet the demands of the situation.

Research has reduced leadership to variables that can be engineered to some extent through selection, training, and design of the situation. Yet in the attempt to analyze leadership we are left with the uneasy feeling that the soul of the leadership process has been lost. While the traditional view of leadership may expect too much of the leader, contemporary theories seem to expect too little. In stressing the accommodation of the leader to subordinates and the situation, models of leadership have largely ignored the possibility that leaders also can transform the values, motives, and even the self-concepts of followers. It is too soon to tell whether a useful body of literature will eventually accumulate from the work on transformational, inspirational, and charismatic leadership, but these approaches promise to put some of the romance and excitement back into the study of leadership.

Changes confronting organizations will require that we reconsider many of our traditional conceptions of leadership. In the traditional, bureaucratic organization (Chapter 1), a strict hierarchy exists in which managers at each level have the authority to tell those below what to do and how to do it. Employees are assigned clearly defined duties and report to a boss who makes sure that these duties are adequately performed. In a stable, orderly world this bureaucratic structure made sense, but rapid technological and societal changes require greater innovation and flexibility than the traditional organization can provide. These trends suggest that managers of tomorrow will not be able to rely on the formal authority that comes with their positions but will need to be able to shift their leadership to fit the situation. Participative and charismatic skills will be especially important in the organization of the future. To successfully deal with the changes that confront today's institutions, leadership will be needed that can provide solutions to problems and build the commitment to implement those solutions.

## DISCUSSION QUESTIONS

1. The trait, behavioral, and situational approaches to leadership were presented as if they were incompatible views. In what ways can these three perspectives be linked to understand leader effectiveness?

2. Some have argued that psychologists do not need to study leadership because it can be reduced to communication, motivation, influence and power, and other basic behavioral processes. Do you agree? Why?

3. Can an effective leader ever be effective by being low on both consideration and initiation of structure? Why?

4. Do you believe power can corrupt any leader or only specific types of leaders? Describe the personal characteristics that might make some leaders abuse power.

5. Should leaders engage in impression management tactics and strategies? Explain.

6. What would the different theories of leadership have to say about how we should go about teaching leaders to lead?

7. What personal characteristics would a leader need to possess to effectively use a contingency model of leadership?

8. Have you ever observed a transformational leader? What did the leader do that transformed followers?

9.  We described a model in which leaders' expectations for their followers were described as self-fulfilling. Describe how followers' expectations for leaders also might be self-fulfilling.

10.  Is leadership overemphasized as the cause of organizational success and failure? Why?

# LEADERSHIP AT NUCOR

Over the last decade the American steel industry has declined and now careens toward bankruptcy. During 1977–1987 the large steel companies lost 50 million tons of capacity and one fourth of the companies went bankrupt. By 1980, 75% of steelworkers had lost their jobs. In the midst of this economic disaster, one steel company, Nucor Corporation, has been remarkably successful. Production has gone from 1.4 million tons in 1981 to 3.5 million in 1990. The profit per ton of steel shipped was $26.80 in 1990 compared with only $2.94 for Inland Steel, one of the big steel producers. The 1990 return on equity of Nucor was 11.5%.

Much of the credit for Nucor's remarkable success has gone to its founder and chief executive officer (CEO), Ken Iverson. Iverson grew up in Downers Grove, Illinois, where his father was an electrical engineer for Western Electric Company. After serving in the Navy during World War II, Ken Iverson attended Purdue University, where he received a master's degree in mechanical engineering. In 1962 he became general manager of Nuclear Corporation's Vulcraft division, which manufactured steel beams for roofs. Three years later he became president of the Nuclear Corporation, "by default" as he puts it. The Nuclear Corporation had run out of money and was on the verge of bankruptcy. Vulcraft was the most profitable part of the business, so Iverson sold off other parts of the company and focused his efforts on the beams business. At that time the steel for making these beams was purchased from U.S. Steel, but steadily increasing prices led Iverson to build his own small mill to supply the bar steel. On June 26, 1969, a minimill opened in Darlington, South Carolina, and by 1980, there were four such mills. Iverson stresses innovation and the use of the latest technology and has consistently succeeded in ventures that were widely thought to be reckless.

Contrary to what one might expect given Nucor's success, corporate headquarters occupy about half of the fourth floor of a rented building in Crawfordsville, Indiana. Although Nucor owns over twenty-two manufacturing plants all over the United States, there are fewer than 20 employees at the headquarters, including secretaries and Iverson. He is probably the only CEO of a major corporation who answers his own telephone. When he flies, he travels tourist class. Unlike most of the big steel corporations, there are only four management levels in Nucor: foreman, department head, plant manager, and Iverson, who is the president/CEO. Moreover, he is adamant in his resistance to increasing the number of managers at Nucor.

Iverson has located his Nucor plants in rural areas. The plants are all nonunion, with the steelworkers consisting mostly of young, inexperienced men hired from the surrounding areas. Plant operations are run by production teams of about eight or nine. These teams are richly rewarded with production bonuses that can amount to 100–150% of the base salary. Iverson was alarmed when bonuses grew larger than 100% of base pay, but he decided not to tamper with the system because of the large gains in productivity. Steelworkers earn as much as triple the annual wage of workers in the rural areas in which the plants are located. As an additional benefit, employees receive $1,800 in tuition for a child attending college or technical school.

Iverson regularly tours plants, asking workers their opinions, and also conducts formal surveys to gauge worker opinion on specific issues. Workers are allowed to make many decisions that in the larger mills would be reserved for management. For instance, workers were asked what they believed the policy for drug offenses should be and their opinions were followed in implementing policy. According to Iverson, "We give the worker the training and furnish the equipment, and then, in a real sense, the team is in business for itself" (Rohan, 1991, p. 30). There has never been a layoff, although Iverson does not promise that there never will be. One plant manager laid off 40 workers in a minimill, but Iverson ordered the manager to rehire the workers and then fired the plant manager. In slow years, employees often cut back to three or four days a week.

The teams of workers in each plant are responsible for maintaining efficiency, but there are strict rules imposed by management. If a steelworker is 15 minutes late for work, he or she loses the production bonus for the day, which often amounts to half his or her pay. Those late 30 minutes or more lose the bonus for the whole week. Employees are not paid when machines break down and production is halted. Also, employees who are out sick for less than three days are not paid at all. Much of the enforcement of work rules comes from the workers themselves. "The reaction to absenteeism at Nucor is swift and unpleasant, and comes from other members of the production team rather than from managers. People who become sick may try to struggle through a day's work for fear of hurting or irritating their fellow team members. If a person on a team is thought to be lazy by the others, they nag him and lecture him, and if he doesn't take to lectures, they get him fired" (Preston, 1991, p. 84).

The operators of the factories have the title of vice president–general manager and have considerable latitude in running all aspects of the operations in their plants. "In many ways they are like presidents of their own operations. . . . I let the general managers rattle around in their own cages. Some of them are a bit like dictators" (Preston, 1991, p. 840). General managers receive bonuses that are directly tied to corporate profits according to a program he calls "Share the Pain." Iverson's own salary is 70% bonus, which means that his salary can drop dramatically during bad years, as was the case during the recession in 1982 when his compensation fell from $450,000 to $108,000. According to one of his officers, "Ken can come down on your neck with the sheer brute power of his authority, when he wants to. Most of the world conceives of Ken Iverson as a hands-off manager, but that is not strictly true. Ken wants to stick his fingers into things and get involved with them. He preaches differently, but he will dictate to people. He will step into the fray several levels down" (Preston, 1991, p. 89).

High performance has been at a cost. Nucor has averaged one death per year and has been accused of cutting corners and pressuring workers to take risks. Another concern is that Nucor is becoming too big to be managed in the informal manner that has been the hallmark of Iverson's leadership style. The suggestion has been made to create an extra layer of management in the form of group vice presidents. But Iverson insists that any layer of management between himself and the operating plants would only get in the way and would reduce his contact with employees.

## CASE QUESTIONS

1. From the information presented, how would you describe the leadership style of Nucor's CEO, Ken Iverson?
2. Do you believe that he will be able to continue managing in this manner as Nucor grows in size?
3. What would the theories of leadership discussed in this chapter say about why he has been successful or unsuccessful?

## Chapter 6 Appendix

| | Pow | Ach | Aff | Inh | Chr3 |
|---|---|---|---|---|---|
| Franklin Roosevelt | 61 | 53 | 44 | −1.80 | 2.5 |
| Harry Truman | 78 | 56 | 65 | .26 | 0.0 |
| Dwight Eisenhower | 49 | 43 | 57 | −4.67 | .6 |
| John F. Kennedy | 77 | 50 | 85 | .79 | 1.3 |
| Lyndon Johnson | 49 | 55 | 59 | −1.11 | 1.5 |
| Richard Nixon | 53 | 66 | 76 | 4.74 | .3 |
| Gerald Ford | nd | nd | nd | −.52 | −.1 |
| Jimmy Carter | 59 | 75 | 59 | 0.00 | −.4 |
| Ronald Reagan | 63 | 60 | 51 | Nd | 1.2 |

Pow, Ach, and Aff were the needs for power, achievement, and affiliation, respectively, and were measured using procedures described in House, Spangler, and Woycke (1991). Inh was activity inhibition, reflecting constraint on the coercive, exploitative, and self-interested use of power. Nd indicates that no data were available. Chr3 was a measure of behavioral charisma taken from a study of presidential style conducted by Simonton (1986). The higher and more positive the number on these measures the higher the president's standing on the variable.

# CHAPTER

7

# Organizational Stress

If you are like most people, you think your life is often stressful, and you think you do not handle stress very well. Many health care professionals echo these sentiments. According to the American Academy of Family Physicians, two thirds of all office visits to family physicians stem from stress-related disorders. Stress has been implicated either directly or indirectly in such life-threatening illnesses as cancer, heart disease, diabetes, cirrhosis of the liver, stomach and intestinal ulcers, arthritis, and lung disease. Among the most widely consumed prescription drugs in the country are a tranquilizer, an ulcer medication, and a drug to treat high blood pressure. The widespread acknowledgment of this "stress epidemic" has prompted many people to try jogging, meditation, diets, counseling, support groups, and even new lifestyles.

This concern has spread to industry, where business leaders have openly expressed alarm about the spiraling costs their organizations incur from stress-related absenteeism, decreased productivity, and medical expenses. Various estimates of the costs of job-related stress range from $50 billion to $75 billion per year. In response, corporations have offered stress management workshops, "wellness" or health maintenance programs, and exercise facilities to their harried employees.

It is rather obvious that, at both a personal and organizational level, there exists a very real interest in decreasing the amount of stress in our lives. To eliminate or even reduce stress, we need to understand exactly what it is. Unfortunately, that is not such an easy task. For years, stress researchers have been trying to agree on a definition of stress (Ivancevich & Matteson, 1980; Mason, 1975; Monat & Lazarus, 1985). Although we still cannot fully resolve this debate, we explore what medical and behavioral scientists have discovered about stress, particularly job-related stress.

Much of the information on organizational stress that we discuss has a decidedly medical and clinical emphasis. This orientation emanates from its historical roots in medicine and clinical psychology. Very simply, people under stress experience both physical and psychological distress. The focus of much research and application, therefore, has targeted the individual, not the organization. Similar to the micro orientation of other topics discussed earlier, such as job attitudes, it may be difficult initially to see how such an orientation fits into a systems model that includes the individual and the environment. However, as the preceding paragraphs demonstrate, the very real distress currently experienced by many organizations in the form of spiraling medical costs and absenteeism has forced stress researchers to assume a broader based perspective. Although the individualistic emphasis predominates in the following pages, we attempt to discuss the impact of job-related stress on other system components when possible.

The chapter is organized into three major sections. The first introduces some of the major issues of stress research. The second deals specifically with the sources and outcomes of job-related stress. The last section is concerned with the management of stress, both at the individual level and organizational level of intervention.

# INTRODUCTION TO THE STUDY OF STRESS

## What Is Stress?

If you were asked to think of synonyms for "stress," what would you say? Anxiety, tension, and pressure? Chances are that at least one of these words would be on your list. How about challenge, excitement, and stimulation? Probably not. If you are typical, you consider taking final exams, having a spat with a significant other, and being involved in an accident stressful events in your life. Do you consider getting that coveted job promotion, falling in love, or taking a European vacation stressful? Probably not, at least not until you have thought about these events. Then you may decide that they can also be stressful. We are sure you would agree that undergoing major surgery and having your car stolen can both be stressful. However, your responses to a major illness and temporarily losing your means of transportation would differ, and the implications of each event in your life would differ drastically.

So, what is stress? Is it something good or bad? Minor or major? The answer is all of the above. Before we offer a more precise definition of stress, we need to examine some popular misconceptions about it (Selye, 1974).

1. You should strive to eliminate all stress from your life.

Definitely not! You would not run that extra mile, sign up for a difficult course, or accept a tough job assignment if you tried to completely avoid stress. The right amount of stress can make life challenging and exciting. Stress can be the spice of life.

2. Stress is just "in your head." It cannot really hurt you.

Not true. We now know that stress predisposes us to illnesses from the common cold to cancer. We will explore this relationship in detail shortly.

3. Stress is really just anxiety or nervous tension. If you could calm down, then you would not be stressed.

No. Anxiety or nervous tension can be a response to the experience of stress. However, stress is much more than anxiety or tension. In fact, people can exhibit a physiological reaction to stress (e.g., increased heart rate and blood pressure) while asleep or unconscious.

4. The experience of stress only implies an excess, such as over-stimulation or overexcitement.

Not true. Being bored or understimulated can also be stressful. Some jobs require workers to sit idle for long periods of time, waiting for some event to occur, such as the appearance of enemy aircraft on a radar screen. Many of these workers report that their jobs are stressful.

Now that we know a little bit more about stress we are ready to develop a definition of stress: *Stress* is any circumstance that places special physical and/or psychological demands on a person such that an unusual or out-of-the-ordinary response occurs. The circumstance, technically termed a *stressor,* can be, for example, a final exam, financial problems, or a difficult boss. The unusual or out-of-the-ordinary response, more appropriately called a *stress response,* may culminate in a variety of physiological or psychological manifestations (e.g., headache, increased alcohol consumption, or depression).

The key to understanding this definition of stress is to realize that some circumstance, typically in the environment, provokes an atypical response. These stressors can take a myriad of forms: chemical fumes, a bad marriage, or work overload. The outcomes of stress responses can be as diverse as the stressors that provoked them, from respiratory disorders to performance deficits. Using our definition, the experience of stress, then, involves a stressor, a stress response, and a stress outcome. Any reference to stress in the balance of this chapter refers to this total experience. Our definition is consistent with the current thinking of stress researchers (Beehr & Franz, 1987).

Historically, stress research, particularly organizational stress research, has attempted to link stressors with fairly long-term outcomes. These long-term outcomes, often labeled *strains,* can be categorized as either behavioral (such as drug addiction or performance deficits), psychological (such as depression or anxiety), or medical (such as heart disease or ulcers). Strains occur along a time continuum, from fairly short-term to long-term. For example, experiencing a stressor may quickly trigger an upset stomach. Experiencing stressors over several years may produce an ulcer. Therefore, our definition of stress implies a process that includes both a stimulus (stressor) and a set of short-term and (potentially) long-term outcomes. (Figure 7.1).

To really understand what happens when we experience stress, we need to look at what happens before we develop that upset stomach or ulcer. We need to start at the beginning of any stressful experience and examine what happens to the body at the very moment of encounter with a stressor.

## The Physiology of Stress

In addition to the short-term and chronic outcomes, responses to a stressor can be very short-term and almost instantaneous. Surprisingly, unlike the longer-term outcomes, these immediate stress responses are always highly similar, regardless of the stressor that provoked them. The intricate chain of physiological events that occurs when an organism (human or animal) encounters a stressor was first investigated early in the twentieth century by a famous American physiologist, Walter Cannon (1929). In his Harvard laboratory, Cannon exposed dogs and cats to a variety of stressors but found that their responses, regardless of the source of the stress, always

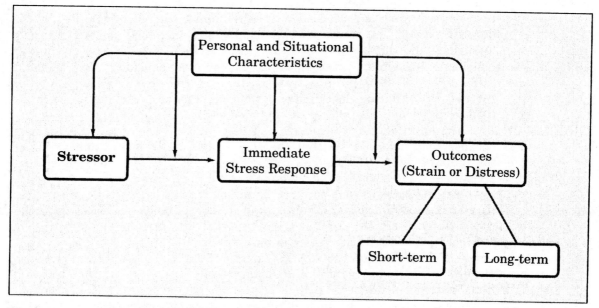

**Figure 7.1**   *Simple stress model*

followed the same pattern. Cannon called this response pattern the *fight or flight response* because, when faced with a threat (stressor), the organism's body prepares for combat or flight to safety.

The fight or flight response, a train of changes in nerves and glands in the body, maps a sequence of events that scientists believe is the result of millions of years of evolution. When the animal or human perceives a stressor, the message is sent to the brain. The brain then simultaneously activates the nervous system and the adrenal glands (one of which rests on top of each kidney). The adrenal gland activation produces two hormones, or chemicals that regulate body functions: adrenaline (epinephrine) and noradrenaline (norepinephrine). These hormones are collectively called catecholamines. Activation of the nervous system and the effects of adrenaline and noradrenaline produce a host of changes, physiologically and biochemically, in the body. These changes, such as increased heart rate and elevated blood pressure, are commonly associated with the experience of stress.

Several years after Cannon mapped the biochemical sequence called the fight or flight response, a young medical researcher by the name of Hans Selye (1952) conducted experiments on rats in hope of discovering a new sex hormone. Instead, he made an infinitely more significant discovery by extending Cannon's work on the stress response. In addition to the fight or flight response, Selye discovered another brain pathway involved in the body's response to stress. Through this pathway, the pituitary gland in the brain activates the adrenal glands to produce other types of hormones in addition to the catecholamines. One of the end products of this activation is the production of a second set of powerful hormones, the glucocorticoids, by the adrenal glands. The glucocorticoids include steroids, such as cortisol. Their immediate and short-term function is primarily to facilitate the conversion of nonsugars, particularly protein, into sugar (glucose) for energy. In the longer term, especially at high concentrations, these steroids can be very harmful to the body by inhibiting the immune system, weakening muscle tissue, ulcerating the stomach lining, and provoking undesirable mental changes.

The implications of Cannon's and Selye's discoveries present a paradox because they demonstrate that the short- and longer term implications of these biochemical reactions can differ. One of the effects of nervous system activation is to stimulate the immune system (e.g., through increased white blood cell production). The enhanced immune response provides extra protection for the body in case of injury. However, steroid hormones build up as the result of stress-related adrenal activation and concentrations of steroid hormones in the body over time can suppress immune functioning. Therefore, it seems obvious that how our bodies successfully adapt to stress in the short-term can be very detrimental in the longer term.

Selye called the second chain of physiological events, which culminates in steroid production, the *stage of resistance*. During the experience of stress, the fight or flight response occurs almost instantaneously. For example, your first responses when you experience a near-miss auto accident (such as a wildly beating heart and rapid breathing) are the result of the fight or flight response, which Selye also called the *alarm stage*. The stage of resistance occurs shortly thereafter. According to Selye, the body at this point seems to be recovering. However, if the stressor is not eliminated, this appearance is only illusory. As discussed above, the costs of longer term adaptation are high, and if continued, can result in long-term or chronic strains, such as heart disease.

Eventually, the body enters the *stage of exhaustion*. In many ways, at least initially, the stage of exhaustion mimics the alarm stage, with the body rallying its last round of defenses. If the stressor remains or returns too frequently, the eventual outcome is death of the organism. Autopsies Selye performed on animals revealed the effects of this progression of biochemical events: adrenal glands enlarged from overstimulation, lymphatic tissue shrunken from the effects of the steroid hormones, and bloody, ulcerated stomachs. Selye called this sequence of events (the alarm stage, the stage of resistance, and the stage of exhaustion) the *general adaptation syndrome*.

It is indeed a bitter irony that responses so adaptive for primitive humans can be so maladaptive for modern humans. Without the fight or flight response or stage of resistance, primitive humans could not have escaped from predators or speared their food. In a confrontation with an irate supervisor, however, modern humans are usually not aided by an elevated heart rate or rapid breathing. They can neither fight nor flee. All too often they must endure stressors over time, with dire consequences.

The physiology of stress presents a complex array of events for the stress researcher to consider. However, at this point, the story is only partially told.

How you perceive and feel about your stressors can also greatly affect your experience of stress. Next, we examine these psychological influences.

## The Psychology of Stress

Referring to the stress model introduced earlier (Figure 7.1), we can use two examples to illustrate how the process of experiencing stress works. Suppose you are working unprotected outside on a scalding August afternoon. How would your body react to that environmental stressor? First, you may feel uncomfortably warm and start to perspire profusely. If you are exposed to extreme heat for an extended period, you may develop a heat stroke; continued exposure would probably lead to death. What about a stressor that is more psychological and social in nature, for example, a difficult job? Your short-term reaction to this stressor might be tension headaches and irritability. Your concern over your job may also disrupt your sleep, so you might start drinking alcohol to relax yourself. If your situation continues unchanged for weeks, months, or years, you may develop a host of strain symptoms, such as poor performance, alcoholism, and finally, cirrhosis of the liver. Liver disease, of course, could eventually be fatal.

How are these two scenarios different? The tragic outcomes are certainly identical. The first involves an environmental stressor, heat, which emanates from the natural environment. The eventual outcome of experiencing this type of stressor is well understood and fairly predictable; the effects of heat stress are universally experienced by all humans. The second example, however, involves a very different type of stressor, a stressor influenced by several psychological and social factors. Unlike heat stress, a difficult job is not a universal stressor. For some people, a difficult job is viewed as a challenge and not a threat. In addition, although prescribed coping responses are available for dealing with heat stress (e.g., increased fluid intake, frequent rest breaks), coping responses for dealing with a difficult job can be as varied as the people who experience this stressor. Identical coping responses for dealing with a difficult job also may be differentially successful across situations and people. Another distinguishing feature between the two scenarios is that the person coping with a difficult job may be just as likely to develop heart disease or ulcers as liver disease.

Your reaction to an environmental stressor, such as extreme heat, depends on such factors as the number and strength of the stressors you must cope with and your ability to cope. For example, suppose you must breathe highly noxious chemicals while enduring extreme heat, and your general health is poor. You will not cope as successfully as someone who must handle exposure to only the heat or the chemical fumes and who is in excellent health.

Your reaction to a psychosocial stressor, however, depends not only on the number and strength of the stressors you must cope with and your ability to cope, but also on how you perceive or evaluate the stressor. Lazarus (1966) coined the term *cognitive appraisal* to describe this evaluative process. For stressors such as a difficult job, you must appraise the situation as being stressful or it is not a stressor for you. Stress is indeed in the eye of the beholder. Lazarus believed that an appraisal occurs both when the situation is perceived as stressful and when some method of coping with the stressor is chosen. The person must first decide the job is difficult and then decide how to cope with it, such as working longer hours.

This two-part appraisal process can have profound effects. For example, you can perceive the existence of a stressor that does not exist in objective reality, such as imagining your boss hates you. Therefore, the stressor has reality only in your imagination. The effects of an environmental stressor can also be compounded by stressful appraisals associated with it. For example, a person exposed to chemical fumes can become very agitated and fearful about his exposure, thus experiencing stress responses beyond those triggered by the environmental stressor.

In addition to the appraisal process, other personal characteristics, such as personality type and amount of social support, can affect the experience of stress. You have no doubt begun to appreciate the enormous task facing the stress researcher: The complex interactions among stressors, stress responses, and outcomes make the appraisal process tricky indeed. For that reason, researchers have developed models or theories of stress that attempt to organize this knowledge in systematic and meaningful ways. We next examine some of these stress models.

## Models of Stress

We define a *model* as a systematic organization of knowledge on some topic. A stress model therefore represents an attempt to organize systematically what we know about stress. A good model should have the capacity for enhancing both prediction and understanding. For example, a model of stress should help us predict if specific stressors will influence the development of specific stress responses or outcomes. To satisfy the criterion of understanding, however, a stress model must be able to explain how and why specific stressors influence the development of certain stress responses. Does our extended definition of stress as represented in Figure 7.1 qualify as a model? It does attempt to organize knowledge about stress. It also explicitly implies that the existence of a stressor allows us to predict the development of stress responses and outcomes. It does not have much to say about how or why this process occurs.

The link between stressor and stress responses is often difficult to specify. For example, if your stressor is a difficult job, you may, in general, be as likely to develop cardiovascular as gastrointestinal disease. If we can rely only on predictive relationships between stressors and stress responses and outcomes, then we have no means of determining when and why one response or outcome would develop over the other. If the stress model incorporates certain explanatory variables, such as age, previous medical history, and personality type, then we can place more confidence in its ability to predict responses from stressors. Modern models of stress attempt to do just that. Many of them have elaborated on the simple framework presented in Figure 7.1 to describe the process by which the experience of stress occurs. However, depending on the focus of the particular model, stressors, stress responses and outcomes, or explanatory (process) variables may be differentially emphasized.

Several stress models have been developed to understand how people handle specific types of stressors. Examples include models to predict how people react when they must make life-and-death decisions in emergency situations, such as a fire or earthquake (Janis & Mann, 1977) and how people react when faced with an important, impending life event, such as students facing a critical exam (Mechanic, 1962). Even Selye's model was somewhat narrow insofar as it was concerned specifically with the physiological and biochemical bases of the stress response. We will examine in detail two well-known models of job-related stress that provide a general understanding of the processes involved in stress. These two models differ considerably in the variables they emphasize and the degree of their specificity, but they also share some common perspectives on stress.

## THE PROCESS MODEL OF TASK PERFORMANCE

McGrath (1976) developed a model to explain the stress related to task performance, particularly work-related task performance (Figure 7.2). This model is based on the premise that task performance is a function of actual task ability and difficulty, and perceived stress. The stress experienced also depends on the perceived consequences of task performance and the uncertainty associated with it. Actual task difficulty depends on the objective situation (stressor), which affects perceptions of task difficulty (perceived situation). In turn, this appraisal process results in a perception of the stressfulness of the task. The person then engages in a decision process to decide how to cope with the stressor. These responses result in the performance process, in which selected behaviors are evaluated on quality, quantity, and speed. The last link is the outcome process, which indicates whether the behaviors produced the desired outcomes. The outcome process feeds back into the original situation and may influence future situations.

For example, suppose your supervisor asks you to prepare a proposal to bid on an important contract. You appraise the situation as attainable, although difficult to accomplish in the allotted time. You also appraise this situation as highly important for your career advancement. Consequently, you decide to drop other projects (if possible) and work overtime and weekends to produce a quality proposal. You submit the finished proposal before the specified deadline. The contracting organization (client) reviews your work and acknowledges that the proposal has considerable merit and potential. However, the client eventually awards the contract to another firm. Because your proposal was unsuccessful, your supervisor gives the next

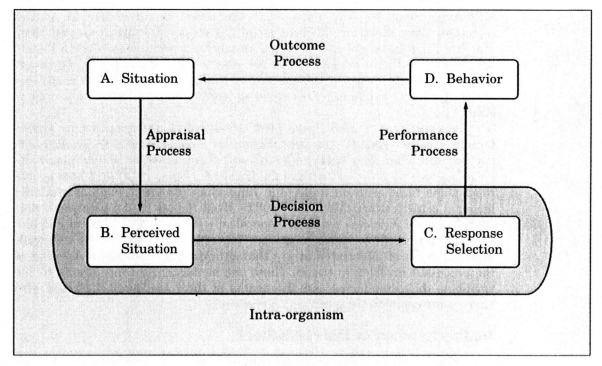

**Figure 7.2** *McGrath's process model of task performance*

Source: McGrath, J.E. (1976). Stress and behavior in organizations. In M.D. Dunnette (Ed.) *Handbook of Industrial/and Organizational Psychology*. Chicago: Rand McNally.

important assignment to one of your coworkers. (You later learn that the nephew of the contracting organization's president works for the firm that was awarded the contract.)

This rather unfortunate example illustrates two important points that McGrath emphasizes in his model: Often performance does not match the outcome, and the outcome affects future situations. McGrath's model also satisfies our criterion of understanding, and perhaps to a lesser extent, prediction. From knowledge about the situation (stressor), we can predict future behavior and, perhaps with less certainty, outcomes. The appraisal, decision, performance, and outcome processes describe how and why the experience of task-related stress occurs. You might also have noticed that McGrath uses several concepts introduced earlier, particularly the influence of psychological factors (cognitive appraisal) on the perception of and response to the stressor. However, McGrath intended this stress model to pertain only to task performance, so it does not address psychological or medical outcomes.

### THE INTEGRATIVE TRANSACTIONAL PROCESS MODEL OF STRESS

Schuler (1982) proposed a complex model of stress in organizations (Figure 7.3). Schuler explained that the rather lengthy title describes the intent

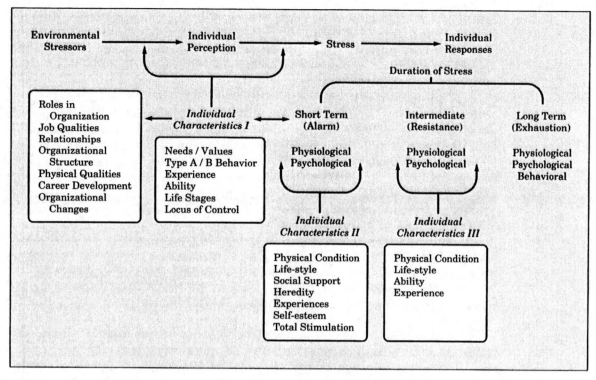

**Figure 7.3** *Schuler's integrative transactional process model of stress in organizations*

*Source:* Schuler, R.S. (1985). Integrative transactional process model of coping with stress in organizations. In T.A. Beehr, & R.S. Bhagat (Eds.) *Human Stress and Cognition in Organizations: An Integrated Perspective.* New York: John Wiley & Sons.

and focus of the model. "Integrative" refers to the fact that the model was developed by considering diverse areas of research. "Transactional" means that (similar to McGrath's model) the relationships in the model are reciprocal, or both a cause and effect of each other (see Chapter 2). "Process" indicates that the relationships implied by the model occur over time and across stressors.

In Schuler's model, some environmental work stressor (for example, a difficult relationship with a coworker) is appraised by the worker as being stressful. This individual perception of stress results in a series of stress responses and outcomes. The model conceives of stress responses and outcomes in terms of Selye's general adaptation syndrome. After the individual perception of stress, the alarm reaction (immediate response) occurs, followed by the resistance stage (intermediate response). Both of these responses have physiological (e.g., elevated blood pressure, heart rate, and respiration) and psychological (e.g., anger or anxiety) components. The exhaustion stage (long-term outcome), which has physiological, psychological, and behavioral components (e.g., heart disease, depression, and drug abuse, respectively) eventually terminates the process. At the individual perception, short-term response, and long-term outcome stages, personal characteristics, such as ability, experience, social support, or physical condition, are hypothesized to influence the relationships in the model. For example, a worker who has low social or affiliative needs may not perceive interpersonal problems with a coworker as very stressful.

The integrative model meets both our prediction and understanding criteria. Knowledge of job stressors allows us to predict individual stress responses. The inclusion of mediating variables, such as individual perception and the general adaptation syndrome, aids our understanding of the process of stress. This model is quite different from McGrath's model of performance stress because it emphasizes the total experience of stress, perhaps throughout a worker's lifetime. It incorporates other, more limited perspectives, such as Selye's research and the concept of cognitive appraisal, to present a broad-based overview of the total stress experience. Schuler's model also makes a unique contribution to stress theory by not only emphasizing the duration of stress, but also the pervasive influence of explanatory variables (individual characteristics) at various stages of the stress experience. Paradoxically, the model's comprehensiveness also may be a source of criticism. Eulberg, Weekley, and Bhagat (1988) criticized similar models for being too vague and all inclusive.

Each of these two representative theories of job-related stress, the process model of task performance and the integrative transactional process model of stress in organizations, has served admirably to provide a springboard for future research, a major goal of any model. Indeed, by studying models such as these, researchers can develop testable hypotheses to examine in future research. The results of such empirical or data-based research provide the fuel for future model building, and thus the cycle of scientific inquiry continues.

Next, we briefly examine the methods of stress research, that is, how stress research is designed; then we examine the measures of stress, or what types of variables are collected to study stress.

## Methods and Measures of Stress

Although there are notable examples of experimental research in the laboratory (Sales, 1969) and in the field (Jackson, 1983), most organizational stress studies are nonexperimental field studies. Very real constraints on the stress researcher have contributed to the predominance of this type of research. The relative merits of laboratory versus field methods are not typically at issue in stress research. For ethical reasons, researchers cannot place workers under stress to study the effects on their behavior and attitudes. Job stress also usually reflects an ongoing or chronic situation, which is extremely difficult to create in the laboratory. For these reasons, organizational stress researchers typically study stress as it naturally occurs in the work environment. Comparisons are made among employees, groups of employees, or organizations as they naturally differ in their levels of stress and stress-related outcomes.

Three types of diagnostic procedures or measures are used to collect data on job-related stress: self-report, behavioral, and physiological measures. Self-report measures, which include questionnaires, surveys, and interviews, require people to report the stress they experience. Self-report measures can inquire both about the nature of stressors and the stress responses and outcomes. Usually people are asked to indicate if the stressor or stress outcome applies to them, and, if so, how frequently or intensely they experience it. Because the easiest and most straightforward way to determine if people are stressed is to ask them, this is the most commonly used method to collect job stress data. Although self-report measures are fairly easy to collect, they are not without problems (Chapter 2).

Behavioral measures usually involve measurement of actual behavior. In field studies, such measures could include job-related absences (number of days per year lost from work), number of accidents at work over the last 12 months, or number of cigarettes smoked per day. Although researchers often believe that these "objective" measures are less prone to response biases than self-report measures, they can be biased if the behaviors are misinterpreted or estimated inaccurately (Chapter 2).

Physiological measures (Table 7.1) can include any index of nervous system activation, such as increased sweating, breathing, heart rate, blood pressure, and muscle tension. Blood pressure and heart rate are most frequently used because the training and equipment requirements necessary to collect them are minimal. The stress hormones produced by the adrenal glands, the catecholamines (adrenaline and noradrenaline) and corticosteroids (for example, cortisol), are the primary biochemical measures of stress. Estimates of these hormones can be obtained from both blood and urine samples. These two types of measures are increasingly being used in organizational stress research, typically in conjunction with self-report and behavioral measures.

The physiological and biochemical measures appear to be perfect stress measures because they are not subject to the response biases of the self-report and behavioral measures. However, the physiological and biochemical measures have their own weaknesses. Natural variability in the levels of these variables occurs over a 24-hour period; they are influenced by exercise, diet, posture, drugs, and general health. This implies that all of these factors must be considered when collecting and interpreting physiological and biochemical data. Within normal limits, large individual differences also exist in the levels of these measures. (For example, regardless of whether you are stressed, your blood pressure always may be higher than your friend's blood pressure.) This large variability frequently demands taking multiple measurements from each person to establish baseline or normal levels. Expensive equipment and trained medical personnel are often required to collect and interpret these types of data. Finally, the procedures, particularly blood sampling, can be invasive and stressful for many people; in such cases, the procedures themselves may affect the measurement process.

**Table 7.1**

---

## PHYSIOLOGICAL AND BIOCHEMICAL MEASURES USED IN STRESS ASSESSMENT

**Physical measures**
- Pulse
- Blood pressure
- Body weight
- Respiratory rate

**Measures with specialized electronic equipment**
- Muscle tension (facial muscles, neck muscles, and others)
- Galvanic skin response (GSR) (sweating or cutaneous conduction)
- Blood flow (measured by plethysmography)
- Electrocardiogram
- Electroencephalogram (brain waves)

**Hormone levels***
- Catecholamines (adrenaline, noradrenaline, and metabolites)
- Cortisol, related hormones and metabolites
- ACTH
- Glucagon
- Other hormones (thyroid, angiotensin, growth hormone, renin, etc.)

**Glucose, lipids, and related metabolites**
- Glucose
- Cholesterol
- Triglycerides
- Lipoproteins
- Free fatty acids

---

*May be measured in blood or urine, depending on the hormone and assay involved.

*Source:* Quick, J.C., & Quick, J.D. (1984). *Organizational Stress and Preventive Management.* New York: McGraw-Hill.

---

To add to the confusion, different types of stress measures sometimes do not agree. After controlling for all the potential biases mentioned above, a recent study (Stefy & Jones, 1988) compared self-reports of job-related stress with several physiological and biochemical stress measures and found little relationship between the subjective and objective measures. Stress researchers are uncertain why there is little evidence of convergent validity among the different types of stress measures. Perhaps each type of measure taps a different part of the stress continuum (see Schuler's model in Figure 7.3). For example, physiological measures may be sensitive to the immediate or very short-term stress response, whereas self-report measures may be sensitive to long-term stress outcomes. Future research needs to address these inconsistencies.

# THE NATURE OF JOB-RELATED STRESS

Our discussions about organizational stress have taken a broad perspective. This overview encompassed the whole stress continuum, from the initial encounter with the stressor to long-term consequences, and the myriad influences in between. Now we examine each part of the stress experience in detail: the various sources of job-related stress (the stressors); the short- and long-term outcomes (the strains); and the intervening personal characteristics that influence the process. To a large extent, we cannot separate discussions of stressors, outcomes, and intervening characteristics. However, each section focuses primarily on one of these three parts of the stress experience.

## Sources of Job-Related Stress (Potential Stressors)

Potential stressors include the occupation or job itself, environmental and organizational stressors, and stressors external to the job that may influence effectiveness at work.

### THE JOB OR OCCUPATION

Would you consider some occupations to be inherently stressful regardless of the organizational or personal circumstances experienced by workers in these occupations (Figure 7.4)? If you were a stress researcher, do you think you would want to study one type of worker over another? Are some jobs or occupations more stressful than others?

From a study of 22,000 workers, the National Institute for Occupational Safety and Health (NIOSH) compiled data on the stressfulness of over 100 occupational groups. According to NIOSH, laborers, secretaries, lab technicians, first-line supervisors, managers, waitresses or waiters, and machine operators belong to the most stressful occupations. The helping professions are also considered to be stressful, especially the jobs of police officers, fire fighters, nurses, and social workers. In a study of more than 2,000 workers across 23 occupations, French, Caplan, and Van Harrison (1982) found occupational differences not only in the amount of stress, but also in the type of stress experienced by workers.

The law enforcement profession is so universally recognized as stressful that a magazine, *Police Stress,* has been published dealing specifically with occupational stress in police work. Because of the often erratic nature of police work, police officers report both work overload (too much to do) and work underload (too little to do) as stressors. Faulty equipment, shiftwork, dealing with the court system, and the physical dangers of the job are additional sources of stress (Davidson & Veno, 1980). Police officers have very high rates of divorce (Hurrell, 1977) and alcoholism (Heiman, 1975), both of which are common strains.

# Post offices too stressful? Inquiry is urged

FROM BLADE STAFF AND WIRE REPORTS

ROYAL OAK, Mich.—U.S. Postmaster General Anthony Frank yesterday called for an investigation into a series of deadly shootings at post offices in the last few years and suspended the man in charge of the Royal Oak post office, saying Daniel Presilla was a dictatorial manager.

"Maybe there's been too much change too soon" brought on by financial cutbacks that burdened both workers and their managers across the system, Mr. Frank told a news conference here.

He spoke 24 hours after a former letter carrier went on a rampage at the post office, killing four people and himself.

Thomas McIlvane, 31, of Oak Park, Mich., who had been fired from his letter carrier's job last year, died early yesterday from a self-inflicted gunshot wound. Police said he entered the post office at 8:48 a.m. Thursday, shot nine employees, and then turned the semiautomatic 22-caliber rifle on himself.

Three people were dead at the scene and a fourth, Rose Proos, 33, of Sterling Heights, Mich., died about 10 a.m. yesterday.

Five other people, one of whom broke her heel after jumping from a window, remained hospitalized yesterday in good to stable condition. Two others were released from the hospital after being treated for injuries they suffered when jumping from windows.

Mr. Frank called for an investigation into the postal shootings as well as other acts of random violence that have plagued the country in recent times. Thirty-four people have died in nine such incidents at postal facilities across the country since January, 1981.

He did not elaborate on who should conduct the investigation, but the largest U.S. postal union called for a congressional investigation.

"There's got to be something wrong with the environment of the post office that would lead to this cluster of massacres in this particular industry," Tom Fabey, spokesman for the 360,000-member American Postal Workers Union, said.

"We're trying to get to the bottom of it. We have asked the chairman of the House Post Office and Civil Service Committee to launch a congressional investigation into what is fundamentally a troubled labor-management climate," he said.

Although Michigan abolished capital punishment in the mid 1800s, federal officials might have been able to seek the death penalty against McIlvane, a University of Toledo law school professor said.

Frank Merritt said yesterday it is a federal crime to murder a postal worker in the performance of his or her duties. Federal law imposes the death penalty for first-degree murder, which is defined as being premeditated or in the commission of certain other crimes, he said.

Thomas Secor, U.S. assistant attorney in Toledo, said that if a similar situation were to occur in Ohio, the local prosecutor and U.S. attorney would work out the issue of whether the suspect would be charged under state or federal law.

**Figure 7.4**  *Newspaper article on stress in the post office*
Source: The *Toledo Blade*, November 1991.

Medical personnel, particularly nurses, have been the focus of much stress research. In general, nurses report that patient deaths, uncertainty about patient treatment, inability to meet patient needs, and interpersonal problems with other medical staff, such as physicians, are common job stressors (Lee, 1987). A recent study (Motowidlo, Packard, & Manning, 1986) of 171 nurses across five hospitals also found that work overload, little support from supervisors, and negligent or incompetent coworkers were sources of stress that were related to depression and decreased work performance.

One surprisingly stressed medical professional is the dentist. Cooper (1980) attempted to identify dentists' job-related stressors by interviewing a group of dentists gathered for a dental association meeting. He found that coping with difficult patients, building a practice, administrative duties, and public opinion of the dentist as an inflictor of pain were identified as job stressors. Cooper also found that those dentists who indicated that some of these stressors were a problem for them showed increased blood pressure and abnormal heart recordings (electrocardiograms). A similar study conducted several years later in Great Britain (Cooper, Watts, Baglioni, & Kelly, 1988) replicated many of these findings.

If you examine the work stressors listed by both nurses and dentists, you will observe that these stressors typically involve interpersonal interactions or interdependency on others (usually coworkers). Medical professionals are thoroughly trained to be skilled scientists and problem solvers but are often woefully unprepared to deal with people and administrative issues. These types of issues are also quite frequently beyond individual control; for example, some patients will die regardless of the quality of care they receive. Lack of control over the work environment is universally perceived as stressful and undoubtedly contributes to the stress experienced by medical professionals.

According to NIOSH, blue-collar and clerical workers, such as laborers and secretaries, are considered to have the most stressful jobs. Psychologists believe that the reported stressfulness is due, in large measure, to the small amount of control these workers have over their daily work activities and working conditions (Fisher, 1985; Sauter, Hurrell, & Cooper, 1989). A national study that examined the relationship between coronary heart disease and employment (Haynes, Feinlieb, & Kannel, 1980) found that the incidence of coronary heart disease was much higher in female clerical workers than in any other group of women studied. The women at highest health risk reported they had little control over their job mobility and nonsupportive bosses.

One occupation NIOSH lists as very stressful but that is typically characterized by considerable control and discretion is managerial work. An important job stressor for most managers is quantitative work overload (Glowinkowski & Cooper, 1986). Work overload in managers has been associated with increased alcohol consumption and lower motivation (Margolis, Kroes, & Quinn, 1974), anxiety and depression (Cooper & Roden, 1985), and coronary heart disease (Russek & Zohman, 1958).

Interestingly, some occupations can be considered stressful not because they require too much in terms of the quantity of work, but because they require too much in terms of the quality of work. This aspect of work overload is called qualitative work overload, or having work that is too difficult. Not surprisingly, qualitative work overload has been identified as a problem for engineers and scientists, who typically work in highly technical jobs (French & Caplan, 1973).

Stressful jobs span the organizational ladder from the bottom rung to the very top, although many of the most stressful jobs, such as laborer and clerical worker, are concentrated in the lower levels of organizations. Given that such a diversity of jobs is stressful, it is logical to assume that some stressors cut across job boundaries and apply to many different occupations. Next, we examine some of these common job stressors.

## ENVIRONMENTAL STRESSORS

Because many blue-collar or working-class jobs involve activities in traditional industrial environments, such as foundries or factories, blue-collar stressors are somewhat different from those experienced by office workers. Blue-collar workers are frequently exposed to environmental stressors, such as high levels of noise and extreme temperatures. The jobs of many factory workers also involve repetitive activities that may lead to feelings of boredom and monotony. (Blue-collar workers also frequently work different shifts, another job-related stressor; see Chapter 12.)

Many workers in foundries and factories are exposed to noise created from the operation of machinery, such as jackhammers or drill presses. The most obvious concern with such noise in work environments is the potential for hearing loss. Initially, the hearing loss is usually temporary, and returns after the worker leaves the job for a few hours or days. However, with continued exposure over time, the temporary loss can become permanent. This occurs because exposure to high intensity noise actually kills the auditory receptors in the inner ear, and nerve impulses cannot be transmitted to the brain. This type of hearing loss is not correctable surgically or with a hearing aid. For these reasons, the Occupational Safety and Health Administration (OSHA) has set standards for exposure times of workers at different noise intensities. A permissible noise exposure for a noise level of 110 decibels, which is equivalent to being six feet from an amplifier at a rock concert, is only 30 minutes.

Apart from hearing loss, you might also think that noise can affect performance, as anyone who has tried to concentrate in a noisy environment can attest. There is clear evidence that high-intensity noise is related to a generalized stress response (Jansen, 1969; Burns, 1979). However, the effects of noise on performance are far from clear-cut. In general, task performance is only impaired at very high noise intensities. Performance deficits are particularly obvious for difficult or demanding tasks. Simple or routine tasks, on the other hand, are typically not affected by noise, and sometimes noise increases performance on simple tasks (Sanders & McCormick, 1987). This enhancement effect probably occurs because the noise acts as a stressor, raising the person's arousal level and therefore overcoming the boredom associated with the task. Unfortunately, most of the evidence we have on task performance under noisy conditions comes from laboratory experiments. We do not know how well these findings generalize to less controlled conditions in real work settings.

As anyone who has stood near a blast furnace in a steel mill can tell you, working under extreme temperature conditions can be very stressful. Because of the potential health effects of enduring extreme heat, heat exposure limits have been set by OSHA. These standards vary according to air temperature, air flow, air humidity, workload levels (light, moderate, and heavy work), and work-rest schedules (for example, one-half work and one-half rest pauses). Similar to the effects of noise on performance, the effects of heat on performance are complex. In general, performance on physical tasks, such as typical factory work, deteriorates only under the hottest temperatures (above 100°F) (Meese et al., 1984). For demanding mental tasks, performance deteriorates under heat exposure, but particularly when two or more tasks are timeshared or performed simultaneously (Hancock, 1981). Unfortunately, most of the data on heat performance has been distilled from laboratory experiments and may not generalize well to industrial environments (Sanders & McCormick, 1987).

Although cold exposure is less common than heat exposure in contemporary work environments, sometimes workers must endure exposure in refrigerated chambers or in winter weather. Apart from the health risks associated with cold exposure, such as frostbite, little is known about performance in frigid conditions. Similar to performance under heat exposure, performance under cold exposure is affected by, for example, such factors as air temperature, air humidity, air flow, and length of exposure to cold conditions. In general, however, we know that manual performance is severely affected by cold exposure. Finger dexterity decreases at temperatures below 55°F, with much greater decreases at lower temperatures (Riley & Cochran, 1984). Performance data on demanding or mental tasks under cold conditions are very limited and inconclusive (Sanders & McCormick, 1987).

In addition to the affects of extreme environmental conditions, other job characteristics of industrial work are considered stressful, such as the repetitive, routinized tasks associated with many assembly-line jobs in factories. This type of work is often experienced as boring and monotonous. In fact, boredom is associated both with decreased physiological arousal and negative attitudes toward work. These two states lead to feelings of repetitiveness, unpleasantness, and constraint (Barmack, 1937). The jobs that are totally machine-paced (i.e., a machine totally controls the flow of the work) are usually the most stressful. In these jobs, workers have no control over work and often have difficulty consistently pacing themselves with the machine. Workers in machine-paced jobs have been found to have high levels of physiological stress (adrenaline), anxiety, depression, somatic (body) complaints, and job dissatisfaction (Smith, 1985).

Many environmental stressors, particularly at high or sustained levels, can adversely influence the physical health of workers. The federal government (OSHA) therefore regulates the exposure levels of many of these stressors in industrial settings. Unfortunately, our knowledge of how these environmental stressors affect task performance is mostly limited to the results of laboratory studies under controlled conditions. More research investigating how these stressors affect performance in industrial settings is clearly needed.

## ORGANIZATIONAL STRESSORS

Whereas blue-collar stressors frequently involve characteristics of the industrial environment or the work itself, white-collar stressors are usually more related to the worker's role in the organization, or the tasks, duties, and expectations that identify the worker's position in the organization. For example, a clerk-typist's work role might be identified by such tasks and duties as typing correspondence, filing papers, making ledger entries, sorting mail, and so on. The clerk-typist has his or her own expectations concerning which of these duties are most critical in performing the job. The clerk-typist's coworkers and supervisor also have expectations concerning the clerk-typist's role (in terms of tasks and duties) at work.

Much organizational stress research in the last 25 years has investigated what happens when workers experience difficulties with their work role demands. In Chapter 5 we discussed the process by which organizational roles emerge and their influence on social behavior. Failures in role-sending and role-taking constitute an important variety of organizational stressor. The role-based stressors most frequently studied are role conflict and role ambiguity. *Role conflict* occurs when role demands are in conflict. This can be illustrated by examining three common types of role conflict. *Intrasender conflict* occurs when one person (often called a role sender) communicates mixed or conflicting messages. For example, a department manager asks her subordinates to increase productivity but to cut back on overtime. Your mother tells you to be popular but to keep up your grades. *Intersender conflict* implies that two or more people send conflicting messages. An example would be if your mother demands that you do one thing, your father the opposite. This type of role conflict is commonly found in organizations when a worker has more than one supervisor; often, satisfying one supervisor neglects the demands of the other. *Interrole conflict* occurs when two or more roles conflict for one person. For example, women today frequently find that the multiple demands of their roles as parent, worker, wife, and student conflict.

*Role ambiguity* results whenever role demands are unclear or unknown. Role ambiguity can occur if there is inadequate or confusing information about how to perform certain tasks related to one's role (as a worker, student, etc.). The new employee who does not understand how to operate the copy machine or computer suffers from ambiguity concerning these activities. Your inability to solve your calculus problem is also an example of task ambiguity.

Table 7.2

---

## ITEMS FROM RIZZO, HOUSE, & LIRTZMAN'S (1970) ROLE CONFLICT AND ROLE AMBIGUITY QUESTIONNAIRE

Listed below are statements that represent possible feelings people might have about their jobs. For each statement below, circle the response (from 1 to 5) that best indicates how you feel about your job.

| | Extremely False | Somewhat False | Neither True Nor False | Somewhat True | Extremely True |
|---|---|---|---|---|---|
| **Role Ambiguity** | | | | | |
| I have clear, planned goals and objectives in my job | 1 | 2 | 3 | 4 | 5 |
| Explanation is clear of what has to be done | 1 | 2 | 3 | 4 | 5 |
| **Role Conflict** | | | | | |
| I receive incompatible (conflicting) requests from two or more people | 1 | 2 | 3 | 4 | 5 |
| I have to do things that should be done differently | 1 | 2 | 3 | 4 | 5 |

*Source:* Rizzo, J.R., House, R., & Lirtzman, S. (1970). Role conflict and role ambiguity in complex organizations. *Administrative Science Quarterly, 15,* 150–163.

---

In addition, role ambiguity can result from inadequate or confusing information about how you will be evaluated in your role. The worker who does not know what behaviors are important for success in the organization (e.g., punctuality, working overtime) suffers from evaluation ambiguity. When your professor does not tell you exactly how she will determine your course grade, you experience evaluation ambiguity. See Table 7.2 for items from a common organizational role conflict and role ambiguity questionnaire.

In 1964, Kahn, Wolfe, Quinn, Snoek, and Rosenthal conducted one of the first investigations of role conflict and role ambiguity in organizations through intensive interviews with workers and surveys distributed to a representative working sample. They found that these role stressors were associated with substantial strains, such as job tension, job dissatisfaction, and lack of trust, confidence, and respect. Twenty years and hundreds of studies later, Jackson and Schuler (1985) completed a quantitative review, or meta-analysis, of the research literature on role conflict and role ambiguity. They reported that increased levels of these role stressors were associated with, among other things, lower worker participation, lower organizational commitment, higher tension and anxiety, and higher propensity to leave the organization. Thus, Jackson and Schuler reaffirmed the negative consequences of role conflict and role ambiguity that Kahn and his colleagues first documented.

Other role-related variables are also potentially important white-collar stressors. By definition, the manager typically manages the work of people in the organization. This implies that the manager's work role includes *responsibility for other people*. Responsibility is esteemed in society. However, the risks of failure are often great, resulting in personal and professional trauma. Surprisingly, very few researchers have investigated this stressor. Caplan (1971), who studied the risk factors associated with coronary heart disease in a group of NASA employees, discovered that those workers who had responsibility for people also smoked more heavily. (Smoking is a risk factor for heart disease.)

A manager's role is characterized by constant interactions with people, both internal and external to the organization (Mintzberg, 1973). Therefore, *interpersonal problems with coworkers* is another possible work role stressor. French and Caplan (1970) reported an association between role ambiguity and poor interpersonal relationships at work. According to the authors, this finding suggests that interpersonal problems stifle effective communications, which lead to role ambiguity and other problems, such as low job satisfaction. Another study (Smith & Sulsky, 1992) also found that interpersonal problems with coworkers was a frequently cited stressor across three diverse groups of workers.

I/O psychologists have intensely researched the influence of role-based stressors in work settings over the last few decades and have consistently found that these stressors exert negative effects on both personal and work-related outcomes. Much interest has recently focused on whether these organizational stressors interact with nonwork stressors. These nonwork stressors are discussed next.

## NONWORK STRESSORS

Most people have noticed that their performance at work or school deteriorates when they have personal problems, such as financial pressures, illness of a family member, or the breakup of a relationship. We know that many factors outside of work can influence effectiveness at work. Researchers have investigated work-nonwork relationships from three general perspectives that resemble the attempts to explain the relationships of job and life satisfaction (Chapter 4). The first is called *spillover,* in which problems outside of work spill over into work life, such as in the examples given previously. Difficulties at work (e.g., receiving a poor performance review) can also affect other aspects of life, such as the ability to concentrate on school assignments. The second is *compensation,* in which one environment compensates for deficiencies in the other. For example, a man who has marital conflicts may immerse himself in projects at work; another who fears being fired may concentrate instead on his family activities. The third is *independence,* in which problems in one environment do not affect the other. For example, personal problems, such as illness of a loved one, do not affect individual work effectiveness (and vice versa). Some evidence supports all three perspectives

(Kabanoff, 1980), although considerable research (Bacharach, Bamberger, & Conley, 1991; Greenhaus & Parasuraman, 1986) and popular opinion favor the spillover perspective.

Most of the research concerning work-nonwork issues has focused on the problems of *dual career couples*. When both partners have a job or career outside the home their lives often become a juggling act to balance the needs of both home and work simultaneously. Achieving this balance becomes even more difficult when children are involved. For example, job demands may require both partners to work late on a certain day. The dilemma becomes one of determining who will watch the children and who will work. Because these types of situations tend to occur frequently, the professional advancement of dual career couples can suffer.

Gupta and Jenkins (1985) identified three general classes of stressors that affect most dual career couples. The first (discussed above) occurs because of conflicts between personal and social and/or job-related expectations. The second arises from ambiguity about effective role-related behaviors. That is, role ambiguity occurs because dual career couples do not know how to satisfy all of the demands placed on them. The third involves the extreme overload that arises from having too many personal, family, and work demands.

The plight of the dual career couple seems pretty dismal. Not so, according to Gupta and Jenkins (1985); there are some compensations for "having it all." These couples often report great satisfaction with their marriages, and children of dual career couples show more independence and flexibility.

## Effects/Outcomes of Stress (Strains)

When discussing different types of stressors, we frequently mentioned the relationships between stressors and stress outcomes, such as job dissatisfaction and poor performance. Our interest focused on specific types of stressors and their effects. Now we turn our attention to health and organizational outcomes.

### HEALTH EFFECTS

Early stress research was conducted by medical researchers such as Walter Cannon and Hans Selye, and health is still an important strain measure in stress research. Several areas of research have evolved because of their specific emphasis on health issues.

**Stressful Life Events**   One of the earlier attempts to link stressors to health was by Holmes and Rahe (1967). They examined the association between the number of stressful life events experienced by a person and the development of illness. The rationale is that, by enduring multiple stressors, people repeatedly experience the stress response. The body is therefore subjected to undesirable physiological changes that often culminate in illness.

Initially, only a global change score, or the total number of life events experienced in a specified time interval, was used. However, Holmes and Rahe were also interested in the relative impact of each of these life stressors. Their research resulted in a weighted or mean value given to each event (Table 7.3). This scoring scheme was achieved by assigning an arbitrary value to marriage and then asking people to scale all other events relative to marriage. Life events scales (also called social readjustment rating scales and schedule of recent life events) have been used in many settings and with various types of people. From this research, we know that when people report they have experienced a large number of events, they also frequently will suffer from a variety of health-related problems. More recently, Naismith (1975) developed a stressful life events scale that deals only with the job setting (e.g., a new boss, job transfer), but this scale has not yet been used widely by stress researchers.

Although the life events approach is very appealing in its simplicity, total life events have not proven overall to be very good predictors of health problems. Stress researchers such as Kasl (1981) have discussed several reasons for the scale's poor predictive validity. Much life events research is retrospective, that is, it asks people about these events and their health after the fact. However, disease often develops in stages over time. If a person is not followed over time (longitudinally), then we do not know if he or she was already experiencing health problems. Researchers need to establish individual health status, document life changes, and then determine what health decrements follow. According to Kasl, life events are also not separable from a person's environment and stage of life. For example, alcoholics experience many life events, and the elderly experience relatively few. (One aspect of aging is that as people age, they experience fewer changes.) In the same vein, no change can be more stressful than change. For example, for many married couples, not experiencing pregnancy or the gain of a new family member is stressful.

An additional criticism has been voiced by Lazarus and his associates (DeLongis et al., 1982; Ivancevich, 1986; Kanner et al., 1981). They maintain that everyday stressors or *daily hassles,* such as misplacing car keys and concern about dieting, have stronger relationships with health problems than stressful life events. Finally, some recent job-related research (Bhagat, McQuaid, Lindholm, & Segovis, 1985) found that negative life events predicted organizational outcomes and withdrawal behavior better than the positive or total (positive and negative) life events. The bright side of all of these criticisms is that the stressful life events approach has stimulated much fruitful research over the past 20 years. Today, the consensus is that stressful life events provide the stress researcher with a small, but important, link between stressors and illness.

**Type A Behavior** Life events research is concerned with the relationship between life events and general health problems. Now we turn to another perspective that examines the relationship between a particular individual or

**Table 7.3**

| STRESSFUL LIFE EVENTS SCALE | |
| --- | ---: |
| **Life Event** | **Rank** |
| Begin or end school | 27 |
| Business readjustment | 15 |
| Change in church activities | 35 |
| Change in eating habits | 40 |
| Change in financial state | 16 |
| Change in health of family member | 11 |
| Change in living conditions | 28 |
| Change in number of arguments with spouse | 19 |
| Change in number of family get-togethers | 39 |
| Change in recreation | 34 |
| Change in residence | 32 |
| Change in responsibilities at work | 22 |
| Change in schools | 33 |
| Change in sleeping habits | 38 |
| Change in social activities | 36 |
| Change in work hours or conditions | 31 |
| Change to different line of work | 18 |
| Christmas | 42 |
| Death of close family member | 5 |
| Death of close friend | 17 |
| Death of spouse | 1 |
| Divorce | 2 |
| Fired at work | 8 |
| Foreclosure of mortgage or loan | 21 |
| Gain of new family member | 14 |
| Jail term | 4 |
| Marital reconciliation | 9 |
| Marital separation | 3 |
| Marriage | 7 |
| Minor violation of the law | 43 |
| Mortgage or loan less than $10,000 | 37 |
| Mortgage over $10,000 | 20 |
| Outstanding personal achievement | 25 |
| Personal injury or illness | 6 |
| Pregnancy | 12 |
| Retirement | 10 |
| Revision of personal habits | 29 |
| Sex difficulties | 13 |
| Son or daughter leaving home | 23 |
| Trouble with boss | 30 |
| Trouble with in-laws | 24 |
| Vacation | 41 |
| Wife begin or stop work | 26 |

*Source:* Adapted from Holmes, T.H., & Rahe, R.H. (1967). The social readjustment rating scale. *Journal of Psychosomatic Research, 11*, 213–218.

personality characteristic and a specific illness, coronary heart disease. Type A behavior has become a widely discussed and popularized topic in recent years. The study of this individual characteristic originated in the 1950s with the clinical observations of two physicians, Drs. Friedman and Rosenman. They noticed distinct behavior differences between patients with heart disease and patients free of heart disease. Because the traditional risk factors of coronary heart disease (CHD), such as smoking, high blood pressure, and cholesterol levels, predict no more than 50% of all CHD cases, Friedman and Rosenman decided to investigate these behavioral differences as potential, independent predictors of CHD.

Friedman and Rosenman found that a constellation of behaviors distinguishes the CHD patient. These behaviors include explosive, accelerated speech, impatience with slowness, heightened pace of living, self-preoccupation, evaluation in terms of numbers (amount), engaging in multiple activities simultaneously, extreme competitiveness, and generalized hostility and dissatisfaction. These behaviors can be summarized in four general categories: *aggressiveness, hostility, time urgency, and competitiveness* (Figure 7.5). According to Friedman and Rosenman, these overt behaviors are most frequently observed in a person with these predispositions (tendencies) when the person is in a challenging or stressful environment (Mathews, 1982). These behaviors run on a continuum from extreme A to extreme non-A, or B. Type B people, the opposite of Type A, are easygoing and much less prone to CHD.

Researchers believe that Type As are more prone to CHD because people with these characteristics experience stress with much greater intensity than Type Bs. Of course, this greater intensity leads to a heightened stress response, with resulting health consequences. Motowidlo, Packard, and Manning (1986) developed a stress model that extended these ideas. They demonstrated that Type As experience greater intensity (and frequency) of stressful events, which lead to greater perceived stress, anxiety, hostility, depression, and lower job performance. Interestingly, Kushnir and Melamed (1991) found that Type As in a sample of Israeli factory workers showed higher stress symptoms *and* higher job satisfaction than Type Bs.

The update on Type A research is not as positive as it may first appear, however. Many researchers are dissatisfied with the construct validity of measures of Type A (Edwards & Baglioni, 1991; Matthews, 1982). Type A is a complex construct, composed of at least four dimensions. The several instruments that classify people on the Type A-B continuum each tap different dimensions of the construct. The oldest measure of Type A is the Structured Interview, a 25-question interview administered by a trained interviewer. Both behaviors during the interview (e.g., the interviewee rushing through the interview questions) and the answers to the interview questions are scored for Type A behavior. The Structured Interview seems to pick up the general reactivity (time urgency) dimension, characterized by rapid speech and multiple activities. The most widely used self-report instrument or questionnaire, the Jenkins Activity Survey, consists of 50 questions with content

**Figure 7.5** *Type A behavior includes aggressiveness, hostility, time urgency, and competitiveness*

similar to the Structured Interview; both an adult and student form exist (Table 7.4). The Jenkins, in contrast to the Structured Interview, appears to measure the dimension of competitiveness best (Matthews, 1982). Therefore, a person who is highly competitive might be classified as Type A with the Jenkins but not with the Structured Interview.

To confuse the situation further, a recent quantitative review of Type A and a large, multi-organization study found that negative affect, such as anger, hostility, and depression, is a better predictor of CHD and

**Table 7.4**

## THE MEASUREMENT OF THE TYPE A BEHAVIOR PATTERN

The Type A construct was originally conceived as a pattern of behavior consisting of an aggressive and continual struggle to achieve more and more in less and less time. Type A has been measured with two alternative scales. With the Structured Interview (SI) an interviewer infers Type A from not only answers to questions but also the interviewee's behavior (e.g., attempts to control the conversation and the speed, explosiveness, and volume of speech). The Jenkins Activity Scale (JAS) is a self-report questionnaire. The following are two items from the JAS:

DIRECTIONS:
For each of the following items, please circle the number of the ONE best answer.

Would people who know you well agree that you tend to get irritated easily?
1. Definitely yes          3. Probably no
2. Probably yes            4. Definitely no

Would people who know you well agree that you tend to do most things in a hurry?
1. Definitely yes          3. Probably no
2. Probably yes            4. Definitely no

*Source:* Jenkins, C.D., Zyzanski, S.J., & Rosenman, R.H. (1979). *The Activity Survey for Health Prediction.* Form N. New York: Psychological Corp., Items 29, 30.

health-related variables (e.g., blood pressure) than the multidimensional measures of Type A (Booth-Kewley & Friedman, 1987; Ganster, Schaubroeck, Sime, & Mayes, 1991). The final verdict on the best way to measure Type A, however, is still unresolved. Like the life events approach, Type A has sparked considerable research within the last 20 years. As researchers unravel the Type A phenomenon, we learn increasingly more about the link between this individual characteristic, the situational demands (stressors) that provoke Type A behavior, and resulting illness.

## Organizational Effects

**Job-related Attitudes**    We can classify the organizational effects or outcomes of stress as either attitudinal or behavioral. Attitudinal effects include job satisfaction, organizational commitment, job involvement, propensity (inclination) to leave the organization, and job-related tension or anxiety. The relationships among these work-related attitudes and stressors are some of the strongest and most consistent in stress research, particularly for the white-collar stressors role conflict and role ambiguity (Jackson & Schuler, 1985). People who report stressful work situations also report that they are tense, anxious, dissatisfied, uncommitted, uninvolved at work, and seriously considering seeking employment elsewhere.

Some research on job stress and attitudes suggests that the relationships among stress and attitudes may be complex. For example, Netemeyer,

Johnston, and Burton (1990) tested a model of role stress and job attitudes originally proposed by Bedeian and Armenakis (1981). This model hypothesizes that greater role conflict and ambiguity lead to increased job tension, which results in lower job satisfaction. Lower job satisfaction, in turn, increases the intention (or propensity) of the worker to leave the organization. In addition to hypothesizing an indirect influence of role conflict and ambiguity on propensity to leave, the model also hypothesizes a direct influence of these two variables in which role conflict and ambiguity directly lower job satisfaction and increase the propensity to leave (Figure 7.6).

Netemeyer and colleagues mailed surveys that assessed role conflict, role ambiguity, job tension, job satisfaction, and propensity to leave the organization to the field sales force of a national manufacturer of consumer goods. They received responses from 183 of these sales people. Statistical analyses of the data indicated that role conflict and role ambiguity effects were mostly indirect; that is, increased role conflict and role ambiguity increased the propensity to leave by increasing job tension and lowering job satisfaction. The direct effects of role conflict and ambiguity on job satisfaction and propensity to leave were much weaker. Therefore, the hypothesized relationships in the Bedeian and Armenakis model were only partially supported.

**Job-related Behaviors**   Although stress researchers have had a long-standing interest in the stress-performance relationship (e.g., McGrath's process model of performance), the relationships found between job-related stressors and behavioral outcomes, such as absenteeism and job performance, are often weak. For instance, Jackson and Schuler (1985) reported that the relation-

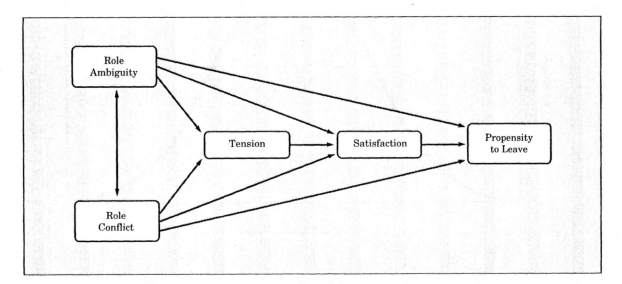

**Figure 7.6**   *A path-analytic study of the consequences of role conflict and ambiguity*

*Source:* Bedeian, A.G., & Armenakis, A.A. (1981). A path analytic study of the consequences of role conflict and ambiguity. *Academy of Management Journal, 24,* 417–424.

ships of role ambiguity and role conflict to performance were very low, especially for objective performance measures such as quantity of output. These low correlations may reflect, in part, the problems that so often plague objective measures of performance (Chapter 9). However, the weak link between job-related stressors and behavioral outcomes also may reflect the complex relationship between stress and performance. Surprisingly, research on this topic began early in the twentieth century, even before Cannon's and Selye's pioneering work on physiological stress responses.

In 1908, Robert Yerkes and John Dodson demonstrated that performance increased with increasing arousal up to a point. Beyond that point, performance decreased with increasing arousal (Figure 7.7). Arousal here refers to a general stress response characterized by alertness or activation. This complex relationship between arousal (the stress response) and performance is often called the inverted-u relationship. This relationship can be generally explained by saying too little stress is just as detrimental as too much. For example, if you were feeling extremely stressed when you took your calculus exam, your score was probably not as high as you could have achieved if less stressed. However, if you were totally relaxed, even lethargic, when you took the exam, you probably did not achieve your highest possible

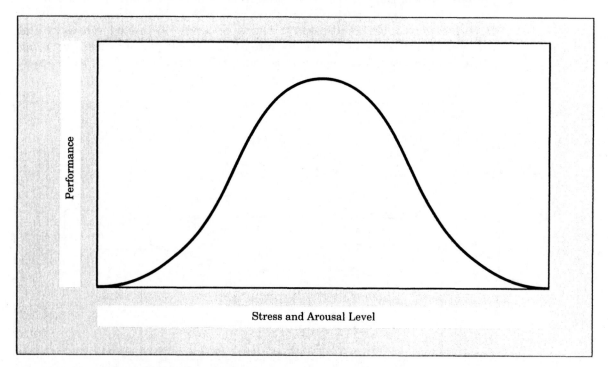

**Figure 7.7** *The Yerkes-Dodson Law*

*Source:* Yerkes, R.M., & Dodson, J.D. (1908). The relation of strength of stimulus to rapidity of habit-formation. *Journal of Comparative Neurology and Psychology, 18,* 459–482.

score either. This is why workers who perform dull or monotonous tasks are often aided by the addition of a stressful stimulus, such as loud noise or music. (Recall the earlier discussion on noise as a blue-collar stressor.) The noise or music can increase the worker's arousal level to the point that performance actually increases.

These relationships conjure up all types of interesting possibilities in which stressors could be used to enhance performance. The addition of a stressor such as noise might increase performance on assembly line jobs (which are often monotonous and repetitive), and when workers suffer from a lack of sleep, which is frequently the case for shift or night workers. Unfortunately, the optimum stress level associated with peak performance varies with people and tasks, so it is difficult to specify how much of any stressor will produce a particular level of performance for a specific individual.

**Burnout**   One type of job-related stress outcome that has both behavioral and attitudinal components and has been the focus of attention in recent years is *burnout.* You have probably used the term to describe yourself, particularly after final exam week. Burnout has received media attention, and is often used in reference to the frustration, exhaustion, and cynicism experienced by human service professionals, such as policemen, social workers, and teachers. Why does burnout most often affect human service professionals? Researchers believe that these jobs frequently require workers to accommodate the extreme needs and dependencies of clients, patients, or students. These extreme demands can be emotionally debilitating for the worker.

In the late 1970s, the psychological and medical community began to realize that the array of symptoms called burnout was a serious health problem beyond the normal experience of stress at work. In fact, burnout technically consists of three specific types of stress responses, usually found in professionals who work in people-intensive jobs. The three types of responses that define burnout are (Jackson, Schwab, & Schuler, 1986):

1. *Emotional exhaustion,* or feelings of being drained or used-up, unable to face a day's work, totally unenthusiastic.
2. *Depersonalization,* or the act of putting psychological distance between the individual and others, creating feelings of callousness and cynicism.
3. *Decreased personal accomplishment,* or the feeling of not living up to former goals and expectations; wasted efforts.

These three dimensions of burnout paint a picture of a worker who brings no enthusiasm to his or her work, who treats others in a cynical and calloused manner, and who seems to accomplish little regardless of the effort expended. The inevitable longer term responses are decreased worker motivation and performance. Specific organizational outcomes (Jackson, 1984) are that clients, such as welfare recipients, patients, or students, receive poor service; relationships with coworkers suffer; and job involvement decreases.

The most widely used measure of burnout is the Maslach Burnout Inventory (Maslach & Jackson, 1981). This questionnaire consists of items that measure each of the three dimensions of burnout: emotional exhaustion, depersonalization, and decreased personal accomplishment (Table 7.5).

Research on burnout has been generally supportive of the three dimensions of burnout and the negative consequences associated with them (Jones & DuBois, 1987). Jackson, Turner, and Brief (1987) reported that although the three dimensions of burnout were each related to different outcomes, all three were associated with feelings of decreased organizational commitment. Another study (Firth & Britton, 1989) found that emotional exhaustion was related to increased absenteeism, and depersonalization to leaving the organization. Because the experience of burnout is yoked to specific occupational stressors, one of the side benefits of burnout research has been the accumulation of knowledge about the stressors and strains in numerous occupational groups. For example, burnout research has been conducted with nurses (Firth & Britton, 1989; Garden, 1989), physicians (Lemkau, Rafferty, Purdy, & Rudisill, 1987), teachers (Russell, Altmaier, & Van Velzen, 1987), lawyers (Jackson, Turner, & Brief, 1987), and managers (Garden, 1989).

## Moderators of Stress: Personal Characteristics

We have examined a variety of stressors emanating both from within and outside the organization; we also examined the potential health and organizational outcomes of experiencing these stressors. Unfortunately, we cannot understand the stress process by simply investigating associations between stressors and stress outcomes. We all know people who lead stressful lives and yet rarely become ill or perform poorly; we know other people who crum-

**Table 7.5**

### ITEMS FROM THE MASLACH BURNOUT INVENTORY (EDUCATOR VERSION)

Emotional Exhaustion
   I feel like I'm at the end of my rope.

Personal Accomplishment
   I feel I'm positively influencing other people's lives through my work.

Depersonalization
   I feel I treat some students as if they were impersonal objects

Source: Maslach, C., Jackson, S.E., & Schwab, R.L. (1986). *The Maslach Burnout Inventory (Educator Survey)*. Palo Alto, CA: Consulting Psychologists Press, Items 5, 9, 20.

ble at the mere suggestion of adversity. For these two extreme types of people, the stress process works quite differently. What distinguishes these opposite types? To examine this issue, we must discuss individual differences.

*Individual differences* are variables that allow us to distinguish among people on such bases as gender, race or ethnicity, age, social status, past experiences, heredity, intelligence, and personality types. These and other individual differences pose special problems for the stress researcher because these variables seem to be important determinants of how people perceive and react to stressors and the types of stress outcomes they experience. Specifically, individual differences can change or *moderate* the stressor-strain relationship (see Chapter 2 for a definition of moderator variable). For example, you may have a hypothesis that women perceive stressors differently and respond differently from men. If this is true, then you could say that gender moderates the stressor-strain relationship.

## GENDER

Gender is one individual difference that may distinguish how people perceive and respond to the stress experience. From birth, females live in a different world from males. They are taught to behave differently and to have different expectations than their male peers. It would therefore not be surprising if they experience stress differently.

An interesting gender difference reported by some researchers (Davidson & Cooper, 1987; Jick & Mitz, 1985) is that women tend to develop psychological stress responses, such as depression and fatigue, whereas men tend to develop physical or physiological stress responses, such as high blood pressure. These findings imply that men and women may experience stress differently. A recent quantitative review of gender differences in occupational stress (Martocchio & O'Leary, 1989), however, found no evidence of differences between men and women in either psychological or physiological stress across nineteen studies. Do women experience stress similarly to men, as Martocchio and O'Leary's results suggest?

Compared with their male counterparts, women suffer distinct occupational disadvantages. For example, women are overrepresented in low-paying jobs with limited promotion opportunities, high job insecurity, and weak or nonexistent labor unions (Brief, Schuler, & Van Sell, 1981). Such jobs include elementary school teacher, clerk/secretary, and nurse. Women also experience some unique job-related stressors. In traditional female occupations, the work itself is often reported to be boring and repetitive. If women cross sex role boundaries into traditionally male blue-collar work, such as factory or foundry jobs, they can suffer excessive physical demands from the work itself. Women may also lack the technical training to compete successfully in these jobs. In traditionally male white-collar or managerial work, women are often not privy to the mentoring or social networks central to managerial career advancement. For example, they are probably not invited to play golf with their male coworkers on Saturday, when business is discussed. Women are also frequently placed in peripheral or lower level management positions (regardless of merit) with little access to the mainstream career track in the organization (Morrison & Von Glinow, 1990; Terborg, 1985).

In addition to the general and specific sources of job-related stress, women with families often suffer the role conflict, ambiguity, and overload that characterize the dual career couples discussed earlier. This dismal picture may lead you to assume that women do not function as well as men on the job. However, existing data seem to contradict this assumption. National statistics generally indicate that the turnover and absenteeism rates for women are similar to rates for men. Although a few studies found some gender differences, particularly in blue-collar jobs, those differences are quite small (Terborg, 1985; U.S. Department of Labor, 1974; 1978). Similarly, when jobs between sexes are equated, women and men show comparable levels of job satisfaction, particularly in managerial and professional work (Smith, Scott, & Hulin, 1977; Weaver, 1980).

Even though few differences exist for job-related outcomes, there are larger gender differences in health outcomes. Working women show more psychosomatic ailments, such as tiredness, irritation, and anxiety, than men (Cooper & Davidson, 1982). Ivancevich and Matteson (1980) also reported that women managers and professionals suffer a higher incidence of drug-related abuse (e.g., abuse of tranquilizers and sleeping pills) and a higher suicide rate than men.

Unfortunately, we cannot definitively answer the question posed at the beginning of this section; it is unclear whether women experience stress differently from men. We know that they experience some unique stressors and that some of their responses to stress (strains) differ from men's responses. However, these antecedent and outcome differences may not have been reflected in the data assessed in Martocchio and O'Leary's (1989) review.

## RACE

Because of differences in lifestyles, experiences, and heritage, people who are members of ethnic minorities may perceive and respond to stress differently from the white majority. However, very little research exists on racial differences in job-related stress. Ford (1985) believes this deficit has occurred because most stress researchers do not belong to minority groups. The few studies do suggest that minority groups suffer greater stress than the white majority. Many of the stressors that afflict working women, such as overrepresentation in lower level jobs and lack of access to training and promotion opportunities, also apply to minority workers (Morrison & Von Glinow, 1990).

Ramos (1975) studied 202 minority professionals (both ethnic minorities and women) at an aerospace organization and found that minority professionals experienced more job-related stress than comparable nonminorities. Another study (Ford, 1980) of minority professionals in a large manufacturing and sales organization found that black subordinates of black supervisors were less stressed than black and Mexican-American subordinates of white supervisors. In addition, Mexican-American women reported even higher levels of stress than their Mexican-American male counterparts.

## PERSONALITY

We all know people we would describe as shy, outgoing, anxious, overbearing, or cheerful. When we use such terms, we are describing a person's personality traits. It is not difficult to imagine that some personality characteristics might influence how people experience stress. For example, a person who is generally anxious would probably perceive a stressor as more threatening and respond more intensely than a person who is usually easygoing and calm.

A personality variable that has received attention in recent years is the Type A behavior pattern. As you recall, Type As are identified by certain personality traits, such as impatience, competitiveness, and hostility. We covered Type A behavior when discussing health outcomes because Type A people are more likely to develop cardiovascular disease.

Another personality variable that has captured the interest of stress researchers is hardiness. Kobasa (1979) defined *hardiness* as a personal characteristic possessed by people who think they control their environment, who are deeply committed to certain aspects of their lives (work, family, etc.), and who view change as a challenge. She found that individuals high on this constellation of personal traits (control, commitment, and challenge) are less apt to experience illness. For example, two studies (Kobasa, Maddi, & Kahn, 1982; Kobasa, Maddi, Puccetti, & Zola, 1985) found that male managers who scored high on hardiness and reported high levels of stress in their lives experienced less illness than low hardiness and high stress managers. These results, however, were not replicated in a sample of female secretaries (Schmied & Lawler, 1986). Unfortunately, too little data on hardiness currently exist to determine if the results with male managers generalize to other groups of workers.

*Negative affectivity* (NA; discussed in Chapter 4 because of its association with job satisfaction) has also generated much interest among stress researchers. As you recall, NA is the personal tendency to experience a wide range of negative emotions, such as tension, worry, dissatisfaction, and sadness. In a sample of teachers, Parkes (1990) found that high NA subjects showed greater reactivity to work demands than low NA subjects. Because NA often correlates highly with stress scales, some researchers have suggested that both NA and stress may measure a predisposition to respond negatively (Watson, Pennebaker, & Folger, 1987; Brief, Burke, George, Robinson, & Webster, 1988). Although Chen and Spector (1991) presented evidence that NA and stress are independent constructs, this debate has not been resolved.

## SOCIAL SUPPORT

Perhaps you have several close, supportive friends (or family members) whom you can count on when life is stressful; on the other hand, perhaps you feel that you have few close relationships. People who identify with either of these two extremes differ in the amount of social support they experience in their lives.

Within the past 15 years, researchers have investigated the effects of work-related social support, or social support from coworkers and supervisors, on strains (primarily job attitudes and health). In these studies, the types of social support provided by coworkers and supervisors have varied, ranging from emotional comfort to support in the form of feedback, information, or financial aid. Many of these studies have found effects of work-related social support on attitudes and health, although the strength and nature of these effects often differed.

Some researchers have found a direct or *main effect* of social support on strain. For example, in a sample of workers from five different organizations, employees who reported low supervisor (emotional) support also reported the presence of strains, such as dissatisfaction with work and depression (Beehr, 1976). Another study (Blau, 1981) examined social support in a sample of bus drivers and discovered that drivers with supportive supervisors and coworkers were more satisfied with their jobs.

Other researchers have found a more indirect link between social support and strains. For example, House and Wells (1978) studied work-related social support in a sample of white male employees in a chemical plant. They found that only the highly stressed employees who reported high supervisor support also reported fewer mental and physical health problems. A similar type of relationship also existed between extraorganizational (wife, family, and friends) support and strain. The type of relationship House and Wells found has been called the *buffering effect* of social support on stress and strains, which means that the beneficial effects of social support are found mostly for highly stressed workers.

Etzion (1984) investigated the relative effects of both work-related and extraorganizational support on male and female workers. Etzion reasoned that social support may be differentially effective for men and women because women are socialized in childhood to be more relationship-oriented than men. She asked 657 male and female professionals to answer a survey on social support, job and life stressors, and burnout. The women reported experiencing more stress (in the form of stressors and burnout) but also more social support than men (Table 7.6). Interestingly, these results also suggested that women tended to rely on extraorganizational sources of social support, whereas men tended to rely on work-related sources of social support.

Etzion's study illustrates the importance of individual differences, such as gender and social support, in understanding how the experience of stress affects strains. Indeed, stress is definitely not egalitarian: some people suffer more than others when stressed. From the previous discussions, you might conjecture that a minority woman high on negative affectivity, low on hardiness (control, commitment, and challenge), and low on social support at work and home might perceive more stress and respond to it more severely than some other types of people.

**Table 7.6**

## COMPARISON OF MEN AND WOMEN: SOCIAL SUPPORT AND THE STRESS-BURNOUT RELATIONSHIP

| Variable | Total ($n = 630$) | | Women ($n = 357$) | | Men ($n = 273$) | | Comparison by Sex |
|---|---|---|---|---|---|---|---|
| | M | SD | M | SD | M | SD | t-test |
| Burnout | 2.97 | .60 | 3.08 | .60 | 2.83 | .58 | 5.23** |
| Life Stress | 3.37 | .95 | 3.50 | 1.00 | 3.20 | .85 | 4.00** |
| Work Stress | 3.98 | .96 | 3.97 | 1.00 | 3.98 | .90 | −.12 |
| Life Support | 5.53 | .79 | 5.58 | .83 | 5.46 | .74 | 1.78* |
| Work Support | 5.13 | .72 | 5.14 | .79 | 5.12 | .62 | .51 |

*$p<.05$, one tailed test. **$p<.001$.
M= mean; SD= standard deviation

*Source:* Etzion, D. (1984). Moderating effect of social support on the stress-burnout relationship. *Journal of Applied Psychology, 69*, 615–622.

# THE MANAGEMENT OF STRESS

We have examined the physiological and psychological facets of the stress process and dissected the model in Figure 7.1 by investigating the various stressors and strains that researchers have identified for different types of workers. How, you may ask, do people deal with these (mostly) everyday work stressors? Latack (1986) developed a scale that measures three types of job-related coping: control, escape, and symptom management. *Control coping* consists of behaviors and cognitive appraisals that are proactive or take-charge; *escape coping* consists of behaviors and cognitive appraisals that are escapist or avoidant; *symptom management coping* consists of strategies that manage the symptoms of stress (Table 7.7). In a sample of hospital managers and professionals, Latack reported that use of control coping was related to high job satisfaction and low anxiety, whereas escape and symptom management coping were related to increased health problems. Recently, Leiter (1991) found that control coping was associated with decreased burnout, whereas escape coping was related to increased burnout. Other researchers (Smith & Sulsky, 1992) discovered that frequent use of all three types of coping strategies was associated with strains, such as job dissatisfaction and health problems, in three independent samples. Both blue- and white-collar workers also reported using control strategies more frequently than the other types of coping strategies.

**Table 7.7**

### EXAMPLES OF ITEMS FROM LATACK'S COPING SCALES

**Control Strategies**
  Get together with my supervisor to discuss this.
  Tell myself that I can probably work things out to my advantage.

**Escape Strategies**
  Remind myself that work isn't everything.
  Separate myself as much as possible from the people who created this situation.

**Symptom Management Strategies**
  Take tranquilizers, sedatives, or other drugs.
  Do physical exercise (jogging, exercycle, dancing, or other participative sports).

*Source:* Latack, J.C. (1986). Coping with job stress: Measures and future directions for scale development. *Journal of Applied Psychology, 71,* 377–385.

The control and escape coping scales consist of coping strategies that individuals probably use on a daily or frequent basis in handling stressful situations at work. However, the symptom management scale includes items that people turn to when the stress in their lives exceeds their ability to cope with it (e.g., seeking professional counseling). Some of these stress management strategies have been used in stress management workshops or programs sponsored by organizations. These programs or workshops typically target the individual or the organization (or a combination) for change. Next, we examine each of these.

## Changing the Person: Individual Methods

### EXERCISE

The 1980s definitely could be called the health decade. One of the consequences of this health consciousness was that people of all ages and lifestyles incorporated exercise programs into their daily routines. Many organizations, such as Coors Brewing Company, Kennicott Copper, Hewlett-Packard, and Johnson & Johnson, followed suit by developing in-house exercise facilities and programs. Some organizations, such as Mesa Petroleum, even offer incentives in the form of cash and fringe benefits to employees who use these facilities on a regular basis (Bailey, 1990).

Beyond the overall health benefits, does the personal and organizational emphasis on physical fitness have any merit as a stress-reduction aid? The answer is a resounding yes! Physical fitness experts agree that a consistent exercise routine is one of the easiest and most reliable ways to reduce the harmful effects of stress as well as to achieve physical fitness. These beneficial effects can include increased physical as well as mental health.

Positive outcomes are typically observed only when the exercise is aerobic. *Aerobic exercise* is any physical activity that produces an elevated respiration, heart rate, and metabolic rate for 20–30 minutes. Examples of aerobic exercise include jogging, swimming, tennis, and bicycling. The reason aerobic exercise is effective seems almost paradoxical. Both the experience of stress and vigorous exercise increase physiological activation (e.g., elevated heart rate, respiration) and hormonal activation (e.g., increased adrenaline levels). However, physically fit people show lower physiological and hormonal activation at rest and under stress (Falkenberg, 1987; Ivancevich & Matteson, 1980; Selye, 1974). In other words, the bodies of physically fit individuals generally maintain a much lower baseline of arousal and depart relatively less from their (lower) baseline than unfit individuals. Engaging in aerobic exercise soon after experiencing stress also seems to have additional benefits. One of the immediate effects of vigorous exercise is to metabolize or burn off the harmful by-products of the stress response quickly (Falkenberg, 1987).

The reasons behind the mental health benefits, however, are less easy to determine. The exercising individual's mental health may improve because he or she is doing something positive. Exercise may also serve as a break or diversion in the day. One of the most interesting explanations is the presence of endorphins, natural, morphine-like chemicals, in the bodies of people who are vigorously exercising. Endorphins are naturally occurring painkillers produced by the brain. Scientists have measured significant elevations of endorphins in the bloodstreams of exercising people. Increases in the levels of these natural substances are also thought to be associated with the phenomena of runner's high and getting a second wind reported by athletes (Falkenberg, 1987; Ivancevich & Matteson, 1980).

The positive benefits of exercise also have been linked to organizationally relevant outcomes, such as task performance, although there is little research (Falkenberg, 1987). People who exercise regularly seem to perform better on some physical and cognitive tasks, especially under stressful conditions. The rationale is that those who exercise regularly are generally less physiologically aroused. This finding is particularly applicable if performance decreases when a person is excessively aroused. In addition, fit people recover from stressful events more rapidly. In those situations in which a person must make judgments or decisions under stress, the ability to recover from the effects of stress may be a crucial determinant of performance.

## RELAXATION/MEDITATION TECHNIQUES

The techniques we refer to are structured relaxation or meditation exercises, not simply resting or thinking pleasant thoughts. The history of these techniques dates back to antiquity; in the sixth century B.C. Eastern scriptures mention mental and physical relaxation achieved through meditative practices. One of the most well-known forms of meditation today, *Transcendental Meditation* (TM), gained recognition in this country when the Maharishi Mahesh Yogi introduced it to America in the early 1960s. TM is a simple type of meditation that requires minimal instruction, although it does have a spiritual emphasis. Secular or nonspiritual techniques have also been popularized; one of the most widely used secular techniques is the *relaxation response* (Benson, 1975). Herbert Benson, a Harvard cardiologist, developed the relaxation response for his patients by distilling the essential components of TM. He claims it produces the same effects as TM.

Meditative and relaxation practices differ not only in the amount of spiritual or religious emphasis, but also in the amount and focus of the training. Many (e.g., TM) require some degree of formal training and others, such as the relaxation response, can be self-taught. Some, such as TM and the relaxation response, emphasize primarily mental relaxation. Others, such as a technique known as *progressive relaxation,* emphasize physical and muscular relaxation. (Progression relaxation exercises attempt to systematically relax each of the 16 major muscle groups in the body.)

Whether ancient meditative practices steeped in religious tradition or modern secular ones are used, the proponents of meditation and relaxation claim all techniques achieve relaxation through a reversal of the stress response: Consistent practice of meditation or relaxation reduces metabolic rate, heart rate, and respiration. Proponents also claim that one long-term effect is reduction of blood pressure. However, a review of the research on the health effects of meditation and relaxation (Holmes, 1984) was not very encouraging. According to this review, relaxation and meditation are no more effective than simply resting. However, these conclusions were based on results from only a few, well-designed experiments; many relevant studies were omitted because they did not allow cause-and-effect conclusions to be drawn.

## OTHER STRESS MANAGEMENT TECHNIQUES

Other stress management techniques that target the individual are biofeedback and therapy. *Biofeedback* involves the electronic measurement of physiological (body) processes that are converted to light or sound signals to provide feedback on how these processes function. For example, a person hooked up to a biofeedback machine can receive feedback about the muscle tension in her neck or forehead in the form of soft tones. Using this auditory feedback, she can learn to control the tension in her forehead or neck. Hopefully, after practice, the person can control her muscle tension without the biofeedback machine.

*Psychotherapy* involves counseling with a trained clinical psychologist or psychiatrist in either an individual or group setting. Typically, the goal of such therapy is to cognitively restructure the way a person thinks so life does not seem so threatening or stressful. Therapy can also include coping skills training, such as time management and assertiveness training. Both biofeedback and therapy are useful and effective stress management practices, although both can be fairly expensive, long-term options.

An operator monitors biofeedback equipment that provides the subject with auditory feedback. The changes in the auditory signals are used to regulate body functions.

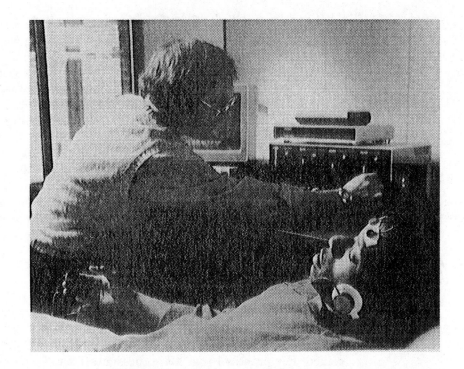

## Changing the Environment: Organizational Methods

Stress management programs sponsored by organizations often include relaxation training and exercise regimens that target the individual as the level of change. In addition to these individually oriented techniques, organizations can implement changes at a macro level, for example, at the level of the work group or the total organization. Instead of helping workers manage the stress they experience, these organizational-level techniques are designed to reduce the sources of stress (stressors). In fact, any intervention or change that creates an improved work setting, such as a better selection or performance appraisal system, can be labeled a stress management technique. However, these types of changes are usually not considered to be stress management tools, although they may indeed reduce employee stress. We next discuss examples of some commonly used stress management techniques that target the larger organizational environment for change.

### TEAM BUILDING: INTERVENTIONS FOR WORK GROUPS

OD consultants often are called upon by organizations to improve work group functioning (Chapter 5). The reason typically given for desiring these changes is not stress within the work group, but poor group performance or functioning. However, the source of these performance problems is frequently stress-related, usually in the form of conflict among work group members.

When conflict arises within a work group because members are unclear about work roles, a technique called *role analysis* (Dayal & Thomas, 1968; French & Bell, 1984) can be helpful. The purpose of role analysis is to clarify the role expectations and obligations of work group members. Initially, a group coordinator or consultant asks the worker (or a representative of a group of workers in similar jobs) to list the duties, behaviors, responsibilities (e.g., balance the budget, meet with upper management, supervise clerical staff), and position (e.g., middle management) in the organization that he or she perceives as defining the work role. This focal work role is discussed in the group until consensus is reached. The end product of this discussion is the *role profile,* a document that defines the work role in terms of duties, behaviors, and responsibilities. This exercise often dramatically clears up confusion about why someone is not doing his or her job correctly; the reason is usually differing perceptions among workers about their and others' work-related responsibilities and obligations.

Some exercises also have been introduced to reduce conflict between or among different work groups (e.g., marketing and sales). The *organizational mirror technique* (French & Bell, 1984) is a set of activities in which a work group receives feedback from one or more groups about how the group is perceived. For practical reasons, representatives of each group, rather than the whole group, meet with a group coordinator. During the meeting, one of the groups "fishbowls" to discuss the issues; the fishbowl is composed of an inner circle of people who talk and an outer circle of people who only listen and observe. The outside circle cannot interrupt the inner circle for any reason. Next, the groups reverse positions. The total group then re-forms (composed of both work groups), discusses the dialogue, and charts a course of action for solving the problem(s).

## STRUCTURAL INTERVENTIONS: CHANGING THE ORGANIZATION

This type of stress management intervention reduces stress by changing the structure of the organization itself or the nature of the jobs or work within the organization. As with the team building interventions, the structural interventions are frequently implemented to increase productivity or general functioning. However, they also typically decrease stress and increase satisfaction.

A commonly used structural intervention is a *quality circles program* (see Chapter 5), a specific type of *participative management* (i.e., worker input into managerial decision making). A quality circles program is a specialized type of participative management because it targets the enhancement of product quality (e.g., making a better car, providing better service to clients). A quality circles group is composed of 10 or fewer employees from a work group that meets regularly to analyze production-related problems. Their recommendations are forwarded to management for support and/or assistance in carrying out the recommendations. Many organizations report dramatic increases in product quality and organizational effectiveness after implementing such a program. As a consequence of their participation in the program, workers also usually feel more invested and involved in their jobs and the organization.

Other types of structural changes in the organization can be used to reduce job-related stress. *Job or task redesign* is one such technique. Many jobs can be changed to increase, for example, the amount of variety, skill, and significance the worker experiences. (See Chapter 3 on the job characteristics model for task redesign.) For example, an assembly line worker's job might be changed so that he or she receives additional training to work on two or three assembly tasks.

## Stress Management Programs: Do They Really Work?

Industry spends millions of dollars annually on stress management programs that incorporate many of the strategies previously discussed. The bottom line is: Do they really work? After participating in such programs do employees feel less stressed? The evidence is mixed, although promising. The most common approach in organizational stress management programs is some combination of general information about stress, relaxation or meditation training, exercise, and therapy/coping skills training. Organizations rarely measure the impact of structural interventions in assessing stress management efforts, probably because structural interventions typically focus on other factors, such as productivity and turnover.

Some well-designed assessments of organizational stress management programs have reported decreases in physiological stress responses, such as pulse rate and blood pressure (Bruning & Frew, 1987) and psychological stress responses, such as burnout (Higgins, 1986). One assessment (Larsson, 1987) even reported increased cognitive performance in military personnel after they participated in a stress management program. Another program helped recently unemployed workers to effectively cope with job loss and attain higher motivation and better quality reemployment (Caplan, Vinokur, Price, & van Ryn, 1989).

However, Ganster and his colleagues (Ganster, Mayes, Sime, & Tharp, 1982) warn against being overly optimistic about the long-term effectiveness of these programs. They assessed the effectiveness of eight weeks of stress management training, which consisted of therapy and relaxation exercises, in a group of public agency employees. Physiological (adrenaline and noradrenaline) and psychological (depression, anxiety, irritation, and body complaints) measures were administered before and after the training and at four months. Although decreases in both physiological and psychological stress responses were found in program participants relative to a control group, the researchers judged these effects to be of minimal practical value, particularly over time. They suggested that, instead of training employees to better endure stress at work, a potentially healthier and more ethical approach would be to make the organizational environment less stressful.

Where do we go from here? Ivancevich, Matteson, Freedman, and Phillips (1990) offered some specific suggestions to improve the quality of worksite stress management programs. For example, most programs have focused on short-term, individual outcome improvements, such as relaxation and coping skills training, in managerial and white-collar employees. As Ganster and his colleagues warned, these types of programs may prove to be minimally effective in the long-term. We also know little about the impact of stress management programs on blue-collar employees, such as factory or foundry workers. At a minimum, future worksite stress management programs should consider long-term outcome improvements and the influence of the type of worker.

# A FINAL SUMMATION AND A LOOK AT THE FUTURE

The experience of stress is composed of environmental sources, or stressors, immediate physiological responses, and short-term and longer term outcomes, or strains. The physiological responses present a paradox because, although they are adaptive in the short-term, they can be very destructive as chronic responses to stress. The perception of stress, or cognitive appraisal, also occupies a central role in the stress experience. Indeed, depending on one's appraisal, the effects of a stressor may be negated or a stressor may be perceived where none actually exists. These complexities inherent in the study of stress have prompted researchers to develop models to organize information about stress.

The occupation itself can be a source of stress, particularly in lower level jobs and jobs in service professions, such as law enforcement and medicine. Environmental stressors, such as noise and heat, are common stressors for many blue-collar workers. Organizational stressors, often called white-collar stressors, have been extensively studied by researchers. The work role–based stressors, role conflict and role ambiguity, have been associated with strains in hundreds of studies. Regardless of whether a worker experiences environmental or organizational stressors or both, all workers are subject to various sources of nonwork stressors. Stressors apart from work settings are believed to influence or spill over into work and vice versa.

Because job-related stressors are considered to be associated with health deficits, much research has focused on these types of strains. The experience of many stressful life events, such as divorce or promotion, has been linked to health problems. One of the more serious of these problems, coronary heart disease, has been related to the Type A behavioral pattern. In addition to health, organizational strains also have been widely studied. The relationships among work-related attitiudes and work-related stressors are some of the most consistent in stress research. The experience of job stressors also can affect job-related behaviors. An example is the phenomenon of burnout, which has been associated with feelings of emotional exhaustion, depersonalization, and decreased feelings of personal accomplishment.

Variables that moderate or change the relationships among stressors and strains have been the focus of much research. Common moderator variables include gender, race, personality characteristics, and social support.

People cope with stress in a variety of ways. Coping strategies can be proactive and take-charge or escapist and avoidant. These coping strategies have often been the focus of stress management programs in industry that typically target the individual or the organization as the focus for change. Individual stress management techniques include exercise, relaxation/meditation, biofeedback, and psychotherapy. Organizational stress management techniques include work group interventions, such as team building, and structural interventions, such as participative management and job or task redesign.

Several current trends in the workplace suggest that work stress will be an increasingly important topic in I/O psychology as the 1990s and beyond bring a host of new stressors to employees. As women continue to enter the work force, demands will continue to be placed on working parents and dual career couples to juggle both work and domestic commitments. Other stressors include job insecurity, job loss, and part-time employment. Although psychologists have little knowledge about these stressors at this time, they are thought to seriously influence worker attitudes, health, and behavior. Within the last 10 years, everyone has become acutely aware of major structural and personnel changes in organizations in the form of downsizing, reductions in manpower, restructuring, and corporate takeovers. These changes have deeply affected American industry and, for many workers, have had a devastating impact on individual jobs and careers (Ivancevich, Matteson, Freedman, & Phillips, 1990). In fact, job insecurity and concern about potential job loss have been associated with decreased personal well-being and negative work-related behaviors and attitudes (Roskies & Louis-Guerin, 1990).

Job loss and unemployment (or their threat) are real and critical issues for many American workers today. While everyone acknowledges the negative effects of job loss and unemployment on the terminated individual (Jahoda, 1982), psychologists only recently have begun to study the personal and organizational impact of job loss on survivors (i.e., those workers who were not terminated). Among the pioneers in this research are Brockner and his colleagues who addressed this issue both in the laboratory (Brockner, Davy, & Carter, 1985) and in the field (Brockner, Grover, & Blonder, 1988). They found that survivors invoked an equity theory explanation (Chapter 3) to reconcile their conflict; that is, the survivors derogated their terminated coworkers and believed that they deserved their fate (Brockner et al., 1985).

In a field study of job loss in several organizations, Brockner studied the influence of layoffs on survivors' job attitudes (Brockner et al., 1985). Results indicated that individual work ethic and prior role ambiguity predicted survivors' job involvement after layoffs. Specifically, those workers with a strong work ethic and low role ambiguity experienced higher job involvement after layoffs than other survivors. However, these relationships held only for those survivors in the mild layoff group (2–5% terminations in the workforce) but not in the severe layoff group (25–70% terminations in the workforce). The researchers reasoned that the severe condition was so stressful, even for the survivors, that personal perceptions had little influence on job attitudes.

A related issue is the proliferation of part-time employees in the American workforce. Because current personnel reductions in industry may be long-term or permanent, management relies increasingly on part-time or temporary workers to maintain productivity levels. However, I/O psychologists know little about these employees' job perceptions. Do part-time and temporary workers experience more job-related stress because they are not full-time, permanent members of some organization? Another problem is the continued impact of the technological explosion on organizational stress. In the last 10 years, American industry has witnessed the automation and computerization of many jobs, which have profoundly changed the nature of work. I/O psychologists have little knowledge regarding how to effectively introduce these changes or the effects that altering the nature of work will have on large segments of the workforce. Workers who observe their jobs being transformed into a set of machine-dependent activities that they are not trained to perform must surely experience a great deal of stress. Because of the implications for total system functioning, we discuss such issues as alternative work schedules and automation/computerization in Chapter 12.

## DISCUSSION QUESTIONS

1. Drawing from your knowledge of stress physiology, explain how a person can become ill from experiencing a stressor. Your explanation should begin with the first encounter with the stressor.
2. What differentiates environmental stressors from psychosocial stressors? Why are psychosocial stressors often considered to be more difficult to study than environmental stressors?
3. What types of organizational or white-collar stressors might affect a secretary? A manager? A sales clerk? Also, what strains might develop from experiencing these stressors?
4. Why has it been said that individual differences pose special problems for the stress researcher? What individual differences have proven to be important moderators of stressor-strain relationships?
5. Drawing on your knowledge of stressors, stress responses, strains, and individual differences, speculate why a hard-driving business executive might suffer a heart attack from enduring stress at work.

## STRESS IN THE POST OFFICE

Earlier in the chapter we cited a newspaper article about the November 1991 shooting massacre in Royal Oak, Michigan, which left four postal employees and the killer, a former postal employee, dead from gunshot wounds (Figure 7.4). Even more shocking is the fact that the Michigan shootings were not an isolated incident; since 1981, 36 people have been killed in eleven other incidents. The third worst massacre in U.S. history occurred in an Oklahoma post office in 1986 when 15 people were killed by a postal employee. Two recent episodes both occurred on the same day at two separate post offices. On May 7, 1993, a disgruntled postal worker in California and another in Michigan went on rampages that in each case resulted in the death of a fellow employee (Barringer, 1993).

Why have these slayings occurred in the post office? It could be argued that with an organization as large as the Postal Service (more than 750,000 employees) there are bound to be a few violent employees. The former U.S. Postmaster Anthony Frank recently commented that the problems reflect the type of worker that the Postal Service has been required to hire—veterans and the mentally disabled. Frank was cited as saying that "When you mandate that...in a tiny, tiny minority of cases you're going to have people slip through who are basically unbalanced people trained to kill....It's a lousy thing to say, but I think it needs to be said" (Barringer, 1993, p. A6).

Contrary to these views, comments of current and former postal workers and management suggest that these were not random events and that the stressful nature of the work environment is driving some workers to the breaking point. An episode of the TV news show *20/20* reported that violent acts by coworkers in the post office were common-

place events (ABC News *20/20*, February 14, 1992). One postal worker said, "Every day I go to work, I wonder if maybe somebody will be there with a gun. That's how bad it is where I work." One retired postmaster described the environment in the post office as having "an aura of fear."

What could possibly be creating such an aversive work environment? The analyses of these events published in newspaper and magazine articles reveal three major sources of job-related stress in the post office of the 1990s: 1) pressure from above (supervisors), 2) monotony of work, and 3) job insecurity.

The pressure from supervisors refers to pressure to improve productivity. Since Congress stopped subsidizing the Postal Service, it has been forced to compete with private postal services, such as United Postal Service. To be competitive and profitable, the mail must move quickly and efficiently. According to an official of the American Postal Workers Union, "You have an extremely high-stress, machine-paced work environment, managed by supervisors who are doctrinaire, quasi-military, and breathe down workers necks" (Barringer, 1993, p. A6).

The second stressor, the monotony of work, has been created by the rapid automation of postal work. Postal employees talk of "huge mail factories" with high-speed letter-sorting machines. A postal employee who operates one of these machines must sort 3,600 letters per hour at the rate of one per second for a full work day. Supervisors keep track of each worker's error rate through computer monitoring while, through one-way windows, postal inspectors watch for mail theft.

The post office is rapidly achieving full automation by introducing a new machine, the optical reader, which can read 35,000 letters

# CASE

per hour. One of these machines will replace 35 workers sorting mail by hand and 17 workers manning the letter-sorting machines. The new system is expected to be fully operational within a few years. This newest trend in automation is expected to eventually reduce the post office's work force by 100,000. Hence, the third stressor, job insecurity, is indeed very salient to many postal employees.

What is the post office doing to help employees deal with the stress? At the time of the Royal Oak shootings a 1-800 number was installed for workers to call if they had complaints or problems. Hundreds of stressed workers tried to call this help number. However, only one person had been assigned to answer these phone calls, so most went unanswered.

## CASE QUESTIONS

1. Recall Ganster, Mayes, Sime, and Tharp's (1982) suggestion that, instead of training employees to endure stress, a better approach would be to make the organizational environment less stressful. Would their suggestion be applicable to the post office's situation?
2. If you were designing a stress management program for postal employees, what would you include in the program? What would be the specific targets of change?

# SECTION 3

## PERSONNEL PSYCHOLOGY:
## IMPROVING THE PERSON-WORK FIT

In this section we cover topics that are usually lumped under the title of personnel or industrial (the I in I/O) psychology. Included in our discussion are job analysis and employee selection, training, and performance appraisal. In contrast to the theoretical slant of organizational psychologists, personnel psychologists tend to be more practically oriented, with much of their research concerned with developing techniques that can be used to improve the fit between employees and the organization.

Providing a good fit is in part an *attraction* problem in that you want to entice the most qualified people to seek employment in your organization. It is a *selection problem* in that once you interest people in applying, you want to be able to choose the best qualified people. It is a *placement problem* in that once hired, you want to put people where they belong. It is a *training problem* in that once hired and placed, you want to instruct your employees so that they can perform the work properly. It is not always the case that providing a good fit requires finding the right people and changing them to fit the organization. The emphasis in *engineering psychology* has been on modifying the work environment

to fit the capabilities and preferences of the people who use that environment.

We begin with the topic that is fundamental to all the other topics covered in this section: job analysis. Observing and describing what people do in their jobs is an essential first step in providing a better match between people and work. Some job analysis techniques are worker oriented and describe jobs in terms of general behavioral processes and human attributes. Other techniques describe work in terms of the specific tasks that are performed. As we demonstrate, how information on the job is to be used should determine which technique is used. We examine several specific applications of job analysis, with special emphasis on their use in the management of wage and salary compensation.

Another important step in providing a good fit is determining the standards of performance that employees are expected to attain in their work. Chapter 9 deals with alternative measures of employee performance and their uses in an organization. Measures of performance can be used in a variety of human resource management activities, including the rewarding, punishing, promoting, firing, and developing of employees. They also are used as criteria in research that evaluates human resource management interventions. We discuss the many options that are available to employers seeking to appraise performance. Performance appraisals can be objective or subjective, can be conducted by supervisors, peers, subordinates, customers, or the employees themselves, and can focus on results, process, or traits of the employees. Much of the performance appraisal in organizations relies on subjective ratings. The large amount of research on subjective rating scales has provided insight into the pros and cons of specific scales such as Behavioral Anchored Rating Scales (BARS). We emphasize, however, that more attention needs to be given to the process of judging performance as opposed to developing the right scale. A particularly important application of performance appraisals is in providing feedback to employees. In concluding, we give special consideration to some of the methods of providing feedback that appear to have great potential for improving performance effectiveness.

Staffing, the focus of Chapter 10, is the chief activity of many I/O psychologists. A variety of selection techniques have been developed during this century that have proven valuable in screening prospective employees and predicting their future performance. These include measures of mental and physical abilities, biodata, personality questionnaires, work samples, assessment centers, structured interviews, and others. A major point in this chapter is that organizations should conduct research to evaluate the sensitivity, reliability, and validity of selection techniques. In actually using a selection instrument in making decisions about potential employees, other factors need to be taken into account, including how many people currently succeed, how many applicants can be rejected out of those who apply, the cost of

the procedure, and the fairness of the decisions. Much of this chapter concentrates on selection, but in closing we also consider employee placement and recruitment.

No matter how good staffing procedures are in a company, the employees that a company attracts and selects will still have rough edges that need to be smoothed to provide a good fit to the work. We come then to training, a personnel function that is aimed at instilling the knowledge, skills, abilities, and attitudes needed to perform the organization's work. As important as training is to the organization, it is often implemented in a haphazard and wasteful way. Chapter 11 is organized around a systems model that is presented as an ideal approach to training. An essential point of this model is that training is a subsystem within the organization and should be evaluated on the basis of how well it fulfills the needs of the larger organization. According to this model, training programs should be designed to fulfill objectives that are derived from a careful assessment of needs, evaluated against how well they fulfill these needs, and modified accordingly. A variety of on-the-job and off-the-job training techniques currently exist, each with advantages and disadvantages. We cover the pros and cons of these various techniques, along with interventions to improve acquisition and transfer of what is learned. Although the training literature is not as well-developed as the work on staffing, this is changing. Chapter 11 covers some of the exciting new developments that are likely to have dramatic effects on the future practice of training.

Most of this section is concerned with changing the person to fit the environment. Chapter 12 considers the other side of the coin, that is, how the environment can be changed to fit the person. This is the domain of engineering psychologists, who have often taken the person as a given and have focused on changing the environment to improve efficiency, productivity, and well-being. One aspect of the work environment is the human-machine interface. Incompatibilities between machines and their human operators can lead to tragic errors, which can be avoided if equipment is designed to take into account the limitations of human auditory, visual, and information-processing abilities. For instance, it has been repeatedly shown that errors can be dramatically reduced through proper construction of displays and controls. Other areas of research have focused on the best ways to design physical work spaces, automation, and work schedules to optimize productivity and efficiency. Finally, we review the contributions that engineering psychologists have made in their research on industrial accidents.

# CHAPTER

8

# Analyzing Work

- What Is a Job?

- Why Conduct a Job Analysis?

- What Is Measured in a Job Analysis?

- How Is a Job Analysis Conducted?

- Specific Methods of Job Analysis

- Job Evaluation as the Basis for Wage and Salary Administration

- A Final Summation and a Look at the Future

- Case: San Jose Tries Comparable Worth

To understand *why* people behave as they do in the workplace and to improve their job effectiveness, we must know *what* they do. The systematic process of collecting and interpreting information on work-related activities is *job analysis*. Contrary to the common perception of job analysis as dull, observing and talking to people about their work can be both fun and challenging. The analyst frequently must act as a Sherlock Holmes, going beyond titles and other surface features to ferret out the essential nature of an employee's activities. But regardless of whether you might enjoy doing a job analysis, it is an activity that is crucial to understanding most of the topics in this text. In Chapters 3 and 4, for example, we found that the work itself is an important source of satisfaction, motivation, and stress. Task variables again emerged in Chapter 5, in which the cooperative nature of work was shown to determine the relative effectiveness of rewarding the group for its collective efforts versus rewarding individuals for their individual efforts and in Chapter 6, in which the relative effectiveness of participative versus autocratic leadership was shown to depend on task structure. Job analysis is the first step in the design of employee selection, training, performance appraisal, and other personnel programs that are the focus of the next chapters. In summary, the pivotal role of the job and the task in personnel and organizational issues makes the analysis of work activities one of the most important topics discussed in this text.

## WHAT IS A JOB?

Something as familiar as "job" would seem to need no definition, but several terms are frequently confused that we must clarify. The terms element, task, position, job, occupation, job family, and career each refer to a different aspect of work. Assume that you are given the responsibility of analyzing the job of a worker in a fast food restaurant. You observe an employee perform the following activities:

1. Requests customer order and depresses keys of multicounting machine to simultaneously record order and compute bill.
2. Selects requested food items from serving or storage areas and assembles items on serving tray or in takeout bag.
3. Notifies kitchen personnel of shortages or special orders.
4. Prepares cold drinks, using drink-dispensing machine, or frozen milk drinks or desserts, using milkshake or frozen custard machine.
5. Prepares hot beverages using automatic water heater or coffeemaker.
6. Serves beverages and food to customers at their tables.
7. Presses lids onto beverages and places beverages on serving tray or in takeout container.

8. Receives payment.
9. Cooks and apportions french fries and performs other minor duties to prepare food, serve customers, or maintain an orderly eating or serving area.

The smallest components of these work activities are called *elements.* "Requests customer order" and "depresses key of multicounting machine" are two elements of the first task statement. One or more elements go together to form a *task,* which we define as a work activity performed to accomplish a specific objective or goal. Work is essentially the performance of tasks. Teachers teach, physicians provide medical care, window washers clean windows, and so it goes through the thousands of jobs that constitute the world of work. Not surprisingly, a large amount of effort is devoted to preparing task statements in job analysis. A task statement usually begins with an action verb and the object of that verb (e.g., presses lids, receives payment, serves cold drinks) and frequently specifies what the person uses in the way of tools or machines (e.g., use drink-dispensing machine, serve tray, use automatic water heater or coffeemaker) as well as the objective of the act (to maintain orderly eating area, to compute bill).

The tasks performed by an individual in an organization define that person's *position.* There are as many positions as there are employees in an organization. Moreover, the tasks performed by any one individual occupying a position are unique to some extent. This is not as likely to be the case with highly routine positions (e.g., a fast food worker) as with less routine positions (e.g., managerial and professional work). A middle-level manager in a larger organization, for instance, will perform some tasks that differ from tasks performed by other managers in the same company, despite the fact that they have the same title.

Now we come to the primary focus of this chapter, the *job.* The U.S. Department of Labor *Handbook of Job Analysis* defines a job "as a group of positions which are identical with respect to their major or significant tasks and sufficiently alike to justify their being covered by a single analysis. There may be one or many persons employed in the same job" (p. 3). Deciding whether a collection of positions should be classified as the same or different jobs ultimately requires human judgment. In some cases this may involve no more than eyeballing the tasks contained in the various positions. In other cases more rigorous analyses are required. For example, employees' descriptions of their tasks could be subjected to complex statistical procedures, and if positions are shown to be very similar in the tasks performed, then this group of positions can be considered a job. A job is in many respects similar to a psychological construct, defined in Chapter 2 as an abstract concept defined by a cluster of behaviors (see Binning & Barrett, 1989, for an interesting discussion of this). A job is a cluster of positions that are explicitly designed by the organization to go together. If jobs always corresponded to the way the organization designed them, there would be little need for job analysis. Of course, what people actually do in a job often deviates in many respects from what

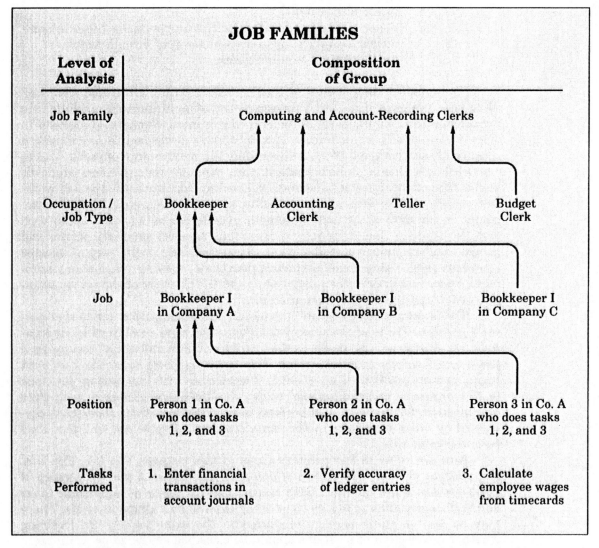

**Figure 8.1** *Example of different types of job groupings at different levels of analysis*

*Source:* Pearlman, K. (1980). Job families: A review and discussion of their implications for personnel selection. *Psychological Bulletin, 87*, 1–27.

was intended, thus requiring that we carefully examine positions to ensure that they deserve to be classified under the same job title.

If we find a group of jobs in several different organizations that are quite similar in the tasks performed, then these jobs are called an *occupation*. For example, there are many jobs in many different schools that involve different types of teaching (math, science, literature, biology), but all of these jobs belong to the teaching occupation. At the highest level of analysis is the *job family*, which is a group of similar occupations.

Thus, the analysis of work yields a hierarchy of work activities. This was illustrated by Pearlman (1980) with the job of bookkeeper. The three bookkeeper positions shown in Figure 8.1 undoubtedly involve different tasks to some extent, but there is enough commonality to place them in the same job. In turn, similarity in bookkeeper jobs across organizations defines the occupation of bookkeeper, and the similarity in the activities of accounting clerk, teller, and budget clerk define a job family of computing and account-recording clerks.

A *career* is a sequence of positions held by an individual employee over time. One employee begins as an accountant in a firm, moves up to manager of a department, is promoted to vice-president, and eventually becomes president of the firm. In this case the employee's career progresses in an upward direction, but careers also may move in a downward direction, as in the case of an employee who starts out as a blue-collar worker, is promoted to foreman, and then goes back to nonsupervisory duties. Those careers that do show an upward progression may not follow a straight, unbroken path in the direction of increased responsibility. An employee might begin in a nonsupervisory position, progress to a managerial position, drop out for several years to raise a family, and then go back to renew his or her earlier career. Charting the various ways that careers can unfold is an intriguing area of research that is likely to receive an increasing amount of attention from I/O psychologists.

This chapter examines under the general term of job analysis the methods that are used in describing and analyzing tasks, jobs, occupations, and careers. The first question we address is *why* we conduct job analyses. Next we focus on *what* we measure, *who* serves as a source of information on work activities, and *how* we perform the analysis. There is no single best approach but much depends on *why* we attempt the job analysis in the first place. Consequently, we first consider several of the major uses of job analysis.

# WHY CONDUCT A JOB ANALYSIS?

The importance of job analysis in an organization cannot be underestimated. When human resource management is done right, invariably the first step is collecting some sort of information on the elements and tasks of the work performed. There are a variety of approaches to job analysis, and which approach we take depends on the use that we will make of the information.

## Reducing Role Conflict and Ambiguity

In Chapter 7 we noted that there is often a discrepancy between what incumbents describe as their position and what the organization and other people say they should do. An immediate benefit of job analysis is that it can clarify and reduce these misunderstandings. A well-written and current job description can help immensely to reduce conflict and ambiguity, especially if those in the jobs are involved in writing the descriptions. The payoffs can include reduced stress (Chapter 7) and increased job satisfaction (Chapter 4) and work motivation (Chapter 3).

## Design and Evaluation of Training

In preparing a training program, the content of the training usually should reflect the content of the job. A job analysis can help in this regard by identifying the major content areas that should be covered in the course material (Faley & Sundstrom, 1985; Glickman & Vallance, 1958). We will discuss behavior description techniques such as the Position Analysis Questionnaire that can be useful in identifying the most important dimensions of the job that should be the focus of the training. If a job is found to involve mainly decision making and communication, for example, and relatively little in the way of public and customer contact, then this would suggest that the training should emphasize the former more than the latter. Finding that several jobs are high on some dimensions would suggest a core curriculum in the training of people performing these different jobs.

## Performance Appraisal and Criterion Development

The performance criteria that are used as the basis for evaluating an individual's job performance should be derived from important dimensions of the job. If the job primarily involves working with people but very little handling of data and information, then the measures of performance should focus primarily on how well the employee deals with people. The job analysis techniques discussed in this chapter all can be used to identify important dimensions of the job. The critical incident technique is among the most common methods because it specifically focuses on the crucial behaviors in the job (Chapter 9).

## Job Design

If an analysis reveals that jobs are high on dimensions likely to be related to dissatisfaction and poor motivation (Chapters 3 and 4), then the job may need to be enriched to increase its motivational potential. If the job analysis reveals that certain job characteristics cause inefficiencies, then work simplification may be needed. Job analysis also can be used to identify sources of discomfort resulting from muscular and physiological stress, environmental demands, and problems with the human-machine interface. Two job analysis techniques that are particularly effective for this purpose are instruments discussed in Chapter 2, the Multimethod Job Design Questionnaire (MJDQ; Campion & Thayer, 1985; Campion, 1988) and the Job Diagnostic Survey (JDS; Hackman & Oldham, 1975). We discussed in Chapter 3 how the JDS could be used to assess job components that appear to be crucial determinants of employee satisfaction and motivation. The MJDQ taps some of the same motivational components of the job as the JDS, but also allows an assessment of whether there are aspects of the job that need simplification to increase efficiency.

## Personnel Selection

In deciding what to look for in new hires, the first step is to carefully analyze the requirements of the job. The beneficial effects of job analysis for selection were shown by Wiesner and Cronshaw (1988), who found that interviews that were based on formal job analysis did a much better job in the selection of employees than those without formal job analyses. Some job analysis procedures provide direct assessments of job requirements (e.g., Fleishman's Ability Requirement Scales). Others provide job information that then can be used to generate the requirements (e.g., the Position Analysis Questionnaire).

Once the knowledge, skills, abilities, and orientations (KSAOs) required in a job have been determined through either direct or indirect means, selection procedures measuring these KSAOs can be used in screening applicants. For instance, if a job analysis shows that a job demands a high degree of general intelligence, physical stamina, and assertiveness, then tests of these characteristics could be used to screen and select applicants. The organization should in most cases consider the job analysis results to be *hypotheses* that must be verified through research (Chapter 10). For instance, if a job seems to require a high level of reading ability, then research will be needed to assess whether currently employed workers high in reading ability actually perform better. Some psychologists argue that not every potential selection procedure needs to be tested in each situation it is used (see the discussion of validity generalization in Chapter 10).

Job analysis is particularly important when a content validation strategy is used to develop and evaluate the selection procedures (Levine, Ash, & Bennett, 1980). For example, if clerical applicants were expected to have specific knowledge, skills, and abilities at the time they were hired, a test might be designed to assess these factors. Items in the test could be based on the important activities of the job identified through job analyses.

## Wage and Salary Administration

A major application of job analysis (discussed in more detail at the end of this chapter) is to decide how much money to pay people in various jobs in the organization. It is often difficult to both successfully compete with other firms in attracting and retaining qualified personnel and at the same time maintain internal equity in the wage system. Wages depend to a large extent on supply and demand factors, but an organization that pays purely on the basis of the external labor market is likely to provoke widespread feelings of inequity. By providing an assessment of the relative worth of jobs to the organization, job evaluation helps maintain some balance between internal equity and external competitiveness in the wage structure.

### Compliance with Civil Rights Legislation

Perhaps the most important stimulus for job analysis has been the civil rights legislation passed since the mid-1960s, including the Civil Rights Acts of 1964 and 1991, the Age Discrimination Act, and the Americans with Disabilities Act. The regulatory guidelines as well as the interpretation of the laws in court cases have made job analysis a very important part of the strategy that organizations use in attempting to comply with these laws. If there is discrimination against minorities, older employees, the disabled, women, and other groups protected by these laws, then the employer must justify the job relatedness of the personnel practices responsible for the discrimination. While job relatedness is subject to various meanings and is not without ambiguity, the courts have generally looked with favor on employers who can back up their decisions with formal job analyses (Kleiman & Faley, 1985; Cascio & Bernardin, 1981).

The Americans with Disabilities Act was signed into law in July 1990 and specifically states that "No covered entity shall discriminate against a qualified individual with a disability because of the disability of such individual in regard to job application procedures, the hiring, advancement, or discharge of employees, employee compensation, job training, and other terms, conditions, and privileges of employment." A "qualified individual with a disability" is defined as "an individual with a disability who, with or without reasonable accommodation, can perform the *essential functions* of the employment position." If employers use a hiring procedure that eliminates disabled applicants from consideration, they must show that the rejected applicant was unable to perform the "essential functions of the position." Although it is not entirely clear how to define "essential functions," employers have scrambled to redo their job descriptions to clarify job requirements. This act will undoubtedly increase the importance of job analysis as a human resource activity in organizations and will lead to more research by I/O psychologists on how to conduct these analyses.

## WHAT IS MEASURED IN A JOB ANALYSIS?

Job analysis involves subdividing the work performed into fundamental elements. But what are these fundamental elements? Fleishman and Quaintance (1984) distinguished among four types of job analyses on the basis of their content: behavior description, behavior requirements, ability requirements, and task characteristics. With the *behavior description* approach, the job analyst generates a list of behaviors describing the most frequent or typical actions of the employee. This is the approach used to generate the typical job description. When data are needed on the task activities necessary to perform the job, a *behavioral requirement* approach to job analysis is preferred. For example, you might not be interested so much in the fact that the fast food worker in the previous example "Makes and serves hot beverages" as in the correct way of performing these activities. A third approach is the *personal characteristics* or *ability requirements* analysis. This is similar to the behavioral requirement approach in that the focus is on what is needed to perform the job effectively. Rather than focusing on behaviors, however, the focus is on the knowledge, skills, abilities, and orientations (KSAOs) required to perform the job. The *task characteristics* approach treats the job as a set of stimuli external to the worker. Stimuli include the work load, the rate at which work is performed, the degree of job variety, the extent to which the person receives feedback on his or her performance, the working conditions (heat, lighting, noise), and the kinds of hardware involved in the job (e.g., rotary knobs, joy sticks, indicator lights, digital readouts). The Job Diagnostic Survey (JDS) of Hackman and Oldham (1975) discussed in Chapter 3 is an example of this approach.

An issue that cuts across these various content areas is whether the analyst should focus on elements that are specific to the job or on general behavioral and cognitive dimensions that can span different jobs. The former alternative is *job-oriented*, whereas the latter is *worker-oriented*. McCormick (1976) defined job-oriented activities as "the description of the work activities performed, expressed in 'job' terms, usually indicating what is accomplished, such as galvanizing, weaving, cleaning, etc.; sometimes such activity descriptions also indicate how, why, and when a worker performs an activity" (p. 652). Worker-oriented activities refer to "behaviors performed in work, such as sensing, decision making, performing physical actions, communication" (p. 653). For example, a job-oriented approach to describing the typical or frequent behavior of a surgeon would include statements such as "makes incisions in skin of patients using scalpel," "closes incision after surgery with sutures," and so forth. A worker-oriented approach would focus on general behavioral dimensions (e.g., performs fine finger movements, uses sharp instruments) or human abilities and other personal characteristics needed to perform the work (e.g., finger dexterity, high intelligence). The job-oriented language in the above example applies only to the job of the surgeon, whereas the worker-oriented language could be used to describe and compare a variety of jobs.

Still another distinction is between a *chronological* and a *functional* organization of tasks. When a job involves a sequence of tasks, the job analysis should include a listing of these tasks in the order in which they are performed. Consider the tasks performed by a baker in baking bread: mixes dough, forms dough into loaf, places loaf in oven, removes loaf. In contrast, many jobs do not involve particular sequences of activities. A teacher might prepare lectures, grade papers, hold student/parent conferences, supervise field trips, and monitor recess. These activities could be grouped into functional areas such as classroom instruction, advising and counseling, and supervision.

# HOW IS A JOB ANALYSIS CONDUCTED?

So far we have discussed work content, the "what" of job analysis activities. Now we turn to three questions related to "how" job analyses are conducted: Which method should be used to collect the information? Who should be the source of the information? How much information is needed to analyze a job?

## Methods of Collecting Job Information

The approach taken to gathering task information is crucial to the accuracy of job analysis. A common dilemma is whether to choose methods that allow a lot of information to be collected cheaply (e.g., self-report questionnaires) or methods that are more expensive but allow more intensive examinations of individual jobs (observation and interviews). The best advice is to avoid reliance on one approach and instead to use multiple methods. Each of the alternatives has advantages and disadvantages, but through using more than one method we can compensate for the weaknesses of one with the strengths of the other.

With *observation,* the analyst watches the employee at work and records the work activities as they are performed. The prototype of the observational method is the classic time-and-motion specialist at work with stopwatch in hand, recording the various elements of the worker's activities. While analysts always should observe the work to some extent, observation can be disruptive of work activities and has limited usefulness in describing jobs with a heavy cognitive component. For instance, the processes by which a manager weighs alternatives and reaches a decision are not very accessible to observation. Because of these and other problems in observation, job analyses are often based on *interviews* with people familiar with the job (either incumbents or supervisors). An interview with a group of experts is called a *technical conference* or *jury.* Another common alternative is *self-report,* in which the employees themselves describe what they do. An intriguing variation on self-report that has been used relatively little by I/O psychologists is to have incumbents keep a daily *diary* of their activities. The *self-report questionnaire* involves retrospective self-reports of work activities by incumbents, sometimes by checking off tasks performed from a list of tasks (the inventory checklist method). Questionnaires are perhaps the most efficient manner of collecting information. Their primary limitation is the tendency of respondents to embellish their work by reporting more responsibilities or demands than really exist. This type of bias is not surprising given that a job analysis can lead to important changes such as the revision of the pay structure and the elimination or restructuring of jobs. Despite its problems, self-report is an effective means of collecting a large amount of job information at a relatively low cost.

As there are no perfect methods of gathering information on jobs, the best approach is to use a combination of approaches. As a first step, a job analyst will want to observe the work firsthand. Following this, a questionnaire might be given to employees and others familiar with the job so that additional data can be gathered on job duties. To verify, elaborate, and clarify information gathered in the self-report phase, the analysts may wish to conduct group or individual interviews.

## Who Provides the Information?

There are several alternative sources of job information, including incumbents, supervisors, and trained job analysts. As in the case of the various methods of collecting job information, each source has advantages and disadvantages, and the best advice is to use more than one source.

Incumbents (those currently performing the work) know more about what they do than anyone else, but not all incumbents provide accurate and reliable data. It is not uncommon to find that incumbents embellish their activities. Incumbents also can be careless as they proceed through a long, tedious questionnaire. Regardless of which occurs, the result may be mistakes in the job description. A demonstration of these problems was provided in a study in which job information was collected from mental health workers who provided direct care to patients (Green & Stutzman, 1986). A clever aspect of this study was the inclusion of five tasks in the inventory that were irrelevant to the job and could not have been performed. Among the five irrelevant tasks were "Prepare budget for facility" and "Complete yearly evaluation of other employees." An example of a relevant task was "give bed-bath to bedridden residents." Interestingly, 57% of the incumbents said that they spent time performing tasks that they could not possibly have performed. Seventy-two percent of these respondents even stated that these tasks were at least somewhat important to their jobs. The authors recommend that a procedure such as this be used to screen incumbents for careless and embellished responding. They also suggest that a large number of incumbents be used when jobs are not well-defined and there is large variation in tasks performed across incumbents.

If you were responsible for conducting a job analysis, you probably would want to choose as your sources those people who would provide the most accurate job information. Common sense suggests that you should pick the best performers and those who are trained in job analysis procedures. Are these the best people to conduct job analyses? We know relatively little about the characteristics that distinguish effective from ineffective job analysts, but the research so far suggests that some of our common sense notions may be wrong. The research generally has shown that employees who are poor performers are no less accurate in how they respond to job analysis questionnaires than employees who are high performers (Wexley & Silverman, 1978; Conley & Sackett, 1987). Other research has shown that sex, race, occupation, or tenure of the incumbent make little difference in the ratings they provide in job analyses (Schmitt & Cohen, 1989; Arvey, Passino, & Lounsbury, 1977). Some findings even cast doubt on whether training and expertise improve job analyses. Much of the research so far has involved the Position Analysis Questionnaire (PAQ), a job analysis technique discussed in more detail later in this chapter. Smith and Hakel (1979) found that ratings by untrained college students were as reliable as ratings by trained analysts, supervisors, and students. In explaining these findings, the authors speculate that experts and nonexperts shared a common stereotype of the jobs used in the study, and that consequently, expertise in job analysis made little difference in how well analysts could describe their jobs.

This surprising finding probably strikes fear in the hearts of many consultants whose living depends on their expertise in job analysis, but the Smith and Hakel study has not gone without criticism (Cornelius, DeNisi, & Blencoe, 1984; DeNisi, Cornelius, & Blencoe, 1987). The high correlations were likely distorted somewhat because a large number of the PAQ items were irrelevant to the jobs and were not rated. One study found that when the job analysis technique was used with jobs that were more relevant to the technique, experts differed from nonexperts in the reliability of their ratings (DeNisi, Cornelius, & Blencoe, 1987). The differences found in this study were not as large as might be expected, however, and depended on the job that was analyzed. For the job of hairdresser, for example, the reliability of naive raters was .63 and for experts, .68. For electrician the reliability was .69 for naive raters and .79 for experts.

A crucial factor influencing differences between experts and nonexperts is the familiarity of the judges with the dimensions and tasks that are analyzed. College students can estimate physical requirements as accurately as specialists (Hogan, Ogden, Gebhardt, & Fleishman, 1980; Hogan & Fleishman, 1979), a finding that probably reflects the fact that expertise provides little advantage in this familiar domain. With less familiar jobs and more complex job analysis procedures, the differences between trained and experienced analysts are likely to be more pronounced.

## How Much Information Is Needed?

Closely related to the question of how much training and expertise raters should have is how much job-related information is needed to obtain accurate and reliable job ratings. Some evidence suggests that less information may be needed than often thought (Smith & Hakel, 1979; Arvey, Davis, McGowen, & Dipboye, 1982; Hahn & Dipboye, 1988). Cornelius, Schmidt, and Carron (1984) compared the accuracy of two approaches to classifying jobs into occupational groups. In one approach, supervisors and incumbents rated their jobs on a 130 item job inventory. With the other approach supervisors and incumbents simply indicated the occupational group to which the title belonged. The second approach was 96% accurate in making this classification, which led the authors to conclude that when the job analysis is intended to determine the similarity of jobs, "any procedure other than simple judgments by incumbents and supervisors is likely to be quantitative overkill" (p. 259). Similar results are reported by Sackett, Cornelius, and Carron (1981). They compared a laborious behavioral description approach requiring hundreds of hours to conduct with a simple global judgment that required about 15 minutes. The two methods yielded almost identical results.

There is undoubtedly some point of diminishing returns at which more information fails to improve the analysis. Determining when the point of diminishing returns is reached is an important area for future research. Until this research is conducted, legal considerations suggest that the analyst use as much information as possible, even if he or she risks overkill. Hiring and other human resource management practices are more defensible against claims of unfair discrimination if they are  based on thorough job analyses by experts.

*Summary*

Information on jobs can be gathered using a variety of methods and drawing from a variety of sources. Interviews, questionnaires, diaries, and observation are among the most common means of gathering the data. The subject matter experts (SMEs) who provide the information could be trained analysts, people in the job, supervisors, or other people knowledgeable about the work. Some people are probably better sources of job information than others, but research has yet to identify the characteristics of a good analyst. Although it seems to make good sense to use analysts who are well-acquainted with the work and trained in the technique, there is little evidence that the demographic characteristics of the analysts or their performance in the job is related to the quality of their job analyses. With some jobs, less information and expertise may be needed than is commonly believed to be necessary.

# SPECIFIC METHODS OF JOB ANALYSIS

Industrial and organizational psychologists and others in the field of human resource management have developed numerous techniques of job analysis. Some of these are standardized techniques that can be used with a wide range of jobs; others are tailored to specific jobs. Some of the techniques are eclectic in combining a variety of methods and content; others use a narrower range of methods and content to gather data on jobs.

## Behaviorally Oriented Techniques

Most of the efforts of I/O psychologists have been devoted to behavioral descriptions of jobs. The most job-oriented of these approaches is the task inventory. Other approaches, such as Functional Job Analysis and the Position Analysis Questionnaire, describe work in terms of basic behavioral processes.

### THE TASK INVENTORY

The Air Force has conducted most of the work on the task inventory approach to job analysis (Archer & Fruchter, 1963; Gael, 1983); an example of one of their task inventories is shown in Figure 8.2. Three basic steps are involved in the construction and administration of a task inventory. First, through observing the work, examining existing job descriptions, and talking to experts, supervisors, and incumbents, the analyst generates a list of task statements that can be used to describe a particular field of work. This list is reviewed by people knowledgeable about the work and then administered to a group of workers who are asked to delete, add, and modify the task statements. The final version will usually contain at least 100 task statements and may include as many as 400 to 500 statements. Often space is provided on the inventory for respondents to add tasks so that the inventory can keep pace with changes that occur in the job. The final version is administered to incumbents, who check off those tasks performed. The beauty of this method is that it also allows a variety of quantitative ratings for each task: relative time spent, the difficulty of learning, importance, criticality, difficulty, and frequency. There is some controversy as to whether tasks really need to be rated on several different scales or whether these scales provide redundant information. Friedman (1990) examined the intercorrelations among ratings of tasks on a seven-point scale on *relative time spent* (1 = I spend a very small amount of time on this task as compared with most tasks I perform and 7 = I spend a very large amount of time on this task as compared with most other tasks I perform); *frequency* (1 = about once every year and 7 = about once each hour or more often); and *importance* (1 = very minor and 7 = extreme importance). He found that time and importance ratings were redundant and should not be included together in an inventory. However, frequency ratings did not appear redundant with either of the other two ratings.

### FUNCTIONAL JOB ANALYSIS

The task inventory method is tailored to the specific job, but Functional Job Analysis (FJA) is a standard technique that can be used to compare very different jobs (Fine, 1988). In this procedure, the analyst begins by generating task statements and then rates *each of the task statements* on its orientation and level with regard to data, people, and things. *Orientation* is measured by allocating 100 percentage points across these three functional areas to

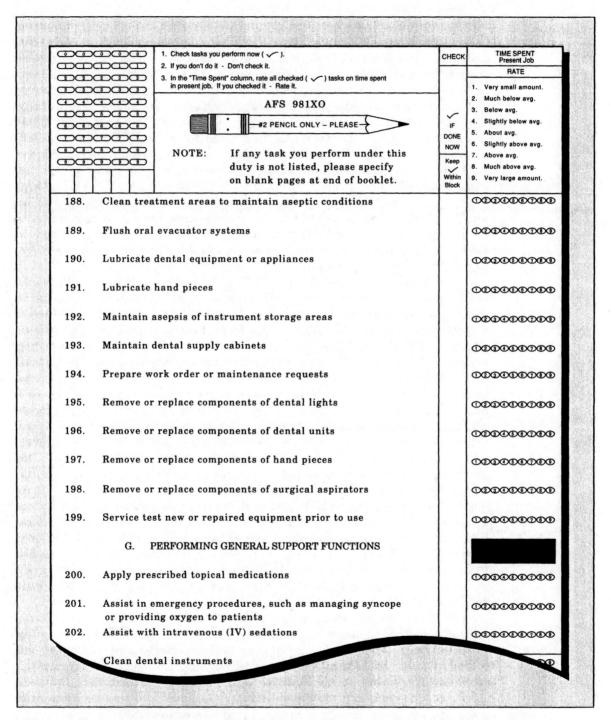

1. Check tasks you perform now ( ✓ ).
2. If you don't do it - Don't check it.
3. In the "Time Spent" column, rate all checked ( ✓ ) tasks on time spent in present job. If you checked it - Rate it.

AFS  981XO

#2 PENCIL ONLY – PLEASE →

NOTE:   If any task you perform under this duty is not listed, please specify on blank pages at end of booklet.

| CHECK | TIME SPENT Present Job |
|---|---|
| | RATE |
| ✓ IF DONE NOW | 1. Very small amount. |
| | 2. Much below avg. |
| | 3. Below avg. |
| | 4. Slightly below avg. |
| | 5. About avg. |
| | 6. Slightly above avg. |
| Keep ✓ Within Block | 7. Above avg. |
| | 8. Much above avg. |
| | 9. Very large amount. |

188.   Clean treatment areas to maintain aseptic conditions

189.   Flush oral evacuator systems

190.   Lubricate dental equipment or appliances

191.   Lubricate hand pieces

192.   Maintain asepsis of instrument storage areas

193.   Maintain dental supply cabinets

194.   Prepare work order or maintenance requests

195.   Remove or replace components of dental lights

196.   Remove or replace components of dental units

197.   Remove or replace components of hand pieces

198.   Remove or replace components of surgical aspirators

199.   Service test new or repaired equipment prior to use

        G.   PERFORMING GENERAL SUPPORT FUNCTIONS

200.   Apply prescribed topical medications

201.   Assist in emergency procedures, such as managing syncope or providing oxygen to patients

202.   Assist with intravenous (IV) sedations

        Clean dental instruments

**Figure 8.2**   *A sample page from U.S. Air Force job-task inventory booklet for dental assistants, AFS 981XO*

*Source:* Christal, R. E., & Weissmuller, J. J. (1988). Job-task inventory analysis. In S. Gael (ed.) *The Job Analysis Handbook for Business, Industry, and Government.* New York: John Wiley, pp. 1036–1050.

indicate how much of each is involved in the task. The level of each dimension refers to the degree of complexity with which a person engages in each function. The data function scale measures the degree of complexity with which the individual handles "information, ideas, facts, and statistics." At the lowest level of complexity is simple comparing, in which the incumbent selects or sorts on the basis of simple judgments of similarity or differences and copying, in which the incumbent transcribes, enters, or posts data. The highest level of complexity is synthesizing, in which the incumbent "Takes off in new directions on the basis of personal intuitions, feelings, and ideas to conceive new approaches." According to Fine, data are always involved to some extent, even when jobs are primarily concerned with things or people. The things scale ranges from precision working at the highest level of complexity to simple handling at the lowest level. The people scale ranges from leading and mentoring at the highest level of complexity to taking instructions at the lowest level. After the rating of each task on all three dimensions, an overall rating of the job is derived through an integration of task ratings.

The U.S. Employment Service (USES) has used a variation of Fine's system. Rather than considering each task in a job separately, however, an entire occupation is rated on data, people, and things. Also, the scales used to measure these three dimensions differ from those used in FJA and are listed in Figure 8.3. Despite these deviations from the FJA procedure, the ratings generated by the USES illustrate how various occupations compare on levels of data, people, and things. (Note that the scale used by the USES is reversed so that a lower number reflects greater complexity.) For instance, the job of fast food worker, which is described at the beginning of the chapter, received a rating of 4 on data, indicating the computing responsibilities of this type of job. A rating of 7 was assigned on the people dimension indicating a relatively low complexity (serving) in relationships with people. Finally, a 2 was assigned on the things dimension, indicating that many of the activities involve operation and control of equipment and other tangibles (see Figure 8.4 for additional examples). Research on the *Dictionary of Occupational Titles (DOT)* has shown that the reliabilities of experts' judgments of occupations on the three dimensions in FJA are generally acceptable (Geyer, Hice, Hawk, Boese, & Brannon, 1989). Nevertheless, it is important to remember that the ratings provided in the *DOT* are for *occupations,* not jobs. A specific job in an organization having the same title as one listed in the *DOT* could receive quite different ratings.

Perhaps the greatest advantage of FJA is that it allows very different jobs to be compared on the same general dimensions. Still another advantage is its simplicity. The extent of training and experience required to use this method is much less than that required for many of the other job analysis techniques we discuss in this chapter. As useful as this procedure is, however, FJA is far too general for many objectives. Also, there is little research evaluating the construct validity of Fine's (1988) FJA or the USES version. The few studies that exist have cast doubt on the hierarchical structure of the three dimensions (Harvey, 1991).

A job's relationship to *data, people* and *things* can be expressed in terms of the lowest numbered function in each sequence. Lower numbers indicate higher complexity on these scales. These functions taken together indicate the total level of complexity at which the worker performs.

## Data

Information, knowledge, and conceptions, related to data, people, or things, obtained by observation, investigation, interpretation, visualization, and mental creation. Data are intangible and include numbers, words, symbols, ideas, concepts, and oral verbalization.

0 Synthesizing (Integrating analyses of data to discover facts and/or develop knowledge)

1 Coordinating (Determining time, place, and sequence of operations or action)

2 Analyzing (Examining and evaluating data)

3 Compiling (Gathering, collating, or classifying information about data, people, and things)

4 Computing (Performing arithmetic operations and reporting on and/or carrying out a prescribed action in relation to them. Does not include counting)

5 Copying (Transcribing, entering, or posting data)

6 Comparing (Judging the readily observable functional, structural, or compositional characteristics — whether similar to or divergent from obvious standards—of data, people and things)

## People

Human beings; also animals dealt with on an individual basis as if they were humans.

0 Mentoring (Advising, counseling, and/or guiding others)

1 Negotiating (Working with others to arrive jointly at decision, conclusions, or solutions)

2 Instructing (Teaching subject matter to others or training others)

3 Supervising (Determining work procedures, maintaining harmony, promoting efficiency)

4 Diverting (Amusing others)

5 Persuading (Influencing others in favor of a product, service, or point of view)

6 Speaking-Signaling (Includes giving assignments and/or directions to helpers)

7 Serving (Immediately responding to the needs or requests of people or animals)

8 Taking instructions-helping (No responsibility involved and involves non-learning helpers)

## Things

Inanimate objects. A thing is tangible and has shape, form, and other physical characteristics.

0 Setting up (Adjusting machines or equipment to prepare them to perform their functions)

1 Precision working (Involves use of body members or tools and considerable judgment)

2 Operating-Controlling (Involves setting up and adjusting the machine as work progresses)

3 Driving-Operating (Involves controlling a machine that must be steered or guided)

4 Manipulating (Using body members, tools, or devices and involves some judgment)

5 Tending (Starting, stopping, and observing machines and equipment. Little judgment)

6 Feeding-Offbearing (Inserting, throwing, dumping, or placing materials in or removing from machines or equipment which are automatic or tended by other workers)

7 Handling (Using body members, hand tools, and/or special devices to work, move, or carry objects or materials. Involves little or no latitude for judgment)

**Figure 8.3**   *Data, People, and Things Scales Used by the United States Employment Service in Analyzing Occupations*

Source: U.S. Department of Labor. (1977). *Dictionary of Occupational Titles.* Washington, DC: U.S. Government Printing Office, 1369–1371.

**Short Order Cook** Prepares food and serves restaurant patrons at counters or tables. Takes orders from customers and cooks foods requiring short preparation time. Completes order from steamtable and serves customer. Accepts payment or writes charge slip. Carves meats, makes sandwiches, and brews coffee. Usually found in small establishments, such as lunch counters and snack bars.

**Choral Director** Conducts vocal music groups, such as choirs and glee clubs. Auditions and selects members of groups. Selects music to suit performance requirements and accommodate talent and ability of group. Directs group at rehearsals and performance to achieve desired effects, such as utilizing knowledge of conducting techniques and music theory. May schedule tours and performances and arrange for transportation and lodging. May transcribe musical compositions and melodic lines to adapt them to or create particular style for group. May conduct group with instrumental accompaniment.

**Hair-stylist** Specializes in dressing hair according to latest style or period, following instructions of patron. Questions patron to determine hairdressing requirements. Studies facial features of patron or performing artist and arranges, shapes, and trims hair to achieve desired effect, using fingers, combs, barber scissors, hair-waving solutions, hairpins, and other accessories. Dyes, tints, bleaches, or curls or waves hair as required. May create new style especially for patron. May clean and style wigs and hairpieces.

**Airline Reservations Agent** Makes and confirms reservations for passengers on scheduled airline flights. Arranges reservations and routing for passengers at request of ticket agent or customer, using timetables, airline manuals, reference guides, and tariff book. Types requested flight number on keyboard of on-line computer reservation system and scans screen to determine space availability. Telephones customer or ticket agent to advise of changes in flight plan or to cancel or confirm reservation. May maintain advance or current inventory of available passenger space on flights. May advise load control personnel and other stations of changes in passenger itinerary to control space and insure utilization of seating capacity on flights.

**Figure 8.4** *Illustration of Functional Job Analysis*

How would you rate each of the above occupations on the complexity with which an incumbent of the occupation relates to people, data, and things? Rate on the scales depicted in Figure 8.3. See the appendix at the end of the chapter for the ratings made by the USES.
*Source:* U.S. Department of Labor. (1977). *Dictionary of Occupational Titles.* Washington, DC: U.S. Government Printing Office.

## THE POSITION ANALYSIS QUESTIONNAIRE

The Position Analysis Questionnaire (PAQ) is a behavioral description method that provides a much more detailed analysis than FJA but like FJA still allows for comparison of very different positions. The development of this procedure by the late Ernest J. McCormick and his students at Purdue University represents the most important contribution to job analysis in the last two decades. The latest version of the PAQ consists of 194 items. These *job elements,* as McCormick calls them, are organized into six divisions that follow a stimulus–organism–response (SOR) model of human behavior. Table 8.1 lists the six original divisions of the PAQ as well as 32 divisional dimensions and 13 overall dimensions uncovered through factor analysis. The first of the six original divisions contains behaviors relating to the *input of information.* Once information is obtained, something must be done with it. The second division is concerned with the *mediational processes* involved. The third division, *work output,* reflects the fact that the employee must act on the information and produce some service or product. These three divisions represent the heart of the SOR model that guided the construction of the PAQ. Two other divisions that represent more of the work context are *interpersonal activities* (e.g., negotiating, persuading, instructing, etc.) and the *work situation and job context* (e.g., outdoor/indoor, noise, frustrating situations, strained personal contacts). The final division is a grab bag of *miscellaneous aspects* including work schedule, pay, time pressures, and responsibilities. In describing a job with the PAQ, the analyst first determines whether each element applies to the job. For most jobs, a large proportion of the elements falls in the "does not apply" category. Of the elements that are involved in the job, the analyst rates the extent of involvement using such scales as the extent of use, amount of time spent, importance to the job, possibility of occurrence, and applicability.

In the early research, McCormick, Jeanneret, and Mecham (1972) used the PAQ to describe a large number of jobs on 184 of the job elements. Statistical analyses of these ratings revealed that jobs can be differentiated along more dimensions than reflected in the initial six divisions found in Table 8.1. In one analysis, the ratings within each of the six divisions were analyzed separately. This yielded 32 *divisional dimensions,* with six found for information input, two for mediational processes, eight for work output, five for relationships with other people, three for job context, and eight for the miscellaneous division. These divisional dimensions are also listed in Table 8.1. A separate analysis performed on all the PAQ items used in the description of 2,200 jobs yielded 13 *overall dimensions* (Table 8.1) and are the most frequently used in practical applications of the PAQ.

The PAQ has proven valuable in both research and practice and has been translated into numerous languages. Similar to Functional Job Analysis, the PAQ's behavioral dimensions allow a wide range of applications. The PAQ has been adopted for use in the design of a variety of personnel functions including compensation, selection, training, and vocational counseling. As data have accumulated on thousands of jobs, it has been possible to use the PAQ to see how even markedly different jobs compare on general dimensions. In one of the more interesting studies of this nature, Arvey and Begalla (1975) adminstered the PAQ to 48 homemakers and found that the homemaker's job was most similar across the divisional dimensions to the job of patrolman. Other jobs with PAQ profiles that were similar to the homemaker included

**Table 8.1**

| DIMENSIONS OF THE POSITION ANALYSIS QUESTIONNAIRE | |
| --- | --- |
| **No.  Technical Title** | **Operational Title** |

Division Dimensions

Division 1: Information Input

| | |
| --- | --- |
| 1. Perceptual interpretation | Interpreting what is sensed |
| 2. Input from representational sources | Using various sources of information |
| 3. Visual input from devices/materials | Watching devices/materials for information |
| 4. Evaluating/judging sensory input | Evaluating/judging what is sensed |
| 5. Environmental awareness | Being aware of environmental conditions |
| 6. Use of various senses | Using various senses |

Division 2: Mental Processes

| | |
| --- | --- |
| 7. Decision making | Making decisions |
| 8. Information processing | Processing information |

Division 3: Work Output

| | |
| --- | --- |
| 9. Using machine/tools/equipment | Using machine/tools/equipment |
| 10. General body versus sedentary activities | Performing activities requiring general body movements |
| 11. Control and related physical coordination | Controlling machines/processes |
| 12. Skilled/technical activities | Performing skilled/technical activities |
| 13. Controlled manual/related activities | Performing controlled manual/related activities |
| 14. Use of miscellaneous equipment/devices | Using miscellaneous equipment/devices |
| 15. Handling/manipulating/related activities | Performing handling/related manual activities |
| 16. Physical coordination | General physical coordination |

Division 4: Relationships with Other Persons

| | |
| --- | --- |
| 17. Interchange of judgmental/related information | Communicating judgments/related information |
| 18. General personal contact | Engaging in general personal contacts |
| 19. Supervisory/coordination/related activities | Performing supervisory/coordination/related activities |
| 20. Job-related communications | Exchanging job-related information |
| 21. Public/related personal contacts | Public/related personal contacts |

home economist, airport maintenance chief, kitchen helper, and fire fighter. In another interesting study, Shaw and Riskind (1983) found that ratings of occupations on the PAQ's 32 divisional dimensions were predictive of a variety of stress indicators, including hypertension, ulcers, cirrhosis, suicides, and anxiety/depression. The PAQ is particularly useful in determining the abilities and traits required in a job. McCormick and his students (Marquardt &

**Division 5: Job Context**

| | |
|---|---|
| 22. Potentially stressful/unpleasant environment | Being in a stressful/unpleasant environment |
| 23. Personally demanding situations | Engaging in personally demanding situations |
| 24. Potentially hazardous job situations | Being in hazardous job situations |

**Division 6: Other Job Characteristics**

| | |
|---|---|
| 25. Nontypical versus typical day work schedule | Working nontypical versus day schedule |
| 26. Businesslike situations | Working in businesslike situations |
| 27. Optional versus specified apparel | Wearing optional versus specified apparel |
| 28. Variable versus salary compensation | Being paid on a variable versus salary basis |
| 29. Regular versus irregular work schedule | Working on a regular versus irregular schedule |
| 30. Job-demanding responsibilities | Working under job-demanding circumstances |
| 31. Structured versus unstructured job activities | Performing structured versus unstructured work |
| 32. Vigilant/discriminating work activities | Being alert to changing conditions |

**Overall Dimensions**

| | |
|---|---|
| 33. Decision/communication/general responsibilities | Having decision, communicating, and general responsibilities |
| 34. Machine/equipment operation | Operating machines/equipment |
| 35. Clerical/related activities | Performing clerical/related activities |
| 36. Technical/related activities | Performing technical/related activities |
| 37. Service/related activities | Performing service/related activities |
| 38. Regular day schedule versus other work schedules | Working regular day versus other work schedules |
| 39. Routine/repetitive work activities | Performing routine/repetitive activities |
| 40. Environmental awareness | Being aware of work environment |
| 41. General physical activities | Engaging in physical activities |
| 42. Supervising/coordinating other personnel | Supervising/coordinating other personnel |
| 43. Public/customer/related contact activities | Public/customer/related contacts |
| 44. Unpleasant/hazardous/demanding environment | Working in an unpleasant/hazardous/demanding environment |
| 45. Nontypical work schedules | Having a nontypical schedule and opportunity to wear optional work clothing |

*Source:* McCormick, E.J., & Jeanneret, P.R., (1988). Position Analysis Questionnaire (PAQ). In S. Gael (Ed.), *The Job Analysis Handbook for Business, Industry, and Government.* New York: John Wiley & Sons, p.829.

McCormick, 1973; Mecham & McCormick, 1969a, 1969b) asked psychologists to estimate the relevance of each of 76 human attributes for performing well on each element in the PAQ. This research provided equations that make it possible for an analyst to describe a job using the PAQ and then statistically generate the profile of the attributes typical of people in the job.

Despite its many advantages, the PAQ has several drawbacks. In describing a specific job, many of the items in the PAQ are irrelevant, and the high rate with which the "does not apply" option is checked can distort the results of the statistical analyses. For instance, a large proportion of items involve the use of machines and equipment and are inappropriate for use with professional and managerial jobs and other jobs involving a large cognitive component. To correct this deficiency, the Professional and Managerial Position Questionnaire (PMPQ) was developed by McCormick and his colleagues. Still another potential drawback is the difficulty of the language. Ash and Edgell (1975) found that the reading level of an earlier version of the PAQ was so difficult that a college degree would be required to interpret many of the instructions and questions. Recent revisions of the PAQ have made the instrument more readable. Still, the PAQ is sufficiently complex to require a trained analyst, thus making it costly to administer.

## Techniques Focused on Requirements

The PAQ, FJA, and task inventory describe jobs in terms of the activities that are performed. Job analysts must often go beyond describing job activities to pinpoint the behaviors and personal attributes that are *required* to perform the work successfully. Two other techniques that are focused on identifying the crucial components of the work are the critical incident technique and the Ability Requirements Scales.

### CRITICAL INCIDENT TECHNIQUE

Of all the methods that emphasize behavioral requirements, no other procedure is as frequently employed as the critical incident technique. This method was developed by John C. Flanagan (1954) for use in the U.S. Army Air Corps during World War II. A typical set of instructions used in the critical incident method is presented in Table 8.2. Employees are asked to think of a specific incident involving an example of extremely effective or extremely ineffective performance. Extreme behaviors are seen as more easily remembered and described than average behaviors. Once the critical incidents are generated, the next step is to determine the dimensions of performance reflected in these incidents. The usual procedure is to have employees sort the incidents into piles, each pile representing a critical dimension of job performance.

As with all the techniques we have discussed, the critical incident technique is limited in some respects. The method is best suited to determining the crucial factors in a job, but it does not provide a good picture of what is typically involved. A dimension may be crucial to performance but only rarely occurs. Another potential problem is a tendency to attribute events in the job to the traits of the person. Flanagan gives an example of a study in which supervisors were asked "Tell just how this employee behaved which caused a noticeable decrease in production." Almost all incidents provided in response

**Table 8.2**

## SAMPLE OF A FORM USED BY AN INTERVIEWER IN COLLECTING EFFECTIVE CRITICAL INCIDENTS

Think of the last time you saw one of your subordinates do something that was very helpful to your group in meeting their production schedule. (Pause till he indicates he has such an incident in mind.) Did his action result in increase in production of as much as one per cent for that day? . . . or some similar period?

(If the answer is "no," say) I wonder if you could think of the last time that someone did something that did have this much of an effect in increasing production. (When he or she indicates that such a situation is in mind, say)

1. What were the general circumstances leading up to this incident?

2. Tell me exactly what this person did that was so helpful at that time.

3. Why was this so helpful in getting your group's job done?

4. When did this incident happen?

5. What was the person's job?

*Source:* Flanagan, J. C. (1954). The critical incident technique. *Psychological Bulletin, 51,* 327-358.

to this question had to do with personality and attitudes rather than behaviors. They subsequently changed the question to "Tell just what this employee did which caused a noticeable decrease in production." This second question produced a much broader range of more behavioral incidents. To the foremen who were reporting incidents, "how this employee behaved" sounded as if personality and attitudes were being studied. Subtle biases are not so easily anticipated and are best avoided by pretesting the questions ahead of time. The question must be posed so that respondents take into account situational factors.

### ABILITY REQUIREMENTS SCALES

A more structured approach to determining ability requirements than the critical incident method is a set of rating scales presented by Fleishman and his associates (Fleishman & Quaintance, 1984). The *Ability Requirements Scales* listed in Table 8.3 were derived from extensive research and include not only psychomotor and physical abilities but also a variety of cognitive abilities. A scale was developed for each of these abilities to allow the rating of the extent to which each ability is required in a task. Take, for example, the

**Table 8.3**

## TRAITS RATED IN THE ABILITY REQUIREMENTS SCALE

| | | | |
|---|---|---|---|
| 1. Oral comprehension | 14. Category flexibility | 27. Arm-Hand steadiness | 40. Stamina |
| 2. Written comprehension | 15. Speed of closure | 28. Manual dexterity | 41. Near vision |
| 3. Oral expression | 16. Flexibility of closure | 29. Finger dexterity | 42. Far vision |
| 4. Written expression | 17. Spatial orientation | 30. Wrist-Finger speed | 43. Visual color discrimination |
| 5. Fluency of ideas | 18. Visualization | 31. Speed of limb movement | 44. Night vision |
| 6. Originality | 19. Perceptual speed | 32. Static strength | 45. Peripheral vision |
| 7. Memorization | 20. Selective attention | 33. Explosive strength | 46. Depth perception |
| 8. Problem sensitivity | 21. Time sharing | 34. Dynamic strength | 47. Glare sensitivity |
| 9. Mathematical reasoning | 22. Control precision | 35. Trunk strength | 48. Hearing sensitivity |
| 10. Number facility | 23. Multilimb coordination | 36. Extent flexibility | 49. Auditory attention |
| 11. Deductive reasoning | 24. Response orientation | 37. Dynamic flexibility | 50. Sound localization |
| 12. Inductive reasoning | 25. Rate control | 38. Gross body coordination | 51. Speech recognition |
| 13. Information ordering | 26. Reaction time | 39. Gross body equilibrium | 52. Speech clarity |

*Source:* Fleishman, E.A., & Mumford, M.D. (1991). Evaluating classifications of job behavior: A construct validation of the ability requirement scales. *Personnel Psychology, 44,* 523–575.

rating scale used to evaluate a task on static strength (see Figure 8.5). A task would be rated as high on requiring static strength (a 6 or 7) if the task required a great amount of lifting, pushing, pulling, or carrying of objects. Each point on the scale is behaviorally illustrated to anchor the various levels of static strength: "reach over and lift a 70 lb. box onto a table" versus "lift a package of bond paper." An *anchor* is the behavior used to represent a numerical scale value. Another example is the scale used to rate the extent of verbal comprehension required in the task. In this case the anchors for the high and low ends of the scale are "understanding in entirety a mortgage contract" versus "understanding a comic book."

### Eclectic Techniques

We have discussed techniques that focus on one of four types of content: behavior description, behavior requirements, trait requirements, and task characteristics. A few other methods go even farther in the direction of using diverse work content in job analysis.

## STATIC STRENGTH

This is the ability to use muscle force to lift, push, pull, or carry objects. It is the maximum muscle force that one can exert for a brief period. This ability can involve arms, back, shoulders, or legs.

---

### How Static Strength is Different from Other Abilities:

| *THIS ABILITY* | | *OTHER ABILITIES* |
|---|---|---|
| Use muscle to exert force against *objects*. | vs. | ***Dynamic Strength:*** Use muscle power repeatedly to hold up or move the body's own weight. |
| Use continuous muscle force, without stopping, up to the amount needed to lift, push, pull, or carry an object. | vs. | ***Explosive Strength:*** Gather energy to move one's own body or to propel some object with *short bursts* of muscle force. |
| Does *not* involve the use of muscle force over a long time. | vs. | ***Stamina:*** *Does* involve physical exertion over a long time. |

---

Requires use of all the muscle force possible to lift, carry, push, or pull a very heavy object.

    ⎱  ┌─ 7
       │           — Reach over and lift a
       ├─ 6           70 lb. box onto a table.
       │
       ├─ 5
       │
       ├─ 4       — Walk a few steps on flat terrain
       │             carrying a 50 lb. back pack.
       ├─ 3
       │
       ├─ 2
       │           — Lift one package of bond paper.
    ⎰  └─ 1

Requires use of little muscle force to lift, carry, push, or pull a light object.

**Figure 8.5**  *Definition and ability rating scale for static strength*

*Source:* Fleishman, E. A., & Mumford, M. D. (1991). Evaluating classifications of job behavior: A construct validation of the ability requirement scales. *Personnel Psychology, 44,* 523–575.

The *Multimethod Job Design Questionnaire* (MJDQ; Campion & Thayer, 1985; Campion, 1988), which was mentioned in Chapter 3, was designed to reflect the job characteristics, mechanistic, biological, and perceptual/motor approaches to describing jobs. Items in the questionnaire deal with factors as diverse as the autonomy allowed in the job, degree of task specialization, noise, and workplace lighting.

Another eclectic approach is that of the U.S. Employment Service (USES; U.S. Department of Labor, 1972). With this method the job is described in terms of five categories of information:

1. What the worker does in relation to data, people, and things (Work Functions).
2. The methodologies and techniques employed (Work Fields).
3. The machines, tools, equipment, and work aids used (MTFWA).
4. The materials, products, subject matter, or services which result (MPSMS).
5. The traits required of the worker (Worker Traits).

In addition to rating the job on each of the five content areas, the job analyst provides several open-ended descriptions of such things as the job duties, primary tasks involved in the job, vocational preparation required, relation to other jobs and workers, and materials and products. The USES job analysis procedures have resulted in the gathering of a tremendous amount of information on thousands of occupations in the United States. Much of this information is summarized in the *Dictionary of Occupational Titles* (U.S. Department of Labor, 1977), which included 17,500 job titles in the fourth edition. Each job title contains a brief description of the primary tasks along with ratings on work function (data, people, things) and the occupational group to which the job belongs. The information gathered and collated by the USES cannot substitute for a job analysis performed on site in an organization, but it is an excellent place to start.

## Summary

Jobs consist of people performing activities and several techniques exist for describing these activities. Task inventories describe the work in terms of the specific tasks contained in positions. Although quite useful for many purposes, they do not allow comparisons of different jobs because of the task-oriented content. Other techniques describe work in terms of fundamental behavioral processes. An example is Functional Job Analysis, which focuses on orientation to, and complexity of involvement with, people, data, and things. The Position Analysis Questionnaire is the most notable of these and has received the most attention in the research literature.

Other procedures are dedicated to specification of the requirements of the job. In the critical incident technique, subject matter experts generate specific episodes of effective and ineffective performance. Through sorting these incidents into categories, the dimensions of performance that are crucial to successful performance are identified. Fleishman's Ability Requirements Scales provide a means of rating individual tasks in a job on cognitive, physical, and psychomotor abilities. Finally, a variety of different types of work content is used in such techniques as Campion's Multimethod Job Design Questionnaire and the job analysis procedures of the U.S. Employment Service.

# JOB EVALUATION AS THE BASIS FOR WAGE AND SALARY ADMINISTRATION

Earlier we described wage and salary administration as an important application of job analysis. *Job evaluation* can be defined as a type of job analysis used to judge the relative worth of jobs in an organization for the purpose of setting fair and equitable compensation rates. It is important to note that jobs, not individual employees, are evaluated with these procedures. There are four primary means of job evaluation: ranking, classification, factor comparison, and point systems. One way of distinguishing among these methods is whether they evaluate the job as a whole or evaluate on the basis of separate dimensions of the job. Another distinction can be made between job evaluation procedures that evaluate the job against other jobs or against some absolute standard (McCormick & Ilgen, 1980, p. 379).

## Ranking

This procedure is perhaps the simplest and involves ordering a group of jobs on the basis of their relative worth from the highest valued jobs to the least valued jobs. With this method the job is evaluated as a whole and against other jobs. This method is suitable for small organizations, but for most large organizations the number of jobs to be ranked makes this a crude and unrealistic approach.

## Classification

Another approach is to judge the whole job against some absolute standard. A classification system consists of a series of classes or grades, the jobs included in a given class are considered substantively similar in their worth to the organization. The most widely used classification procedure is the General Schedule (GS) used by the U.S. Office of Personnel Management. The jobs of most employees of the U.S. federal government are classified into one of 18 grades. The lowest of these, GS 1, involves jobs with the simplest routine activities requiring immediate supervision. GS 9 involves positions requiring general supervision and special technical, supervisory, or administrative experience. Classification systems are generally crude and can be biased by job titles. Moreover, an organization faced with legal challenges to its compensation system may be hard pressed to defend a classification system.

## Factor Comparison

This procedure was originally developed by Benge, Burk, and Hay (1941) and involves evaluating a job on several dimensions called *compensable factors*. With this method, jobs are compared with other jobs on each compensable factor. The steps involved can be outlined as follows:

1.  *Conduct job analysis.* All jobs to be included under the compensation plan are analyzed on the same set of factors. Benge, Burk, and Hay (1941) proposed five factors: mental requirements, skill requirements, physical demands, responsibility, and working conditions.
2.  *Select benchmark jobs.* Once all jobs are analyzed, then 15–20 are chosen that are believed to be paid appropriately and that reflect a range of values along the factors.
3.  *Rank the benchmark jobs on each factor.* For each factor, the benchmark jobs are next ranked from those that are highest to those that are lowest.
4.  *Distribute existing wage of benchmark jobs across factors.* The current wage (usually the hourly rate) of each is divided to reflect how much the pay reflects the various factors.
5.  *Application of the system.* In using the final system, nonbenchmark jobs are evaluated one factor at a time on the basis of the dollar value believed most appropriate. For example, on mental requirements the job of secretary might be seen as above the level of a receptionist but below the level of a paralegal. The dollar values allocated to the benchmark jobs help in assigning a specific numerical value to the job along this scale. The final wage assigned to the job can be broken down into the amount dependent on each factor.

## Point Systems

This is the most frequently used type of job evaluation procedure and involves evaluating jobs a factor at a time on an absolute rating scale. The specific factors used depend on the particular system. The number of factors can range from only one in the case of Jaques' (1963) *time span of discretion* (TSD) approach to 20 or more in other systems. Jaques' TSD method focuses on the time lag between an incumbent's actions and when the consequences of these actions become known. Jobs deserving of higher wages are those in which the TSD is long; those in which the TSD is short are deserving of relatively lower wages.

One of the most widely used point systems is the Hay Guide Chart-Profile Method (Hay & Purves, 1954), which is used to evaluate jobs against

**Table 8.4**

| A POINT SYSTEM USED IN THE EVALUATION OF HOURLY PAID JOBS | | | | | | | | |
|---|---|---|---|---|---|---|---|---|
| **Factors and Subfactors** | **%** | **Degrees and Points** | | | | | | **Weight in Per-Cent** |
| | | **1st Deg.** | **2d Deg.** | **3d Deg.** | **4th Deg.** | **5th Deg.** | **6th Deg.** | |
| <u>Skill</u> | 50 | | | | | | | |
| 1. Education & Job Knowledge | | 12 | 24 | 36 | 48 | 60 | 72 | 12 |
| 2. Experience & Training | | 24 | 48 | 72 | 96 | 120 | 144 | 24 |
| 3. Initiative & Ingenuity | | 14 | 28 | 42 | 56 | 70 | 84 | 14 |
| <u>Effort</u> | 15 | | | | | | | |
| 4. Physical Demand | | 10 | 20 | 30 | 40 | 50 | 60 | 10 |
| 5. Mental and/or Visual Demand | | 5 | 10 | 15 | 20 | 25 | 30 | 5 |
| <u>Responsibility</u> | 20 | | | | | | | |
| 6. Equipment or Tools | | 6 | 12 | 18 | 24 | 30 | 36 | 6 |
| 7. Material or Product | | 7 | 14 | 21 | 28 | 35 | 42 | 7 |
| 8. Safety of Others | | 3 | 6 | 9 | 12 | 15 | 18 | 3 |
| 9. Work of Others | | 4 | 8 | 12 | 16 | 20 | 24 | 4 |
| <u>Job Conditions</u> | 15 | | | | | | | |
| 10. Working Conditions | | 10 | 20 | 30 | 40 | 50 | 60 | 10 |
| 11. Unavoidable Hazards | | 5 | 10 | 15 | 20 | 25 | 30 | 5 |
| TOTAL | 100% | 100 | 200 | 300 | 400 | 500 | 600 | 100% |

*Source:* Zollitsch, H.G., & Langsner, A. (1970). *Wage and Salary Administration.* Cincinnati: South-Western.

three factors: know-how, problem solving, and accountability. *Know-how* refers to the "sum total to every kind of skill, however acquired, required for acceptable performance" (Milkovich & Newman, 1984, p. 150). This encompasses vocational and specialized technical training as well as human relations skills. *Problem solving* refers to "original, 'self-starting' thinking required in the job for analyzing, evaluating, creating, reasoning, arriving at and making conclusions" (Milkovich & Newman, p. 151). *Accountability* refers to "answerability for action and for the consequences thereof" (Milkovich & Newman, p. 152). Another point system was developed by the National Electric Manufacturers Association (NEMA) that uses an 11-factor system grouped under four general areas: skill, effort, responsibility, and job conditions. A rating scale is designed to measure each factor, with the scale values reflecting the relative weight of the factor. Table 8.4 shows the point values used in the NEMA system for rating hourly jobs. In this specific example, the experience factor is most heavily weighted, whereas such factors as mental and/or visual demand and responsibility for work of others are weighted the least.

The assumption of the Hay and NEMA systems is that their respective sets of factors can be universally applied. However, organizations would want to modify these systems to fit their circumstances. The first step would be to conduct a job analysis to determine the major dimensions of the job and those that should serve as "compensable factors." Next, a scale would be constructed for each factor that reflected the degree to which a job might require or possess each factor; the resulting factors would be assigned weights to show their relative importance to the organization. One way of determining these weights is to allocate 100 points among the factors, with a higher number of points assigned the factors that are believed more important in determining wages. For instance, if the factors were responsibility, effort, work conditions, and skill, the organization might decide to allocate 40 points to responsibility, 30 to effort, 20 to skill, and 10 to work conditions.

## Establishing the Pay Structure

After evaluating jobs by using one of the above procedures, the next question concerns how to assign wages. Informed employers will want to conduct surveys of the going rates of pay to determine whether they wish to match, surpass, or fall below the going rate. In managing internal equity, the employer constructs a *pay policy* line such as the one in Figure 8.6. The line is constructed by plotting the wage of each job in the organization against the numerical value resulting from the job evaluation. Linear regression procedures (see Chapter 2) can indicate the best fitting line that can be used to predict current wages from knowledge of the job evaluation values attached to the job. Where jobs deviate from this line, the wage may need to be changed. In some cases this involves reclassifying the job into a lower wage rate or upgrading the wage. The pay line is a useful tool to track and maintain internal equity. It is not uncommon to find that some jobs appear overpaid as the result of falling far above the pay line, whereas other jobs appear underpaid as the result of falling below the line. It is tempting to correct the discrepancy by adding or deleting job evaluation points to bring things back in line. Such a practice may be politically expedient, but unless real changes in the job accompany these modifications in points, this practice makes a sham of the whole process.

### THE POLICY-CAPTURING APPROACH

It is possible to bypass the job evaluation procedures we have discussed and use a *policy-capturing approach*. With this method, jobs are analyzed on general dimensions with a method such as the PAQ. Using multiple regression (Chapter 2), a statistical equation is generated that can be used to predict current salaries from job dimensions (Robinson, Wahlstrom, & Mecham,

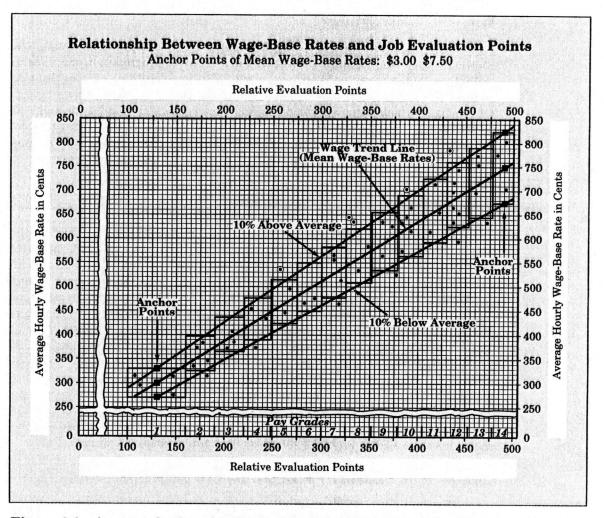

**Figure 8.6**   *An example of a pay policy line used in constructing salary structure*

Source: Zollitsch, H. G., & Langsner, A. (1970). *Wage and Salary Administration.* Cincinnati: South-Western.

1974). The equation can then be used to set the salaries for other jobs in the future. For instance, if the PAQ were used for this purpose, scores on the 13 overall dimensions (see Table 8.1) previously discussed would be computed for a job and entered into the equation determined from the multiple regression analysis of a large number of jobs. The equation would generate the salary that people in that job should receive to maintain consistency with the current salary structure. Policy capturing appears to apply more to lower level jobs than to professional and managerial jobs (Harvey, 1991). Also, an overreliance on policy capturing may perpetuate discriminatory wage practices such as paying women less than men.

## WHICH IS THE BEST METHOD?

Little research has been done to provide direct comparisons among the methods of job evaluation. An exception is a study conducted by Gomez-Mejia (1982), in which a comparison was made of three traditional job evaluation methods (i.e., point systems, factor comparison, and ranking), three policy-capturing methods, and a hybrid method that combined traditional and policy-capturing approaches. Few differences were found in the accuracy of the approaches, but a panel of compensation specialists liked the hybrid method better than the others.

## Comparable Worth Controversy

In recent years, job analysis and evaluation procedures have been the focus of a raging controversy over how to reduce the discrepancies between men and women in their pay. In 1990, the median earnings of American women working full time was slightly more than 70% of the earnings of men working full time, an improvement over the 1960–1970 decade, during which working women received only about 59% of what men were paid. The gap is less pronounced among younger workers. Among full-time workers (four or more years of college, 24 years old or younger), men earned a median of $22,333 while women earned a median of $20,500. This represents earnings of 92 cents by a woman for every dollar earned by a man of the same age and education. The gender gap widens, however, as women age. Between the ages of 24–34, a college-educated woman earned 75% of the earnings of college-educated men. The percentages were 65% for those between 34–44, 59% for those between 45–54, and 54% for those between ages 55–64 (Bovee, 1991).

### ORIGINS OF THE GENDER GAP IN WAGES: THE CASE OF SECRETARIAL WORK

The data clearly indicate that women tend to be paid less than men and part of the reason is the tendency of jobs to become sex-typed. The sex-typing of work appears to result from a complex interplay of technological, organizational, cultural, and demographic forces. Rather than staying constant, radical shifts in the sex-typing of a job can occur as these factors change. An interesting example of this is the job of secretary, which changed from a male to a female job during this century (Davies, 1982; Lowe, 1987). In the early 1800s the typical clerical worker was a man (over 97%) who performed a variety of duties in managing the office of the business. At the bottom of the hierarchy were the office boys. Another job was that of the clerk who did odd jobs, errands, sweeping, and some copying of correspondence. The bookkeeper kept the financial records of the firm. The copyists, as they were called, would take the rough drafts of the owner/manager of the firm and then put them into final form. The private secretarial position was the top of the clerical hierarchy, and those occupying this position often moved up to executive positions.

After the Civil War, the large corporation emerged, characterized by separation of management and ownership and the division of the business into departments and divisions. To handle the increased paper work generated by these larger organizations, clerical work became increasingly specialized. With the introduction of the typewriter in the late 1800s, the skilled occupation of copyist became obsolete and the typist emerged as a new job. Women provided a large pool of cheap labor that could fill the demand for these new, more specialized clerical jobs, and schools began training women to fill this demand. Clerical work ceased to be a career path toward management and became a low-paid, largely female, occupation. In 1870, women constituted 4.5% of stenographers and typists. By 1930, women constituted 95.4% of these jobs. The private secretarial position also became a female position. While it retained the variety and many of the same responsibilities found in the past, the position was no longer a stepping stone to management. The duties of the private secretary depended to a large extent on the personal relationship of the secretary and boss. Moreover, the secretarial job became stereotyped as a position that required stereotypic feminine attributes.

## THE CONCEPT OF COMPARABLE WORTH

Legal attempts to eliminate the gap in wages between men and women were taken as far back as 1963 when the Equal Pay Act was passed by Congress. According to this law, employers are prohibited from paying women less than men if they perform work that is essentially equal in the content of the job on the dimensions of skill, responsibility, effort, and working conditions. Critics of this act note that requiring *equal content* is far too stringent to make it an effective tool for eliminating sex discrimination in wage and salary administration.

A different doctrine of fairness states that women should be paid the same if they perform work of *comparable worth.* The means of determining comparable worth is to evaluate or analyze jobs using procedures that provide comparisons on broad dimensions, such as the PAQ, functional job analysis, and point systems of job evaluation. According to the principle of comparable worth, if an executive secretary's job involves similar behavioral processes and demands as a manager's job, then the secretary should be paid the same as the manager despite the obvious differences in the content of the jobs. Wages are seldom based solely on job analysis procedures, in that employers must pay wages that allow them to compete with other firms in hiring the most qualified employees. As of this date, the notion of comparable worth has not fared well in gaining acceptance at the federal level, although some states and municipalities have adopted comparable worth policies.

## BIASES IN JOB EVALUATION

The comparable worth controversy has brought attention to the possibility that job analysis and evaluation procedures are biased against women. A report on job evaluation commissioned by the National Research Council in the late 1970s concluded that there are serious problems (Treiman & Hartmann, 1981). These claims lacked an empirical basis, however, and are only beginning to receive the attention of researchers. It is difficult to conduct field research on sex bias in job evaluation because of the extreme sex segregation of so many occupations. As a result, it is very difficult to compare the wages of men and women while holding the content of the work constant. Controlled experiments are perhaps the only alternative, and the few that have been conducted have failed to reveal dramatic differences in the evaluation of jobs as a function of the sex of the incumbent.

One such experiment was conducted by Schwab and Grams (1985), who asked compensation specialists to rate three banking jobs using the Midwest Industrial Management Association (MIMA) point system for office jobs. Information was provided on the bank and the specific jobs evaluated, along with background information on the tenure, sex, and current average salary of current jobholders. The sex ratio of the incumbents and average current pay were manipulated so that half the respondents believed that the job of banking representative was predominantly female and the other half believed it was predominantly male. Also, half believed the average salary was currently $22,590 while the other half believed it was $33,880. The information on current salary had a large and significant effect on job evaluations. The higher the current pay of the job, the higher the ratings given to the jobs by the compensation specialists. No differences were found as a function of the sex of the incumbents. The authors warn, however, that this particular group may have exceeded the professionalism and training of the typical job evaluator in industry.

Although sex bias did not appear to influence the evaluations in this study, it is important to recognize that the effects of wage in the above study reflect a serious problem. Ideally, job evaluation provides a profile of the job on characteristics divorced from market value of the job. Contrary to this ideal, job analysts seldom are unaware of how incumbents in a position are paid relative to other incumbents. It may be impossible using current job evaluation procedures to completely separate external factors from internal factors.

## A FINAL SUMMATION AND A LOOK AT THE FUTURE

Job analysis is the method by which the components of work are identified and studied. Jobs result from the interactions of people with the work environment and the characteristics of the people performing the work. Through observation, interviewing, and self-report of the incumbents themselves, job analysts attempt to capture the essence of positions along one or more of these dimensions. If the activities of people in positions are similar enough in important respects, the positions are classified as belonging to the same job.

Research in I/O psychology has yielded a variety of job analysis techniques. Some of these provide job-oriented descriptions that are specific to the tasks performed. Others are more worker-oriented and allow broad comparisons among all sorts of work. Much of the research in recent years has focused on the latter approach as exemplified by such standardized, worker-oriented techniques as the Position Analysis Questionnaire. Different methods of job analysis are needed, depending on the specific use that will be made of the information. If the intent is to clarify the duties of people in the organization, to design a performance appraisal system, or to design a training program, highly specific information may be needed that can only come through task-oriented approaches such as task inventories and the critical incident technique. If the intent is to decide which jobs are sufficiently similar to be combined for purposes of validating selection procedures, or if the intent is to use the procedure to establish a wage structure, then a worker-oriented technique such as the Position Analysis Questionnaire may be of more value.

Jobs are occasionally viewed as static entities that are akin to tools, machinery, and other physical aspects of the organization. Jobs change, however, as a function of changes in technology, culture, work force composition, and organizational structure. Three trends that have great implications for job analysis are the participation of women in traditionally male jobs, the computerization of work, and the increasing use of teams in organizations.

The dramatic increase in the number of women in traditionally male occupations is one of the factors that may have an important influence on the nature of work activities. Lunneborg (1990), for instance, speculates that women will change male-dominated work such as management in the direction of being "humane, less competitive, and less hierarchical" (p. ix). It is also possible, however, that the work will influence those performing it rather than vice versa or that neither jobs nor people will change as more women enter traditionally male occupations. Only time will tell which of these hypotheses has more merit.

While we can only speculate on the impact of women on occupations, it seems clear that computerization of the workplace is fundamentally changing the nature of some jobs. Take, for example, secretarial work. Just as the introduction of the typewriter played a role in changing the secretarial job, the coming decades will see changes for clerical work and the job of secretary as the computer replaces the roledex, the typewriter, and other secretarial tools. Some have speculated that the long-term effects will be in the direction of narrower, more specialized, and less interesting work. In some cases, however, the introduction of computer technology seems to have upgraded the job of secretary. For instance, in many universities the ease with which word processing on the computer allows writing and rewriting has resulted in faculty typing their own manuscripts. This has allowed the secretary to take over other functions involving more responsibility, such as overseeing the budget and supervising other clerical people. In contrast to the job of secretary, Gutek and Larwood (1987) argue that in professional and managerial occupations, the computer tends to be seen as just another tool and is having a relatively minor impact on the fundamental nature of the work.

A third factor to consider is the move toward team-based management in organizations. As more organizations use teams at all levels of the organization, the boundaries between some jobs have become blurred. For instance, in manufacturing it is increasingly common to see teams of workers assigned to assemble a product with members of the teams rotating through different tasks. The cross-functional teams that are being used to develop new products are another example. An important issue that is likely to receive more attention in the future is how to compensate individual employees when work is team based. One alternative is to base compensation on the skills of the employee rather than on the nature of the job (Lawler & Ledford, 1985).

These changes will require new job analysis techniques. For instance, the introduction of high technology has increased the complexity and skill requirements of many jobs (Zuboff, 1988). Current job analysis methods seem unsophisticated in their attention to the cognitive components of work, however. For instance, the *Dictionary of Occupational Titles* is badly in need of revision to incorporate these and other neglected components (Adler, 1992). New job analysis procedures also are needed to capture the team component of work, which has been largely neglected in the individual emphasis of traditional methods. Another need is for methods of analyzing and anticipating future changes in work. Such methods may be crucial in human resource planning to meet future demands.

## DISCUSSION QUESTIONS

1. What is the difference between job-oriented and worker-oriented job analysis procedures? What are the best uses of each approach?
2. Distinguish among task, job, occupation, and career.
3. Job analyses on manual work can be conducted by observing the activities of the position's incumbent. How could you collect data on more cognitive jobs, such as a manager, a research scientist, or a computer programmer?
4. What is the model of work underlying the PAQ?
5. How do job analysis and evaluation enter into the comparable worth issue?
6. What effects, if any, do you believe that the increasing number of women managers will have on the job of manager?

# SAN JOSE TRIES COMPARABLE WORTH

In the summer of 1981, Local 101 of the American Federation of State, County, and Municipal Employees (AFSCME) declared a strike against the city of San Jose, California (Farnquist, Armstrong, & Strausbaugh, 1983). The strike was unusual in that it was intended to eliminate the gap in salaries between men and women working for the city. In the final settlement of this dispute the city of San Jose incorporated a version of comparable worth in deciding salaries of men and women.

Originally a group of women had pressed the city to eliminate inequities in salaries. After the city failed to take action, these women obtained the support of the AFSCME in promoting their cause. In 1979, the city agreed to hire a consulting firm, Hay & Associates, to conduct job evaluations and to study the salary structures of men and women. The study began with a revision of the classification system that was currently in use. The 540 city jobs were reclassified into approximately 300 job classes representing similar positions. A nine-member committee studied the job descriptions and other documents relevant to each job class and then rated the jobs on the four factors used in the Hay method: know-how, problem solving, accountability, and working conditions (see the discussion of these factors earlier in this chapter). The sum of the four ratings (total points) on these factors was taken as a measure of the job's value to the organization.

A scattergram similar to Figure 8.5 was constructed in which the weekly salary of each job was plotted against the total points assigned to the job. Jobs that were outside the 15% band above and below the overall trend (the regression line or best fitting line; see Chapter 2) were considered to need adjustments to achieve internal equity. Of overcompensated classes, 27 of 32 were male

dominated and only one was female dominated. Of undercompensated classes, 30 of 46 were female dominated, whereas 7 were male dominated. A perusal of individual jobs illustrates the disparities. Clerk typist II, a female-dominated job, received $550 a month, whereas aircraft refueler, a male-dominated job, received $729 a month. Both jobs were assigned 140 total points in the job evaluation, however. Senior legal secretary, a female-dominated job, received a salary of $665 a month whereas senior carpenter, a male-dominated job, received a salary of $1,119 a month. Both received 226 points in the job evaluation study.

Both the city and the union agreed that there was a problem but disagreed on the causes and solution. The pure comparable worth solution would have been to pay all jobs at the trend line. In other words, those jobs above the trend line would have their salaries cut, whereas those below would be given raises. Although the union did not press for this radical approach, they did advocate adjustments in the salaries of female-dominated jobs to bring them up to the level of male-dominated jobs. The union argued that these adjustments were needed because of sex discrimination that created wide gaps in the salaries of men and women. City officials, on the other hand, counterargued that a variety of factors were at work besides discrimination against women. Moreover, they argued that the city had to take into account the going market wages for jobs. If the city raised the salaries to restore internal equity and ignored the market, it would be unduly costly and would put the city at a disadvantage in recruiting skilled workers. The union went on strike and after eight days reached an agreement. According to the settlement, special equity adjustments were implemented in which female-dominated classes below the regression line would receive 5–15% increases in salary over two years to bring them within 5–6% of the trend line. For instance, clerk typist II, which was 6.91% below the 10% band, would receive special increases of 2.5% in each of the next two years. Almost all the adjustments were in the female-dominated job classes. None of the male-dominated classes would receive special adjustments over this period.

The critics of this comparable worth solution have argued that it is unreasonable to ignore the market place in setting wages. Moreover, basing wages solely on the results of job evaluation without taking into account the ability to pay risks financial ruin. Still another argument is that jobs should receive equal pay if the occupants perform equal work. Thus, two jobs might be comparable in their value to the organization in that they receive the same overall points, but they may not be equal in that different points are assigned to different factors. For example, a clerk typist might receive more points from know-how but an aircraft refueler might receive more points from working conditions. The higher salaries paid to the aircraft refueler may reflect the relative short supply of people willing to work under the undesirable conditions. Consequently, a premium is needed to get people to work under the undesirable conditions, whereas there may be an ample supply of people with the type of know-how required in the clerk typist job. Supporters of the comparable worth solution argue that the marketplace has held women down and drastic solutions are needed to reduce the large gaps that continue to separate the wages of men and women.

## CASE QUESTIONS

1. Do you believe the comparable worth approach taken in the San Jose case was a reasonable solution to reducing the gap in salaries between men and women? Why?

2. A senior legal secretary in San Jose received $665 a month while a senior carpenter received $1,119. Is it fair to pay the secretary less in light of the fact that they received the same number of Hay points? Present arguments for and against the fairness of paying the carpenter more.

3. What are the possible problems that can result from attempts to impose a comparable worth solution to reducing pay inequities between men and women?

## Chapter 8 Appendix, Answers to Figure 8.4

Short Order Cook

     Data =       6 (Comparing)

     People =    7 (Serving)

     Things =    1 (Precision working)

Choral Director

     Data =       0 (Synthesizing)

     People =    4 (Diverting)

     Things =    7 (Handling)

Hair Stylist

     Data =       2 (Analyzing)

     People =    7 (Serving)

     Things =    1 (Precision working)

Airline Reservations Agent

     Data =       3 (Compiling)

     People =    6 (Speaking-Signaling)

     Things =    7 (Handling)

# Performance Appraisal and Feedback

The topics of performance appraisal and feedback should be very familiar to you. All your life you have been evaluated by teachers, parents, coaches, friends, and a host of other people. As you probably already know, this does not end when you enter the world of work. In an organization the list of evaluators expands to include supervisors, coworkers, subordinates, and customers. Appraisal and feedback in an organization are typically casual, such as occurs in a colleague's pat on the back or the passing smile of a supervisor. Concerns over lawsuits and the need to improve productivity in an increasingly competitive business environment, however, have prompted employers to develop more systematic and quantitative appraisal systems. I/O psychologists have contributed to these efforts by developing rating techniques and by exploring the cognitive and social processes involved in appraisals.

To understand and improve performance appraisals we need to first consider the functions that they can fulfill within an organization. There are many specific uses of appraisals (Cleveland, Murphy & Williams, 1989), but most of these fall within three general functions. Appraisals can be used for *administrative* purposes, such as in deciding on monetary rewards, transfers, layoffs, and assignments, and for documenting these decisions. They are also used in *employee development* to counsel, coach, and in other ways improve the performance of individual employees. Finally, they are used as criteria in *research,* such as in the validation of selection instruments and the evaluation of training programs.

We organize our discussion around the what, how, and who of appraisals. What is appraised? How should organizations go about conducting these appraisals? Who conducts the appraisal? The answers to these questions depend on which of the three functions the appraisal is intended to fulfill.

## WHAT ARE THE CHARACTERISTICS OF A GOOD APPRAISAL MEASURE?

Regardless of their purpose, all appraisals can be evaluated on the extent to which they are reliable, practical, relevant, fair, and discriminative. *Reliability* was discussed in Chapter 2 and is covered again in Chapter 10. *Practicality* was defined by Patricia Cain Smith (1976) as being "available, plausible, and acceptable to those who want to use it for decisions" (p. 746) and needs no further discussion. Perhaps the most important basis for evaluating a performance measure is *relevance,* which is how well it reflects important criteria of performance. Schneider and Schmitt (1986) define *criteria* as "those behaviors and outcomes at work that competent observers can agree constitute necessary standards of excellence to be achieved in order for the individual and the organization to both accomplish their goals" (p. 77). The first step in defining criteria is to identify the goals against which the effectiveness of the organization and its subunits are judged. This is easier said than done given that the various constituencies of an organization are often in conflict over what the organization should be maximizing. For instance, customers may want an inexpensive, high-quality product. Government regulatory agencies may want compliance with rules and regulations. Labor unions may want high wages, job security, and safe working conditions for the workers. The issue becomes even more complex as we examine the often conflicting goals of subunits within the organization. Nevertheless, it is a valuable exercise for an organization to set forth what it stands for and what it is attempting to achieve. These values and goals can then set the framework for defining the criteria for various subunits and individual jobs. The *ideal criteria* (sometimes called the ultimate criteria) are all the important goals that the organization wishes the employee to achieve in his or her work.

In addition to reliability, practicality, and relevance, it is often important that appraisal measures possess *discriminability*, which is the ability to distinguish among employees. If everyone tends to get the same appraisal, then the evaluation is unlikely to be of much value in administering salary increases or evaluating personnel programs. Another important requirement for appraisals is that they are *fair*. This means that they not only are free of bias against women, minorities, and other factors irrelevant to performance but that they also are perceived as fair. Allowing appraisees to participate in the design of the system is one way of avoiding the feelings of inequity that so often plague performance appraisal.

If we assume that criteria are theoretical constructs and performance appraisals are attempts to measure these constructs, then evaluating a performance appraisal measure becomes a type of construct validation (Chapter 2). In this case, relevance of a measure becomes essentially construct validity, which we illustrate in Figure 9.1 as the degree of overlap between the measure and the ideal criteria. The ideal criteria for salespeople might include maximizing gross sales, following policies, and providing service to existing customers. In the example, performance is actually measured on number of sales, enthusiasm with which the salesperson participates in meetings, the accuracy with which the salesperson fills out forms, and whether the salesperson initiated and answered calls to clients. Enthusiasm in meetings is irrelevant to the ideal criterion and is thus a source of *contamination*. Another problem in the measure illustrated in Figure 9.1 is that the measure of client service leaves out important dimensions of providing service, such as solving problems and the politeness with which the salesperson interacts with the client. To the extent that a measure fails to reflect important dimensions of the ideal criterion, it is *deficient*. Relevance can also suffer because of *opportunity biases* in the form of information that is beyond the control of the employees. Imagine a salesperson who is evaluated on the number of lawnmower sales but who is assigned a territory that includes mostly apartment complexes. If this salesperson were evaluated lower than another salesperson who has mainly residential customers, then the performance measure would suffer from an opportunity bias.

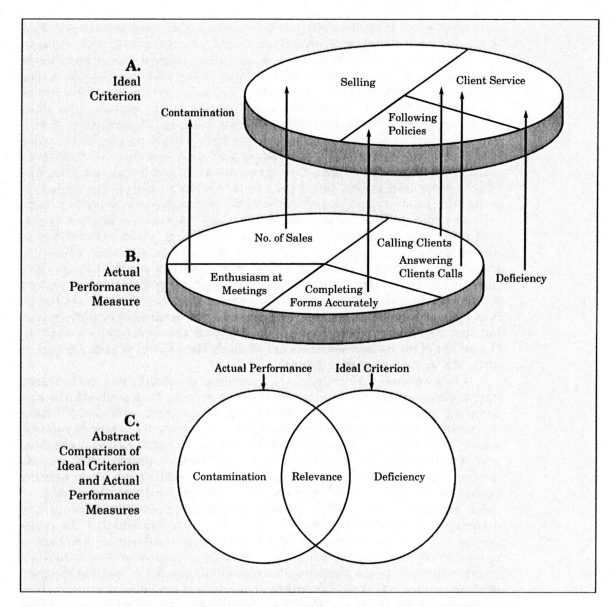

**Figure 9.1** *Conceptualization of criterion relevance, contamination, and deficiency*

*Source:* Schmitt, N., & Klimoski, R. J. (1991). *Research Methods in Human Resources Management.* Cincinnati: South-Western

## WHAT IS EVALUATED?

The answer to the question "What is evaluated?" depends on the functions that an appraisal serves. Traditionally, organizations have focused on the personal characteristics of the employee, with the typical performance evaluation form emphasizing traits such as integrity, conscientiousness, appearance, energy, ambition, etc. Although traits may be warranted when they are used as the basis for promotions or placement, the problems with this type of evaluation have been recognized for many years (McGregor, 1957). In using trait rating scales, supervisors are prone to rating effects such as halo and leniency (discussed later in this chapter). They also provide a poor basis for giving feedback to employees. How, for instance, does a supervisor tell an employee that he or she is a "3" on "conscientiousness"? If an organization must defend an appraisal system against claims of unfair discrimination, a trait system may be hard to legally justify.

An alternative to evaluating traits is to evaluate employess on the *outcomes* of their labor. At first glance, this seems to be the best approach. Why should we care if an employee has a bad attitude or is deficient with regard to some personality attribute as long as he or she gets the work done? It is often difficult, however, to assign responsibility for the outcomes of an individual employee in the complex and interdependent tasks characteristic of so many organizations. Another danger is that organizations may focus on what is measurable and neglect important performance factors that are not as easily measured.

Focusing solely on the visible and quantifiable elements of performance not only threatens relevance but can create conflict, as units or people in an organization attempt to achieve personal goals at the cost of overall organizational goals (Chapter 5). Telling salespeople that the only thing that counts is the dollar value of their sales might increase the sales of individual salespeople in the short-term, but could adversely affect customer service and cooperation among members of the salesforce. Other unintended consequences of an overemphasis on outcomes are illegal and unethical acts. For instance, a large retail chain was accused of cheating customers on car repairs that were unneeded or not done. The scandal has resulted in more than 10 million dollars so far in fines, with incalculable losses in future business. The main culprit appears to have been a performance appraisal system that placed emphasis on the dollar value of repair work performed (Kelly & Schine, 1992). Similar problems have occurred in Wall Street brokerage firms, in which pressures to meet unrealistically high sales quotas to keep their jobs can encourage brokers to engage in illegal and unethical trading practices (Power & Siconolfi, 1991). When outcomes in the form of sales revenue become a primary focus of evaluation there is always a risk that employees will interpret this as "anything goes."

We come then to an approach that for some I/O psychologists is the method of choice: the evaluation of *behavioral process*. In this case, employees are evaluated on *what they do* to produce outcomes. Salespeople, for example, might be evaluated on their courtesy in dealing with clients, their integrity, whether they follow up on customer complaints, or how much they cooperate with peers. This approach also can be carried to extremes, however, if the means become the ends and the employee loses sight of final objectives. In the worst cases it can engender a rigidity in which employees stick to past procedures even as task requirements change. This becomes a greater problem on complex, changing tasks for which there is more than one method of accomplishing the same objective. Rating a productive employee down because he or she does not conform to the right procedures is ill-advised in many situations. To give a high evaluation to an unproductive employee just because he or she makes all the right moves makes even less sense.

There is evidence that managers are likely to emphasize outcome measures when they may be least appropriate, that is, when the tasks are complex, interdependent, and the managers lack expertise (Ouchi & Maguire, 1975). In these conditions managers may feel pressure from their superiors to show evidence of good performance, but it is in these same conditions that the quality of performance information is poorest. Despite the pitfalls, many of the problems in appraisal can be avoided if attention is first given to the uses that are to be made of the appraisal and an approach is taken that fits these intended uses. Even using traits can make sense, according to Kavanagh (1971), if it can be shown that the traits are related to success on the job and if the approach is intended to predict future performance. If feedback and employee development are the main uses, however, then some mix of behavioral process and outcomes is needed. Determining whether processes or outcomes are emphasized requires a careful study of the jobs and technology. With a relatively simple technology, employees can be held accountable for the products of their labor, and the evaluation of outcomes is warranted. In complex situations, however, the products of employee efforts are often far removed from their individual actions and the success of each employee depends on what fellow employees do. In these cases the evaluation needs to emphasize behavioral process.

# HOW DO WE MEASURE PERFORMANCE?

Once a decision is made on *what* to evaluate, attention shifts to the best method to use. Two alternatives to performance measurement are distinguishable: objective and subjective (judgmental) measures of performance.

## Objective Measures of Performance

Using *objective measures* of behavioral process and outcomes often is touted as the best approach. A typist's performance can be measured with the number of lines typed and the number of errors made. A salesperson's performance can be measured with dollar value of sales. A forester can be evaluated on the number of trees cut.

Despite the hard numbers that objective measures provide, this approach can fall short on all three of the attributes of good appraisals. Objectivity of measurement does not necessarily ensure reliability (Klemmer & Lockhead, 1962; Rothe, 1978). Objective measurement of performance may not be practical in complex and interdependent jobs for which obtaining hard outcomes is expensive and time consuming. Also, dimensions that are highly quantifiable and open to objective measurement may lack relevance because of deficiency, opportunity bias, and contamination.

An overemphasis on what can be measured objectively and the neglect of dimensions that are harder to measure can have unfortunate consequences both for the organization and clients. For instance, hospitals have been criticized for appraisal systems that emphasize the number of patients seen by temporary nurses rather than quality of care, an approach that apparently has led to shortcuts in patient care and tragic consequences (Bogdanich, 1991). Another example comes from a unit in a major telecommunications corporation that evaluated the speed with which its service representatives dealt with customers by recording the duration of their phone conversations (Rigdon, 1990). Although employees were expected to provide a high level of customer service, the goal for many became to end their phone conversations quickly. Attempts to change these perceptions seem to have had only limited success. Although "employees now believe that the customer comes first, they remain confused by [the] continued emphasis on speed" (p. B4). Focusing on objective measures of productivity and efficiency can discourage employees from taking the risks that must be taken to come up with new ways of doing things. The best companies, according to one article, encourage "employees to use the expertise of the whole company, giving workers incentives for successful innovation, and refusing to punish those whose gambles don't pay off" (Dumaine, 1991, p. 57).

A possible advantage of objective measures is that they are seen as fairer than subjective measures in many cases. There are exceptions, however. Technological advances have made it possible for organizations to gather large amounts of information on objective measures of performance in some jobs. Invasion of privacy is likely to become more of an issue as this technology is increasingly used in the surveillance of employees. An example is the "active badge" that Olivetti has developed. These clip-on IDs contain computer chips that transmit infrared signals to sensors placed around the workplace. Thus, at any time the location of an employee can be instantaneously determined (Coy, 1992, p. 38). A technology that is currently in use is computer monitoring of the efficiency and accuracy of keyboard operators. Chalykoff and Kochan (1989) describe a system used in a collection agency that was part of the U.S. Internal Revenue Service. Supervisors monitored employees' work-related calls and evaluated their handling of the conversations. Additionally, there was computer tracking of the performance of average time spent talking, number of calls completed, and number of calls attempted. Contrary to what you might expect, little evidence was found that computer monitoring was detrimental to employee satisfaction and morale. Some critics would still argue, however, that such obtrusive methods are inherently unethical, violate human rights, and place employees under undue stress (Chapters 7 and 12). The debate is likely to continue as more organizations use computer technologies for surveillance purposes.

## Judgmental Measures of Performance

Because of the problems of using objective measures, organizations rely mainly on judgments of supervisors in appraising performance (Lent, Aurbach, & Levin, 1971). The most common of all rating scales for performance appraisal is the *graphic rating scale,* an example of which is provided in Figure 9.2. If you ever have been asked "On a scale of 1 to N how would you rate X?" you have used a graphic rating scale. Anchors can come in a variety of forms, but the most common types indicate whether the ratee possesses a high to low amount of the dimension, is poor to excellent, or is far below average to far above average. Very little guidance is usually given on how the rater is to judge where the person is on the scale. The result is that raters must struggle with what particular points on a scale mean. One rater's "2" on a 1 to 5 scale might be another person's "3" or "4." The ambiguities in interpreting the scale steps on a graphic scale have been blamed for a variety of rating effects, including halo, leniency, contrast, and so on. Also, if the rater has difficulty understanding the scale, then he or she will probably have difficulty conveying feedback to ratees on the dimension in question. Imagine the problems you might encounter in explaining to an employee that he or she is a "3" on dependability and a "1" on initiative?

Much of the research of I/O psychologists on performance appraisal ratings can be seen as a search for alternatives to graphic rating scales. We first

|  | Unsatisfactory | Marginal | Average | Above Average | Outstanding |
|---|---|---|---|---|---|
| Cooperativeness | 1 | 2 | 3 | 4 | 5 |
| Quality of Work | 1 | 2 | 3 | 4 | 5 |
| Work Habits | 1 | 2 | 3 | 4 | 5 |
| Initiative | 1 | 2 | 3 | 4 | 5 |
| Creativity | 1 | 2 | 3 | 4 | 5 |
| Dependability | 1 | 2 | 3 | 4 | 5 |
| Attitude | 1 | 2 | 3 | 4 | 5 |
| Adaptability | 1 | 2 | 3 | 4 | 5 |
| Resourcefulness | 1 | 2 | 3 | 4 | 5 |

**Figure 9.2** *Example of a graphic rating scale*

review some of the common rating effects that can lessen the value of judgmental measures of performance and then review alternative rating methods that have been used to improve accuracy.

## RATING EFFECTS

The research on judgmental measures of performance has revealed several systematic tendencies to rate in a certain direction. These tendencies are often called rating biases, a term that seems to imply that they are always in error. However, halo, leniency, and other similar tendencies are not always wrong. Consequently, we prefer to call them *rating effects* to distinguish them from the concepts of rating error and accuracy.

<u>Halo</u>   The most common of the rating effects is halo (Cooper, 1981). Halo occurs when the rater tends to give the same level of rating across all dimensions. Halo can occur at any point along the scale, although the most frequent tendency is for people to give uniformly positive ratings across dimensions. For example, an employee who is seen as having a good attitude might be evaluated positively on not only attitude but other dimensions, such as quantity and quality of performance. Another example would be a student evaluating his or her instructor on such things as knowledge of the subject matter, enthusiasm in lecturing, availability to students, and fairness of tests. A student who rates the teacher's enthusiasm negatively might then give low ratings to the teacher on all of the other dimensions. In many cases halo represents an error in that the rater incorrectly generalizes from performance on one dimension to other dimensions rather than carefully considering each separate aspect of performance. Still, it is possible that halo in ratings can reflect a true correlation among the various dimensions. As a consequence, some have argued that a distinction needs to be made between "true halo" and "halo error" (Cooper, 1981).

<u>Central Tendency, Severity, and Leniency</u>   Another tendency is for a rater to use only part of the scale in evaluating different ratees. Raters may show *central tendency,* in which they assign most ratees to the middle of the rating scale. This could reflect a conservative strategy in which a rater attempts to avoid mistakes by giving everyone an average appraisal. *Severity* occurs when a rater gives mainly negative evaluations, such as an instructor who grades all students down in an effort to appear tough. The more common tendency is *leniency,* in which raters assign all subordinates to the positive end of the scale. There are a variety of reasons this might occur. For instance, an easy instructor might give all As because of easy grading standards, because he wants to receive good teacher ratings from students, or because he likes his students, to name only a few possible reasons. As in the case of halo, we should not necessarily assume that these rating tendencies represent errors. A teacher could show leniency because the students in a class actually deserve good grades. Perhaps the most serious problem with these types of effects is that they do not allow a differentiation among employees. This could

be a serious problem if the appraisals are to be used for such purposes as assigning rewards for individual performance.

**Context Effects**    This refers to the influence that group performance can have on the ratings of an individual member of the group. Assume that two employees both have achieved the same, moderately good, level of performance. One is in a group in which the level of performance of coworkers is awful. The other is in a group of high performers. A *contrast effect* would occur for the employee in the low-performing group if that person were rated higher when in the context of the other employees than when rated alone. Likewise, contrast effects would occur for the employee in the high-performing group if that employee were rated lower when in the context of the other employees than when rated alone.

Another type of context effect that is not observed as frequently is *assimilation*. In this case, the rating is drawn *toward* the levels exhibited by others. Thus, more positive evaluations could be given to an employee who is in a group of star performers than if that employee were evaluated outside that context. Assimilation effects are more likely when the person rated is fairly close to the level of performance of others in the situation. Contrast effects are more likely when large differences are found between the person rated and others in the situation.

**Order Effects**    Information about performance seldom comes all at once but usually becomes available over time. The order in which information appears can influence appraisals. A commonly observed effect is the *primacy* effect, in which the first information about a ratee influences the final evaluation more than information appearing later. A student who on the first day of class comes late and then falls asleep in class may never recover in the eyes of some instructors. On the other hand, students who on the first day listen attentively and answer the instructor's questions may evoke a warm feeling that lasts the rest of the semester.

It is also possible to find *recency* effects in which the last information on the person influences final ratings more than information appearing earlier. The research suggests that primacy effects are more likely when one overall evaluation is made after observing information on the ratee, whereas recency effects are more likely when the rater evaluates the ratee on each item of information as it occurs (Farr, 1973). The typical evaluation in an organization is more conducive to primacy than recency.

**Negativity Effects**    A type of rating effect observed in a wide range of tasks is the tendency to place more weight on negative information than on positive or neutral information (Bolster & Springbett, 1961). Performance appraisals can become a search for negative evidence rather than a search for a representative sample of performances that could allow for an accurate assessment. To counteract this tendency, it is frequently suggested that supervisors should make a special effort to catch their subordinates performing well.

**Similar-to-Me Effects**    Still another type of effect occurs when the rater evaluates the other person on the basis of the similarity of that person to the rater

(Wexley, Alexander, Greenawalt, & Couch, 1980). For instance, if you were a manager you might tend to give higher ratings to individuals who share your political beliefs, graduated from your college, and grew up in your region of the country.

**Physical Attractiveness**  The physical appearance of the employee seems a questionable factor on which to base the evaluation of performance in most cases. Nevertheless, research has shown that persons who are physically unattractive receive lower ratings than those who are attractive (Stone, Stone, & Dipboye, 1992). A recent example of this effect that received widespread attention was the firing of a ticket agent by one of the major airlines for not wearing makeup. In this case, the employee was reported to be a highly effective performer, but her lack of makeup violated the norms of the organization. The employee in this case threatened a lawsuit and was reinstated, but other victims of this type of discrimination may not have been as fortunate.

Although most research has shown attractive people receive higher evaluations, there is evidence that attractive women may be at a disadvantage in some situations. One study found that an unattractive woman received higher performance ratings than an attractive woman when they performed a traditionally male job but that the attractive woman received higher ratings when they performed a traditionally female job (Heilman & Stopeck, 1985). This has been called the "beauty is beastly" effect. According to one explanation, attractiveness increases the influence of sex stereotypes so that an attractive woman is seen as possessing stereotypic feminine traits to a greater extent than an unattractive woman.

**Personal Liking**  Somewhat related to the similar-to-me and attractiveness effects is a tendency for ratings to be influenced by the evaluator's personal liking for the ratee. Those responsible for appraising performance should be able to rise above their personal feelings. Still, it is not uncommon to hear supervisors express something along these lines: "He (she) is performing just fine, but there is something about him (her) that I just don't like." Empirical evidence that raters' liking for a ratee can reduce accuracy comes from research showing student bias in the evaluations of teachers as the result of personal liking (Cardy & Dobbins, 1986; Dobbins & Russell, 1986). One study found that students are more accurate in judging the performance of teachers when the teachers are equally likable than when the teachers differ in likability (Cardy & Dobbins, 1986).

Similarly, supervisors have been shown to give higher ratings to subordinates with whom they have a high degree of personal acquaintance (Kingstrom & Mainstone, 1985). However, the findings suggest that personal liking may do more than just influence ratings. In this particular study, the relationship of acquaintance and employee performance was mediated by supervisor treatment of the employee. Thus, acquaintanceship results in preferential treatment which then leads to higher performance (see the discussion of LMX theory in Chapter 6.

**Demographic Effects** Also related to the similar-to-me effect is the tendency to rate people of a particular age, gender, or race higher or lower than people in other groups. These effects can violate civil rights legislation protecting the employment rights of older employees (those above 40), women, and minorities.

*1. Age.* The dramatic rise in the number of age discrimination suits in the U.S. over the last decade suggests that appraisals are lower for older employees. The extent to which this is a problem varies across organizations. For instance, there appears to be a strong preference for the hiring of younger employees in advertising, which traditionally has been thought of as a young person's industry (Lipman, 1991). There is evidence, however, that the negative perceptions of older employees extend beyond specific industries (Rosen & Jerdee, 1976). Empirical confirmation that age influences appraisals comes from a survey showing that supervisors tended to evaluate older employees less positively (Waldman & Avolio, 1986). Age effects were more pronounced for nonprofessional employees than professional employees. Interestingly, the same study found that the older employees were more productive (as measured by objective indicators) than younger employees, regardless of whether they were in professional or nonprofessional occupations.

*2. Gender.* Women in traditionally male roles can also be at a disadvantage in the appraisals of their performance, but research so far has been neither clear nor consistent in demonstrating that women receive lower ratings. The findings appear to vary considerably across laboratory studies, but research conducted with actual appraisals in organizations tends to show an effect in favor of women (Smith,Olsen,& Falgout,1991). But questions can be raised about the generalizability of both types of research. Are findings with college students (the predominant subjects in lab studies) really appropriate for drawing conclusions about managerial decisions? On the other hand, are the organizations that are willing to permit a study of sex effects truly representative of organizations in general? Questions such as these can only be answered by conducting both lab and field research and then comparing the results (Chapter 2).

Whether performance appraisal is to blame is open to debate, but the evidence seems fairly clear that women and minorities are not being promoted to the highest levels at the same rates as white men ("Throwing stones at the 'glass ceiling,' " *Business Week,* August 19, 1991; "Study says women face glass walls as well as ceilings," *Wall Street Journal,* March 3, 1992). The U.S. Department of Labor released a report in 1991 showing that in nine large corporations the careers of minorities and women appeared to reach a plateau lower than that of the typical white male. This has been called the "glass ceiling" and could reflect a variety of factors other than performance appraisals, including differences in task assignments, training opportunities, and mentoring relationships. Nevertheless, some corporations have taken a careful look at their appraisal procedures in the attempt to weed out subtle and not-so-subtle sources of sexism. An example is the Xerox Corporation which asked a panel of senior executive women to look at the wording contained in appraisal procedures (Lublin, 1991c). The committee recommended that the definitions attached to the leadership dimension on the appraisal form be changed from "intense desire to win," which seemed stereotypically male, to "intense desire to succeed," which seemed more gender neutral.

*3. Race.*    While sex effects are not particularly clear from previous research, research on ratee race has shown that black employees tend to receive lower ratings than white employees (Kraiger & Ford, 1985; Sackett & DuBois, 1991; Waldman & Avolio, 1991). Race effects appear to vary considerably with the situation, however. Kraiger and Ford (1985) concluded from their analysis that black raters rated whites lower than blacks, whereas white raters rated blacks lower than whites. They also found that blacks received the lowest evaluation where they represented a small proportion of the work force. Studies conducted by Sackett and DuBois (1991) and by Waldman and Avolio (1991) failed to confirm these results, however. Another issue that remains unresolved is whether differences in appraisals represent real differences in performance or unfair discrimination. It may be that the tendency for black employees to receive lower ratings not only reflects supervisory prejudice but also reflects employee deficiencies in knowledge, skills, or abilities that stem from past educational disadvantages.

*4. Are Demographic Effects Changing?*    The problem with attempting to determine the extent to which age, gender, and race influence ratings is that there is continuing pressure to eliminate these effects. Consequently, effects found in some studies may soon become obsolete as stereotypes diminish and organizations are held more accountable. A large study in the U.S. Army (Pulakos, White, Oppler, & Borman, 1989), for example, found little evidence that black, Hispanic, and women soldiers received lower ratings from their officers. We can only hope that these findings reflect a genuine trend in the direction of less discrimination.

**Rating Error Versus Rating Effect**    Although rating effects such as halo and leniency are frequently considered equivalent to rating errors, this is not always the case. An *error* presumes some standard that we use for comparison (Gordon, 1970). Thus, if we had a supervisor judge the typing speed of a secretary we could use as a standard the actual typing speed of the secretary to measure error in the judgment. The actual typing speed would be the true score and the degree of error committed in estimating speed would be measured by taking the difference between the estimated and the true score.

Somewhat more controversial is the attempt to measure error in the appraisal of performance on subjective dimensions. For instance, Murphy, Garcia, Kerkar, Martin, and Balzer (1982) had students watch videotaped lectures and evaluate the lecturer's performance on two scales: (1) the frequency with which each of 12 behaviors occurred in the lectures (e.g., uses blackboard), and (2) the performance of the lecturers on each of eight dimensions that included poise, interest, and thoroughness of preparation. For each videotape, true scores were obtained for the two types of ratings from 13 expert raters who rated the tapes on the same two scales after repeatedly watching the tapes. The true score for each dimension was the mean rating of the experts on the dimension. The results revealed that subjects who were accurate in estimating the frequency of the behaviors were also accurate in appraising performance. Once the true scores of a taped performance are computed in this manner, factors can be manipulated in experiments (e.g., order of presentation, delay between stimulus presentation and rating, type of rating scale) to determine the effects on the accuracy of judgments (Borman, 1979a; Borman, 1979b; Murphy & Balzer, 1986; Murphy, Garcia, Kerkar, Martin, & Balzer, 1982). Although laboratory research on rating accuracy has been useful in theoretical explorations of rating behavior, such research is difficult to conduct in organizational settings because true scores of performance for people in actual jobs in an organization cannot be readily obtained. Consequently, researchers in organizational settings often must rely on traditional rating effect measures such as halo and leniency when they explore performance appraisal in field settings.

## ALTERNATIVE MEASURES OF PERFORMANCE

Graphic scales are vulnerable to all of the rating effects and errors that we have described so far. As a consequence, I/O psychologists have developed alternatives that attempt to eliminate the problems associated with graphic scales. In describing these alternatives, we distinguish among three types of judgmental measures in terms of the task presented to the rater: absolute judgments, behavioral description procedures, and comparative procedures.

**Absolute Judgments**   With this type of measure, the task is to evaluate the ratee on the level of performance shown on a dimension. In other words, the evaluator is to rate how much of the dimension the ratee has demonstrated in the performance of the job. Two examples are the Behavioral Anchored Rating Scale (BARS) and the Mixed Standard Scale (MSS).

*1. Behavioral Anchored Rating Scale (BARS).*   This method of appraisal was presented as a means of improving the anchors on graphic scales (Figure 9.3). Rather than relying on vague anchors such as "high" or "good," a BARS anchors various points along the scale with behaviors that reflect what would be *typical* or *expected* of a person with that level of performance.

The procedures for developing BARS were first set forth by Smith and Kendall (1963) and consist of five steps. First, people knowledgeable about the job generate critical incidents of performance. In the second step, the same or different persons sort the incidents into 5 to 10 performance categories to determine the dimensions on which performance is to be evaluated. In the third step, the incidents are scrambled and other experts reallocate them to the performance dimensions generated at the second step. If a high percentage of the experts agree on the reallocation of an incident (50% to 80% or higher), the incident is retained; otherwise, it is discarded. In the fourth step, still other experts rate each of the remaining incidents on the level of performance it represents. Finally, incidents with low standard deviations (indicating high agreement among the experts) are chosen to anchor several levels of

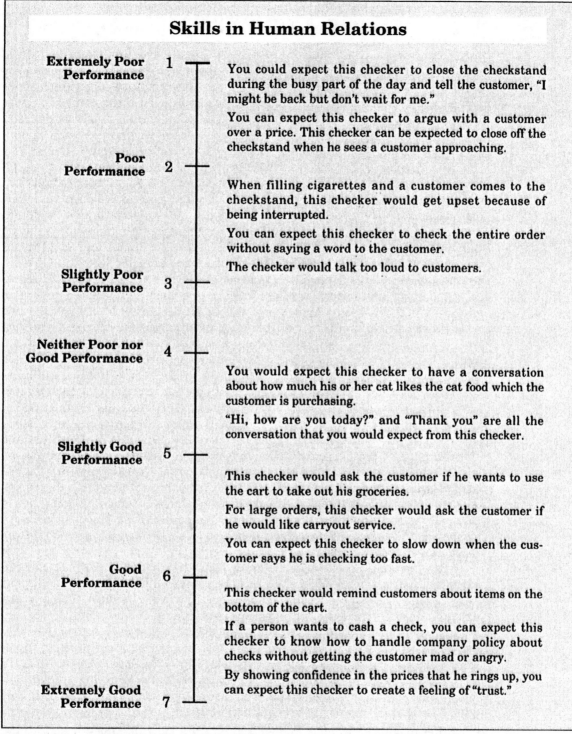

**Figure 9.3** *A Behaviorally Anchored Rating Scale used in evaluating a supermarket cashier*

*Source:* Fogli, L. (1988). Supermarket cashier. In S. Gael (Ed.) *The Job Analysis Handbook for Business, Industry, and Government.* New York: John Wiley & Sons, pp. 1215–1228.

performance on each dimension. In using the scale, the rater is instructed to evaluate the employee's performance on a dimension. Specifically, the rater is to pick a scale value on a dimension if the past performance of the employee is typical of the behavior represented by the anchor, even if the employee never actually exhibited the specific behavior. A variation on these instructions is to have the rater indicate what the employee is *expected* to do on each dimension. This version sometimes is called a *Behavioral Expectation Scale* (BES).

*2. Mixed Standard Scale (MSS).* A BARS provides clearer anchors than the typical graphic scale, but raters still know the dimension (e.g., dependability) on which they are evaluating an employee at the time they are making their ratings. Consequently, evaluations on BARS are still subject to halo, leniency, and other rating effects because it is obvious what is high and what is low on the scale. The Mixed Standard Scale (MSS) hides the dimensions and focuses the evaluation on what would be the anchors in a BARS (Blanz & Ghiselli, 1972). The MSS is developed in a manner similar to a BARS. Experts generate dimensions and examples of performance on each dimension. There is an allocation step in which experts sort the items according to dimensions and retain those for which there is a high amount of agreement. Experts also rate each example on the level of performance represented by the item. Unlike a BARS, however, the actual instrument on which an employee is evaluated lacks dimension labels and has no anchored rating scales. Rather, examples are chosen to represent good, average, and poor performance for each dimension, and these examples are listed in random order. The rater conducting the appraisal indicates for each item whether the person's performance is better than, the same as, or worse than the performance indicated in the statement. The rater is told neither the dimension associated with the statement nor the level of performance that the statement represents. A scale value is assigned on the basis of the pattern of responses to the three items for a dimension (Figure 9.4). For instance, if the person who is rated is seen as doing better than all three items, the person's performance on the dimension is transformed into a rating of 7. A person who is seen as performing poorer than all three items receives a rating of 1.

How well does the MSS do in improving the quality of performance ratings? Evaluations of the MSS show both benefits and liabilities of the method. Early research presented some evidence that a MSS reduces leniency and halo (Blanz & Ghiselli, 1972; Finley, Osburn, Dubin, & Jeanneret, 1977; Saal & Landy, 1977). Subsequent research, however, has not been as positive. This scale-type is not well-received by raters and is seen as more difficult to use than a BARS or graphic rating scale (Dickinson & Zellinger, 1980). Also, the disguising of the dimensions, a primary feature of the MSS, may make little difference in the quality of ratings. This was shown in an experiment conducted by Dickinson and Glebocki (1990) in which the dimensions on the MSS were either disguised or made known to the raters. No differences in halo and leniency were found between the two conditions. A third potential problem with the MSS is that the format may confuse raters rather than help them make judgments. Some indication of this is the high rate of logical error that

| Favorability of the Behavioral Incident | | | Derived Rating |
|---|---|---|---|
| Positive | Average | Negative | |
| + | + | + | 7 |
| 0 | + | + | 6 |
| - | + | + | 5 |
| - | 0 | + | 4 |
| - | - | + | 3 |
| - | - | 0 | 2 |
| - | - | - | 1 |

**Figure 9.4**   *Patterns of logically consistent responses in the Mixed Standard Scale (MSS) and the rating derived from each pattern*

Note: Raters are presented with one positive, one average, and one negative behavioral incident for each performance dimension evaluated. Their task is to indicate whether the ratee's performance is better than (+), the
same as (0), or poorer (−) than each incident. The performance evaluation is the derived rating associated with
each pattern. All other patterns are considered errors. See Saal (1979) for how to treat errors.

has been found in some research with the MSS (Barnes-Farrell & Weiss,
1984; Prien & Hughes, 1987). A logical error can be detected by examining the
pattern of responses on a MSS. Assume, for example, you used a MSS to measure performance of a supermarket cashier on the dimension of "skill in
human relations" and that three of the anchors from the BARS illustrated in
Figure 9.3 were the items presented to raters. If the rater indicated that the
cashier performed at a level that was better than the positive item (e.g., "You
can expect this checker to create a feeling of trust") but also poorer than the
negative item (e.g., "You can expect this checker to argue with a customer
over a price"), then this pattern would be considered a logical error on the
part of the rater. Realize, however, that the rater is not describing whether
the checker showed the specific behavior in the item. Rather, the rater is to
evaluate whether the checker's typical performance would be better than, the
same as, or poorer than the level of performance represented by the item.

**Behavioral Description Procedures**   The BARS and MSS are quite sophisticated, but neither has been shown to eliminate rating errors. Although both
approaches focus the attention of raters on specific behaviors to a greater
extent than graphic rating scales, the primary task of the rater is still evaluative. The idea underlying behavior description procedures is that rating

errors can be reduced if the rater's primary task is to observe and describe, rather than to evaluate, the behavior of the employee. With this approach, once behaviors have been recorded, then an evaluation is *derived* from the description on the basis of prescaled values of the behaviors used in the description. Descriptive measures include the Behavioral Observation Scale (BOS), the weighted checklist, and the forced choice method.

*1. Behavioral Observation Scale (BOS).* In a behavioral observation scale (BOS) the frequency with which each behavior has been observed for the employee is rated, and the evaluation of the employee on a dimension is the sum or mean of these ratings (Figure 9.5). The steps followed in developing a

---

### Report your observations of the cook on the behavior listed under waiter / waitress plus the following:

**Is careful not to waste food**
Almost never  1  2  3  4  5  Almost always

**Keeps grease off floor and counters**
Almost never  1  2  3  4  5  Almost always

**Uses tongs or spatula to handle food rather than hands**
Almost never  1  2  3  4  5  Almost always

**Cooks meat that looks and/or smells bad**
Almost always  1  2  3  4  5  Almost never

**Comes up with new recipes or ideas for modifying existing recipes**
Almost never  1  2  3  4  5  Almost always

**Prepares for the next shift so that the next cook has minimum rather than maximum work to do**
Almost never  1  2  3  4  5  Almost always

**Consults other cooks for suggestions on ways to help one another**
Almost never  1  2  3  4  5  Almost always

**Customers complain about the quality of the food**
Almost always  1  2  3  4  5  Almost never

**Is open to suggestions from management and employees**
Almost never  1  2  3  4  5  Almost always

**Keeps sink clean**
Almost never  1  2  3  4  5  Almost always

**Runs out of supplies, for example: clams, potatoes, forks, napkins, milk, ketchup, and the like**
Almost always  1  2  3  4  5  Almost never

**Anticipates busy and slow days in terms of how much fish to cut and how many potatoes to peel**
Almost never  1  2  3  4  5  Almost always

| 60-192 | 193-222 | 223-252 | 253-282 | 283-300 | |
|---|---|---|---|---|---|
| very poor | unsatis-factory | satis-factory | excellent | superior | Total = _____ |

**Figure 9.5** *Example of a behavioral observation scale used to evaluate a cook*

Note: These are 12 of 60 items used in this scale
*Source:* Latham, G. P., & Wexley, K. N. (1981). *Increasing Productivity through Performance Appraisal.* Reading, MA: Addison-Wesley.

BOS, according to Latham and Wexley (1981), are similar in several respects to the development of the BARS. The first step is to identify the crucial dimensions of job performance by asking experts to provide critical incidents of effective performance. The behavioral items generated are then allocated to the various dimensions, and those items that judges agree belong to a dimension are retained. A chief aim in the development of a BOS is *high internal consistency* (see Chapter 2). To achieve this, the correlation of the response to each item with the total score on a dimension is computed. Items are retained that have the largest correlations with the total score.

A BOS appraisal consists of ratings of the frequency with which the employee demonstrates the specified behavior. Although there is little consensus on how to structure frequency ratings, Latham and Wexley (1981) recommend a 5-point scale in which 1 represents 0–64% of time, 2 is 65–74%, 3 is 75–84%, 4 is 85–94%, and 5 is 95–100%. The danger in relying on frequency judgments is that an infrequent event may be an extremely important performance. A tanker captain does not spill oil on a frequent basis but just one spill is enough to constitute a bad performance of catastrophic proportions.

*2. Weighted Checklist.*    In this rating procedure the rater is given a list of various performances and is told to check off those that are applicable to the employee. One version starts by obtaining a pool of critical incidents of performances. Judges indicate the level of performance reflected in each item, and those incidents on which judges can agree are retained. The median of the rated values of the items checked is the performance appraisal assigned to the ratee. Still another variant of the weighted checklist is to take the items and through statistical means determine the extent to which each item distinguishes exceptional from poor performance.

Figure 9.6 is an example of a weighted checklist. The values in the first column are the scaled values of each item. These were obtained by having supervisors rate a large group of items on a nine-step scale to describe whether the items reflected a highly favorable (9) to highly unfavorable (1) performance. Only those items for which supervisors could attain a high degree of agreement were retained. The value attached to each item was the median of the supervisor ratings. In using this weighted checklist the rater checked off those items that were descriptive of the ratee and the median of the scale values associated with the checked items was the performance appraisal. Jurgenson (1949) found a problem in using this procedure, however. Take, for example, the three employees rated in Figure 9.6. Employee C was described with all the items yet received a lower appraisal than employees A and B, who were described with only the most favorable items. To correct this problem, Jurgenson recommended subtracting each scale value from the midpoint of the scale (i.e., 5). The performance appraisal was then calculated by taking the sum of the revised scale values of those items checked.

*3. Forced Choice Methods.*    In the attempt to get supervisors to differentiate among subordinates in appraisal ratings, psychologists developed a variant of the weighted checklist method called forced choice appraisal (Berkshire & Highland, 1953). With this method the supervisor chooses from among performance items that are matched on how good they sound but actually differ in

| Item | Scale Values* | | Employee | | |
|---|---|---|---|---|---|
| | | | A | B | C |
| Is one of the best employees in the department. | 8.6 | 3.6 | X | X | X |
| Has unusually good quality. | 8.4 | 3.4 | X | X | X |
| Carries through on all jobs. | 8.2 | 3.2 | X | X | X |
| Is extremely loyal. | 8.0 | 3.0 | X | X | X |
| Gives close attention to instructions of the supervisor. | 7.8 | 2.8 | X | X | X |
| Plans work well. | 7.6 | 2.6 | X | X | X |
| Has good judgment | 7.4 | 2.4 | X | X | X |
| Learns new work easily. | 7.2 | 2.2 | | X | X |
| Is enthusiastic. | 7.0 | 2.0 | | X | X |
| Reacts favorably to corrections. | 6.8 | 1.8 | | X | X |
| Starts work earlier than others. | 6.6 | 1.6 | | X | X |
| Is a steady worker. | 6.4 | 1.4 | | | X |
| Gets help when in difficulty. | 6.2 | 1.2 | | | X |
| Profits from past mistakes. | 6.0 | 1.0 | | | X |
| Is pleasant and courteous. | 5.8 | .8 | | | X |
| Does fair share of work. | 5.6 | .6 | | | X |
| Does not give excuses when corrected. | 5.4 | .4 | | | X |
| Total score based on median | | | 8.0 | 7.6 | 7.0 |
| Revised scale value | | | 21.0 | 28.6 | 34.0 |

*\* Values in second column were revised values computed by subtracting 5 from the original scale values in the first column.*

**Figure 9.6** *Example of a weighted checklist used in evaluating employee performance*

Source: Jurgenson, C. E. (1949). A fallacy in the use of median scale values in employee checklsts. *Journal of Applied Psychology, 33,* 56–58.

the extent to which they discriminate effective from ineffective performance (Figure 9.7). This method presents raters with a set of behaviors that have been prescaled using the same procedures as those used in developing a weighted checklist. Unlike the weighted checklist method, however, items are not only scaled on how well they distinguish the effective from the ineffective performers but also on how good they seem. One form of the forced choice method presents the rater with four items; the four items represent all combinations of ability to discriminate between good and poor performance and social desirability. Thus, two items distinguish between performance, with one representing good performance and the other bad performance. Two other items do not distinguish between high and low performers despite the fact that one sounds very good and the other sounds bad. The final performance appraisal is the sum of the value of those items chosen across all these quartets that actually differentiate between different levels of performance. The forced choice procedure has been found to be reliable and to yield measures of performance that are consistent with other measures (King, Hunter, & Schmidt, 1980). Unfortunately, supervisors appear to detest forced choice procedures. Another potential problem is that many supervisors will eventually determine which alternatives yield the most favorable ratings. An organization would continually need to add new items to be able to use a forced choice system for routine purposes.

**Comparative Procedures**   Despite the sophistication of the various rating methods, none can guarantee that leniency, severity, or central tendency will not enter into the evaluation of employees. This is a major problem if the primary use of the appraisal is to differentiate among employees for such purposes as allocating rewards or deciding which employees to promote, lay off, transfer, and so on. The surest method of avoiding these biases is to force evaluators to compare the performance of each ratee with those of others. The comparative approach includes rankings, paired comparison, and forced distribution.

*1. Ranking.*   Employees are ranked from the best to the worst on each dimension and/or on overall performance. While this may seem simple, the task can become quite difficult as the number of employees to be ranked increases. *Alternation ranking* is a procedure that can help simplify the task and involves assigning a 1 to the best performer and a value of $N$ to the worst performer in a group of size $N$. Next, the best and worst of the remaining people are ranked. This continues until all are ranked. Although ranking can allow the organization to distinguish among employees, their true performance is unlikely to match the rectangular distribution that ranking procedures assume to exist. Nevertheless, a ranking approach can force supervisors to distinguish among employees when tough decisions must be made.

*2. Paired Comparison.*   The ranking procedure yields a crude measure that can range from 1 to $N$. Paired comparison can yield a much more precise estimate of performance and consists of taking all possible pairs of employees and asking the judge to pick the better performer in each pair. The percentage of

**Examples of four item blocks containing either all favorable or two favorable and two unfavorable items.**

**1. Instructions** Pick the two statements which are most descriptive

    a. Patient with slow learners (FI 2.82, DI 1.15)
    b. Lectures with confidence (FI 2.75, DI .54)
    c. Keeps interest and attention of class (FI 2.89, DI 1.39)
    d. Acquaints classes with objective for each class in advance (FI 2.85, DI .79)

**2. Instructions** Pick the statement which is most descriptive and the one which is least descriptive in each block

    a. Fine personal bearing (FI 3.01, DI 1.21)
    b. Adapts readily to new duties (FI 2.98, DI .59)
    c. Is not well qualified to instruct in all phases of subject (FI .65, DI −.75)
    d. Does not put class at ease (FI .78, DI −.13)

**Examples of triads containing either all favorable or all unfavorable items.**

Instructions: Pick the statement which is most descriptive and the one which is least descriptive in each block

**1. All unfavorable triad**

    a. Does not answer all questions to the satisfaction of the students (FI 1.43, DI −.20)
    b. Does not use proper voice volume (FI 1.47, DI −.80)
    c. Supporting details are not relevant (FI 1.40, DI −.15)

**2. All favorable triad**

    a. Conducts class in orderly manner (FI 2.22, DI 1.20)
    b. Repeats questions to the whole class before answering them (FI 2.29, DI .57)
    c. At ease before class (FI 2.35, DI .53)

*FI = favorableness index, computed as the mean supervisor rating on a five point scale of how favorable each statement was when used with reference to an instructor.*

*DI = discrimination index and indicates the extent to which a statement distinguished between instructors identified as highly effective and ineffective. The larger the value, in either a positive or negative direction, the more the item discriminated between these groups.*

**Figure 9.7** *Excerpts from forced choice measures used in rating Air Force instructors*

Source: Berkshire, J. R., & Highland, R. W. (1953). Forced-choice performance rating: A methodological study. *Personnel Psychology, 6,* 355–378.

times each employee is chosen as the better performer can be used to derive a measure of performance. This procedure becomes exceedingly complex as the number of employees increases. With 10 employees the number of comparisons is 45; with 20 it is 190; and with 30 it is 435. Another potential problem is intransitivity. An example would be if employee A is judged better than B, and B better than C, but then C is evaluated as better than A. Intransitivity becomes a greater problem when the number of comparisons is large and the differences in performance among employees are fairly small. One possible solution to the intransitivity problem is to provide appraisers with well-defined, specific components of performance rather than having appraisers compare employees on their overall (global) performance.

*3. Forced Distribution.*     Still another comparative procedure is to sort employees into categories using predetermined quotas. In some cases the distribution might approximate a normal curve: 10% receiving a 1; 20% a 2; 40% a 3; 20% a 4; and 10% a 5. More common is a curve with a negative skew, for example, 5% receiving a 1; 10% a 2; 50% a 3; 25% a 4; and 10% a 5. An example with which you are probably familiar is the grading curve in a class. An instructor might give no more than 10% As, 25% Bs, 50% Cs, and 15% Ds. IBM Corporation is an example of a company in the process of implementing a forced distribution–type procedure. They began what they call an R&R (rating and ranking) system of appraisal in which employees doing similar work in a group are not only rated on a 1 to 4 scale but are also ranked ("New R&R doesn't give executives any rest," *Wall Street Journal,* December 13, 1991). According to one description of this system (Gabor, 1992), only 10% can get the top and bottom ratings, with the remainder falling at the middle two scale points. Those who receive the lowest ratings and rankings are fired if they do not improve within three months. Those receiving the top ratings could receive very large bonuses.

Problems can occur with a forced distribution procedure when quotas do not match the true distribution of performance. A concern that has been expressed about IBM's R&R system, for example, is that some units may have more or fewer than 10% of their employees at the top and bottom of the scale. Forced distribution procedures can also hurt cooperation as employees in an organization compete against each other for top ratings. The consequence is that employees may take a win-lose orientation to their work when they should be cooperating.

## Conclusions

The first rating scales in performance appraisal were graphic scales that typically measured employees on various traits. The rating biases and errors found with graphic scales led to a search for better scales that would eliminate these problems. As a result of these efforts, organizations seeking numerical scales to use in employee evaluation have a variety of methods to choose from. With all the effort expended on developing more sophisticated rating methods, none of the alternatives we have discussed seem sufficiently superior to justify unqualified use across all situations. This conclusion is supported by three recent meta-analyses. Heneman (1986) found no differences among various rating scales in agreement achieved between outcome measures and subjective ratings. Kraiger and Ford (1985) found that the type of scale did not moderate race effects. Finally, Harris and Schaubroeck (1988) found that rating scale type did not influence extent of agreement among self, peers, and supervisors.

Each of the evaluation methods has strengths and weaknesses. A direction for future research is to explore the contingencies under which one method is preferred over the others. Feldman (1986b) has speculated that the type of instrument that is best depends on the appraisal task. If there is an objective performance model specifying the relationship between task behavior and task outcome and the appraiser is essentially an observer and recorder of behaviors, then a BOS or BARS is most appropriate. If objective performance is absent and the appraiser must be an interpreter of behavior and outcomes, then a MSS or a well-anchored graphic scale is best suited. There is also some evidence that a BARS is a better means of providing feedback to instructors on their teaching (Hom, DeNisi, Kinicki, & Bannister, 1982), but there are too few data at this time to justify a strong conclusion.

## OTHER ATTEMPTS TO IMPROVE RATINGS

The type of scale used in performance appraisal is important, but more must be done to improve the rating process than to provide a good scale. Raters may need to be involved in the development of scales and may need training in how to accurately evaluate performance.

**Participation in the Development of the Measure**   It may be that the scale itself is not as important as the process followed in its development. Some evidence of this was provided by Friedman and Cornelius (1976) in a study in which Air Force ROTC students at a large university were assigned randomly to one of three conditions. In one condition they participated in the construction of a BARS to be used in rating their instructors following the steps described earlier for the construction of a BARS. A second group participated in the development of a graphic rating scale. A third group used a graphic scale but did not participate in its development. Subjects in all three groups were asked to rate their instructors. Participation in scale construction, apart from the type of scale, was found to reduce rating effects. The most reduction was found for the scale that was constructed with direct student involvement.

**Training Raters**   Training aimed at reducing rating effects can reduce halo, leniency, and other rating effects (Bernardin & Buckley, 1981; Spool, 1978; Smith, 1986). Unfortunately, eliminating these rating effects does not guarantee increased accuracy. Training to reduce rating effects can, in fact, reduce accuracy of rating by replacing one effect with another (Bernardin & Buckley, 1981). For instance, if raters are instructed to avoid leniency and, in response, they become very severe in their ratings, then the training might increase, not reduce, rating error. Bernardin and Buckley (1981) recommend three types of training to replace the traditional focus on changing rating sets. First, training should focus on increasing the accuracy of the rater's observations, perhaps through having the rater keep a diary of the ratee's performance. Another recommendation is to use training to give raters a *common frame of reference* for observing and rating. A third recommendation is to give special coaching in how to cope with situations in which the evaluator must give negative evaluations. Smith (1986) concludes from his review that the best way to improve rating accuracy is to use a combination of performance standards and performance dimensions training. "Before raters are asked to observe and evaluate the performance of others, they should be allowed to discuss the performance dimensions on which they will be rating. They should also be given the opportunity to practice rating sample performance. Finally, they should be provided with 'true' or expert ratings to which they can compare their own ratings" (p. 37).

The success of any training program is likely to depend on the nature of the tasks that the ratees perform. Lee (1985) distinguished among four types of tasks and proposed the type of training needed for each. If there are valid and reliable performance appraisal measures and knowledge of how processes translate into outcomes (e.g., how assembly line workers should assemble the product), then raters should be trained to record performances and translate these observations into ratings according to whatever guidelines are set forth in the appraisal system. For instance, raters could be shown videotapes of effective and ineffective performances and given feedback on how accurately they evaluate these performances. If there is incomplete knowledge of how task behaviors lead to outcomes but there are reliable and valid measures of performance (e.g., sales positions), then more emphasis should be placed on frame-of-reference training in which raters meet as a group and reach some consensus on their standards. A third type of task involves work for which there is understanding of how task behaviors translate into task outcomes but there are few valid and reliable measures of outcomes (e.g., a bank teller). In this situation, raters should be trained to observe and keep a diary of employee performance. Finally, if the task lacks outcome measures and there is also incomplete understanding of how task behaviors translate into outcomes, then frame-of-reference training should first be used "to develop and to observe 'reliable' performance behaviors" (p. 329). Next, "raters should be trained to recall instances of the identified behaviors and to justify or attribute the relevance of the rated behaviors" (p. 329). It also may be important on tasks for which there is a lack of clear understanding of how task behaviors translate into outcomes to improve the rater's self-efficacy as a rater (Lee, 1985). In other words, raters appear to do a better job in rating if they feel confident that they can make accurate judgments.

# WHO SHOULD JUDGE PERFORMANCE?

In evaluating performance, an organization has at least four possible sources of information: supervisors, peers, self-appraisals, subordinates, and customers. Each of these sources has its own strengths and weaknesses.

## Supervisors

Not surprisingly, supervisors are the most common source of performance appraisals. Indeed, surveys indicate that the immediate supervisor is the primary evaluator in over 95% of appraisal programs in industry (Lazer & Wilkstrom, 1977) and in municipal government (Lacho, Stearns, & Villere, 1979). The use of supervisors is predictable given the hierarchical structure of the typical organization, but organizations are experimenting with other potential sources of evaluations including peers, subordinates, the employees themselves, and customers. An example is the Powertrain division of General Motor's "big car" group which uses input from subordinates and peers as well as supervisors to evaluate employee contributions to the firm (Gabor, 1992). Let us examine the evidence on these other, less traditional sources of information and how they might compare with supervisor appraisals.

## Peers

Most organizations have been reluctant to use peer ratings. One fear is that peers will be overly lenient, but the evidence is mixed, with some studies showing that peers are more lenient than supervisors (Schneier, 1977; Zedeck, Imparto, Krausz, & Oleno, 1974) and other studies showing no difference in this regard (Holzbach, 1978; Klimoski & London, 1974). Another fear is that a peer evaluation system may evoke competition and distrust among coworkers (DeNisi, Randolph, & Blencoe, 1983). This seems especially likely when peers do not trust each other and perform their tasks under a competitive reward system (Brief, 1980).

Although there is a case to be made against peer ratings, the evidence seems clear that peer evaluations (especially peer nominations) can be reliable and valid predictors of future performance (Kane & Lawler, 1978; 1980). These findings are not surprising because peers often have the opportunity to observe first hand the performances of their fellow employees. Moreover, peer evaluations agree substantially with those of supervisors, with one survey finding a correlation of .62 (Harris & Schaubroeck, 1988). As organizations move away from the traditional hierarchical approaches to management and increasingly use teams (Chapter 5), peer evaluations are likely to be used even more. An example is Digital Equipment Corporation in Colorado Springs, Colorado, which has attempted to encourage employee involvement and participation as key elements of its corporate culture. Consistent with this culture, they have implemented an appraisal system in which team members evaluate each others' performance (Norman & Zawacki, 1991).

## Self-Appraisals

Another option is to ask employees to evaluate their own performances. Self-appraisals tend to show somewhat less halo than either peer or supervisor ratings. A person rating his or her own performance is probably more knowledgeable and complex in distinguishing levels of performance on different dimensions than external observers, but the downside of self-appraisals is that they are more lenient than either peer or supervisory ratings (Beatty, Schneier, & Beatty, 1977). Also, the employee's ratings of his or her own performance do not appear to agree very well with either supervisor ratings ($r$ = .35) or peer ratings ($r$ = .36) (Harris & Schaubroeck, 1988). By leading the employee to believe that self-appraisals will be scrutinized for accuracy, it is possible to reduce leniency (Farh & Werbel, 1986). Nevertheless, the primary value of self-appraisals in most organizations will not be to replace other sources of evaluations but to stimulate reflection and to start a dialogue between the supervisor and subordinate (Campbell & Lee, 1988).

## Subordinates

A few organizations such as IBM, Ford, and RCA (Bernardin & Beatty, 1984) have used subordinates to evaluate managers, but this is probably the least used of all the sources. Perhaps the most extensive use of this source is by universities in the form of student ratings of instructors. A major concern with this approach is that people in subordinate positions may be influenced in their evaluations by the evaluation that they expect to receive from the supervisor. The research on teacher evaluations, however, suggests that student ratings of teachers are only weakly related to the expected grade (Feldman, 1976; Howard & Maxwell, 1980, 1982). On the basis of research in business organizations, Mount (1984) concluded that subordinates are a better source for some dimensions than for others. Subordinates were in the best position to evaluate "delegation" and "work direction" because they were able to directly observe performance in these areas. On the other hand, dimensions such as "know-how," "administration," and "innovation" were better evaluated by the supervisor since they were directly observable and the supervisor had the expertise to evaluate them.

## Customers

With an increasingly service-oriented economy, organizations are likely to make more use of client and customer opinions. Indeed, some consulting firms specialize in monitoring services rendered in restaurants and other customer-intensive industries. The authors know of a phone company that randomly calls customers to check on their satisfaction with the services provided by the firm. These data are used to evaluate the employees who are responsible for providing service to customers. Unfortunately, there is little research on customers as a source of performance appraisals. One possibility is that customers are less tolerant of extenuating circumstances than are peers, subordinates, or supervisors. If this is the case, their ratings may be much less lenient and more discriminating than ratings by other sources. This hypothesis will need to be tested in future research.

# PROCESSES INVOLVED IN PERFORMANCE RATING

The discussion so far has had a decidedly practical slant. Improving judgmental appraisals will require, however, a better understanding of why people form the appraisals they do. To understand the dynamics involved, I/O psychologists in recent years have developed theories of the appraisal process. The model presented by DeNisi, Cafferty, and Meglino (1984) in Figure 9.8 specifies six essential steps involved in performance appraisals (DeNisi, Cafferty, & Meglino, 1984, p. 362):

1. Observation of the behavior by a rater.
2. Formation of some cognitive representation of the behavior by a rater.
3. Storage of this representation in memory.
4. Retrieval of the stored information needed for a formal evaluation.
5. Reconsideration and integration of the retrieved information with other items of information available.
6. Assignment of a formal evaluation to a ratee using a suitable rating instrument.

## Cognitive Processes in Ratings

Throughout the process depicted in Figure 9.8, raters attempt to reduce the information on ratees to make the information more meaningful and manageable. There are three subsystems involved in the processing of all types of information, including performance information (Chapter 12). First, auditory and visual information is held for a few seconds in the *sensory store.* This information is lost unless it passes through the second subsystem, the *short-term* or *working memory,* where information is encoded and stored. This process includes the pre-encoder, memory bins, and the causal attributions presented in Figure 9.8. Finally, some information is entered into the *long-term memory* of the individual and is permanently retained. Guiding the process in which information is encoded and stored are the cognitive structures of the rater in the form of cognitive categories and schemas. We dis-

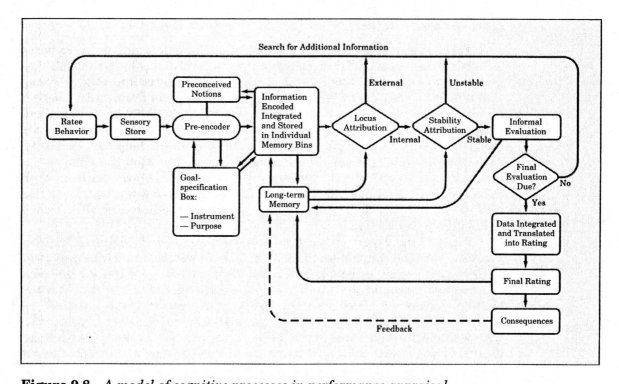

**Figure 9.8**   *A model of cognitive processes in performance appraisal*

*Source:* DeNisi, A. S., Cafferty, T. P., & Meglino, B. M. (1984). A cognitive view of the performance appraisal process: A model and research propositions. *Organizational Behavior and Human Performance, 33,* 360–396.

cussed these concepts in Chapter 6 in the context of leadership. Let us examine them again before applying them to the performance appraisal context.

*Cognitive categories* refer to a collection of things, entities, or people that are considered to be equivalent. Once a person is labeled as belonging to a category of people (e.g., labeled as a typical salesperson), there is a tendency to view that individual as sharing all the other characteristics possessed by members of that category (e.g., the person is just like other salespeople: outgoing, aggressive, brash). The process of categorization is guided by another form of cognitive structure, the *schema,* which can be defined as a set of perceived relationships among beliefs or ideas. An important type of schema is the *implicit personality theory,* which is a belief about how a set of personal traits are interrelated (e.g., the belief that people who are intelligent are also cold and aloof). A rater might first label an individual on the basis of category membership (e.g., a typical lazy worker), and then schemata relating that label to other attributes lead to an inference of other characteristics (e.g., a lazy worker is also unreliable, dishonest, unintelligent). Cognitive structures can influence the encoding, integration, storage, causal attributions, recall, and evaluations of those conducting performance appraisals. We now give these separate cognitive processes a closer examination.

## THE ENCODING, INTEGRATION, AND STORAGE OF RATEE BEHAVIOR

There is a huge amount of raw data that can potentially serve as bases for evaluations in even the simplest of jobs. Appraisers cannot remember or make sense of all the information that could possibly enter into an evaluation. Encoding is the process by which the observer interprets the raw data once it leaves the sensory store in Figure 9.8. A supervisor is likely to observe thousands of acts on the part of a subordinate, such as standing around the water cooler, working late at night, joking with fellow workers, helping a customer. From the raw data, the supervisor develops an idea of what the employee is like. This idea is called a *mental representation* and can exist in more than one form, such as a general impression (Fred is a lousy worker), a specific trait (Fred is lazy), or a visual image (a mental picture of Fred lounging around the water cooler).

An essential aspect of encoding is *cognitive categorization,* in which the appraiser assigns the employee to collections of people whom the appraiser believes are similar to the ratee. A rater might categorize a specific behavior (e.g., lounging around the water cooler is categorized as a lazy behavior) or the total person (e.g., Fred is categorized as a lazy person). Once an employee is categorized, the rater tends to see the ratee as sharing many of the attributes of members of the category. A male manager might believe, for example, that the typical "old" person is overly conservative, moody, and dull. On the basis of a single bit of evidence such as gray hair, a manager lumps an employee into the general category of "old person." The employee is consequently labeled an "old person" and all sorts of characteristics believed possessed by "old people" are then attributed to this employee.

The mental representations of a ratee are integrated and then stored in memory. When the time comes to evaluate the ratee using formal appraisal procedures, these mental representations are recalled in judging the ratee's performance. One implication is that the processing of information is inherently inaccurate in that no human rater can possibly take into account all the actions of a ratee. A key to improving the appraisal process is to use procedures that force the rater to attend to specific behaviors rather than general categories and that encourage a more deliberate and thoughtful processing of information. This is exactly the objective of several of the rating procedures we have discussed in this chapter.

## CAUSAL ATTRIBUTIONS

In encoding information, raters eventually must ask why an employee shows a particular level of performance. Why does Fred lounge around the water cooler? Why did he do so poorly on that last project? Why was he late to work last Monday? Attribution is the process by which appraisers attempt to dig into underlying causes. At one level, the rater determines whether the behavior or outcome of the behavior was caused by the person (internal locus) or something outside the person (external locus). At another level, the rater determines whether what happened is the consequence of some stable personality characteristic and whether the situation is likely to be repeated (e.g., Fred is a lazy person and is likely to remain lazy), or some unstable, temporary factor (e.g., Fred was just having a bad day). A general tendency is to assign more responsibility to the person than is warranted by failing to recognize the importance of the situation (Ross, 1977). If an employee has an accident on the job, for example, the supervisor might ask what the employee did wrong without paying careful attention to the workplace as a possible cause of the accident.

One solution is to train raters to acknowledge situational factors. Another solution is suggested by evidence that raters with task experience are more likely to take into account situational factors than inexperienced raters (Mitchell & Kalb, 1982). Thus, it may be wise to use raters who have prior task experience and who can understand the situational factors that can influence performance. Perhaps the best alternative is to encourage evaluators to approach performance appraisal as a problem-solving process rather than as a foregone conclusion. Later in this chapter we discuss Maier's notions of the problem-solving approach to conveying performance feedback.

## INFORMATION GATHERING

A crucial determinant of the quality of a performance appraisal is the rater's search for additional information. DeNisi et al. (1984) propose that there is a general tendency for raters to search for incidents of performance that they can attribute to internal, stable causes. To the extent that they uncover incidents that are attributable to external or unstable causes, raters continue to search for information. The way this search proceeds depends to a large extent on the raters' preconceived notions. Some research suggests that raters tend to look for information that confirms their prior opinions of the ratee. If Fred's supervisor already has formed a negative opinion of his performance, then he may tend to look only for additional negative information. If the supervisor has a more positive impression, however, he may focus on positive information to the neglect of negative information. The consequence can be a self-fulfilling prophecy in which the supervisor's treatment of the subordinate encourages the expected behavior (Feldman, 1986a). (See Chapter 6 on self-fulfilling prophecies in leadership.) For example, supervisors who suspect that subordinates are lazy, untrustworthy souls may supervise them closely. The unintended consequence, however, is that subordinates who are treated like children may eventually act like children.

## RECALL

Ideally, for the final, formal evaluation of performance, the rater recalls all the important items of information about the ratee observed since the last appraisal. The actual process deviates from this ideal, however. As shown in Figure 9.8, the rater continually makes informal evaluations of the ratee's performance. According to DeNisi et al. (1984), there is a tendency to recall the evaluations and not the specific information associated with them. Thus,

Fred's supervisor may see him standing around the water cooler one day and might label this behavior "lazy." Later the act of standing around the water cooler may be forgotten, but the impression of Fred as lazy is remembered. As time passes, the tendency to recall the label and not the behaviors associated with the label becomes even more pronounced.

An obvious solution is to require more frequent performance appraisals to reduce the delay between the performance and its appraisal. Not surprisingly, appraisals conducted soon after the performance are more accurate than when they are delayed (Heneman & Wexley, 1983; Rush et al., 1981; Murphy, Gannett, Herr, & Chen, 1986). Another solution to the memory loss in appraisals is to have supervisors keep a running record of the ratee's behavior. In an experiment demonstrating the effectiveness of this procedure, Bernardin and Walter (1977) had one group of students in a general psychology class keep an observational diary by recording critical incidents of teacher behavior related to each of the dimensions on which they were to evaluate the teacher. The group that was trained in the use of the scale and kept a diary tended to be less lenient, more reliable, and less prone to halo than the untrained students who did not keep a diary. Findings such as these leave little doubt that keeping a diary would improve the accuracy of ratings. Still, this approach may be impractical because of the reluctance of the typical, busy manager to take the time to record observations.

## DATA INTEGRATION AND FINAL EVALUATION

At some point in the process the rater combines the information recalled on the ratee and forms a final evaluation of the ratee's performance. The hope is that raters rationally take each item of information, attach some weight to the item, and then combine these various components in an algebraic fashion. This process is often short-circuited, however, as raters form judgments and then recall and integrate information in a manner that is consistent with the conclusion. A solution may be to require a rating of specific performance dimensions prior to, or instead of, forming an overall judgment of the performance. With many of the rating procedures discussed in this chapter, such as the BARS and BOS, the overall evaluation is formed by averaging or summing the ratings on individual dimensions.

## THE COGNITIVE STRUCTURES OF RATERS

Raters differ in the cognitive structures (i.e., the cognitive categories and schemas) that they bring to the appraisal of performance. A basis on which to distinguish among raters is in the complexity of these structures. For instance, one rater may possess a very elaborate and detailed set of beliefs about successful performance, whereas another might have a much cruder notion of what constitutes successful performance. Schneier (1977) suggests in his *cognitive compatibility theory* that appraisal systems need to be matched to the complexity of the rater. Specifically, he predicts that a complex performance appraisal format, such as a BARS, is more effective if the rater has a high degree of cognitive complexity than if the rater has a low level of cognitive complexity. Although an initial study supported his theory (Schneier, 1977), little support has been found in subsequent research (Borman, 1979b; Lahey & Saal, 1981; Sauser & Pond, 1981; Bernardin & Boetcher, 1978; Bernardin, Cardy, & Carlyle, 1982). An exception is a study by Cardy and Kehoe (1984), in which it was found that those who were complex in their processing of information achieved greater accuracy in their performance appraisals than those who were holistic in their information processing.

Differences in cognitive structures can provide an explanation for why more experienced raters have been found in some studies to provide better ratings (Jurgenson, 1950; Cascio & Valenzi, 1977). Kozlowski, Kirsch, and Chao (1986) found that fans who lacked knowledge about baseball or specific baseball players relied more on their conceptual schemata of baseball performance and less on the actual performance of the players. The result was that the least halo in ratings of baseball players was found for those who were knowledgeable about baseball and the players, whereas the most halo was found for those low in both types of knowledge.

## Organizational Determinants of the Rating Process

As the process model in Figure 9.8 shows, performance ratings depend on more than the cognitive processes of the rater. A variety of factors external to the rater and ratee influence the ratings assigned to ratees and the effectiveness of the process.

### PURPOSE OF THE RATING

Appraisals are conducted for a variety of reasons (Cleveland, Murphy, & Williams, 1989). The specific purpose as perceived by the rater can have a major impact on the outcome of the appraisal, as the "goal-specification box" in Figure 9.8 shows. A common finding is that ratings gathered for experimental purposes (e.g., test validation, training) are less lenient (Taylor & Wherry, 1951; Sharon & Bartlett, 1969) and more accurate (Dobbins, Cardy, & Truxillo, 1988) than ratings that are gathered for administrative purposes (e.g., to determine pay increases, layoffs). Similarly, ratings gathered to develop and improve employees appear to differentiate more among ratees than ratings gathered to determine merit raises or to decide which employees to retain (Zedeck & Cascio, 1982).

### DIFFERENCES IN ORGANIZATIONAL CULTURE/CLIMATE

Organizations vary in the patterns of norms, roles, and values expressed in their cultures/climates (Chapter 5). The culture/climate of the organization affects the accuracy and fairness of performance appraisals. Evidence of this was reported by Zammuto, London, and Rowland (1982), who compared the bases for performance appraisals of resident advisors in university dormitories. Although the same evaluation scales were used in four halls, raters in two emphasized understanding students' problems; raters in another emphasized efficiency in planning and conducting meetings; raters in the remaining dorm gave approximately equal emphasis to understanding student problems and availability for advising students.

An organizational culture/climate can also support or discourage discrimination in appraisals against employees on the basis of race, age, sex, and other factors. In other words, supervisors may tend to rate some employees down because others in the organization expect them to give lower evaluations to these employees. Lawrence (1988) found some evidence of this in a study of age bias. Managers in an electric utility were asked to estimate the typical age of employees at a particular level of the organization and to indicate the age range at each level. Using these data, the managers were grouped into those whose careers were ahead of schedule, on schedule, and behind schedule relative to the typical age of those at the employee's level. The managers who were perceived as young for their position (so-called fast trackers or water walkers) were evaluated more positively than those who were seen as older relative to the normative age at their level. Similar norms may account for bias against women, blacks, and other groups. The implication is that eliminating bias may require changing the norms of the organization through active interventions (Chapter 5).

Among the most important elements of culture/climate are the beliefs of employees that they can trust management to act fairly and competently. Lawler (1971) suggested that if there is a lack of trust in management, an organization should not even attempt to use formal performance appraisal unless highly objective performance data can be used. Kane and Lawler (1979) further suggested that performance appraisal systems are more effective in improving performance when tasks and goals are clear than when they are ambiguous.

## ACCOUNTABILITY OF THE RATER FOR THE APPRAISAL

A major factor in the accuracy of performance appraisals is the extent to which the organization requires appraisers to justify their decisions and judgments. A possible means of increasing accountability of supervisors for their appraisals is to set up a review panel to oversee the performance appraisal system and give feedback to managers on their implementation of appraisals (Bernardin, 1986).

Social psychological research suggests that accountability leads to greater vigilance in the monitoring of performance, more complex judgment and decision strategies, greater self-awareness of cognitive processes, and more data-driven processing of evidence (Tetlock, 1985). Although holding evaluators accountable has some obvious benefits, a high degree of accountability can lead to bad judgments. For instance, one study found that age bias was greater when the evaluators believed that they would have to convey their ratings to experts (Gordon, Rozelle, & Baxter, 1988). In this case, evaluators appeared to comply with what they believed were the expectations of the experts that low ratings be given to older employees. According to the authors, accountability can lead to an information overload and the reliance on stereotypes to deal with this overload. These findings clearly demonstrate that improvements in performance appraisal require that the person to whom the evaluator is accountable values accuracy and fairness.

## POLITICS OF THE ORGANIZATION

We have assumed that appraisals represent a sincere attempt to come up with an accurate assessment of how well an employee is doing. Anyone who has seen performance appraisals as they are actually conducted in the organization knows that appraisals can serve as political tactics that are used to win or maintain power relative to others in the organization. Disturbing evidence of this was provided in a study conducted with 60 upper level executives (Longenecker, Sims, & Gioia, 1987). A surprising number of these respondents admitted that they deliberately manipulated formal appraisals for political purposes. Executives indicated that organizational politics were almost always a factor. A surprising number of respondents indicated that they intentionally inflated appraisals (1) to maximize the merit increases that could be given to a subordinate, (2) to protect or encourage an employee whose performance was suffering because of personal problems, (3) to avoid hanging out dirty laundry, (4) to avoid creating a written record of poor performance, (5) to avoid a confrontation, (6) to give a break to a subordinate who had improved, and (7) to justify promotion and thereby rid themselves of a poorly performing subordinate. Poor appraisals were not frequent but were sometimes given to shock a subordinate, teach rebels a lesson, send a message that a subordinate should consider leaving, and to build a case against a subordinate. Whether managers approach the appraisal process as a game to be played or as an important task to be performed well is likely to depend on the attitude of top management. If higher management takes appraisal seriously, the lower levels of management seem much more likely to do the same.

## Summary

The early research on performance appraisal was directed at finding a scale or procedure that worked and was not concerned with why it might or might not work. It is becoming increasingly clear, however, that improvements in performance appraisal will require a better understanding of the psychological processes involved. At the heart of performance appraisal is information processing. The rater observes, encodes, interprets, stores, and later recalls information on the performance of the ratee. This information is then integrated in some fashion to form a judgment of performance. Another way of expressing the process depicted in Figure 9.8 is that valid appraisals are likely to follow the dictums of good science (Chapter 2). The essence of good science is that in testing hypotheses investigators are data driven, meaning that they rigorously gather information and then base final decisions on an objective analysis of these data. In contrast to good scientific practice, however, the appraisal of performance is often theory driven, meaning that the raters' ideas about what constitutes a good performance and their views of specific ratees bias data gathering and analysis. In addition to the rater's cognitive processing, appraisals are influenced by organizational factors in the form of the purpose of the appraisal, the norms of the organization or the subunit, organizational politics, and the extent to which raters are held accountable for the quality of their ratings.

# FEEDBACK OF PERFORMANCE APPRAISAL

In some cases appraisals are used solely as criteria in the validation of tests or for some other research purpose and are not communicated to the person appraised. If they are used to develop the employee and to improve his or her performance, however, they must be communicated. Few other actions have as much potential for positive change. The management of the Universal Card division of AT&T attributes much of its success to its feedback system (Rowland, 1992). The quality of customer service is measured daily on 150 measures and then communicated to employees on color monitors. Testimonials such as this are consistent with the research on feedback. One review of this literature found that objective feedback usually worked, with 87% of the laboratory studies and 100% of the field studies showing performance improved when people received feedback (Kopelman, 1986). Feedback has both an informational and motivational function (Chapter 10). In the former case, feedback can inform the recipient of what works and doesn't work and can possibly allow the recipient to develop a cognitive model of the task. In the latter case, feedback can increase the motivation of the recipient through reinforcing correct behaviors and punishing wrong behaviors, satisfying psychological needs (e.g., needs for recognition and self-esteem), increasing expectancies that effort will pay off, and encouraging goal setting (Chapter 3). Despite the consistent support for the effectiveness of feedback, it is important to note that most of this evidence comes from research involving simple tasks. In the complex tasks that people often perform in organizations, feedback still can be beneficial but also has great potential for harm (Becker & Klimoski, 1989). One example is feedback in the form of destructive criticism which survey results show to be among the most important causes of conflict in organizations (Baron, 1988). To understand the factors determining whether feedback succeeds or fails we need to examine feedback as a process that starts with the source who communicates information in some form and the recipient who seeks or avoids feedback. Once feedback is communicated, attention shifts to the recipient's processing of the information on performance and the response to the feedback.

## Feedback Giving and Seeking

For feedback to have any benefits, those evaluating performance must be willing to give the feedback in an undistorted form. The problem is that supervisors are generally reluctant to give feedback. They do not like playing God. They wish to avoid arguments with those whom they evaluate. They may fear lowering the self-esteem of those who are performing poorly or giving a false sense of confidence to those who are performing well. When they must give feedback, supervisors appear more likely to respond to negative performance than to positive performance (Feild & Holley, 1977; Fisher, 1979). This feedback may be so distorted, however, that recipients fail to see it as negative (Benedict & Levine, 1988; Feild & Holley, 1977; Fisher, 1979). There may be a tendency for supervisors to give feedback that they think the recipients want to hear. Klimoski and Inks (1990) demonstrated this in a laboratory experiment in which they had students in the role of supervisor provide face-to-face feedback, written feedback, or no feedback to a fictitious worker on the basis of that worker's performance on a clerical task. The worker's self-perceived performance was described as either high or low for some of the subjects, while others were given no information on the worker's self-perceived performance. Subjects who anticipated giving face-to-face feedback were more likely to conform to the worker's self-assessment in their feedback than those giving anonymous or no feedback.

Just as feedback giving often fails, feedback *seeking* is also less than ideal in many situations. Ashford and Cummings (1983) proposed that there are two strategies for seeking feedback. People may *monitor* their own performance or they may directly *inquire* how they are doing from others. Because directly asking others for feedback has greater potential for threatening self-esteem, it is less likely to be used than monitoring. Larson (1989) proposed that when individuals believe they have performed poorly, they tend to seek feedback in a way that minimizes negative feedback from others. Underlying these strategies is the "deep-seated motivation to maintain a positive self-esteem" (p. 408).

The employee's natural tendency to seek positive feedback and the supervisor's natural discomfort with giving negative feedback can lead to a conspiracy (Larson, 1989). The employee attempts to avoid negative feedback, and in response to these attempts the supervisor softens the feedback so that it does not seem as negative. Supervisor and employee may never confront performance problems, although both may recognize that problems exist. It seems doubtful, however, that this can go on forever. More than one employee has been abruptly dismissed after a crisis finally brings performance deficiencies to the attention of those above the immediate supervisor. A much more satisfying situation for an organization and its employees occurs when employees feel free both to give and seek feedback.

## Processing of Feedback

Once feedback is communicated, the next crucial question is how recipients process the information and respond to it. Ilgen, Fisher, and Taylor (1979) conceptualized the feedback process as a three-part communication process similar to that described in Chapter 5 (Figure 9.9). The first issue is whether the recipient accurately perceives the message. The next issue is whether the feedback is accepted. The final issue is whether the recipient desires to comply with the feedback. Conceived in these terms, there are numerous opportunities for feedback to succeed or fail. Take, for example, the response to negative feedback. You could view these various steps as alternative lines of defense. First, employees may see their performance as more favorable than it really is, a distortion that is more apt to occur when the feedback is ambiguous than when it is specific and clear. If the feedback is unequivocally negative and cannot be distorted, then they may tend to deny responsibility. They may attribute the performance to extenuating circum-

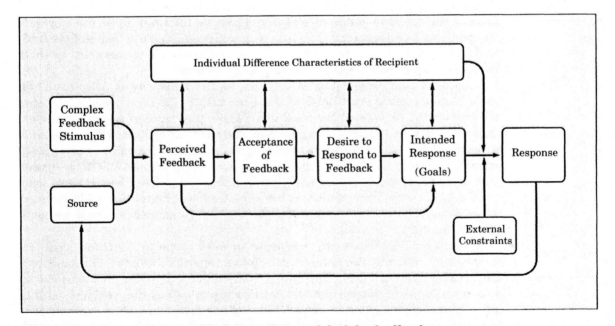

**Figure 9.9** *Ilgen, Fisher & Taylor's (1979) model of the feedback process*

Source: Ilgen, D. I., Fisher, C. D., & Taylor, M. S. (1979). Consequences of individual feedback on behavior in organizations. *Journal of Applied Psychology, 64,* 349–371.

stances or the unfairness of the source of appraisal. Once employees accept responsibility for the failure, they might devalue the importance of achieving the performance goals that they failed to achieve. Assuming the source of the negative feedback can break through all these lines of defense, the person may finally set a goal to improve the deficiencies. How well he or she actually improves performance depends on external constraints such as coworkers, tools, and work environment.

Ilgen et al. proposed that the characteristics of the message and the characteristics of the recipient should determine whether feedback is accurately perceived and accepted. The accuracy with which recipients perceive feedback should increase as the psychological distance between the source and the recipient decreases. Thus, people should be more likely to accept feedback from themselves than from supervisors or coworkers (Herold & Greller, 1977; Herold & Parsons, 1985; Greller, 1980; Greller & Herold, 1975). Feedback from sources having credibility and power also should be more acceptable. Immediate, positive, and frequent feedback should be perceived more accurately than delayed, negative, and infrequent feedback. The most powerful message characteristic is the sign (positive or negative) of the feedback. Not surprisingly, positive feedback is accepted more than negative feedback (Stone, Gueutal, & McIntosh, 1984).

Employees may accurately perceive feedback and accept it as valid, but the feedback still may not influence their intentions or goals. The next step in the process is the desire to respond. Recipients should be most willing to respond when the feedback conveys information that they are competent and in control of the task. The key to providing negative feedback, then, is to do so in a manner that maintains the self-esteem of the recipient.

## Feedback in the Formal Appraisal Session

Most organizations try to ensure that subordinates receive feedback from their supervisors by requiring supervisors to hold an annual appraisal session in which they are to share the appraisal with subordinates and inform them of salary increases. Herb Meyer and his associates documented some of the problems of this type of appraisal session in a series of studies at General Electric (Meyer, Kay, & French, 1965). Ninety-two appraisal sessions with a variety of salaried employees were observed. The typical session was 30–90 minutes long and covered 32 performance items. In the average session, praise was given on 19 items and criticisms were conveyed on 13. Praise tended to be general, whereas criticisms tended to be much more specific. According to Meyer et al., there were few constructive responses to criticism, with the average number observed being less than one per interview. Employees tended to view their own performance very positively prior to the sessions and subsequently tended to see their manager's evaluation as being less positive than their self-appraisal. The more criticisms employees received, the lower they performed 10–12 weeks later. Meyer concluded that the traditional comprehensive annual performance appraisal does more harm than good. Praise appeared to have little effect, whereas criticism appeared to lessen future performance, especially for those with low self-esteem.

In light of all the dysfunctional consequences observed by Meyer, how can feedback sessions be conducted so that the problems are avoided? Meyer advised a *split role appraisal system* in which one set of appraisal procedures is used for the purpose of developing employees and another set of procedures is used for wage and salary administration. The developmental appraisal would be characterized by goal setting and frequent feedback. The other system would be quantitative and possess more of the characteristics of the traditional appraisal. Although many organizations have adopted some variety of the split-role appraisal, research has not provided much support for this approach. There is reason to question whether employees can ever *not* think of the possible implications of feedback for salary, even if salary discussions are put off until other meetings (Ilgen & Feldman, 1983). Also, contrary to Meyer's findings, there is evidence that developing employees in an appraisal session is not necessarily incompatible with discussing salary (Prince & Lawler, 1986; Dorfman et al., 1986).

So what can be done to improve the appraisal feedback session? Maier (1958) distinguished three styles of conducting appraisal sessions. In the *tell and sell approach* a supervisor starts by telling the employees just where they stand and then proceeds to sell the employees on the accuracy of the appraisal. While this method may be appropriate with new hires or with experienced employees who are used to such directive methods (Latham & Wexley, 1981, p. 152), it can degenerate quickly. Much depends on the existing relationship of the manager and the subordinate and the manager's persuasive skills. An alternative is *tell and listen.* Here the manager conveys the appraisal and then listens with understanding to the appraisee's thoughts and feelings. The success of this style depends on the ability of the manager to counsel and advise. The best method, according to Maier, is what he calls the *problem-solving* interview. The manager starts by recognizing areas of performance in which the employee has done well and then asks if there are areas in which the manager could provide assistance. Hopefully, the employee will mention some relevant problem areas and the discussion can then focus on potential solutions.While discussing the problems, the manager avoids talking too much and instead carefully listens to the appraisee. The problem-solving appraisal ends with specific goals set for future improvements in performance.

Past research supports the effectiveness of several aspects of Maier's problem-solving approach to giving feedback. Attitudes toward appraisal sessions appear more favorable if the appraisal is aimed more at *goal accomplishment* than traits of the ratee (McConkie, 1979). Another element of successful appraisal sessions is *participation*. Individuals who believe that they have the opportunity to present their ideas or feelings and who believe that the supervisor actively sought their views are more accepting of appraisals than those who are not allowed to participate (Bassett & Meyer, 1968; Burke, Weitzel, & Weir, 1978; Burke & Wilcox, 1969; Dipboye & dePontbriand, 1981; Greller, 1975; Landy, Barnes, & Murphy, 1978). Also, feedback that consists of constructive criticism and praise is better received and more likely to benefit performance than destructive criticism (Baron, 1988; 1990).

While the problem-solving approach makes sense, it requires the most interpersonal skill of all the feedback styles to successfully implement and presumes that the supervisor is open to suggestions. If the recipient believes that the supervisor already has reached a conclusion and is using participation as a manipulative technique, the whole attempt could backfire. Moreover, problem-solving appraisals seem unlikely to have much of an effect on performance if they occur only once a year in the formal appraisal session (Dorfman, Stephan, & Loveland, 1986). One of the best ways to improve formal appraisals is to increase the *frequency* with which they occur (Landy, Barnes, & Murphy, 1978). Much can happen in one year, and it is probably unrealistic to expect to cover all aspects of the employee's performance in a single half-hour session.

# A FINAL SUMMATION AND A LOOK AT THE FUTURE

As useful as performance appraisals are, you have seen how they often fail in their implementation because of inherent conflicts in the appraisal process. Supervisors often do not relish the thought of evaluating employees, and employees certainly do not look forward to being appraised. To succeed, measures of performance are needed that are relevant to the work, reliable, and practical. A variety of options exist; which is chosen depends on the objectives of the appraisal system. Appraisals can focus on the traits of the employee, behaviors exhibited in performing the work, and outcomes achieved. The various aspects of performance can be measured through either objective or subjective procedures, although practical concerns have led to a reliance in most organizations on supervisory judgments. If subjective measures are used, these can be either direct (graphic scales, BARS, MSS), indirect (weighted checklist, forced choice), or comparative (ranking, paired comparison, forced distribution). The judgments can be made by supervisors, peers, subordinates, and customers. Given the variety of approaches that can be taken in measuring performance, organizations would be well advised to use a diversity of techniques and to draw from a variety of sources. The correct combination of sources and techniques depends on the demands of the situation.

In recent years, researchers' attention has turned from a search for the best rating scale to understanding the processes underlying accurate appraisal. Raters possess cognitive structures that guide their observation, encoding, interpretation, retrieval, and integration of information and the final judgment of performance. For example, raters tend to assign ratees to categories of employees on the basis of their similarity to some stereotype (e.g., the typical good employee, the typical bad employee) and this categorization can bias subsequent information processing. Although the attempt to simplify through categorization and other cognitive shortcuts can never be entirely eliminated, appraisal systems should encourage the rater to emphasize the facts available on the employee's performance and to rely less on the prior beliefs about the way things should be or might be.

In discussing the cognitive factors involved in the rating process it is easy to think of appraisal as limited to what goes on between rater and ratee. But the effectiveness of appraisal systems also depends on organizational factors. A good appraisal system requires effective leadership, motivation, and teamwork and must become a natural part of the culture of the organization. Becoming a part of the culture requires that higher level management supports the system and that supervisors are held accountable for the quality of their ratings. It also requires that the appraisal system fits the nature of the technology.

An effective appraisal system and an effective feedback system go hand-in-hand. Improving feedback skills and implementing feedback systems presume (perhaps incorrectly) that the original appraisals are accurate. Likewise, sound measures of performance are of little use in developing employees unless the information contained in these measures is received, accepted, and acted on by the employee. Research generally suggests that feedback discussions are more beneficial if they are participative, goal-oriented, and supportive rather than tell and sell lectures. Although it is common for organizations to conduct appraisal sessions only once a year, it is unlikely that any style of feedback will be effective if it occurs this infrequently.

Performance appraisals have played an important role in the management of work in organizations, and changes currently underway in the workplace suggest that this role will only grow in importance. There are two trends, however, that are pushing performance appraisal in somewhat different directions. One trend is toward increasing formality and accountability in appraisals. As organizations attempt to succeed in an increasingly competitive world, it has become more important to measure the performance of employees so that their successes can be rewarded and their deficiencies corrected. Civil rights legislation, such as the Americans with Disabilities Act and the Civil Rights Act of 1991, will impose even heavier demands on organizations to document the rationale behind important decisions such as the firing, transfer, or promotion of employees. Somewhat inconsistent with the pressures on organizations to bureaucratize their appraisal procedures is the movement toward team-based organizational structures and worker participation. These trends will require appraisal procedures that are conducive to the development of individual employees and the building of effective teams (Chapter 5). The development of performance appraisal systems that can fulfill these two competing needs is a crucial issue that will require the attention of I/O psychologists in the future.

## DISCUSSION QUESTIONS

1. Why are most performance appraisal measures judgmental rather than objective?

2. What are advantages and disadvantages of evaluating traits, process, and outcomes?

3. If you were to develop a performance appraisal instrument to measure the teacher performance of college instructors, what approach would you use? Why? Describe the steps you would take in the development of the instrument.

4. Why is job analysis so crucial to the development of performance appraisal measures?

5. Describe the various rating effects that can enter into rating procedures.

6. In what circumstances do you believe comparative judgments would be most appropriate? Why?

7. What are the implications of the culture/climate of an organization (Chapter 5) for who should judge performance and the method of appraisal that should be used?

8. Describe how each of the rating effects could result from either the rater's cognitive processes or organizational factors.

9. Is it realistic to conduct performance appraisals according to a split-role model? Why?

10. What are the implications of the various rating methods and appraisal sources for how to give appraisal feedback?

11. The suggestion has been made that if there is no trust between employees and management, then an organization should not even use formal performance appraisals. What do you think?

## TEACHER EVALUATION IN TEXAS

In the early 1980s a presidential commission published *A Nation at Risk* (National Commission on Excellence in Education, 1983), a report that brought attention to the many problems plaguing United States schools, including illiteracy, an alarmingly high drop-out rate, crime, and declining test scores. This report spawned attempts to reform schools across many of the 50 states. An important part of these reforms has been the development of procedures for evaluating teacher performance in the classroom. The teacher evaluation system used in Texas elementary and secondary schools is typical of the new teacher appraisal systems that have been introduced over the last decade.

Around the same time that *A Nation at Risk* was released, a task force headed by Texas tycoon Ross Perot was created by Governor Mark White to draft a blueprint for school reform in Texas. One of the task force's suggestions was to create a career ladder that would reward teachers who perform well with salary increases. In 1984, Texas House Bill 72 instituted a four-level career ladder for all elementary and secondary school teachers. Beginning teachers would start at level one, with promotion to the second, third, and fourth levels bringing salary increases of $1,500–$2,000. The decision to promote a teacher would depend mostly on classroom performance.

Under the system that was implemented in the mid 1980s, assessors enter the classroom to observe and evaluate teachers' performance. These evaluations are performed on 29 specific behaviors using a three-point scale: unsatisfactory, satisfactory, and exceptional. The behaviors represent the five major performance categories listed below (Texas Education Agency, 1986/87):

1. *Uses instructional time efficiently* (e.g., follows prepared lesson plans based on curriculum and objectives, focuses the students' attention at the beginning of the lesson, starts lesson immediately, uses models or illustrates what students are to learn).

2. *Motivates students successfully* (e.g., relates learning activities to student interests, offers varied learning activities, uses pleasant-sounding tone).

3. *Increases productive student behavior* (e.g., varies praise words, informs students of their progress).

4. *Demonstrates proficiency in subject area* (e.g., demonstrates sound knowledge of subject matter in lesson presentations).

5. *Demonstrates proficiencies in oral/written language* (e.g., pronounces words correctly, uses gramatically correct English)

The ratings on the 29 behaviors are performed by two assessors (typically the principal and a teacher) who visit each teacher once a year and observe for a minimum of 30 minutes that teacher's performance during a class. The teacher is forewarned of when these visits will occur. Assessors are given detailed guidelines and extensive training in the use of these guidelines. Within five days of observing the classroom performance, a conference is held in which each assessor seeks additional information and shares his or her impressions with the teacher. Afterward, each assessor makes a final rating that is made known to the teacher. Finally, the assessors meet to reach a consensus on their evaluation of the teacher on the five major categories and decide on an overall evaluation of the teacher's classroom performance. The assessment team also completes a Growth/Improvement Professional Refinement Plan in which the teacher is given suggestions as to how to improve performance on specific behaviors. Promotion of a teacher to the next rung on the career ladder requires that the teacher achieve a specific numerical evaluation on the overall assessment and then maintain this for several years.

This system of appraisal has proven to be controversial. Defenders argue that a system such as this is a means of holding teachers accountable to the public that pays their salaries. Incompetent teachers can be identified and actions taken to either correct their deficiencies or dismiss them. Moreover, an objective, rational system of appraisal will allow the best teachers to be recognized and rewarded. Rather than relying on subjective and highly politicized judgments of principals and other administrators, teachers know specifically what is required of them to qualify as excellent teachers. Another argument in favor of the system is that it can provide the basis for financial incentives to keep the most talented teachers in the teaching profession. Fairfax County schools in Virginia have used an appraisal system similar in several respects to the Texas system (Brown, 1992). The Fairfax system allowed the dismissal of over 500 teachers who were performing poorly. According to the county school board chairman, "Even with a changing demography, our SAT scores are up, minority achievement is up, dropouts are down, the rate of students going to college is up. . . . People who say it hasn't helped aren't using all the data" (p. B7). According to one teacher with 25 years experience, the merit pay "gave me back the fire . . . I really can't say in honesty that it was the money. . . . It was more simply the challenge, something to shoot for, a way to be recognized" (p. B7).

There are also many criticisms of teacher appraisal systems such as the one found in Texas. One complaint is that teachers are forced into an artificial performance on the day the assessors visit. Given that teachers have the list of 29 specific classroom behaviors that the assessors will be rating, there is always the danger that teachers will simply give the assessors what they want rather than providing a representative sample of their teaching performance. One teacher described with disgust the theatrics of one of her fellow elementary school teachers to win the approval of the assessors (authors' personal communication). These antics, which included on one occasion dressing in a clown suit, were only exhibited during the visits of the assessors. Another potential problem is divisiveness between teachers who receive recognition and promotion and those who do not. Rather than motivating the "losers" to try harder, the appraisal may only lead to feelings of inequity and favoritism. Other complaints are that the checklist does not take into account the individual attention that a teacher might give to students with special problems or variations in teacher style. According to one critic, "Uncertainty is at the heart of all real teaching. We never know exactly what to teach, how to teach, or what our students will make of our teaching" (McNeil, 1987, p. 212). Yet, the system assumes that assessors have a clear understanding of what distinguishes an effective teacher from an ineffective teacher. The system has been accused of only adding to the stress and frustration of teachers who already are faced with adverse work conditions such as low pay and lack of control. Moreover, the effectiveness of the system in tying pay to performance depends to a large extent on the commitment of taxpayers to providing the funds. The size of merit pay increases in Texas has suffered as the result of lack of funds, and recently the Fairfax schools suspended merit pay as a budget-tightening measure (Brown, 1992).

## CASE QUESTIONS

1.   What would you look for in evaluating whether the Texas system of teacher evaluation is an effective system of performance evaluation?
2.   What are the unintended consequences of an appraisal system such as this?
3.   What would you do to improve this system of appraisal?
4.   There are those who would argue that an activity such as teaching cannot be subjected to a standardized, behaviorally specific evaluation. Do you agree with this assertion? Why?

**10**

# Staffing: Attraction, Selection, and Placement

- **Staffing and the Matching Strategy**

- **Attraction and Job Search**

- **Selection**

- **Placement**

- **Selection and Placement Tools: Predictors**

- **A Final Summation and a Look at the Future**

- **Case: Selection of Firefighters in Cleveland**

Staffing is a continuing activity in every organization. People leave or retire and must be replaced; reorganization, growth, and modernization create new jobs to be filled. How well this function is carried out goes a long way toward determining the organization's level of success. Take, for example, the software company Microsoft Corporation, which has achieved phenomenal success in recent years. Much of their success may be the consequence of the huge number of people who seek employment with Microsoft and the firm's ability to select the best and the brightest of these applicants (Rebello & Schwartz, 1992). In 1991, for instance, over 120,000 people applied for employment. After face-to-face interviews with over 7,000 applicants, about 2,000 were finally employed.

For many years, I/O psychology has developed techniques to help employers make these important decisions. In fact, much of the field's popular reputation—and notoriety—stems from tools such as the selection and classification tests that are so evident in modern society. Unfortunately, the public in general and employers in particular do not understand these techniques very well. As a result, many mistakes are made in applying them, and much misdirected controversy surrounds their use. For example, some political activist groups have gone so far as to advocate the outright *banning* of all employment tests, a move that would have catastrophic implications for the American economy and society.

While the net contribution of psychological techniques to the staffing function has been positive, it could be considerably more so were the public and the primary users better informed. The purpose of this chapter, therefore, is to give you a clear understanding of the principles that underlie the development, evaluation, and proper use of techniques for making staffing decisions. These techniques usually involve the strategy of fitting people to jobs, with the goal of obtaining a good match. They do it through recruiting, selection, and assignment or placement decisions. There are, of course, other ways of achieving a good fit, notably *training* and *job redesign;* these are discussed in other chapters.

# STAFFING AND THE MATCHING STRATEGY

The first of the three main strategies for achieving a good fit between people and work assumes that neither individuals nor job requirements change very much. In contrast to *training,* which is aimed at changing people, and *job redesign,* which changes the work itself, the *matching* strategy consists of getting the best qualified people you can find for the jobs you now have and seeing to it that they are allocated properly. The assumption is that people are happiest and most productive doing what they do best, a condition that would seem to benefit everyone.

## Strategy Complications

The logic of striving for a good match rather than filling positions with whomever is handy seems almost too obvious to mention. It turns out, however, that neither the strategy nor its justification is as simple as it seems.

### THE DEFINITION PROBLEM

In the first place, it is not easy to define what a good match is or to recognize one when we see it. Suppose, for example, that employers filled all their highest paying positions with male college graduates on the premise that these applicants were best qualified for such work. Can we accept this idea of a good match without question? If not, on what basis would we challenge it? Probably we would demand some explanation of the job requirements and the qualities that they think make male college graduates so uniquely qualified. Now, suppose they answer that such people are just brighter than others, and their top jobs require the best minds they can get. Few of us would buy this explanation, and we would demand that they offer some proof. When we saw it, however, we would probably be just as unhappy with their evidence as we were with their explanation.

In short, we would discover that there is room for argument over what constitutes a good match at every level of analysis. In this chapter we explore ways of pinning the matching concept down to its most objective form, thereby leaving as little room for argument as possible. Nevertheless, it will always be subject to interpretation, and as a result, no technique can guarantee a match that everyone will consider ideal or even appropriate.

### THE FAIRNESS ISSUE

Suppose that we could agree on an approach that does fit people to jobs effectively. Moreover, suppose we could *prove* that it produces happier, more productive employees. Would this satisfy everyone? Once again, the answer is "no." In this case, the argument involves the larger impact of the strategy on society and the question of whether the strategy is *fair*. Happy and productive employees are unquestionably beneficial both to themselves and their employers, and to some extent, to society at large. But what about the people who lose out in the matching process, especially if they are little, if any, less qualified than the others? More importantly, what if those people are disproportionately women, ethnic minorities, older people, or some other group that has been discriminated against in the past? Certainly *they* are not happier and more productive than they would have been had they been hired, and if they remain unemployed or underemployed in large numbers, one could argue that society is not better off either.

Thus the issue boils down to who benefits how much from the attempt to achieve a good person-job match, and who suffers how much as a result. In other words, it becomes a question of social values, and in particular, *fairness.*

Fairness is highly prized in American society. Therefore, if our society thinks matching is the fairest way to fill jobs, as it did without question for many years, it would tend to prefer that strategy. However, not everyone in our society sees matching as fair, and since the advent of the civil rights movement in the 1960s, this point of view has posed a serious challenge to the conventional wisdom. The argument goes as follows. If some segment of the population (say women or minorities) has been systematically denied the same chance as others to become qualified, then filling all jobs with today's most qualified candidates merely perpetuates an existing bias. If, for economic or other social reasons, whites had a greater opportunity than blacks or Hispanics to attend college, they would be much more likely to meet the college degree qualification and hence to be chosen for high-level jobs. Since these are the highest paying jobs, the selected (white) employees would make more money, send more of their children to college, thereby qualifying more of them for future jobs of the same sort, and the cycle would repeat. According to this view, fairness demands deviating from a strict matching strategy in order to break the cycle. It requires a strategy such as that commonly referred to as *affirmative action,* in which disadvantages are explicitly taken into account when hiring decisions are made.

Fairness, then, is no easier to pin down than the idea of a good match. However, I/O psychology has played a leading role in making explicit the various ways this difficult concept can be interpreted. It is impossible to settle on a definition of fairness that would please everyone, but in the case of personnel decisions, I/O psychologists can spell out with considerable precision what the different definitions are so that arguments over fair employment can focus on real issues rather than misunderstandings.

The material in this chapter should enable you to understand these emotionally charged issues as well as, or better than, the politicians and judges who define social justice for society. It may not change your mind about fair employment, but it should at least help you appreciate why people hold different views on the subject. A case *can* be made for hiring people on bases other than "the best person for the job," unfair though that strategy may appear, just as it can for the best match strategy. Of course, establishing that someone really is "the best person," or more generally, measuring individual differences reliably and validly, poses its own set of problems. These too should become much clearer as the chapter unfolds.

## Implementation Substrategies or Tactics

A final complication for the matching strategy is that it is composed of three somewhat distinct but interrelated components or substrategies: *attraction* (mainly, *recruiting*), *selection,* and *placement.* For example, the more people you can interest in joining your organization (attraction), the more likely you are to find some with superior qualifications from whom to choose (selection). But unless you do a good job of allocating them to specific positions (placement), you may not realize their full benefit.

Logically, the processes are sequential and dependent: You cannot place what you have not recruited or selected. From a practical standpoint, however, an employer may choose to emphasize one approach over the others, and that can make a big difference in overall strategy and results. For example, a company might select people on the basis of considerations other than proven capability (say, affirmative action goals and motivation to learn) and then do an extremely careful job of matching those selected with the existing job openings (a *placement* emphasis). Or, by contrast, a company might precisely define the requirements of a job and then look for exactly the right person to fill that job (an *attraction-selection* emphasis). It is perhaps worth noting that employers, particularly in the private sector, have tended to view selection as the key process even when placement might offer considerably more promise. The most effective approach usually depends on an accurate reading of the situation and proper implementation of the preferred approach.

As we examine the various approaches to matching people and jobs, then, you should not lose sight of the overall strategy and the fact that it poses a number of important questions for human resources professionals. Some of these issues have direct implications for individuals such as yourselves who are about to enter the workforce. For example, widespread honesty testing or drug screening could put your career at risk, and affirmative action programs could positively or negatively affect your chances of landing that perfect job. Are such policies and programs fair and reasonable or just another reflection of an irrational socio-political climate? Understanding the foundations on which recruiting, selection, and placement techniques rest should help you decide.

# ATTRACTION AND JOB SEARCH

Organizations have a fair amount of control over the pool of applicants for their jobs, just as individuals have some control over their list of potential employers. In both cases that control is exercised through a variety of familiar promotional techniques. For example, a company can attract more applicants by advertising in more media, presenting itself and its job openings in a more favorable light, expanding the geographical scope of its promotion efforts, and offering incentives for application. Job seekers can do many of the same things to market themselves, and both parties can restrict or target the candidate pool by following the opposite strategies. In other words, each can intentionally regulate the kind and distribution of information that reaches the other and thereby influence the other's level of interest (Porter, Lawler, & Hackman, 1975).

## Misrepresentation and Realistic Job Previews (RJP)

There are also, however, more subtle control mechanisms that sometimes produce unintended or unrecognized consequences. In the worst cases they *are* recognized and the consequences *are* intended, but because they are socially unacceptable, they are not admitted publicly. Most of these involve misrepresentation in one form or another. For example, a recent segment of the television program "60 Minutes" explored the practice of circumventing antidiscrimination laws by using employment agencies to screen out qualified minority candidates. The hiring organization would instruct the agency to refer only attractive Caucasian women for particular job openings, thereby withholding the information entirely from black or Hispanic applicants. The hiring organization could not be accused of illegal discrimination against minorities since its records would show that no such individuals appeared in the applicant pool.

Similar results have been obtained by simply discouraging minority applicants from applying (e.g., circulating the message that they are not welcome, or adopting selection practices that are known to make them feel uncomfortable). A municipal fire department in West Texas was highly successful in discouraging black applicants by emphasizing its redneck image. This stereotype, which was well recognized in the black community, had what is called a *chilling effect* by discouraging potential black applicants from applying for firefighter positions.

Not all forms of misrepresentation and influence are so blatant or malicious. Both organizations and applicants tend to emphasize their positive over their negative features in the understandable effort to attract the best candidates. Both also make decisions that affect their attractiveness to the other. For example, how a job is defined (what its legitimate requirements are) and what skills an applicant has developed in preparation for entering the labor market obviously affect their mutual attractiveness.

Sometimes, however, these decisions can have unintended consequences, such as the unnecessary exclusion of an entire class of candidates. Only recently have we come to realize that people with disabilities are often prevented from gainful employment simply because so many jobs were designed, rather arbitrarily, for the more fortunate majority. Certainly these decisions were not made with the *intent* of discriminating against the disabled; it was just not customary to consider this population when requirements were being set. Federal legislation has heightened society's awareness of this problem and clarified employers' responsibility for addressing it, particularly with the passage of the Americans with Disabilities Act in July 1990 (O'Keeffe, 1993). There will probably always be some jobs for which some disabilities are problematic, but the number is rapidly shrinking. Tools developed by I/O psychology, such as job analysis and specialized training, have contributed to the shrinkage.

One issue associated with the initial attraction process that has received research attention involves the tendency to oversell. It has been suggested that a company's positive misrepresentation, intentional or not, may set the stage for subsequent dissatisfaction when reality overtakes illusion (Wanous, 1976). A company's success in attracting the desired candidate may thus be short-lived as disillusionment leads the employee to perform poorly or to quit. The logical way to avert this unhappy situation would be to provide a more realistic picture of the job at the outset, an approach that has been labeled *realistic job preview* (RJP).

In RJP, the employer attempts to convey to the applicant exactly what he or she will do under what conditions; what opportunities there are for growth and advancement; what it takes to realize these opportunities; what risks there are; and so on. Frequently, the description includes selected illustrations presented on videotape or even through direct observation of people doing the job. The key is that such job samples be *representative* and *honest* rather than biased to show only the good features.

There is a risk, of course, that presenting even a few negative features might put the would-be employer at a competitive disadvantage. Unfortunately, overselling is the norm in modern society, whether the product is toothpaste, presidential candidates, or potential employers. We have come to expect it. Thus, even minor disadvantages could loom large in a job candidate's decision among employers, particularly if the choice is otherwise a close call. On the other hand, the contrast could favor the RJP employer by conveying an image of integrity, and if a job candidate joined a firm despite the realistic preview, there is a greater chance that it was for the right reasons.

So, which is it? Is honesty the best policy, or are the advertisers right when it comes to the practical matter of attracting job candidates? The answer provided by the literature is not as clear-cut as we might like. Early research seemed to support the virtue of RJP (Ilgen & Seely, 1974; Reilly, Tenopyr, & Sperling, 1979; Wanous, 1973), but later studies found little evidence for any of the presumed benefits (Reilly, Brown, Blood, & Malatesta, 1981; Guzzo, Jette, & Katzell, 1985). The opinions as to whether RJPs work are somewhat mixed. In a meta-analysis of 21 experiments evaluating RJPs, Premack and Wanous (1985) concluded that "RJPs tend to lower initial job expectations, while increasing self-selection, organizational commitment, job satisfaction, performance, and job survival" (p. 706). Other reviewers are not nearly as encouraging. McEvoy and Cascio (1985) conducted a meta-analysis of 20 experiments and found very small effects of RJPs in reducing turnover. They concluded that "managers might do well to look elsewhere when seeking turnover reduction strategies to implement prior to hiring" (p. 35). Most recently, attention has shifted to the search for conditions under which RJP is most likely to work and attempts to understand why it works (McEvoy & Cascio, 1985; Meglino & DeNisi, 1987).

## Moral/Ethical versus Scientific Questions

In the final analysis, honesty in recruiting is a moral/ethical rather than an empirical issue, and as such raises an important question about the role of science in such dilemmas. We believe that organizations should make every effort to provide an honest description of what a job entails, whether or not they use a formal RJP approach and whether or not it scares off applicants, because it is the right thing to do. Scientific research should focus on how best to accomplish this goal rather than whether its tangible benefits outweigh its costs.

There is a serious danger in trying to apply science to moral/ethical questions of this sort because science can produce apparent justification for immoral or unethical acts. If lying turned out to produce a clear benefit to its perpetrator in some context, for example, it would be no less dubious a practice even though it might gain credibility as a business practice. A society that misuses science in this way may find itself in deep trouble. Because of the sensitive position I/O psychology enjoys at the intersection of science and business, it must be extremely careful not to contribute to misuses. Throughout this text you can find numerous instances in which the opportunity (and indeed, the temptation) for such misuse is great. Fortunately in the case of RJP, the evidence does not seem to be in serious conflict with the moral/ethical answer: Doing the right thing poses little risk and a reasonable chance of paying off, but what if it did not?

# SELECTION

If, through successful recruiting or a favorable labor market, an organization finds itself with a number of applicants for each of its job openings, it is faced with a selection problem. How it chooses can obviously affect the success of the outcome. Just as obviously, every employer faced with such choices tries to pick candidates who have a good chance of working out, that is, ones who will show up at work reliably, learn quickly, work hard, get along well, and be trustworthy. Employers use different techniques for making these hiring decisions, such as interviews, work histories, background checks, tests, and personal references. Some practice these techniques formally and scientifically; others do so informally and rely heavily on their intuition.

## The Logic of Selection

What is less obvious is that all selection approaches involve much the same underlying logic. Personnel selection is a forecasting problem. Implicitly or explicitly, the employer gathers information on candidates to try to foretell how well they will do if hired. Generally, the prediction is based on an explicit or implicit theory as to what determines success and failure. Let us consider two hypothetical examples: one informal and implicit, the other formal and explicit.

## CONTRASTING EXAMPLES: IMPLICIT VERSUS EXPLICIT (SCIENTIFIC) APPROACHES

J.P. Megabucks, president of a local bank, hires all his employees personally. He relies heavily on personal references from people he knows plus an informal interview. He claims to have an uncanny ability for judging people. What he looks for in a candidate are what he calls "the old-fashioned values": honesty, loyalty, dedication, the work ethic. He points with pride to several employees whom he hired as tellers over 20 years ago who have worked their way up to senior management positions.

Amalgamated Microchip, by contrast, is a large manufacturing firm that hires hundreds of new employees each year through its 30-person HRM department. All its positions are described clearly in written staffing documents that include detailed specification of necessary qualifications that are updated periodically through a comprehensive job analysis program. The selection process is managed by HRM professionals who use a variety of techniques, including test batteries and structured interviews, to measure candidate qualifications. Each employee who is hired is evaluated after three months on the job, and annually thereafter, using a formal appraisal system. The HRM department conducts periodic studies of its selection process to see how well the predictive information it uses actually does in forecasting employee success as indicated by the annual appraisals. It occasionally makes changes in its predictors (e.g., adds, deletes, modifies a test) on the basis of these studies.

**Common Features**   With these contrasting cases in mind, consider the analysis of their common forecasting problem as illustrated in Figure 10.1. In each case there is an underlying theory of what constitutes a good match of people to jobs and how it relates to success. For the bank, this theory consists of a set of beliefs in Mr. Megabucks' head. For Microchip, the theory is an empirically based model of explicit job requirements and personal characteristics, the matching of which can be related to explicit outcome criteria (appraisal results). Both the bank and Microchip, however, are trying to achieve the same goal (they share the "best fit" philosophy), and both think their respective methods will get it for them. Both believe that the information they gather on each applicant (their *predictors*) will predict the chances of that applicant's success if hired. Both select on that basis, albeit in very different ways.

There are other similarities as well. One is the individual differences assumption that we encountered earlier. Unless people have enduring characteristics or *traits* that distinguish them from one another, an employer would have little hope of doing better than chance in selective forecasting. What a person is like today would have no bearing on what he would be like tomorrow; the best candidate today could be the worst tomorrow. Even a perfect measure of qualifications would be of no predictive value. Megabucks thus assumes that people differ on "old fashioned values," and the ones they hold now will always be a part of them. Lazy people will always be lazy; dumb ones

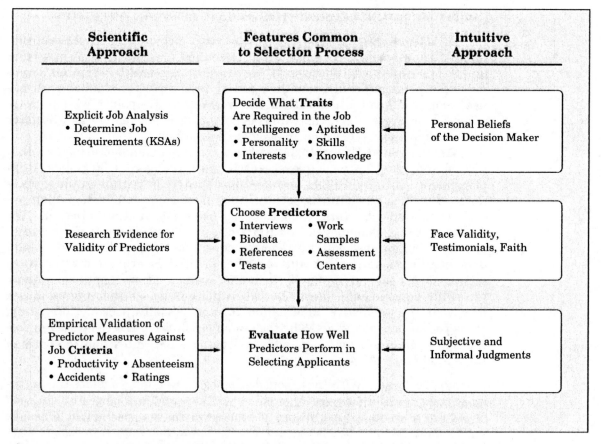

**Figure 10.1** *A summary of the major components involved in the scientific and intuitive approaches to selection*

will never get smart. Microchip makes much the same assumption, but not necessarily about the same traits. It believes that people who score high (or low) on its tests will maintain pretty much the same relative standing on those tests.

Another similarity involves confidence in how the traits are identified and measured. Both believe that their ways of estimating the important traits on which people differ are *valid*. Megabucks needs only his own intuition to be convinced of it. Microchip relies on research and scientific evidence. If the predictive information that either uses was not, in fact, indicative of the identified traits, the whole logic would disintegrate. The predictors would provide misleading information about traits and would thus be *invalid* trait indicators. For example, if the information Megabucks got from a former employer about a candidate's dedication was actually just a reflection of their past friendship, it would not be a valid measure of the candidate's *dedication* trait. It might or might not be a good predictor of *job success,* however, despite its failure as an index of dedication. Megabucks' theory about the importance of dedication could be wrong. If *friendliness* rather than *dedication* were actually what counted most in being a successful bank employee, the good personal reference could be a highly valid predictor of *job success* even though it was an invalid *trait measure* for dedication.

If you are a bit puzzled by this distinction between predictiveness and trait measurement, you are not alone. The difference between these two meanings of validity causes confusion among professionals as well as students. We return to it later in a discussion of the different ways validity can be viewed. The point here is that both intuitive (Megabucks) and scientific (Microchip) approaches to selection assume that the predictors are valid trait indicators, that the traits are important for job success, and that the predictors are therefore also valid for predicting job success.

**Important Differences** Despite their logical similarity, however, there are vast differences in the precision and usefulness of the two extreme cases illustrated. The purely intuitive approach is usually inaccurate and lends itself to the kinds of biases discussed earlier. Since the employer is confident of his judgment, he does not bother to check his track record for picking winners. In fact, people generally remember successes more readily than failures when contemplating their own past judgments (Fischhoff, 1975), so whatever thought Megabucks might give to his record would only reinforce his already inflated self-confidence. The employers who hired only male college graduates (clearly intuitive types) undoubtedly believed that their theory about who has superior qualifications was correct. So they never saw the need to test it by hiring women and non–college graduates to see how they fared relative to the college-educated men. The intuitive approach may succeed in some cases, and there may even be an occasional employer who can judge human traits reasonably well. There is no inherent reason why this nonscientific approach could not be validated against the success rates of hires, just as the more explicit scientific approach is. In reality, however, that almost never happens. From available evidence and from what we know about the nature and accuracy of judgments of this sort, it is a safe bet that intuitive selection is rarely accurate (Zedeck, Tziner, & Middlestadt, 1983). Even when it is accurate, there is usually no way to verify this.

By contrast, the kind of explicit, scientific approach used by Microchip has accuracy checks built into its every step. Important selection requirements are not taken on faith, but are established through systematic job analysis. Trait measures are carefully matched to these requirements, and the whole system is validated against measures of on-the-job success. If any or all of the predictors give useless or false information, that failure can be detected and corrected. In short, an approach of this kind, properly implemented, tells you exactly how well it is doing in selecting people, and with at least some precision, lets you understand the reasons why.

## I/O PSYCHOLOGY'S ROLE

The contribution of I/O psychology to the selection process is essentially that of providing employers the techniques and information for implementing an explicit scientific approach. It offers specific predictors, such as well-researched tests and structured instruments for gathering background information on people, and techniques for developing the employer's own predictors. It provides job analysis tools (Chapter 8) and ways of measuring *criteria* such as job performance (Chapter 9). But most of all, I/O psychology substitutes scientific thinking and objectivity for subjectivity, speculation, and undetectable error. That is, I/O psychology advocates an approach to selection in which the logic outlined in Figure 10.1 is made explicit and the various steps can be checked empirically.

## ADAPTATION TO SPECIAL CIRCUMSTANCES

Many employers are too small to undertake all the elaborate techniques described in the Microchip illustration. A firm of 25 or 30 people would hardly be able to afford a whole HRM department, and it would take years to carry out a meaningful test of its predictors against performance criteria. Still, even a "mom and pop" operation can benefit from the scientific approach. For example, it can take advantage of research done elsewhere to establish the validity of certain predictors for measuring traits or forecasting success in similar kinds of jobs (Schmidt & Hunter, 1977), and it can define job requirements and evaluate work performance systematically rather than in a hit-or-miss fashion. It also can keep performance or other criterion records so that it can estimate how well its personnel decisions are working out (Arvey & Faley, 1988). The point is, a small company can implement the logic of the scientific approach to selection without incorporating all its tools. Doing so requires a bit more imagination when there are size or resource limitations.

## ALTERNATIVE USES

Many of the tools involved in selection have other uses as well, like the tools for job analysis (Chapter 8) and performance appraisal (Chapter 9). Predictor information also can have multiple uses. A test of mechanical knowledge, for example, could be just as helpful in *placing* people, or in deciding what *training* they need, or even in *designing* a job for them as for choosing them in the first place.

Because this chapter focuses on matching people and jobs, we limit our discussion to matters involving selection and placement techniques. Since much of the discussion applies to both, and since the logic is a bit easier to follow in the case of selection, we explain how measures are evaluated and used in selection before getting into placement. We spend most of our time on the *processes* rather than the *tools themselves*. It is more important for you to understand the principles by which selection and placement techniques should work than it is to memorize a list of specific techniques. We conclude the chapter with a brief look at the available tools: interviews, biographical data, and tests.

## Evaluation of Measurement Techniques

Without realizing it, you are already well on your way to understanding how selection tools are evaluated. In thinking through the selection logic and examples, you laid the conceptual groundwork for the more technical material that you must now absorb. In general, the key techniques involve the three main attributes of selection tools: *sensitivity, reliability,* and *validity.* We have discussed these in previous chapters, especially Chapter 2. All three can apply to any kind of measures, but here we focus on their relevance in evaluating the *predictors* and *criteria* used in selection.

*Sensitivity* is the ability of the measuring instrument to detect and read out differences in whatever you are trying to measure. A thermometer that was only capable of distinguishing hot from cold would be much less sensitive than one that registered temperature in degrees, irrespective of how consistently and accurately it responded to heat. Thus, the idiot light in your car that tells you that your engine is overheating is less sensitive than the temperature gauge in your friend's car. Similarly, an intelligence test that had only bright and dumb categories would be less sensitive than one that read out IQ points.

*Reliability,* on the other hand, is the extent to which the instrument gives you a consistent reading irrespective of its sensitivity. If the idiot light tells you you're in trouble every time the engine temperature exceeds the normal operating range, and that you are not in trouble whenever it is within that range, it is perfectly reliable. In fact, it would be reliable even if it told you *exactly the opposite:* reliability, like sensitivity, has nothing to do with being right. In contrast, an intelligence test that set your IQ at 120 today and 75 tomorrow would not be reliable (assuming, as we usually do, that intelligence is a trait that doesn't change from day to day).

*Validity* differs from the other two attributes in that it is *only* about being right. More specifically, it is the extent to which the instrument gives you a reading of whatever it is you are trying to measure rather than something else. If the wires to the idiot light or temperature gauge were connected by mistake to the car's electrical system, they would give bad information no matter how precisely and reliably they did so. If these readings were taken at face value, money could be wasted on unnecessary repairs and serious harm could be done to the engine in the process. Similarly, if an intelligence test really measured how hard you tried rather than how bright you were, it could mislead you into making some bad career decisions. Moreover, it would be an *invalid* test of intelligence.

Considered together, sensitivity, reliability, and validity go a long way toward defining the quality and usefulness of the information we use in the selection (or placement) process. Applied to predictors like tests or interviews, they tell us how well we can expect to do in forecasting success. Applied to criteria such as performance appraisal measures, they tell us how well we can expect to do in recognizing success or failure once we have it. Think, once again, about the difference between the instruments used by Mr. Megabucks and the Microchip company in their respective approaches to selection. Which do you think provide the most sensitive, reliable, and valid information? Perhaps now you can appreciate more why Megabucks' intuitive measures are suspect and difficult to evaluate.

Even when we have explicit measures such as those used by Microchip, however, it is no simple matter to tell how accurate they are; this usually requires inferences and the use of statistics. Moreover, while *conceptually* different, the three attributes are related in important ways when it comes to estimating each one for a particular instrument.

Take validity and reliability. If the temperature gauge is unreliable, any reading is likely to be inaccurate. You can estimate *how* unreliable it is by taking a number of readings before the engine has cooled and describing the range of obtained temperatures. The best estimate of the true temperature would be the average reading (a statistical inference). But how can you tell whether you are hooked up to the right system and that what you measure is actually engine temperature? One way would be to wait for the engine to cool (a criterion change) and then look for a corresponding change in the average reading. But the more unreliable the measures were, the harder it would be to tell whether the expected change had occurred. Again, you can make a statistical inference, but your confidence in that inference would decline as the variability (unreliability) of the measures increased. Thus, reliability constrains the validity estimates you can get for a predictor or criterion measure. Validity, however, does not limit reliability estimates since reliability has nothing to do with *what* you measure.

We have established, then, that the key evaluative attributes of predictor and criterion instruments can only be estimated, and that doing so involves inferences. You can make different kinds of inferences, particularly with respect to reliability and validity, and each calls for a somewhat different method and interpretation. Let us consider reliability first.

## RELIABILITY INDEXES

You can get variation in readings for many reasons other than real changes in what you are trying to measure and all of them contribute to unreliability. In the temperature example, variations in temperature readings could be caused by a variety of factors: momentary changes in the gauge's internal circuits, the angle at which you read the meter, your visual acuity, the humidity in the air, or some temporary change in your engine.

In the case of human trait measures, such as the aptitude tests you took to get into college, you might score higher than your true score because a particular form of the test was easier than it was supposed to be, because you got lucky, or you had a really great prep course that inflated your score. On the other hand, you might score lower than your true score because the test was unduly difficult, you were unlucky, you were out late the night before, or you were distracted by noise in the building.

As you can see, these distorting influences are a mixed bag. Some have to do with the test itself (difficulty, representativeness of items); some involve circumstances (your health, testing conditions). Some are transient conditions (distraction, luck), while others are persistent (difficulty). Thus, if we took multiple readings in order to estimate test reliability, our results would be influenced by how we took the reading. Having you take *exactly* the same form of the test twice, say a week apart, would allow the transient things to change, but not the persistent things. Moreover, you would probably do better on the second administration because of your experience with the first. Taking two *forms* of the same test at once (e.g., by alternating items from both tests) would let the persistent factors (e.g., specific items) change, but not the transient ones. You would be just as tired and distracted on Form A as on Form B.

What we have, then, are several reliability indexes, each aimed at controlling different factors and involving different inferences. All are based on the logic of comparing two or more readings of the same thing (a fixed temperature; a human trait), and all rely on the statistical method of correlation that you encountered in Chapter 2. A *reliability index,* therefore, is the number (0.0–1.0) you get when you correlate two sets of readings (call them $X_1$ and $X_2$) that you obtain from the same source (e.g., people) using the same basic measuring instrument (e.g., test). It is usually expressed as $r_{xx}$. The different kinds of indexes reflect different ways of getting the two sets of readings. They fall roughly into three categories.

**Test–Retest Indexes**   These involve getting both readings from the same people on exactly the same test, either right away *(immediate test–retest reliability)* or with a time interval separating the two administrations *(delayed test–retest reliability)*. Because of its focus on variations over time, the test–retest estimate is often called the *coefficient of stability.* Giving the same test a second time means that there is no chance to pick up variation due to unusual test items, unusual difficulty, or other features of the test itself. Thus, if it has such peculiarities, no test–retest index will reflect them, and the result will overestimate the true reliability accordingly.

Giving the test right away does the same for many transient factors (e.g., distractions), whereas delaying the second administration allows these factors to vary. Obviously, the degree of opportunity depends on how long the interval is: A few hours might allow the distraction to go away, but probably not your tiredness; a year would overcome both of these and also give you a chance to forget most of the specific items (or look up answers to those that gave you the most trouble). The bottom line is, the test–retest method can give you an inflated estimate of stability the more you reduce the delay interval. Immediate test–retest coefficients are often in the range of .90–.99.

**Parallel Forms Indexes**    Here, the two readings are taken using different versions of the same test, either right away *(immediate parallel forms reliability)* or after a time interval *(delayed parallel forms reliability)*. Because the two forms are supposed to be comparable even though they contain different items, the term *coefficient of equivalence* is often applied to these indexes.

The logic in this case is exactly the same as for the test–retest method. The only difference is that factors having to do with the *test itself* (difficulty, particular items) can also vary. Thus it is a more conservative, but in our view, a more complete, estimate of reliability, particularly in its delayed form. It requires having enough items to make up two versions of the test and some way of equating them. For purely statistical reasons, test length has an important bearing on how large a correlation coefficient you can get. Thus, comparing two short forms gives a lower estimate of reliability than two long forms even if both pairs are equally reliable. Noting this, you can understand the difference between two versions of the parallel forms approach: *split-half* and *alternate-forms* methods. Split-half methods simply consider half the items on a full-length test that you take at one sitting as one form of the test and the other half as a second form. It is actually an immediate administration of *half-length* parallel forms. The alternate-forms method compares two full-length tests, usually taken as delayed parallel forms.

The statistical means by which you can correct the reliability coefficient for short length is the Spearman-Brown formula (Murphy & Davidshofer, 1991, p. 96):

$$\text{new } r_{xx} = \frac{n(\text{old } r_{xx})}{1 + (n - 1)\text{old } r_{xx}}$$

In this formula, n is the factor by which the test is increased in length. For instance, if the number of items is doubled, then n = 2. The "old $r_{xx}$" is the reliability of the shorter test and the "new $r_{xx}$" is the reliability of the lengthened test.

With this index you can estimate what the split-half index would have been for a longer test (e.g., the full-length alternate forms). It can be argued, however, that this correction *overestimates* true reliability, a sin that some regard as just as serious as the *underestimation* you get with the uncorrected shorter tests. Alternate-forms reliability is more commonly in the .80s than the .90s, even for measures that are corrected for length, just as you would expect now that you understand what goes into them.

**Internal Consistency Indexes and Item Response Theory (IRT)**    One source of error is that associated with the particular items that make up a test. Because of the way it is worded, or how hard it is, or what exact knowledge it requires, an item may or may not represent the same domain as others designed to measure the same thing. For example, an algebra test might include both word problems and numerical problems, all involving the same general algebraic principles. Some people, however, have more trouble with one kind of problem than the other. Thus, there would be some variation in scores due to item format. In other words, the verbal problems measure something different from the numerical problems, even though both may also measure knowledge of algebraic principles.

*The internal consistency* index estimates the extent to which the various items all measure the same thing. It is essentially the combined (average) correlation of scores on every item with every other item in the test. In this sense it is much like split-half reliability reduced to the individual-item level. Consequently, it too is sensitive to the number of items, only here the correction is built right into the formula for estimating internal consistency:

$$r_{xx} = \frac{k(\bar{r}_{ij})}{1 + (k - 1)\bar{r}_{ij}}$$

where k is the number of items and $\bar{r}_{ij}$ is the average intercorrelation among items. If you think about it, the notion of internal consistency begins to sound very much like *validity:* measuring what we want to measure rather than something else. If you try to measure algebra proficiency and format preferences inadvertently creep in, internal consistency will be reduced. However, you could get perfect internal consistency and still measure the wrong thing.

When you get down to the level of evaluating individual items, then a lot of questions arise that extend beyond internal consistency and into the validity domain. Not only is it important to know that an item is consistent or inconsistent with others; it is useful to know *on what basis* it differs from them. Is it more difficult, or does it tap different traits? The attempt to answer such questions has led to a whole new approach to test evaluation, *item response theory (IRT).* While an explanation of this complex approach is beyond the scope of this book (see Lord, 1980, for a full discussion), suffice it to say that IRT enables the test developer to analyze the relationship between the traits being measured and people's responses to individual items.

### VALIDITY INDEXES

Estimating the extent to which a measuring instrument such as a test is measuring what you want it to also can be done in various ways, and once again, each involves different kinds of inferences. The three main approaches estimate *construct validity, content validity,* and *criterion-related* validity. We discussed these in Chapter 2 as bases for evaluating psychological measures and return to these concepts now to apply them to the evaluation of selection instruments.

**Construct Validity**   As discussed in Chapter 2, all three approaches to validity are types of construct validity. Construct validity is in many respects the most fundamental of the three, and refers to how well your measures reflect the characteristic you are interested in (temperature, intelligence, algebra proficiency). Because they cannot be observed directly, traits on which people differ are called *constructs.* The only way you can be confident they exist is by making inferences from what people do (which you *can* observe). If a person answers algebra questions correctly, you infer that she has "algebra knowledge," particularly if another person who has never been exposed to algebra gets them wrong. If she does well on many different kinds of mathematical items on which people are known to differ, you may infer that she has a high "quantitative aptitude." "Algebra knowledge" and "quantitative aptitude" are constructs. They are valid to the extent that you have made the right inferences.

Estimating the construct validity of an instrument such as a test is not easy since you have no direct access to the construct itself. The available indirect approaches, which involve statistical techniques, are too advanced to go into here. We can, however, describe the logic of these techniques. In general, they consist of testing *theories* about how the construct operates. For instance, a person who just took an intensive course in algebra should have more "algebra knowledge" than one who has not, other things being equal. If the scores on a test presuming to measure the "algebra knowledge" construct do not differentiate between these two individuals, you would have to assume that your test has low construct validity.

Another approach involves using different measuring instruments (e.g., different tests) to index the same construct and then comparing the resulting measures (test scores). The theory here is that if a construct exists, different measures of it should *converge*. Hence, the more convergence, the higher the construct validity. If you think this sounds like parallel-forms reliability, you are right: The two have much in common. Obviously these are gross oversimplifications of how one would actually do a construct validation study, but they illustrate the concept. How one expresses construct validity, therefore, depends on what kind of study was done; there is no simple index, such as a correlation coefficient, to convey this information.

**Content Validity**   This is best thought of as coverage or representativeness. Content validity concerns the extent to which your measures cover the full range of the domain you are interested in rather than just a portion of it or some other domain. If, for example, your algebra test failed to include questions on geometric functions and substitution rules, it would be less content valid than if it did cover this material. Similarly, if it included questions on English grammar, it would be less content valid than if it did not: Such questions represent a different, and irrelevant, content domain.

Since it involves the idea of sampling from a larger domain, content validity is sometimes expressed as a proportion. To do so, however, requires that you have a clear indication of what the relevant domain is, and some way of measuring what is and is not covered. In practice neither of these requirements is easily met, so content validity is often reduced to a matter of expert judgment. For example, one way to objectify a relevant job domain is through job analysis (Chapter 8). If 100 critical task or function elements were identified in a maintenance job, the content validity of a test for that job could be expressed in terms of how many of the 100 were represented. A 50% sampling would be rather poor; 90% would be rather good. You probably realize at this point that how precisely content validity can be expressed depends on how specifically the content elements can be defined. If the content is a well-defined set of observable *behaviors*, such as task elements, it can be described much more explicitly than if it is a set of unobservable mental *constructs*, such as traits. Thus it is easier to define the content validity of a test for auto mechanics than a test of mechanical aptitude. You can *describe* what auto mechanics do; you can only *infer* what constructs underlie the ability to be a good auto mechanic. This example illustrates how content and construct validity are conceptually different, yet related. The better you can define the constructs of interest, the better you can do in judging how much of the relevant domain is covered with the measuring instruments.

**Criterion-Related Validity**   This is, in many respects, the most practically significant of the three concepts. It invokes the bottom line question of how much proven capability your instrument has in forecasting some criterion measure, such as job performance. Under ideal circumstances, it is the key to successful use of tests and other predictive devices in selection and placement.

Criterion-related validity is based on the premise that you try to measure constructs or other content for a purpose: to improve your forecasting ability. You care about mechanical aptitude or the content of the mechanic's job because you want to predict who will make the best performing mechanics before you put them into mechanic jobs. You tell how valid your measures are by relating individual scores to actual job success. If the test is a valid measure of whatever it takes to be a good mechanic, people who score high should be more successful on the job than those who score low. As in the case of reliability estimation, the best way to express relations of this sort is through correlation. Thus, the most common index of criterion-related validity is the *validity coefficient,* the correlation of predictor (X) with criterion (Y) measures (or $r_{xy}$). Since the general public has trouble understanding correlation, however, the relation is often expressed directly in terms of *expected success rate* (Figure 10.2). This index shows the likelihood of a person's succeeding (surpassing some prespecified level of performance) on the criterion for each predictor score or range of scores. There are two common ways of obtaining criterion-related validity estimates: the *predictive* and the *concurrent* approaches. They are similar in both the underlying logic and mode of expression (i.e., $r_{xy}$ or expectancy) that we have just explored. They differ, however, in one important respect. The predictive approach uses job *candidates,* whereas the concurrent approach uses job *incumbents*.

In both cases, the instrument (test) you wish to validate is given to a number of people for whom you compare test and criterion scores. For incumbents, you already have your criterion measures (you know who has worked out well and who has not), whereas for candidates, you must wait until you have made your choices and they have had a chance to show something. This difference is important for several basic reasons. First, the incumbent sample may be quite different from the candidate sample, if only because they have already been selected on *some* basis. Second, even if they are basically alike,

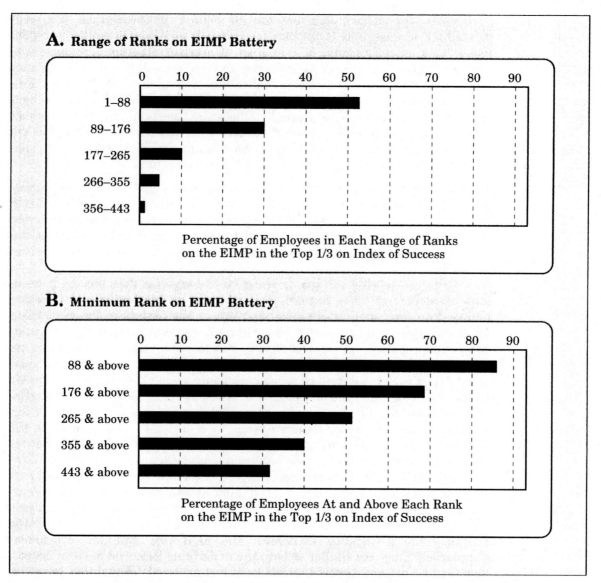

**Figure 10.2** *Illustration of (A) an individual expectancy chart and (B) an institutional expectancy chart showing the percentage of managers in the top one-third on managerial success as a function of scores on the Early Identification of Management Potential (EIMP) test battery*

*Source:* Adapted from Sparks, C.P. (1983). Paper and pencil measures of potential. In G. Dreher & P. Sackett (Eds.) *Perspectives on Employee Staffing and Selection.* Homewood, IL: Richard D. Irwin, pp. 349–368.

the two samples take the test under very different circumstances. The security of knowing that you have a job is not the same as the pressure and uncertainty in trying to get one. Third, the criteria may be different. Many times the predictive approach relies on very early performance indicators (often *training* evaluations). Incumbents, on the other hand, generally have established some sort of track record.

Ideally, the predictive model is the most appropriate for selection and placement purposes. However, for that potential to be realized, certain conditions must exist that rarely do in practice. For example, candidates should be hired without regard for their scores on the test you are trying to validate (i.e., until the validity has been established). Few employers, however, are willing to spend time and money testing candidates, and then ignore the results just to get a better reading on the value of the test. Thus, the more valid the test actually is, the less variability there will be in the criterion measures of those hired using it, and the harder it becomes to demonstrate its true validity. Also, of course, the predictive model faces the criterion problem that employers generally go with early performance measures rather than waiting five or ten years to see how well the predictions really turned out.

The point is, the predictive approach can be very costly to do *right*; and as it is compromised in the interest of economy, its potential advantage over the concurrent approach diminishes. For this reason the concurrent approach is often preferable despite its limitations as a forecasting index. Sometimes it is used on an interim basis while the data necessary for a good predictive study are being collected.

**Practical Comparison of Validation Measures**    Now that you understand the three main ways of validating predictors such as tests, you may wonder which is best. Technically, the answer is *none:* Each focuses on a different attribute and thus gives you a different perspective on an instrument's validity. Usually these perspectives are related, but the connection can be loose.

For example, you might have a valid test of the mechanical aptitude *construct,* but because mechanics have to read technical manuals, it might not cover all the *content* required for success as a mechanic (in this case, reading ability). Thus it might or might not have a high *concurrent* or *predictive* validity against a performance criterion. If you went only by a criterion-related index, you might make a bad mistake. Suppose the $r_{xy}$ was .60, a high value, and you decided to use the test to screen all your applicants for mechanic positions. Everything goes well until the new edition of the technical manual comes out, whereupon half your mechanics start making serious mistakes due to their poor reading ability. On the other hand, suppose the $r_{xy}$ was only .20 and you decided not to use the test. By failing to understand that the problem was merely a content deficiency, and that by adding a simple verbal test you could raise the predictiveness substantially, you would have missed the chance to significantly improve your selection process.

Even if a test has both construct and content validity, and therefore should be a good selection device, it may not appear valid on a predictive or concurrent validity index because a criterion is involved. Criterion-related validity estimates are no better than the criterion measures that the predictors are intended to predict. The less sensitive, reliable, or valid these measures are, the less meaningful any $r_{xy}$ becomes. Truly valid predictors can yield low $r_{xy}$ values; truly invalid ones can yield high $r_{xy}$ values. Unreliability can limit validity estimates and thereby underpredict criterion scores. Overprediction can also occur when the criterion measure is not what you think it is. A common example is the situation in which the *job performance* criterion is measured using a seriously biased subjective rating. Suppose that raters give friendly people better ratings than unfriendly ones irrespective of their actual performance. A test might show a high $r_{xy}$ against this false performance criterion, when in fact it really predicted *sociability* rather than performance *and did it well.* Hakel (1986) complained that I/O psychology has given far more attention to the development of predictors and validation techniques than to the criteria they hope to predict. Unfortunately, his complaint is still valid.

Ideally, you should take all validity perspectives into account—at least implicitly—in evaluating a predictor. But there is yet another perspective to be considered: *face validity*, or the extent to which a predictor looks relevant. An ordinary typing test is face valid because it is obviously job-related. You sit at a typewriter and type. Personality tests commonly used in selecting police officers are not as face valid because they ask questions (such as whether you dream a lot or like to play golf) that have little apparent connection to law enforcement. While not a substitute for the other kinds of validity, face validity can have a bearing on how test takers react to the test, and therefore, how meaningful their scores are (Schmitt & Robertson, 1990). In any case, even though you should consider all these perspectives, including face validity, there is still the practical question of what to make of it all. Is there a *practical* answer to which index is best? If the goal is predicting performance for the purposes of selecting or placing people, then obviously predictive validity is the most useful provided that it is based on a defensible criterion and developmental sample. Concurrent validity is sometimes a reasonable alternative when these conditions are lacking. However, if the criterion is seriously deficient or highly suspect, even the concurrent index should be avoided in favor of some combination of content and construct strategies.

This is an important point because of the common tendency among unsophisticated test users to view predictive and/or concurrent indexes as inherently better than the others. That criterion-related validation yields a handy number, $r_{xy}$ or expectancy, is probably part of the reason. Unscrupulous test marketers capitalize on this ignorance in promoting their wares. Now that you are more sophisticated on the subject, however, you realize that numbers alone can be grossly misleading. You already know how difficult it is to get a good measure of criteria such as job performance (Chapter 9). Therefore, whenever you see validity coefficients used to document the worth of a predictor, you should immediately look for the criterion measures. Can you accept them as appropriate and complete? Were they taken on enough of the right kinds of people to convince you that the prediction will hold for the people you want to attract? If you have serious doubts, look into the content and construct evidence.

**Other Validity Considerations**    Although conditions are rarely ideal for estimating criterion-related validity, the potential usefulness of this index for selection and placement has led researchers to look hard for ways to compensate for its major drawbacks, generally through statistical means. The technical details of these techniques are much too involved to go into here, and virtually all of them have controversial features. Nevertheless, you should at least understand them conceptually.

*1. Reliability Corrections.*    If the predictor and/or criterion measures used to calculate validity coefficients are unreliable, what the validity *would have been* with reliable measures can be estimated using what is known as a *correction for attenuation:*

$$\text{corrected } r_{xy} = \frac{\text{obtained } r_{xy}}{r_{xx} \cdot r_{yy}}$$

As we saw earlier, unreliability due to the shortness of either the test or criterion can itself be corrected using the Spearman-Brown formula.

*2. Validity Generalization.*    Unreliability is but one of several potential sources of error that can combine to depress the obtained $r_{xy}$ and thus underestimate true validity. Sampling errors and range restriction, or an artificially narrow spread of scores on one or both measures, are other common sources. Most validity studies carried out in work settings suffer from a combination of these deficiencies, a situation that has led some researchers to argue that we have grossly underestimated the true predictive power of mental tests (Schmidt & Hunter, 1977).

Since there are statistical corrections for all these errors that can be applied if data from a number of roughly comparable validity studies are available, it is possible to estimate *generalized* validity for a type of test by implementing all the corrections at once. Several different *validity generalization models* have been proposed for doing this, and when applied to actual data, all have tended to produce dramatic increases in validity estimates—often on the order of double or triple the values reported in the original (component) studies. Although some researchers believe that this approach overestimates true validity (Zedeck & Cascio, 1984), it has now been used in validating a variety of selection tests, including those for computer programming, clerical, oil field, and life insurance jobs (Murphy & Davidshofer, 1991).

Validity generalization, however, is more than a collection of statistical corrections. It represents an important shift in thinking about evaluation and use of tests for prediction. The traditional view was that to do a good job of selecting or placing people, you had to validate a test in the *specific context* in which it was to be used: the same organization, job, worker population. It was assumed that the more you deviated from local conditions, the less faith you could put in your validity estimates. By contrast, the generalization concept (and evidence) suggests that you should put more faith in validity estimates obtained over a *variety of contexts,* since this enables you to make the appropriate corrections and get closer to the true predictiveness.

These contrasting philosophies have several practical implications. For example, the federal guidelines on the fair use of tests in selection were written from the traditional local-validation perspective (EEOC, 1978), whereas current professional guidelines accept the generalization model (American Psychological Association, 1985; Society for Industrial-Organizational Psychology, 1987). In reality, of course, each has its limits. If you are a very small employer, you have little chance of doing a meaningful local validation study and would be much better off relying on generalized validity estimates. If you are the U.S. Air Force and wish to predict pilot success, you can probably do better validating locally (Carretta, 1989). The area between these extremes offers plenty of room for both judgment and argument.

*3. Synthetic Validity.* An alternative but rarely used way of dealing with the problem of validation for small employers involves decomposing jobs into component dimensions (e.g., supervision, physical requirements, etc.) and validating tests *for each component* against criteria *for that component* as represented in a number of different jobs. This is called *synthetic* validation because it uses somewhat abstract (dimensional-composite) measures as criteria rather than straight forward whole-job measures. It relies heavily on dimensional job analyses, such as the PAQ (Chapter 8), for the components. If you want to learn more about this approach, see Guion (1965) or Mossholder and Arvey (1984).

*4. Shrinkage and Cross-validation.* When you conduct a criterion-related validation study, part of the correlation you obtain will be due to the particular sample of people from whom you gathered predictor and criterion scores. The estimated predictiveness may not prove to be as great for a different sample, and hence may overstate the true validity. It is possible to estimate how inflated $r_{xy}$ actually is by determining how much it shrinks when a sampling correction is applied. *Shrinkage* can be estimated either by applying a formula to the original data (Schmitt, Coyle, & Rauschenberger, 1977) or by using the prediction equation developed on the original sample to make predictions for another sample and seeing how they turn out. The latter approach, which is known as *cross-validation,* is generally considered to be the more conservative (i.e., to show the most shrinkage). Debate continues as to which is better (Murphy, 1983; Zedeck & Cascio, 1984).

The important point for our purposes is to recognize that uncorrected validity estimates must be taken with a grain of salt—in some cases, a whole shaker full—when evaluating a predictor. Test publishers are fond of reporting the highest values they can get away with to promote their products. If close scrutiny reveals that no correction was made in the original validity estimates for shrinkage, you can expect less predictiveness than advertised, often much less, when you try to use such tests in your selection system.

Summing up the topic of validity and validation, it is important to recognize that there is no *single* way to establish that a test or criterion is a true index of what you want to measure, nor is there a uniformly *best* way. This is so because there are different, yet equally meaningful, virtues that a measurement can have. Which is most appropriate depends on a practical context: what you plan to use it for and what constraints there are on the validation process. We have belabored this point, and the discussion of validity, because a little understanding of validity is a dangerous thing. Unfortunately, there are many people in our society, some in very powerful positions, who have just that. It is our sincere intent not to add you to their number.

### PERSONNEL DECISION MAKING: USE OF SELECTION TOOLS

Having explored the features that make tests and other predictors potentially useful, we now consider how they are actually used. The quality of these instruments is a necessary, but not sufficient, condition for successful selection or placement. A number of factors besides validity must be considered, such as the supply of the needed talent, the cost of mistakes in hiring, and the importance of maintaining work standards. Both selection and placement are complex, although manageable, decision problems. Because it is the nature of the decision problem that distinguishes selection from placement, this will lead us naturally into the *placement* topic.

**Selection Ratio (SR) and Validity**    Three major considerations determine whether it is a good idea to use a selection strategy at all, and if so, how to use a particular selection device to implement that strategy. The first is a comparison of your need with the available labor supply, usually expressed as a ratio (*selection ratio,* or number of vacancies you want to fill over the estimated number of potential candidates). A distinction has been drawn between two different meanings of SR, the present version being more appropriately referred to as *hiring rate* (Alexander, Barrett, & Doverspike, 1983). For present purposes, however, the more commonly used term, selection ratio, will suffice. As the ratio approaches or exceeds 1:1 it makes no sense to select: You will need to hire everyone you can drag in the door. As the ratio gets smaller, the potential utility of selection goes up. If it were 1:10, for example, you would have a good chance of getting a superior crop of recruits, provided you could identify them. That, of course, is where your predictor comes in. The more valid it is, the better your chances of picking the superior candidates. So *validity* is the second consideration.

**Base Rate of Success (BR)**    The third is your definition of what constitutes a superior (or successful) employee, and this one gets a little complicated. The basic idea is that how valuable any particular quality of selection is to you depends on how much it matters that the person selected do well. If you are trying to fill a job that requires little more than a warm body, and where virtually everyone is successful, investing in a fancy selection system makes little sense. If, however, poor performance can ruin you, and those who can perform well are rare, good selection becomes extremely valuable.

Thus, how satisfactory an unselected set of hires would be by whatever standards you normally employ represents a baseline against which the value of selection can be judged. Usually it is expressed in terms of the actual or estimated proportion of hires whom you have considered successful before using an explicit selection system, a value known as the *base rate of success* (BR). If 80% of your previous hires were successful (or you estimated that 90% of your usual applicants would succeed), it would take an extremely valid selection test to make much difference. If the base rate were 20%, even a moderately valid test might help, assuming a favorable selection ratio.

**Selection Decisions**    Selection ratio (SR), base rate of success (BR), and validity ($r_{xy}$), therefore, combine to establish the potential usefulness of a selection strategy. Tables have been developed to help employers apply this logic to various kinds of selection decisions (Taylor & Russell, 1939; Naylor & Shine, 1965). Thus, you could estimate SR and BR and then consult a table to see how much improvement a selection system of a given $r_{xy}$ would be likely to provide. The principles involved can best be summarized using a graphic illustration of a simple hypothetical selection problem (Figure 10.3). Suppose you need to fill 10 clerical positions, the SR for applicants has been running about 1:10 (i.e., ten applicants for every position), and about half the clerks you hire are rated satisfactory or better on their annual appraisals (BR = 50%). Your decision is whether to add a test battery to your selection process. As illustrated in the scatterplot in Figure 10.3, the test has an estimated validity against some relevant criterion of $r_{xy} = .60$. If we draw a horizontal line at the criterion level that distinguishes success from failure (e.g., a *satisfactory* rating), we can see how a selection strategy will fare using any test score we choose as a decision cutoff (that is, a cut score above which we hire and below which we do not). Drawing a vertical line at this score, we can read our expected success and failure rates from the quadrants formed by the intersection of these lines.

In the example shown, the selection cut score is located at a point that will give you the 10 hires you need (i.e., such that 10 of the 100 expected applicants will score to the right of the line and thus fall in quadrant I or IV). Given the other parameters in this case, you can expect about eight of them to succeed (quadrant I) and two to fail (quadrant IV). Although not perfect, the result would be considerably better than the five successes (50% BR) you could expect without the test: about 30% better, in fact.

Once you have grasped the principles involved in this simple example, you can use the diagram to explore a variety of alternative decisions and cases. Consider what would happen if you shifted your performance standards (horizontal cut-off line) up or down. With a lower standard, you could move your cut score to the right and still get your 10 people; with a higher standard, you would have to accept some with lower test scores to fill your slots. What if the test were less valid (closer to a round scatterplot), or the SR were .5 rather than .1 (i.e., you would have only 20 applicants scattered over the space and would have to take 10 of them)? In either case, you would have to move your cut score on the test to the left to get your 10 people, and more of them would fail. Even under the conditions shown, you might decide to set the decision cutoff at a point that would ensure 10 *successes* rather than 10 *hires*, thereby requiring several overhires.

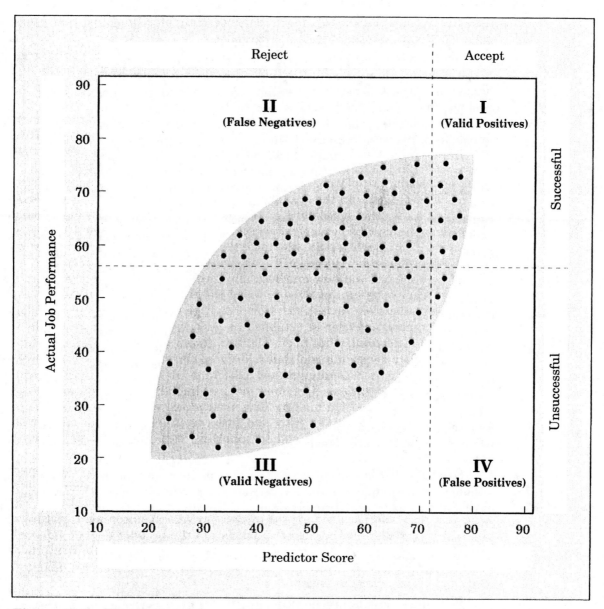

**Figure 10.3**  *Illustration of the traditional selection model (cutoffs set at rating of 56 and predictor score of 72)*

<u>**The Broader Decision Problem**</u>    While it is a convenient way to conceptualize selection problems, neither the diagram nor its underlying principles provide enough information to tell you what to *do* about them. Should you hire just the 10 people you need, or 13 so as to ensure 10 successful ones? Does the test battery save you enough by screening out likely failures to offset the cost of

using it? And what if the test is suspected of being biased against minorities, older applicants, or other "protected" groups?

To answer such questions requires that you consider a much broader range of factors than just SR, BR, and $r_{xy}$. In fact, it brings us back to the fundamental fairness issue raised earlier: Who benefits from trying to get the best possible person-job fit, who is hurt by it, and by how much?

We concluded that fairness and other value-related issues have no unequivocal answers because there is always a subjective element involved. We also promised to explain how I/O psychology has helped clarify such issues, and the time has come to make good on our promise. The key is to think of selection, or placement, or promotion, or any other personnel action as a *decision problem.* In the example we just gave, you saw how an employer can clarify a selection problem (e.g., whether to use a predictive instrument, or which one to use) by estimating what it will add to the expected success of hires. This is obviously a help, and until the last few decades, it was about all the help we could offer. However, it leaves out the whole *value* dimension.

It does not tell you how much the improvement in the people you hire is *worth,* or what *costs* are involved in using the test with any particular set of cut scores and success definitions. Nor does it give you a clue as to what factors you ought to consider in establishing such values, or how you ought to weigh them in deciding what to do. The traditional selection model, therefore, is an incomplete decision model, but additional clarification has become available in recent years. Techniques now exist that enable the estimation of the collective value of various personnel actions, including selection and placement, and help in decision making. The basic ideas, which have been around for decades (Brogden, 1949), attracted little attention until the mid 1970s, when procedures were developed for applying cost estimates to employee behavior (Cascio, 1987).

Since the 1970s a number of these cost estimation tools have appeared, although their complexity and the variability in the estimates they produce have limited their practical acceptance (Schmitt & Robertson, 1990). You should understand that even these models provide an incomplete picture of most personnel decision problems. Advances in the broader field of *judgment and decision making* (Stevenson, Busemeyer, & Naylor, 1990; von Winterfeldt & Edwards, 1986; Yates, 1990), mostly ignored by I/O psychology, offer considerable promise for the future.

Personnel actions are no different, in a formal sense, from any other kind of business decision (e.g., whether to undertake a new product line) or consumer decision (e.g., who to vote for or what toothpaste to buy). Thus, the same principles that have been developed and used in other decision contexts apply here. We examine some of these principles with enough detail to give you a conceptual, but not a technical, understanding.

*1. Rational Decision Models.*     The common feature of any decision problem is that a choice must be made among options that differ in attractiveness. Buying toothpaste, casting votes, or selecting employees all have this feature, and if we behave rationally when making such choices, we pick the one that offers us the most of whatever we value (the brightest smile, the lowest taxes, the best workers). In most cases, however, the choice is not as simple as it seems because (1) the options have multiple facets or *attributes* that we care about (in the toothpaste example, price, taste, and decay-fighting capability, as well as a bright smile), (2) we may value some attributes more than others, and (3) we cannot be sure that a particular option will actually deliver a particular attribute as advertised (e.g., politicians tend to forget their campaign promises). Furthermore, (4) we may not even be aware of all the relevant attributes unless someone brings them to our attention (e.g., the "womanizing" issue in Gary Hart's ill-fated bid for a 1988 presidential nomination).

Due to these complications, we are not likely to make the best possible choices, nor even to realize that we have come out short on the things we wanted (Fischhoff & Johnson, 1990). The more complex the problem, the less well we are likely to fare unless we can find some way to handle the complexity. That is where decision theory, more specifically *utility* and *choice* models, come in.

*2. Utility Models.*    These approaches help decision makers spell out and evaluate their options in a systematic way. Consider, for example, a general approach known as *multiattribute utility theory (MAUT)*. First, you identify all the attributes that matter to you (e.g., in the case of toothpaste, cost, health benefits, taste, and smile). Next, you identify your choice options (brands). Finally, you estimate how much each option offers of each attribute using a common *(utility)* scale, add up the component values, and compare the results. Estimating some of these values is no easy matter, particularly given the requirement of a common scale. One approach is to convert everything, including the subjective features, to dollars; another is to use some neutral scale such as rating points or "utiles."

*3. Choice Models.*    This approach tells you which option to pick. If in the above example one brand scored higher than the others overall, it would be the obvious choice. Usually, however, the choice is not so obvious because of the uncertainty in some of the attribute-option combinations. You do not know for sure that your smile will be improved with Brand X. So you must estimate how *likely* each option is to produce each attribute, and figure this into your overall evaluation. A choice model commonly applied to this kind of problem is the *expected utility maximization* model, which weights the collective value of an option's attributes by the chances of getting them and then looks for the option with the highest expected utility.

*4. Personnel Selection Application.*    In the case of personnel selection decisions, the expectation part of the problem is solved by the traditional selection approach. The simple case depicted in Figure 10.3 tells you, for any possible decision cutoff, what the chances are of (1) hiring successful employees (quadrant I), (2) hiring unsuccessful ones (quadrant IV), (3) not hiring ones who could have succeeded (quadrant II), and (4) not hiring ones who would have failed (quadrant III). These expectancies are represented by the proportions of cases falling within each of the four quadrants (.08, .02, .42, and .48, respectively). More sophisticated versions of this general approach let you estimate expected changes in *performance* rather than just gross success-failure criteria. Still, expectation is all they tell you.

Utility models, on the other hand, enable you to get beyond mere expectations to the *worth* of each of these kinds of outcomes by using whatever attributes you consider important. You would probably include estimates of such things as what a highly successful performer (or some increment in performance) is worth, how much a failure costs you (in training, mistakes, morale, or frustration), and what the testing program would cost to implement and administer. All these are values connected with the people you *hire* using the program (quadrants I and IV). To complete the utility estimate, you would have to include values for the *not hired* quadrants as well. This is where social values (e.g., the desire to be fair) or related costs (e.g., the risk of discrimination lawsuits) would be registered.

Finally, after estimating the overall utility of each decision option (using vs. not using a test battery, alternative cut scores for the battery, alternative testing programs, etc.), you could use a choice model to help you make the best decision.

*5. Costing Personnel Decisions.*    Business tends to reduce everything to a dollar value, including such societal considerations as polluting the environment, employee welfare, and fairness. For example, a decision on whether to implement costly air pollution controls might be cast in the form of $X for the controls versus $Y for the combined cost of penalties, litigation, and bad publicity multiplied by the risk of getting caught. If X = $5 million and Y = $10 million times .10 (risk), there would be a $4 million advantage in continuing to pollute.

Thus, by dividing a complex decision into its estimated cost elements, a company can make economically rational choices. The values used here are hypothetical, of course, but they illustrate the sad reality that penalties levied by society on antisocial behavior such as pollution and hiring discrimination are often too small to act as effective deterrents; this becomes apparent in decision analysis. The example also illustrates the point we made earlier about the danger of applying science to moral and ethical issues. Doing so can make socially irresponsible behavior look like a wise business practice, particularly if no attempt is made to factor in social costs.

While there are thus obvious disadvantages to putting all the utility attributes on a common economic scale, it has the advantage of using a language that everyone understands and even the most hard-nosed executive can appreciate. It is much easier to sell managers on a human relations program expressed in dollar savings from reduced turnover and waste than it would be on the inherent social virtues of responsible management. Therefore, recent applications of decision theory to human resource management have featured the strategy of estimating costs and benefits of management tools (selection devices, training programs, performance appraisal systems, etc.) in dollar terms (Arvey & Faley, 1988; Cascio, 1991). Limited though it is, this is one of the main ways I/O psychology has helped to clarify the true nature of selection problems.

A good example of this application of multiattribute utility analysis is the *Cascio-Ramos estimate of performance in dollars* (CREPID). If you wanted to convince management that they should adopt a particular selection battery or some other HRM tool, you could help your case by telling them how much the improved performance they could expect would be worth. The CREPID model enables you to estimate this value by (1) decomposing each job into *major activities* (attributes); (2) *weighting* each attribute for each job by a combination of its importance, difficulty, frequency (or time spent on it), and seriousness of errors; (3) putting a *dollar value* on the attributes by apportioning current salaries for the job category according to the attribute weights (e.g., if the *responsibility* attribute were weighted .10 in a job category, and the average salary were $30,000 for that category, the value of responsibility would be set at $3,000); (4) rating performance of incumbents on each of the attributes on a 0–200 point scale; and (5) multiplying each employee's performance points for each attribute by its dollar value (as determined in step 3) and adding them up (Cascio, 1991). The resulting dollar figure tells you how much the individual employee's performance is worth. With this estimate set, you can easily compute mean performance values for any job category and variability around these means (the standard deviation of performance). By attaching these performance values to the estimate of how much you expect performance to improve as a result of the HRM tool, you can make your case in the dollar language that managers appreciate.

*6. Fairness Revisited.*    Before leaving the topic of selection as decision making, we need to bring to a conclusion a theme woven throughout the chapter: the fairness issue. How has the logic of decision analysis helped clarify this inherently subjective problem, and could it do more?

To answer the first part of the question, return to the situation depicted in Figure 10.3. Suppose that our valid ($r_{xy} = .60$) test actually does screen out a disproportionate number of minority applicants (i.e., it has what the law calls *adverse impact* against these groups). In practice, minorities score lower on the test, on the average, than whites do. This could occur because of a real difference between the groups in whatever traits are important for success or because of bias (a difference due to some unrelated factor or factors). One way to tell would be to compute the validity or prediction equations *separately* for the two groups and compare the results, an approach called the *moderator variable* design or *moderated validity*. Race in this case would constitute the moderator variable, a factor that is suspected of influencing the relation of test to criterion scores. If predictiveness shows up for only one group (*single-group* validity) or is much different for the two groups (*differential* validity), then we suspect bias.

Any reasonable person would agree that it would be grossly unfair to screen minority candidates out using biased test scores. At one time it was suspected that many of our most common predictors were differentially biased against minorities, a fear that has proven largely unfounded (Boehm, 1977). However, the possibility of differential validity and potential bias in a specific predictor for minorities, women, or any other group can never be ruled out without empirical evidence. From a moral-ethical standpoint it is incumbent upon employers to make sure a selection device is valid whenever it is shown to have *adverse impact* (see Table 10.1) against an identifiable group. Until very recently, it was also a *legal* requirement.

Suppose, on the other hand, it turns out that the predictiveness is comparable for the two groups even though one scores lower. We would have to assume that the lower scores are due to less actual capability, and that those screened out have less chance of success. In this case, we would be well within our legal rights in using the predictor (Arvey & Faley, 1988). However, one could still question its *fairness* on grounds that we explained earlier: The success criterion could be biased, or even if it were not, social patterns of discrimination could account for the lower scores. In short, we are back to the subjective realm of social values.

How, then, has the fairness issue been clarified? Mainly it has been by distinguishing the components of the selection process that contribute to adverse impact and suggesting options for dealing with them. In fact, a number of explicit fairness models have been specified, each of which amounts to a decision rule based on a different set of utility assumptions (Arvey & Faley, 1988). The traditional model (Figure 10.3), for example, considers only the people *hired,* and only the *employer's* utilities: Costs to people *not hired* and to society at large are disregarded. A strict quota model in which the goal is to hire the right number of each identified group (women, minorities, older people, etc.), considers only the broad *social* utilities without regard for the employer or the qualified people who are not hired. The other models fall somewhere between these extremes. Clarification, therefore, spells out the options rather than proclaiming which concept of fairness is the right one, but even this level of clarification is a substantial improvement over uninformed argument.

It may seem harsh to characterize the ongoing public debate over fair employment policy as uniformed, but the patchwork of laws, regulations, and court rulings (collectively known as case law) that have evolved suggest strongly that our legislators and judges do not fully understand the technical issues. We will not recount the sequence of twists and turns that public policy has taken over the years, nor the contradictions and ambiguities that it has produced, except to say that it has tended to reflect the political views of the party in power and has left employers and employees quite confused. A good account of the critical events may be found in Arvey & Faley (1988). Table 10.1 summarizes some of those events.

During the 1970s, the social and legal emphasis was on ensuring that employers did not blatantly discriminate against minorities and women, a practice called *disparate treatment,* nor indirectly discriminate by using employment procedures that are biased against such groups, a practice called *disparate (or adverse) impact.* It was fairly easy for those who believed that they were victims of such practices to bring suit against their employers. Even in the more subtle disparate impact case, all the employee had to do was show that the employer's *stock* of employees or *flow* of new hires was not rep-

**Table 10.1**

## U.S. LAWS AND SUPREME COURT CASES HAVING IMPLICATIONS FOR RECRUITING AND SELECTING EMPLOYEES

**Civil Rights Act of 1964:** Federal law that declared many forms of racial and sexual discrimination illegal. Title VII of this act made it illegal "to fail or refuse to hire or to discharge any individual, or otherwise to discriminate against any individual with respect to his compensation, terms, conditions, or privileges of employment because of such individual's race, color, religion, sex, or national origin." A federal agency, the Equal Employment Opportunity Commission (EEOC), was created to administer the law.

**Executive Order 11246 (1965).** President Lyndon Johnson issued an executive order in which all employers having contracts with the federal government in excess of a specified amount were prohibited from discriminating on the basis of race, religion, color, sex, or national origin. This order also requires employers to take *affirmative action* to ensure that women and minorities are hired. Employers were required to file timetables and goals in which they report areas of underutilization of protected groups and steps they will take to remedy these deficiencies. The Department of Labor was given authority to investigate and monitor compliance with the order.

**The EEOC Uniform Guidelines (1978).** Rules set down by a panel of experts from industry, government, and education for fair employment practices. The guidelines called for systematic record keeping on employment decisions (e.g., tabulation of who is and isn't hired, validity studies). According to the *four-fifths rule,* a hiring procedure has "adverse impact" against a group when the selection rate for the group is less than 80 percent of the group with the highest rate of selection. If there is adverse impact, the employer must show that the hiring procedures are valid.

**Age Discrimination in Employment Act (ADEA).** The original act was passed in 1967 and later amended in 1978 and protects employees between the ages of 40 and 70 from discrimination on the basis of age. Employers may use age as a qualification but only if it is a legitimate and necessary qualification (also called a bona fide occupational qualification or BFOQ).

**Griggs v. Duke Power (1971).** The Duke Power Co. in North Carolina had a policy of only promoting employees out of the labor pool to higher skill jobs if they had a high school degree and passing scores on two aptitude tests. Black applicants tended to score lower on the two tests and were less likely to have a high school degree. Consequently, they were more likely to be passed over for promotion. The Supreme Court ruled that if selection procedures have an adverse impact on the hiring of a protected group, the employer must show that the procedures are valid even if the discrimination was unintentional.

**Albermarle Paper Company v. Moody (1975).** As in Duke Power, the company's use of tests led to discrimination against black employees in hiring and promotion. Unlike Duke Power, the company in this case presented evidence for the validity of the selection procedures. The Supreme Court ruled against the employer largely on the basis of the poor technical quality of the validation research. Employers were expected to adhere to the technical guidelines set forth in the Uniform Guidelines of the EEOC.

**Americans with Disability Act (1990).** This act makes it unlawful to discriminate against a qualified person with a disability. Disability is defined broadly as including a physical or mental impairment that substantially limits one or more of the major life activities, a record of such an impairment, or being regarded as having such an impairment. The act states that employers may not discriminate against a qualified individual in employment decisions, including selection, promotion, and placement. A qualified individual with a disability is defined as an individual with a disability who, with or without reasonable accommodation, can perform the essential functions of the employment position. This act has yet to be interpreted in the courts.

**Table 10.1 (Continued)**

**Civil Rights Act of 1991.** During the 1980s the U. S. Supreme Court in several court decisions made it much harder for a person filing a suit (the plaintiff) to prove discrimination. Griggs v. Duke made it clear that if there is adverse impact against a protected group, the burden would be on the employer to show that selection procedures are valid. In Wards Cove Co., Inc. v. Atonio et al (1989), however, the U. S. Supreme Court placed much more of a burden on the plaintiff. In the Civil Rights Act of 1991 Congress stated that "the decision of the Supreme Court in Wards Cove Packing Co. v. Atonio, 490 U. S. 642 (1989) has weakened the scope and effectiveness of Federal civil rights protections." Consequently, the act made into law the concepts set forth in Griggs v. Duke Power (1971) and also extended the Civil Rights Act of 1964 by allowing the plaintiff to have a jury trial and to claim punitive damages.

resentative of the available labor pool in terms of sex, race, or whatever was the basis of the complaint (Ledvinka, 1982). Then the burden of proof was on the employer to show that his hiring practices, individually or collectively, were justifiable for reasons of *business necessity*. Often this meant demonstrating the validity of a selection device and showing that it had as little adverse impact against the group in question as any available alternative.

With the conservative shift of the 1980s, however, came a succession of changes in the legal climate that is still in full sway. Without going into the complicated legal issues involved, it has become much harder for an aggrieved party to bring suit and win (Potter, 1989). For one thing, purely statistical data such as the representation of minorities in the population and the rate at which they are hired are less acceptable as evidence of disparate impact. For another, the courts made it easier for employers to justify business necessity in defending their hiring practices: in essence, loosening the validation requirements in cases of disparate impact. The burden of proof shifted from defendant to plaintiff: Employees must go to more trouble to prove that they are being treated unfairly than employers do to prove that they are not treating employees unfairly. Congress recognized this shift and passed the Civil Rights Act of 1991 to shift the burden back toward the organization, but it is too early to tell whether this act will make it easier to sue for discrimination or will increase the amount of such litigation.

Is further improvement possible for bringing some coherence and rationality to arguments over hiring practices and other related issues? Of course. One way would be to extend multiattribute utility theory to the social policy realm. Legislators, judges, and employers could thrash out their differences using a common set of explicit value dimensions rather than vague generalizations. For example, the issue of how much adverse impact is tolerable in a valid selection process could be resolved with reference to the estimated utilities for employees, protected groups, society at large, or any other relevant constituency rather than using emotionally charged and nebulous concepts such as social justice. When existing rules encourage practices that are clearly at variance with the best interests of society, as in the air pollution example, it would be a sign that the rules (laws) need to be reexamined. Stiffer penalties would encourage a more equitable representation of social values. None of this is likely to receive wide acceptance, however, because it would force politicians to do what they hate to do most: get specific on controversial issues. Moreover, if employers resist models that consider only cost factors because the models are too complicated (Schmitt & Robertson, 1990), it is doubtful they would welcome models of even greater complexity, especially when current trends operate in the employers' favor. Still, this is an area in which I/O psychology could contribute to society's well-being in an important way by promoting defensible strategies for decision making.

## COMPENSATORY AND NONCOMPENSATORY SELECTION STRATEGIES

We have limited our attention to one kind of selection scenario: the case in which there is a single predictive score for each candidate, a selection cut score, and a single choice point. Actually, even the simplest cases generally involve *multiple* predictors, such as background information and an interview. If testing is used, it often consists of a *battery* of tests, each aimed at a different trait or job component. All this information must be combined if a decision is to be reached. How this is done matters a great deal insofar as effectiveness, fairness, or any other outcome is concerned.

The most common strategy, particularly when a test battery is involved, is the *compensatory* approach, whereby a low score on one predictor can be offset by a high score on another. The aggregate is the basis for prediction, and the statistical tool of *multiple regression* (Chapter 2) is often used to combine measures. Even when the process is done intuitively (remember Mr. Megabucks) and there are no real scores, compensatory logic tends to dominate. We may be inclined to overlook experience deficiencies, for example, in a person who is obviously motivated to learn.

Most other decision strategies involve *noncompensatory* elements. In the *multiple cutoff* approach, each predictor is considered separately, each has its own cut score, and a candidate must exceed the cutoff on *all* scores to qualify. This approach is most appropriate when success requires at least a minimal amount of certain key characteristics. For example, you cannot compensate for lacking intelligence by having a pleasant personality and great physical strength if selection to medical school is at issue.

Sometimes the decision proceeds in stages, each having its noncompensatory cutoff, rather than being determined all at once. This is referred to as a *multiple hurdle* strategy. It makes good sense in cases that involve a long, costly development process and for which ultimate success requires exceptional capability. Selection of combat pilots for the U.S. military forces is a case in point. You would not want to entrust a multimillion dollar aircraft and the lives of an entire crew to someone who failed to meet performance standards at any stage in the training process regardless of how well he or she did at earlier stages.

# PLACEMENT

While much of the selection logic applies to placement as well, several noteworthy differences stem from the fact that a number of individuals and jobs must be considered *at once* to achieve the best *overall* fit. In some cases all the people must be assigned to jobs; in others, some can be screened out (making one of the placement categories "elsewhere"). In very large organizations, such as the military, there are two sequential decisions: identification of a cadre of acceptable recruits (selection) followed by assignment (placement) into existing specialization categories. Gross initial assignment is generally followed by specific job placement, and a succession of subsequent placements, as the person's career unfolds.

Just as in the case of selection, placement strategy depends on the utilities you accord the various outcomes. If, for example, you were only concerned with giving everyone an equal chance at every job and did not care about performance, you might assign them randomly. If you were mainly concerned about a few critical jobs, you might want to fill those with your top candidates, irrespective of how the others were assigned. Since there are so many possible methods and so many possible attributes to consider, placement decisions can be complicated. This is probably the main reason placement has received less attention in either research or practice than selection (Zedeck & Cascio, 1984).

Once again, decision models can help you organize your preferences and pick a strategy that best suits your objectives. We illustrate how such models work rather than getting into the technical details of specific models. Let us assume that your goal is to assign people to get the highest collective performance from the group. Assume, further, that you have classified all the jobs according to the personal qualities (knowledge, skills, abilities, etc.) that contribute to successful performance and that you have measured all your candidates on all of these qualities. Finally, assume that you have an estimate of how sensitive performance is to different levels of the various personal qualities. At this point, it would be a simple matter for a computer to calculate which assignment pattern would yield the highest expected performance aggregate. Undoubtedly many of the jobs would be filled by someone other than the most qualified people, since the best candidates would probably turn out to be the most qualified for several jobs, and even the worst candidates would have to be placed somewhere. Nevertheless, a uniquely best placement strategy could be specified to achieve the stated goal.

In the workplace it is rarely possible to satisfy all these assumptions, so the kind of approach illustrated is seldom fully implemented. However, various approximations can be used (Landy, 1989). For our purposes it is enough that you understand the principles involved so you can appreciate (1) the importance of specifying your placement objectives, (2) the kinds of information you need to optimize assignment for those objectives and, (3) the way decision models can be used to help you approach that optimum. The more completely you can describe these decision elements, the closer you can come to the ideal placement.

# SELECTION AND PLACEMENT TOOLS: PREDICTORS

The main purpose of this chapter has been to acquaint you with the basic ideas that underlie the philosophy and practice of matching people and jobs. We have asked you to think through the logic of the matching philosophy itself as well as the various strategies for implementing it, and most of all, we have asked you to think about the implications of these strategies for the employee, the employer, and society at large. If we have succeeded, you have a good understanding of how tools such as predictors, validation techniques, and decision models work, what they are good for, and how they should be used. We have not been very specific about the tools themselves because they are too numerous, and most require more background than we can provide here.

In the rest of this chapter, we take a brief look at the predictors (interviews, biographical information, and tests) around which the matching philosophy is built. Each is best thought of as a source of information about an individual. The information obtained from one predictor often can be verified by using other predictors that yield related information. If somebody reports having had experience as a mechanic (biodata) and does well on an appropriate test, we can put more faith in both. Also, each source has its strengths and weaknesses. Thus, it is usually advisable to use multiple predictors. One of the most serious mistakes in the use of tests is overreliance on a single predictor, even when it is a reasonably good predictor.

## Interviews

Interviews can be conducted in a variety of ways for a variety of purposes. They can be highly *structured* or *open ended*, focused on selling the job, sizing up the candidate, or getting some specific piece of information (e.g., how a person handles stress). Many are done simply because company rules require it or the employer feels more comfortable seeing the candidate in the flesh.

Not surprisingly, interviews vary considerably in the extent to which they are useful as predictors. As typically conducted, they are subject to many interviewer biases and distortions associated with the interaction between interviewer and interviewee (Dipboye, 1992; Harris, 1989). Nevertheless, they are by far the most commonly used kind of predictor and managers have great faith in them, particularly managers who operate in the intuitive mode. A great deal of interview research has been done over the years in an effort to understand the distortions and to develop ways to improve the process. Some work has sought to establish actual reliability and validity estimates, although in practice such data are rarely gathered.

The most current generalizations to be drawn from this work are that (1) interviews can have respectable predictive validity, particularly if they are carefully structured and corrected for unreliability (Wiesner & Cronshaw, 1988); (2) using multiple interviews can improve their reliability (although it is costly) as can training in and structuring of the interview process (Arvey & Campion, 1982); (3) it is still not clear whether interviews give us unique information about the interviewee or whether the same information can be obtained more easily and accurately through tests or biographical inventories (Dipboye, 1989); and (4) each interview is a dynamic social process that evolves as a function of the unique interaction between the interviewee and the interviewer(s) (Dipboye & Macan, 1988). Taken together, these conclusions suggest that the interview may hold more promise than it has traditionally been given credit for, but much still remains to be learned before we can make the best use of it. A particularly important area for future research is to determine why structured interviews have higher predictive validity than unstructured interviews (Dipboye & Gaugler, 1993).

## Biographical Information

This category includes demographic, work history, and other personal data. It can be gathered using application blanks, reference checks, resumes, and other familiar techniques. Since biodata are usually obtained in the hiring process and written records of them tend to be retained, they have lent themselves readily to validation research. Although the results have been mixed, some studies have reported quite reasonable predictive validities (mostly in the $r = .20 - .40$ range). Naturally, validity and usefulness depend on exactly what information is included, what predictions are desired, and a number of other factors (Mumford & Owens, 1987).

The main weakness in this source of information, as in the structured interview, has been that it is difficult to tell why a biographical item is predictive (i.e., what construct it taps). Recent work seems to be overcoming this problem through various construct validation efforts (Zedeck & Cascio, 1984; Schmitt & Robertson, 1990; Mumford & Owens, 1987). Also in common with the interview, there is the obvious potential for biodata to be culturally biased. Questions about arrest record, parents' education level or marital status, and number of brothers and sisters, for example, could be surrogates for *ethnicity*. This potential problem has been mitigated somewhat by the appearance of various advisories listing appropriate and inappropriate questions (Arvey & Faley, 1988), but there is virtually no research assessing bias in specific items. If such research were conducted it might show that biodata and structured interviews offer less risk of cultural bias overall than do other kinds of predictors (Huffcut, 1990).

Biodata must tap many of the same constructs as interviews and tests. One could easily develop a structured interview from the items on a biographical inventory, and many of these items would look similar to items on a test of personality traits. The real issue, then, is one of underlying constructs. Once we have a better grasp of the traits that are most predictive of important criteria and of how the various sources of predictive information map onto them, we will be in a better position to know when to use each predictor.

## Tests

Tests have been devised for virtually every trait you can imagine. Collections of them have been assembled into predictive *batteries* for specific jobs (e.g., mechanic) or job families (e.g., clerical occupations). They vary in format from the familiar *paper-and-pencil* variety that you have come to know and love, including both objective and essay forms, to ones that measure physical abilities or other skills through some kind of manual *performance*. Some are derived from theoretical constructs such as cognitive abilities or dispositions, while others are empirically based and face valid. At the latter extreme are those consisting of actual samples of the jobs or tasks for which people are being selected (*work sample tests* or *simulations*). An increasingly popular version of this approach is known as the *assessment center,* a comprehensive and intensive simulation of an entire work situation (Gaugler, Rosenthal, Thornton, & Bentson, 1987).

### STANDARDIZATION AND NORMING

Most of the tests used in personnel decision making are *standardized,* which means that they were professionally developed under carefully controlled conditions using a particular sample of people (a *developmental* sample). How this sample performed is the basis for interpreting the scores when a test is applied to other people. The distribution of scores in the developmental sample, or test *norms,* constitute the frame of reference, much as if your grade on an American history test were set by the curve established in a previous class. You might, for example, get an A by scoring at a level that would place you in the top 10% of that class (distribution) even though you missed 30% of the questions.

Pursuing this example, it should be apparent why it is important that the developmental sample, hence the norms for the test, be appropriate for you and your class. Imagine how you would feel if the previous class consisted of honors history majors, and your class was comprised largely of Hispanic immigrants whose cultural background was very different from that of the previous class. You probably would question the fairness of these norms. Many standardized tests specify norms for the various populations represented in their developmental sample (e.g., women and men, ethnic groups, age groups, the general U.S. population). The employers must decide for themselves how appropriate the norms are for the applicant pool.

Some tests, like the ones you take in most of your courses, are not standardized, but are home grown. Usually the instructor's emphasis is on ensuring adequate representation of the material for which you are responsible, an implicit content validity orientation. The same is true of many tests used by employers to evaluate learning or achievement. What matters most is coverage, irrespective of who is taking the test. A pilot who does not know emergency procedures is a hazard no matter how his overall flying performance compares with other trainees.

When home-grown tests are used *predictively* they should be subjected to the same kinds of developmental processes and quality checks as standardized tests, developing *local* norms, and reliability and validity statistics. When this approach is followed, comparability of developmental and application populations (hence appropriateness of norms) is assured since they are one and the same. Unfortunately, however, employers often fail to follow through on the costly evaluation of home-grown tests, so reasonable content validity is about the best you can hope for. In the context of academic courses, when content mastery is the goal, this is usually enough. In the context of making critical personnel decisions, when predicting success is the goal, it clearly is not.

## TYPES OF TESTS

Tests used in selection and placement can be classified on many dimensions. For our purposes, however, it is sufficient to distinguish four broad categories: achievement, specific aptitude, general intelligence, and personality measures.

**Achievement Tests**   These tests measure a person's present level of knowledge or proficiency in a content area, usually resulting from some educational experience. Typing tests, your final exam in history, and the Scholastic Aptitude Test (SAT) for physics competency are good examples. Because they attempt to provide a representative sample of content from a topical area, the typical approach to validating achievement tests is to use a content validation strategy. However, criterion-related and construct validation approaches also may be appropriate approaches to validating achievement tests, depending on the inferences that are made from test scores.

**Specific Aptitude Tests**   In contrast to achievement tests, which attempt to measure what a person has learned in specific areas, aptitude tests attempt to measure what a person is *capable* of learning in these areas. Thus, achievement tests focus on the past and measure knowledge and skills that are assumed to be open to change, while aptitude tests measure relatively stable traits that are assumed to predict how a person is likely to perform in the future. *Specific aptitude tests* attempt to measure traits that involve a person's potential or capability to be knowledgeable or proficient in some specific area. The quantitative and verbal parts of the SAT are examples with which you may be familiar. Illustrated in Figure 10.4 are items used to measure

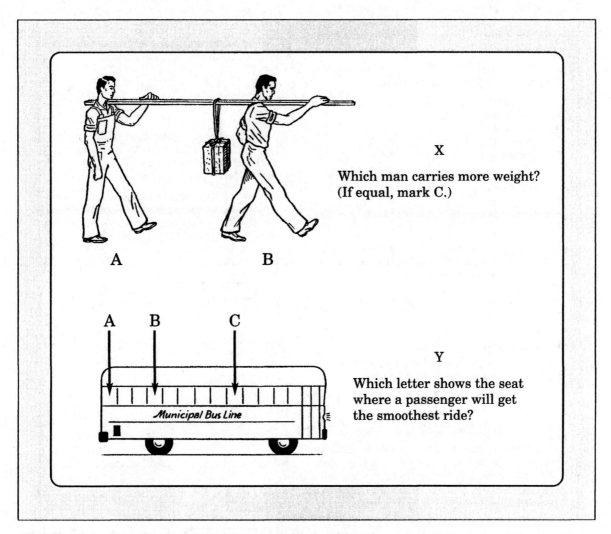

**Figure 10.4**   *Item used to measure mechanical ability*

*Source:* From the Bennett Test of Mechanical Comprehension (Reproduced by permission. Psychological Corporation, New York, N.Y. All rights reserved).

mechanical ability. Figure 10.5 shows items used to measure the seven primary mental abilities originally identified by Thurstone (1938): verbal comprehension, word fluency, number aptitude, inductive reasoning, memory, spatial aptitude, and perceptual speed. These types of tests often contain items that are more abstract and less bound to specific content than the typical achievement test. Consequently, criterion-related or construct validation strategies are often more appropriate in evaluating aptitude tests than content validation strategies.

*Verbal comprehension:* to understand the meaning of words and their relations to each other; to comprehend readily and accurately what is read; measured by test items such as:

Which one of the following words means most nearly the same as *effusive?*

1. evasive
2. affluent
3. **gushing**
4. realistic
5. lethargic

*Word fluency:* to be fluent in naming or making words, such as making smaller words from the letters in a large one or playing anagrams; measured by test items such as:

Using the letters in the word *Minneapolis,* write as many four letter words as you can in the next two minutes.

_____
_____
_____
_____

*Number aptitude:* to be speedy and accurate in making simple arithmetic calculations; measured by test items such as:

Carry out the following calculations:

| 346 | 8732 | 422 x 32 = _____ |
|---|---|---|
| + 722 | − 4843 | 3630 : 5 = _____ |

*Inductive reasoning:* to be able to discover a rule or principle and apply it to the solution of a problem, such as determining what is to come next in a series of numbers or words; measured by test items such as:

What number should come next in the sequence of the following five numbers?

1 5 2 4 3

1. 7
2. 1
3. 2
4. 4
5. 3

*Memory:* to have a good rote memory for paired words, lists of numbers, etc.; measured by test items such as:

The examinee may be given a list of letters paired with symbols such as:

| A * | E ? |
|---|---|
| B , | F ; |
| C ★ | G : |
| D ! | H . |

He is given a brief period to memorize the pairs. Then he is told to turn the page and write the appropriate symbols after each of the letters appearing there.

*Spatial aptitude:* to perceive fixed geometric relations among figures accurately and to be able to visualize their manipulation in space; measured by test items such as:

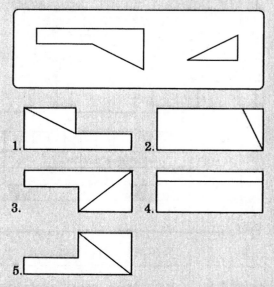

Which figure would result if the two pieces in the picture above were put together?

*Perceptual speed:* to perceive visual details quickly and accurately; measured by test items such as:

Make a check mark in front of each pair below in which the numbers are identical.

1. 367773_____367713
2. 471352_____471352
3. 581688_____581688
4. 324579_____334579
5. 875989_____876898

**Figure 10.5** *Items used in measuring seven primary mental abilities*

*Source:* Dunnette, M.D. (1966). *Personnel Selection and Placement.* Monterey, CA: Brooks/Cole.

As discussed in Chapter 2, psychological constructs are often easier to conceive than to measure. While achievement and aptitude constructs can be easily distinguished in theory, in practice it is impossible to completely distinguish between aptitude and achievement. It would be very hard to measure your math aptitude, for instance, without relying to some extent on your experience with quantitative concepts. Likewise, experience with language is invariably confounded with verbal aptitude. Rather than imposing rigid distinctions, it is perhaps best to think of the distinction in terms of emphases rather than absolute differences. Aptitude tests emphasize abilities and potential more than achievement tests do.

**General Intelligence Tests**   These measure mental aptitude more broadly than do any of the specific aptitude tests. Their purpose is to indicate overall capability for acquiring and using knowledge, in essence *learning* ability, and while not without problems (Murphy & Davidshofer, 1991), their record in forecasting a wide variety of learning and performance outcomes (e.g., academic grades, training completion, job success, etc.) has been good (Guion, 1965; Schmidt & Hunter, 1981; Walsh, 1989). From a predictive standpoint, therefore, intelligence tests are among the most valid tools we have.

Somewhat paradoxically, they also have been among the most vehemently criticized on both technical and social grounds. Indeed, intelligence testing has been at the heart of a host of major social controversies, including the civil rights movement, fair employment practices, and our national education policy. Even the debate over minimum admissions standards for college athletes is an intelligence testing issue. From a technical standpoint, experts continue to argue over the appropriate content and interpretation of such tests (Murphy & Davidshofer, 1991).

If you consider the different concepts of validity and the conflicting values surrounding the concept of fairness, you can easily see why intelligence testing generates controversy. There is no universal agreement, even among the experts, on the precise definition of the intelligence *construct*. Some see it as an aggregate of all the specific aptitudes; others see it as a superordinate *G factor* that governs the individual's intellectual prowess; still others see it somewhere in between: broader than specific aptitudes but comprising several somewhat independent components (e.g., verbal, quantitative, spatial capabilities).

Among the more prominent current theories is one that distinguishes reasoning ability (*fluid* intelligence) from skill content and the ability to store knowledge (*crystallized* intelligence) (Cattell, 1963). Interestingly, fluid intelligence seems to drop off as people get older, whereas crystallized intelligence is more resistant to aging (Horn, 1985). Modern theories of human *cognition* have introduced a whole new perspective on the intelligence construct and how best to measure it (Sternberg, 1977). For example, individuals differ greatly in their ability to hold items in working (short-term) memory as well as to manipulate those items quickly. Since both of these traits are related to how well people learn, they are obvious candidates for intelligence testing (Kyllonen, 1991).

So long as there is disagreement over the intelligence construct, therefore, the construct validity of any intelligence test can be challenged. If we do not know what it is, how can we trust any tool that purports to measure it? While there is some merit to this criticism in a narrow technical sense, it is more than offset by the massive evidence of *convergence* among different intelligence test results. Correlation or agreement among different measures of the same thing (temperature, intelligence, mechanical aptitude) is a principal way of showing that a construct exists, and of indexing its *construct validity*. Thus, even though a detailed understanding of what intelligence consists of is still evolving, any of the more commonly used tests will give a good account of a person's overall learning ability. Intelligence is as valid a construct as any we have.

The other main criticism of intelligence testing, the social values and fairness argument, is the more emotionally charged and difficult to resolve. There tend to be large, stable differences between the average scores for whites and certain minority groups on intelligence tests, favoring the former group by as many as 15 IQ points or one standard deviation (Murphy & Davidshofer, 1991). Thus, when used to select people for jobs, academic admission, or any other socially valued opportunity, these tests tend to have adverse impact against protected groups. The debate centers around what these differences mean and whether it is fair to use them in selection.

The most inflammatory part of the argument focuses on whether there is a genetic component involved, an issue that cannot be resolved to everyone's satisfaction with existing evidence and would be of little practical value if it could. A more fruitful issue is whether bias is involved, because if it is, there is the possibility of correcting for it. Since many intelligence tests were originally developed on predominantly white, urban samples, there was reason to question the norms. However, research on race as a moderator of validity has not produced much evidence for differential or single-group validity. Moreover, efforts to produce culturally fair tests, that is, to eliminate items that would favor a particular ethnic background, have if anything increased rather than reduced the discrepancy in average scores (Jensen, 1980). Therefore, whatever its basis, the difference appears to be real.

The preceding discussion of test fairness brings us back to the question of what to do about it. The answer is that it all depends on your particular idea of fairness. While there is no commonly accepted solution, federal and state officials have wrestled mightily with the problem in the context of defining and enforcing fair employment practices. They have tried, without much success, to write a clear set of rules fostering the idea that if a test (or other selection device) has adverse impact, it must be proven valid. The most noteworthy of these is a set of guidelines published by the federal government in 1978 to interpret Title VII of the Civil Rights Act of 1964, the law that prohibited discrimination in employment (EEOC, 1978). Although they helped somewhat at the time, these rules also proved to be subject to varying interpretations, and newer evidence on validity generalization and other technical issues has eroded their value. Moreover, the political winds have altered the philosophy that the rules were designed to clarify.

Issues and rules surrounding fair employment practices are not limited to the adverse impact of intelligence tests on minority groups, nor to tests or even selection per se. Included are personnel decisions and tools of any kind that affect the treatment of groups protected under the law. Employers must be as careful about how they evaluate or promote people, for example, as about how they hire them. We discuss these matters here only because intelligence testing, with its widely recognized disparate impact, has been at the core of the controversy from the beginning. Ironically, it still commands much more attention in the press and in the courts than techniques such as interviews and biodata, which are considerably easier to use in an unfair, biased way (Arvey & Faley, 1988).

**Personality Tests**   These are aimed at measuring dispositions or tendencies rather than capabilities. Personality tests are based on the idea that people have stable mental and behavioral patterns that they use in making their way through life, and these patterns can be described in terms of a relatively small number of traits. While there are many different tests, each with its own list of traits, the consensus view is that there are five basic underlying dimensions: *extraversion, agreeableness, conscientiousness, emotional stability,* and *openness to experience* (Tupes & Christal, 1961; Digman, 1990).

Even if this concept of personality is correct, getting measures that are useful for predictive purposes is no easy task. In the first place, traits are only part of the story. Situational characteristics and their interaction with traits are viewed by some theorists as considerably more important (Pervin, 1985). Thus, for example, you might be high on the *extraversion* trait, but if you found yourself in a work setting in which you were viewed as an outsider and your coworkers resented show-offs, you might not act extraverted.

Second, it is harder to measure dispositions than capabilities, particularly in the context of selection or placement. When you take an intelligence or aptitude test your sole aim is to do as well as you can. When you take a personality test, however, there are no right answers, and your strategy depends on the purpose of the test. If it is to help you understand yourself, as in a counseling session, you may answer with total honesty in hope of making a good career choice. If it is to help you get a job, as part of the selection process, you may answer to put yourself in the best possible light. For instance, you probably would not admit to some of the crazy or borderline dishonest things you did as a teenager if you were applying for a job in a bank!

Most personality tests used in selection are of the *self-report* variety; their items are *transparent* (easy to figure out), and they are thus subject to faking. Some try to overcome the problem by forcing you to choose between equally desirable or undesirable self-descriptions or by including special items that reflect your tendency to "fake good" (so-called *lie scales*). None can completely eliminate faking. An alternative to self-report gets around the problem by having you interpret ambiguous (hence nontransparent) stimuli such as ink blots, open-ended sentences, or incomplete stories (see the discussion of the TAT in Chapter 3). Unfortunately these so-called *projective* techniques present other problems. True, their lack of transparency makes them hard to fake, but interpreting what your responses say about you is problematic. At best, it requires a somewhat subjective analysis by a trained professional; at worst it is a dark art. Except for the TAT, such tests rarely have been validated in the workplace against relevant criteria.

In fact, personality measures have not fared well in the practical business of predicting work criteria (Guion, 1965). Typical validities rarely exceed .20, and when combined with other measures, personality scores seldom add more than a few percentage points to overall predictiveness. Nevertheless, one should not dismiss such measures too quickly. Even slight improvements in selection can be valuable if the cost of mistakes is high and large numbers of hiring decisions are being made. Moreover, personnel decision making is not the only reason to give personality tests. Provided they have good *construct* validity, they can provide useful information for competent professionals to use in counseling employees or for researchers to use in studying organizational behavior. There is always the possibility that validities are spuriously low because we have chosen the wrong criteria. Maybe personality measures would perform better if they were used to predict job satisfaction, commitment, or turnover indexes rather than performance measures.

The growing consensus on a five-factor model of personality plus recent evidence that measures on at least some of the traits are stable over long periods of time (Costa & McCrae, 1988) have stimulated a renewed interest in their predictive possibilities. Recent meta-analyses of the personnel selection research on personality have shown more impressive evidence for the validity of personality tests than revealed in earlier reviews (Tett, Jackson, & Rothstein, 1991; Barrick & Mount, 1991). Perhaps the most encouraging results have come from studies on large samples of military recruits (Hough, Eaton, Dunnette, Kamp, & McCloy, 1990). These researchers were able to show that measures of six personality constructs predicted important job-related criteria with uncorrected validities that in some cases reached as high as the .30s and .40s. Interestingly, the inventory used to measure these constructs *(ABLE, or Assessment of Background and Life Experiences)* is biographical in nature, supporting our earlier point about the potential similarity of biodata and personality constructs.

One criterion for which growing numbers of employers hope to find predictive help in personality measures involves the problem of employee dishonesty. Theft and other forms of dishonest behavior are becoming a major cost factor that employers want to combat through better selection (Chapter 1). A recent review of the research on paper and pencil tests of honesty has provided support for the validity of these measures in predicting theft and other forms of dishonesty (Ones, Viswesvaran, & Schmidt, 1993). From what we know about personality tests, however, it should be apparent that such devices offer limited protection against crooks, and even that may be offset by their notorious false alarm rate or tendency to misidentify good people as dishonest (Murphy & Davidshofer, 1991). The same is true for other kinds of honesty tests such as the polygraph which, ironically, though now largely illegal for hiring, has often been used as the *criterion* for validating honesty tests.

**Directions**

If you agree with a statement, or feel that it is true about you, answer TRUE.  If you <u>disagree</u> with a statement, or feel it is not true about you, answer FALSE.

People often expect too much of me.

The idea of doing research appeals to me.

It is hard for me to just sit still and relax.

I enjoy hearing lectures on world affairs.

I read at least ten books a year.

I like parties and socials.

**Figure 10.6**  *Sample items from the California Psychological Inventory*

*Source:* Gough, H.G. (1986). *California Psychological Inventory.* Palo Alto, CA: Consulting Psychologists Press.

This is just one example of the many flaws that characterize the development and validation of honesty tests. We repeat our admonition: Honesty testing may have its place, but only in the hands of the ethical, competent professional (Chapter 1). Unfortunately, those are often not the hands in which you find it.

In the strictest sense, global personality tests are those that try to present a complete picture of an individual's trait profile. A good example is the California Personality Inventory (Figure 10.6). There are also a number of more focused self-report inventories that exclusively measure interests, attitudes, temperaments, or various other facets of the broader personality. In all likelihood you have had firsthand experience with an interest inventory as part of a career or academic counseling program (Figure 10.7).

Virtually all the information about the global tests applies equally to these focused ones. Global or focused personality tests are designed to measure a specified set of constructs. Whether they do for the *person taking the test* is heavily dependent on the usage context. An interest inventory like the one shown lets you compare your interest profile against norms for people who have succeeded in specific fields. Used for counseling, it probably does a good job of disclosing relevant traits. Used for selection, however, it probably reveals something very different: your *perception* of what a successful person

**Directions:** This inventory is used to help you understand your work interests in a general way, and to show you some kinds of work in which you might be comfortable. The following pages list many jobs, activities, school subjects, and so forth, and you are asked to show your liking and disliking for each. Your answers will be compared with the answers given by people already working in a wide range of jobs, and your scores will show how similar your interests are to the interests of these people. But this is not a test of your abilities; it is an inventory of your *interests.* Your scores will be presented to you later, on a special sheet called a profile, with information on how to understand the scores.

**Part I. Occupations**

For each occupation listed below, show how you would feel about doing that kind of work.

Mark in the space labeled "L" if you think you would like that kind of work.

Mark in the space labeled "I" if you are indifferent (that is, if you think you wouldn't care one way or another).

Mark in the space labeled "D" if you think you would dislike that kind of work.

| L | I | D | 1. Actor / Actress

**Part II. School Subjects**

Show in the same way whether you are interested in these school subjects even though you may not have studies them.

| L | I | D | 1. Agriculture

**Part III. Activities**

Show in the same way as before. Give the first answer that comes to mind.

| L | I | D | 1. Making a speech

**Part IV. Leisure Activities**

Show in the same way how you feel about these ways of spending your leisure time. Work rapidly. Do not think over various possibilities. Give the first answer that comes to mind.

| L | I | D | 1. Golf

**Part V. Types of People**

Most of us choose jobs where we can work with people we enjoy. Show in the same way as before how you would feel about having day-to-day contact with the following types of people. Work fast. Don't think about specific examples. Just give the first answer that comes to mind.

| L | I | D | 1. Highway construction workers

**Part VI. Preference Between Two Activities**

Show which activity or occupation of each pair you like better: if you prefer the one on the left, mark in the space labeled "L;" if you prefer the one on the right, mark in the space labeled "R;" if you like or dislike both the same, or if you can't decide, mark the space labeled "=." Work rapidly. Mark one space for each pair.

1. Airline pilot | L | = | R | Airline ticket agent

**Part VII. Your Characteristics**

Show here what kind of person you are: if the statement describes you, mark in the space labeled "Y" (for "Yes"); if the statement does not describe you, mark the space labeled "N" (for "No"); if you cannot decide, mark in the space labeled "?." (Be frank in pointing out your weak points, because these are as important as your strong points in choosing a career.)

| Y | ? | N | 1. Usually start activities of my group

**Figure 10.7**   *Sample items from the Strong Vocational Interest Blank (SVIB)*

*Source:* The Board of Trustees of the Leland Stanford Junior University. (1985). *Strong Interest Inventory of the Strong Vocational Interest Blanks.* Palo Alto, CA: Consulting Psychologists Press.

in a specific field is interested in, and perhaps, your inclination to respond honestly.

<u>Assessment Centers</u>  In most assessment centers, people are assessed in groups, partly on the basis of their individual performance on tasks and partly on how they interact with other members of the group. Their assessment is carried out by a team of assessors specially trained in assessment center procedures. An assessment center could be located either within the organization or at some physical site outside the organization. Although psychologists may be involved in running the center, employees of the organization most often serve as assessors. Any type of employee could be evaluated with this method, but managerial applicants are most often the assessees. All of the selection instruments we have discussed (biographical data, interviews, and tests) could be included in an assessment center. Some instruments are unique to assessment centers, however. In one of these, the in-basket exercise, the assessees are presented with problem situations to which they respond by writing memos. Another common exercise is the leaderless group discussion, in which a group of assessees is given a topic to discuss and is observed to see how each person handles himself or herself in the discussion. On the basis of the various exercises, the team of assessors rates the assessees on a variety of dimensions, such as leadership, creativity, flexibility, motivation, and interpersonal skills.

Assessment centers are among the most predictive of selection instruments. Gaugler, Rosenthal, Thornton, and Bentson (1987) conducted a meta-analysis of 47 validation studies and found an average validity weighted by sample size of .29 in the prediction of various job criteria. After accounting for the unreliability of the criteria and restriction in range, a corrected validity of .37 was found. Despite the apparent success of assessment centers, there is little understanding of why they are predictive. Klimoski and Brickner (1987) proposed five possible reasons:

1. *Assessment center ratings contaminate criteria.* In some cases assessment evaluations may be known to the supervisors rating assessee performance on the job or making promotion decisions.
2. *Common stereotypes.* Those rating assessment center performances and those rating performance of the assessee on the job may possess similar stereotypes of a successful employee. Thus, assessment centers may capture the biases of those providing criterion ratings. Contrary to this interpretation, Gaugler et al. (1987) found that higher validities were obtained when psychologists were the assessors as opposed to managers. One would expect that psychologists would not be as familiar with stereotypes influencing personnel decisions as managers.
3. *Self-fulfilling prophecies.* Those doing well in assessment centers may experience feelings of self-efficacy and competence

that then carry over to the performance of the job. Likewise, those doing poorly might have low expectations for future success and subsequently fail on the job.

4. *Assessment center evaluations capture past performance.* Because assessors are exposed to a variety of information about past performances, assessor ratings may not reflect traits revealed in the assessment center as much as past performances of the assessee. One way that this might operate is if assessors review biographical data that reveal past accomplishments. Another possible manifestation of this bias would be if assessment center tasks sample actual tasks on the job. For instance, assessees with management experience could be expected to do better on an in-basket exercise than assessees without management experience.

5. *Assessment center evaluations as tests of managerial intelligence.* Assessees with higher levels of intelligence generally receive higher ratings in assessment centers than those with lower intelligence. This suggests that those who do better in the assessment center later do well on the job because of their intelligence.

Unfortunately we do not have the data to allow us to choose from among these alternative explanations. Sufficient data have been collected to allow us to conclude that assessment centers are useful tools in the selection and development of managers. Now researchers need to search for an explanation of why this technique succeeds.

**Work Samples**    The most direct method of testing applicants is to give them actual job tasks to perform and see how they do. Work samples are often used in organizations, such as when secretarial applicants are given dictation or material to type, firefighter applicants are told to carry a ladder, an auto mechanic applicant is told to adjust some car brakes, or a computer programmer applicant is given a program to write. The typical, informal work sample often suffers from a lack of standardization. One applicant for a secretarial position might be asked to take dictation of a very difficult letter from a reader who mumbles, and under noisy conditions, whereas another applicant might be faced with much more favorable test conditions. A second problem with informal work samples is that they may not provide a representative sample of the tasks in the job (i.e., they lack content validity). Consider, for instance, if secretaries were hired on the basis of how well they took dictation but this task was performed infrequently in the job. In this case, the work sample would not provide a very sound basis for selection decisions. A third problem can occur if new hires are not expected to have a specific task skill but to develop the skill through training. The applicant with prior experience would have an advantage, but you might overlook an inexperienced but highly capable applicant who could do the job well after training. A work sample could lead to unfair discrimination against minorities and women who might lack the experience of white male applicants (e.g., women might not have the experience in working on cars) but with training could do just as well as white males.

Despite the problems, there are advantages to properly designed work samples. High criterion-related validities are frequently associated with work samples. There is some evidence that smaller differences are found between majority and minority applicants on work sample tests than on paper-and-pencil tests of ability (Schmidt, Greenthal, Hunter, Berner, & Seaton, 1977). There is also evidence that applicants are more accepting of work samples, possibly because of their face validity (Robertson & Kandola, 1982). If work samples are used they should be based on formal job analyses. Using content validation strategies, an evaluation should be made of whether the tasks included in the sample are representative of important or critical tasks in the job. A work sample should be implemented in the same way for all applicants. Performance in the sample should be scored with objective measures of results and/or behaviorally anchored ratings (e.g., BARS or BOS; Chapter 9) rather than with casual observations (Brugnoli, Campion, & Basen, 1979). Moreover, work samples only should be used to measure those skills that applicants are expected to bring with them to the job.

## COMPUTERIZED PSYCHOLOGICAL TESTING

Like everything else in modern society, testing is becoming increasingly computer based, a development that poses many serious risks to accompany its immense advantages and opportunities. To do justice to this topic would require a whole chapter (Burke, 1993). To illustrate the point, however, let us consider a few pros and cons.

On the plus side, there are the obvious efficiencies to be realized in item presentation, scoring, and data processing. Perhaps more importantly, computer display and response capabilities (e.g., graphics and direct manipulation of icons) may allow us to measure traits that are inaccessible to standard paper-and-pencil instruments or to measure the standard traits better. Current research by the U.S. Air Force, for example, has uncovered some new cognitive ability dimensions responsible for learning through the use of computer-based testing (CBT) methods (Kyllonen, 1991). On the minus side, there are considerations such as cost and the potential for misuse and overselling. No gadget, however sophisticated, can compensate for lack of sound conceptual development, but potential test users do not always appreciate that. The seemingly limitless capability of high technology tends to fool people into believing that computers can do anything. Opportunists have been quick to capitalize on this ignorance by marketing unproven CBT software and by making exaggerated claims. The problem has become serious enough to prompt the American Psychological Association to develop a set of guidelines explicitly aimed at CBT (COPS & CPTA, 1986), but this is far from a total solution. The only real safeguard is an informed consumer.

# A FINAL SUMMATION AND A LOOK AT THE FUTURE

This chapter is about the age-old problem of staffing, and the equally venerable solution of trying to match human qualities to job requirements. Although outwardly a simple and reasonable approach, the matching strategy leads us into a variety of complications. It poses serious and unanswerable questions regarding the definition of a good match and the nature of social justice. It raises a host of implementation questions, from what tactics to emphasize to how best to evaluate specific tools. Some of these questions have answers and some do not, but regardless of how difficult the issues may be, I/O psychology has improved the situation considerably by making them more explicit. We cannot say what is *fair,* but we can give a clear account of the alternatives in any particular staffing controversy.

The most important contributions of I/O psychology, however, have come in the development and refinement of procedures for carrying out recruitment, selection, and placement tactics in a systematic, unbiased fashion. Not only with tools such as standardized predictors, but with technologies for validating them and for evaluating their worth, I/O psychology has been and continues to be a leading force in the pursuit of responsible staffing. Our principal goal has been to make sure you understand why these predictors are valuable and how they work.

Nowhere is the connection between I/O psychology and its societal and organizational contexts more apparent than in staffing and the issue of fairness, clearly the dominant theme of the past two decades. It is hard to see how society's demand for more equitable staffing practices could possibly have been implemented without I/O psychology's contribution.

This is not to say that all fair employment issues have been resolved. New ones appear with each shift in society's priorities, and society tends to be fickle. From demographic projections (Chapter 1), it appears that fairness questions involving age, gender, and ethnicity will command the attention of the next generation of I/O psychologists. When, for example, do physical and cognitive changes associated with aging justify terminating or reassigning an employee? How should such changes be measured to protect the rights of both the individual and the organization? What accommodations should be made for the special requirements of women or individuals for whom English is a second language?

Not all future staffing issues, however, will directly involve fairness. Projected shortages in the supply of skilled labor and technology-driven increases in the demand for certain skills will make effective recruiting, selection, and placement doubly important. So the search for demonstrably better tools will continue, but there is more. Employers also will need to invest more heavily in skills training. Thus, each individual hired who has trouble learning or who decides to leave after acquiring the skills will represent a substantial cost. What this means for I/O psychology is that greater attention will need to be given to the overall *systems* perspective on staffing rather than the piecemeal approach that is so evident today.

By systems perspective we mean projecting how many of what kinds of people will be needed over the next $N$ years (say, 1–5), and determining how best to achieve that goal using all available tools. The cost and effectiveness of each component, from recruiting to retention, will be considered together in developing an overall strategy. Naturally the success of this approach depends on how well you can estimate the capability of the component tools as well as the costs and benefits associated with each. It also requires a way of modeling the overall staffing process.

Modern computer technology provides the computational power to address such complex problems, and indeed progress has been made toward developing human resource planning software. Much remains to be done, however, in the matter of establishing precise evaluative estimates for the component tools. It may well turn out that we need to upgrade some of them substantially or emphasize them more. For example, employee commitment and retention will probably command greater attention as the skilled-labor shortage materializes: Ways to measure, predict, and enhance these outcomes will grow in importance.

The systems perspective is an extension of our discussion of decision making applied to staffing decisions. Human resource managers have only begun to realize the potential in this kind of global thinking. Applications to date have been limited to the simplest decision models applied to narrowly defined staffing problems (Schmitt & Robertson, 1990). We believe there is much to be gained by expanding the decision-modeling approach to include multiple processes, and I/O psychology has much to contribute to this endeavor.

Personnel selection, if done properly, can contribute significantly to an organization's effectiveness. But even with the best selection, employees learn much of what they need to perform their jobs as the result of their experiences in the work place after they are hired. A large part of the learning comes from trial-and-error, but organizations seldom leave the process entirely to chance. Instead, they are likely to formalize the learning process by training employees in the knowledge, skills, and attitudes needed to perform their jobs. We move on, then, to the second strategy for achieving a good fit, the training approach.

## DISCUSSION QUESTIONS

1.  For many highly skilled jobs there is a limited supply of qualified applicants, and organizations must compete to attract them. Is it justifiable for corporate recruiters to emphasize the positive aspects of the job and play down the negative, or should they be completely honest in describing the job?

2.  Compare and contrast selection and placement. Describe the situations in which each strategy would be the preferred approach.

3.  How does the scientific approach to selection resemble an intuitive approach and in what ways do they differ?

4. Why is reliability a necessary but not sufficient condition for criterion-related validity?

5. Why should the nature of the predictor and its intended use determine which of the approaches to estimating reliability is most appropriate?

6. Describe how a test with a low validity might still be useful as a result of the selection ratio and the base rate of success.

7. Show how one might use a rational decision model to choose among applicants for a job.

8. Discuss the evidence for and against the various predictors that can be used in selection and placement.

9. How does a compensatory strategy differ from a noncompensatory strategy? When might the latter be more appropriate?

10. Are hiring quotas for minorities and women fair? What are the arguments for and against the use of quotas?

## CASE
## III

### SELECTION OF FIREFIGHTERS IN CLEVELAND

In 1983 a group of women applied for firefighter positions in the City of Cleveland but were rejected. They filed a lawsuit against the city claiming that in rejecting them for employment, the city had violated Title VII of the 1964 Civil Rights Act. At the time they were rejected, the city had never hired a woman as a firefighter.

The selection process consisted of two tests, with applicants required to first pass a written test before taking a physical abilities test. These exams had been developed by a psychologist who had conducted job analyses to determine the tasks required of entry-level firefighters. From an examination of the frequency and importance of the tasks, a determination was made of the knowledge, skills, and abilities required for entry-level firefighters. Based on this research, a written test was developed to assess reading comprehension, the ability to follow directions, mathematical skills, and other forms of cognitive reasoning. The physical test consisted of three parts:

1. *Event 1: Overhead Lift.* Using a 33-pound barbell, candidates must lift the barbell overhead repeatedly for one minute or up to a maximum of 35 lifts.

2. *Event 2: Fire Scene Set-up and Tower Climb.* While wearing a custom-tailored self-contained breathing apparatus, candidates must drag two lengths of standard $2\frac{1}{2}$-inch hose 180 feet (90 feet one way, drop coupling, run to the other end of the hose, pick up and return 90 feet, drop coupling in designated area), run 75 feet to pumper, remove a one-person ladder (approximately 35 pounds) from the side of the pumper, carry the ladder into the fire tower, place it against the back rail of the first landing, and continue up the inside stairwell to the fifth floor where a moni-

tor observes the candidates' arrival. Then, candidates return to the first landing, retrieve the ladder, and place it on the pumper.

3. *Event 3: Dummy Drag.* Still wearing their self-contained breathing apparatus, candidates must drag 100-pound bag 70 feet (40 of which includes low headroom), turn and, still dragging the bag, return to the starting point.

The written test was worth a maximum of 100 points. An adjustment was made by awarding five extra points if the applicant was a qualified veteran, ten extra points if the applicant was a city resident, and six points if the applicant was a minority. The minority adjustment was made as the result of a previous court case involving racial discrimination. Those applicants who received an adjusted score of 35 points or higher were allowed to take the physical abilities test.

Of 285 women who took the written test, 122 passed and took the physical exam. Only 29 women scored high enough on both tests to be placed on an eligibility list. A total of 1,927 men took the written exam, with 1,206 passing. Of these, 1,069 scored high enough on both tests to be placed on the eligibility list. Those on the eligibility list were rank ordered on their test totals. The woman with the highest score ranked 334 on the eligibility list.

Previous Supreme Court decisions in cases involving the Civil Rights Act of 1964 (Griggs v. Duke Power, 401 U.S. 424, 429–431; Albemarle Paper Co. v. Moody, 422 U.S. 405) had established that those filing a suit must first show that one group was hired at a significantly lower rate than other groups as the result of the hiring procedures. In this case, the large differences in the rate at which men and women had been hired enabled the plaintiffs (the women) to make what is known as a prima facie case of discrimination. Once shown to have an adverse impact, the employer must then produce evidence that the procedures have "a manifest relationship to the employment in question." EEOC guidelines dictate that showing a manifest relationship involves providing evidence of the criterion, construct, and content validity of the hiring procedures.

The plaintiffs claimed that the tests lacked in all three respects. The physical tests lacked content validity because the three events only superficially replicated the actual sequence of tasks in the firefighter job. They also argued that the city had failed to show a substantial relationship between the test scores and criteria of success in the jobs. The physical tests lacked construct validity because they tested only anaerobic performance. In other words, the physical tests reflected traits such as strength and speed, and ignored stamina.

The lawyer representing the City of Cleveland submitted research findings that they claimed supported the validity of the selection procedures. The city claimed that the fact that the tests were constructed on the basis of a thorough job analysis was evidence of their content validity. Criterion-related validity was supported in a technical study showing a positive correlation between test scores and supervisor ratings of performance in the firefighter job. Although the aerobic capacity of applicants was not tested, the city argued that "speed and strength were most critical at the initial stages of a fire where matters of life and death are most acute."

The plaintiffs also argued that women were placed at a disadvantage by the scoring system that gave minority and veterans extra points. Although the elimination of these bonus points would raise the rank of women applicants, the city argued that the elimination of these adjustments would do little to improve the chances of the women applicants, given that the highest ranked woman was still only 334 on the eligibility list.

## CASE QUESTIONS

1. If you were the judge in this case, would you find the City of Cleveland guilty or innocent of discrimination against women? Why?

2. If you were a consultant for the city in this case, how would you go about evaluating the content, construct, and criterion validity of the selection tests?

3. What would you do to provide more opportunity for women wishing to become firefighters? Would these procedures be fair to male applicants?

4. One argument has been that requiring an employer to prove the validity of selection procedures when adverse impact has been shown is equivalent to requiring a person accused of murder to prove that he or she is innocent. Do you believe that the burden of proof should be on the employer to show that what they are using in selection is valid? Why?

# Training and Development

- Needs Assessment

- Training and Development Phase

- Evaluating Training Effectiveness

- Special Training Needs

- A Final Summation and a Look at the Future

- Case: Developing Leaders and Teamwork Through Outdoor Adventure Training

After years of education, you may think that you will be finished with school once you receive your academic degree. If you believe this, you are probably wrong. In all likelihood, your degree is a prelude to a lifetime of continuous training and retraining as you and the organizations for which you work try to keep abreast of rapidly changing and increasingly complex technologies. Indeed, training has become an integral part of the strategy that corporations use to maintain competitiveness (Cooper, 1992). According to one estimate, U.S. corporations with 100 or more employees invested 43.2 billion dollars for training in 1991 (*Quality Digest,* January, 1992, p. 6). For example, General Electric's Management Development Institute in Crotonville, Illinois, offers a menu of courses to its employees that rivals the four-year programs in university business schools (Stewart, 1991a). The Polaroid Corporation gives raises not just to employees who are promoted, but also to those who acquire the skills that their departments need (Stewart, 1991b). Motorola spent more than $60 million on training and expects its more than 100,000 employees to continuously upgrade their knowledge and skills (Therrien, 1989).

Some evidence suggests that these large investments in training and development lead to better organizational performance (Russell & Terborg, 1985), but the sad truth is that the large sums spent on training are often wasted as the result of the haphazard manner in which these efforts are undertaken. In the present chapter we describe a systems approach that is likely to yield a greater return than the typical approach. The best known of these is Goldstein's (1993, p. 15) systems model of training (Figure 11.1). The basic assumption of this model is that training achieves the best results when it consists of an orderly, planned sequence of events. The process starts with an assessment of needs and the specification of training objectives, followed by the careful design and implementation of a program, and culminating in the evaluation of how well the training achieves the objectives. The model also presents training as a *subsystem* that cannot stand alone but must take into account the larger organization and the world outside the organization. Several other key characteristics of this model are:

1. *Continual evaluation and modification.* From a systems perspective the design of a training program is never finished. The organization is continually involved in updating and revising to better achieve objectives.
2. *Different methods are needed to meet different conditions.* The specific methods of training (e.g., lecture, role playing) depend on the objectives, the trainees, the task, and a variety of other variables.
3. *A research orientation.* An investigative approach is taken in which the program is evaluated scientifically and the training is continued only if it achieves the program's objectives.
4. *Training is part of a larger set of interacting systems.* The criteria used in evaluating training programs are not absolute

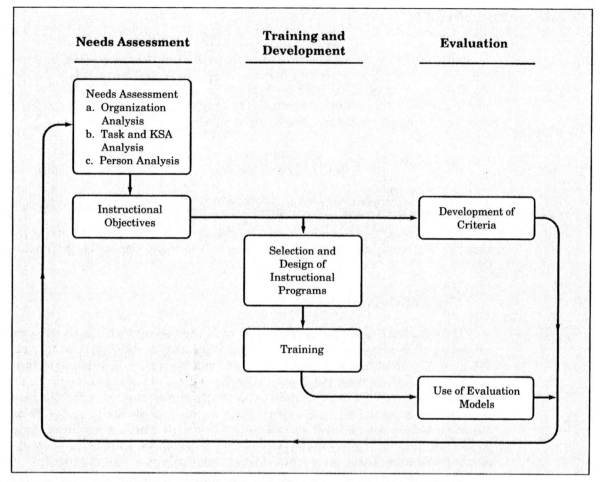

**Figure 11.1**   *A systems model of instruction*

*Source:* Adapted from Goldstein, I.L. (1993). *Training in Organizations: Needs Assessment, Development, and Evaluation.* Monterrey, CA: Brooks/Cole, p. 21.

but are determined by the other subsystems within the organization. For instance, a change in the management philosophy of the organization or in the values of society will change the type of training needed.

Although many questions remain unanswered, past work has provided some clues on the best way to train employees. Let us examine each of the phases in Figure 11.1 and some of the lessons to be learned from past research.

# NEEDS ASSESSMENT

The first step in the model is the most important in many respects but is also the most neglected (Ostroff & Ford, 1989). To make the best use of training dollars, a careful analysis is required to determine where changes are needed and whether training can fulfill these needs. Moore and Dutton (1978) offer the following equation to guide these efforts.

$$\text{Training Need} = \frac{\text{Standard or}}{\text{Desired Performance}} - \frac{\text{Present or}}{\text{Actual Performance}}$$

The more the present or actual performance falls below the standard or desired performance, the greater the need for training.

In assessing training needs, information should be gathered on the organization, the task, and the people performing the tasks (McGehee & Thayer, 1961).

## Organization Analysis

*Organization analysis* is concerned with the "objectives, resources, and allocation of those resources" of the whole organization (McGehee & Thayer, 1961, pp. 25–26). Consistent with the idea that training is a subsystem that must fulfill objectives of the larger system, the logical place to begin is by assessing how well the organization is currently performing. A variety of data could be used, including how well the organization performs in terms of its major goals (profits, service) and the efficiency with which it achieves these goals (cost of labor, cost of materials, quality of products, utilization of equipment, distribution costs, waste, down time, late deliveries, and repairs).

An organization analysis should take into account not only the *current* state of affairs but what the organization will need to do to handle *future* technologies and markets, as well as changing characteristics of workers. An example comes from a carpet manufacturer in Dalton, Georgia (Cooper, 1992). Like most other employers in the carpet industry in Dalton, workers were traditionally hired with little regard to their level of education. "For decades, a strong back and nimble hands were enough. A high-school diploma was nice, but certainly not necessary. Personnel officers simply smiled to themselves when applicants who were asked to fill out forms suddenly would say, 'Can I take this home? I forgot my glasses.' Then, because they actually were unable to read or write, they'd get someone else to fill it out for them" (p. A5). In the 1980s, to compete with increasing competition from foreign textile industries as well as increased demand for customized carpets tailored to the specific preferences of customers (e.g., more colors and carpets with logos), the company bought more sophisticated, computerized manufacturing equipment. This new technological environment required not only basic mathematical and reading skills but also the ability to analyze problems and make production decisions. Unfortunately, only 8% of the employees were estimated to possess these skills. To survive, the company launched a massive effort to provide basic training in reading, writing, science, social studies, and math to employees. The lesson of this example is that employers need not only to inventory the *current* skills and knowledge possessed by employees but also to project *future* needs. As part of this analysis, the number of employees that can be expected to leave should be estimated so that an evaluation can be made of the skill gaps that will need to be met through hiring, transfers, and training.

## Task Analysis

Knowing where the organization succeeds and fails in achieving its objectives sets the stage for a task analysis to determine what must be done to perform the work effectively. A typical beginning point is to describe tasks in the job using procedures discussed in Chapter 8. From these descriptions an analyst decides what knowledge, skills, abilities, and orientations (KSAOs) are required for performance of the tasks. *Knowledge* can be defined as an organized body of factual or procedural information that is applied in performing the job. *Skill* is the psychomotor capability to perform job operations. *Ability* is the cognitive capability necessary to perform the job. Employee *orientations* refer to specific temperaments or attitudes that are needed in the job. For instance, a child care worker might be expected to like children or a sales clerk might be expected to tolerate rude customers.

A useful technique in task analysis is the critical incident method (Chapter 9). By asking employees to describe incidents in which they failed to perform well, deficiencies can be identified and then targeted for training (Folley, 1969). Goldstein, Macey, and Prien (1981) recommended forming a panel of five to eight experts and asking them to answer the following questions:

1.  What are the characteristics of good and poor employees on (name of task)?

2.  Think of someone you know who is better than anyone else at (name of task). Why do they do so well?

3.  What does a person need to know to (name of task)? Recall concrete examples of effective and ineffective performance and discuss the causes or reasons.

4.  If you hire a person to perform (name of task), what kind of KSAOs do you want the person to have?

5.  What do you expect the person to learn in training that would make him or her effective at (name of task)?

Answers to these questions provide the basis for writing descriptions of the KSAOs required in the job.

## Person Analysis

The task analysis identifies how the work should be done, whereas the person analysis evaluates whether employees are fulfilling the requirements of the task. Among the ways of performing this assessment are (1) have supervisors or others rate the employees on their KSAOs; (2) have employees rate themselves on their KSAOs; (3) gather objective data on employee performance, such as sales volume or quantity produced; and (4) test employee proficiency with written tests (Wexley & Latham, 1981). The person analysis can provide a variety of information that feeds directly into the later design and implementation of training. The data gathered can suggest what the content of the training program should be, the methods used to present this content, who is likely to benefit from training, and possible actions that can be taken to gain trainees' acceptance.

An important type of data that a person analysis can provide concerns the *trainability* of potential trainees. Trainability is the likelihood of the person's benefiting from a program and is a function of the trainee's task ability, motivation, and perceptions of the work environment (Noe, 1986). An assessment of trainability could indicate that different types of training will be needed for different types of trainees, that some intervention will be needed prior to the training to prepare the trainee for the program, or that training should not even be attempted with some trainees because of their low ability or motivation. Measures of trainability could come from test scores, performance in minicourses that sample content of the entire course (Reilly & Israelski, 1988; Reilly & Manese, 1979), and performance of trainees on early training trials (Gordon & Cohen, 1973; Gordon & Kleiman, 1976).

## An Example of a Needs Assessment

To illustrate a typical needs assessment, we describe a study that was conducted with 200 managers and their supervisors in a hospital (McEnery & McEnery, 1987). The managers rated the level of performance required in the job and the level of performance they actually exhibited in the job for each of 29 knowledge, skills, and abilities areas. Each manager's superior also rated him or her on the same scales. Whenever the manager's performance on the KSAOs fell below the level required, a training need was said to exist (Table 11.1).

This study not only illustrates a typical needs assessment, but also demonstrates the limitations of relying on subjective reports in making these assessments. As Table 11.1 shows, managers reported less need for training than did their superiors on 25 of the 29 KSAOs. The correlations between the rating of the manager and the superior also indicate a very low level of agreement. Other evidence from this study suggested that superiors allowed their own needs for training to color their perceptions of their subordinates' training needs. No one method is free from problems; the best recommendation is

**Table 11.1**

| RESULTS OF A TRAINING NEEDS ANALYSIS CONDUCTED BY McENERY & McENERY (1987) | | | |
|---|---|---|---|
| *Identification of subordinates' needs* | | | |
| | Percentage identifying need | | Correlation of supervisors' and subordinates' needs identification |
| Dimension | Supervisor | Subordinate | Correlation |
| | % | % | |
| 1. Prioritizing | 41 | 24 | 0.03 |
| 2. Scheduling | 33 | 21 | 0·03 |
| 3. Following up | 39 | 35 | 0·20* |
| 4. Recognizing problems | 42 | 29 | 0·07 |
| 5. Gathering information | 35 | 29 | 0·22* |
| 6. Analysing problems | 38 | 30 | 0·08 |
| 7. Making decisions | 42 | 28 | 0·00 |
| 8. Adopting new approaches | 44 | 30 | 0·08 |
| 9. Coordinating | 29 | 22 | 0·03 |
| 10. Keeping up to date | 27 | 36 | 0·04 |
| 11. Achieving results | 29 | 30 | 0·13* |
| 12. Enforcing rules | 22 | 21 | 0·02 |
| 13. Writing | 32 | 25 | 0·11 |
| 14. Presenting verbally | 32 | 34 | 0·12* |
| 15. Being aware of structure | 33 | 30 | 0·04 |
| 16. Selecting employees | 34 | 31 | 0·00 |
| 17. Conducting performance reviews | 32 | 23 | 0·00 |
| 18. Developing subordinates | 39 | 24 | −0·04 |
| 19. Instructing employees | 28 | 24 | 0·12* |
| 20. Assigning work | 31 | 22 | −0·06 |
| 21. Delegating tasks | 38 | 22 | 0·10 |
| 22. Involving subordinates | 31 | 16 | −0·06 |
| 23. Handling grievances | 44 | 26 | −0·10 |
| 24. Maintaining good atmosphere | 34 | 24 | 0·06 |
| 25. Maintaining job knowledge | 27 | 22 | 0·00 |
| 26. Handling problem subordinates | 43 | 30 | 0·05 |
| 27. Providing feedback to subordinates | 38 | 30 | 0·05 |
| 28. Making non-discriminatory decisions | 18 | 8 | −0·04 |
| 29. Providing safe environment | 17 | 18 | −0·12 |

*Statistically significant at the 0·05 level.

*Source:* McEnery, J., & McEnery, J.M. (1987). Self-rating in management training needs assessment: A neglected opportunity? *Journal of Occupational Psychology, 60,* 49–60.

to use more than one method in gathering data on the tasks, the person, and the organization.

## Specification of Instructional Objectives

A needs assessment sets the stage for specifying the objectives of the training program. Goldstein (1993) observes that the needs assessment "tells the trainer where to begin, and the specification of the objectives tells him the completion point of the program" (p.79). Prior to stating instructional objectives, organizations should enter into a problem-solving process in which they consider the deficiencies in performance identified in the needs assessment and decide whether training is required (Mager & Pipe, 1970). Assuming that training is the preferred solution, then the next step is to set specific objectives for instruction.

### Learning Outcomes

In setting objectives the first concern is to identify the learning outcomes that are to be the target of the training. Gagne (1984) distinguished five types of learning outcomes:

**Verbal Information**   This is also referred to as *declarative knowledge* and exists in the form of "facts" that allow a person to declare or state something. Such information often comes as meaningful packages of items. If you could identify or recall the various parts of an automobile (e.g., steering wheel, brake, shift stick), then this would be a demonstration of verbal information.

**Intellectual Skills**   This is also referred to as *procedural knowledge* and consists of a chain of concepts, rules, and principles tied together through "if, then" statements. In learning to identify different geometric shapes, one rule might be "if there are three sides, then the geometric shape is that of a triangle; if there are four equal sides and four right angles, then the geometric shape is that of a square." Learning to identify different geometric shapes (e.g., rectangles, triangles) would be an intellectual skill, whereas repeating verbatim a definition of each would be verbal information. As stated by Gagne, Briggs, and Wager (1988, p. 44), learning an intellectual skill is learning "*how to* do something of an intellectual sort" whereas learning verbal information is learning "*that* something exists or has certain properties." Learning intellectual skills presumes that you have learned the concepts that constitute the procedures (what the terms in the above example mean such as side, angle, equal, and three). Learning intellectual skills involves more than memorizing strings of words, however, because the learning of a principle is demonstrated only when you can apply it in a variety of situations (e.g., can use the rule to correctly spell a variety of words containing i and e).

**Cognitive Strategies**   This type of learning consists of the strategies that allow you to learn, think, and solve problems. The primary difference between this and intellectual skills is that intellectual skills are concerned with structured problems, whereas cognitive strategies are concerned with novel problems. An example of a cognitive strategy would be solving an algebra problem. The learner would need first to identify the essential aspects of the problem and recall the relevant intellectual knowledge (e.g., procedures of multiplication, subtraction, division). The recalled procedures are then combined to form a new, higher order principle that allows the solution of the problem. In studying the materials of a history course, students recall what was said in class and written in the text (e.g., important dates) as well as learn intellectual skills in the form of procedures associated with the course (e.g., how to use economics to understand historical trends). They also learn strategies for how to understand and retain the material. One student might associate events in history with visual images of these events or the people involved. Another student might organize the material chronologically.

In both examples, the students use a *strategy* to master the material that may generalize to the learning of other material. Essentially they *learn how to learn,* and the cognitive strategies involved may be more important than the specific facts or procedures acquired in the course. The learning of cognitive strategies does not stand alone, however, but presumes that the learner has acquired the intellectual skills and verbal information that are prerequisite to acquiring these strategies.

**Motor Skills**    These are the abilities to perform organized motor activities such as riding a bicycle, tying your shoes, or driving a car. An important characteristic of a motor skill that distinguishes it from other types of skills is that practice results in gradual improvement over time.

**Attitudes**    These are predispositions to make certain choices or to engage in particular acts. Commercials are oriented to changing our attitudes toward products. Schools attempt to instill certain attitudes about hard work and respect for others. Likewise, companies often attempt to instill in employees a common set of values, such as providing high quality services to clients. As more organizations have become concerned with managing their cultures (see Chapter 5), the objectives of training programs have widened to include not only the teaching of technical skills but also the attitudes and values appropriate to the organizational culture (Feldman, 1989). Indeed, training in many corporations has become the primary socialization process for new hires. An example is McDonald's Hamburger University in Oak Brook, Illinois, where new franchise owners are taught not only a variety of skills crucial to running the business but also are indoctrinated in the McDonald's philosophy. Other examples can be found at Disney Land and Disney World where the training program for new employees stresses the importance of maintaining the magic of the theme park in interactions with guests.

## STATING INSTRUCTIONAL OBJECTIVES

The trainer should avoid expecting too much or too little of trainees. A common error is to claim that the training will achieve all sorts of lofty goals, including greater insight, appreciation, and understanding. While the objective may sound good, both instructor and trainee are likely to be confused about what constitutes successful completion of the training.

An objective should specify what the trainees need to do to demonstrate that they have acquired the KSAOs that are the focus of the training. Objectives come in two general forms. A *performance objective* states what the trainee will be able to *do* at the end of the training, whereas a *learning objective* states what the trainee will *know* (Mager, 1972, 1973; Mager & Pipe, 1970). In training an auto mechanic to clean and repair a carburetor, a performance objective might be to "replace worn and defective parts of a carburetor," whereas a learning objective might be to "list the parts of the carburetor from memory." Both types of objectives should be written using "doing" verbs (say, count, place, point out, install, complete, fix, replace, solve) rather than "knowing" verbs (understand, appreciate, develop an attitude for, see the value of, increase, grow, recognize). Rather than stating "The student will understand the causes of accidents in the workplace," the trainer might state "The student will list the top reasons for accidents in the workplace." According to Mager (1972), an instructional objective should not only state something that is observable, but it should also define the level of performance needed to achieve the objective. In stating objectives for a training program to improve safe work practices, for example, the objective might be that the trainee correctly identify three out of four solutions to work practices that result in back injuries. It should be noted that some training experts disagree with Mager and advise against always stating the performance criterion when writing instructional objectives (Gagne, Briggs, & Wager, 1988).

While we believe that most training interventions could benefit from stating specific instructional objectives, it is important to avoid being overly narrow. A common problem is focusing in the statement of objectives on mastery of verbal information to the neglect of intellectual skills and cognitive strategies. For instance, becoming proficient in the scientific method requires the acquisition of skill in designing experiments to test hypotheses. If an instructor of a research methods course limited the objectives to successful recall of specific information or the definition of terms and overlooked the problem solving that is required in research, the instructional objectives for this course would be overly narrow. The solution is to carefully assess the learning outcomes (i.e., verbal information, intellectual skills, cognitive strategies, motor skills, attitudes) that are the desired target of the program and make sure the objectives reflect all of the outcomes.

*Summary*

A needs assessment shows where the deficiencies are and whether training offers viable solutions. In a needs assessment data are gathered on the organization, the tasks that are the focus of the training, and the specific individuals who are the potential trainees. The heart of the analysis is assessing what is required and then judging the extent to which people in the situation are deficient in these requirements. The most important products of the needs assessment are instructional objectives. Specific, measurable objectives for what the trainee will know and be able to do are essential in designing the training program and evaluating its effectiveness and are a source of goals that can be used to motivate the trainees to learn (Chapter 3). The final outcome of a properly conducted needs assessment could be a decision to *not* conduct training. For instance, if performance problems result from such things as low motivation and inadequate equipment, training is not the appropriate intervention. In conducting needs analyses, it is important to keep an eye on the future and not be overly fixated on the present.

# TRAINING AND DEVELOPMENT PHASE

Four crucial issues should be addressed in the design of an instructional environment. The first is how to maximize performance in the training itself. This requires knowing the research on motivation and learning. The findings of this research provide useful guidelines for ensuring that trainees acquire KSAOs as efficiently as possible and retain what they learn. Performance in the training is not as important, however, as whether trainees take what they learn in the classroom and use it in the work place. Thus, the second issue that we consider is how to facilitate *transfer* of training to the work environment. A third issue is the on-the-job and classroom training methods that can be used in the training program and the factors that should be considered in the choice among these alternative methods. Finally, because well-conceived training programs can still fail as the consequence of the way trainers conduct them, we consider the factors influencing the implementation of training.

## Incorporating the Findings of Learning Research

A huge amount of research conducted over the last century has provided useful insights into how people learn. Unfortunately, the laboratory experiments allowing for the rigorous testing of hypotheses have provided a weak basis for generalizing to complex organizational tasks. Those conducting research on training also bear some of the responsibility by not attempting to build bridges between life and lab. Despite the dangers of generalizing the findings of basic research to organizational training, however, learning research has generated useful insights that can serve as a source of suggestions on how to improve employee instruction (Glaser, 1990). Much of what we discuss here concerns the conditions that facilitate initial acquisition of what is learned. As we will show later, the same factors do not necessarily ensure what is learned will transfer to the work place.

### PRACTICE AND RECITE

The old adage "practice makes perfect" is applicable here. Basic research has demonstrated repeatedly that if the material to be learned is *information* (e.g., memorize the parts of a machine), then students should be asked to recite. Similarly, if the training is focused on acquisition of skill, then the students should not just learn about what to do but should be asked to demonstrate the skills. The learning curves are likely to differ from job to job, with steep acquisition possible for easy jobs and slow accumulation for difficult jobs (McCormick & Ilgen, 1980, pp. 234–235). Also, learning curves are likely to vary in shape with the type of response measured (e.g., speed of response, quantity, errors).

Some research has shown that practice should continue to the point of *overlearning*. In other words, practice should continue past the point at which no additional gains are made (the asymptote on the learning curve). The benefits of overlearning were clearly shown in an experiment in which reserve soldiers were trained to disassemble and reassemble an M-60 machine gun (Schendel & Hagman, 1982). A training trial was a complete disassembly and reassembly of the gun, and soldiers received training until they could perform the task without error (the criterion). The soldiers were assigned at random to one of three groups. One group received 100% overtraining. For example, if two training trials were required for an individual to reach criterion (one errorless trial), then that soldier would receive two additional training trials after reaching criterion. Another group received the same amount of additional training as the overtrained group, but they received this additional training in the form of a refresher course midway through an eight-week period. Thus, if a soldier in this group took two trials to achieve criterion then two additional refresher trials were provided four weeks later. A control group was simply trained to criterion and then received a retention test at the end of eight weeks. After eight weeks, soldiers in all three groups were tested by having them disassemble and reassemble the machine gun until they achieved one errorless trial.

The overtrained group performed better than the refresher and control groups. The findings of this experiment showed that overtraining can be highly effective and efficient in the learning of complex skills. A recent survey of over 50 experiments confirms that overlearning is an effective strategy, although more so for cognitive than for physical tasks (Driskell, Willis, & Copper, 1992). There are potential problems with an overlearning strategy. A point of diminishing returns is likely to be reached at which increasing the number of overlearning trials eventually fails to improve retention. Overlearning may even harm performance on simple tasks if repetition leads to boredom and a decline in motivation. Also, Driskell, Willis, and Copper (1992) found that if refresher training is not provided, the benefits of overlearning on retention "dissipate to zero after 5 to 6 weeks" (p. 621).

## USE DISTRIBUTED PRACTICE

A basic issue in designing a training program is whether practice should be massed or distributed. In the former case, the whole course is thrown at trainees in one or a few intensive sessions, whereas in the latter, the sessions are spread out over time. An example of *distributed practice* is the three-hour college course, with two or three classes per week over the course of 10–15 weeks. An example of *massed practice* would be an intensive summer course that meets six to nine hours per day for two or three weeks. The total amount of time spent is the same, but the courses differ in the spacing of the presentation of material and the opportunity for rehearsal.

Massing practice sessions often leads to better short-term performance than does spacing, but massed practice leads to poorer long-term performance of the task. If you have ever crammed for an exam and then found that a week after the exam you have forgotten most of what you knew, you have some sense of this effect. Although you can find exceptions to the rule in the large body of research on spacing (Adams, 1987), the best advice is to provide distributed practice and generally avoid massed practice.

## USE WHOLE-TASK LEARNING FOR TASKS HIGH ON COMPLEXITY AND ORGANIZATION

The issue of distributed practice leads naturally to the question of whether it is better to teach the whole task or to use part learning. The latter involves subdividing the task into separate components, teaching them separately, and then later bringing these components together in a separate session. Pure part training occurs when each component is taught in a separate phase of the training and then all components are combined in a final phase. Progressive part training occurs when new components are combined with the previously taught components in each successive phase of training until all parts are put together in the final phase.

Blum and Naylor (1968) proposed that task complexity and organization are crucial in determining the relative effectiveness of whole and part training. Task complexity refers to the difficulty of each task component considered separately. Task organization refers to the extent to which components of the task are interrelated. Blum and Naylor proposed that whole-task training becomes more efficient than part-task methods when the task is both highly organized and complex. The part method becomes increasingly superior to whole-task training with tasks that are low in organization and high in complexity.

An example of a task of high organization and relatively high complexity would be driving a standard transmission automobile. Given that the task involves an interrelated sequence of actions, it would be more efficient to learn these acts as sequences rather than learning them as individual tasks (e.g., using the brake, using the clutch, steering the car, shifting gears). An example of a low organization task would be the game of baseball. In this case the trainee needs to learn the various subtasks of baseball independently (e.g., catching, batting, pitching), although each subtask (e.g., batting) is a highly organized task that is best learned as a single interrelated sequence of acts. For example, if you were learning to bat, you would practice the entire activity rather than devote separate sessions to standing at the plate, keeping the eye on the ball, swinging at the bat, and so on.

## GIVE KNOWLEDGE OF RESULTS

Feedback can either come from the task itself or can be augmented by providing external sources of information on performance (Chapter 9). Performance during training is usually better if trainees are provided with specific feedback on how well they are doing rather than with no feedback. The benefits seem to derive from the effects on acquisition of the correct responses as well as the effects on motivation of the recipient. In other words, feedback seems to improve performance as the result of providing information on correct performance as well as increasing the motivation of the person to succeed on the task (Chapter 9).

Research provides some insight into the types of feedback most likely to be helpful in improving task learning and performance (Annett, 1961). Feedback on successes tends to be more effective than feedback on failure. Specific knowledge of results is more effective than general feedback. Feedback should be provided immediately after the response rather than delayed. Similar to overlearning, there is probably a point of diminishing returns in providing feedback. Learning can suffer if feedback is so specific and so frequent that it overloads the recipient with information. Imagine, for instance, if you were learning to play golf and the instructor provided detailed feedback on every single move you made. Continuous feedback of this nature would be distracting and might arouse considerable anxiety and self-consciousness.

## SET GOALS

One of the more consistent findings in the I/O literature is the effect of goal setting. Individuals exhibit higher levels of performance when they are given specific or hard goals than when they are given ambiguous or easy goals (Chapter 3). The facilitative effects of a goal require, however, that the individual accept the goal. Also, feedback appears to be necessary for goal setting to have beneficial effects. According to Locke et al. (1981), goals direct attention, mobilize effort, encourage task persistence, and facilitate the development of task strategies. All of these consequences would have obvious benefits for the learning of a task. Despite the benefits, we must refrain from claiming that hard, specific goals are universally effective (Chapter 3). Some evidence suggests that goals specifying how well the trainee should perform are most beneficial in the later stages of learning when the responses are so well learned that they are automatic (Kanfer & Ackerman, 1989). Earlier in the process, when the trainee must devote attention to task demands, difficult goals actually could be distracting.

## GIVE POSITIVE REINFORCEMENT

On the basis of research on instrumental conditioning (also known as operant conditioning), it has been proposed that the best approach to ensure that trainees learn is to give them positive reinforcement immediately after every acceptable response. In the case of complex skills, the behavior of the trainee may need to be shaped through reinforcing successive approximations to the desired response. The first response may be a crude approximation of what is wanted, but the trainer would provide positive reinforcers (e.g., praise) for those behaviors that at least approximate the correct response. With each trial, the reinforcement becomes more selective and contingent on producing a closer approximation to the desired response. Once a response is mastered, research on instrumental conditioning suggests that higher rates of responding can be maintained by shifting to intermittent or partial schedules of reinforcement.

While there are useful applications to training that can be drawn from the research on operant conditioning, it is now generally accepted that reinforcement does not facilitate learning through a simple stamping-in process but is instead mediated by complex cognitive events. Moreover, administering reinforcement in the same manner that a pigeon or rat would be reinforced in the lab is often impractical in organizational training environments. If your instructor tossed candy to you to reward good comments you might initially be stimulated to talk more, but you would probably eventually see this "contingent reinforcement" as manipulative or at best silly.

## PROVIDE MODELS

Research on behavioral modeling was stimulated largely by criticisms of a radical behavioral view that described all human learning as under the control of reinforcement. Among the most influential of these critics has been Albert Bandura (1986), whose social learning theory was discussed in Chapter 3. Although Bandura believes that the most powerful way of enhancing learning is to directly reinforce behavior, he proposes in his theory that people most often learn through observing others. The technique of behavioral modeling is based on social learning theory and consists of providing trainees with models who exhibit the desired performances. An assumption underlying this technique is that observational learning is largely an "information-processing activity in which information about the structure of behavior and about environmental events is transformed into symbolic representations that serve as guides for action" (Bandura, 1986, p. 51). Consequently, models should be provided that catch the attention of trainees and that allow the learner to convert what they observe into symbols. Essential learning points should be summarized and presented in a form that facilitates the trainees' encoding, storage, and retrieval of what they observe (Chapter 9). Learning points are similar to instructional objectives and are the key behaviors to be acquired. Some evidence shows that trainees who generate their own learning points may be able to process information more deeply and derive greater benefits from observing the model than trainees who are given learning points by the instructor (Hogan, Hakel, & Decker, 1986).

## MAKE LEARNING A TEAM EFFORT

Research has accumulated over the last three decades on the relative effects of rewarding people for their individual efforts and rewarding them for their collaborative efforts. These findings have been applied to the classroom in the form of *cooperative learning.* The essential characteristic of this method is that students work in small groups and are expected to help each other learn. Beyond this essential element, however, there are many variations. Cooperative learning appears to be more effective than individual approaches to learning if individual trainees are held accountable and group rewards are provided (Slavin, 1983). This approach appears to be successful because of the high performance norms that emerge as the result of rewarding the group for its collective performance (Chapter 5). These norms support group members in encouraging and assisting each other in learning the task.

Most of the work on cooperative learning has used elementary and secondary school children. In one of the few demonstrations with adults, soldiers who had been trained with computer-assisted instruction (CAI) were compared with those who had been trained in pairs with the same CAI materials (Dossett & Hulvershorn, 1983). The group learning in this case was identical to the individual learning except that in the former a pair of trainees sat at each terminal rather than an individual. Training in pairs resulted in 25% faster learning of the material than individual training. In a second study, the training of pairs was found to be most effective when one member of the pair was highly competent.

## GAGNE'S MODEL OF INSTRUCTIONAL DESIGN

Although the guidelines discussed above can be useful, their applicability to organizational training is highly limited. Gagne (1984) proposed that the conditions you incorporate in a training program to facilitate learning depend on which of the five learning outcomes previously discussed are of greatest concern. The learning of cognitive strategies, for example, requires knowledge of certain principles and factual knowledge. In turn, learning of procedures requires that the learner first know specific verbal information. Practice is more important in the learning of motor skills, where acquisition is more gradual, than in the learning of intellectual skills, where acquisition often comes as a flash of insight. On the other hand, if acquisition of cognitive strategies is the primary objective, it is more important to provide the learner with a variety of novel problems to solve than it is to have the learner engage in rote practice. All five of the learning outcome categories are likely to be involved in the planning of a course, except when motor skills are the primary focus (Gagne, Briggs, & Wager, 1988, p. 51).

The designer of a course should keep in mind the cognitive and behavioral events that define the learning process and structure the program to support this process. Learning involves the following eight steps in Gagne's model:

1. Attention determines the extent and nature of reception of incoming stimulation.
2. Selective perception (sometimes called pattern recognition) transforms this stimulation into the form of object features for storage in short-term memory.

3. Rehearsal maintains and renews the items stored in short-term memory.
4. Semantic encoding prepares information for long-term storage.
5. Retrieval, including search, returns stored information to the working memory or to a response generator.
6. Response organization selects and organizes performance.
7. Feedback provides the learner with information about performance and sets in motion the process of reinforcement.
8. Executive control processes select and activate cognitive strategies; these modify any or all of the previously listed internal processes.

*Instructional events* are external conditions incorporated in the training that support and facilitate each of the internal learning processes listed above. The nature of the instructional events that need to be incorporated in a program will differ according to the learning outcomes that are the objectives of the training. Take, for example, the instructional events used to aid retrieval (step 5). If the objective is to convey intellectual skills, then you would want to give examples of how the intellectual skills could be applied in different contexts. If the objective is to impart verbal information, then you would want to relate the information to larger bodies of knowledge and provide images and mnemonics to facilitate later recall. If motor skills were the focus, then you would want to give the trainees feedback on their performance and have them practice the material.

## Transfer and Maintenance of Training

The most important issue in designing a training program is whether what is learned in the training environment generalizes to the workplace and is maintained. Transfer can be positive, zero, or negative. The most desirable state of affairs is *positive transfer,* in which what is learned in the training improves learning or performance in the work setting. *Zero transfer* occurs when training does not affect the individual's performance when he or she returns to the work setting. The worst state of affairs is *negative transfer,* in which training hinders learning and performance in the work setting. Take, for example, a course in which managers are taught human relations skills. Such training could have zero transfer if the managers returned to an organization that did not support a human relations approach. Some research indicates that this training might even have negative transfer if the supervisor returned to a work place in which nonparticipation and insensitivity to workers were the norm (Fleishman & Harris, 1962).

An issue related to transfer is *maintenance* of training, which is the length of time that skills and knowledge are retained once the trainee returns to the job. Numerous potential maintenance curves are possible; a few of the more likely curves are illustrated in Figure 11.2 (Baldwin & Ford, 1988). Type

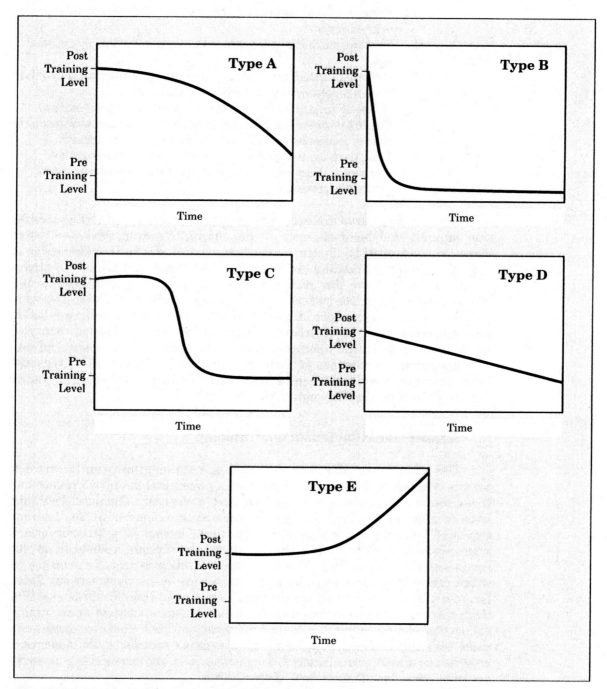

**Figure 11.2**  *Types of transfer maintenance curves*

*Source:* Baldwin, T.T., & Ford, J.K. (1988). Transfer of training: A review and directions for future research. *Personnel Psychology, 41,* 63–105.

A in this figure seems the most likely. This curve describes a situation in which there is a decline in skills that begins slowly but accelerates over time. This pattern may indicate the need for a refresher course at some point after the training session. Other patterns are possible, such as an immediate and complete loss of the trained behavior upon return to the work place (Type B) or a dynamic in which a moderate-to-low level of the skill is demonstrated at the beginning but the skill accelerates over time (Type E).

A general principle that has been set forth for achieving positive transfer is that the stimulus and response elements in the training should correspond to the stimulus and response elements in the work situation. The *model of identical elements* of Thorndike and Woodworth (1901) proposes that the greatest transfer is achieved when both the stimuli and responses are the same as those in the work setting (Table 11.2). In this situation, trainees would practice the actual task they will perform in the work environment (Goldstein, 1993). Somewhat less transfer is achieved when the task stimuli differ but the responses are the same. This is common to many training programs. An example is a leadership program in which the leader behaviors taught in the class are similar to those that are exhibited in the work setting (e.g., using a participative style in leading employees), but the conditions under which the behaviors are exhibited are different (e.g., describing how one would be participative in a written analysis of a case as opposed to actually demonstrating participation in a face-to-face interaction). Where the task stimuli and the responses both differ from what is found in the work setting, no transfer occurs. Finally, negative transfer occurs if the task stimuli are the same but the response requirements differ.

Generally, those practices that enhance learning during initial training should also improve transfer and maintenance. Several exceptions, however, were recently noted in a review by a National Research Council committee (Druckman & Bjork, 1991). The authors of this report concluded that in

**Table 11.2**

### TYPE OF TRANSFER BASED ON STIMULUS AND RESPONSE SIMILARITY

| Task Stimuli | Response Required | Transfer |
|---|---|---|
| Same | Same | High positive |
| Different | Different | None |
| Different | Same | Positive |
| Same | Different | Negative |

*Source:* Goldstein, I.L. (1993). *Training in Organizations: Needs Assessment, Development, and Evaluation.* Monterrey, CA: Brooks/Cole, p. 125. Adapted from Holding, D.H. (1965). *Principles of Training.* London: Pergamon Press.

addition to improving the original learning and increasing similarity of the training and work place task, transfer can be enhanced by (1) providing contextual interference during training, (2) introducing some typical on-the-job messiness by increasing the variability and variety of the examples given during training, and (3) reducing feedback. These conclusions are interesting because all three are likely to decrease performance in the training itself but are likely to improve transfer by involving trainees in the learning process and encouraging a deeper level of information processing. Let us consider each of these three interventions in more detail.

The use of *contextual interference* reflects the fact that the *ease* with which material is acquired during training is not always a good indicator of how much has been learned. You undoubtedly have taken courses that you disliked because of their difficulty or the poor presentation of the material. In some cases you may have been surprised to discover later that, although you seemed to be performing poorly throughout the course, you remembered and could apply the material. If this has happened to you, you may have experienced firsthand the beneficial effects of contextual interference. Research demonstrating this typically has presented trainees with problems that must be overcome during the training and that require them to think deeply about the information. In an experiment demonstrating the effectiveness of providing contextual interference, subjects were given a technical article, with half the subjects receiving an outline that was consistent with the article and the other half receiving an inconsistent outline (Mannes & Kintsch, 1987). Although subjects given the consistent outline did better on a test of verbatim knowledge, those with an inconsistent outline actually did better in applying what they learned to the solution of problems.

A second suggestion for improving transfer has been to provide a *variety of examples* during training. Assuming that the examples provided are representative of what will be found in the work place, varied examples should lead the trainee to derive rules or principles that facilitate transfer. Through applying principles to many different problems, trainees supposedly learn general task strategies that they can then apply to the world outside the classroom (Ellis, 1965; Duncan, 1958; Shore & Sechrest, 1961).

The third suggestion, *reduce the amount of feedback* during training, is more concerned with what *not* to do and conflicts with one of the principles of learning we discussed earlier. Although the initial acquisition of learning is enhanced by providing frequent knowledge of results, trainees may develop a dependency on the feedback and fail to acquire information-processing strategies. Providing only occasional feedback may force the trainees to develop the strategies needed after completing the training.

All three of these methods of enhancing transfer force trainees to become more involved in the training and to process information more deeply. The underlying assumption is that transfer is largely a matter of developing the correct cognitive strategies. Transfer also can fail, however, if trainees are confronted in the workplace with barriers to using what they have learned. Trainees typically give little thought in the training itself to how they can overcome factors on the job that prevent transfer. Two other means of ensuring transfer and maintenance are to directly address this issue in the training course by *setting goals* for applying what is learned in the workplace and *developing means of coping* with barriers to transfer.

An example of an attempt to improve coping with barriers is *relapse prevention* (RP) (Marx, 1982). RP programs were originally developed to help drug addicts and alcoholics cope with situations that lead to relapses. Marx (1982) believed that some of the components of these programs could help trainees in management development courses transfer what they learn to the workplace and then maintain this learning. In these programs participants identify the situations that are likely to lead to relapse and consider possible means of coping with them. For instance, if you are trained to be participative with your subordinates and you then confront your autocratic boss, how do you deal with this?

To our knowledge, only one experiment attempted to evaluate the effectiveness of RP, and the findings failed to support the technique (Wexley & Baldwin, 1986). In this research students were trained to effectively manage their time by using such techniques as establishing and writing down long-term goals, linking short-term objectives and activities to long-term goals, using a daily planner, and constructing a daily to-do list. The question was whether students would actually use the time-management techniques they learned in their daily lives. Students in the RP condition developed possible coping responses for dealing with situations in which relapse was likely by having subjects brainstorm individually and as a group high-risk situations that might prevent them from using their time management skills. They then developed methods of coping with these situations. A control group received time-management training but did not receive any transfer training. In the other two conditions, goal setting was used to ensure transfer. Trainees either set or were assigned goals for specific time-management practices they would attempt (e.g., "plan my day using a daily planner and refer to it several times"). The two goal-setting conditions led to greater use of time-management skills than the RP and control sessions. Although the findings do not support RP, it might have been that a combination of goal setting and RP training would have led to even better results. Until such research is conducted, we have little basis for concluding whether RP is effective.

A potentially important determinant of whether learning in a training session carries over to the workplace is the effect of the training on the trainee's motivation. A trainee who walks out of a training session fired up to use what he or she learned back on the job seems more likely to show transfer than a trainee who rejects the training. At the least, efforts should be made to ensure that the training meets the expectations of trainees (Tannenbaum, Mathieu, Salas, & Cannon-Bowers, 1991). One approach is to induce *realistic expectations* by providing a realistic preview of the course at the beginning of or prior to the training program. It also may mean recruiting trainees whose expectations are consistent with the program (Noe & Schmitt, 1986). Attempts could be made to heighten pretraining motivation through such means as incentives for learning or persuading trainees of the benefits. Allowing trainees to choose the type of training they receive is still another way of enhancing motivation, but this option should be used only if it is possible to match preferences. Asking for the relative preferences of trainees and then assigning them to a course that is not their top choice can backfire (Baldwin, Magjuka, & Loher, 1991).

We have discussed what can be done in the training itself to support transfer and maintenance, but equally important to consider is what can be done in the workplace. Supervisory and peer support are perhaps the most important factors. If you learn a new skill and then return to a work environment in which your supervisor or coworkers will not allow you to practice what you have learned, you are unlikely to transfer your learning to the workplace; if you do, you are unlikely to maintain what you have learned. One possible way of increasing positive transfer is to inform supervisors of the nature of the training and solicit their support prior to the training. Supervisors also could set goals for trainees related to the training and reinforce the application of the training in the workplace. Another means of inducing positive transfer is to have supervisors serve as examples or models of what was taught. Finally, peer support of learning could be enhanced with a buddy system in which coworkers participate in the training together so that they can reinforce each other for using what they learned when they return to the workplace (Baldwin & Ford, 1988, p. 98).

A workplace factor that can influence transfer and maintenance but is much more difficult to modify is *organizational climate* (Chapter 5). Some organizations appear to possess climates that support transfer of training, whereas other climates are much less supportive. Goldstein (1986) cited evidence that trainees in organizations that support risk taking, experimentation, and personal development were more likely to apply what they learned when they returned to the workplace. If an organizational analysis conducted in the needs assessment phase shows that training of a certain type conflicts with the climate, then it would be futile to proceed with implementing the training. A possible alternative is to change the organizational climate using the organizational development interventions discussed in Chapter 5. Changing an entire climate is extremely difficult, however, and may take years to accomplish.

*Summary*

Some attention should be given in the design of a training program to creating conditions that enhance the performance of trainees in the training program. Basic learning research suggests several guidelines that can help in this regard, but there are limitations to applying them to organizational training. Gagne suggested analyzing the extent to which five learning outcomes are involved in the training: verbal information, intellectual skills, cognitive strategies, attitudes, and motor skills. Instructional events are then provided to facilitate each stage of the learning process. The basic issue is not so much how people perform in the course, however, as whether they transfer what they learn to the workplace. Although better performance in training can generaly facilitate transfer, there are important exceptions. Transfer can be improved by actively involving participants in the learning of the material, requiring deep processing of the information, and providing support in the workplace for what is learned.

## Alternative Training Media

General principles of learning and transfer can provide guidance in the design of training programs, but specific techniques must be used in the actual training of employees. Training techniques consist of both on-the-job and off-the-job methods. Either of these can be approached in a systematic manner but on-the-job training is most often unsystematic and seldom attends to all the elements presented in Figure 11.1, that is, assessment of needs for training, planned design of the training, and evaluation. On-the-job and off-the-job methods differ not just in the location of the training but in their philosophies.

### ON-THE-JOB TECHNIQUES

The most common means of training employees is to use on-the-job methods; one survey showed over 93% of companies used this approach for managers and supervisors (Saari, Johnson, McLaughlin, & Zimmerle, 1988). Obviously this is a very general category consisting of methods that can be informal and spontaneous in nature or very formal and planned. Most on-the-job training is the informal type. For instance, the Xerox Corporation conducted a study in which it was found that repairmen learned the most about repairing copiers from "hanging around swapping stories" (Stewart, 1991c, p. 50). Somewhat more formal on-the-job techniques exist in the form of mentoring, internships, apprenticeships, and job rotation and transfers.

**Mentoring**  Mentoring can occur in the form of an intense relationship in which a senior employee (the mentor) gives guidance to a junior employee (the protégé). Employees who have mentors appear more likely to receive promotions and higher pay than those who do not (Whitely, Dougherty, & Dreher, 1991). The danger of this method is that it depends so much on one person's choosing to form a personal relationship with another. Employees who are dissimilar to potential mentors on sex, race, and other personal characteristics may have less opportunity to be mentored than those who fit the mold. An indication of this comes from a study showing that employees from higher socioeconomic status backgrounds were more likely to receive mentoring and were more likely to benefit from it than those from lower socioeconomic backgrounds (Whitely, Dougherty, & Dreher, 1991). Additional concerns have been raised about the tendency of white, male senior managers to choose other white, male employees as their protégés, to the disadvantage of women and minorities (Noe, 1988a; Ragins & Cotton, 1991). Mentoring can be of benefit in the training of employees, but organizations need to administer the process to avoid these biases and to maximize the benefits.

**Internships**    Internships were defined by Taylor (1988) as "structured and career-relevant work experiences obtained by students prior to graduation from an academic program" (p. 393). While these are often praised as an effective means of preparing students for work, the effects of internship experiences have received little attention in research. An exception was a study reported by Taylor (1988) in which university students who participated in internships were compared with those who did not. Interns appeared to benefit more than those who had no internships, with those whose internships allowed autonomy reaping the greatest benefits. Students who had been interns had a clearer conception of their own vocational abilities, interests, and values. In their search for employment they were more likely to use informal job sources and were evaluated more favorably by recruiters. Once employed, they achieved higher salary positions and were more satisfied with their salaries.

Unfortunately, little attention has been given so far to whether interns acquire job-related skills that transfer to their first job. That internships are not always beneficial was demonstrated in a study with psychiatric residents in a medical school (Lindy, Green, & Patrick 1980). Those who had one year of internship experience were inferior in their psychotherapy skills to residents who had no internship experience. The authors of this study suggest that humiliating experiences in the internship may have lessened the interns' empathy. As in the case of mentoring, internships vary widely in the quality of the experience.

**Apprenticeships**    This type of on-the-job training is used in teaching skilled trades and typically consists of having a trainee spend time on the job assisting a more senior employee in addition to classroom training. The lack of a coherent national apprenticeship program has been viewed by some observers as a major source of low productivity in the United States (Kolberg & Smith, 1992; McKenna, 1992). American apprenticeships are used mainly for adults entering specific skilled jobs, with fewer than 2% of high school graduates entering apprenticeships. In contrast, over 70% of non–college-bound German high school graduates enter the work force by way of a national apprenticeship system. In the German system, students spend one or two days a week taking classes comparable to what would be found in a U.S. junior college.

Despite the potential value of these programs, they are not without problems (Strauss, 1967). The opportunities for learning may depend largely on the motivation and skill of the senior employee to whom the apprentice is assigned. Having to put in a full day's work can lessen the efficiency with which apprentices learn in the classroom. Apprentices may learn incorrect or inefficient work methods from senior employees. Also, overreliance on apprenticeships ignores the intellectual component that is an important part of many skilled jobs. Relying on apprenticeship training to the neglect of learning basic principles may only lead to technological obsolescence. Interestingly, a current trend in German apprenticeships is to place more emphasis on theory relative to hands-on experience to meet the demands of increasingly complex technologies ("Experts in overalls," *Business Week / Reinventing America,* 1992).

**Job Rotation and Transfers**    In these types of on-the-job training, the employee supposedly benefits from being moved to different types of positions or different locations. Job rotation is typically short-term, such as when management trainees in a grocery store spend as part of their orientation to the business a week as a sacker, another as a cashier, and still another as a stocker. Transfers are usually of longer duration and involve a geographic relocation for the employee and his or her family. Large corporations, for example, often reassign professional and managerial employees every few years. One reason for this is to expose the employees to a variety of jobs and different parts of the organization so that they can acquire a better conception of different functions and the interrelations of these functions. The belief is that those who have a sense of the big picture will manage better than those who know only their special function (e.g., accounting, finance, production). Although frequently used in large organizations to develop managerial employees, there is little research evaluating whether job rotation and transfer are effective in achieving this objective (Pinder & Walter, 1984). Anecdotal evidence suggests that transfers and rotations can have dysfunctional as well as beneficial consequences. Increasingly, employees appear to be turning down transfers, even at the cost of upward mobility (Shellenbarger, 1991; Shireman, 1991). If transfers involving relocation are to be effective, organizations need to provide support that includes recognition on the job and help to families in adjusting to new communities (Pinder & Walter, 1984).

**The Hidden Costs of On-the-Job Training**    All of the on-the-job training methods discussed here are attractive because they appear clearly relevant to the job, and the trainee is producing while learning. These visible and immediate advantages may divert attention from the drawbacks in such programs. The time that must be devoted to training a novice can detract from the trainer's own productivity. The lost use and possible damage to equipment incurred by the trainee are other potential costs that can quickly outweigh any advantages of the on-the-job approach. Unfortunately, most organizations never carefully evaluate the costs and benefits of their on-the-job training. If they did, many would probably find that off-the-job methods offer many advantages over on-the-job approaches.

Despite the potential problems, much can be done to increase the benefits of this familiar approach to training. Efforts should be made to pick good teachers, and those chosen should be instructed in how to train. Most importantly, on-the-job trainers should be evaluated in how well they provide instruction and should be rewarded for effective performance of this role.

Rather than relying solely on on-the-job training, organizations may wish to consider *vestibule training,* which combines on-the-job and classroom training. The advantages of this approach were demonstrated in an experiment in which the performance of sewing-machine operators given vary-ing lengths of off-the-job training was compared with the performance of oper-ators given vestibule training (Lefkowitz, 1970). Vestibule training in this case consisted of classroom instruction part of the day in a room located adja-cent to the assembly line and on-the-line coaching from supervisors the remainder of the day. The highest productivity and lowest rate of quitting was found for the group given both on-site and off-site training. An aspect of the off-site training that may account for its success was that trainees discussed solutions to various job problems that had been responsible for the high turnover. The fact that employees talked about job problems in the classroom also appeared to encourage supervisors to give greater attention to trainees.

Another means of taking the best of on-the-job experience and combining it with classroom instruction is to identify the expert performers of a specific task, determine what they do in performing the task, and then teach this knowledge to novices. One variation of this is called *cognitive modeling*. The first step is to use elicitation methods to capture the knowledge of the expert, possibly through the use of the critical incident technique (Klein, 1990). Specifically, an expert is asked to describe nonroutine performances and the skills he or she employed in accomplishing the task. The rules and procedures derived from the information provided by the expert can then be imparted to the novice by having the experts or instructors think out loud as they solve or diagnose a problem and make a decision. The success of cognitive modeling of expertise appears to depend on whether the experts can convey their processes and whether they are sensitive to the strategies being used by the trainee. Cognitive modeling techniques have been successful in teaching read-ing and writing and hold considerable promise for job training (Druckman & Bjork, 1991).

## OFF-THE-JOB TECHNIQUES

In attempting to convey specific skills, knowledge, or attitudes the designer of a training program has several alternatives available. We con-sider these alternatives and some of the research related to each.

**Lecture**   The classroom method with which you are undoubtedly most famil-iar is the lecture. Perhaps because it is so familiar, the lecture has become the favorite target of many critics of traditional approaches and advocates of innovative instruction. Typical of the charges leveled against the lecture is that it (1) places the trainee in a passive role, (2) too often consists of one-way communication from lecturer to trainee, (3) provides little opportunity for the trainee to receive feedback on what he or she is learning, (4) relies too heavily on the style of the individual instructor, and (5) ignores individual differences among trainees in their abilities, interests, and learning styles. Moreover, the lecture has been accused of evoking negative feelings on the part of the trainee that disrupt the learning of the material and the transfer of skills to the work place. Although these criticisms are probably appropriate to many lectures, forgotten in the attacks are the many benefits of this approach. A primary advantage is that a lecture allows a large number of people to be instructed at a relatively low cost. A skilled lecturer can reduce anxiety and promote positive attitudes toward the material. Moreover, the lecture is flexible enough that it can be combined with a variety of other methods (e. g., audiovisuals, role playing, case discussions).

There are many opinions about the pros and cons of the lecture but surprisingly few hard facts. Past research has tended to include the lecture as a control condition against which more innovative methods are compared. Unfortunately, researchers rarely provide control conditions in which the lecture is compared with no training, and even less frequently examine the relative costs of lecture and the alternative methods. If researchers were to take into account the lower cost and learning achievement relative to no training, research findings might present a more positive view of the lecture. Another important but often neglected factor is the lecturer's skill. Given the eagerness to show the advantages of the new method over the old, researchers may not use the best possible lecturers. Also, the lecture may appear deficient as the result of a Hawthorne effect, in which any new method is preferred as the result of its novelty.

Although the deck is probably stacked against the lecture, a close examination of the research reveals that the lecture is more effective than commonly thought (Burke & Day, 1986). There is little to justify relying solely on the lecture in all training situations, but there is even less support for the position that the lecture is useless and should be avoided.

**Taped Presentations**   Rather than using a live lecture, an alternative approach is to present material via films, audio tapes, and videotapes. The widespread availability of video and audio recorders has created numerous opportunities for instruction. One of the authors is familiar with a chemical plant that contracted with several departments in a university to produce videotapes of lectures on specific topics. Engineers and scientists wishing to update their skills and stay current with the field could view the tapes during breaks in their work. A second example is a colleague of the authors who videotaped her psychology class lectures and put them on reserve in the library. Students could check these tapes out to go back over points covered in the lectures. Commuters can now acquire audiotaped lectures on various topics that they can play en route to work and home.

An obvious advantage of a taped lecture is that it is less memory based. By replaying the tape trainees can ensure that they have received the information that the instructor intended to convey rather than relying on their memory of what was said or their notes. Material can be presented in a dramatic and attention-catching manner through the use of professional actors, carefully prepared scripts, special effects, and editing. The most stimulating lecturers can be videotaped so that all students can benefit from their instruction. Taped presentations also have the advantage of allowing the standardization of the instruction, thus ensuring that all trainees are exposed to the same material.

The primary disadvantage is that there is even less opportunity for feedback and two-way communication with a canned lecture than there is with a live lecture. Also, once the film, videotape, or audiotape is produced, it may be difficult and costly to modify. One large state university decided to teach many of its introductory courses by showing taped lectures via closed circuit TV. Unfortunately, after going through an expensive process of taping numerous lectures, the tapes were discovered to be amateurish and boring. There is little research on this approach, but one generalization seems warranted: Taped presentations are a useful adjunct to other methods but are seldom enough to carry an entire program.

**Programmed Instruction**    The ideal learning environment has been described as one in which trainees (1) are required to be actively involved in the learning process rather than serving as passive recipients of information, (2) can progress at their own pace, (3) are given immediate feedback on their responses, and (4) are rewarded frequently with success experiences. In the 1920s programmed instruction was first offered as the technique that could incorporate all these features. Pressey (1950) developed auto-instructional programs in which students read questions, chose an answer from alternatives, and received immediate feedback in the form of a light or buzzer. Programmed instruction did not become widely known, however, until a 1954 *Harvard Educational Review* article by psychologist B.F. Skinner introduced a type of programmed instruction called the *linear program.*

The first step in developing a linear program is to define the field to be covered in the program and to organize the material in a developmental order. The material is then presented in frames, each of which consists of one or a few sentences. An overt response is required for each frame through filling in a blank to indicate a missing item of information. Trainees are provided with immediate feedback on whether their responses are correct or incorrect and then proceed to the next frame, moving on a single path through the material at their own pace. An example of a linear program is provided in Figure 11.3. As shown here, concepts are slowly introduced by first presenting them in simple terms before adding more complex material. After answering each question, the trainee is told the correct answer and often is given an explanation. The idea is to make the material so easy that most trainees succeed at each step of the process.

The *branching program* has been proposed as an alternative to the linear program. In this case multiple routes are provided to complete the material, with the learner allowed to skip steps or take accelerated routes based on past success. If the learner makes a correct response to a frame, he or she can proceed to the next frame. If the learner makes an incorrect response, then he or she is directed to a set of frames intended to provide remedial instruction (Figure 11.4). Branching programs often allow greater tailoring to individual differences by permitting the fast learner to skip ahead while the slower learner is given smaller steps to master.

Research on programmed instruction has provided the following generalization: Trainees acquire material faster with this type of instruction, but

This is a lesson on the use of tests in the selection of applicants for a job. To be useful, a test should be *sensitive* in that it allows you to distinguish among applicants, and *reliable*, in that it is consistent in the distinctions made among applicants.

distinguish

1. A test that is sensitive is able to_____among applicants.

sensitivity

2. If all the applicants receive the same score on a test, the test lacks_____.

consistent

3. With a test that is reliable we can make_____distinctions among applicants.

unreliable

4. If we retest a group of applicants and find that the applicants with the highest scores on a test become the lowest scorers and the applicants with the lowest scores become the highest scorers, then this test is probably _____.

invalid

5. A test that allows us to correctly measure what we are trying to measure is valid. If the test does not allow you to measure what you are trying to measure, it is_____.

valid, reliable

6. A test can be highly reliable without being valid but a test cannot be_____unless it is also_____.

verbal ability

7. If a psychological test is called a measure of verbal ability, then it should be highly correlated with performance on jobs that require_____. Performance on these jobs serves as a criterion, or standard, for determining validity of the test.

criterion

8. The validity of the test is measured with the correlation coefficient between scores on the test and scores of the same individuals on the _____. This coefficient is called the validity coefficient.

sales performance

9. To determine the validity coefficient of a test of verbal ability we need a criterion with which to compare the scores made on the test. The criterion for a test of verbal abilities is usually verbal performance. The criterion for a test of sales ability would be_____.

• The answer to each frame of this program is found in the left hand column. Keep the answer for each frame covered until you have answered the item in the frame.

**Figure 11.3**   *An example of a linear instructional program*

**Page 1**

To be useful in selecting applicants, a test must be *sensitive* in that it distinguishes among applicants. It must be *reliable* in that it makes consistent distinctions among applicants. It must be *valid* in that it accurately measures what it is supposed to measure. A reliable test may or may not be valid, but a valid test must be reliable.

Now, based on these three standards, consider the following situation. Applicants for a job take two tests, test A and test B.

On test A, they are found to differ considerably on their scores with some showing very low scores, and still others high scores. When retested on test A, the lowest scoring applicants are still found to have the lowest scores; the average applicants still have average scores; the highest applicants still have the highest scores.

On test B, they are found to also differ considerably on their scores, with the same spread found for the other test. When retested on test B, however, the relative positions of the applicants on the test change. The lowest scoring applicants are found to be among the highest scorers; some of the average applicants now score high while others score low; the highest applicants now have average and low scores.

Which of these statements is correct:

A. Test A has higher validity than test B (Turn to page 7)

B. Test B has higher validity than test A (Turn to page 8)

C. Test B is more reliable than test A (Turn to page 9)

D. Test A is more reliable than test B (Turn to page 10)

**Page 7**

Not necessarily. Even though test A consistently distinguishes among applicants, it may not measure what it is intended to measure. On the other hand, test B is unlikely to have higher validity than A given the inconsistency with which it distinguishes among applicants.

*Please read the question on page 1 again and select another alternative*

**Page 8**

You are incorrect. A test that fails to make consistent distinctions among applicants cannot be more valid than a test that makes consistent distinctions.

*Please read the question on page 1 again and select another alternative*

**Page 9**

You are incorrect. Although the two tests have similar sensitivity, test B is less consistent in distinguishing among applicants than test A.

*Please read the question on page 1 again and select another alternative*

**Page 10**

You are right! Test A is more consistent in distinguishing among applicants than test B and is thus more reliable. They are similar in their sensitivity, however, and test A's reliability does not guarantee that it has high validity. Although test B cannot have higher validity than test A, test A and test B could both have low validity.

*Now proceed to the second question on page 2*

**Figure 11.4** *Example of an intrinsic branching instructional program*

there is little evidence that they *retain* the material any better than students taught with more traditional techniques, such as the lecture (Nash, Muczyk, & Vettori, 1971). There are problems with past research, however, that limit the conclusions that can be drawn from its findings. Goldstein (1993) observed that the self-paced nature of programmed instruction makes it difficult to compare with more traditional techniques that impose a fixed time period. If students in the traditional method were allowed to stop and have their knowledge tested whenever they felt ready, the differences between programmed instruction and traditional instruction might not be as large as found in some studies. Other problems in research on programmed instruction are the lack of adequate comparison groups and the nonrandom assignment of trainees to the conditions.

Regardless of the ambiguities of past research, programmed instruction seems quite effective as an instructional method, particularly in presenting factual material. A major advantage is its portability, as it can be used in instructing employees who are geographically separated. As with all methods, there are potential pitfalls. Preparing a good program is expensive and time consuming. Several rounds of pretesting are usually needed to refine the program. Also, not all trainees relish the solitude of a course that consists solely of programmed instruction. Some evidence shows that the best approach to achieving acceptance is to combine programmed instruction with other techniques involving more personal contact, such as discussion, lecture, or tutoring (Patten & Stermer, 1969).

**Simulation**   This technique consists of having trainees perform in the context of a model of an on-the-job situation. On-the-job training maximizes transfer but at a cost to efficient acquisition, whereas classroom techniques can ensure that certain material is taught in an efficient manner but may not carry over to the job. A simulation seems to be an ideal compromise that combines the best of both techniques.

Simulation training can come in the form of business games in which teams of players operate a simulated business, competing against each other or some optimal model. The trainees deal with a large number of contrived problems under realistic assumptions about the business and the outside world. Participants receive feedback on the results of their decisions (e.g., a profit-and-loss statement) as well as critical analyses of their behavior. Illustrative of mechanical simulations are the flight simulators used in the training of aircraft pilots. Not surprisingly, both commercial airlines and the military have invested heavily in flight simulators.

Simulations frequently are designed to closely resemble the tasks in the job situation. The degree of similarity in surface features achieved, the *physical fidelity*, is often the primary basis for evaluating the effectiveness of a simulation. For example, flight simulators attain a high degree of physical fidelity by incorporating not only the controls, lights, and instruments of a cockpit, but even the physical motions of the aircraft. Although physical fidelity may be important in motivating the trainee, a more important

Flight simulators attain a high degree of physical fidelity by incorporating not only the controls, lights, and instruments of a cockpit, but even the physical motion of the aircraft.

consideration is *psychological fidelity,* which is the extent that performance on the simulator involves the same behavioral and information-processing requirements as the job task. Unfortunately, surprisingly little attention has been given to the evaluation of the psychological fidelity of simulations.

An example of how a simulation could be evaluated was provided in an examination of automobile driving simulators used to train taxicab drivers (Edwards, Hahn, & Fleishman, 1977). The on-the-street driving behavior of a sample of taxi drivers was recorded by having observers pose as riders and evaluate their performance on a structured evaluation form. The drivers later performed two different driving simulations. The correlation between driving performance on the street and performance in the simulators was very low, casting doubt on the psychological fidelity of these simulators.

**Conference Discussion**   A variety of approaches could be included under this method, but they all involve a few key characteristics. A relatively small group (5–10 people) meets under the guidance of an instructor to discuss the material. Rather than lecturing, the instructor organizes the material, stimulates discussion, poses questions, summarizes key points, steers the discussion into productive directions, and generally orchestrates the discovery process. A key attribute of conference discussions is two-way communication among participants and between participants and the instructor. Often the discussion is in the form of problem solving in which the group tackles an issue, generates alternative solutions, and arrives at conclusions. The main advantages of conference discussion are often stated as (1) developing problem-solving and decision-making skills, (2) modifying attitudes, and (3) teaching human relations skills. There is little evidence to allow conclusions as to the merits of this approach relative to other methods, given the wide variety of forms that the conference method can assume. There is evidence, however, that discussion, which is an essential aspect of this approach, enhances learning (Brown & Palincsar, 1989; Lampert, 1986; Minstrell, 1989).

**Case Method**   This involves presenting a hypothetical or real situation to a group of trainees and having them analyze the causes of problems and suggest solutions. The case method can be useful in teaching general principles that can be applied in diagnosing problems and making decisions. Also, it is an inexpensive method of applying abstract ideas to practical problems. Given that there is often no one best answer to many complex problems, an important objective of the case method is to give students experience in dealing with the ambiguity of real problems. The style of the case discussion leader can vary widely. Some instructors use a highly unstructured approach in which they attempt through challenges and questions to get the students to arrive at principles themselves. Other instructors are much more structured and lecture on their own views of the case. Although widely used in business schools, there are critics of this approach (Argyris, 1980). Unfortunately, there is little research to show the advantages of the case method over other methods or to allow conclusions as to the best style of presenting case materials.

**Role Playing**   With this method trainees are given a scenario and a role to play and then act out what they believe they would do given the facts in the role. A potential drawback of role playing is that some trainees feel more comfortable with role playing than others. Consequently, some may resist adopting the role and reject the whole experience, while others go too far and overact. Nevertheless, role playing has been found effective in teaching interpersonal skills such as salesmanship, communication, giving feedback, and conflict resolution (Solem, 1960).

This method also can be of value in changing attitudes. When people must act out a position that is contrary to their beliefs, their beliefs may change to be consistent with the role (Kidron, 1977). Authoritarian managers might be asked, for instance, to take the role of a participative manager in the hope that playing this role will soften their attitudes toward participation. Role playing also can be useful in getting people to understand the positions of others with whom they have poor relations. For instance, a trainee playing the supervisor's role might switch and play the subordinate role to gain some insight into how it feels to be on the receiving end of an appraisal. Bass, Cascio, McPherson, and Tragash (1976) described a program called PROSPER that was used in increasing managers' awareness of black employees' problems. Participants are given a case involving an insubordinate black engineer and a managerial role in which they are required to express positive attitudes toward black employees and attempt to develop the potential of the engineer in the role play. Research with over 2,000 managers has shown that the attitudes of managers are more positive toward black employees after the role play than before. The attitudinal changes appeared to be maintained when tested 3–5 months later.

**Behavior Modeling**   This technique is based loosely on Albert Bandura's social learning theory, discussed in Chapter 3 and earlier in this chapter. Bandura asserts that learning can occur vicariously as the consequence of an observer's noticing and remembering a model's actions. If the observer is capable of enacting the model's behavior and appreciates the potential payoff to be gained from it, then the observer is likely to perform the model's behavior.

Goldstein and Sorcher (1974) were the first to apply Bandura's concepts to industrial training. Five key steps are involved in behavior modeling training:

1. The trainer brings the attention of the trainees to some key points to be learned in the session.
2. A videotape or film is shown that depicts the enactment of the points to be learned.
3. To further enhance retention, the group of trainees discusses the modeled behavior shown in the films or tapes.
4. Trainees role play the behaviors to be learned in the presence of the other trainees and the instructor.
5. Trainees receive feedback on how well they adopted the learning points in their role play. Verbal reinforcement (i.e.,

praise) is given for successful enactments of the desired behaviors.

6. Trainees discuss how they will transfer what they have learned in class to the work situation.

Goldstein and Sorcher (1974) reported several studies supporting the use of behavioral modeling training programs in improving managers' skills in orienting new employees, teaching job skills, motivating poor performers, correcting inadequate work quality and quantity, conducting performance reviews, and handling discrimination complaints. Although the initial returns from research on behavioral modeling suffered from poor research design (McGehee & Tullar, 1978), subsequent research with better designed experiments has provided fairly consistent support for the effectiveness of behavioral modeling (Latham & Saari, 1979; Gist, Rosen, & Schwoerer, 1988; Gist, Schwoerer, & Rosen, 1989).

## CHOOSING AMONG ALTERNATIVE METHODS

As should be obvious by now, there is a wide variety of training methods you could use in designing a training program, and none is superior on every count. Each has its positive and negative features, and the decision as to which to use should be based on a careful analysis of the instructional objectives, the trainees, the resources available, and other attributes of the situation. Randolph and Posner (1979) proposed a decision model to guide this choice that is similar to the Vroom/Yetton/Jago leadership model (Chapter 6).

Some insight into the relative effectiveness of the various methods can be gained by asking training directors to evaluate them. Carroll, Paine, and Ivancevich (1972) asked training directors to rank order various methods in the order of their effectiveness for achieving the following objectives: knowledge acquisition, changing attitudes, problem-solving skills, interpersonal skills, participant acceptance, and knowledge retention. Lectures were ranked last or next to the last across all these dimensions. The best method of ensuring knowledge acquisition and retention was seen as programmed instruction. Role playing was seen as one of the best for changing attitudes and developing interpersonal skills. In terms of participant acceptance, the case study and the conference discussion were seen as best.

Although trainer opinion is a weak basis on which to judge the relative merits of training methods, research findings are generally consistent with the above opinions, with the notable exception of the lecture method. The lecture appears to be much more effective as an instructional method than commonly thought. In perhaps the most comprehensive survey of the training research, Burke and Day (1986) examined 70 studies that evaluated the effectiveness of managerial training. The studies covered six different training content areas: general management training, human relations/leadership, self-awareness, problem solving/decision making, rater training, and motivation/values. The analysis also compared seven methods: lecture, lecture/group discussion, a specific programmed learning package on leadership called Leader Match, sensitivity training, behavioral modeling, lecture/group discussion with role playing or practice, and those training programs that combined three or more methods. A major conclusion of this study was that trained managers were more effective on objective results than untrained managers. Of the various methods, behavioral modeling seemed to be the most effective approach, but surprising support was found for the lecture.

## Implementation

Even if a training program is designed that has content and methods that fit the objectives, the program must still be put in place. The final effectiveness of a program will depend on how well it is implemented. Where a training program is dependent on a trainer for its implementation, the trainer's attitudes and expectations can be crucial to whether the program succeeds or fails. If the trainer has a low opinion of the trainees and believes that the program will not succeed, these negative expectancies may become self-fulfilling prophecies. In this case, programs that should work may fail because of the trainer's casual implementation of the training or poor treatment of the trainees. On the other hand, a trainer who has high hopes for a training program could make it work even though it is not the best approach.

Evidence of the effects of the trainer's prior expectations were demonstrated by Eden and Ravid (1982) in an experiment conducted in a military training program. The researchers led some of the instructors to believe that their trainees had high success potential whereas others were given no information on their trainees. Despite the fact that their expectations were unrelated to the actual success potential of the trainees, trainees described as having high success potential performed better than the other trainees. The higher performance appeared to have resulted from the better treatment received from the instructor. The message seems fairly clear from these results: In addition to picking the best method, trainers should be confident that the training will succeed and must communicate this confidence to the trainees.

In addition to the expectations and attitudes of the trainer, the trainer's skill as an instructor is likely to influence learning as well. As you well know, not all instructors are equally endowed with the ability to teach. Common sense is supported by scientific evidence as shown in a review of teacher influences on student achievement (Brophy, 1986). According to this review, "students achieve more when their teachers emphasize academic objectives in establishing expectations and allocating time, use effective management strategies to ensure that academic learning time is maximized, pace students through the curriculum briskly but in small steps that allow high rates of success, and adapt curriculum materials based on their knowledge of students' characteristics" (p. 1069).

*Summary*

A variety of training methods and media are available for instructing trainees. The most widely used approach is on-the-job training in the form of sink-or-swim, that is, throw the person into the job and hope that he or she learns from successes and failures. Other on-the-job methods include mentoring, internships, apprenticeships, job rotation, and transfers. On-the-job training appears to have many advantages, but there are hidden costs. The alternative is to use classroom methods such as the lecture, audiovisual presentations, programmed instruction, simulations, conference discussion, case analyses, role playing, and behavioral modeling. None of these approaches should be considered inherently effective or ineffective. Each appears better suited for achieving some learning outcomes than others. When methods must be implemented by a trainer, important factors to consider are the attitudes, expectations, and skills of the trainer. There is some evidence that trainers who have high expectations for trainees will do a better job instructing than trainers with lower expectations.

# EVALUATING TRAINING EFFECTIVENESS

The systematic approach to training that has been followed in this chapter emphasizes evaluation of the effectiveness of the training. Although this is an essential component of the model presented in Figure 11.1, evaluation is the most poorly performed of all the phases. A survey of over 600 companies revealed that a large percentage did not evaluate their management training programs at all (Saari, Johnson, McLaughlin, & Zimmerle, 1988). Of those companies that did, most relied on often casual surveys of trainee opinions. The systematic approach to training requires rigorous research procedures that follow the same guidelines used in any basic or applied research (Chapter 2). Rather than repeating Chapter 2, here we devote attention to special concerns that need to be considered when evaluating training.

## Criteria for Evaluation

The criteria or standards against which the effectiveness of the training will be evaluated should be considered early in the process of designing the program. Indeed, Figure 11.1 suggests that a direct outcome of the needs assessment and specification of instructional objectives is the choice of criteria.

A popular approach to training evaluation criteria is Kirkpatrick's (1977) four-step model of evaluation. In step 1, trainee *reactions* are assessed, usually by asking how much they liked the program. This is by far the most frequently employed means of evaluating training programs. The typical student evaluation of instructors in a college course is a good example. In step 2, *learning* is assessed by evaluating the extent to which trainees understand and absorb the principles, facts, and techniques conveyed in the course. This is also common and is usually measured with paper-and-pencil tests of achievement. The criteria described in the next two steps of the model are less frequently used in evaluating programs. In step 3 an assessment is made of how much the training *changes behavior* in ways that transfer to the job. Step 4 involves the measurement of *results*. These could include such outcomes as reduction in costs, turnover, absenteeism, and grievances and increases in the quantity and quality of performance.

Most evaluations of training in industry never go beyond step 1, on the assumption that if trainees like the training, then there must be corresponding benefits on the other three criteria. This assumption is incorrect. Alliger and Janak (1989) reviewed research that examined the interrelationships among the four Kirkpatrick levels and found that, although learning was moderately related to both results and behavior, and behavior was strongly related to results, trainee reactions were unrelated to the other evaluation criteria. Clearly, organizations should not rely as they currently do on trainee attitudes as an indicator of how much was learned, the degree of behavioral change, and results. If these other criteria are important, they need to be directly measured.

Kirkpatrick's model has dominated thinking about criteria development and can provide alternatives for measuring training effectiveness, but the model of systematic training set forth in Figure 11.1 requires that criteria be based on a needs assessment. In other words, the choice of criteria should be guided by the analysis of organizational needs, task requirements, and current position of trainees in relation to these needs. A needs assessment may lead to a focus on only one or two of the criteria, rather than all the criteria. You might decide in a particular situation, for instance, that trainee reactions are the only relevant criteria (e.g., a training program aimed at improving morale) and that behavior change, learning, and organizational performance are irrelevant.

## Summative versus Formative Evaluations

It is not uncommon for an evaluation of a training program to find differences in trainee reactions, learning, behavior, or results without attempting to explain these differences. A more efficient approach to conducting an evaluation is to consider not only final outcomes but also process factors that might influence the success of the training. Process measures can be gathered by monitoring the training at frequent intervals, perhaps through observing trainees and trainers, testing for mastery and retention of the material, or surveying reactions to the program. An analysis of these data can allow a determination of why a program succeeded or failed in the attempt to achieve objectives, thus suggesting modifications in the program. Evaluation of a program on the basis of nothing but outcome measures is sometimes referred to as *summative evaluation,* whereas evaluation that incorporates mediating processes is referred to as *formative evaluation* (Scriven, 1967). Both types of evaluations are needed. The formative evaluation allows for the modification and fine tuning implied in Figure 11.1, but eventually a summative evaluation is needed in deciding whether to continue the training or shift to an alternative.

## Research Design in Training Evaluation

Chapter 2's discussion of the alternative approaches to conducting research applies to the evaluation of training programs. The chief purpose of a research design is to allow the elimination of alternative explanations for the results. Thus, if a training program is found to yield higher performance than no training, can we actually attribute this effect to the program or could it be due to other factors? The best way to eliminate the alternatives is to conduct true experiments in which trainees are assigned at random to the conditions of the experiment (e.g., the training and no training groups). If people are assigned nonrandomly, it is difficult to determine if differences on the criteria between the experimental and control conditions are actually due to training or some extraneous factor. For instance, if participants are selected for a program by asking for volunteers, and if those who do not volunteer are used as the control, any difference between the experimental group and the control group might be the result of volunteering and not the training.

True experiments are the best way to evaluate a training program (Chapter 2), but the difficulties of conducting experimentation in an actual organization should not be underestimated. Trainees seldom submit in a completely passive manner to experimental procedures. Instead, they are likely to look around at coworkers to see if they are receiving the same treatment, and these comparisons can threaten the validity of a field experiment. One possibility is that those who are assigned to the no training control will be jealous of those who are assigned to the training condition. In some situations the opposite could occur, such as when trainees interpret assignment to a training session as punishment or as being deficient in some respect. Another possibility is that supervisors of the control (no training) groups will compensate by giving them special attention. Other threats to the validity of an experiment occur if information in the training leaks out to other groups or if the training and control groups compete against each other. The result may be that differences between the trained and the untrained groups are minimized. Consequently, a training program that is in fact effective may appear ineffective.

In addition to considering possible threats to the internal validity of the research evaluating the training program, an examination also should be made of whether the findings are likely to generalize to other situations. When considered in the context of a training design, Goldstein (1993) proposed that attention be given to at least three factors. *Performance validity* refers to whether performance in the training program carries over to performance in the job. *Intraorganizational validity* refers to whether results of training shown with one group of trainees in the organization will extend to new groups of trainees within the same organization. *Interorganizational validity* is concerned with whether results with a training program in one organization will extend to other organizations.

## Individual Differences Among Trainees

Measures of trainee differences (e.g., ability, personality) should be built into training evaluations (Ackerman & Humphreys, 1990). The inclusion of such measures should allow an examination of the relative effects of variations in the training and trainee characteristics. Mumford et al. (1988) conducted perhaps the most comprehensive study of this issue. They used six characteristics of trainees (aptitude, reading level, academic achievement motivation, educational level, educational preparation, and age) and 16 course content characteristics (e.g., reading difficulty, instructional quality, student-faculty ratio) to predict the performance in training of 5,078 Air Force trainees. The characteristics of the trainees were better predictors than the course content variables of performance in training. Both trainee and course characteristics predicted negative outcomes, such as having to repeat sections of the course and remedial counseling, but student characteristics were the stronger predictors for these criteria.

It is important to note that Mumford et al. (1988) examined performance in training, not the more important variable of how well training transferred to the work place. Another question that Mumford et al. did not address but that is likely to receive attention in future research is whether some types of students do better in some courses than in others. Cronbach (1975) argued that evaluations of training should use an *aptitude–treatment–interaction* (ATI) approach to assess whether the effects of the training differ as a function of the characteristics of the trainee. In the context of this chapter, the *treatment* (T) is the training program whereas *aptitude* (A) is used very generally to encompass any individual difference, including not only what we defined as aptitude in Chapter 10, but also personality traits and demographic characteristics such as age and gender. *Interaction* (I) refers to the possibility that one variation of training may affect one type of trainee differently than another type of trainee. With an ATI design we might test the hypothesis that behavioral modeling is more useful with older employees, whereas programmed instruction is more effective for younger employees. This pattern of results would constitute an interaction of our two independent variables: type of training and age of trainee. Evaluations using ATI could be a crucial source of data that is later used in the person analysis phase of needs assessment to determine who should be trained and the method of training. Although current knowledge is too meager to provide guidelines, this situation will change as more research using ATI designs is conducted.

*Summary*

Regardless of how well a training program is conceived, its effectiveness remains an open question until it is evaluated. A summative evaluation can provide the basis for deciding whether the training achieved its intended objectives and whether modifications should be made or the entire program should be discarded. A formative evaluation allows for the tracking of factors that possibly account for success or failure and that can be used to fine tune the program.

In designing an evaluation of a program, the instructional objectives are used to determine the criteria on which the training is later evaluated. Through random assignment of trainees to experimental conditions and through the observation and measurement of potential confounding factors, research can allow alternative interpretations of results to be eliminated. Another useful addition to an evaluation is consideration of individual differences among trainees in an ATI design. Research evaluating training programs in an actual organizational context can seldom eliminate with certainty all the alternative possibilities. Evaluating training is as much art as science.

# SPECIAL TRAINING NEEDS

We have examined general principles that can guide the design, implementation, and evaluation of any training program. We now examine in more detail three specific training issues that are likely to receive more attention from organizations as we approach the twenty-first century.

## Retraining

An implication of some of the changes confronting organizations is that the average employee will need to undergo retraining throughout his or her career. Higher order thinking skills will be demanded in more and more jobs as technologies become increasingly complex. For instance, the U.S. Department of Labor (1987) in *Workforce 2000* estimated that 60% or more of the jobs in the 1990s will require the equivalent of four years of high school mathematics. To meet these demands, London and Bassman (1989) offer the following recommendations:

> Individuals and organizations should view training as a way to prepare for future contingencies. Updates in technological advancements, management development courses, and programs to help people learn how to learn provide individuals with the abilities and confidence (resilience) to meet unforeseen changes in the midcareer and late-career stages. Continuous learning should be the central

policy of an organization, supported by rewards for self- and subordinate development. (p. 368)

While lifelong learning will become the norm, not all employees are likely to be receptive. Research will be needed to understand the process by which employee skills become obsolete (Fossum, Arvey, Paradise, & Robbins, 1986) and the special training needs of the older employee (Sterns & Doverspike, 1989). Although little is known at the present about the best ways to proceed, it seems that organizations will need to provide support in the form of counseling, goal setting, and feedback to build career resilience, insight, and identity (London & Bassman, 1989). In addition to psychological support, more organizations will need to provide financial support in the form of tuition assistance and bonuses.

## Training for Work Force Diversity

The increased participation of minority and female employees in the work force and the globalization of business will bring fresh ideas and creativity to organizations but is also likely to add new tensions and conflicts. To cope with these pressures, organizations are implementing training programs to impart the skills, knowledge, abilities, and attitudes needed to deal with the challenges of a diverse work force and a global economy.

One type of training focuses on employee appreciation for ethnic and racial diversity (Jackson and Associates, 1992). For instance, Alderfer (1992) describes a race relations competence workshop conducted with managers in a large corporation that consists of three days of lectures, role playing, and cross-race conference discussions. Another type of training that has become more common focuses on relations between men and women. With passage of the Civil Rights Act of 1991, victims of sexual harassment can for the first time sue for punitive and compensatory damages. There is also increased awareness of this problem, largely as the result of highly publicized charges of harassment in the Clarence Thomas hearings and the Navy Tailhook incident. The number of harassment charges filed with the Equal Employment Opportunity Commission increased from about 5,500 in 1988 to almost 10,000 in 1992 (Segal & Kelly, 1992). To deal with this problem, an increasing number of organizations are attempting to increase the sensitivity of their employees to sexual harassment. Program objectives include conveying to employees company policies on harassment, showing them what behaviors are appropriate and inappropriate, and informing them about what to do if they are victims of harassment. In a survey of 495 companies conducted in 1991 by the American Management Association, over 60% of firms with 500 or more employees said that they had provided training to reduce sexual harassment in the workplace (Lublin, 1991a). The root of the problem may not be so much the behavior of individuals as an organizational climate or culture that fosters harassment (Chapter 5), but training can be an important first step in eliminating a hostile work environment.

With the globalization of business, training is also needed in how to effectively deal with people from other countries. One study found that 20–40% of managers working in foreign countries failed in their assignments (Black and Mendenhall, 1990). To avoid these problems, an increasing number of U.S. companies have their employees participate in cross-cultural training in which they are provided instruction in the language, culture, and history of the country where they will be working (Lublin, 1992b). Earley (1987) found that U.S. managers who were transferred to South Korea were better able to adjust to the assignment if they had received this type of training than if they had not received such training. Most of the research in this area has focused on the *culture assimilator* (Fielder, Mitchell, & Triandis, 1971), a particular type of training that uses programmed learning to instill in the trainee the concepts, attitudes, role perceptions, customs, and values of a culture that differs from that of the trainee. The development of an assimilator should start with critical incidents in which Americans and host nationals describe events that made a difference in their attitudes toward the other culture. Around 100 of these are collected and then turned into items in the program. One incident collected in the development of a Greek assimilator is the following (Fieldler, Mitchell, & Triandis, 1971, pp. 97-98):

> Sharon Hatfield, a school teacher in Athens, was amazed at the questions that were asked her by Greeks whom she considered to be only casual acquaintances. When she entered or left her apartment, people would ask her where she was going or where she had been. If she stopped to talk she was asked question like "how much do you make a month?" or "Where did you get that dress you are wearing?" She thought the Greeks were very rude.

Four alternative responses are written for each episode, one stating the correct response and the other three stating some ethnocentric view. For each response, trainees are directed to an explanation for why the response is correct or incorrect. In the case of Sharon Hatfield, the following question was posed: "Why did the Greeks ask Sharon such 'personal' questions?" and the following four alternatives are presented:

1. The casual acquaintances were acting as friends do in Greece, although Sharon did not realize it.
2. The Greeks asked Sharon the questions in order to determine whether she belonged to the Greek Orthodox Church.
3. The Greeks were unhappy about the way in which she lived and they were trying to get Sharon to change her habits.
4. In Greece such questions are perfectly proper when asked of women, but improper when asked of men.

If the trainees respond with one of the incorrect answers (2, 3, 4), they receive some explanation as to why the response was incorrect. The research evaluating the effects of the culture assimilator have been generally favorable in showing that those who go through this training perform better when interacting with those of the target culture (Fiedler et al., 1971; O'Brien, Fiedler, & Hewett, 1971; Worchel & Mitchell, 1972). The danger of the culture assimilator and other forms of cultural training is that these programs can promote stereotypes. While learning the rules of a culture, trainees must simultaneously appreciate the individual differences that exist in even the strongest cultures. Despite the potential pitfalls, a survey of the research on cross-cultural training has shown that it is effective in improving the adjustment and performance of foreign-based managers in their assignments (Deshpande & Visweswaran, in press).

## Training the Chronically Unemployed

Projections indicate that a large proportion of new entries into the work force will be minority youth, often from disadvantaged groups that may find it difficult to assimilate to working life. Possible evidence of the growing isolation of minority youth from the world of work is data showing that a declining percentage of inner city youth even attempt to find employment (Duke, 1991). As a possible solution for this critical problem, private organizations as well as federal, state, and local governments have provided job training for the disadvantaged and unemployed worker. This involvement is likely to increase in the future as relatively unskilled minorities constitute an increasingly large proportion of the labor market. In the 1960s and 1970s training of the hardcore unemployed received a large amount of attention in the research literature. Unfortunately, many of the programs appeared to fail miserably, and their apparent lack of success was partly responsible for the drastic drop in federal funds invested in such training over the last decade. An overall assessment is difficult because of the wide variations of these programs in content, method, and organizational backing. Several features have been shown to differentiate the successful programs from the unsuccessful programs, however, and can serve as a guide to the design of future programs.

1. The most effective training programs combine actual employment with academic training. Trainees in these programs are less likely to drop out if they feel that the program is likely to lead to a job.
2. The jobs should provide opportunities for advancement rather than being dead-end positions.
3. Trainees in these programs are likely to lack confidence and need special attention both during and after the training in the form of feedback, reinforcement, encouragement, and counseling.
4. Training should consider motivational and attitudinal factors as well as job skills. An exclusive focus on one to the neglect of the other is likely to lead to failure and frustration. For

example, changing attitudes toward work without also imparting skills necessary to do the work is likely to be ineffective. Likewise, an exclusive concern with job skills without attempting to modify attitudes toward work may be equally ineffective.

5. Many programs fail as the result of simple breakdowns in communication. For example, inner city, minority trainees can have difficulty communicating with a suburban, white trainer.

Some programs designed with these general principles in mind seem to be working. The Lockheed Aircraft Company has reported low drop-out rates and on-the-job performance levels comparable with regular hires for hard-core trainees enrolled in two such programs. Another success was a military program known as Project 100,000 (Sticht, Armstrong, Hickey, & Caylor, 1987). Instruction in basic skills such as reading, writing, and arithmetic was most effective when combined with material relevant to the intended job field. Also, teaching basic literacy and job skills together was more effective than first teaching basic literacy, followed by training in job-relevant skills.

The key to progress is for the organization to realize that the problem of the hard-core unemployed is not simply a problem residing in deficiencies of the trainee. Rather, the organization also must be willing to make changes. For example, in addition to training new hires from deprived backgrounds, their superiors and peers may need to be trained as well to increase their appreciation for diversity and to eliminate prejudicial beliefs. The organization may even need to revise rules and procedures (e.g., dress codes). In short, successful assimilation of the hard-core unemployed into the organization may require some degree of accommodation of the system to the trainee as well as accommodation of the trainee to the organization.

# A FINAL SUMMATION AND A LOOK AT THE FUTURE

To maximize the benefits of training, this chapter proposes that employers use a systems model (Goldstein, 1993). Many of the suggestions in this model are consistent with common sense. The first step is to conduct a needs assessment to determine where the deficiencies are in the organization and whether training can correct these gaps. A well-done needs assessment not only provides information on what should be the target of the training and who should be trained, but the process itself may have some important benefits. For example, the participation involved in surveying employees regarding their own needs for training can be a means of building commitment to the training program.

The needs assessment lays the groundwork for the design of the training program. We can overemphasize current needs in these assessments, however. An example is a recent survey of 1,400 jobs showing that 78 percent of them did not require algebra (Bracey, 1992). These findings led to a recommendation to reduce the number of years of algebra required in school. This would be a foolish act, however, as pointed out by Albert Shanker (1992) who suggested that the lack of algebra-use on the job "reflects employers' belief that American workers couldn't handle a Japanese-style workplace where highly skilled jobs require workers to know math and use it. . . . Maybe the fact that so few of our workers use math is a symptom of something wrong with the way our workplace is structured rather than something wrong with teaching algebra to our youngsters" (p. E7). Moreover, to only look at current needs and to ignore the future is to risk obsolescence in the rapid technological change characterizing today's world.

Instructional events should be built into the training program to facilitate each step of this learning process. Basic research suggests useful principles for facilitating learning, but careful consideration should be given to the specific type of learning outcomes associated with the trainees' tasks. Likewise, a variety of instructional methods are available; the choice should be dictated by the nature of the learning task. Efforts should be made to ensure that trainers have attitudes and skills conducive to effective implementation of the training program. The final stage is the evaluation of training against the specific instructional objectives set for the program. An investigative approach is recommended in which the training is evaluated, modified as needed, and finally discarded if nothing can be done to achieve the objectives or if better approaches are available.

Despite the value of a systems approach to training, this model is more an ideal than a reality. In a survey of over 600 employers, Saari, Johnson, McLaughlin, and Zimmerle (1988) found that only 27% indicated that they conduct formal needs assessments in determining needs for management training. Rather than selecting instructional methods that fit learning objectives, organizations too often choose a method on the basis of superficial considerations, such as the current fad or an attractive brochure. Once implemented there is often little follow up or evaluation to ensure that the program is doing what it was intended to accomplish.

As more research accumulates, sufficient data eventually may be available to allow training methods to be tailored to specific objectives and specific types of trainees. Until that time, the best advice for organizations is to use logic, careful planning, and empirical research to guide training efforts.

Goldstein and Gilliam (1990) noted five major trends that will require organizations to invest in employee training and development. First, the pool of available workers is expected to shrink dramatically, and employers will be forced into a much greater reliance on training to ensure a qualified work force. Second, organizations will need to draw increasingly from the ranks of women and disadvantaged or older people, and training will need to be shaped to the special needs of these groups. Third, as technologies become increasingly complex, a highly trained work force will be needed that is capable of "inferences, diagnoses, judgment, and decision, often under severe time pressures" (p. 139). Fourth, the continuing shift from manufacturing to service jobs will require that employees be trained in people-handling skills, such as interpersonal communication and leadership. Fifth, the increasing globalization of commerce will require a greater understanding and ability to deal with other cultures. As organizations face these pressures, school systems are under increasing criticism for failing to impart the knowledge and skills needed to function in the increasingly demanding work environment. Business organizations will need to fill the void with their own training programs.

The training function is likely to become more important in the management of human resources as companies attempt to meet the skill requirements of increasingly complex jobs. Employers will need to rely on training to upgrade the skills of present employees and to provide basic skills for the disadvantaged and immigrant employees who will become a larger proportion of the work force in future years. Training also will be used to prepare employees for the cultural diversity associated with changing demographics and the globalization of commerce.

## DISCUSSION QUESTIONS

1. The systems model of training is more an ideal than a reality. Why do you believe that human resource managers and others responsible for training often do not follow the individual stages in this model?
2. In what ways could you combine on-the-job and off-the-job training techniques to increase the benefits and reduce the disadvantages of each approach?
3. The lecture is much maligned as a technique of instruction but may be underrated. What do you think? Explain.
4. There is evidence that some of the factors that facilitate performance during training may actually hurt transfer of the training to on-the-job application. What occurs in these situations? How could performance in training be improved without harming transfer?
5. The basic assumption of the ATI approach is that some training techniques will be much more effective for some trainees than for others. What types of people do you believe would benefit most and least from each of the training techniques discussed in this chapter?
6. The top management of an organization is alarmed by claims of sex discrimination that have been filed against them. They approach you to help them to plan a training program to reduce discriminatory actions on the part of their male managers. In responding to this request, how would you use the systems model outlined in this chapter?
7. The employee in the organization of the future will need to be continually involved in retraining to keep pace with changing technologies. What can be done to encourage employees to engage in lifelong learning?
8. The typical evaluation of college instruction never goes beyond student evaluations of the course and instructor. Is this enough? Why? What other criteria could be used in evaluating a course?

**CASE**

### DEVELOPING LEADERS AND TEAMWORK THROUGH OUTDOOR ADVENTURE TRAINING

Throughout this text we have described how many of the largest American corporations are attempting to change their organizational cultures and the leadership styles of their managers and executives. These organizations are replacing bureaucratic methods with teamwork, collaboration, and risk taking. An increasingly popular but controversial type of program used in implementing these changes is outdoor adventure training.

There are many varieties of outdoor adventure training, but all typically involve presenting a group with physical barriers that they must overcome either as a group or individually. After attempting to overcome these challenges, trainees discuss what they learned about themselves, others, and working together, and how they can apply what they have learned back at work.

In wilderness training, the group undergoes training in a secluded and rugged setting. Challenges can include climbing vertical mountain walls, rappelling down cliffs, rafting in whitewater rapids, hiking over rugged terrain, and crossing deep ravines on ropes. In an example of such a program, the University of Michigan business school brought together 21 senior executives from Japanese, American, and Indian companies for five weeks (Main, 1989). Part of their time together was spent on an island off the coast of Maine where the participants were presented with "physical tests that sane middle-aged men normally avoid." (Main, p. 74). For instance, participants were faced with squeezing blindfolded at night through the Crack, "a passage narrower than a normal human body, between two enormous boulders." In the raft race, teams had to construct a raft from a collection of barrels, rope, and other materials, navigate to a buoy off-shore, and dismantle the buoy. In working together to overcome these barriers, the various executives supposedly broke through language and cultural barriers to understand something about themselves and others.

In another version of adventure training, the trainees stay at a permanent site. A common type of challenge involves climbing a ladder and leaping to another location. In the "leap of faith," trainees are attached to a harness, climb to the top of a tall pole, stand on a small wobbly plate at the top of the pole, and then leap to catch a trapeze. In the "trust fall" trainees fall backward from a ledge and other trainees catch them. In the spiderweb all trainees except for one are blindfolded and must pass other members through without touching a web of ropes hung between two posts. The group is instructed by the one trainee who can see. Other exercises are foot races, rope climbing, and wall climbing.

According to one observer, "Most individuals going through the program move through predictable mental opening-up stages. They start off looking around and are nervous about how they're going to do. Then after they've completed a task, their energy starts to shift—and by the end of the day, they're often in a more spontaneous, hugging, high-fiveing, cheering mode—and are excited, hoarse and thrilled about the future. . . . Often, participants begin to question: Where else in my life have I been performing less than is really possible? Where have I been settling for less? . . . By examining what happens to oneself under duress in a controlled situation, employees can learn and build on that self-knowledge so they're much more grounded in the relationship between what they think and what they do, when they return to work" (Laabs, 1991, pp. 59–60).

Anecdotal evidence provides mixed support for the effectiveness of outdoor adventure training. A director of marketing who participated in a wilderness program stated that "Every time I climbed over a rock, I needed someone's help. . . . There's a valuable lesson to be learned in being able to ask for help and graciously accept it, but the reality is I don't have a 40-pound pack on my back in the office. . . . Do I think that everything we did translates to the office environment as well as other activities would? Probably not" (Laabs, 1991, p. 56). In another example, a 16-member staff participated in a one-day team building program in the attempt to increase the harmony with which they worked together. A member of this team felt that the lack of harmony reflected deeper problems that the training would not correct. "I've seen no improvement whatsoever. In fact, things are worse. . . . The people who went were outdoorsy-types anyway. So to them, it was just an activity. . . . Many of my co-workers are somewhat intimidated by our boss. They feel that in order to keep their jobs, they had to do this" (Laabs, 1991, pp. 56–57). Others are more positive. One participant described her experience in the leap of faith challenge as restoring her self-esteem and as leaving her with a concrete reminder that at some point in any project she must take risks and act on faith (Conlin, 1988, pp. 31–32).

The typical evaluation is anecdotal. A representative of a company that sent 400 of its 12,000 employees on wilderness training claimed that "The response has been quite favorable. People come back enthused and say they've got increased confidence" (Laabs, 1991, p. 62). Occasionally questionnaires or interviews are used to determine how trainees reacted to their experience. One human resources manager of a company that sent employees to an outdoor adventure says that he "is planning to send a questionnaire to all the participants and then assemble a one- to two-day follow-up session this month to get feedback about the seminar's overall results" (Laabs, 1991, p. 63).

## CASE QUESTIONS

1. If you were in charge of deciding what type of training to use to improve employee leadership skills and to improve teamwork, would you seriously consider outdoor adventure training? Why?
2. How would you evaluate the effectiveness of an outdoor adventure training program in improving leadership skills and teamwork?
3. What do you think might be some of the legal considerations in this type of training?
4. Outdoor adventure training and other types of experiential training are often aimed at changing trainee values. For instance, organizations may attempt to instill in trainees the need to be risk takers and to be team oriented in their working relationships. Do you believe that an organization has the right to require employees to participate in training that is directed at changing their values? Should training be restricted to changing knowledge, skills, and abilities directly related to the job? Justify your answer.

# The Work Context

- Background and Systems Orientation

- Psychological and Behavioral Factors in the Work Context

- Physical and Temporal Factors in the Work Context

- Safety at Work

- A Final Summation and a Look at the Future

- Case: Safety Issues in the Workplace: United Auto Workers v. Johnson Controls

Have you ever stared in puzzlement at a microwave oven, digital clock, automobile console, or pocket camera? Did your puzzlement grow to exasperation as you attempted to use them? Odds are, whether or not you were successful in operating any of these pieces of equipment, you felt inadequate and perhaps even embarrassed at your ineptness. You may have even muttered to an onlooker that you simply are not mechanically minded. However, regardless of your reaction, you undoubtedly felt you had lost one more battle in the war between man (or woman) and machine. The superior forces of technology had again outsmarted a mere mortal.

Most people seem to misperceive such events in one of two ways. They think they alone are losing ground with the products of the space age (in other words, everyone else is 20 IQ points brighter than they are). Alternately, they complacently accept the inferior status of humankind as the natural order in a world dominated by computer chips and cathode ray tubes.

If you are guilty of the first misperception, you should read Donald Norman's book, *The Psychology of Everyday Things* (Norman, 1988). In the opening paragraphs, Norman recounts an anecdote about Kenneth Olsen, the engineer who founded and runs Digital Equipment Corporation and who has two engineering degrees from M.I.T. It seems that Olsen confessed that he had not figured out how to heat a cup of coffee in the company's microwave oven. One of the authors can truly empathize with Olsen every time she uses a new, state-of-the-art microwave at work; simply heating a cup of soup requires a programming sequence that would baffle a computer expert.

Even those among us (like Kenneth Olsen) who know they are not more stupid or mechanically inept than everyone else still seem to acquiesce to technology. We have been intimidated by our mechanized world so long that we blithely accept our subservience. Fortunately, assistance is at hand. The role of the human factors psychologist is to work with designers and engineers to create machinery, equipment, technology, and environments that are compatible with human abilities and needs. His or her goal is to insure that everything from hammers to shopping complexes are designed so they are simple, safe, and pleasant to use. In recent years, events such as the Three Mile Island accident, the *Challenger* space shuttle disaster, and Ralph Nader's consumer crusades have drawn public awareness to the frequently unsuccessful interactions between humans and machines.

## BACKGROUND AND SYSTEMS ORIENTATION

The birth of human factors psychology as we know it today occurred during World War II (Mark, Warm, & Huston, 1987). Psychologists and engineers collaborated to solve the massive problems presented by training large numbers of relatively unskilled personnel to use sophisticated military hardware. A plethora of incidents arose in the process that illustrated the potentially tragic outcomes of ignoring the human element in equipment design. For example, confusion between the landing gear and flap control (a control that increases lift or altitude) was reputed to be the cause of more than 400 Air Force accidents in a 22-month period during World War II (McFarland, 1946; Sanders & McCormick, 1987).

The acknowledgment that human limitations must be considered in the design of any environment or piece of equipment eventually led to the correction of many flaws, such as the one described above, and improved individual and organizational efficiency (Howell, 1991). The concept of maximizing the fit between the human and the machine is the cornerstone of contemporary human factors. Another way of expressing the idea of fit is to view the human and machine not as separate entities, but as interacting components of a human-machine system (Figure 12.1).

In a human-machine system, the human perceives (senses) the situation and interacts with or directs the machine, typically through some type of control (e.g., switches, wheels, or knobs). The machine acts on or processes this information (e.g., raises the temperature or reduces the speed). The result of this information processing is communicated back to the human, usually through some type of visual or auditory display (e.g., a TV screen or buzzer).

An example might clarify this process. When you turn on your car's ignition, you use a switch to communicate a command to your car. As a consequence, your car engine starts to function. You receive feedback from the

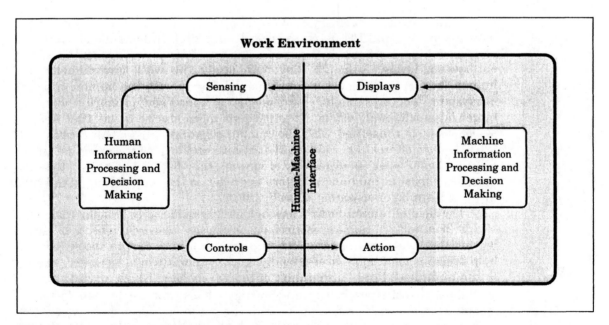

**Figure 12.1** *Model of human-machine system*

*Source:* Howell, W. (1991). Human factors in the workplace. In M. Dunnette & L. Hough (Eds.) *Handbook of Industrial and Organizational Psychology.* 2nd ed., Palo Alto, CA: Consulting Psychologists Press.

engine both auditorially (the sound of the motor running) and visually (the speed indicated on the speedometer). You then use this information to make additional decisions, such as whether to increase or decrease your driving speed.

According to Howell (1991), there are several critical features of any human-machine system.

1.  Systems are composed of several interacting components. As you drive, the relationship between you and your car involves a series of ongoing, complex interactions.
2.  The design of the actual interaction between the human and machine, or the *human-machine interface,* is critical. Obviously, if the controls you use to communicate with your car are not easy to use and if the feedback provided by the instrument panel is not interpretable, you will not be an effective (or safe) driver.
3.  Humans and machines often perform similar functions. This point is illustrated by the fact that both you and your car process information.
4.  Systems are often hierarchical or composed of smaller and larger systems. You and your car are only one of many person-automobile subsystems within a larger system we collectively call traffic.

This last point about system levels provides a link between human factors psychology and I/O psychology (Howell, 1991). In fact, one of the major distinguishing characteristics between the two fields is an emphasis on different system levels. Although they both study the work environment, the human factors psychologist is concerned primarily with the human-machine subsystem, whereas the I/O psychologist is concerned primarily with the larger organizational system. (It is perhaps more precise to say that the I/O psychologist is concerned with the human-organization system because I/O psychologists often study individual attitudes and behavior aggregated at the organizational level.) Another way of viewing this difference is to say that the principal thrust of the human factors approach is through design rather than through training or selection (Howell, 1991).

The field of human factors psychology is considerably broader than that of I/O psychology; human factors encompasses research and application beyond the work environment. For example, a human factors specialist may help design a safer, more user-friendly bathroom or kitchen. However, similar to the multidisciplinary orientation of I/O psychology, which attracts professionals with both psychology and business backgrounds, human factors is peopled largely with professionals from the psychological (mostly experimental) and engineering disciplines. In fact, psychologists constitute less than half of the field's membership, and most of the graduate programs are currently housed in engineering schools (Howell, 1991). This fractionation is similarly reflected in the multiple terms used to identify the discipline: Human factors, engineering psychology, ergonomics, and human engineering have all been used by authorities in the field, who often disagree on the most appropriate label (Chapanis, 1976; Howell & Goldstein, 1971; Wickens, 1984).

Because our interest lies specifically in work-related issues, this chapter deals with those human factors topics that apply primarily to the work environment. The first section covers psychological and behavioral factors in the work context, including human error and capabilities. The second section builds on this to discuss physical and temporal factors in the work context and considers both equipment and environmental design as physical factors of work. A discussion of shiftwork considers the temporal factors of work. The last section draws together the first two sections to illustrate how individual and organizational factors contribute to accident occurrence at work. Current efforts to curtail accidents through mandated safety legislation and legal issues in human factors also are discussed. For a more comprehensive treatment of human factors, see Kantowitz and Sorkin (1983), Sanders and McCormick (1993), or Wickens (1992).

# PSYCHOLOGICAL AND BEHAVIORAL FACTORS IN THE WORK CONTEXT

## Human Error and Reliability

Why is the study of human error so important? Recall our earlier discussion about the historical roots of human factors in World War II. Engineers and psychologists teamed up to reduce the human error that frequently resulted from human-machine incompatibilities; their joint efforts saved countless lives. The cornerstone of human factors has always been a slavish dedication to combating human error. To combat error, you must understand it. To understand error, you must be able to identify and measure it.

### TYPES OF HUMAN ERROR

Error can be identified as belonging to one (or more) of five categories: error of omission, error of commission, extraneous act, sequential error, and time error (Kantowitz & Sorkin, 1983; Swain & Guttman, 1983).

An *error of omission* occurs when someone forgets to perform a task or part of a task; for example, the secretary who forgot to fill the copy machine with toner (and therefore obtained illegible copies) has committed an error of omission. An *error of commission* occurs when someone incorrectly performs a task; for example, an error of commission would occur if the secretary placed a page incorrectly in the copy machine and only part of the page was copied.

The remaining three types of error (extraneous act, sequential, and time) are specific types of errors of commission because they involve incorrect ways of performing some task. An *extraneous act* refers to some behavior that diverts attention from the task being performed, such as when a security guard missed a prowler because he was reading the newspaper. A *sequential error* can occur when a task is performed out of sequence. For example, a sequential error would occur if the driver backed out of the garage before opening the garage door. A *time error* is committed when a task is performed too early or too late, such as the student who performed poorly on an exam because she arrived 30 minutes late.

Identifying and labeling different types of errors can have implications for how they can be reduced or eliminated, and is often a first step in that direction. For example, workers who commit many sequential errors may require additional job skills training (see Chapter 11). If too many extraneous acts are committed, the job environment may need to be redesigned to reduce or eliminate sources of distraction.

## HUMAN RELIABILITY

The flip side of human error is human reliability. To the human factors specialist, the term human reliability denotes something quite different from the meaning of reliability in I/O. Both terms are used generally to indicate the absence of error, but differ considerably beyond this common ground. To the I/O psychologist, reliability indicates either the stability of test scores over time (test–retest reliability) or the consistency of item responses within a test (internal consistency reliability) (Chapter 2). However, in human factors, human reliability is defined as the probability of successful performance of a task or parts of a task (Sanders & McCormick, 1987). Human reliability is always measured as a probability value. For example, if the probability that a worker reads a dial correctly is .88, then in 100 attempts to read the dial, the worker will read the dial correctly 88 times and incorrectly 12 times.

In the 1950s, human factors specialists began creating data bases of human reliability estimates for certain jobs. *Data Store,* one of the earliest data bases, was developed for the electronics industry (Munger, 1962; Munger, Smith, & Payne, 1962). Data Store is composed of 20 pages of tables with performance times and probabilities (Table 12.1). This information can be used to compute the probability of successful performance for many tasks performed with electronic equipment. Most of these estimates have been drawn from expert judgments reported in research studies. More recently, a similar type of human reliability data base, *Technique for Human Error Rate Prediction* (THERP), was developed for the nuclear power plant industry (Swain & Guttman, 1983).

If a comprehensive assessment of reliability is desired, machine as well as human reliability must be considered. The reliability of a piece of equipment, a machine, or a component of a machine can be estimated by observing its failure rate over time. Like the estimates of human reliability, machine reliability is expressed as the probability of successful performance. Both human and machine reliabilities can be combined to provide an estimate of total *system reliability.*

**Table 12.1**

| DATA STORE (HUMAN RELIABILITY) TABLES: OPERATION OF JOYSTICKS BY STICK LENGTH AND MOVEMENT | | |
|---|---|---|
| **Dimension** | **Time in seconds to be added to base time*** | **Reliability** |
| Stick length (inches) | | |
| 6–9 | 1.50 | .9963 |
| 12–18 | 0.00 | .9967 |
| 21–27 | 1.50 | .9963 |
| Stick movement (degrees) | | |
| 5–20 | 0.00 | .9981 |
| 30–40 | 0.20 | .9975 |
| 40–60 | 0.50 | .9960 |
| *Base time, 1.93 seconds. | | |

*Source:* Adapted from Munger, S. (1962). *An Index of Electronic Equipment Operability: Evaluation Booklet.* Washington, DC: American Institutes for Research.

On the surface, it seems that the ability to label and measure error should go a long way toward eliminating the presence of error in the workplace. Unfortunately, the identification and quantification of error (particularly human error or unreliability) have not been very successful. Reasons include difficulties in validating the probability estimates on actual performance data and the availability of data for only a limited number of tasks in specific jobs (Adams, 1982; Goldbeck & Charlet, 1974; 1975; Meister, 1985; Sanders & McCormick, 1987).

## Human Capabilities and Limitations

If we systematically attempt to reduce or eliminate error, we must be able to accomplish more than simply identifying and measuring it. We must be able to understand why human error occurs. To accomplish that end, human factors researchers have extensively studied human limitations and capabilities, traditional domains of the experimental psychologist. What are the boundaries of human functioning that predispose people toward committing error? What human capabilities might enhance human, and therefore system, reliability?

Our historical exploration of human capabilities and limitations proceeds from the early research on human sensory functioning, specifically auditory and visual functioning, to the more current research on human information processing. We also discuss exciting new directions of information processing research in human attention and mental work load.

## AUDITORY FUNCTIONING

Hearing provides you with the means to appreciate some of life's pleasures, such as listening to a beautiful piece of music, and the means to protect yourself from harm, such as the ability to recognize a fire alarm. Because many human-machine interfaces involve auditory stimuli (e.g., alarms, bells, buzzers, and, of course, speech), the human factors specialist must have a working knowledge of the human auditory system.

When a sound originates from a source, such as a tuning fork or a stereo, air molecules move up and down in response to changes in air pressure from the vibrating source. These vibrations create wave-like forms that are continually repeated (Figure 12.2). Each of these individual waveforms constitutes one cycle; most sound sources produce many of these waveforms or cycles every second. This characteristic of sound is called its *frequency* and is expressed in cycles per second or Hertz (Hz). Frequency is associated with the perception of pitch. A high-frequency sound (many cycles per second) is associated with a high-pitched sound; a low-frequency sound (few cycles per second) is associated with a low-pitched sound.

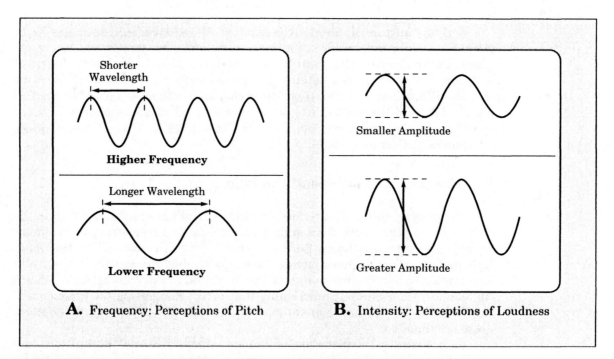

**A.** Frequency: Perceptions of Pitch    **B.** Intensity: Perceptions of Loudness

**Figure 12.2** *Wave form of a pure sound with parameters indicated*

The normal human ear is sensitive to a range of 20–20,000 Hz. Many animals, such as dogs, are sensitive to much higher frequencies than the human ear can distinguish. Dog whistles cannot be heard by the human ear because they produce frequencies above the 20,000-Hz threshold. We also know that the human ear is not equally sensitive to all frequencies between 20 and 20,000 Hz; we are less sensitive to lower frequency sounds (20–500 Hz) and more sensitive to middle and higher frequency sounds (1,000–5,000 Hz). For example, equating all other factors, the human ear perceives a 5,000-Hz sound as louder than a 500-Hz sound. In addition, you can better localize (determine the direction of) higher compared with lower frequency sounds. In other words, you could identify (and localize) an ambulance siren (high frequency) more readily than a foghorn (low frequency).

Another important characteristic of sound is its *intensity*. The intensity of sound refers to the perception of loudness, indicated in Figure 12.2 by the height of the waveform. The higher the waveform, the louder you perceive the sound. Sound intensity is measured with the decibel (dB), a logarithmic unit of measurement; the logarithmic scale means that a 10-dB increase equals a hundredfold increase in sound intensity. For example, if the intensity of an alarm were increased from 80 to 90 dB, the increase would be perceived as one hundred times louder by the human ear (although that perception also varies with the frequency of the sound). Because sustained noise (particularly at high intensities and frequencies) can impair hearing by destroying the nerve cells in the inner ear, noise levels in industrial environments are regulated by law (Chapter 7).

## VISUAL FUNCTIONING

You are a visually oriented being. Your eyes are extremely sensitive to fine detail and an array of colors. Human beings communicate with each other through visual stimuli ranging from prose to paintings, and consider the loss of vision as one of life's greatest tragedies. It is no surprise that many human-machine interfaces include visual stimuli, such as words or color coding. For this reason, the human factors specialist must be knowledgeable about the human visual system.

Your eyes could not function normally without light. Typically, the light we see is either emitted from a light source, such as a light bulb, or reflected off the surfaces of objects in the environment, such as sunlight reflected from buildings and trees. Much as your ears are able to perceive only a small range of sound frequencies, your eyes are sensitive to only a small range of the light spectrum, more appropriately called the *electromagnetic spectrum*. Light also has a waveform similar to that of sound. The amplitude of this waveform mainly affects the perception of brightness; the wavelength, or frequency affects the perception of color. Of the visible spectrum, your eyes can perceive high-frequency light (red) and low-frequency light (violet or blue). You have color receptors in your eyes that are responsible for day vision and black-and-white receptors for dim light and night vision.

Humans are primarily *diurnal,* or day-oriented, organisms. Your sensitive color receptors, which function only in bright light, permit you to perceive a tremendous amount of detail in the environment, from coloration to object form. Because most color receptors are concentrated in the center of the eyeball, day vision is most sensitive when your eyes are focused straight ahead. Peripheral vision is more sensitive at night because black-and-white receptors are located on the periphery of the eyeball. Your day orientation is further illustrated by the fact that, when going from a light to a dark environment, your eyes require 30–40 minutes to completely adapt to the reduced illumination; when reentering the light environment, your eyes adapt to the increased illumination almost immediately.

## SIGNAL DETECTION

An area of research that applies equally well to both human visual and auditory perception is *signal detection theory* (SDT). This theory is most helpful in describing how people make decisions about faint or ambiguous stimuli, or signals. The concepts of signal and noise are fundamental to SDT. *Noise* is any circumstance that can interfere with detection of a signal or stimulus. The noise is usually in the form of some type of environmental interference, and, despite the terminology, does not necessarily refer to auditory interference. Your ability to hear a telephone ringing above the simultaneous clamor of the television, radio, dishwasher, and washing machine, for example, is a signal detection problem; you must detect a signal (the ringing telephone) amid the background noise from your appliances. Similarly, the radar operator tries to discriminate the blip of an aircraft from the static on a radar screen.

Noise generally varies over time and is assumed to approximate a normal distribution (Chapter 2), with values ranging from low to high. When the signal occurs, its intensity is added to the noise. A person attempting to identify the occurrence of the signal must, at any point in time, decide if the signal and noise or only the noise exist. SDT is particularly concerned with the decision errors that human beings make when trying to discriminate a faint or ambiguous signal amid noise. The possible decision errors are *false alarms,* or saying a signal exists when there is no signal, and *misses,* or saying there is no signal when there is one.

These decision errors are committed everyday in work environments with often costly and/or tragic outcomes. The refinery worker must monitor a noisy plant for alarm buzzers triggered by dangerous chemical reactions; the dentist must decide whether the grey area on the x-ray is a cavity. Although these situations differ greatly, both the worker and the dentist must distinguish a faint stimulus (signal) amid a distracting environment. The most obvious way to increase discriminability is to increase the strength of the signal (e.g., a louder buzzer) or decrease the background clutter (e.g., better quality x-ray film). Other options exist, including training people to more accurately make these discriminations. Signal detection theory has been applied to a variety of occupational problems over the past 25 years, such as medical diagnosis and inspection and quality control in industry (Hutchinson, 1981; Kantowitz & Sorkin, 1983; Wickens, 1984).

## Human Information Processing

Human beings not only perceive the environment through their senses, they also use this information in some systematic fashion to interpret their environment. Another way of explaining this capability is to say that human beings process information. Information processing can be very simple, such as finding your way home from school or remembering an acquaintance's name. However, more complex information processing is typically involved in such activities as solving calculus problems or making career decisions. The study of human information processing has long been a central interest of psychologists; over the past 40 years considerable knowledge has accumulated on how people process information (see also chapters 5, 6, and 9).

The human mind can be conceived as an information processing system composed of three subsystems. The first subsystem receives information from the environment (typically visual or auditory information) and holds that information for a very short time interval, varying from milliseconds to a few seconds. This subsystem is called *sensory store* and has been likened to a camera that snaps very brief visual and auditory pictures of the world.

The second subsystem receives the information from sensory store. This subsystem is called *working or short-term memory* and, unlike sensory store, requires purposeful involvement of the human as an information processor. To retain the information transferred from sensory store, the human processor must actively work at encoding, or giving meaning, to the information so it can be permanently stored. We often struggle to keep information from slipping out of short-term memory, such as our frequently futile attempts to rehearse new phone numbers. The ability to retain information in short-term memory can be enhanced if some meaning is attached to the information there. For example, the phone numbers 222-3456 or 374-HELP are fairly easy to remember because they have some meaning beyond a random string of letters or numbers.

Information in short-term memory is thought to be encoded in three ways: visually, acoustically (or phonetically), and semantically. For example, if you read the word *cat* you encode it by visualizing a cat in your mind, by silently repeating the word, and by remembering some of your experiences with a cat. Interestingly, when you read a word, the phonetic coding seems to be salient. As a consequence, errors of recall for written material often reflect acoustic, not visual, errors. The letter A, for example, would more likely be confused with the letter K, which sounds similar to A, than the letter H, which it visually resembles (Conrad, 1964).

One of the most important discoveries about short-term memory is our ability to retain only about seven items in short-term memory at any time

(Miller, 1956). These seven items do not need to be single letters or numbers but chunks of information grouped together. For example, the number 2269500456683 exceeds the capacity of short-term memory and is difficult to commit to memory. However, 226 9500 4566 83 does not exceed the capacity of short-term memory. If you memorize the "chunked" version of the number, you will probably recall it by these four units or chunks. Social security numbers, telephone numbers, and credit card numbers all use the chunking concept.

Information that survives short-term memory is transferred to permanent storage in the third subsystem, *long-term memory*. Transferred information that has some meaningfulness seems to be most effectively coded into long-term memory. That is why, as most students have sadly discovered, rote memorization is not a useful method of study. Effective memory aids all involve imposing salience or meaning on material to be learned, such as the number 374-HELP. Retrieval of information from long-term memory is much more difficult if the information was not initially stored using strong cues.

In addition to the memory deficits that can occur because information was not effectively stored in long-term memory, human beings are susceptible to many cognitive distortions and biases when they process information. These biases are inherent in the manner people seek information, estimate the outcomes of certain situations, and attach values to outcomes (Chapter 9).

Some common examples illustrate these points. People weigh early information more heavily than later information, which is why first impressions can be so difficult to alter. Often, people treat all information as equally reliable and valid. Otherwise, many popular scandal magazines would not be in business. Once they have made a decision, people tend to seek out only confirming information. For example, after you have purchased a Toyota, you probably do not want to listen to your friend praise his Honda. Also, people tend to attribute positive outcomes to themselves and negative ones to other sources. In other words, you more commonly take credit for your successes rather than your failures. These few examples demonstrate that people are typically not very rational and, consequently, not very good, decision makers (Wickens, 1984).

Modern theorists have combined knowledge about human capabilities and limitations to produce general models of human information processing that incorporate both sensory (auditory and visual) functioning and cognitive processing. Wickens (1984) suggested one such model (Figure 12.3). Through your physical senses, you receive information (mostly in a visual and/or auditory form) from the environment. This sensory information is initially processed in sensory store and subsequently in short-term (working) and long-term memory. Many of the cognitive distortions and biases just discussed come into play during the decision and response selection (i.e., when you decide what to do with the information you perceive) and the response execution phases. For example, you may not seek to discover a person's positive attributes if he or she made a bad first impression. From perception to response execution, your motivation and ability to exert and maintain atten-

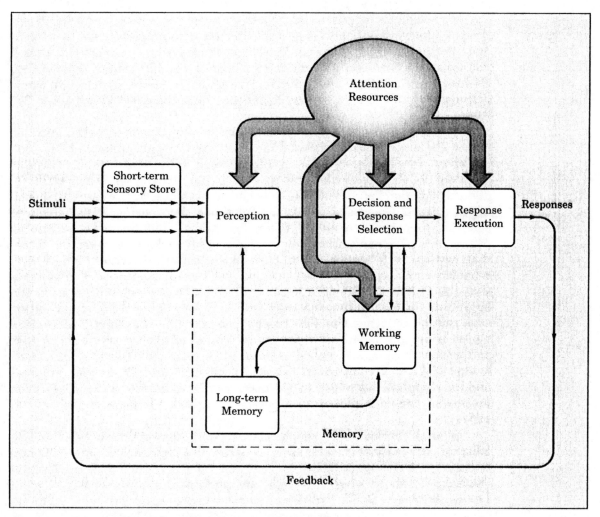

**Figure 12.3**   *Model of human information processing*

*Source:* Wickens, C.D. (1984). *Engineering Psychology and Human Performance.* Columbus, OH: Charles E. Merrill.

tion have a pervasive influence. Because of its significance in human information processing, attention is discussed in detail next.

## Attention and Mental Work Load

Closely related to the concept of information processing is *attention*. Since childhood, we have been admonished by parents and teachers to pay attention. Maintaining attention is often difficult, particularly for boring or tedious information.

Although paying attention implies that you purposefully and selectively process information about some aspect of the environment, that processing can occur in a variety of forms. You maintain *selective or focused attention* if you focus on some specific event or set of events and filter out or ignore other, unrelated events (Broadbent, 1958). The ability to maintain selective attention enables you to talk on the telephone while the radio plays a few feet away.

In today's fast-paced society, however, another type of attention predominates. *Divided attention* refers to the ability to focus attention on more than one event simultaneously (Lane, 1982; Wickens, 1984). An example of divided attention is simultaneously eating lunch and driving. Another term for divided attention is *timesharing*. Timesharing is a descriptive term because it implies sharing mental resources. Sometimes timesharing is not effective, such as when you attempt to study for exams while watching television. Although timesharing attention among several tasks often results in less than optimal performance on any of them, the routine activities of most modern jobs demand constant reliance on divided attention. Anyone who has ever seen the cockpit of a modern jet aircraft or a power plant control room can appreciate the mental timesharing required of the pilot or the operator during even routine activities. For that reason, one of the most currently researched topics in human factors involves the allocation of mental resources in task performance, commonly called *mental work load* (MWL). The basic idea behind MWL is a comparison between a person's limited mental resources and the resources demanded by the task; another definition is the information processing demands placed on a person by a task (Sanders & McCormick, 1987).

Mental workload has been measured with behavioral (task-based), physiological, and subjective (self-report) indexes. The typical behavioral measure assesses performance decrements when the difficulty of one task is increased (Wickens, 1984) or when two tasks are performed simultaneously (Ogden, Levine, & Eisner, 1979). Because humans are hypothesized to have a limited allocation of mental resources, adding additional, competing demands, or greater MWL, should result in lower performance on one or both tasks. As the pilot example indicates, this scenario is very realistic in many jobs. Physiological indexes measure changes in physiological states while performing some task. For example, heart rate variability and a type of brain wave called an evoked potential (Figure 12.4) seem to be very sensitive to changes in mental effort. Physiological measures, particularly the heart rate measures, have shown promise in MWL research (Furedy, 1987; Vincente, Thornton, & Moray, 1987). Heart rate usually becomes less variable with increases in MWL (Mulder & Mulder, 1981). The subjective measures ask the person to indicate, by referring to a response scale, how much mental effort a certain task requires. These subjective measures have been roundly criticized for a relative deficiency of supporting reliability and validity evidence (Boyd, 1983; Smith, 1990).

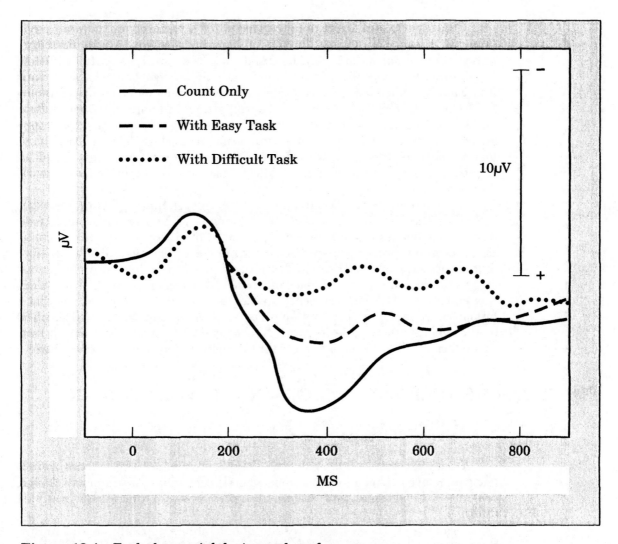

**Figure 12.4**  *Evoked potential during task performance*

Source: Adapted from Kramer, A., Wickens, C.D., & Donchin, E. (1983). An analysis of the processing requirements of a complex perceptual-motor task. *Human Factors, 24,* 605.

Like the behavioral, physiological, and self-report measures of stress discussed in Chapter 7, the three types of MWL measures frequently do not agree in their assessments of MWL levels. Yeh and Wickens (1988) suggested that this lack of agreement may reflect the suitability of specific types of MWL measures for certain situations. For example, when excessive MWL demands exist, people may underestimate their capabilities and potential performance. Therefore, subjective measures may not be as accurate as behavioral measures under difficult task conditions.

There are several direct implications of MWL research for the work environment. If the MWL of specific jobs or parts of jobs can be reliably determined, that information can be used to select workers with sufficient capabilities for mentally demanding tasks and to redesign jobs so certain functions are allocated more appropriately to humans or machines (Sanders & McCormick, 1987). According to Howell (1991), human factors specialists and I/O psychologists may unknowingly be exploring the same turf. Such constructs as job-related stress, work motivation, and job satisfaction may have direct relationships with measures of MWL. For example, a task rated as requiring a great deal of mental effort also may be perceived as a work stressor.

We have covered some fundamental concepts in human factors research, including the identification and measurement of human error and basic human capabilities and limitations in terms of auditory, visual, and information processing properties. In discussing human error (reliability) and information processing (MWI) research we drew direct parallels between human factors topics and the traditional concerns of I/O psychology, such as job selection and stress. The earlier discussions center around basic information about human perception and information processing, which are typically researched in the laboratory by experimental psychologists. We next demonstrate how this information has been translated into practical, job-related applications.

# PHYSICAL AND TEMPORAL FACTORS IN THE WORK CONTEXT

## Equipment Design

Recall the story about Kenneth Olsen's frustrating experiences with a microwave oven. This all-too-common scenario describes an equipment design problem in which the human-machine interface does not function optimally (if at all).

Drawing on the research results about human capabilities and limitations, we now list a few general prescriptions for equipment design. This type of information is the stock in trade of the human factors practitioner and illustrates the well-known stereotype of the human factors specialist as a "knobs and dials" expert. (Although not mentioned here, straightforward engineering considerations, such as maintainability and cost of operation, are also heavily weighted in any design decisions.)

### DISPLAYS

Displays are devices used by an information sender (machine) to communicate with a human receiver (Buck, 1983) and form a critical part of the human-machine interface (Figure 12.1). Typically, displays take two forms, auditory and visual. *Auditory displays* communicate using the auditory modality (sound) and include bells, buzzers, alarms, sirens, or speech in some form (human or computer generated). *Visual displays* communicate using the visual modality (sight) and include signs, billboards, gauges, dials, and screens. Visual information can be unchanging, such as a billboard, or rapidly changing, such as a television screen.

**Auditory Displays**   Much research on auditory displays has focused on emergency alarms because of the safety implications of alarm design; correctly and rapidly perceived alarms can save many lives. From signal detection theory, we know that the signal (alarm) must be sufficiently distinct from background (e.g., traffic or industrial) noise to be easily heard. This can be accomplished by increasing the intensity or duration of the signal or by decreasing the background noise. Consequently, most warning signals and alarms are high intensity (above 80 dB). Warning and alarm signals should use frequencies in the midrange (500–3,000 Hz) because the human ear is most sensitive to this range and because background noise is typically low frequency (well below 500 Hz).

Alarms, however, often must be heard over long distances and easily localized (the direction of the alarm determined by the listener). Maximizing these two criteria, unfortunately, requires some tradeoffs. Because high-frequency sounds cannot travel as far as lower frequency sounds, frequencies over 1,000 Hz should not be used when alarms must be heard over long distances. Relatively high- or midrange-frequency sounds, on the other hand, are better localized than lower frequency sounds. Because research (Caelli & Porter, 1980) has determined that human beings are extremely poor at localizing sound sources such as emergency alarms (often committing errors that include total reversals in direction), a higher frequency alarm is ultimately safer. The dilemma presented here illustrates the difficult design decisions human factors specialists frequently face when attempting to optimize several display features simultaneously.

**Visual Displays**   Although not obvious from the preceding discussion, design issues for auditory displays are usually less complex than for visual displays. The information communicated by auditory displays (e.g., warning alarms) is usually fairly simple; the information you hear is mostly processed in short-term memory and discarded. Visual information, on the other hand, is usually processed on multiple levels (visual, acoustic, and semantic), which increases the number of potential design options and also the potential for confusion.

Because of the importance of color in our visual system, *color coding* is commonly used to enhance visual displays. Research (Hitt, 1961; Smith & Thomas, 1964) has shown that color coding is often superior to other types of coding, such as shapes, symbols, and geometric forms. Color coding seems to be particularly effective when certain objects must be identified among several other, similar objects. For example, files, electric wires, gauges, dials, maps, and charts are more effectively scanned when they are color coded. When choosing specific colors, people respond to red most quickly, followed by green, yellow, and white (Reynolds, White, & Hilgendorf, 1972). Red works especially well under poor visual conditions, such as reduced light, and therefore is a good color choice for such visual displays as road signs and critical industrial gauges. The greater effectiveness of the color red probably evolves from conditioning since birth to regard red as an indicator of extreme importance or danger.

When more sophisticated labeling than color is necessary, *symbolic coding* presents additional options. Symbolic coding has consistently proven to be more efficient than verbal (word) coding, even when language is not a problem. For example, depictions of typical male or female figures on bathroom doors and symbols for fire on fire escape exits in office buildings are recognized faster than the corresponding spoken words (Ellis & Dewar, 1979). The reason for symbol superiority is obvious: Because words must be translated into their corresponding meaning (symbols), encoding time in short-term memory is reduced by initially using symbols. (Of course, the superiority of symbols holds only if they are sufficiently well-designed so that people can recognize their meaning.)

Some additional, important features of visual displays should be considered, particularly when designing industrial gauges and dials (Sanders &

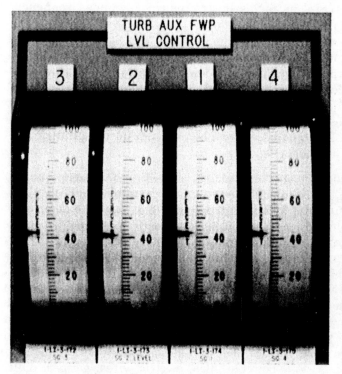

These are examples of equipment design flaws in the Three Mile Island nuclear power plant at the time of the 1979 partial core meltdown. The first photo is another example of "common sense" gone awry. Is this the way people count? The second photo shows another problem. Note the reversal of the "trip-reset" positions.

McCormick, 1987). Numerical scales on gauges or dials should follow some reasonable numeric progression, such as 1-2-3 or 0-10-20. People should not be forced to interpolate values on a scale to obtain a precise reading, such as attempting to estimate a value between 0 and 10 (Whitehurst, 1982). Pointers on gauges or dials should be pointed in form and not overlap with the scale numbers. Pointers on scales should rise for higher values and fall for lower values; similarly, higher numbers should indicate more of some value while lower numbers should indicate less (Roscoe, 1968). When only an estimate or range is needed, displays should not provide superfluous information (precise numeric values) that requires increased information processing. For example, if the worker only needs to determine whether the temperature is within normal range or dangerously hot, the temperature gauge should provide only that (qualitative) type of information.

Such design prescriptions are based on attempts to reduce the user's information processing demands and probably seem like so much common sense. However, these simple design prescriptions have been flagrantly violated many times in industrial settings. Some of the more obvious design flaws found in the Three Mile Island nuclear power plant after the 1979 mishap, for example, are shown in the photographs on the preceding page. Many of these flaws could have been remedied by using modern digital displays, which are commonly found today in watches, clocks, and automotive gauges. Digital displays are effective under many circumstances, and they are being used increasingly in most industrial settings.

## CONTROLS

In addition to displays, controls form another critical link in the human-machine interface (Figure 12.1). A control is defined as any device that allows a human to transmit information to a machine (Kantowitz & Sorkin, 1983). Improving control design was one of the earliest problems tackled by human factors specialists. (Recall the discussion about the confusion between landing gear and flap controls in World War II airplanes.) Control design problems are still common today. One study found that, of the 405 people interviewed, 44% reported inadvertently operating the fingertip controls attached to their car's steering column (Moussa-Hamouda & Mourant, 1981), such as operating the windshield wipers instead of the turn signal.

The technology for control design is fairly well-documented and widely available to the industrial designer (Van Cott & Kinkade, 1972). Controls can vary on several dimensions, such as color, texture, shape, and labeling. When controls are within an operator's field of vision and lighting is adequate, *color coding* controls can be effective.

Human beings can distinguish at least three different categories each of control shape (Jenkins, 1947) and texture (Bradley, 1967). *Shape* and *texture coding* can therefore be functional. Because of an early interest in cockpit control design, the U.S. Air Force expanded shape coding to include *symbolic coding*. The symbolic coding of controls means that controls are shaped similarly

These employees are working in the control room of a modern power plant.

to their function; for example, the landing gear control is shaped like a wheel and the flap control like a wing. Consistent with symbolic coding of displays, symbolic control coding reduces the information processing demands on the user and therefore the potential for error.

*Label coding* is the most common, and often the only, means of coding controls. Power plant control rooms are frequently replete with a sea of controls distinguished only by their labels (Seminara, Gonzalez, & Parsons, 1977). Unfortunately, label coding is subject to the information processing errors discussed previously. For example, in reading labels, we know that acoustic errors are committed more frequently than visual errors. Therefore, adjacent controls should not be labeled with similar *sounding* letters or words. Labels should also be descriptive and short; lengthy, technical labels impose excessive processing demands on the user. Optimal control coding often can be achieved by coding along several different dimensions simultaneously, such as color, shape, texture, and labeling (Bradley, 1967).

## CONTROL-DISPLAY RELATIONSHIPS

Displays and controls do not function separately, but collectively as integral components of a human-machine system (Figure 12.1). Unfortunately, the most well-designed controls and displays may present usability problems when combined into a working unit. Control-display relationships, consequently, create a new set of problems for the human factors specialist to tackle. In designing control-display linkages, one of the most important considerations is determining the population stereotype for that relationship. A *population stereotype* for a control-display linkage is a widely accepted (although not universal) relationship between the control and display. For example, in the United States, you flick a light switch up to turn on the light; in England, the opposite relationship holds. Within each country, however, the population stereotype for this control (switch)–display (light) linkage is very strong.

Many control-display usage problems emanate from those situations in which the population stereotypes are weak or nonexistent. One of the most flagrant examples of a weak population stereotype is the control-display linkage on the front of the range and heating elements on top of the range (Figure 12.5a). The position of the knob corresponding to the appropriate element varies considerably across different brands and models (Shinar, 1978). Human factors researchers solved this design dilemma over 30 years ago (Figure 12.5b; Chapanis & Lindenbaum, 1959), although few, if any, manufacturers have since incorporated this feature into their range designs (Shinar, 1978). This is a sad note given the obvious inconvenience and potential danger afforded by many ranges, particularly electric ranges, which provide little feedback about which burner is operating.

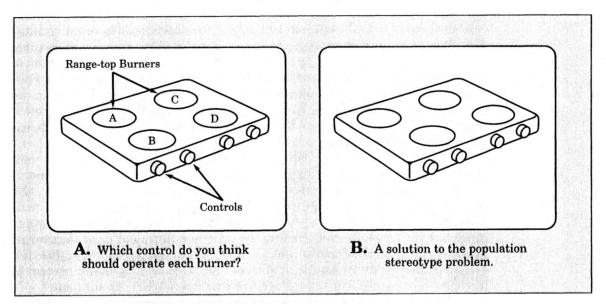

**A.** Which control do you think should operate each burner?

**B.** A solution to the population stereotype problem.

**Figure 12.5 a & b** *Control-display linkage of range top*

*Source:* Kantowitz B., & Sorkin, R. (1983). *Human Factors: Understanding People-System Relationships.* New York: Wiley, p. 329.

## Computers

The modern personal computer provides an excellent example of a human-machine system. The human interacts with the computer through a keyboard or mouse (controls) and the computer processes this information and provides a response on a VDT or visual display terminal (visual display). The human processes the information provided by the computer and uses it as input for the next interaction with the computer. Computers, therefore, can be conceived as consisting of specialized visual displays and controls, with all of the attendant problems of any display or control interfaces.

As anyone who has recently purchased a personal computer can attest, the computer hardware and software options available on the market today are virtually endless. Modern computers can accomplish feats that were considered to be in the realm of science fiction only 10 or 15 years ago. The only real constraints are cost and (possibly) the limits of one's imagination (Howell, 1991). Because computer technology proliferated so rapidly, knowledge about the user-computer interface has lagged seriously behind. As a consequence, users of computer hardware and software (particularly novices) often report extreme bewilderment, which grows to frustration, in their attempts to interface with almost any computer. Assuming they can find the on-off switch, common complaints run the gamut from lengthy, cryptically written software manuals to unintelligible software languages.

One of the fundamental problems in designing user-friendly computers lies not with the users, but with the designers themselves. The designers, typically computer software and/or hardware specialists, produce computer systems that are elegant and efficient but, ultimately, incomprehensible to the average user. This rift has arisen because computer specialists are experts in computers and the users are novices. A growing body of research and theory (Abelson & Black, 1986; Glaser, 1984; Lord & Maher, 1990) indicates that experts differ from novices not only in the amount of information they possess, but also in the way they process information. For example, experts recall relevant information better than novices (McKeithan, Reitman, Rueter, & Hirtle, 1981) and with less distortion or bias than novices (Fiske, Kinder, & Larter, 1983).

Kantowitz and Sorkin (1983, p. 13) recounted a situation in which computer specialists designed computer software for secretaries in a telecommunications company; the secretaries were unable to use it. Interestingly, the only secretaries who were not totally baffled by the system were those with prior computer programming experience. The designers used a computer expert's mental model when creating the software, although most secretaries operate with a novice's mental model. The system succeeded only after the designers created an inelegant, inefficient, but easy-to-understand version of the software, one that was more compatible with a novice's orientation.

Creating an optimal human-machine system by matching the potential users' information processing capabilities with software and hardware specifications has implications for the human factors specialist in designing everything from a small piece of equipment to total organizational systems.

However, many of the everyday human-computer design problems emanate from much more specific, data-driven issues.

A good example of a nuts and bolts question is: How should the information on a VDT be displayed to optimize performance? Tullis (1983) isolated many of the variable features of VDT format design, such as density of characters (print) and groupings of characters. He manipulated these features in controlled laboratory studies and measured user performance (search time to locate some feature in the display) and user acceptance (of the display format). Interestingly, the display formats that people liked were not necessarily the ones associated with the best performance. Differences between objective (performance) and subjective (attitudinal) criteria are frustratingly common in human factors research. The questions raised by these differences, such as the potential long-term implications of choosing to optimize performance over preference, remain unresolved for many situations (Howell, 1991).

If you use a personal computer for such tasks as word processing, you may have noticed that you cannot read the VDT screen as rapidly as a piece of paper. Why do you think this is true? Perhaps people cannot process information (read) as well from a screen as from paper. Alternatively, they may not enjoy reading as much from a screen as paper, and, as a consequence, their reading speed diminishes. This very practical problem has been addressed in recent human factors research (Gould, Alfaro, Finn, Haupt, & Minuto, 1987). In a complex series of laboratory experiments in which proofreading speed was measured after manipulating certain physical properties of the printed page, Gould and his colleagues determined that people cannot see VDT images as well as paper because the image quality of the screen is inferior to paper. Therefore, reading speed could be increased by improving the image quality of the computer display.

The research that examined display format features and display reading speed tackled issues that have real dollars-and-cents implications for organizations. Given the multitude of workers who are daily yoked to VDT screens, even a small savings in time would potentially reap considerable productivity gains for organizations. These studies underscore the fact that the ultimate goals of human factors and I/O research are often more alike than different. The major distinction between the two perspectives may be that I/O places more emphasis on attitudinal or subjective criteria, a legacy of the human relations movement. Human factors research also considers subjective criteria, although often only as secondary variables.

## Environmental Design

In the last section, we discussed human-machine interface issues in the design of equipment displays (visual and auditory), controls, and a specialized type of equipment possessing both displays and controls, the computer. Now we consider a more global or macro issue in the work context, the design of total work spaces. Although not explicitly stated in Figure 12.1,

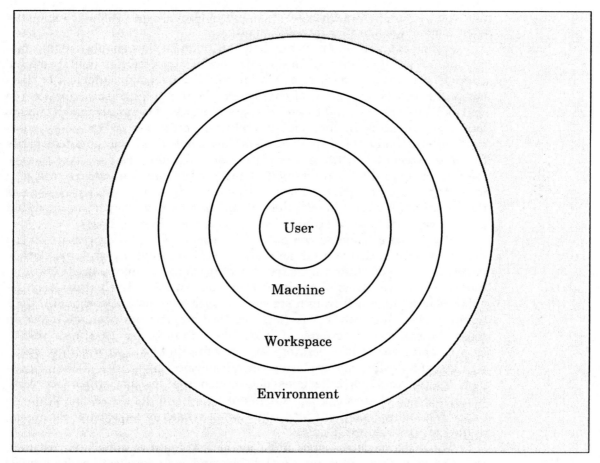

**Figure 12.6** *Extended human-machine system*

*Source:* From Applied Ergonomics. (1974). *Applied Ergonomics Handbook.* Surrey, England: IPC Science and Technology Press, p. 10.

the human-environment interface is an extension of the human-machine interface. Other authors (*Applied Ergonomics Handbook,* 1974) have also conceived of the extension of the human-machine system to larger systems (work spaces and environments) (Figure 12.6). Human beings interact with their environments in predictable ways that can have profound effects on human functioning.

## WORK SPACES

Have you ever paused to consider why your chair or desk is somewhat uncomfortable? Has your mother ever complained that she cannot reach many of her kitchen cabinets without the aid of a stool? Have you ever had to bend your head to pass unscathed through a doorway? These situations touch on person-environment design issues, issues that we typically notice only when they become problems.

To optimize the fit between the human form and the environment, various physical dimensions of the human body must be considered when designing any structure, from a kitchen cabinet to a secretary's office chair. The subspecialty of human factors that deals with these issues is called *engineering anthropometry,* or the application of dimensions and physical characteristics of the human body to optimize human-machine or -environment interfaces (Kantowitz & Sorkin, 1983; Sanders & McCormick, 1987). The dimensions and physical characteristics of the human body have been compiled in comprehensive source books, such as the *NASA Anthropometric Source Book,* which contains almost 1,000 body measurements taken from more than 90 surveys. The measurements run the gamut from height and weight to forearm-hand length and buttock circumference (Table 12.2).

**Table 12.2**

## EXAMPLE OF AN ANTHROPOMETRIC TABLE

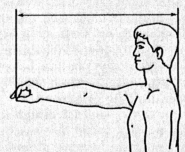

### THUMB-TIP REACH

Definition: The horizontal distance from the wall to the tip of the thumb, measured with the subject's back against the wall, his arm extended forward, and his index finger touching the tip of his thumb.

Application: Workspace layout; Equipment design: a minimum forward thumb-tip reach distance with shoulder and torso restrained.

| Sample & Reference | Survey Date | No. of Subj. | Age Range | DescriptiveStatistics* | | | |
|---|---|---|---|---|---|---|---|
| | | | | X̄ | SD | 5%ile | 95%ile |
| **FEMALES** | | | | | | | |
| USAF Women | 1968 | 1905 | 18–56 | 74.1 (29.2) | 3.9 (1.5) | 67.7 (26.7) | 80.5 (31.7) |
| **MALES** | | | | | | | |
| USAF Flying Personnel | 1967 | 2420 | 21–50 | 80.3 (31.6) | 4.0 (1.6) | 73.9 (29.1) | 87.0 (34.3) |
| RAF Flying Personnel | 1970–71 | 1997 | 18–45 | 80.2 (31.6) | 3.6 (1.4) | 74.4 (29.3) | 85.1 (33.5) |
| Italian Military | 1960 | 1342 | 18–59 | 75.3 (29.6) | 3.7 (1.5) | 69.3 (27.3) | 81.6 (32.1) |
| German AF | 1975 | 1004 | Not Reported | 80.0 (31.5) | 4.3 (1.7) | 73.1 (28.8) | 87.1 (34.3) |

*Data given in centimeters with inches in parentheses.

X̄ = mean; SD = standard deviation.

*Source:* Adapted from *Anthropometric Source Book, Volume 1: Anthropometry for Designers.* NASA Reference Publication 1024 (July, 1978). Washington, DC: National Aeronautics and Space Administration Science and Technical Information Office.

Because people come in all shapes and sizes, these tables are often segmented by sex, age, and national origin. This demographic segmentation is invaluable when designing for special populations, such as children. The human factors literature is replete with horror stories documenting failures to consider appropriate user populations. For example, some of the early Japanese automobile imports were designed for the smaller Japanese torso and could not comfortably or safely accommodate larger American drivers.

The anthropometrist must consider three general design principles when applying anthropometric measurement to the design of any work space: design for the extreme person, such as the very tallest/largest or the very shortest/smallest; design for the average person; or design for a range of persons. The applicability of each principle varies with the particular design feature under consideration.

In many cases, the anthropometrist designs for the tallest, largest, or strongest individual. Designing for the maximum value typically implies the 95th percentile, which means that only 5% of all people are taller or larger than that value. For example, by accommodating very tall or large people, doorways also permit entry of short or average people. Of course, even a 7-foot doorway would not accommodate a very few people. Conversely, the anthropometrist often designs for the shortest, smallest, or weakest individual, which typically implies the 5th percentile. A feature designed for the 5th percentile would be usable by all but 5% of those people who are below that value. For example, the effort required to throw a light switch should be so minimal that almost anyone is capable of operating the switch.

Because most people are not at the extremes, why not design for the average person? Surprisingly, such a design decision would fail to accommodate many, if not most, members of the population because almost every design decision must account for multiple dimensions and characteristics. Body dimensions are often not well correlated; you (like many people) may have long legs, short arms, large feet, and a short torso, which would complicate any design decision. Bittner (1974) compared 13 body dimensions for the extreme values (95th and 5th percentiles) and discovered that 52%, not the expected 10%, of the population would be excluded when simultaneously comparing all 13 dimensions for one situation.

When feasible, the optimal approach may be to design for a wide range of the population, usually the 5th–95th percentiles. This design principle usually requires the piece of equipment or facility to be adjustable, such as automobile seats and office chairs. Designing for an adjustable range becomes a formidable task if multiple populations, such as the 5th–95th percentiles for different races of both sexes, must be accommodated.

## AUTOMATION AND COMPUTERIZATION

Most offices are becoming increasingly automated and/or computerized. How do you think you would feel if your supervisor told you that your job would soon be completely computerized and that your daily activities at work would consist solely of sitting in front of a computer screen? You would probably feel even worse if told that your job was being totally automated and that your services would no longer be needed. Both scenarios are being experienced by increasingly larger numbers of workers. Unfortunately for both workers and organizations, many organizational issues beyond the straightforward implementation of new technology are rarely considered.

One ironic trend of contemporary organizational life is the blurring of barriers between traditional white- and blue-collar work. Computer technology has contributed greatly to the demise of these barriers (Briner & Hockey, 1988; Howell, 1991). For example, office workers seated in front of a computer screen for eight hours every day often find that computerization has resulted in work activities that are simpler, fractionated, less skilled, and more boring than before. White-collar work has, in a sense, assumed many aspects of assembly line or production work, such as specialization and higher speed and accuracy requirements. Computerized production workers, on the other hand, often operate a keyboard and read technical material from a computer screen. They sometimes have computer access to information, such as equipment costs and specifications, formerly available only to management. The necessity for many lower level supervisory positions, consequently, has declined, and low to midlevel managers (often realistically) fear for their jobs (Sinclair, 1986).

Another pressing issue involves complaints about potential health problems associated with computer screens (VDTs). These complaints range from skin rashes to miscarriages. Of particular concern is the potential for visual discomfort or disease from staring at the computer screen for protracted time intervals (Briner & Hockey, 1988) and for neuromuscular disorders of the hand, such as *carpal tunnel syndrome,* caused by repetitive bent-wrist motions when using a computer keyboard. Given the quantity of human factors research on computer displays and controls that has been incorporated into both hardware and software design, these stringent criticisms are indeed surprising.

In 1983, the National Academy of Sciences appointed a panel to study the health risks associated with computer usage. After careful study, the panel reported that there was no scientific evidence that, when designed in accordance with current technology, computers per se were implicated in the development of health problems. However, the panel also indicated that health risks may accrue from the manner in which computers are integrated into the work environment. To quote the final report (Leeper, 1983), "when understanding has advanced to the level that [VDT] guidelines are feasible, the most likely course will be development of different sets of guidelines for different jobs" (p. 2). There have been no new developments over the last decade to justify revisions in the panel's conclusions.

One implication of the panel's statement is that, although we know a good deal about the optimal design of computer systems (e.g., Gould et al., 1987), we know very little about how to introduce computerization into the work force to ensure its acceptance and subsequent success (Turnage, 1990).

Beyond some scattered evidence that prior experience with computers influences attitudes toward computer usage (Rafaeli, 1986) and that these attitudes influence intentions to use computers (Bagozzi, 1981; Hill, Smith, & Mann, 1987), our knowledge base about the subjective component of human-computer interaction is minimal. Unfortunately, there seems to be a mysticism about computers (Norman, 1984) such that inexperienced users often have negative, perhaps even irrational, attitudes about them (Arndt, Clevenger, & Meiskey, 1985). These subjective considerations may outweigh the technical ones because, if people have negative attitudes toward computerization and automation, they cannot (or will not) use them effectively.

An even more generic organizational concern is what should and should not be automated or computerized in the workplace. In other words, which functions should remain with the human and which should be relegated to the machine? In human factors terminology, this is called *function allocation*. To maximize efficiency and minimize error, the prevailing school of thought would automate or computerize every job to the fullest extent, thus creating passive, machine-dependent workers. However, psychologists have warned against such dependency because, in those situations in which automation is unavailable or malfunctions, the human may be too poorly prepared to cope alone (Howell, 1991).

The importance of function allocation was exemplified by the 1988 *Vincennes* tragedy (The Vincennes incident, 1988). As you may recall, the USS *Vincennes* was equipped with one of the most highly sophisticated (intelligent) weapon systems in our naval fleet. During operations in the Persian Gulf, the *Vincennes* accidentally shot down an Iranian commercial airliner after it was mistakenly identified as a hostile military aircraft. Consequently, numerous Iranian lives were lost and the United States found itself in a precarious diplomatic situation. A panel of psychologists testified before the House Armed Services Committee that the automated systems in the *Vincennes* allowed the operators to become less involved in and increasingly dependent on the ship's computer system so that they were unable to make critical decisions when necessary. To quote one of the psychologists on the panel,

> "Research is badly needed to understand when and just how much automation to introduce in situations where the ultimate control and responsibility must rest with the human operator." (*Science News,* October 15, 1988)

Although workers often feel they are competing against a machine, "machines and humans are not really comparable subsystems" (Kantowitz & Sorkin, 1987, p. 359). For Kantowitz and Sorkin (1987), the inherent difference is that "people are flexible and inconsistent whereas machines are consistent but inflexible" (p. 361). These two sets of mutually exclusive attributes imply that humans and machines are suited for different tasks. For example, machines are better adapted for routinized and repetitive work, which requires consistent and unchanging behaviors. Humans, however, are better adapted for such inconsistent and changing behaviors as long-range planning, goal setting, and management (Howell, 1991; Meister, 1985). Successful implementation of automation and computerization in the workplace undoubtedly will be determined by isolating the specific combinations of both machine and human functions that optimize certain situations.

## Temporal Design

### SHIFTWORK

Have you ever pulled an all-nighter when cramming for an important exam? Do you think you scored lower than if you had gotten sufficient sleep the night before the exam? After the exam, did you take an extended nap and then go to bed that night at your regular bedtime? After your nap, were you groggy and unable to concentrate on your evening activities? Were you unable to sleep well throughout the night after napping earlier? The answers to these questions are probably yes. Your all-nighter both deprived you of sleep and disturbed your body's normal sleep-wake cycle.

Human beings are day-oriented creatures. The evidence supporting this statement is abundant in our everyday lives. You mostly work and play during the day. As discussed earlier, your visual system is designed to operate better in daylight than darkness. It is therefore not surprising that many other human functions are oriented toward day activity. The most well-known are physiological variables, such as body temperature, heart rate, and blood pressure, although nonphysiological variables, such as self-rated alertness and simple performance measures, also follow this trend. Levels of these variables in the body typically reach a peak during the day and a trough or low point during the night (Figure 12.7). This cyclic activity repeats itself every 24 hours; such 24-hour cycles are called *circadian cycles*. Theoretically, these 24-hour cycles will change or invert if the sleep-wake period is altered for at least 10–14 days. Circadian cycles are extremely important because they shape human physiological, psychological, and behavioral functioning.

It should be apparent why you do not generally function well at night: Many of your bodily processes are at their lowest, much like an idling automobile. It is not surprising that people who try to work at night and sleep during the day often report they cannot do either very well. Shiftworkers, who comprise approximately 20–25% of the workforce, must cope with changing work and sleep schedules and the problems this type of lifestyle spawns. Shiftwork is defined broadly here, and refers to any regular employment outside the 7 AM–6 PM interval (Monk, 1989). The costs of adaptation to irregular or changing schedules can be high, touching everything from personal relationships to work performance. For these reasons, organizations should be concerned about the potential effects of shiftwork on their employees. The importance of these issues has even been recognized by the federal government in a recent publication by the Office of Technology Assessment (1991).

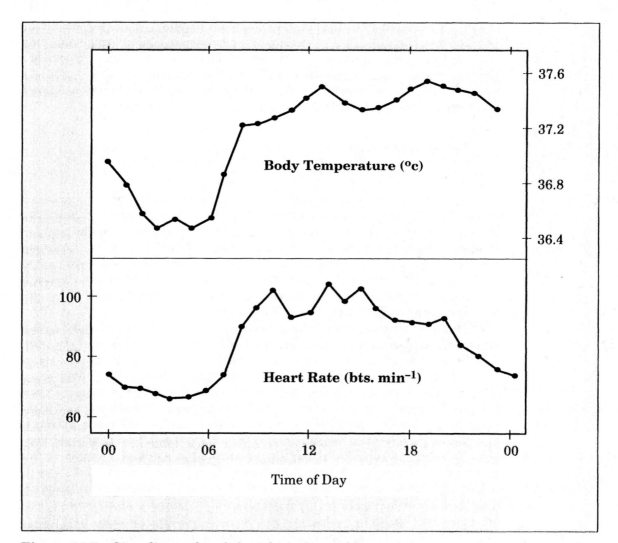

**Figure 12.7** *Circadian cycles of physiological variables*

*Source:* Adapted from Minors, D.S., & Waterhouse, J.M. (1985). Introduction to circadian rhythms. In S. Folkard & T. Monk (Eds.) *Hours of Work: Temporal Factors on Work-Scheduling.* Chichester, England: John Wiley & Sons.

Work schedules are another aspect of the organizational environment; this aspect of the human-environment interface is an extension of the human-machine interface (Figure 12.6). In the case of shiftwork, the human-environment interface is often unpredictable and frequently stressful. We next discuss four areas in which shiftworkers' personal and work lives suffer most from altering work and sleep schedules: job performance, job-related attitudes, personal health, and social and domestic situations. We then discuss some general strategies for managing the negative effects of shiftwork.

**Job Performance** Many industrial accidents involving human error occur between midnight and 6 AM. For example, the Three Mile Island mishap occurred at 4 AM. The nuclear power plant workers who committed the almost tragic errors were weekly rotating shiftworkers (or shiftworkers who changed shift schedules every seven days) and were halfway through their night shift (Ehret, 1981). Knowing that shiftwork disrupts cyclic physiological functions and sleeping patterns, it is obvious why shiftworkers often perform worse than comparable day workers. However, the impact of shiftwork, particularly night work, is not simply to adversely affect all work performance. The nature of the performance differences are complex and seem to depend on the type of work (task) being performed.

Psychologists have long known that levels of arousal in the body parallel the 24-hour body temperature cycle. The performance trends of many simple tasks, such as simple reaction time and visual search, also parallel the body temperature and arousal cycles. Therefore, performance on simple tasks, such as monitoring and inspection, which are common industrial tasks, would be expected to reach their lowest level during the late night and early morning hours (Folkard, 1990; Monk, 1989). These performance decrements, of course, would be further exaggerated by sleep loss.

Paradoxically, some complex mental tasks involving short-term memory are performed fairly well at night. Because complex task performance has been the subject of much circadian performance research, it would be instructive to examine some of this research, such as Monk and Embrey's (1981) field study.

Monk and Embrey (1981) studied six workers who operated a process-control computer in a large automated chemical plant in England. These workers were studied for one month while experiencing one complete cycle of their rapidly rotating shift system (three days on rotating shifts followed by two rest days). Because the shift system rotated so rapidly, these shiftworkers were unable to completely adjust to any particular schedule, and therefore retained their day orientation.

While on shift, each worker took his temperature, rated his alertness, and performed both a simple and complex task every two hours. The tasks were simple and complex (difficult) versions of a visual search task, in which subjects attempted to find a specific target (usually a certain letter or number or sequences of letters or numbers) in pages of written material. As predicted, performance on the complex version of the search task was better on the night shift than on the day shift. A more interesting performance measure, however, was the actual job performance of each of the six workers over the one-month interval. Because they typically worked on a computer, performance could be objectively monitored during the course of the study. The computer tasks were relatively complex cognitively, requiring the aggregation of information about plant operations. As predicted, job performance was also better on the night shift than on the day shift (Figure 12.8).

The mechanism underlying performance trends on complex tasks is unknown at this time. To complicate matters further, some of the research

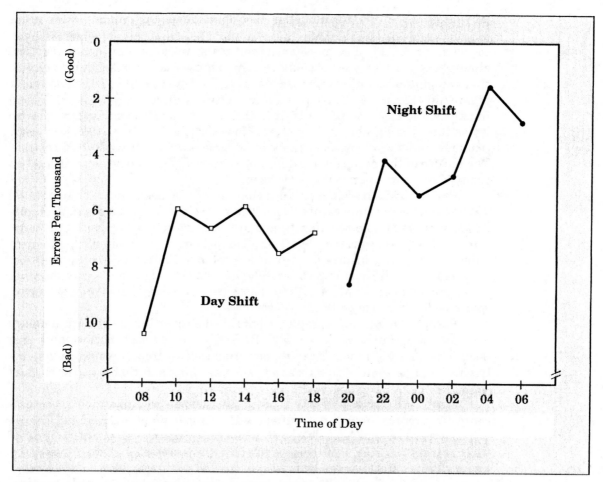

**Figure 12.8**   *Computer task performance as a function of workshift*

Source: Monk, T.H. & Embrey, D.E. (1981). A field study of circadian rhythms in actual and interpolated task performance. In A. Reinberg, N. Vieux, & P. Andlauer (Eds.) *Night and Shift Work: Biological and Social Aspects.* Oxford, England: Pergamon Press.

using complex tasks has not shown the night superiority in performance reported by Monk and Embrey (1981). Researchers are certain, however, that the clock governing complex task performance differs from the body temperature or arousal clock governing simple task performance. Evidence also exists suggesting that the biological clock underlying complex performance adjusts more readily to changes in sleep schedules than the clock underlying simple task performance (Folkard, 1990). The implications of these task-based performance differences for scheduling shiftwork are enormous. For example, routine or monotonous work should be automated or closely monitored at night. Slowly rotating or fixed shifts would also aid simple task performance. Complex tasks, such as those requiring judgment and decision making, might be more effectively performed at night and on rapidly rotating (a rotation every two or three days) shift systems. Unfortunately, industry has largely neglected to consider these issues when designing shift systems (Smith, 1989).

**Job-Related Attitudes**   Little research has explored the job-related attitudes of shiftworkers, but what exists suggests that shiftworkers are more disgruntled than their day-working counterparts. Overall, shiftworkers report lower job satisfaction than day workers (Agervold, 1976; Herbert, 1983). Shiftworkers also demonstrate lower need fulfillment and emotional well-being (Frost & Jamal, 1979). The negative emotional state of shiftworkers can probably be attributed, at least partially, to the increased health and domestic problems they face relative to day workers.

**Personal Health**   Shiftworker researchers do not all agree that shiftwork has deleterious effects on health. In fact, a paradoxical finding is that shiftworkers often report fewer health complaints than regular day workers. Workers who experience the most distress usually leave shiftwork early, and those who stay in shiftwork are undoubtedly a select group (Angersbach et al., 1980). Frese and Okonek (1984) claimed that current statistics are biased because they do not distinguish among the various reasons workers actually left shiftwork and therefore probably underestimate the number of workers who left specifically for health reasons.

Gastrointestinal disorders are the health problems most widely associated with shiftwork (Angersbach et al., 1980; Koller, 1983). Rutenfranz, Knauth, and Angersbach's (1981) review of health statistics for over 30,000 workers found the prevalence of gastric ulcers across various groups to be .3–7% for day workers, 5% for shiftworkers not on the night shift, 2.5–15% for shiftworkers on the night shift, and 10–30% for shiftworkers who had left shiftwork. Angersbach et al. (1980) also found that gastrointestinal disease becomes more prevalent after prolonged exposure to night work, not just shiftwork.

Recent studies have also suggested a possible connection between shiftwork and cardiovascular disease (Koller, 1983; Knutsson, Akerstedt, Jonsson, & Orth-Gomer, 1986). In a carefully controlled study, Koller (1983) found that 19.9% of shiftworkers suffered from cardiovascular disease compared with 7.4% of day workers. In a longitudinal study that spanned 15 years, Knutsson et al. (1986) also reported an increased risk of cardiovascular disease in shiftworkers.

Unfortunately, epidemiological (or archival medical) research is subject to some rather unique confounding factors. In surveying relative differences in the disease rates of shiftworkers and day workers, researchers have been unable to determine if the higher incidence rate in the shiftwork group is due to shiftwork per se or some other factor. For example, workers with poorer health or who are already ill may select shiftwork because the higher pay differentials can help defray medical expenses. Also, many shiftwork positions are relatively unskilled and may attract those workers who, by virtue of their socioeconomic status, do not have ready access to medical care.

To control for these confounding factors, people in the different comparison groups are often matched on such variables as age, socioeconomic status, and job tenure (e.g., Koller, 1983). However, the optimal research design is longitudinal; the worker's health status, personal characteristics, and lifestyle are initially assessed and he or she is tracked over time to determine if disease develops as a function of the work situation (e.g., Knutsson et al., 1986). These types of controlled, longitudinal designs permit the strongest inferences about the effects of shiftwork on health. However, due to practical and financial constraints, such studies are rare.

**Social and Domestic Factors**    The negative impact of shiftwork seems to be greatest in the social and domestic spheres. A frequent complaint of shiftworkers is that shiftwork interferes with their personal lives, particularly their familial roles (Jackson, Zedeck, & Summers, 1985; Staines & Pleck, 1984). This interference is manifested in weekend and evening work, times families usually plan most of their mutual social activities. Shiftwork also appears to contribute to another unfortunate personal outcome: In a survey of over 1,400 hourly workers, Tepas et al. (1985) reported that divorces and separations were 50% more frequent in night workers than in any other group.

A related issue is the excessive domestic load that can accompany shiftwork. Shiftworkers frequently work at night and tend to domestic and child-rearing duties during the day, a lifestyle that does not allow sufficient time for sleep and leisure. In fact, female night shiftworkers with two children sleep on the average nine hours less per week than unmarried female day workers (Gadbois, 1981). (Men sleep approximately eight hours less per week than their day-working counterparts.)

A problem reported by both married and unmarried night workers is the inability to become involved in social, community, and religious activities because of work schedules (Folkard, Minors, & Waterhouse, 1985; Monk, 1989). A survey of shiftworkers in the British steel industry (Wedderburn, 1981) found that shiftworkers' major complaint was their work schedule's effect on social life. This social isolation is endemic to shiftwork, and contributes to the fewer friends and more leisure time in solitary pursuits reported by shiftworkers relative to day workers (Herbert, 1983; Walker, 1985). The exception to this social isolation occurs in company towns in which most citizens are employed by an industry that uses shiftwork (e.g., a steel mill or automobile plant) (Tasto et al., 1978; Wedderburn, 1975). In such cases, local businesses and activities are more attuned to shiftworkers' needs, such as providing restaurants and bars with extended or unusual hours.

**Coping Strategies**    The prognosis for shiftwork seems bleak: Compared with day workers, shiftworkers generally experience less job satisfaction, lower job performance, greater health risks, and greater domestic and social problems. In addition, roughly 20% of all people who experience shiftwork are totally unable to adapt successfully (Monk, 1988). These problems will not diminish in the future. The percentage of the working population on some type of shiftwork will undoubtedly grow as modern industry provides increased automation and computerization, continuous manufacturing operations, and 24-hour service facilities. A number of strategies, both organizational and personal, can potentially ameliorate the negative effects of shiftwork.

From an organizational perspective, shiftwork systems should be selected with some regard for human circadian functions. A fixed shift allows the worker to adapt fully to his or her specific shift schedule, and therefore is potentially the most successful type of shift system for many types of industrial jobs. However, shiftworkers frequently revert to some other schedule on their days off, and their bodies must consistently readjust when they return to work. This situation is equivalent to a self-imposed rotating shift on the body. Formal rotating shift systems are becoming increasingly popular because they do not yoke workers permanently to any one shift.

Most of the controversy about designing shift systems has revolved around which variation of the rotating shift is optimal. All shiftwork experts agree that the shift system with a weekly rotation is most likely to produce performance and health problems (Czeisler, Moore-Ede, & Coleman, 1982; Monk, 1989), because within the 7-day interval, the body only partially adapts to the altered schedule. Unfortunately, weekly rotating shifts are also the most common. Beyond this general prescription against weekly rotations, expert opinion is divided on which type of rotating system is best (Monk, 1989), with some advocating a rapidly rotating system (Akerstedt, 1985) and some a slowly rotating system (Czeisler et al., 1982). Every shift system should be implemented only after a detailed analysis of the specific situation (Monk, 1989). As discussed earlier, the type of work or task being performed is one factor that should be considered when designing shift systems.

Two other factors, circadian type and age, seem to influence adjustment to shiftwork. You are probably familiar with people who feel best in the morning and prefer to go to bed and get up early; they are often called larks or *morning types*. Conversely, you know others people who feel best in the evening or night and prefer to go to bed and get up late; they are often called owls or *evening types*. Extreme morning types, in particular, seem to have difficulty coping successfully with night work and with changing shifts (Hildebrandt & Stratmann, 1979; Smith, Reilly, & Midkiff, 1989). As people age, they generally experience problems adapting to the demands of shiftwork. Because the circadian systems of people in their late 40s and 50s become more morning-oriented and less flexible, older shiftworkers' well-being and sleep often suffer (Foret, Bensimon, Benoit, & Vieux, 1981; Monk & Folkard, 1985). Organizations should make a conscious effort to counsel morning types and older workers about the potential effects of nightwork and the coping strategies that may be most helpful.

Beyond designing shift systems more consistent with circadian functioning and monitoring certain groups of high-risk workers, organizations can facilitate shiftworkers' adjustment by providing employee education and counseling. Information about the effects of altering sleep-wake cycles and the best strategies to cope with such a lifestyle should be incorporated into orientation and employee development programs (Monk, 1988; Smith, Reilly, Moore-Hirschl, Olsen, & Schmieder, 1989).

## Alternative Work Schedules

**Flextime**   A concept that originated in Europe in the 1960s is to provide workers some autonomy in scheduling their working hours. The typical flextime system requires all employees to be on the job during core hours, for example, from 10 A.M.–3 P.M.; the flexible working hours comprise the time before and after the core hours, for example, 8 A.M.–10 A.M. and 3 P.M.–5 P.M.

Not much data are available on the effects of flextime. However, what exist are favorable, although mostly limited to changes in job attitudes and attendance, not performance. It is too soon to draw definite sweeping conclusions, but the following patterns seem to be emerging from the research that has evaluated flextime:

1.   Employees generally prefer flextime programs over traditional work schedules, and are satisfied with these schedules when they are implemented (Golembiewski & Proehl, 1978).
2.   Job satisfaction does not increase as the result of the implementation of a flextime program (Hicks & Klimoski, 1981).
3.   Although little effect on productivity is typically found, there is no evidence that flextime harms productivity (Schein, Maurer, & Novak, 1977).
4.   Flextime reduces absenteeism (Dalton & Mesch, 1990) and tardiness (Ronen, 1981).

Interestingly, Ronen (1981) found that Israeli workers on flextime changed their schedules very little after implementation of the flextime system; their average time to start work was eight minutes later and their average time to end work was 22 minutes later. As Landy (1989) suggested, the enthusiasm employees typically express for flextime may be more related to an increase in perceived control than to any objective changes in their lives provided by flextime.

As previously stated, flextime seems to have few effects on productivity, but there is likely to be some variation in this regard. Clearly, in some jobs flextime would be unsuitable; for example, teachers, police officers, and nurses probably could not serve their clients very effectively under such a system. For other types of jobs, flextime may dramatically improve performance. Ralston, Anthony, and Gustafson (1985) presented one example of enhanced productivity from a flextime program. They collected data from data entry operators and computer programmers in two state agencies, one with and one without flextime. The computer programmers had to share their equipment (the computers) with other programmers; the data entry operators had their own machines. The flextime program increased productivity only for the computer programmers. The researchers suggested that flextime may be more beneficial when workers must share limited resources. Only under these specific circumstances could organizations expect to see improvements in the bottom line (productivity).

**Four-Day Workweek**   Another way to alter the hours of work is to compress the workweek into fewer days. This usually implies four 10-hour days instead of five 8-hour days. Less data exist on the effects of the compressed workweek than on flextime, with the exception of the glowing accolades in the popular press. In groups of pharmaceutical workers (Nord & Costigan, 1973) and clerical and supervisory workers (Goodale & Aagaard, 1975), researchers found that employee support for compressed work schedules was enthusiastic, although some negative effects were reported, such as sleep loss and tiredness. Upon introduction of a 4-day workweek, Ivancevich (Ivancevich, 1974; Ivancevich & Lyon, 1977) discovered some initial improvements in productivity, which disappeared in a two-year follow-up assessment. The use of compressed work schedules has declined slightly in recent years and may eventually be replaced by the increasingly popular flextime programs.

# SAFETY AT WORK

## Occupational Accidents

In 1988, 10,600 fatal industrial accidents were reported in the United States (National Safety Council, 1989). These figures do not reflect nonfatal and near-miss accidents. In fact, researchers (Kjellen, 1984) have estimated that nearly ten million near-miss incidents occur each year in addition to reported job-related accidents. The significance of this statistic lies in the fact that near accidents are excellent predictors of future accidents (Tarrants, 1980).

Do you remember your last accident involving an injury? Perhaps you cut your finger, broke your leg, or suffered a sore back. When friends inquired about your accident, they undoubtedly asked the inevitable question: How did it happen? Chances are, they did not ask *why* it happened. The ultimate cause of your accident may have been obvious to you and others (e.g., you were distracted or speeding). However, in many instances, people are unable to specify the exact reason(s) for an accident's occurrence. According to the National Research Council and the Institute of Medicine, Committee on Trauma Research (Committee on Trauma Research, 1985), the etiology of most accidents is relatively unknown and unresearched.

A case really does not have to be made for studying industrial accidents. Almost everyone would agree that accidents of any type can result in substantial human suffering and losses in manpower, equipment, facilities, and productivity. We can attempt to isolate factors that precipitated the accident in terms of *unsafe acts* (behaviors), such as horseplay or poor judgment, and/or *unsafe conditions,* such as faulty tools or chemical spillage. For example, if, prior to an accident, the worker disregarded the standard safety procedures for handling toxic materials (unsafe act), we know exactly what produced the accident. However, we still do not know why it happened. Why did the worker disregard procedures that could safeguard his health and life? Often we cannot identify causal factors of accidents because there is little theory of accident causation.

We next review some general models of human behavior and physiology that draw upon psychological theory to clarify why people respond in certain ways that predispose them to accidents and how these same models can be used in prevention programs. The organization and content of this section draw heavily from Oborne (1987), to whom the reader is referred for a more comprehensive discussion. With reference to the systems model (Figure 12.1), our focus here is on the person (unsafe behavior) or the person-environment (unsafe behavior-unsafe conditions) interface.

## Learning Models

Most job-related tasks, such as operating a computer or a drill press, involve a series of sequential, learned activities. Simple learning principles, specifically reinforcement, guide our mastery of these tasks. For example, when you flip a series of switches and the computer starts to function, you have been positively reinforced for performing a specific series of activities. That is, your positive reinforcement for activating a sequence of controls is an operational computer. When you activate an incorrect sequence of controls, you do not receive positive reinforcement in the form of an operational computer. Every time you activate the correct sequence of controls and are rewarded with a functioning computer, you are positively reinforced for these actions and increase the probability that these actions will be repeated in the future (see Chapter 3 for a discussion of reinforcement models).

Ironically, the way people learn correct behaviors (through positive reinforcement) is exactly the way they learn unsafe behaviors. Unsafe behavior is frequently less time consuming and more socially acceptable than safe behavior, both of which are very reinforcing. A common example involves the use (or more appropriately, lack of use) of safety goggles in industry. Even though safety goggles can safeguard workers' eyes from injury, many wear the goggles only under duress. Locating the goggles can be time consuming (a "hassle") and wearing them is often uncomfortable and viewed as unmanly or cowardly (for "sissies"). In addition, injuries from accidents are rare. Workers may experience many accident-free years while not wearing the goggles, which reinforces not wearing them even more.

Because learning models are such strong, guiding forces behind human behavior, psychologists have investigated the efficacy of various accident prevention programs based on learning theory. Komaki, Barwick, and Scott (1978) reported dramatic success in reducing industrial accidents through the implementation of simple learning principles. After investigating industrial accidents in two departments of a food manufacturing plant, they discovered that unsafe behavior was less time consuming than safe behavior and rarely resulted in actual injuries. Also, safe behavior was rarely rewarded or even acknowledged by the plant's management.

From observations and interviews, Komaki and colleagues (1978) compiled examples of safe and unsafe behaviors in both departments (Table 12.3). Slides were created of the safe and unsafe behaviors and shown to the workers. After discussing the slides in detail, the researchers asked the workers to set a department goal for percentage of safe behaviors, which was prominently displayed at the work site. The workers were given frequent feedback about their progress in achieving the safety goal. As Figure 12.9 indicates, the percentage of safe behaviors increased immediately after the intervention (safety program). Unfortunately, as Figure 12.9 also indicates, safe behavior decreased dramatically after the program had been formally discontinued.

The rapid reversal to previous levels of unsafe behavior after reinforcement of safe behavior had been terminated clearly illustrates how inherently reinforcing unsafe behavior can be. Komaki and colleagues' research also demonstrates that efforts to increase safety through behavioral change is, by itself, insufficient. To effect a radical change in behavior, it is necessary to change how people think and feel about safety, a goal more appropriately tackled by cognitive theory.

## COGNITIVE MODELS

In addition to sequential learned activities, many job-related tasks involve a sizeable memory component. Workers must remember, for example, how to operate complex machinery and interpret readings on dials and gauges. As discussed earlier, our ability to remember and recall information is limited. Information may be lost because of ineffective processing in short-term memory and may never be encoded in long-term memory. The information may decay over time in long-term memory, or become distorted or inaccessible due to interference from other information. For example, after learning how to operate a new piece of equipment, a worker may confuse the new operating sequence with a previously learned one.

The potential deficits of the memory process are even more probable when unusual or rare events occur, such as a mechanical malfunction. Such circumstances demand out-of-the-ordinary judgments and behaviors, which may have been poorly learned initially and therefore difficult to retrieve from memory. The imperfections of the memory process require most emergency procedures to be overlearned (see Chapter 11), although even this safeguard does not guarantee success.

Unfortunately, accident researchers have not really explored the role cognitive processes play in the etiology of accidents and safety management. One exception is DeJoy (1985), who examined the applicability of cognitive attribution theory to safety management in industry. He maintained that attributional processes largely explain why safety management programs have been relatively ineffective. For example, supervisors and management engage in defensive cognitive biases when attaching blame for accidents and injury. These biases consist of blaming the worker (unsafe behavior) rather than the

**Table 12.3**

┌─────────────────────────────────────────────────────────────────────────┐

### EXAMPLES OF SAFE BEHAVIORS FROM KOMAKI, BARWICK, AND SCOTT'S (1978) OCCUPATIONAL SAFETY STUDY

#### Makeup department

When picking up pans from the conveyor belt, no more than two pans are picked up prior to placing the pans on the pan rack.

Roll pans are stacked no higher than the rear rail of the pan rack.

When lifting or lowering dough trough, hand holds and at no time loses contact with dump chain.

When pulling dough trough away from dough mixer, hands are placed on the front rail of the dough trough and not on the side rails.

#### Wrapping department

There are no cardboard spacers (defined as cardboard 30 mm square or larger) on the floor.

When cutting wire bands from stacks of boxes or spacers, employee cuts with one hand and holds the metal strap above the cut with the other hand.

When moving conveyor, at least one person is on each end.

When handling a skid, employee attempts to break its fall in some manner, for example, sliding it off rather than letting it fall flat on the floor.

#### Both departments

When mechanical problems arise (e.g., pans jam on conveyor belt, belt breaks), the machine is turned off (the machine is off when the on-off switch is in the off position and the machine's moving parts have stopped) or maintenance is notified.

*Source*: Komaki, J., Barwick, K., & Scott, L. (1978). A behavioral approach to occupational safety: Pinpointing and reinforcing safe performance in a food manufacturing plant. *Journal of Applied Psychology, 63*, 434-445.

└─────────────────────────────────────────────────────────────────────────┘

environment (unsafe conditions), regardless of the objective situation (Chapter 9). The results of such attributions can culminate in strained worker-management relationships and chronically unsafe work environments.

## PERSONALITY MODELS

You have undoubtedly known people who seem to be accident prone. You may attribute their unfortunate accident proneness to bad luck, carelessness, or risky behavior. Regardless of the presumed source, however, accident

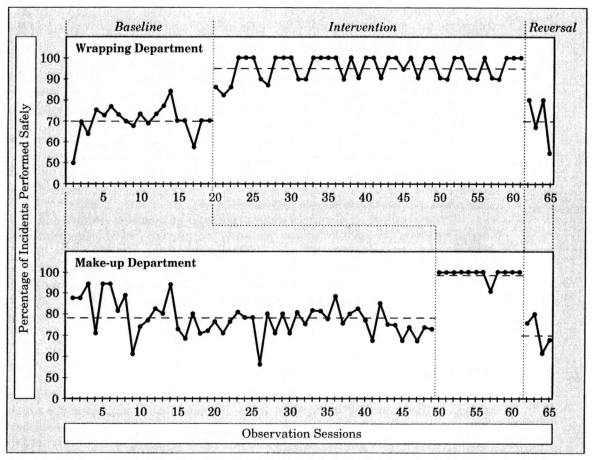

**Figure 12.9**   *Percentage of items performed safely by employees in two departments of a food manufacturing plant during a 25-week period of time*

Source: Komaki, J., Barwick, K., & Scott, L. (1978). A behavioral approach to occupational safety: Pinpointing and reinforcing safe performance in a food manufacturing plant. *Journal of Applied Psychology, 63,* 434–445.

proneness is generally assumed to be a somewhat enduring, dispositional quality.

The concept of accident proneness as a personality characteristic was first suggested from a study of munitions workers in World War I (Greenwood, Woods, & Yule, 1919). An extensive study was conducted later by Newbold (1926), who examined the accident records of 9,000 workers in several manufacturing industries. Farmer and Chambers (1939) investigated the automobile accident records of a large group of drivers. All three studies concluded that a few people accounted for a disproportionately large number of the total accidents.

The implication of the early research is that some dispositional quality of accident repeaters accounted for their inflated accident rates relative to the remainder of the population. If this is the case, industry could use personality tests to exclude accident-prone people from dangerous jobs, such as nuclear power plant operations and demolitions. However, subsequent research has not isolated any single personality dimension that accounts for accident proneness. Mohr and Clemmer (1988) analyzed longitudinal accident data for workers in heavy industry after statistically controlling for job hazards, exposure, age, and changes in job and location. They found that the proportion of accident repeaters over time did not exceed chance. These results suggest that the conclusions of the early research may have been determined more by confounding factors in the data than by any real differences between accident repeaters and accident-free individuals.

Current thinking about accident proneness is that susceptibility to accidents depends on an interaction between the person and the environment, which can vary over time (Reason, 1974). For example, a worker who is anxious over personal problems may be more likely to experience an accident while operating machinery. Although no single personality dimension predicts accident occurrence, Hansen (1989) reported that two personality variables, social maladjustment and neuroticism, were good predictors of accident occurrence in a study involving over 300 chemical plant workers.

## Life Stress Models

You would probably not be surprised to learn that people are more prone to accidents when they experience stress in their lives. People who are under stress, particularly high levels of stress, experience cognitive narrowing and distortion (Chapter 7). This reduced cognitive functioning can severely impair performance.

Hirschfeld and Behan (1963; 1966) reviewed the circumstances of approximately 300 industrial accidents that resulted in disability. They concluded that stress was a precipitating factor in accident occurrence and that it also contributed to longer periods of disability. Brenner and Selzer (1969) also found that drivers who reported recent social stress, including job stress, were five times more likely to cause a fatal automobile accident. Verhaegen, Vanhalst, Derycke, and VanHoeke (1976) compared workers' stressful experiences to accident rates in two plants. In one plant, they found that workers who expressed concern about their children's health and decreased satisfaction with the home were more likely to be responsible for causing an industrial accident.

## Biological Models

The emphasis here is on accident models that focus on the human physiological functions. Two models have been proposed, one dealing with circadian (24-hour) influences and one with biorhythm influences.

The Three Mile Island nuclear power plant mishap occurred on the night shift; many similar industrial accidents have occurred between midnight and 6 A.M. (Mitler et al., 1988). Attempts to tie circadian differences in performance to actual accident occurrence are few, with most studies merely assuming the performance-accident link. Notable exceptions are the studies by Folkard, Monk, and Lobban (1978) and Smith, Colligan, Frockt, and Tasto (1979), both of which found circadian variation in the frequency of minor accidents in a hospital. An increase in accident frequency on the night shift was also reported in a paint manufacturing company (Levin, Oler, & Whiteside, 1985) and in a glass factory and steel plant (Wojtczak-Jaroszowa & Jarosz, 1987).

Although existing data suggest that circadian factors influence accident rates, there is absolutely no evidence that biorhythms have such effects. *Biorhythms* refer to the physical, emotional, and intellectual cycles that occur over 23, 28, and 33 days, respectively. Similar to circadian rhythms, each type of biorhythm cycle is described by a waveform with a peak and a trough. The peaks correspond to positive phases in the cycles and the troughs to negative phases. According to the theory, accidents are more likely to occur when these rhythms are in troughs or crossing over from peaks to troughs or vice versa.

Wolcott, McKeeken, Burgin, and Yanowitch (1977) calculated the three biorhythms for more than 4,000 pilots involved in aviation accidents. The researchers recorded the times of accident occurrence and categorized accidents according to whether they resulted from pilot error. The results of the analyses are unequivocal: No relationship existed between the phases of the pilots' biorhythms and aviation accidents. Other studies have also found no relationship between biorhythm phases and aviation accidents (Khalil & Kurucz, 1977) and vehicular and industrial accidents (Carvey & Nibler, 1977).

Although the learning, cognitive, personality, life stress, and biological models all make contributions to our understanding of the accident process, no single accident model has incorporated variables from all of these models. This is unfortunate because, in reality, accidents undoubtedly result from a myriad of interacting factors. Ramsey (1978) included many of these variables in his accident sequence model (Figure 12.10). This model sequentially maps the process that occurs within the person under potentially dangerous conditions.

From the initial perception of the hazard to the safe or unsafe behavior associated with the hazard, the model traces the process and the underlying skills, cognitive states, personality characteristics, and experiences that guide the process. For example, perception of the hazard depends on human abilities and limitations, such as vision and hearing. Cognition of the hazard is shaped by the person's memories of prior training and previous experience with the same or similar situations. The decision whether or not to avoid the hazard is influenced by certain personality traits of the person and attitudes toward safety practices. The ability to avoid the hazard depends on both characteristics of the person and the physical design of the work setting.

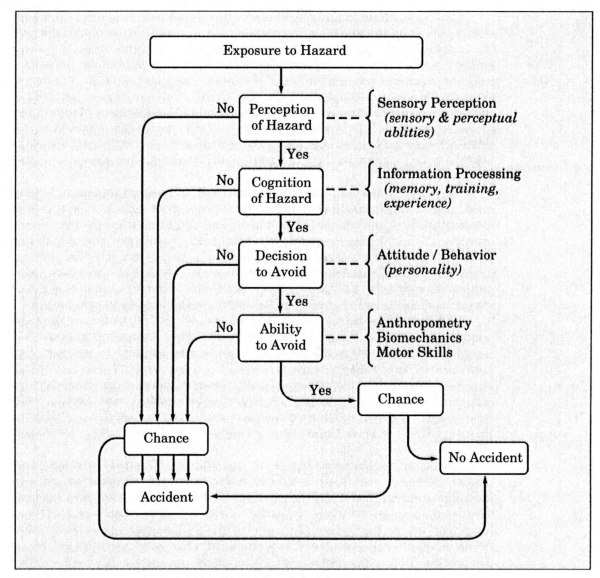

**Figure 12.10**   *The accident sequence model*

Source: Adapted from Ramsey, J. (1978). *Ergonomic Support of Consumer Product Safety.* Paper presented at the American Industrial Hygiene Association Conference.

The accident causation models discussed here (and most others) relate to people issues. We do not deny the practical problems involved in reporting, collecting, and interpreting accident data. (For example, should an accident with no injury or property damage be classified as an accident? How can we determine the cause of accidents when organizational records only document the injured person or outcome of the accident?) We also do not deny the effects of straightforward engineering considerations, such as poorly designed tools and work environments, on accident occurrence. However, both workers and managers ultimately must assume responsibility for safe behavior in the workplace. As Cohen (1977) stated, "Maximally effective safety programs in industry will be dependent on those practices that can successfully deal with 'people' variables" (p. 168).

## Safety Legislation

Occupationally related injury and illness were accepted as integral parts of American industry in the nineteenth century and the first half of the twentieth century. However, a growing social awareness in the 1960s plus a mine explosion in West Virginia that killed 78 miners in 1968 culminated in the passage of the first federal health and safety legislation. The *Occupational Safety and Health Act* (OSHA) took effect on April 28, 1971.

The Occupational Safety and Health Act requires employers to provide a workplace "free from recognized hazards likely to cause death or serious physical harm to [their] employees." Some of the specifications in the act are as follows:

1. The act establishes the process whereby standards, particularly for toxic substances, can be developed.
2. The act authorizes OSHA inspectors to enter any workplace without prior notification. Penalties are specified for violations assessed during these work site inspections. These violations may be appealed by the employer.
3. The act provides for the establishment of the National Institute for Occupational Safety and Health within the Department of Health, Education, and Welfare to conduct research on occupational health and safety issues.
4. The act requires employers to keep consistent records on all occupationally related injuries and illnesses.

The 1970s were stormy years for OSHA. The immediate adoption of almost 400 pages of national consensus standards enraged both industry and labor. Many of these standards were ill-conceived and some were completely ridiculous. For example, one regulation mandated split toilet seats and prohibited round seats. Another regulation required coathooks on bathroom doors. Yet another regulation prohibited employers from providing ice water to employees. (The reason for this regulation had its roots in history: Long ago, ice was cut from blocks in rivers and was frequently unsanitary.) Many badly needed standards, for example, standards for benzene or asbestos toxicity levels, were overly strict or too vague to implement. Fortunately, within recent years, many of the questionable standards have been dropped or altered significantly.

During the past 20 years OSHA has weathered almost insurmountable problems in developing and implementing reasonable industry standards, equitably enforcing health and safety guidelines, and enduring political scandals (Cadis, 1983). Industry complained bitterly during the 1970s' Carter administration that OSHA unfairly discriminated against the employer to protect the worker. The tables turned during the Reagan and Bush administrations of the 1980s; complaints from labor about OSHA's failure to protect the worker to appease the employer were more common. Regardless of the prevailing political climate, OSHA's future as a government entity appears to be secure and, after many reforms over the years, promising.

## Legal Issues

By considering human capabilities and limitations, human factors experts can help design safer and more usable products. It therefore seems sensible to call on them when a legal dispute arises concerning the safety of some product. In recent years, the courts have increasingly turned to human factors specialists to provide expert testimony involving product liability litigation.

Product liability disputes may involve product defects. These defects can result from an improperly designed product, such as an unsafe brake system in an automobile, or from a manufacturing flaw, such as an exploding can of shaving cream. In other cases, the product itself is not defective, but the manufacturer has been negligent or has misrepresented the product. For example, the manufacturer may fail to warn the user that a piece of industrial equipment cannot be safely operated in environmental temperatures over 85°F. The manufacturer of an over-the-counter medicine may also claim that its product is not addictive when, in reality, that claim has not been verified.

The rapidly growing specialty of forensic human factors provides both new professional options and headaches for the human factors specialist. Attempting to assess the safety of a product in a court of law is very different from designing a safe product in the laboratory (Kantowitz & Sorkin, 1983). The legal aspects involved in product liability have assumed so much importance that Kantowitz and Sorkin (1983) devoted a separate chapter to these topics; the interested reader is referred to that source for a comprehensive treatment of legal issues in human factors.

In conclusion, we can confidently state that today's human factors specialist has graduated from his or her former status as a "knobs and dials" expert. Contemporary human factors has been presented with a very complex puzzle, a puzzle composed of a perplexing array of human and technological issues undreamed of even 20 years ago. Fitting together the pieces of this puzzle has required and will require the application of a tremendous amount of knowledge, skill, and effort. We are confident that the discipline can meet this challenge.

# A FINAL SUMMATION AND A LOOK AT THE FUTURE

The birth of human factors psychology occurred during World War II when engineers and psychologists joined forces to train military personnel to use sophisticated military hardware (Chapter 1). Out of this experience grew the concepts of maximizing the fit between the human and the machine and the human and the machine as interacting components of a human-machine system. Multiple terms have been used to identify the discipline, such as human factors, engineering psychology, and ergonomics.

Because human factors specialists are committed to maximizing the fit between human and machine, they are particularly interested in all types of human error. Two major categories of error, errors of omission (forgetting to perform a task or part of a task) and commission (incorrectly performing a task), have been identified. The flip side of human error, human reliability, is the probability of successful task performance. To successfully combat error, the human factors psychologist must understand human abilities, such as auditory and visual properties. Signal detection theory is helpful in describing how people make decisions about faint or ambiguous stimuli or signals. Signal detection theory has been applied to a number of occupational problems, such as medical diagnosis and quality control in industry.

Human beings can process, as well as perceive, information in a variety of ways. The study of human information processing has produced models and theories of human information processing that consider how people receive and process information from their senses. Some of these models also consider cognitive distortions and biases that affect information processing. Research on information processing has led to the development of the concept of mental work load, or the information processing demands placed on a person by a task. Mental work load can help us understand how to more effectively select workers and redesign tasks.

With their knowledge of human capabilities, human factors specialists have tackled important problems involving the interactions of humans with their work environments. They have contributed to the design of optimal auditory and visual displays, which are devices used by a machine to communicate with a human. Another area of application has been in the design of workplaces. For instance, the engineering anthropometrist considers three general design principles when designing any work space: design for the extreme person (such as the tallest or thinnest), design for the average person, or design for a range of people. The selection of one design principle over another is dictated by the situation. Human factors specialists also work on office designs (see Chapter 5 for a discussion of open vs. cellular offices). Workers' adjustment to shiftwork is still another issue of concern in human factors. Shiftwork has been shown to have numerous ill effects: disruption of the human circadian cycles, diminished task performance on some types of tasks, more negative job attitudes, increased health problems, and disruption of personal lives. Coping strategies for managing shiftwork more effectively have been recommended, such as designing shift systems to be compatible with circadian functioning and providing worker education and counseling about shiftwork.

The study of human error and reliability is central to human factors psychology. It is therefore not surprising that human factors specialists have a long-standing interest in industrial accidents. Any accident can be described in terms of the unsafe acts (behaviors), such as horseplay, and/or unsafe conditions, such as chemical spillage, which preceded it. In clarifying why people respond in certain ways that predispose them to accidents, models of human behavior have been proposed. Several have proven useful, including learning (behavioral), cognitive (information processing), personality, life stress, and biological models. All of these have added to our understanding of the etiology of accidents and have been incorporated into general models of accident behavior.

Future trends suggest that human factors psychology will grow in importance. Increasing concern with safety in the workplace is one such trend. Federal legislation has been necessary to protect worker safety. Our most important safety legislation is the Occupational Safety and Health Act of 1971, which established both safety standards for industry and the National Institute for Occupational Safety and Health. The human factors psychologist has frequently had an impact on safety litigation by providing expert testimony in court to resolve allegations of unsafe workplaces, procedures, or products. Much of this testimony has involved specific product liability issues.

Another trend is the automation and computerization of office and industrial environments. One of the products of this trend is a blurring of the distinction between blue-collar (nonmanagerial) and white-collar (frequently managerial) work. Human factors specialists have worked with engineers and programmers in designing user friendly computers; this collaboration will be needed even more in the future. One of the major problems in designing computer software and hardware that are easy to use is that the designers, who are computer experts, differ in their amount of information and way they process information compared with the users, who are mostly novices. The designers, therefore, frequently design computer systems that are incomprehensible to most users. Other research on computers has resulted in improved format features and display qualities. The problems associated with computerization and automation probably emanate from ignorance about how to introduce these technological advances into the workforce to ensure their acceptance and success. This issue even extends to ignorance about exactly what should be automated or computerized. The whole area of research on human-computer interaction has dollars-and-cents implications for organizations and is one of the most promising areas of future research and application in the discipline of human factors.

## DISCUSSION QUESTIONS

1. Why should an organization be concerned about human reliability estimates? What are the practical implications for identifying various sources of error (e.g., sequential errors, time errors) in workplaces?

2.  Why is it important for the human factors specialist to have a thorough understanding of human abilities, such as visual and auditory functioning and information processing? How has this knowledge been applied to the design of visual and auditory displays and controls?

3.  What is mental work load? How can knowledge about mental work load be applied to make work more efficient?

4.  What are the three major design principles the anthropometrist considers when designing any work space? Give examples of situations in which you would choose each of the three principles.

5.  How does shiftwork affect personal and organizational functioning? What are some remedies to these problems?

6.  Think of different situations at work in which knowledge about learning, cognitive, personality, life stress, and biological models of human behavior might help create a safer work environment.

# SAFETY ISSUES IN THE WORKPLACE: UNITED AUTO WORKERS V. JOHNSON CONTROLS

In addition to the human factors issues involved in industrial safety, safety issues in the workplace can have far-reaching personal, societal, and political implications. The recent Supreme Court decision on the controversial case of the United Auto Workers v. Johnson Controls is one such example (Simon, 1990).

Johnson Controls manufactures automobile batteries. Workers involved in the manufacture of batteries must often work in high–lead exposure conditions. Because high lead concentrations in the body of a pregnant woman can harm the unborn child, Johnson Controls adopted a stringent fetal protection policy in 1982 for female workers in its Wisconsin-based battery manufacturing plant. Specifically, the policy stated that all women of childbearing capacity were prohibited from holding any job in the plant in which, within the previous year, any worker had registered a lead level in excess of the level considered safe for children by the U.S. Centers for Disease Control, or if any single air sample taken in the work area had exceeded safe levels. At the time the policy was implemented, eight female employees had become pregnant while maintaining unsafe blood lead levels. (None of the children born to these women appeared to suffer any birth defects.)

Johnson Controls justified this policy to its employees on the basis that lead exposure at very low concentrations poses a risk to an unborn child and that these effects could occur before a woman knew she was pregnant. Prior to implementing this policy, Johnson Controls had considered several other policies, such as a voluntary exclusion program and monitoring blood lead levels of all female workers. The only official policy that had existed before 1982 was a warning to female workers about the risks involved in lead exposure. Johnson Controls also maintained that it was using the safest technology available for the manufacture of automobile batteries. A group of employees affected by the exclusionary policy filed a class action suit in the District Court, claiming sex discrimination under Title VII of the Civil Rights Act of 1964. (In this group of petitioners, one woman had even chosen to be sterilized to retain her job.) Both the District Court and the Court of Appeals maintained that Johnson Controls' policy constituted a business necessity. That is, the courts deemed that exclusion by sex was necessary for the normal (safe) operation of business.

The Supreme Court overturned the earlier court decisions. The Court countered that Johnson Controls' fetal protection policy overtly discriminated against women and qualified as disparate treatment under Title VII of the 1964 Civil Rights Act (Chapter 10). The Court's opinion was based on the fact that lead exposure can also adversely affect the male reproductive system, although no exclusionary policy existed for male employees. The issue of business necessity was also denied by the Court because the potential for becoming pregnant or being pregnant did not interfere with any employee's ability to perform her job. According to the Court [International Union, United Automobile, Aerospace & Agricultural Implement Workers of America, UAW, et al vs. Johnson Controls, Inc. 89 U.S. 1215 (1991)]:

Fertile women, as far as appears in the record, participate in the manufacture of batteries as efficiently as anyone else. . . . Concern for a woman's existing or potential offspring historically has been the excuse for denying women equal employment opportunities. (p. 17) . . . It is no more appropriate for the courts than it is for the individual employers to decide whether a woman's reproductive role is more important to herself and her family than her economic role. Congress has left this choice to the woman as hers to make (p. 22).

## CASE QUESTIONS

1. Who should bear the moral and legal responsibility for the lifetime care of any deformed children borne by these workers?
2. Should manufacturing processes that place workers' health (both female and male) in such danger be allowed even if safer processes are not available?
3. Johnson Controls claims that the manufacturing process it uses is the safest available. What options might a human factors specialist consider to make the work environment even safer?

# Conclusions and Future Trends

- Major Themes

- What Does the Future Hold for I/O Psychology?

- Conclusions

Chapter 1 describes I/O psychology's emergence as a separate discipline in the early part of this century and its development to the present time. Subsequent chapters examine the theory, research, and practice that currently define I/O psychology. All things change, however, and as we make the transition to the next century, irresistible forces will have important consequences for I/O psychology. Chapter 13 reiterates some of the major themes stressed in the previous chapters and provides some glimpse of the challenges that the field of I/O psychology will face in the future.

# MAJOR THEMES

Throughout the text we have stressed that I/O psychology is *interdisciplinary* and draws from a variety of areas of research and theory. Research in social psychology, individual differences, and measurement have had the greatest impact, but we have noted the growing influence of cognitive research and theory. This is a healthy development, but I/O psychologists still need to go further to integrate the contributions of disciplines outside of psychology, including sociology, anthropology, and economics.

Closely related to the interdisciplinary nature of I/O psychology is the emphasis placed on organizations as *open systems*. There are several important implications of this perspective. First, it means that we cannot focus on just psychology or any other single facet of organizational life. Organizations consist of multiple variables in interaction, and attempts to change one variable must take into account the effects of the others. For example, although we typically treat the organizational and personnel topics as if they were completely separate, they are closely interrelated. In attempting to select individual employees with the right abilities (Chapter 10), we need to consider the groups in which these employees work (Chapter 5). In attempting to train employees in job skills (Chapter 11), we need to consider their motivation (Chapter 3) and their work attitudes (Chapter 4). In attempting to change the leadership behavior of managers in an organization (Chapter 6), we need to consider the nature of their jobs (Chapter 8) and the criteria used in evaluating and rewarding them (Chapter 9).

An open system also means that organizations are not islands unto themselves but interact with and are closely bound to their environments. Consequently, we cannot be content with examining only the internal workings of the organization, but must take into account customers, other organizations, laws, cultural changes, technological innovations, and the many other external forces impinging on the organization. One implication of this open-systems view is that organizations must take in more energy than they expend to survive. Another way of stating this is that organizations are subject to *entropy* and must invest in the maintenance of the system to survive. Such investments often do not directly translate into higher productivity, but are still crucial to maintaining the organization. For example, chapters 5 and 6 noted that two basic functions of the group are fulfilling socioemotional needs and fulfilling task goals. An overemphasis on one and the neglect of the other can introduce instability to the system and speed the process of dissolution. For instance, downsizing can achieve improvements in the performance of the organization, but these gains may prove illusory as employee satisfaction and loyalty decline (Chapter 3) and stress increases (Chapter 7).

A third theme is that the *scientific method* is the preferred approach to generating knowledge about organizations. Rather than relying on the current fad or the opinions of the latest guru of industry, rigorous research is needed to evaluate theories and management practices. The idea of using scientific research to solve organizational problems is not new; it was an essential aspect of Frederick Taylor's scientific management (Chapter 1). Despite the fact that it is more than 100 years old, however, subjecting management practices to empirical scrutiny remains a revolutionary concept. While I/O psychology has had a tremendous impact, few organizations use the scientific method as an integral part of their management of human resources. For example, most organizations still adopt training programs on the basis of current fashion rather than on the basis of rigorous evaluation (Chapter 11), and most still rely on unstructured, unvalidated interviews in selecting employees (Chapter 10), despite the evidence in favor of more structured procedures. While differences of opinion continue as to the best approach to conducting research, faith in the scientific method as a means of generating knowledge about organizations remains a unifying theme in I/O psychology.

Perhaps one of the reasons that scientific research is avoided in organizations is that it seldom produces simple answers to organizational problems. From the many studies reviewed here it is clear that the results of scientific research are usually complex and provisional. Often the conclusion is "X works in this situation, but Y is more likely to work in that situation." This point brings us to a fourth theme: The solution of organizational problems requires a *contingency approach*. There is no one best way, and the attempt to improve organizational effectiveness requires that we first diagnose the situation and then choose from among alternative possibilities the one with the highest probability of success. But theorists do not always follow the contingency approach. In Chapter 1 we observed that scientific management, classical management theory, and human relations theory all erred in making universal claims for the one best way of managing. Later, however, we learned how contingency theorists have set forth the type of leadership needed under specific situational conditions, such as unstructured versus structured tasks. We encountered contingency theory again in research on motivation, job satisfaction, and work stress, in which a variety of moderator variables (Chapter 2) have been identified that can radically change the direction of relationships among variables.

# WHAT DOES THE FUTURE HOLD FOR I/O PSYCHOLOGY?

I/O psychology has evolved during the twentieth century in directions that reflect changes in society. This book describes the product of the last 100 years, but I/O psychology will continue to evolve in response to coming changes. Indeed, current societal changes seem likely to dwarf anything that has previously occurred. The realignment of the world powers, technological innovations, shifts in the characteristics of the workforce, the restructuring of large U.S. corporations, the shift to a service-based economy, and the increasing use of team-based management are among the changes that will require different human resource practices. Table 13.1 summarizes how organizations and human resource management practitioners are attempting to meet these new demands. Let us examine what I/O psychology can contribute in helping organizations to cope with the future and the gaps that currently exist in our knowledge that will need to be addressed in future research and theory.

## The Destabilizing of the World Order

At the present writing, a dramatic shift in the political climate in Eastern Europe is underway in response to the dissolution of the U.S.S.R., and the pell-mell dash from totalitarian repression and various forms of socialism to various forms of personal, political, and economic freedom. The magnitude and suddenness of this change is stunning, as are the massive unresolved problems it has introduced. Free elections in the Soviet Union, a unified Germany, noncommunist governments in one after another of the Eastern Bloc nations: Such events could not have been dreamed of a few years ago. Nor could we envision accompanying issues, such as how to make the transition from a controlled to a free-market economy, how to deal with the resulting adjustments, such as mass unemployment and economic collapse, and how to retain political entities such as the U.S.S.R. in the face of demands for independence from its constituent republics.

The decline in hostilities between traditional Eastern and Western antagonists seemed to promise a real possibility for lasting world peace. All too soon, however, came the realization that the clash between superpower philosophies is far from the only threat to world harmony. With Iraq's invasion of Kuwait in 1990, and the consequent military action by U.S. and Allied forces, it became apparent that almost any nation can foment conflict on a global scale. The fact that much of the resource that is vital to the world's economy, oil, is concentrated in one of the world's most unstable regions, the Middle East, where cultural forces that we barely understand, let alone know how to deal with or control, poses immense risks to modern society. Proliferation of nuclear and other advanced weapons in the hands of heretofore insignificant Third World nations can make any despot or terrorist with aspi-

**Table 13.1**

| WORK ENVIRONMENT CHANGES AND HUMAN RESOURCES PRACTICE | | | | |
|---|---|---|---|---|
| | | **Human Resources Areas** | | |
| **Organization Responses** | **Themes of HR Practice** | **Organization Development** | **Training** | **Individual Evaluation** |
| **Constant Training** | Continuous Learning | Link organization renewal to continuous learning | Training and re-training; support external development | Select for learning ability; appraise/reward development |
| **Constant Innovation** | Generating Change | Foster climate supporting new ideas; quality improvement programs | Re-train for new products/services; develop innovativeness | Select for creativity; appraise/reward risk-taking |
| **Rapid Pace of Change** | Responsiveness to change | Team building for responsiveness; Intergroup problem solving; conflict resolution | Re-train for new products/services; develop adaptability; resistance to stress | Select and appraise for adaptability, coping |
| **Strategic Planning** | Coordination of strategy | Team building for goal clarity and agreement | Gap analyses; help develop plans and tie training to them | Environmental scans & force analyses; tie selection to strategic plans |
| **Flexible Structures** | Participation | Survey feedback & employee input; autonomous work groups | Training for empowerment and leadership | Selection for participativeness and leadership |
| **Quality Emphasis** | Excellence | Quality improvement programs | Group problem-solving skills for quality improvement programs | Selection for high work standards |
| **Customer Orientation** | Service | Team building to facilitate customer service | Training for customer service | Selection for interpersonal skills |
| **Constituency Management** | Equitable treatment; flexible HR policies | Foster equitable climate via team building, survey feedback | Training to value diversity; basic skills training; gear training to diverse population | Fair selection practices; drug and honesty testing; wide recruiting |

*Source:* Howard, A. (1991). New directions for human resources practice. In D. W. Bray and Associates (Eds.) *Working with Organizations and Their People.* New York: Guilford, pp. 219–251.

rations of grandeur a major threat virtually overnight. Reduction of East-West tensions, which both sides had at least come to understand, has been replaced by threats that no one really understands.

Although they may appear far removed from the topics we have covered in this book, the fall of communism and the ensuing turbulence in world affairs offer many challenges and opportunities for the application of modern management, OD, and HRM principles. A massive segment of the industrialized world, much of it still operating in the mode of the 1920s and totally adapted to centralized planning and management, must reorient itself. New markets will open up, as will new competitors, and new pleas for foreign aid. In addition, despite Middle East instability and the dramatic Allied success in the Gulf War, it is clear that the U.S. will continue making significant reductions in military spending, but not nearly enough to eliminate the budget deficit or solve domestic problems such as homelessness, drug abuse, crime, and the decline in education. Dramatic as they are, the changes in Eastern Europe are but one part of an increasingly complex international scene insofar as American business is concerned. Foreign ownership of American business is becoming commonplace, as is the multinational corporation (Doktor, Tung, & Von Glinow, 1991). Much of the manufacturing that was once the backbone of American industry is now done abroad, and all signs point to our eventually becoming a strictly "service economy," with even that threatened by decline (Offerman & Gowing, 1990; Quinn & Gagnon, 1986).

The upshot of all these events is that it is becoming increasingly important for the workforce in general and aspiring managers in particular to familiarize themselves with other societies and cultures. Surveys of the American public's general knowledge show consistently that the United States is abysmally ignorant of other countries' geography, political systems, languages, cultures, and people. The disciplines concerned with organizations and management must take an active role in alleviating this ignorance. The instruments used by I/O psychologists to measure work satisfaction or organizational climate in U.S. firms, for example, may not be suitable for application in Southeast Asia or Eastern Europe without substantial modification. The values that I/O psychology is committed to promoting in American culture, such as fair and humane treatment of the workforce, seem to have little meaning in some Middle Eastern and African cultures, where human rights and the treatment of women and minorities are still in the dark ages. What is our proper role under these circumstances?

International and intercultural issues of this sort are largely unexplored in I/O psychology. Indeed, the body of knowledge presented in this text is dominated by research from the United States and Western Europe. There is a small, productive program of I/O research in Japan, but I/O psychology is a rare commodity in most Asian countries, the Middle East, Eastern Europe, and Latin America. Because the basic cognitive and motivational processes at work in organizational behavior are likely to generalize across cultures, it seems doubtful that a whole new I/O psychology is needed for each culture. Nevertheless, culture is a tremendously important moderator that must receive more attention in the future. Eventually the body of evidence in other cultures may be sufficiently large that we can present a truly universal I/O psychology in a textbook such as this. Until then, however, I/O psychology remains a mostly American undertaking.

## Technological Change

Not all the noteworthy trends in society are international in scope. Technological change, driven largely by the continuing evolution of computer-based systems, continues to revolutionize the nature of work and job requirements (Howell, 1991; Turnage, 1990). This technology not only creates new types of jobs but may fundamentally change the way people relate to one another in organizations; it may, eventually, change the basic nature of organizations. According to one estimate, by the year 2000 workplace computer terminals will be as common as the telephone, and these computers will be integrated into networks that will allow employees separated by long distances to collaborate (Turnage, 1990). Automation of the workplace will require higher levels of education and cognitive ability. All indications point to a future in which service and skilled occupations will increase while the demand for relatively unskilled labor will shrink dramatically. Coupled with this demand picture is a disturbing set of trends on the supply side. Demographic projections and education trends foretell a decline in the numbers of new entrants into the work force, particularly in skilled areas. Thus, there promises to be a severe shortage in the personnel required to operate our sophisticated technologies, and a corresponding glut in the unskilled, unemployable segment of the population (Johnston & Packer, 1987).

What all this suggests is that we must either learn to live with chronic high unemployment or find more efficient and effective ways to train people in the required skills. Among those skills are the fundamental "three Rs," on which the students of our public education system have been declining for over a generation. Innovations in training technology may offer a partial solution (Goldstein & Gilliam, 1990; Howell & Cooke, 1989). The potential of the computer for efficient instruction has been recognized for a long time, but for a variety of reasons, has not yet lived up to expectations. One consistent problem has been the fact that the technology has led psychology. Our understanding of human knowledge and mental skill acquisition has, until fairly recently, been quite primitive.

Now, however, thanks largely to the reorientation of psychology toward an emphasis on cognition and to developments in the field of educational technology, the picture is considerably brighter. A recent survey conducted by the U.S. Department of Education indicated that more than 70 research organizations are actively engaged in efforts to put what we already know about computer-based training to work on specific training problems (personal communication). For I/O psychology, the message is clear. In the coming years training, particularly the application and evaluation of new educational technologies, will occupy much more of the field's attention than it has in the past.

Computer technology also has important implications for social behavior in the organization. Electronic mail systems, videoconferencing, and computer-mediated meetings are among the technological innovations that promise to change the nature of collaborative work in organizations. Unfortunately, the potential gains in productivity from using these technologies is seldom realized because of the failure to design systems that people feel comfortable with and want to use. Naisbitt (1982) referred to the need for high tech/high touch, meaning that at the same time sophisticated technologies are introduced, attention needs to be given to the needs and abilities of the human users. In the future I/O psychologists will become increasingly involved not only in selecting and training people to use computer technologies, but also in designing these systems for optimal human use.

## Demographic Change

The projected shortfall in skilled labor is not the only demographic trend with implications for I/O psychology. The baby boomers are passing through middle age, which means that the workforce is aging. The proportion of women and ethnic minorities in the workforce continues to grow (Johnston & Packer, 1987). Whites as a percentage of the civilian work force are projected to decline by 9.3% during 1986 to 1995, whereas minorities (black, Hispanic, Asian, and others) are projected to increase by 21.7% during this same period (U.S. Department of Labor Statistics, 1988). The net result will be a much more diverse work force than in the past. As women continue to enter the workforce, tensions between family and work demands (Zedeck & Mosier, 1990), as well as other sources of stress, can be expected to command increased attention in the workplace (Ivancevich, Matteson, Freedman, & Phillips, 1990). It is not hard to think of ways that I/O psychology might help organizations and individuals adapt to these changes. However, the impact will not be great unless the field makes a more proactive stance than it has in the past. As London and Moses (1990) suggest, I/O psychologists must reorient their role in the organization from *analyst/technician* to *change agent/strategist*. We are only beginning to see this transformation.

## Restructuring of the Large Corporation

The drastic changes occurring in the world economy have forced many of the largest American corporations to radically restructure in the attempt to cope. They have downsized through layoffs, early retirements, shortened workweeks, and job transfers, and as a consequence, no one feels as secure in their jobs as they did previously. In the past years, blue-collar employees were the primary victims of layoffs, but now professional and managerial employees are the target. Not only failing organizations use downsizing; even highly successful firms lay off workers in the attempt to increase their competitiveness. For instance, Ameritech, one of the so-called Baby Bell companies created from the breakup of AT&T, has eliminated almost 2,000 white-collar jobs since 1984 and plans to cut 12% of its managers despite record profits (Sherman, 1993).

We also see more organizations adopt structures that allow collaboration and quick responses to new technologies, shifts in customer preferences, and other environmental changes. The hierarchical structure of the classical management theorists is mutating into forms that are so radical that we lack the theories and metaphors to describe them. The dominant type of organization in the future may be a temporary network, formed to accomplish a specific objective and then dissolved when this objective is achieved. Early signs of this are in the computer industry, in which competitors have joined together in temporary partnerships to design and manufacture new computers. For instance, Apple Computer teamed up with Sony to produce the first 100,000 of its PowerBook notebooks in 1991. Approximately 13% of Corning's earnings in 1992 resulted from partnerships with other companies. One visionary predicts the emergence of "a national information infrastructure linking computers and machine tools across the U.S. This communications superhighway would permit far-flung units of different companies to quickly locate suppliers, designers, and manufacturers through an information clearinghouse. Once connected, they would sign electronic contracts. . . . Teams of people in different companies would routinely work together, concurrently rather than sequentially, via computer networks in real time. Artificial-intelligence systems and sensing devices would connect engineers directly to the production line" (Byrne, 1993, pp. 100–101).

There are numerous implications of this restructuring of corporations for I/O psychology. We need to understand how to maintain the loyalty and motivation of employees who can no longer count on secure employment. We need research on alternative career paths. Although vertical paths, in which people rise to higher and higher levels of responsibility, were the dominant career paths in the past, horizontal career paths, in which people stay at the same level of responsibility but do different things, are becoming more common. We also need research on alternatives to downsizing. Although individual companies may profit from reducing the ranks of employees, the long term consequences for the whole economy are frightening. If unemployed people cannot buy the products and services that organizations provide, then we will all suffer the consequences. Organizations need creative alternatives to mass layoffs; I/O psychologists can contribute to the generation and evaluation of these alternatives (Francis, Mohr, & Andersen, 1992; Faltermayer, 1992; Greenhalgh, Lawrence, & Sutton, 1988).

The corporation of the past was characterized by stability and security. In contrast, employees of the future will need coping skills in which they respond to continual change by giving up their routine practices, exploring alternatives, and adopting new practices. What can organizations do to prepare employees for this type of environment? Training offers one possible solution, and I/O psychologists will need to become involved in generating and evaluating training programs that attempt to instill flexibility and adaptability. One recent study provided some clues as to what such programs may need to include: "to be truly prepared to learn new work skills in the future, a person must possess positive self-attitudes (identity and adaptability) as well as positive attitudes toward work" (Doeringer et al., 1991, p. 186). Work is also needed on methods of increasing adaptability and flexibility through selection, leadership, and motivation. There is little research in I/O on these issues, but the future will not allow us to ignore these important questions.

## The Shift to Services

About two-thirds of the employed population in the United States work in service jobs, and, according to one projection, nearly three fourths of American workers will be involved in providing various services by the year 2000 (Johnston & Packer, 1987). Mechanic, welder, steelworker, seamstress, and other jobs involving transformation of physical material into products are declining while teacher, waiter, counselor, customer representative, and other jobs involving the providing of services are increasing. Many service jobs require not only technical skills but also interpersonal competencies such as the ability to communicate, negotiate, persuade, and lead. Indeed, the Secretary's Commission on Achieving Necessary Skills (SCANS), appointed by the U.S. Department of Labor, issued a 1990 report citing skills involved in the serving of others as among the core proficiencies needed for entry-level work of the future (Offerman & Gowin, 1993). Much of the knowledge base of I/O psychology was produced when manufacturing was the dominant sector in American industry. The focus of I/O research was on the relationship of the individual employee and a physical or intellectual task. Consequently, we know very little about interpersonal skills in the work force relative to what we know about cognitive and motor skills. As organizations attempt to select, train, and evaluate employees who provide services, we are likely to see much more research on this neglected topic.

## The Increasing Use of Team Management

Chapter 5 discussed the increasing reliance of organizations on work teams, a trend that will probably accelerate in coming years. The move toward team management is partly driven by new technologies that allow collaboration even when people are separated by large distances. Another impetus is the elimination of managerial and professional positions in some large corporations. To take up the slack, workers themselves are expected to make decisions and assume responsibilities that were formerly reserved for management. We have accumulated a large amount of data on the determinants of team effectiveness (Chapter 5), but as mentioned in several previous chapters, there are still noticeable gaps in our knowledge. Much of our current understanding is based on a model of the individual employee. A pressing issue for future I/O research and application is to generate possible methods of selecting, training, evaluating, and leading teams. We also need job analysis tools for measuring the components of teamwork comparable to the tools that are currently used in the analysis of individual work activities (Chapter 8).

# CONCLUSIONS

These are but a few of the societal trends that I/O psychology and related disciplines need to consider as we approach the twenty-first century. The worldwide drug problems and the closely related growth in crime, proliferating (often irreversible) environmental abuses, the health-care crisis, the spread of AIDS, are other widely publicized social issues that will have an impact on the workplace. I/O psychology cannot solve all these problems, but it most certainly cannot remain untouched by them, either. Will we, for example, contribute to or discourage the testing of employees and job applicants for the AIDS virus and for drug use? How? Will we continue to focus on helping organizations and managers become more successful in achieving their goals, or will we become more involved in evaluating the societal validity of these goals? Like the organizations it seeks to serve, I/O psychology faces hard choices. Remember, however, that in the past I/O has made some of its greatest advances during times of social upheaval and crisis (e.g., World War II). In meeting the challenges of the future, I/O seems likely to flourish as a profession and as a science.

# References

Abelson, R. P., & Black, J. B. (1986). Introduction. In J. A. Galambos, R. P. Abelson, & J. B. Black (Eds.), *Knowledge structures* (pp. 1-18). Hillsdale, NJ: L. Erlbaum.

Ackerman, P., & Humphreys, L. G. (1990). Individual differences theory in industrial and organizational psychology. In Marvin D. Dunnette & Leanetta M. Hough (Eds.), *Handbook of industrial and organizational psychology* (2nd ed., pp. 223-283). Palo Alto, CA: Consulting Psychologists Press.

Adams, J. A. (1982). Issues in human reliability. *Human Factors, 24,* 1-10.

Adams, J. A. (1987). Historical review and appraisal of research on the learning, retention, and transfer of human motor skills. *Psychological Bulletin, 101,* 41-74.

Adams, J. S. (1963). Toward an understanding of inequity. *Journal of Abnormal and Social Psychology, 67,* 422-436.

Adams, J. S. (1965). Inequity in social exchange. In L. Berkowitz (Ed.), *Advances in experimental social psychology* (Vol. 2, pp. 267-299). New York: Academic Press.

Adler, S., Skov, R., & Salvemini, N. (1985). Job characteristics and job satisfaction: When cause becomes consequence. *Organizational Behavior and Human Decision Processes, 35,* 266-278.

Adler, T. (1992, November). Labor department hires APA to help revise job title book. *The APA Monitor,* Vol. 23, p. 16.

Agervold, M. (1976). Shiftwork: A critical review. *Scandinavian Journal of Psychology, 17,* 181-188.

Air Florida 737 voice recorder transcribed (1982, January). *Aviation Week & Space Technology, 116,* 81-91.

Akersted, T. (1985). Adjustment of physiological circadian rhythms and the sleep-wake cycle to shiftwork. In S. Folkard & T. Monk (Eds.), *Hours of work: Temporal factors in work-scheduling.* Chichester, England: Wiley.

Aldag, R., Barr, S., & Brief, A. (1981). Measurement of perceived task characteristics. *Psychological Bulletin, 90,* 415-431.

Alderfer, C. P. (1969). An empirical test of a new theory of human needs. *Organizational Behavior and Human Performance, 4,* 142-175.

Alderfer, C. P. (1972). *Existence, relatedness, and growth: Human needs in organizational settings.* New York: Academic Press.

Alderfer, C. P. (1992). Changing race relations embedded in organizations: Report on a long-term project with the XYZ corporation. In Susan E. Jackson & associates (Eds.), *Diversity in the workplace: Human resources initiatives.* New York: The Guilford Press.

Alexander, R. A., Barrett, G. V., & Doverspike, D. (1983). An explication of the selection ratio and its relationship to hiring rate. *Journal of Applied Psychology, 68,* 342-344.

Allen, M. P., Panian, S. K., & Lotz, R. E. (1979). Managerial succession and organizational performance: A recalcitrant problem revisited. *Administrative Science Quarterly, 24,* 167-180.

Allen, N. J., & Meyer, J. P. (1990). The measurement and antecedents of affective, continuance and normative commitment to the organization. *Journal of Occupational Psychology, 63,* 1-18.

Alliger, G. M., & Janak, E.A. (1989). Kirkpatrick's levels of training criteria: Thirty years later. *Personnel Psychology, 42,* 331-342.

Altman, I. (1987). Centripetal and centrifugal trends in psychology. *American Psychologist, 42,* 1058-1069.

American Psychological Association (1985). *Standards for educational and psychological testing.* Washington, DC: American Psychological Association.

*American Psychologist.* (1987). Resolutions approved by the National Conference on Graduation Education in Psychology. *American Psychologist, 42,* 1070-1084.

Andrews, I., & Valenzi, E. (1970). Overpay inequity or self-image as a worker: A critical examination of an experimental induction procedure. *Organizational Behavior and Human Performance, 53,* 22-27.

Andrisani, P. J., & Shapiro, M. B. (1978). Women's attitudes toward their jobs: Some longitudinal data on a national sample. *Personnel Psychology, 31,* 15-34.

Angersbach, D., Knauth, P., Loskant, H., Karvonen, M., Undeutsch, K., & Rutenfranz, J. (1980). A retrospective cohort study comparing complaints and diseases in day and shift workers. *International Archives of Occupational Environment and Health, 45,* 127-140.

Annett, J. (1961, May) The role of knowledge of results in learning: A survey. (U.S. NAVTRADEVCEN, Technical Document Report 342-3), Cited in M. Blum & J. C. Naylor. (1968). *Industrial psychology: Its theoretical and social foundations.* New York: Harper & Row.

*Applied ergonomics handbook.* (1974). Guilford, Surrey, England: IPC Science and Technology Press.

Archer, W. B., & Fruchter, D. A. (1963, August). *The construction, review, and administration of Air Force job inventories.* Lackland AFB, Texas: 6570th Personnel Research Laboratory, Aerospace Medical Division.

Argyle, M. (1991). *Cooperation: The basis of sociability.* London: Routledge.

Argyris, C. (1968). Some unintended consequences of rigorous research. *Psychological Bulletin, 70,* 185-197.

Argyris, C. (1980). Some limitations of the case method: Experiences in a management development program. *Academy of Management Review, 5,* 291-296.

Arndt, S., Clevenger, J., & Meiskey, L. (1985). Students' attitudes toward computers. *Computers and the Social Sciences, 1,* 181-190.

Arvey, R. D., & Begalla, M. E. (1975). Analyzing the homemaker job using the Position Analysis Questionnaire (PAQ). *Journal of Applied Psychology, 60,* 513-518.

Arvey, R. D., Bouchard, T. J., Jr., Segal, N. L., & Abraham, L. M. (1989). Job satisfaction: Environmental and genetic components. *Journal of Applied Psychology, 74,* 187-192.

Arvey, R. D., & Campion, J.E. (1982). The employment interview: a summary and review of recent research. *Personnel Psychology, 35,* 281-322.

Arvey, R. D., Davis, G. A., McGowen, S. L., & Dipboye, R. L. (1982). Potential sources of bias in job analytic processes. *Academy of Management Journal, 25,* 618-629.

Arvey, R. D., & Faley, R.H. (1988). *Fairness in selecting employees.* Reading, MA: Addison-Wesley.

Arvey, R. D., & Ivancevich, J. (1980). Punishment in organizations: A review, propositions, and research suggestions. *Academy of Management Review, 5,* 123-132.

Arvey, R. D., Passino, E. M., & Lounsbury, J. W. (1977). Job analysis results as influenced by sex of incumbent and sex of analyst. *Journal of Applied Psychology, 62,* 411-416.

Ash, R. A., & Edgell, S. L. (1975). A note on the readability of the Position Analysis Questionnaire (PAQ). *Journal of Applied Psychology, 60,* 765-766.

Ashford, S. J., & Cummings, L. L. (1983). Feedback as an individual resource: Personal strategies of creating information. *Organizational Behavior and Human Performance, 32,* 370-398.

Ashour, A. S. (1973). The contingency model of leadership effectiveness: An evaluation. *Organizational Behavior and Human Performance, 9,* 339-355.

Atkinson, J. (1964). *An introduction to motivation.* New York: Van Nostrand Reinhold.

Bacharach, S. B., Bamberger, P., & Conley, S. (1991). Work-home conflict among nurses and engineers: Mediating the impact of role stress on burnout and satisfaction at work. *Journal of Organizational Behavior, 12,* 39-53.

Bagozzi, R. (1981). Attitudes, intentions, and behavior: A test of some key hypotheses. *Journal of Personality and Social Psychology, 41,* 607-627.

Bailey, C. N. (1990, November). Wellness programs that work. *Business and Health, 8,* 28-40.

Baldwin, T. T., & Ford, J. K. (1988). Transfer of training: A review and directions for future research. *Personnel Psychology, 41,* 63-105.

Baldwin, T. T., Magjuka, R. J., & Loher, B. T. (1991). The perils of participation: Effects of choice of training on training motivation and learning. *Personnel Psychology, 44,* 51-65.

Bandura, A. (1982). Self-efficacy mechanism in human agency. *American Psychologist, 37,* 122-147.

Bandura, A. (1986). *Social foundations of thought and action: A social cognitive theory.* Englewood Cliffs, NJ: Prentice-Hall.

Barmack, J. E. (1937). Boredom and other factors in the physiology of mental effort: An exploratory study. *Archives of Psychology, 218,* 1-83.

Barnard, C. (1938). *The functions of the executive.* Cambridge, MA: Harvard University Press.

Barnes-Farrell, J. L., & Weiss, H. M. (1984). Effects of standard extremity on mixed standard scale performance ratings. *Personnel Psychology, 37,* 301-316.

Baron, R. A. (1988). Negative effects of destructive criticism: Impact on conflict, self-efficacy, and task performance. *Journal of Applied Psychology, 73,* 199-207.

Baron, R. A. (1990). Countering the effects of destructive criticism: The relative efficacy of four interventions. *Journal of Applied Psychology, 75,* 235-245.

Barrick, M. R., & Mount, M. K. (1991). The big five personality dimensions and job performance: A meta-analysis. *Personnel Psychology, 44,* 1-27.

Barringer, F. (1993, May 8). Anger in the post office: Killings raise questions. *The New York Times,* pp. A1, A6.

Bass, B. M. (1990). *Bass & Stogdill's handbook of leadership* (3rd ed.). New York: The Free Press.

Bass, B. M., Cascio, W. F., McPherson, J. W., & Tragash, H. J. (1976). Prosper-training and research for increasing management awareness about affirmative action in race relations. *Academy of Management Journal, 19,* 353-369.

Bass, B. M., & Dunteman, G. (1963). Behavior in groups as a function of self, interaction, and task orientation. *Journal of Abnormal and Social Psychology, 66,* 419-428.

Bass, B. M., & Valenzi, E. R. (1974). Contingent aspects of effective management styles. In J. G. Hunt & L. L. Larson (Eds.), *Contingent approaches to leadership.* Carbondale, IL: Southern Illinois University Press.

Bassett, G. A., & Meyer, H. H. (1968). Performance appraisal based on self-review. *Personnel Psychology, 21,* 421-430.

Bateman, T. S., & Strasser, S. (1984). A longitudinal analysis of the antecedents of organizational commitment. *Academy of Management Journal, 17,* 95-112.

Beatty, R. W., Schneier, C. E., & Beatty, J. R. (1977). An empirical investigation of perceptions of ratee behavior frequency and ratee behavior change using behavioral expectation scales (BES). *Personnel Psychology, 30,* 647-658.

Becker, H. S. (1960). Notes on the concept of commitment. *American Journal of Sociology, 66,* 32-42.

Becker, T. E., & Klimoski, R. J. (1989). A field study of the relationship between the organizational feedback environment and performance. *Personnel Psychology, 42,* 343-358.

Bedeian, A. G. (1980). *Organizations: Theory and analysis.* Hinsdale, IL: Dryden.

Bedeian, A. G., & Armenakis, A. A. (1981). A path analytic study of the consequences of role conflict and ambiguity. *Academy of Management Journal, 24,* 417-424.

Beehr, T. A. (1976). Perceived situational moderators of the relationship between subjective role ambiguity and role strain. *Journal of Applied Psychology, 61,* 35-40.

Beehr, T. A., & Franz, T. M. (1987). The current debate about the meaning of job stress. In J. M. Ivancevich & D. C. Ganster (Eds.), *Job stress: From theory to suggestions.* New York: The Hawthorne Press.

Benedict, M. E., & Levine, E. L. (1988). Delay and distortion: Tacit influences on performance appraisal effectiveness. *Journal of Applied Psychology, 73,* 507-514.

Benge, E. J., Burk, S. L. H., & Hay, E. N. (1941). *Manual of job evaluation* (4th ed.). New York: Harper & Row.

Benne, K., & Sheats, P. (1948). Functional roles of group members. *Journal of Social Issues, 4,* 41-49.

Bennis, W. G. (1966). Organizational developments and the fate of bureaucracy. *Industrial Management Review, 7,* 41-55.

Bennis, W. G. (1989). *Why leaders can't lead: The unconscious conspiracy continues.* San Francisco: Jossey-Bass.

Benson, H. (1975). *The relaxation response.* New York: Avon Books.

Berkowitz, L., & Donnerstein, E. (1982). External validity is more than skin deep. *American Psychologist, 37,* 245-257.

Berkshire, J. R., & Highland, R. W. (1953). Forced-choice performance rating: A methodological study. *Personnel Psychology, 6,* 355-378.

Bernardin, H. J. (1986). A performance appraisal system. In Ronald A. Berk (Ed.), *Performance assessment: Methods and applications*. Baltimore: The Johns Hopkins University Press.

Bernardin, H. J., & Beatty, R. (1984). *Performance appraisal: Assessing human behavior at work*. Boston: Kent-PWS.

Bernardin, H. J. , & Boetcher, R. (1978, August). The effects of rater training and cognitive complexity on psychometric error in ratings. Paper presented at the meeting of the American Psychological Association, Toronto.

Bernardin, H. J., & Buckley, M. R. (1981). Strategies in rater training. *Academy of Management Review, 6*, 205-212.

Bernardin, H. J., Cardy, R. L., & Carlyle, J. J. (1982). Cognitive complexity and appraisal effectiveness: Back to the drawing board? *Journal of Applied Psychology, 67*, 151-160.

Bernardin, H. J., & Walter, C. S. (1977). Effects of rater training and diary-keeping on psychometric error in ratings. *Journal of Applied Psychology, 62*, 64-69.

Bettman, J. R., & Barton, A. W. (1983). Attributions in the boardroom: Causal reasoning in corporate annual reports. *Administrative Science Quarterly, 28*, 165-183.

Bhagat, R. S., McQuaid, S. J., Lindholm, H., & Segovis, J. (1985). Total life stress: A multimethod validation of the construct and its effects on organizationally valued outcomes and withdrawal behaviors. *Journal of Applied Psychology, 70*, 202-214.

Binning, J. F., & Barrett, G. V. (1989). Validity of personnel decisions: A conceptual analysis of the inferential and evidential bases. *Journal of Applied Psychology, 74*, 478-494.

Birnbaum, P., Farh, J., & Wong, G. (1986). The job characteristics model in Hong Kong. *Journal of Applied Psychology, 71*, 598-605.

Bittner, A., Jr. (1974). *Reduction in user population as the result of imposed anthropometric limits: Monte Carlo estimation* (TP-74-6). Point Mugu, CA: Naval Missile Center.

Black, J. S., & Mendenhall, M. (1990). Cross-cultural training effectiveness: A review and a theoretical framework for future research. *Academy of Management Review, 15*, 113-136.

Blake, R. R., & Mouton, J. S. (1964). *The managerial grid*. Houston, TX: Gulf.

Blanz, F., & Ghiselli, E. E. (1972). The mixed standard scale: A new rating system. *Personnel Psychology, 25*, 185-199.

Blau, G. J. (1981). An empirical investigation of job stress, social support, and job strain. *Organizational Behavior and Human Performance, 27*, 279-302.

Blau, G. J. (1985). The measurement and prediction of career commitment. *Journal Occupational Psychology, 58*, 277-288.

Blau, G. J. (1986). Job involvement and organizational commitment as interactive predictors of tardiness and absenteeism. *Journal of Management, 12*, 577-584.

Blau, G. J. (1988). Further exploring the meaning and measurement of career commitment. *Journal of Vocational Behavior, 32*, 284-297.

Blau, G. J. (1989). Testing the generalizability of a career commitment measure and its impact on employee turnover. *Journal of Vocational Behavior, 35*, 88-103.

Blau, G. J., & Boal, K. B. (1987). Conceptualizing how job involvement and organizational commitment affect turnover and absenteeism. *Academy of Management Review, 12*, 288-300.

Blau, P. M. (1954). Cooperation and competition in a bureaucracy. *American Journal of Sociology, 59*, 530-535.

Block, L., & Stokes, G. (1989). Performance and satisfaction in private versus nonprivate work settings. *Environment and Behavior, 21*, 277-297.

Bluen, S. D., Barling, J., & Burns, W. (1990). Predicting sales performance, job satisfaction, and depression by using the achievement strivings and impatience-irritability dimensions of Type A behavior. *Journal of Applied Psychology, 75*, 212-216.

Blum, M. L., & Naylor, J. C. (1968). *Industrial psychology: Its theoretical and social foundations.* New York: Harper & Row.

Boehm, V. R. (1977). Differential prediction: A methodological artifact? *Journal of Applied Psychology, 62*, 146-154.

Boehm, V. R. (1980). Research in the "real-world": A conceptual model. *Personnel Psychology, 33*, 495-504.

Bogdanich, W. (1991). *The great white lie.* New York: Simon & Schuster.

Bolster, B. I., & Springbett, B. M. (1961). The reaction of interviewers to favorable and unfavorable information. *Journal of Applied Psychology, 45*, 97-103.

Booth-Kewley, S., & Friedman, H. S. (1987). Psychological predictors of heart disease: A quantitative review. *Psychological Bulletin, 101*, 343-362.

Borman, W. C. (1979a). Format and training effects on rating accuracy and rater errors. *Journal of Applied Psychology, 64*, 410-421.

Borman, W. C. (1979b). Individual difference correlates of accuracy in evaluating others' performance effectiveness. *Applied Psychological Measurement, 3*, 103-115.

Bouchard, T. J., Jr., & Hare, M. (1970). Size, performance, and potential in brainstorming groups. *Journal of Applied Psychology, 54*, 51-55.

Bourne, B. (1982). Effects of aging on work satisfaction, performance and motivation. *Aging and Work, 5*, 37-47.

Bovee, T. (1991, November 14). Pay gap between men, women widening with age. *Houston Post*, pp. A1, A19.

Bowers, D. G., & Seashore, S. E. (1966). Predicting organizational effectiveness with a four-factor theory of leadership. *Administrative Science Quarterly, 11*, 238-263.

Boyd, S. (1983). Assessing the validity of SWAT as workload measurement instrument. In A. Pope & L. Haugh (Eds.), *Proceedings of the Human Factors Society 27th Annual Meeting.* Santa Monica, CA: Human Factors Society.

Bracey, G. W. (1992, June 12). Cut out algebra. Mostly it's a useless impractical exercise. *The Washington Post*, p. C5.

Bradley, J. (1967). Tactual coding of cylindrical knobs. *Human Factors, 9*, 483-496.

Brass, D. J. (1985). Men's and women's networks: A study of interaction patterns and influence in an organization. *Academy of Management Journal, 28*, 327-343.

Brayfield, A. H., & Crockett, W. H. (1955). Employee attitudes and employee performance. *Psychological Bulletin, 52*, 396-424.

Breaugh, J. A. (1981). Relationships between recruiting sources and employee performance, absenteeism, and work attitudes. *Academy of Management Journal, 24*, 142-147.

Brenner, B., & Selzer, M. (1969). Risk of causing a fatal accident associated with alcoholism, psychopathology, and stress: Further analysis of previous data. *Behavioral Science, 14*, 490-495.

Brenner, M. H., & Sigband, N. B. (1973). Organizational communication: An analysis based on empirical data. *Academy of Management Journal, 16*, 323-325.

Brief, A. P. (1980). Peer assessment revisited: A brief comment on Kane and Lawler. *Psychological Bulletin, 88*, 78-79.

Brief, A. P., & Aldag, R. (1975). Employee reactions to job characteristics: A constructive replication. *Journal of Applied Psychology, 60*, 182-186.

Brief, A. P., Burke, M. J., George, J. M., Robinson, B. S., & Webster, J. (1988). Should negative affectivity remain an unmeasured variable in the study of job stress? *Journal of Applied Psychology, 73*, 193-199.

Brief, A. P., & Motowidlo, S. J. (1986). Prosocial organizational behavior. *Academy of Management Review, 11*, 710-725.

Brief, A. P., Schuler, R. S., & Van Sell, M. (1981). *Managing job stress*. Boston: Little, Brown.

Briner, R., & Hockey, R. J. (1988). Operator stress and computer-based work. In C. L. Cooper & R. Payne (Eds.), *Causes, Coping and Consequences of Stress at Work*. New York: John Wiley & Sons.

Broadbent, D. E. (1958). *Perception and communication*. London: Pergamon.

Broadbent, D. E. (1982). Task combination and selective intake of information. *Acta Psychologica, 50*, 253-290.

Brockhaus, R. H., Sr. (1980). Risk taking propensity of entrepreneurs. *Academy of Management Journal, 23*, 509-520.

Brockner, J., Davy, J., & Carter, C. (1985). Layoffs, self-esteem, and survivor guilt: Motivational, affective, and attitudinal consequences. *Organizational Behavior and Human Decision Processes, 36*, 229-244.

Brockner, J., Grover, S. L., & Blonder, M. D. (1988). Predictors of survivors' job involvement following layoffs: A field study. *Journal of Applied Psychology, 73*, 436-442.

Brogden, H.E. (1949). When testing pays off. *Personnel Psychology, 2*, 171-183.

Brooke, P. P., Jr. (1986). Beyond the Steers and Rhodes model of employee attendance. *Academy of Management Review, 11*, 345-361.

Brooke, P. P., Jr., Russell, D. W., & Price, J. L. (1988). Discriminant validation of measures of job satisfaction, job involvement, and organizational commitment. *Journal of Applied Psychology, 73*, 139-145.

Brophy, J. (1986). Teacher influences on student achievement. *American Psychologist, 41*, 1069-1077.

Brown, A. L., & Palincsar, A. S. (1989). Guided, cooperative learning, and individual knowledge acquisition. In L. B. Resnick (Ed.), *Knowing, learning and instruction: Essays in honor of R. Glaser* (pp. 393-443). Hillsdale, NJ: L. Erlbaum.

Brown, D. L. (1992, February 20). Merit pay fallout has two sides. *The Washington Post*, pp. B1, B7.

Brugnoli, G. A., Campion, J. E., & Basen, J. A. (1979). Racial bias in the use of work samples for personnel selection. *Journal of Applied Psychology, 64,* 119-123.

Bruning, N. S., & Frew, D. R. (1987). Effects of exercise, relaxation, and management skills training on physiological stress indicators: A field experiment. *Journal of Applied Psychology, 72,* 515-521.

Brush, D. H., Moch, M. K., & Pooyan, A. (1987). Individual demographic differences and job satisfaction. *Journal of Occupational Behaviour, 8,* 139-156.

Buck, J. (1983). Visual displays. In B. Kantowitz & R. Sorkin (Eds.), *Human factors: Understanding people-system relationships*. New York: John Wiley & Sons.

Bulkeley, W. M. (1992, January 28). Computerizing dull meetings is touted as an antidote to the mouth that bored. *The Wall Street Journal*, pp. B1, B8.

Buller, P. F., & Bell, C. H., Jr. (1986). Effects of team building and goal setting on productivity: A field experiment. *Academy of Management Journal, 29,* 305-328.

Burke, M. J. (1993). Computerized psychological testing: Impacts on measuring predictor constructs and future job behavior. In N. Schmitt, W. C. Borman, & Associates (Eds.), *Personnel selection in organizations*. San Francisco: Jossey-Bass.

Burke, M. J., & Day, R. R. (1986). A cumulative study of the effectiveness of managerial training. *Journal of Applied Psychology, 71,* 232-245.

Burke, R. J., Weitzel, W., & Weir, T. (1978). Characteristics of effective employee performance review and development interviews: Replication and extension. *Personnel Psychology, 31,* 903-919.

Burke, R. J., & Wilcox, D. S. (1969). Characteristics of effective performance review and development interviews. *Personnel Psychology, 22,* 291-305.

Burke, W., & Hornstein, H. A. (1972). *The social technology of organization development*. Fairfax, VA: Learning Resources.

Burns, J. M. (1978). *Leadership*. New York: Harper & Row.

Burns, T. (1954). The direction of activity and communication in a departmental executive group. *Human Relations, 7,* 73-97.

Burns, W. (1979). Physiological effects of noise. In C. M. Harris (Ed.), *Handbook of noise control*. New York: McGraw-Hill.

Byrne, J. A. (1993, February 8). The virtual corporation. *Business Week*, pp. 98-102.

Cadis, P. (1983). Occupational safety and health administration. In D. R. Whitman (Ed.), *Government agencies* (pp. 400-407). Westport, CT: Greenwood Press.

Caelli, T., & Porter, D. (1980). On difficulties in localizing ambulance sirens. *Human Factors, 22,* 7 19-724.

Calder, B. J. (1977). An attribution theory of leadership. In B. M. Staw & G. R. Salancik (Eds.), *New directions in organizational behavior* (pp. 179-204). Chicago: St. Clair Press.

Calder, B. J., & Staw, B. (1975). Self-perception of intrinsic and extrinsic motivation. *Journal of Personality and Social Psychology, 31,* 599-605.

Caldwell, D. F., & O'Reilly, C. A. (1982). Task perceptions and job satisfaction: A question of causality. *Journal of Applied Psychology, 67*, 361-369.

Campbell, D. J., & Lee, C. (1988). Self-appraisal in performance evaluation: Development versus evaluation. *Academy of Management Review, 13*, 302-314.

Campbell, D. T., & Fiske, D. W. (1959). Convergent and discriminant validation by the multitrait-multimethod matrix. *Psychological Bulletin, 56*, 81-105.

Campbell, J. P. (1968). Individual versus group problem solving in an industrial sample. *Journal of Applied Psychology, 52*, 205-210.

Campbell, J. P., Dunnette, M. D., Lawler, E. E., & Weick, K. E. (1970). *Managerial behavior, performance, and effectiveness.* New York: McGraw-Hill.

Campbell, J. P., & Pritchard, R. (1976). Motivation theory in industrial and organizational psychology. In M. D. Dunnette (Ed.), *Handbook of industrial and organizational psychology.* Skokie, IL: Rand McNally.

Campion, M. (1988). Interdisciplinary approaches to job design: A constructive replication with extensions. *Journal of Applied Psychology, 73*, 467-481.

Campion, M., & Thayer, P. (1985). Development and field evaluation of an interdisciplinary measure of job design. *Journal of Applied Psychology, 70*, 29-43.

Cannon, W. (1929). *Bodily changes in pain, hunger, fear, and rage.* Boston: C. T. Branford.

Caplan, R. D. (1971). *Organizational stress and individual strain: A social-psychological study of risk factors in coronary heart disease among administrators, engineers, and scientists.* Unpublished doctoral dissertation, University of Michigan.

Caplan, R. D., Vinokur, A. D., Price, R. H., & van Ryn, M. (1989). Job seeking, reemployment, and mental health: A randomized field experiment in coping with job loss. *Journal of Applied Psychology, 74*, 759-769.

Cardy, R. L., & Dobbins, G. H. (1986). Affect and appraisal accuracy: Liking as an integral dimension in evaluating performance. *Journal of Applied Psychology, 71*, 672-678.

Cardy, R. L., & Kehoe, J. F. (1984). Rater selective attention ability and appraisal effectiveness: The effect of a cognitive style on the accuracy of differentiation among ratees. *Journal of Applied Psychology, 69*, 589-594.

Carlson, E. (1991, September 9). Mediators are flourishing on anti-litigation sentiments. *The Wall Street Journal*, p. B2.

Carlson, S. (1951). *Executive behavior.* Stockholm: Stromborgs.

Carretta, T.R. (1989). USAF pilot selection and classification systems. *Aviation Space and Environmental Medicine, 60*, 46-49.

Carroll, P. B. (1991, May 29). Akers to IBM employees: Wake up! *The Wall Street Journal*, pp. B1, B2.

Carroll, S. J., Jr., Paine, F. T., & Ivancevich, J. J. (1972). The relative effectiveness of training methods: Expert opinion and research. *Personnel Psychology, 25*, 495-510.

Carsten, J. M., & Spector, P. E. (1987). Unemployment, job satisfaction, and employee turnover: A meta-analytic test of the Muchinsky model. *Journal of Applied Psychology, 72*, 374-381.

Cartwright, D., & Zander, A. (1968). *Group dynamics: Research and theory* (3rd ed.). New York: Harper & Row.

Carvey, D., & Nibler, R. (1977). Biorhythmic cycles and the incidence of industrial accidents. *Personnel Psychology, 30,* 447-454.

Cascio, W. F. (1991). *Costing human resources: the financial impact of behavior in organizations* (3rd ed.). Boston: PWS-Kent.

Cascio, W. F., & Bernardin, H. J. (1981). Implications of performance appraisal litigation for personnel decisions. *Personnel Psychology, 34,* 211-226.

Cascio, W. F., & Valenzi, E. R. (1977). Behaviorally anchored rating scales: Effects of education and job experience of raters and ratees. *Journal of Applied Psychology, 62,* 278-282.

Cattell, R. B. (1963). Theory of fluid and crystallized intelligence: A critical experiment. *Journal of Educational Psychology, 31,* 161-179.

Chadwick-Jones, J. K., Nicholson, N., & Brown, C. (1982). *The social psychology of absenteeism.* New York: Praeger.

Chalykoff, J., & Kochan, T. A. (1989). Computer-aided monitoring: Its influence on employee job satisfaction and turnover. *Personnel Psychology, 42,* 807-834.

Chapanis, A. (1976). Engineering psychology. In M. D. Dunnette (Ed.), *Handbook of industrial and organizational psychology.* Chicago: Rand McNally.

Chapanis, A., & Lindenbaum, L. (1959). A reaction time study of four control-display linkages. *Human Factors, 1,* 1-7.

Chen, P. Y., & Spector, P. E. (1991). Negative affectivity as the underlying cause of correlations between stressors and strains. *Journal of Applied Psychology, 76,* 398-407.

Cherrington, D. J. (1980). *The work ethic: Working values and values that work.* New York: Amacom.

Cherrington, D. J. (1983). *Personnel management.* Dubuque, IA: William C. Brown.

Cherrington, D. J. (1989). *Organizational behavior.* Needham Heights, MA: Allyn & Bacon.

Cherrington, D.J., Reitz, H.J., & Scott, W. E., Jr. (1971). Effects of contingent and noncontingent reward on the relationship between satisfaction and task performance. *Journal of Applied Psychology, 55,* 531-536.

Christal, R. E., & Weissmuller, J. J. (1988). Job-task inventory analysis. In S. Gael (Ed.), *The job analysis handbook for business, industry, and government* (pp. 1036-1050). New York: John Wiley.

Chusmir, L. H. (1982). Job commitment and the organizational woman. *Academy of Management Review, 7,* 595-602.

Chusmir, L. H., & Parker, B. (1984, August). *Gender differences in personalized and socialized power among managerial women and men.* Paper presented at the annual meeting of the Academy of Management, Boston, MA.

Cleveland, J. N., Murphy, K. R., & Williams, R. E. (1989). Multiple uses of performance appraisal: Prevalence and correlates. *Journal of Applied Psychology, 74,* 130-135.

Cohen, A. (1977). Factors in successful occupational safety programs. *Journal of Safety Research, 9,* 168-178.

Committee on Trauma Research, Commission of Life Sciences, National Research Council and the Institute of Medicine (1985). *Injury in America, a continuing public health problem* (p. 164). Washington, DC: National Academy Press.

Conger, J. A., & Kanungo, R. N. (1988). Training charismatic leadership: A risky and critical task. In J. A. Conger, R. N. Kanungo, & associates (Eds.), *Charismatic leadership: The elusive factor in organizational effectiveness* (pp. 309-323). San Francisco: Jossey-Bass.

Conley, P. R., & Sackett, P. R. (1987). Effects of using high-versus low-performing job incumbents as sources of job-analysis information. *Journal of Applied Psychology, 72,* 434-437.

Conlin, J. (1988, December). The making (or brainwashing) of a manager. *Successful Meetings, 37,* 30-36.

Conrad, R. (1964). Acoustic comparisons in immediate memory. *British Journal of Psychology, 55,* 74-84.

Conrath, D. W. (1973). Communication patterns, organizational structure, and man: Some relationships. *Human Factors, 15,* 459-470.

Cook, J. D., Hepworth, S. J., Wall, T. D., & Warr, P. B. (1981). *The experience of work.* New York: Academic Press.

Cook, T. D., & Campbell, D. T. (1979). *Quasi-experimentation: design and analysis issues for field settings.* Chicago: Rand McNally.

Cooper, C. L. (1980). Dentists under pressure: A social psychological study. In C. L. Cooper & J. Marshall (Eds.), *White collar and professional stress.* New York: John Wiley & Sons.

Cooper, C. L., & Davidson, M. J. (1982). The high cost of stress on women managers. *Organizational Dynamics, 10,* 44-53.

Cooper, C. L., & Roden, J. (1985). Mental health and satisfaction among tax officers. *Social Science and Medicine, 21,* 747-751.

Cooper, C. L., Watts, J., Baglioni, A.J., Jr., & Kelly, M. (1988). Occupational stress amongst general practice dentists. *Journal of Occupational Psychology, 61,* 163-174.

Cooper, H. (1992, October 5). Carpet firm sets up an in-house school to stay competitive. *The Wall Street Journal,* pp. A1, A5.

Cooper, W. H. (1981). Ubiquitous halo. *Psychological Bulletin, 90,* 218-244.

COPS & CPTA. (1986). *Guidelines for computer-based tests and interpretations.* Washington, DC: American Psychological Association.

Cornelius, E. T., III, DeNisi, A. S., & Blencoe, A. G. (1984). Expert and naive raters using the PAQ: Does it matter? *Personnel Psychology, 37,* 453-464.

Cornelius, E. T., III, Schmidt, F. L., & Carron, T. J. (1984). Job classification approaches and the implementation of validity generalization results. *Personnel Psychology, 37,* 247-260.

Costa, P. T., Jr., & McCrae, R. R. (1988). Personality in adulthood: A six-year longitudinal study of self-reports and spouse ratings on the NEO Personality Inventory. *Journal of Personality and Social Psychology, 54,* 258-265.

Coy, P. (1992, August 17). Big brother pinned to your chest. *Business Week,* p. 38.

Cronbach, L. J. (1957).The two disciplines of scientific psychology. *American Psychologist, 12,* 671-684.

Cronbach, L. J. (1975). Beyond the two disciplines of scientific psychology. *American Psychologist, 30,* 116-127.

Cronshaw, S. F., & Lord, R. G. (1987). Effects of categorization, attribution, and encoding processes on leadership perceptions. *Journal of Applied Psychology, 72,* 97-106.

Curry, J. P., Wakefield, D. S., Price, J. L., & Mueller, C. W. (1986). On the causal ordering of job satisfaction and organizational commitment. *Academy of Management Journal, 29,* 847-858.

Cyert, R., & March, J.G. (1963). *A behavioral theory of the firm.* London: Prentice-Hall.

Czeisler, C., Moore-Ede, M., & Coleman, R. (1982). Rotating shift work schedules that disrupt sleep are improved by applying circadian principles. *Science, 217,* 460-463.

Daft, R. L., & Lengel, R. H. (1984). Information richness: A new approach to managerial behavior and organizational design. In B. Staw & L. L. Cummings (Eds.), *Research in organizational behavior* (Vol. 6, pp. 191-234). Greenwich, CT: JAI Press.

Dalton, D. R., & Mesch, D. J. (1990). The impact of flexible scheduling on employee attendance and turnover. *Administrative Science Quarterly, 35,* 370-387.

Davidson, M. J., & Cooper, C. L. (1987). Female managers in Britain: A comparative perspective. *Human Resource Management, 26,* 217-242.

Davidson, M. J., & Veno, A. (1980). Stress and the policeman. In C. L. Cooper & J. Marshall (Eds.), *White collar and professional stress.* New York: John Wiley & Sons.

Davies, M. W. (1982). *Woman's place is at the typewriter: Office work and office workers 1870-1930.* Philadelphia: Temple University Press.

Davis, B., & Milbank, D. (1992, February 7). If the U.S. work ethic is fading, 'laziness' may not be the reason. *The Wall Street Journal,* p. A1.

Davis, K. (1968). Success of chain of command oral communications in a manufacturing management group. *Academy of Management Journal, 11,* 379-387.

Dayal, I., & Thomas, J. M. (1968). Operation of KPE: Developing a new organization. *Journal of Applied Behavioral Science, 4,* 473-506.

deCharms, R. (1968). *Personal causation.* New York: Academic Press.

Deci, E. (1971). Effects of externally mediated rewards on intrinsic motivation. *Journal of Personality and Social Psychology, 18,* 105-115.

Deci, E. (1972). The effects of contingent and noncontingent rewards and controls on intrinsic motivation. *Organizational Behavior and Human Performance, 8,* 202-210.

Deci, E. (1975). *Intrinsic motivation.* New York: Plenum Press.

DeJoy, D. (1985). Attributional processes and hazard control management in industry. *Journal of Safety Research, 16,* 61-71.

Delbecq, A. L., Van De Ven, A. H., & Gustafson, D. H. (1976). *Group techniques for program planning: A guide to nominal group and delphi processes.* Glenview, IL: Scott, Foresman.

DeLongis, A., Coyne, J. C., Dakof, G., Folkman, S., & Lazarus, R. S. (1982). Relationship of daily hassles, uplifts and major life events to health status. *Health Psychology, 1,* 119-136.

DeNisi, A. S., Cafferty, T. P., & Meglino, B. M. (1984). A cognitive view of the performance appraisal process: A model and research propositions. *Organizational Behavior and Human Performance, 33,* 360-396.

DeNisi, A. S., Cornelius, E. T., III, & Blencoe, A. G. (1987). Further investigation of common knowledge effects on job analysis ratings. *Journal of Applied Psychology, 72,* 262-268.

DeNisi, A. S., Randolph, W. A., & Blencoe, A. G. (1983). Potential problems with peer ratings. *Academy of Management Journal, 26,* 457-464.

Deshpande, S. P., & Viswesvaran, C. (in press). Is cross-cultural training of expatriate managers effective? A meta-analysis. *International Journal of Intercultural Relations.*

Dessler, G. (1980). *Organization theory: Integrating structure and behavior.* Englewood Cliffs, NJ: Prentice-Hall.

Deutsch, M. (1949). An experimental study of the effects of cooperation and competition upon group process. *Human Relations, 2,* 199-232.

Dickinson, T. L., & Glebocki, G. G. (1990). Modifications in the format of the mixed standard scale. *Organizational Behavior and Human Decision Processes, 47,* 124-137.

Dickinson, T. L., & Zellinger, P. M. (1980). A comparison of the behaviorally anchored rating and mixed standard scale formats. *Journal of Applied Psychology, 65,* 147-154.

Diehl, M., & Stroebe, W. (1987). Productivity bias in brainstorming groups: Toward the solution of a riddle. *Journal of Personality and Social Psychology, 53,* 497-509.

Dienesch, R. M., & Liden, R. C. (1986). Leader-member exchange model of leadership: A critique and further development. *Academy of Management Review, 11,* 618-634.

Digman, J. M. (1990). Personality structure: emergence of the five-factor model. *Annual Review of Psychology, 41,* 417-440.

Dipboye, R. L. (1987). Problems and progress of women in management. In K. S. Koziara, M. H. Moskow, & L. D. Tanner (Eds.), *Working women: Past, present, future.* Washington, DC: Bureau of National Affairs.

Dipboye, R. L. (1989). Threats to the incremental validity of interviewer judgments. In R. W. Eder & G. R. Ferris (Eds.), *The employment interview: Theory, research, and practice.* Newbury Park, CA: Sage.

Dipboye, R. L. (1990). Laboratory vs. field research in industrial and organizational psychology. In C. L. Cooper & I. T. Robertson (Ed.), *International Review of Industrial and Organizational Psychology* (Vol. 5, pp. 1-34).

Dipboye, R.L. (1992). *Selection interviews: Process perspectives.* Cincinnati: South-Western.

Dipboye, R. L., & de Pontbriand, R. (1981). Correlates of employee reactions to performance appraisal systems. *Journal of Applied Psychology, 66,* 248-251.

Dipboye, R. L., & Gaugler, B. B. (1993). Cognitive and behavioral processes in the selection interview. In N. Schmitt & W. C. Borman (Eds.), *Personnel selection in organizations.* San Francisco: Jossey-Bass.

Dipboye, R. L., & Macan, T. (1988). A process view of the selection/recruitment interview. In R. S. Schuler, S. A. Youngblood, & V. L. Huber (Eds.), *Readings in personnel and human resource management.* St. Paul, MN: West.

Dobbins, G. H., Cardy, R. L., & Truxillo, D. M. (1988). The effects of purpose of appraisal and individual differences in stereotypes of women on sex differences in performance ratings: A laboratory and field study. *Journal of Applied Psychology, 73*, 363-370.

Dobbins, G. H., & Russell, J. M. (1986). The biasing effects of subordinate likeableness on leaders' responses to poor performers: A laboratory and a field study. *Personnel Psychology, 39*, 759-777.

Doeringer, P. B., Christensen, K., Flynn, P., Hall, D. T., Katz, H. C., Keefe, J. F., Ruhm, C. J., Sum, A. M., & Useem, M. (1991). *Turbulence in the American workplace.* New York: Oxford University Press.

Doktor, R., Tung, R.L., & Von Glinow, M.A. (1991). Incorporating international dimensions in management theory building. *Academy of Management Review, 16*, 259-365.

Dorfman, P. W., Stephan, W. G., & Loveland, J. (1986). Performance appraisal behaviors: Supervisor perceptions and subordinate reactions. *Personnel Psychology, 39*, 579-597.

Dossett, D. L., & Hulvershorn, P. (1983). Increasing technical training efficiency: Peer training via computer-assisted instruction. *Journal of Applied Psychology, 68*, 552-558.

Dossett, D. L., Latham, G., & Mitchell, T. (1979). The effects of assigned versus participatively set goals, KR, and individual differences when goal difficulty is held constant. *Journal of Applied Psychology, 64*, 291-298.

Drake, B. H., & Moberg, D. J. (1986). Communicating influence attempts in dyads: Linguistic sedatives and palliatives. *Academy of Management Review, 11*, 567-584.

Drescher, S., Burlingame, G., & Fuhriman, A. (1985). Cohesion: An odyssey in empirical understanding. *Small Group Behavior, 16*, 3-30.

Driskell, J. E., Willis, R. P., & Copper, C. (1992). Effect of overlearning on retention. *Journal of Applied Psychology, 77*, 615-622.

Druckman, D., & Bjork, R. A. (1991). *In the mind's eye: Enhancing human performance.* Washington, DC: National Academy Press.

Dubin, R. (1956). Industrial workers' worlds: A study of "Central Life Interests" of industrial workers. *Social Problems, 3*, 131-142.

Duke, P., Jr. (1991, August 14). Urban teenagers, who often live isolated from the world of work, shun the job market. *The Wall Street Journal*, p. A10.

Dumaine, B. (1991, December 2). Closing the innovation gap. *Fortune*, pp. 56-62.

Duncan, C. P. (1958). Transfer after training with single versus multiple tasks. *Journal of Experimental Psychology, 55*, 63-72.

Dunham, R. B. (1976). The measurement and dimensionality of job characteristics. *Journal of Applied Psychology, 61*, 404-409.

Dunham, R. B., Aldag, R., & Brief, A. (1977). Dimensionality of task design as measured by the Job Diagnostic Survey. *Academy of Management Journal, 20*, 209-221.

Dunham, R. B., & Herman, J. B. (1975). Development of a female faces scale for measuring job satisfaction. *Journal of Applied Psychology, 48*, 161-163.

Dunnette, M. D. (1966). *Personnel selection and placement.* Monterey, CA: Brooks/Cole.

Dunnette, M. D., Campbell, J., & Hakel, M. (1967). Factorial contributions to job satisfaction in six occupational groups. *Organizational Behavior and Human Performance, 2*, 143-174.

Dutton, J. M., & Walton, R. E. (1972). Interdepartmental conflict and cooperation: Two contrasting studies. In J. W. Lorsch & P. R. Lawrence (Eds.), *Managing group and intergroup relations* (pp. 285-309). Homewood, IL: Irwin and Dorsey.

Dyer, W. G. (1987). *Team building: Issues and alternatives.* Reading, MA: Addison-Wesley.

Eagly, A. H., & Johnson, B. T. (1990). Gender and leadership style: A meta-analysis. *Psychological Bulletin, 108*, 233-256.

Earley, P. C. (1987). Intercultural training for managers: A comparison of documentary and interpersonal methods. *Academy of Management Journal, 30*, 685-698.

Earley, P. C., Connolly, T., & Ekegren, G. (1989). Goals, strategy development, and task performance: Some limits on the efficacy of goal setting. *Journal of Applied Psychology, 74*, 24-33.

Earley, P. C., & Kanfer, R. (1985). The influence of component participation and role models on goal acceptance, goal satisfaction, and performance. *Organizational Behavior and Human Decision Processes, 36*, 378-390.

Easterbrook, J. A. (1959). The effect of emotion on cue utilization and the organization of behavior. *Psychological Review, 66*, 183-201.

Eden, D. (1984). Self-fulfilling prophecy as a management took: Harnessing pygmalion. *Academy of Management Review, 9*, 64-73.

Eden, D. (1990). *Pygmalion in management: Productivity as a self-fulfilling prophecy.* Lexington, MA: Lexington Books.

Eden, D., & Ravid, G. (1982). Pygmalion versus self-expectancy: Effects of instructor- and self-expectancy on trainee performance. *Organizational Behavior and Human Performance, 30*, 351-364.

Education and Training Committee, SIOP (1982). *Guidelines for education and training at the doctoral level in industrial/organizational psychology.* College Park, MD: Society for Industrial and Organizational Psychology.

Edwards, D. D., Hahn, C. P., & Fleishman, E. A. (1977). Evaluation of laboratory methods for the study of driver behavior: Relations between simulator and street performance. *Journal of Applied Psychology, 62*, 559-566.

Edwards, J., & Bagolini, A. (1991). Relationship between Type A behavior pattern and mental and physical symptoms: A comparison of global and component measures. *Journal of Applied Psychology, 76*, 276-290.

Ehret, C. (1981). New approaches to chronohygiene for the shift worker in the nuclear power industry. In A. Reinberg, N. Vieux, & P. Andlauer (Eds.), *Night and shift work: Biological and social aspects* (pp. 263-270). Oxford, England: Pergamon Press.

Eisenberg, E. M., & Witten, M. G. (1987). Reconsidering openness in organizational communication. *Academy of Management Review, 12*, 418-426.

Eisenberger, R. (1989). *Blue Monday: The loss of the work ethic in America.* New York: Paragon House.

Eisenberger, R., Huntington, R., Hutchison, S., & Sowa, D. (1986). Perceived organizational support. *Journal of Applied Psychology, 71*, 500-507.

Ellis, H. C. (1965). *The transfer of learning.* New York: Macmillan.

Ellis, J. G., & Dewar, R. E. (1979). Rapid comprehension of verbal and symbolic traffic sign messages. *Human Factors, 21,* 161-168.

Entvisle, D. (1972). To dispel fantasies about fantasy-based measures of achievement motivation. *Psychological Bulletin, 77,* 377-391.

Equal Employment Opportunity Commission. (1978). Uniform guidelines on employee selection procedures. *Federal Register,* 43:38290-38315.

Erez, M., Gopher, D., & Arzi, N. (1990). Effects of goal difficulty, self-set goals, and monetary rewards on dual task performance. *Organizational Behavior and Human Decision Processes, 47,* 247-269.

Erez, M., & Kanfer, F. (1983). The role of goal acceptance in goal-setting and task performance. *Academy of Management Review, 8,* 624-627.

Etzion, D. (1984). Moderating effect of social support on the stress-burnout relationship. *Journal of Applied Psychology, 69,* 615-622.

Eulberg, J. R., Weekely, J. A., & Bhagat, R. S. (1988). Models of stress in organizational research: A meta-theoretical perspective. *Human Relations, 41,* 331-350.

Evans, M. G., & Dermer, J. (1974). What does the least preferred co-workers scale really measure? *Journal of Applied Psychology, 59,* 202-206.

Faley, R. H., & Sundstrom, E. (1985). Content representativeness: An empirical method of evaluation. *Journal of Applied Psychology, 70,* 567-571.

Falkenberg, L. E. (1987). Employee fitness programs: Their impact on the employee and the organization. *Academy of Management Review, 12,* 511-522.

Faltermayer, E. (1992, June 1). Is this layoff necessary? *Fortune,* pp. 71-86.

Farh, J. , & Werbel, J. D. (1986). Effects of purpose of the appraisal and expectation of validation on self-appraisal leniency. *Journal of Applied Psychology, 71,* 527-529.

Farkas, A. J., & Tetrick, L. E. (1989). A three-wave longitudinal analysis of the causal ordering of satisfaction and commitment on turnover decisions. *Journal of Applied Psychology, 74,* 855-868.

Farmer, E., & Chambers, E. G. (1939). A study of accident proneness amongst motor drivers. *Industrial Health Research Board Report* (No. 84). London: Industrial Health Research Board.

Farnquist, R. L., Armstrong, D. R., & Strausbaugh, R. P. (1983). Pandora's worth: The San Jose' experience. *Public Personnel Management, 12,* 358-368.

Farr, J. L. (1973). Response requirements and primacy-recency effects in a simulated selection interview. *Journal of Applied Psychology, 58,* 228-233.

Fayol, H. (1930). *Industrial and general administration.* (J.A. Coubrough, Trans.). Geneva: International Management Institute. (Original work published 1916).

Feild, H. S., & Holley, W. H. (1977). Subordinates' characteristics, supervisors' ratings, and decisions to discuss appraisal results. *Academy of Management Journal, 20,* 315-321.

Feldman, D. C. (1984). The development and enforcement of group norms. *Academy of Management Review, 9,* 47-53.

Feldman, D. C. (1989). Socialization, resocialization, and training: Reframing the research agenda. In I. L. Goldstein, (Ed.), *Training and development in organizations* (pp. 376-416). San Francisco: Jossey-Bass.

Feldman, J. M. (1986a). A note on the statistical correction of halo error. *Journal of Applied Psychology, 71*, 173-176.

Feldman, J. M. (1986b). Instrumentation and training for performance appraisal: A perceptual-cognitive viewpoint. In K. M. Rowland & G. R. Ferris (Eds.), *Research in personnel and human resources management.* (Vol. 4, pp. 45-100). Greenwich, CT: JAI Press.

Feldman, K. A. (1976). Grades and college students' evaluations of their courses and teachers. *Research in Higher Education, 4*, 69-111.

Ferris, G. R., & Gilmore, D. (1985). A methodological note on job complexity indexes. *Journal of Applied Psychology, 70*, 225-227.

Ferris, G. R., & Mitchell, T. R. (1987). The components of social influence and their importance for human resources research. In K. M. Rowland & G. R. Ferris (Eds.), *Research in personnel and human resources management.* (Vol. 5, pp. 103-128). Greenwich, CT: JAI Press.

Ferster, C., & Skinner, B. (1957). *Schedules of reinforcement.* New York: Appleton-Century-Crofts.

Fiedler, F. E. (1978). The contingency model and the dynamics of the leadership process. In L. Berkowitz (Ed.), *Advances in experimental social psychology* (Vol. 11, pp. 59-112). New York: Academic Press.

Fiedler, F. E., Chemers, M. M., & Mahar, L. (1976). *Improving leadership effectiveness: The LEADER MATCH concept.* New York: Wiley.

Fiedler, F. E., & Garcia, J. E. (1987). *New approaches to effective leadership: Cognitive resources and organizational performance.* New York: Wiley.

Fiedler, F. E., Mitchell, T. R., & Triandis, H. C. (1971). The culture assimilator: An approach to cross-cultural training. *Journal of Applied Psychology, 55*, 95-102.

Fiedler, F. E., Murphy, S. E., & Gibson, F. W. (1992). Inaccurate reporting and inappropriate variables: A reply to Vecchio's (1990) examination of cognitive resource theory. *Journal of Applied Psychology, 77*, 372-374.

Field, R. H. G. (1982). A test of the Vroom-Yetton normative model of leadership. *Journal of Applied Psychology, 67*, 523-532.

Field, R. H. G., & House, R. J. (1990). A test of the Vroom-Yetton model using manager and subordinate reports. *Journal of Applied Psychology, 75*, 362-366.

Fine, S. A. (1988). Functional job analysis. In S. Gael (Ed.), *The job analysis handbook for business, industry, and government* (Vol. 2, pp. 1019-1035). New York: John Wiley & Sons.

Finley, D. M., Osburn, H. G., Dubin, J. A., & Jeanneret, P. R. (1977). Behaviorally based rating scales: Effects of specific anchors and disguised scale continua. *Personnel Psychology, 30*, 659-669.

Firth, H., & Britton, P. (1989). Burnout, absence and turnover amongst British nursing staff. *Journal of Occupational Psychology, 62*, 55-59.

Fischhoff, B. (1975). Hindsight: Thinking backward? *Psychology Today, 8*, 70-76.

Fischhoff, B., & Johnson, S. (1990). The possibility of distributed decision making. In National Research Council (Ed.), *Distributed Decision Making*. Washington, DC: National Academy Press.

Fishbein, M., & Ajzen, I. (1975). *Belief, attitude, intention, and behavior: An introduction to theory and research*. Reading, MA: Addison-Wesley.

Fisher, A. B. (1992, November 30). Welcome to the age of overwork. *Fortune*, pp. 64-71.

Fisher, C. D. (1979). Transmission of positive and negative feedback to subordinates: A laboratory investigation. *Journal of Applied Psychology, 64,* 533-540.

Fisher, C. D. (1980). On the dubious wisdom of expecting job satisfaction to correlate with performance. *Academy of Management Review, 5,* 607-612.

Fisher, C. D. (1985). Social support and adjustment to work: A longitudinal study. *Journal of Management, 11,* 39-53.

Fiske, S. T., Kinder, D. R., & Larter, W. M. (1983). The novice and the expert: Knowledge based strategies in political cognition. *Journal of Experimental Social Psychology, 19,* 381-400.

Flanagan, J. C. (1954). The critical incident technique. *Psychological Bulletin, 51,* 327-358.

Fleishman, E. A., & Harris, E. F. (1962). Patterns of leadership behavior related to employee grievances and turnover. *Personnel Psychology, 15,* 43-56.

Fleishman, E. A., & Quaintance, M. K. (1984). *Taxonomies of human performance*. Orlando, FL: Academic Press.

Fogli, L. (1988). Supermarket cashier. In S. Gael (Ed.), *The job analysis handbook for business, industry, and government* (pp. 1215-1228). New York: John Wiley & Sons.

Folger, R. (1984). Emerging issues in the social psychology of justice. In R. Folger (Ed.), *The sense of injustice: Social psychological perspectives* (pp. 3-24). New York: Plenum Press.

Folger, R., & Konovsky, M (1989). Effects of procedural and distributive justice on reactions to pay raise decisions. *Academy of Management Journal, 32,* 115-130.

Folkard, S. (1990). Circadian performance rhythms: Some practical and theoretical implications. *Philosophical Transactions Royal Society of London, Biological Sciences, 327,* 543-553.

Folkard, S., Minors, D., & Waterhouse, J. (1985). Chronobiology and shift work: Current issues and trends. *Chronobiologica, 12,* 31-54.

Folkard, S., Monk, T., & Lobban, M. (1978). Short and long term adjustment of circadian rhythms in 'permanent' night nurses. *Ergonomics, 21,* 785-799.

Folley, J. D., Jr. (1969). Determining training needs of department store sales personnel. *Training and Developmental Journal, 23,* 24-27.

Ford, D. L. (1980). Work, job satisfaction, and employee well-being: An exploratory study of minority professionals. *Journal of Social and Behavioral Sciences, 26,* 70-75.

Ford, D. L. (1985). Facets of work support and employee work outcomes: An exploratory analysis. *Journal of Management, 11,* 5-20.

Ford, R.C., Armandi, B.R., & Heaton, C.P. (1988). *Organization theory*. New York: Harper & Row.

Foret, J., Bensimon, G., Benoit, O., & Vieux, N. (1981). Quality of sleep as a function of age and shift work. In A. Reinberg, N. Vieux, & P. Andlauer (Eds.), *Night and shift work: Biological and social aspects* (pp. 149-153). Oxford, England: Pergamon Press.

Forgionne, G. A., & Peeters, V. E. (1982). Differences in job motivation and satisfaction among female and male managers. *Human Relations, 35*, 101-118.

Fossum, J. A., Arvey, R. D., Paradise, C. A., & Robbins, N. E. (1986). Modeling the skills obsolescence process: A psychological/economic integration. *Academy of Management Review, 11*, 362-374.

Francis, J., Mohr, J., & Andersen, K. (1992, January). HR balancing: Alternative downsizing. *Personnel Journal*, pp. 71-75.

French, J. R. P., Jr., & Caplan, R. D. (1970). Psychosocial factors in coronary heart disease. *Industrial Medicine, 39*, 383-397.

French, J. R. P., Jr., & Caplan, R. D. (1973). Organizational stress and individual strain. In A. J. Marrow (Ed.), *The failure of success*. New York: Amacom.

French, J. R. P., Jr., Caplan, R. D., & Van Harrison, R. (1982). *The mechanisms of job stress and strain*. New York: Wiley.

French, J. R. P., Jr., & Raven, B. (1959). The bases of social power. In D. Cartwright (Ed.), *Studies in social power* (pp. 150-167). Ann Arbor, MI: University of Michigan Press.

French, W. L., & Bell, C. H. (1984). *Organization development: Behavioral science interventions for organization development* (3rd ed.). Englewood Cliffs, NJ: Prentice-Hall.

Frese, M., & Okonek, K. (1984). Reasons to leave shiftwork and psychological and psychosomatic complaints of former shiftworkers. *Journal of Applied Psychology, 69*, 509-514.

Fried, Y., & Ferris, G. (1986). The dimensionality of job characteristics: Some neglected issues. *Journal of Applied Psychology, 71*, 419-426.

Friedman, B. A., & Cornelius, E. T., III (1976). Effect of rater participation in scale construction on the psychometric characteristics of two rating scale formats. *Journal of Applied Psychology, 61*, 210-216.

Friedman, L. (1990). Degree of redundancy between time, importance, and frequency task ratings. *Journal of Applied Psychology, 75*, 603-612.

Frost, P., & Jamal, M. (1979). Shift work, attitudes, and reported behavior: Some associations between individual characteristics and hours of work and leisure. *Journal of Applied Psychology, 64*, 66-70.

Furedy, J. (1987). Beyond heart rate in the cardiac psychophysical assessment of mental effort: The T-wave amplitude component of the electrocardiogram. *Human Factors, 29*, 183-194.

Gabor, A. (1992, January 26). Take this job and love it. *The New York Times*, Section 3, pp. 1, 6.

Gadbois, C. (1981). Women on night shift: Interdependence of sleep and off-the-job activities. In A. Reinberg, N. Vieux, & P. Andlauer (Eds.), *Night and shift work: Biological and social aspects* (pp. 223-237). Oxford, England: Pergamon Press.

Gael, S. (1983). *Job analysis: A guide to assessing work activities*. San Francisco: Jossey-Bass.

Gagne, R. M. (1984). Learning outcomes and their effects: Useful categories of human performance. *American Psychologist, 39*, 377-385.

Gagne, R. M., Briggs, L. J., & Wager, W. W. (1988). *Principles of instructional design* (3rd ed.). New York: Holt, Rinehart & Winston.

Galbraith, J. D. (1977). *Organization design*. Reading, MA: Addison-Wesley.

Ganster, D., Schaubroeck, J., Sime, W., & Mayes, B. (1991). The nomological validity of the Type A personality among employed adults. *Journal of Applied Psychology, 76*, 143-168.

Ganster, D. C., Mayes, B., Sime, W. E., & Tharp, G. P. (1982). Managing organizational stress: A field experiment. *Journal of Applied Psychology, 67*, 533-542.

Garden, A. (1989). Burnout: The effect of psychological type on research findings. *Journal of Occupational Psychology, 62*, 223-234.

Gaugler, B.B., Rosenthal, D., Thornton, G.C., III, & Bentson, C. (1987). Meta-analysis of assessment center validity. *Journal of Applied Psychology Monograph, 72*, 493-511.

Georgopolos, B., Mahoney, G., & Jones, N. (1957). A path-goal approach to productivity. *Journal of Applied Psychology, 41*, 345-353.

Gersick, C. J. G. (1988). Time and transition in work teams: Toward a new model of group development. *Academy of Management Journal, 31*, 9-41.

Gersick, C. J. G., & Hackman, J. R. (1990). Habitual routines in task-performing groups. *Organizational Behavior and Human Decision Processes, 47*, 65-97.

Geyer, P. D., Hice, J., Hawk, J., Boese, R., & Brannon, Y. (1989). Reliabilities of ratings available from the Dictionary of Occupational Titles. *Personnel Psychology, 42*, 547-560.

Gies, J. (1991). Automating the worker. *Invention & Technology, 6*, 56-63.

Gist, M. E., Rosen, B., & Schwoerer, C. (1988). The influence of training method and trainee age on the acquisition of computer skills. *Personnel Psychology, 41*, 255-265.

Gist, M. E., Schwoerer, C., & Rosen, B. (1989). Effects of alternative training methods on self-efficacy and performance in computer software training. *Journal of Applied Psychology, 74*, 884-891.

Gladstein, D. (1984). Groups in context: A model of task group effectiveness. *Administrative Science Quarterly, 29*, 499-517.

Glaser, R. (1984). Education and thinking. *American Psychologist, 39,* 93-104.

Glaser, R. (1990). The reemergence of learning theory within instructional research. *American Psychologist, 45*, 29-39.

Glick, W. H. (1985). Conceptualizing and measuring organizational and psychological climate: Pitfalls in multilevel research. *Academy of Management Review, 10*, 601-616.

Glick, W., Jenkins, G., & Gupta, N. (1986). Method versus substance: How strong are underlying relationships between job characteristics and attitudinal outcomes? *Academy of Management Journal, 29*, 441-464.

Glickman, A. S., & Vallance, T. R. (1958). Curriculum assessment with critical incidents. *Journal of Applied Psychology, 42*, 329-335.

Glowinkowski, S. P., & Cooper, C. L. (1986). Managers and professionals in business/industrial settings: The research evidence. In J. M. Ivancevich & D. C. Ganster (Eds.), *Job stress: From theory to suggestions*. New York: The Hawthorne Press.

Goldbeck, R., & Charlet, J. (1974, June). *Task parameters for predicting plane layout design and operator performance* (WDL-TR-5480). Palo Alto, CA: Western Development Laboratories, Philco-Ford Corp.

Goldbeck, R., & Charlet, J. (1975, November). *Prediction of operator work station performance* (WDL-TR-7071). Palo Alto, CA: Western Development Laboratories, Philco-Ford Corp.

Goldstein, A. P., & Sorcher, M. (1974). *Changing supervisor behavior*. Hawthorne, NY: Aldine.

Goldstein, I. L. (1986). *Training in organizations: Needs assessment, development, and evaluation* (2nd ed.). Monterrey, CA: Brooks/Cole.

Goldstein, I. L. (1993). *Training in organizations: Needs assessment, development, and evaluation* (3rd ed.). Monterrey, CA: Brooks/Cole.

Goldstein, I. L., & Gilliam, P. (1990). Training system issues in the year 2000. *American Psychologist, 45*, 134-143.

Goldstein, I. L., Macey, W. H., & Prien, E. P. (1981). Needs assessment approaches for training development. In H. Meltzer & W. R. Nord (Eds.), *Making organizations humane and productive*. New York: John Wiley.

Golembiewski, R. T., Billingsley, K., & Yeager, S. (1976). Measuring change and persistence in human affairs: Types of change generated by OD designs. *Journal of Applied Behavioral Science, 12*, 133-157.

Golembiewski, R. T., & Proehl, C. W. (1978). A survey of the empirical literature of flexible workhours: Character aand consequences of a major innovation. *Academy of Management Review, 3*, 837-853.

Gomez-Mejia, L. R. (1982). A comparison of the practical utility of traditional, statistical, and hybrid job evaluation approaches. *Academy of Management Journal, 25*, 790-809.

Goodale, J., & Aagaard, A. (1975). Factors relating to varying reactions to four-day workweeks. *Journal of Applied Psychology, 60*, 33-38.

Goodman, P. (1974). An examination of referents used in the evaluation of pay. *Organizational Behavior and Human Performance, 12*, 170-195.

Goodman, P., Devadas, R., & Hughson, T. L. G. (1988). Groups and productivity: Analyzing the effectiveness of self-managing teams. In J. P. Campbell, R. J. Campbell, and associates (Eds.), *Productivity in organizations* (pp. 295-328). San Francisco: Jossey-Bass.

Goodman, P., & Friedman, A. (1971). An examination of Adams' theory of inequity. *Administrative Science Quarterly, 16*, 271-288.

Gordon, M. E. (1970). The effect of the correctness of the behavior observed on the accuracy of ratings. *Organizational Behavior and Human Performance, 5*, 366-377.

Gordon, M. E., & Cohen, S. L. (1973). Training behavior as a predictor of trainability. *Personnel Psychology, 26*, 261-262.

Gordon, M. E., & Kleiman, L. S. (1976). The prediction of trainability using a work sample test and an aptitude test: A direct comparison. *Personnel Psychology, 29*, 243-253.

Gordon, M. E., Slade, L. A., & Schmitt, N. (1986). The "science of the sophomore" revisited: From conjecture to empiricism. *Academy of Management Review, 11,* 191-207.

Gordon, R. A., Rozelle, R. M., & Baxter, J. C. (1988). The effect of applicant age, job level, and accountability on the evaluation of job applicants. *Organizational Behavior and Human Decision Processes, 41,* 20-33.

Gould, J., Alfaro, L., Finn, R., Haupt, B., & Minuto, A. (1987). Reading from CRT displays can be as fast as reading from paper. *Human Factors, 29,* 497-517.

Graeff, C. L. (1983). The situational leadership theory: A critical view. *Academy of Management Review, 8,* 285-291.

Graen, G. B. (1976). Role making processes within complex organizations. In M. D. Dunnette (Ed.), *Handbook of industrial and organizational psychology* (pp. 1201-1246). Chicago: Rand McNally.

Graen, G. B., Alvares, K. M., Orris, J. B., & Martella, J. A. (1970). Contingency model of leadership effectiveness: Antecedent and evidential results. *Psychological Bulletin, 74,* 285-296.

Graen, G. B., & Scandura, T. A. (1987). Toward a psychology of dyadic organizing. In L. L. Cummings & B. M. Staw (Eds.), *Research in Organizational Behavior* (Vol. 9, pp. 175-208). Greenwich, CT: JAI Press.

Green, S. B., & Stutzman, T. (1986). An evaluation of methods to select respondents to structured job-analysis questionnaires. *Personnel Psychology, 39,* 543-564.

Green, S. G., & Mitchell, T. R. (1979). Attributional processes in leader-member interactions. *Organizational Behavior and Human Performance, 23,* 429-459.

Greenbaum, C. W. (1979). The small group under the gun: Use of small groups in battle conditions. *Journal of Applied Behavioral Sciences, 15,* 392-405.

Greenberg, J. (1988). Equity and workplace status: A field experiment. *Journal of Applied Psychology, 73,* 606-613.

Greenberg, J. (1989). Cognitive reevaluation of outcomes in response to underpayment inequity. *Academy of Management Journal, 32,* 174-184.

Greenberg, J. (1990). Employee theft as a reaction to underpayment inequity: The hidden cost of pay cuts. *Journal of Applied Psychology, 75,* 561-568.

Greene, C. N., & Podsakoff, P. M. (1981). Effects of withdrawal of a performance-contingent reward on supervisory influence and power. *Academy of Management Journal, 24,* 527-542.

Greenhalgh, L., Lawrence, A. T., & Sutton, R. I. (1988). Determinants of work force reduction strategies in declining organizations. *Academy of Management Review, 13,* 241-254.

Greenhaus, J. H., & Parasuraman, S. (1986). A work-nonwork perspective of stress and its consequences. In J. M. Ivancevich & D. C. Ganster (Eds.), *Job stress: From theory to suggestions.* New York: The Hawthorne Press.

Greenwood, M., Woods, H., & Yule, G. (1919). A report on the incidence of industrial accidents upon individuals with special reference to multiple accidents (Report No. 4, Industrial Health Research Board). In W. Haddon, E. A. Suchmann, & D. Flein (Eds.), *Accident Research.* New York: Harper.

Greller, M. M. (1975). Subordinate participation and reaction to the appraisal interview. *Journal of Applied Psychology, 60,* 544-549.

Greller, M. M. (1980). Evaluation of feedback sources as a function of role and organizational level. *Journal of Applied Psychology, 65,* 24-27.

Greller, M. M., & Herold, D. M. (1975). Sources of feedback: A preliminary investigation. *Organizational Behavior and Human Performance, 13,* 244-256.

Griffeth, R., Vecchio, R., & Logan, J., Jr. (1989). Equity theory and interpersonal attraction. *Journal of Applied Psychology, 74,* 394-401.

Griffin, R. (1983). Objective and social sources of information in task design: A field experiment. *Administrative Science Quarterly, 28,* 184-200.

Guion, R. M. (1965). *Personnel testing.* New York: McGraw-Hill.

Guion, R. M. (1973). A note on organizational climate. *Organizational Behavior and Human Performance, 9,* 120-125.

Guion, R. M. (1980). On trinitarian doctrines of validity. *Professional Psychology, 11,* 385-398.

Gullahorn, J. T. (1955). Distance and friendship as factors in the gross interaction matrix. *Sociometry, 15,* 123-134.

Gupta, N., & Jenkins, D. (1985). Dual-career couples. In T. A. Beehr & R. S. Bhagat (Eds.), *Human Stress and Cognition in Organizations* (pp. 141-175). New York: Wiley.

Gutek, B. A. (1985). *Sex and the workplace.* San Francisco: Jossey-Bass.

Gutek, B. A., & Larwood, L. (1987). Information technology and working women in the USA. In M. J. Davidson & C. L. Cooper (Eds.), *Women and information technology* (pp. 71-94). Chichester, England: John Wiley & Sons.

Guzzo, R. A., Jette, R. D., & Katzell, R. A. (1985). The effects of psychologically based intervention programs on worker productivity: A meta-analysis. *Personnel Psychology, 38,* 275-291.

Hackett, R. D. (1989). Work attitudes and employee absenteeism: A synthesis of the literature. *Journal of Occupational Psychology, 62,* 235-248.

Hackman, J. R., Brousseau, K. R., & Weiss, J. A. (1976). The interaction of task design and group performance strategies in determining group effectiveness. *Organizational Behavior and Human Performance, 16,* 350-365.

Hackman, J. R., & Morris, C. G. (1975). Group tasks, group interaction process, and group performance effectiveness: A review and proposed integration. In L. Berkowitz (Ed.), *Advances in experimental social psychology* (Vol. 8, pp. 47-95). New York: Academic Press.

Hackman, J. R., & Oldham, G. R. (1975). Development of the Job Diagnostic Survey. *Journal of Applied Psychology, 60,* 159-179.

Hackman, J. R., & Oldham, G. R. (1976). Motivation through the design of work: Test of a theory. *Organizational Behavior and Human Performance, 16,* 250-279.

Hackman, J. R., & Oldham, G. R. (1980). *Work redesign.* Reading, MA: Addison-Wesley.

Hahn, D. C., & Dipboye, R. L. (1988). Effects of training and information on the accuracy and reliability of job evaluations. *Journal of Applied Psychology, 73*, 146-153.

Hakel, M.D. (1986). Personnel selection and placement. *Annual Review of Psychology, 37*, 351-380.

Hall, D. T., & Nougaim, K. E. (1968). An examination of Maslow's need hierarchy in an organizational setting. *Organizational Behavior and Human Performance, 3*, 398-415.

Hall, J., & Watson, W. H. (1971). The effects of a normative intervention on group decision-making performance. *Human Relations, 23*, 299-317.

Halpin, A. W. (1957). The leader behavior and effectiveness of aircraft commanders. In R. M. Stogdill & A. E. Coons (Eds.), *Leader behavior: Its description and measurement* (pp. 52-64). Columbus, OH: Ohio State University, Bureau of Business Research.

Hamner, W. C. (1991). Reinforcement theory and contingency management in organizational settings. In R. Steers & L. Porter (Eds.), *Motivation and work behavior* (pp. 61-86). New York: McGraw-Hill.

Hamner, W. C., & Foster, L. (1975). Are intrinsic and extrinsic rewards additive? A test of Deci's cognitive evaluation theory of task motivation. *Organizational Behavior and Human Performance, 14*, 398-415.

Hancock, P. A. (1981). The limitation of human performance in extreme heat conditions. In R. C. Sugarman (Ed.), *Proceedings of the Human Factors Society, 1981.* (25th Annual Meeting, pp. 74-78). Santa Monica, CA: Human Factors Society.

Hansen, C. (1989). A causal model of the relationship among accidents, biodata, personality, and cognitive factors. *Journal of Applied Psychology, 74*, 81-90.

Harder, J. (1991). Equity theory versus expectancy theory: The case of major league baseball free agents. *Journal of Applied Psychology, 76*, 458-464.

Harris, M. M. (1989) Reconsidering the employment interview. *Personnel Psychology, 42*, 691-727.

Harris, M. M., & Schaubroeck, J. (1988). A meta-analysis of self-supervisor, self-peer, and peer-supervisor ratings. *Personnel Psychology, 41*, 43-62.

Harvey, R. J. (1991). Job analysis. In M. D. Dunnette & L. M. Hough (Eds.), *The handbook of industrial and organizational psychology: Volume 2* (2nd ed., pp. 71-164), Palo Alto, CA: Consulting Psychologists Press.

Harvey, R. J., Billings, R., & Nilan, K. (1985). Confirmatory factor analysis of the Job Diagnostic Survey: Good news and bad news. *Journal of Applied Psychology, 70*, 461-468.

Hay, E. N., & Purves, D. (1954, July). A new method of job evaluation. *Personnel*, 72-80.

Haynes, S. G., Feinleib, M., & Kannel, W. B. (1980). The relationship of psychosocial factors to coronary heart disease in the Framingham study: Eight year incidence of coronary heart disease. *American Journal of Epidemiology, 111*, 37-58.

Hedge, A. (1984). Ill health among office workers: An examination of the relationship between office design and employee well-being. In E. Grandjean (Ed.), *Ergonomics and health in modern offices*. London: Taylor & Francis.

Heilman, M. E., Block, C. J., Martell, R. F., & Simon, M. C. (1989). Has anything changed? Current characterizations of men, women, and managers. *Journal of Applied Psychology, 74*, 935-942.

Heilman, M. E., Hornstein, H. A., Cage, J. H., & Herschlag, J. K. (1984). Reactions to prescribed leader behavior as a function of role perspective: The case of the Vroom-Yetton model. *Journal of Applied Psychology*, *69*, 50-60.

Heilman, M. E., & Stopeck, M. H. (1985). Attractiveness and corporate success: Different causal attributions for males and females. *Organizational Behavior and Human Performance*, *21*, 346-357.

Heiman, M. F. (1975). The police suicide. *Journal of Police Science and Administration*, *3*, 267-273.

Heneman, R. L. (1986). The relationship between supervisory ratings and results-oriented measures of performance: A meta-analysis. *Personnel Psychology*, *39*, 811-826.

Heneman, R. L., & Wexley, K. N. (1983). The effects of time delay in rating and amount of information observed on performance rating accuracy. *Academy of Management Journal*, *26*, 677-686.

Herbert, A. (1983). The influence of shift work on leisure activities: A study with repeated measures. *Ergonomics*, *26*, 565-574.

Herold, D. M., & Greller, M. M. (1977). Feedback: The development of a construct. *Academy of Management Journal*, *20*, 142-147.

Herold, D. M., & Parsons, C. K. (1985). Assessing the feedback environment in work organizations: Development of the Job Feedback Survey. *Journal of Applied Psychology*, *70*, 290-305.

Hersey, P., & Blanchard, K. H. (1982). *Management of organizational behavior: Utilizing human resources* (2nd ed.). Englewood Cliffs, NJ: Prentice-Hall.

Herzberg, F., Mausner, B., Peterson, R. O., & Capwell, D.F. (1957). *Job attitudes: Review of research and opinion*. Pittsburgh: Psychological Service of Pittsburgh.

Herzberg, F., Mausner, B., & Snyderman, B. (1959). *The motivation to work*. New York: John Wiley & Sons.

Hicks, W. D., & Klimoski, R. J. (1981). The impact of flextime on employee attitudes. *Academy of Management Journal, 24,* 333-341.

Hickson, D. J. (1961). Motives of people who restrict their output. *Occupational Psychology, 35,* 110-121.

Higgins, J. M. (1983). *Organizational policy and strategic management: Text and cases*. New York: Dryden.

Higgins, N. C. (1986). Occupational stress and working women: The effectiveness of two stress reduction programs. *Journal of Vocational Behavior*, *29*, 66-78.

Hildebrandt, G., & Stratman, I. (1979). Circadian system response to night work in relation to the individual circadian phase position. *International Archives for Occupational and Environmental Health, 3*, 73-83.

Hill, T., Smith, N., & Mann, M. (1987). Role of efficacy expectations in predicting the decision to use advanced technologies: The case of computers. *Journal of Applied Psychology*, *72*, 307-313.

Hinkin, T. R., & Schriesheim, C. A. (1989). Development and application of new scales to measure the French and Raven (1959) bases of social power. *Journal of Applied Psychology*, *74*, 561-567.

Hinrichs, J. R. (1964). Communications activity of industrial research personnel. *Personnel Psychology*, *17*, 193-204.

Hirschfeld, A. H., & Behan, R. C. (1963). The accident process: I. Etiological considerations of industrial injuries. *Journal of the American Medical Association*, *186*, 193-199.

Hirschfeld, A. H., & Behan, R. C. (1966). The accident process: III. Disability: acceptable and unacceptable. *Journal of the American Medical Association, 197,* 125-129.

Hitt, W. (1961). An evaluation of five different abstract coding methods: Experiment IV. *Human Factors, 3,* 120-130.

Hogan, J. C., & Fleishman, E. A. (1979). An index of the physical effort required in human task performance. *Journal of Applied Psychology, 64,* 197-204.

Hogan, J. C., Ogden, G. D., Gebhardt, D. L., & Fleishman, E. A. (1980). Reliability and validity of methods for evaluating perceived physical effort. *Journal of Applied Psychology, 65,* 672-679.

Hogan, P. M., Hakel, M. D., & Decker, P. J. (1986). Effects of trainee-generated versus trainer-provided rule codes on generalization in behavior-modeling training. *Journal of Applied Psychology, 71,* 469-473.

Holland, D. (1991, December 9). When leaders talk, people listen-and act. *Houston Business Journal,* p. 3.

Hollenbeck, J. R., Williams, C., & Klein, H. (1989). An empirical examination of the antecedents of commitment to difficult goals. *Journal of Applied Psychology, 74,* 18-23.

Hollenbeck, J. R., & Williams, C. R. (1986). Turnover functionality versus turnover frequency: A note on work attitudes and organizational effectiveness. *Journal of Applied Psychology, 71,* 606-611.

Holmes, D. S. (1984). Meditation and somatic arousal reduction: A review of the experimental evidence. *American Psychologist, 39,* 1-10.

Holmes, T. H., & Rahe, R. H. (1967). The social readjustment rating scale. *Journal of Psychosomatic Research, 11,* 213-218.

Holzbach, R. L. (1978). Rater bias in performance ratings: Superior, self and peer ratings. *Journal of Applied Psychology, 63,* 579-588.

Hom, P. W., DeNisi, A. S., Kinicki, A. J., & Bannister, B. D. (1982). Effectiveness of performance feedback from behaviorally anchored rating scales. *Journal of Applied Psychology, 67,* 568-576.

Homans, G. (1961). *Social behavior: Its elementary forms.* New York: Harcourt, Brace, & World.

Hoppock, R. (1935). *Job satisfaction.* New York: Harper & Row.

Horn, J. L. (1985). Remodeling old models of intelligence. In B. Wolman (Ed.), *Handbook of intelligence: Theories, measurements, and applications.* New York: Wiley.

Hothersall, D. (1984). *History of psychology.* Philadelphia: Temple University Press.

Hough, L. M., Eaton, N. K., Dunnette, M. D., Kamp, J. D., & McCloy, R. A. (1990). Criterion-related validities of personality constructs and the effect of response distortion on those validities. *Journal of Applied Psychology Monograph, 75,* 581-595.

House, J. S., & Wells, J. A. (1978). Occupational stress, social support, and health. In A. McLean, G. Black, & M. Colligan (Eds.), *Reducing occupational stress: Proceedings of a conference* (Publication No. 78-140, pp. 8-29). Department of Health, Education, and Welfare (NIOSH).

House, R. J. (1971). A path-goal theory of leader effectiveness. *Administrative Science Quarterly, 16,* 321-328.

House, R. J. (1977). A 1976 theory of charismatic leadership. In J. G. Hunt & L. L. Larson (Eds.), *Leadership: The cutting edge* (pp. 189-207). Carbondale, IL: Southern Illinois University Press.

House, R. J. (1988). Power and personality in complex organizations. In B. M. Staw & L. L. Cummings (Eds.), *Research in Organizational Behavior.* (Vol. 10, pp. 305-357). Greenwich, CT: JAI Press.

House, R. J., & Mitchell, T. R. (1975). Path-goal theory of leadership. In K. N. Wexley & G. A. Yukl (Eds.), *Organizational behavior and industrial psychology* (pp. 177-186). New York: Oxford University Press.

House, R. J., Spangler, W. D., & Woycke, J. (1991). Personality and charisma in the U. S. Presidency: A psychological theory of leader effectiveness. *Administrative Science Quarterly, 36,* 364-396.

House, R. J., & Wigdor, L. A. (1967). Herzberg's dual-factor theory of job satisfaction and motivation: A review of the evidence and criticism. *Personnel Psychology, 20,* 369-389.

Housel, T. J., & Davis, W. E. (1977). The reduction of upward communication distortion. *Journal of Business Communication, 14,* 49-65.

Howard, A. (1990). *The multiple facets of industrial / organizational psychology.* Arlington Heights, IL: Society for Industrial and Organizational Psychology.

Howard, A. (1991). New directions for human resources practices. In D. W. Bray and associates (Eds.), *Working with organizations and their people* (pp. 219-251). New York: The Guilford Press.

Howard, A., & Lowman, R.L. (1985). Should industrial-organizational psychologists be licensed? *American Psychologist, 40,* 40-47.

Howard, A., Pion, G. M., Gottfredson, G. D., Flattau, P. E., Oskamp, S., Pfafflin, S. M., Bray, D. W., & Burstein, A. G. (1986). The changing face of American psychology. *American Psychologist, 41,* 1311-1327.

Howard, G. S., & Maxwell, S. E. (1980). The correlation between student satisfaction and grades: A case of mistaken causation? *Journal of Educational Psychology, 72,* 810-820.

Howard, G. S., & Maxwell, S. E. (1982). Do grades contaminate student evaluations of instruction? *Research in Higher Evaluations, 16,* 175-188.

Howard, J. H., Cunningham, D. A., & Rechnitzer, P. A. (1986). Role ambiguity, Type A behavior, and job satisfaction: Moderating effects on cardiovascular and biochemical responses associated with coronary risk. *Journal of Applied Psychology, 71,* 95-101.

Howell, J. M., & Frost, P. J. (1989). A laboratory study of charismatic leadership. *Organizational Behavior and Human Decision Processes, 43,* 243-269.

Howell, J. P., & Dorfman, P. W. (1981). Substitutes for leadership: Test of a construct. *Academy of Management Journal, 24,* 714-728.

Howell, W. C. (1991). Human factors in the workplace. In M. D. Dunnette & L. M. Hough (Eds.), *Handbook of industrial and organizational psychology* (Vol. 2). Palo Alto, CA: Consulting Psychologists Press.

Howell, W. C., & Cooke, N. J. (1989). Training the human information processor: A look at cognitive models. In I. L. Goldstein (Ed.), *Training and development in work organizations: Frontiers of industrial and organizational psychology* (pp. 121-182). San Francisco: Jossey-Bass.

Howell, W. C., & Dipboye, R. L. (1986). *Essentials of industrial and organizational psychology.* Chicago: Dorsey.

Howell, W. C. , & Goldstein, I. (1971). *Engineering psychology: Current perspectives in research*. New York: Meredith.

Hrebiniak, L. G., & Alutto, J. A. (1972). Personal and role related factors in the development of organizational commitment. *Administrative Science Quarterly, 17*, 555-572.

Huffcut, A. I. (1990). Structural interviews emerge: The new technique of the 1990s? *Industrial-Organizational Psychologist, 27*, 83-84.

Hulin, C. L., Drasgow, F., & Komocar, J. (1982). Applications of item response theory to analysis of attitude scale translations. *Journal of Applied Psychology, 67*, 818-825.

Hulin, C. L., & Smith, P. C. (1964). Sex differences in job satisfaction. *Journal of Applied Psychology, 48*, 88-92.

Hunt, J. W., & Saul, P. N. (1975). The relationship of age, tenure, and job satisfaction in males and females. *Academy of Management Journal, 18*, 690-702.

Hurrell, J. J. (1977). *Job stress among police officers: A preliminary analysis* (Publication No. (NIOSH) 7604228), U.S. Department of Health, Education, and Welfare. Cincinnati: U.S. Government Printing Office.

Hutchinson, T. (1981). A review of some applications of signal detection theory. *Quality and Quantity, 15*, 71-98.

Huselid, M. A., & Day, N. E. (1991). Organizational commitment, job involvement, and turnover: A substantive and methodological analysis. *Journal of Applied Psychology, 76*, 380-391.

Hymowitz, C., & O'Boyle, T. F. (1991, May 29). Two disparate firms find keys to success in troubled industries. *The Wall Street Journal*, pp. A1, A9.

Iaffaldano, M. T., & Muchinsky, P. M. (1985). Job satisfaction and job performance: A meta-analysis. *Psychological Bulletin, 97*, 251-273.

Idaszak, J., & Drasgow, F. (1987). A revision of the Job Diagnostic Survey: Elimination of a measurement artifact. *Journal of Applied Psychology, 72*, 69-74.

Ilgen, D. I., & Feldman, J. M. (1983). Performance appraisal: A process focus. *Research in Organizational Behavior, 5*, 141-197.

Ilgen, D. I., Fisher, C. D., & Taylor, M. S. (1979). Consequences of individual feedback on behavior in organizations. *Journal of Applied Psychology, 64*, 349-371.

Ilgen, D. I., & Seely, W. (1974). Realistic expectations as an aid in reducing voluntary resignations. *Journal of Applied Psychology, 58*, 452-455.

International Union, United Automobile, Aerospace & Agricultural Implement Workers of America, UAW et al. v. Johnson Controls, Inc. 89 U.S. 1215 (1991).

Ironson, G., Smith, P. C., Brannick, M. T., Gibson, W. M., & Paul, K. B. (1989). Construction of a "Job in General" scale: A comparison of global, composite, and specific measures. *Journal of Applied Psychology, 74*, 193-200.

Ivancevich, J. M. (1974). Effects of the shorter workweek on selected satisfaction and performance measures. *Journal of Applied Psychology, 59*, 717-721.

Ivancevich, J. M. (1985). Predicting absenteeism from prior absence and work attitudes. *Academy of Management Journal, 28,* 219-228.

Ivancevich, J. M. (1986). Life events and hassles as predictors of health symptoms, job performance, and absenteeism. *Journal of Occupational Behaviour, 7,* 39-51.

Ivancevich, J., & Lyon, H. (1977). The shortened workweek: A field experiment. *Journal of Applied Psychology, 62,* 34-37.

Ivancevich, J. M., & Matteson, M. T. (1980). *Stress and work.* Glenview, IL: Scott, Foresman.

Ivancevich, J. M., Matteson, M. T., Freedman, S. M., & Phillips, J. S. (1990). Worksite stress management interventions. *American Psychologist, 45,* 252-261.

Jablin, F. M. (1979). Superior-subordinate communication: The state of the art. *Psychological Bulletin, 86,* 1201-1222.

Jacklin, C. N., & Maccoby, E. E. (1975). Sex differences and their implications for management. In F. E. Gordon & M. H. Strober (Eds.), *Bringing women into management* (pp. 23-38). New York: McGraw-Hill.

Jackson, J. (1965). Structural characteristics of norms. In I. D. Steiner & M. Fishbein (Eds.), *Current studies in social psychology* (pp. 301-308). New York: Holt, Rinehart & Winston.

Jackson, J. H., & Morgan, C. P. (1982). *Organization theory: A macro perspective for management* (2nd ed.). Englewood Cliffs, NJ: Prentice-Hall.

Jackson, S. E. (1983). Participation in decision-making as a strategy for reducing job related strain. *Journal of Applied Psychology, 68,* 3-19.

Jackson, S. E. (1984). Organizational practices for preventing burnout. In A. S. Sethi & R. S. Schuler (Eds.), *Handbook of organizational stress coping strategies* (pp. 89-111). Cambridge, MA: Ballinger.

Jackson, S. E., & Associates (1992). *Diversity in the workplace: Human resources initiatives.* New York: The Guilford Press.

Jackson, S. E., & Schuler, R. S. (1985). A meta-analysis and conceptual critique of research on role ambiguity and role conflict in work settings. *Organizational Behavior and Human Decision Processes, 36,* 16-28.

Jackson, S. E., & Schuler, R. S. (1990). Human resource planning. *American Psychologist, 45,* 223-239.

Jackson, S. E., Schwab, R. L, & Schuler, R. S. (1986). Toward an understanding of the burnout phenomenon. *Journal of Applied Psychology, 71,* 630-640.

Jackson, S. E., Turner, J. A., & Brief, A. P. (1987). Correlates of burnout among public service lawyers. *Journal of Occupational Behaviour, 8,* 339-349.

Jackson, S. E. , Zedeck, S., & Summers, E. (1985). Family life disruptions: Effects of job-induced structural and emotional interference. *Academy of Management Journal, 28,* 574-586.

Jacobs, T. O. (1971). *Leadership and exchange in formal organizations.* Alexandria, VA: Human Resources Research Organization.

Jahoda, M. (1982). *Employment and unemployment: A social-psychological analysis.* Cambridge, England: Cambridge University Press.

James, L., & James, L. R. (1989). Integrating work environment perceptions: Explorations in the measurement of meaning. *Journal of Applied Psychology, 74*, 739-751.

James, L., & Jones, A. P. (1974). Organizational climate: A review of theory and research. *Psychological Bulletin, 81*, 1096-1112.

James, L., & Tetrick, L. (1986). Confirmatory analytic tests of three causal models relating job perceptions to job satisfaction. *Journal of Applied Psychology, 71*, 77-82.

Janis, I. (1972). *Victims of groupthink*. Boston: Houghton Mifflin.

Janis, I. (1982). *Groupthink: Psychological studies of policy decisions and fiascoes* (2nd ed.). Boston: Houghton Mifflin.

Janis, I., & Mann, L. (1977). *Decision making*. New York: The Free Press.

Jansen, G. (1969). Effects of noise on physiological state. In W. D. Ward & J. E. Frick (Eds.), *Noise as a public health hazard* (ASHA Report No. 4). Washington, DC: American Speech and Hearing.

Janson, R., & Martin, J. K. (1982). Job satisfaction and age: A test of two views. *Social Forces, 60*, 1089-1102.

Jaques, E. (1963). *Equitable payment*. New York: John Wiley & Sons.

Jenkins, C. D., Zyzanski, S. J., & Rosenman, R. H. (1979). *The activity survey for health prediction*. Form N. New York: Psychological Corp.

Jenkins, W. (1947). The tactual discrimination of shapes for coding aircraft-type controls. In P. M. Fitts (Ed.), *Psychological research on equipment design*. (USAF Research Report No. 19).

Jensen, A. R. (1980). *Bias in mental testing*. New York: The Free Press.

Jick, T. D., & Mitz, L. F. (1985). Sex differences in work stress. *Academy of Management Review, 10*, 408-420.

Johnson, D. P. (1974). Social organization of an industrial work group: Emergence and adaptation to environmental change. *Sociological Quarterly, 15*, 109-126.

Johnson, D. W., Maruyama, G., Johnson, R., Nelson, D., & Skon, L. (1981). Effects of cooperative, competitive, and individualistic goal structures on achievement: A meta-analysis. *Psychological Bulletin, 89*, 47-62.

Johnston, W. B., & Packer, A. E. (1987). *Workforce 2000: Work and workers for the 21st century*. Indianapolis, IN: Hudson Institute.

Jones, J. W., & DuBois, D. (1987). A review of organizational stress assessment instruments. In L. R. Murphy & T. F. Schoenborn (Eds.), *Stress management in work settings* (pp. 47-66). Washington, DC: National Institute for Occupational Safety and Health.

Jorgenson, D., Dunnette, M., & Pritchard, R. (1973). Effects of the manipulation of a performance-reward contingency on behavior in a simulated work setting. *Journal of Applied Psychology, 57*, 271-280.

Jurgenson, C. E. (1949). A fallacy in the use of median scale values in employee checklists. *Journal of Applied Psychology, 33*, 56-58.

Jurgenson, C. E. (1950). Intercorrelations in merit rating traits. *Journal of Applied Psychology, 34*, 240-243.

Kabanoff, B. (1987). Predictive validity of the MODE conflict instrument. *Journal of Applied Psychology, 72,* 160-163.

Kabanoff, B. (1980). Work and nonwork: A review of models, methods, and findings. *Psychological Bulletin, 88,* 60-77.

Kabanoff, B., & O'Brien, G. E. (1980). Work and leisure: A task analysis. *Journal of Applied Psychology, 65,* 596-609.

Kahn, R. L. (1981). *Work and health.* New York: Wiley.

Kahn, R. L., Wolfe, D. M., Quinn, R. P., Snoek, J. D., & Rosenthal, R. A. (1964). *Organizational stress: Studies in role conflict and ambiguity.* New York: John Wiley & Sons.

Kane, J. S., & Lawler, E. E., III. (1978). Methods of peer assessment. *Psychological Bulletin, 85,* 555-586.

Kane, J. S., & Lawler, E. E., III. (1979). Performance appraisal effectiveness: Its assessment and determinants. In B. M. Staw (Ed.), *Research in organizational behavior* (Vol. 1, pp. 425-478). Greenwich, CT: JAI Press.

Kane, J. S., & Lawler, E. E., III. (1980). In defense of peer assessment: A rebuttal to Brief's critique. *Psychological Bulletin, 88,* 80-81.

Kanfer, R. (1991). Motivation theory and industrial and organizational psychology. In M. Dunnette & L. Hough (Eds.), *The handbook of industrial and organizational psychology* (2nd ed.), (Vol. 1, pp. 75-170). Palo Alto, CA: Consulting Psychologists Press.

Kanfer, R., & Ackerman, P. (1989). Motivation and cognitive abilities: An integrative/aptitude-treatment interaction approach to skill acquisition. *Journal of Applied Psychology, 74,* 657-690.

Kanner, A. D., Coyne, J. C., Schaefer, C., & Lazarus, R. S. (1981). Comparison of two modes of stress measurement: Daily hassels and uplifts versus major life events. *Journal of Behavioral Medicine, 4,* 1-39.

Kanter, R. M. (1989). *When giants learn to dance.* New York: Simon & Schuster.

Kanter, R. M. (1991, January-February). Championing change: An interview with Bell Atlantic's CEO Raymond Smith. *Harvard Business Review, 69,* 118-130.

Kantowitz, B., & Sorkin, R. (1983). *Human factors: Understanding people-system relationships.* New York: Wiley.

Kantowitz, B., & Sorkin, R. (1987). Allocation of functions. In G. Salvendy (Ed.), *Handbook of human factors* (pp. 355-370). New York: Wiley.

Kanungo, R. N. (1982). *Work alienation.* New York: Praeger.

Kaplan, A. (1964). *The conduct of inquiry.* Scranton, PA: Chandler.

Kaplan, R. E. (1977). The conspicuous absence of evidence that process consultation enhances task performance. *Journal of Applied Behavioral Science, 13,* 346-360.

Kasl, S. V. (1981). The challenge of studying the disease effects of stressful work conditions. *American Journal of Public Health, 71,* 682-684.

Katz, D., & Kahn, R. L. (1978). *The social psychology of organizations.* New York: John Wiley.

Katz, D., Maccoby, E., & Morse, N. C. (1950). *Productivity, supervision, and morale in an office situation*. Ann Arbor, MI: Institute for Social Research, University of Michigan.

Katz, R. (1982). The effects of group longevity on project communication and performance. *Administrative Science Quarterly, 27*, 81-104.

Katzell, R. (1983). Improving quality of work life. *American Psychologist, 38*, 126.

Katzell, R. (1986). *Essentials of work motivation theories*. Paper presented at the 21st International Congress of Psychology, Jerusalem, Israel.

Katzell, R., & Thompson, D. (1988). *An integrative theory of work motivation*. Unpublished manuscript.

Katzell, R., & Thompson, D. (1990). An integrative model of work attitudes, motivation, and performance. *Human Performance, 3*, 63-85.

Kavanagh, M. J. (1971). The content issue in performance appraisal: A review. *Personnel Psychology, 24*, 653-668.

Keller, R. T. (1989). A test of the path-goal theory of leadership with need for clarity as a moderator in research and development organizations. *Journal of Applied Psychology, 74*, 208-212.

Kelly, K., & Schine, E. (1992, June 29). How did Sears blow this gasket? *Business Week*, p. 38.

Kendler, H. H. (1987). *Historical foundations of modern psychology*. Pacific Grove, CA: Brooks/Cole.

Kerlinger, F. N. (1973). *Foundations of behavioral research* (2nd ed.). New York: Holt, Rinehart and Winston.

Kernan, M., & Lord, R. (1990). Effects of valence, expectancies, and goal-performance discrepancies in single and multiple goal environments. *Journal of Applied Psychology, 75*, 194-203.

Kerr, S., & Jermier, J. M. (1978). Substitutes for leadership: Their meaning and measurement. *Organizational Behavior and Human Performance, 22*, 375-403.

Khalil, T., & Kurucz, C. (1977). The influence of "biorhythm" on accident occurrence and performance. *Ergonomics, 20*, 389-398.

Kidron, A. G. (1977). The effectiveness of experiential methods in training and education: The case of role playing. *Academy of Management Review, 2*, 490-495.

King, L. M., Hunter, J. E., & Schmidt, F. L. (1980). Halo in multidimensional forced-choice performance evaluation scale. *Journal of Applied Psychology, 65*, 507-516.

King, M., Murray, M. A., & Atkinson, T. (1982). Background, personality, job characteristics, and satisfaction with work in a national sample. *Human Relations, 35*, 119-133.

Kingstrom, P. O., & Mainstone, L. E. (1985). An investigation of the rater-ratee acquaintance and rater bias. *Academy of Management Journal, 28*, 641-653.

Kipnis, D. (1976). *The powerholders*. Chicago: University of Chicago Press.

Kipnis, D., Schmidt, S. M., & Wilkinson, I. (1980). Intraorganizational influence tactics: Explorations in getting one's way. *Journal of Applied Psychology, 65*, 440-452.

Kirkpatrick, D. (1992, March 23). Here comes the payoff from PCs. *Fortune*, pp. 93-102.

Kirkpatrick, D. L. (1977). Evaluating training programs: Evidence versus proof. *Training and Development Journal, 31*, 9-12.

Kirmeyer, S. L., & Lin, T. (1987). Social support: Its relationship to observed communication with peers and superiors. *Academy of Management Journal, 30*, 138-151.

Kjellen, U. (1984). The deviation concept in occupational accident control: II. Data collection and assessment of significance. *Accident Analysis and Prevention, 16*, 307-323.

Klauss, R., & Bass, B. (1982). *Interpersonal communication in organizations.* New York: Academic Press.

Kleiman, L. S., & Faley, R. H. (1985). The implications of professional and legal guidelines for court decisions involving criterion-related validity: A review and analysis. *Personnel Psychology, 38*, 803-834.

Klein, G. A. (1990). Knowledge engineering: Beyond expert systems. *Information and Decision Technologies, 16*, 27-41.

Klemmer, E. J. (1971) Prelude to 2001: Explorations in human communication. (Reported in A. Chapanis, 1971). *American Psychologist, 26*, 949-962.

Klemmer, E. J., & Lockhead, G. R. (1962). Productivity and errors in two keying tasks: A field study. *Journal of Applied Psychology, 62*, 230-233.

Klimoski, R. J., & Brickner, M. (1987). Why do assessment centers work? The puzzle of assessment center validity. *Personnel Psychology, 40*, 243-260.

Klimoski, R. J., & Inks, L. (1990). Accountability forces in performance appraisal. *Organizational Behavior and Human Decision Processes, 45*, 194-208.

Klimoski, R. J., & London, M. (1974). Role of the rater in performance appraisal. *Journal of Applied Psychology, 59*, 445-451.

Klinger, E. (1966). Fantasy need achievement as a motivational construct. *Psychological Bulletin, 66*, 291-308.

Knutsson, A., Akerstedt, T., Jonsson, B., & Orth-Gomer, K. (1986, July 12). Increased risk of ischaemic heart disease in shift workers. *Lancet*, pp. 89-92.

Kobasa, S. C. (1979). Stressful life events, personality and health: An inquiry into hardiness. *Journal of Personality and Social Psychology, 37*, 1-11.

Kobasa, S. C., Maddi, S. R., & Kahn, S. (1982). Hardiness and health: A prospective study. *Journal of Personality and Social Psychology, 42*, 168-177.

Kobasa, S. C., Maddi, S. R., Pucetti, M. C., & Zola, M. C. (1985). Effectiveness of hardiness, exercise and social support as resources against illness. *Journal of Psychosomatic Research, 29*, 525-533.

Koch, J. L., & Steers, R. M. (1978). Job attachment, satisfaction, and turnover among public sector employees. *Journal of Vocational Behavior, 12*, 119-128.

Kochan, T. A., & Barocci, T. A. (1985). *Human resource management and industrial relations.* Boston: Little, Brown.

Kohlberg, L. (1968). The child as moral philosopher. *Psychology Today, 2*, 24-30.

Kolberg, W. H., & Smith, F. C. (1992, February 9). A new tract for blue-collar workers. *The New York Times*, p. F13.

Koller, M. (1983). Health risks related to shift work. *International Archives of Occupational and Environmental Health, 53,* 59-75.

Komaki, J. L. (1986). Toward effective supervision: An operant analysis and comparison of managers at work. *Journal of Applied Psychology, 71,* 270-279.

Komaki, J. L., Barwick, K., & Scott, L. (1978). A behavioral approach to occupational safety: Pinpointing and reinforcing safe performance in a food manufacturing plant. *Journal of Applied Psychology, 63,* 434-445.

Komaki, J. L., Coombs, T., & Schepman, S. (1991). Motivational implications of reinforcement theory. In R. Steers & L. Porter (Eds.), *Motivation and work behavior* (pp. 87-108). New York: McGraw-Hill.

Kopelman, R. E. (1986). Objective feedback. In E. Locke (Ed.), *Generalizing from laboratory to field settings* (pp. 119-147). Lexington, MA: Lexington Books.

Kozlowski, S. W. J., Kirsch, M. P., & Chao, G. T. (1986). Job knowledge, ratee familiarity, conceptual similarity, and halo error: An exploration. *Journal of Applied Psychology, 71,* 45-49.

Kraiger, K., Billings, R., & Isen, A. (1989). The influence of positive affective states on task perceptions and satisfaction. *Organizational Behavior and Human Decision Processes, 44,* 12-25.

Kraiger, K., & Ford, J. K. (1985). A meta-analysis of ratee race effects in performance ratings. *Journal of Applied Psychology, 70,* 56-65.

Kramer, A., Wickens, C. D., & Donchin, E. (1983). An analysis of the processing requirements of a complex perceptual-motor task. *Human Factors, 24,* 605.

Kunin, T. (1955). The construction of a new type of attitude measure. *Personnel Psychology, 8,* 65-77.

Kushnir, T., & Melamed, S. (1991). Work-load, perceived control, and psychological distress in type A/B industrial workers. *Journal of Organizational Behavior, 12,* 155-168.

Kyllonen, P. C. (1991). CAM: A theoretical framework for cognitive abilities measurement. In D. Detterman (Ed.), *Current topics in human intelligence: Theories of intelligence.* Norwood, NJ: Ablex.

Laabs, J. J. (1991, June). Team training goes outdoors. *Personnel Journal, 70,* 56-63.

Lacho, K. J., Stearns, G. K., & Villere, M. R. (1979). A study of employee appraisal systems of major cities in the United States. *Public Personnel Management, 8,* 111-125.

Lahey, M. A., & Saal, F. E. (1981). Evidence incompatible with a cognitive compatibility theory of rating behavior. *Journal of Applied Psychology, 6,* 706-715.

Lampert, A. (1986). Knowing, doing, and teaching multiplication. *Cognition and Instruction, 3,* 305-342.

Landy, F. J. (1978). An opponent process theory of job satisfaction. *Journal of Applied Psychology, 63,* 533-547.

Landy, F. J. (1986). Stamp collecting versus science: Validation as hypothesis testing. *American Psychologist, 41,* 1183-1192.

Landy, F. J. (1989). *Psychology of work behavior.* Pacific Grove, CA: Brooks/Cole.

Landy, F. J., Barnes, J. L., & Murphy, K. R. (1978). Correlates of perceived fairness and accuracy of performance evaluation. *Journal of Applied Psychology, 63,* 751-754.

Lane, D. (1982). Limited capacity, attention allocation, and productivity. In W. Howell & E. Fleishman (Eds.), *Human performance and productivity: Information processing and decision making* (Vol. 2, pp. 121-156). Hillsdale, NJ: L. Erlbaum.

Larson, J. R., Jr. (1989). The dynamic interplay between employees' feedback-seeking strategies and supervisors' delivery of performance feedback. *Academy of Management Review, 14,* 408-422.

Larson, J. R., Jr., & Callahan, C. (1990). Performance monitoring: How it affects work productivity. *Journal of Applied Psychology, 75,* 530-538.

Larson, J. R., Jr., Hunt, J. G., & Osborn, R. N. (1976). The great hi-hi leader behavior myth: A lesson from Occam's razor. *Academy of Management Journal, 19,* 628-642.

Larsson, G. (1987). Routinization of mental training in organizations: Effects on performance and well-being. *Journal of Applied Psychology, 72,* 88-96.

Latack, J. C. (1986). Coping with job stress: Measures and future directions for scale development. *Journal of Applied Psychology, 71,* 377-385.

Latham, G. P., Mitchell, T., & Dossett, D. (1978). Importance of participative goal setting and anticipated rewards on goal difficulty and job performance. *Journal of Applied Psychology, 63,* 163-171.

Latham, G. P., & Saari, L. M. (1979). Application of social learning theory to training supervisors through behavioral modeling. *Journal of Applied Psychology, 64,* 239-246.

Latham, G. P., & Steele, T. (1983). The motivational effects of participation versus goal setting on performance. *Academy of Management Journal, 26,* 406-417.

Latham, G. P., Steele, T., & Saari, L. (1982). The effects of participation and goal difficulty on performance. *Personnel Psychology, 35,* 677-686.

Latham, G. P., & Wexley, K. N. (1981). *Increasing productivity through performance appraisal.* Reading, MA: Addison-Wesley.

Latham, G. P., & Yukl, G. (1975). A review of research on the application of goal setting in organizations. *Academy of Management Journal, 18,* 824-845.

Lawler, E. E., III. (1968). Effects of hourly overpayment on productivity and work quality. *Journal of Personality and Social Psychology, 10,* 306-313.

Lawler, E. E., III. (1971). *Pay and organizational effectiveness: A psychological view.* New York: McGraw-Hill.

Lawler, E. E., III. (1973). *Motivation in work organizations.* Monterey, CA: Brooks/Cole.

Lawler, E.E., III, Koplin, C., Young, T., & Fadem, J. (1968). Inequity reduction over time in an induced over-payment situation. *Organizational Behavior and Human Performance, 3,* 253-268.

Lawler, E. E., III, & Ledford, G. E. (1985). Skill based pay. *Personnel, 62,* 30- 37.

Lawler, E. E., III, & Suttle, J. (1972). A causal correlational test of the need hierarchy concept. *Organizational Behavior and Human Performance, 7,* 265-287.

Lawler, E. E., III, & Suttle, J. (1973). Expectancy theory and job behavior. *Organizational Behavior and Human Performance, 9,* 482-503.

Lawrence, B. S. (1988). New wrinkles in the theory of age: Demography, norms, and performance ratings. *Academy of Management Journal, 31,* 309-337.

Lawrence, P. R. (1958). *The changing of organizational behavior patterns*. Boston: Division of Research, Harvard Business School.

Lawrence, P. R., & Lorsch, J. W. (1967). *Organization and environment: Managing differentiation and integration*. Boston: Harvard University Graduate School of Business.

Lawrence, P. R., & Lorsch, J. W. (1969). *Developing organizations: Diagnosis and action*. Reading, MA: Addison-Wesley.

Lawshe, C. H. (1975). A quantitative approach to content validity. *Personnel Psychology, 28*, 563-575.

Lazarus, R. S. (1966). *Psychological stress and the coping process*. New York: McGraw-Hill.

Lazer, R. I., & Wilkstrom, W. S. (1977). *Appraisal managerial performance: Current practices and future directions*. New York: Conference Board.

Ledvinka, J. (1982). *Federal regulation of personnel and human resource management*. Boston: Kent.

Lee, C. L. (1985). Increasing performance appraisal effectiveness: Matching task types, appraisal process, and rater training. *Academy of Management Review, 10*, 322-331.

Lee, C. L. (1987). Professionals in medical settings: The research evidence in the 1980's. *Journal of Organizational Behavior Management, 8*, 195-213.

Lee, R., & Klein, A. (1982). Structure of the Job Diagnostic Survey for public sector occupations. *Journal of Applied Psychology, 67*, 515-519.

Leeper, P. (1983). VDTs and vision: Workplace design is the key. *Human Factors Bulletin, 26*, 1-3.

Lefkowitz, J. (1970). Effect of training on the productivity and tenure of sewing machine operators. *Journal of Applied Psychology, 54*, 81-86.

Leiter, M. P. (1991). Coping patterns as predictors of burnout: The function of control and escapist coping patterns. *Journal of Organizational Behavior, 12*, 123-144.

Lemkau, J. P., Rafferty, J. P., Purdy, R. R., & Rudisill, J. R. (1987). Sex role stress and job burnout among family practice physicians. *Journal of Vocational Behavior, 31*, 81-90.

Lengel, R. H., & Daft, R. L. (1988). The selection of communication media as an executive skill. *The Academy of Management Executive, 11*, 225- 232.

Lent, R. H., Aurbach, H. A., & Levin, L. S. (1971). Predictors, criteria, and significant results. *Personnel Psychology, 24*, 519-533.

Leon, F. (1981). The role of positive and negative outcomes in the causation of motivational forces. *Journal of Applied Psychology, 66*, 45-53.

Leventhal, G. (1976). Fairness in social relationships. In J. Thibaut, J. Spence, & R. Carson (Eds.), *Contemporary topics in social psychology*. Morristown, NJ: General Learning Press.

Levin, I., & Stokes, J. P. (1989). Dispositional approach to job satisfaction: Role of negative affectivity. *Journal of Applied Psychology, 74*, 752-758.

Levin, L., Oler, J., & Whiteside, J. (1985). Injury incidence rates in a paint company on rotating production shifts. *Accident Analysis and Prevention, 17*, 67-74.

Levine, E. L., Ash, R. A., & Bennett, N. (1980). Exploratory comparative study of four job analysis methods. *Journal of Applied Psychology, 65*, 524-535.

Lewin, K. (1951). *Field theory in social science*. New York: Harper & Row.

Lewin, K., Lippitt, R., & White, R. K. (1939). Patterns of aggressive behavior in experimentally created climates. *Journal of Social Psychology, 10*, 271-299.

Lieberson, S., & O'Connor, J. F. (1972). Leadership and organizational performance: A study of large corporations. *American Sociological Review, 37*, 117-130.

Likert, R. (1961). *New patterns of management*. New York: McGraw-Hill.

Lincoln, J. R., & Miller, J. (1979). Work and friendship ties in organizations: A comparative analysis of relational networks. *Administrative Science Quarterly, 24*, 181-199.

Lindy, J. D., Green, B., & Patrick, M. (1980). The internship: Some disquieting findings. *American Journal of Psychiatry, 137, 1,* 76-79.

Lipman, J. (1991, August 27). As layoffs increase, so do age-bias suits. *The Wall Street Journal*, p. B8.

Lipset, S. M. (1992). The work ethic, then and now. *Journal of Labor Research, 13*, 45-54.

Locke, E. A. (1968). Toward a theory of task motivation and incentives. *Organizational Behavior and Human Performance, 3*, 157-189.

Locke, E. A. (1970). Job satisfaction and job performance: A theoretical analysis. *Organizational Behavior and Human Performance, 3*, 157-189.

Locke, E. A. (1975). Personnel attitudes and motivation. *Annual Review of Psychology, 26*, 457-480.

Locke, E. A. (1976). The nature and causes of job satisfaction. In M. D. Dunnette (Ed.), *Handbook of industrial and organizational psychology*. Skokie, IL: Rand McNally.

Locke, E. A. (Ed.). (1986). *Generalizing from laboratory to field settings*. Lexington, MA: D. C. Heath.

Locke, E. A. (1991). The motivation sequences, the motivation hub, and the motivation core. *Organizational Behavior and Human Decision Processes, 50*, 288-299.

Locke, E. A., & Latham, G. (1990). Work motivation and satisfaction: Light at the end of the tunnel. *Psychological Science, 1*, 240-246.

Locke, E. A., Shaw, K., Saari, L., & Latham, G. (1981). Goal setting and task performance: 1969-1980. *Psychological Bulletin, 90*, 125-152.

Lodahl, T. M., & Kejner, M. (1965). The definition and measurement of job involvement. *Journal of Applied Psychology, 49*, 24-33.

Loher, B., Noe, R., Moeller, N., & Fitzgerald, M. (1985). A meta-analysis of the relation of job characteristics to job satisfaction. *Journal of Applied Psychology, 70*, 280-289.

London, M., & Bassman, E. (1989). Retraining midcareer workers for the future workplace. In I. L. Goldstein (Ed.), *Training and development in organizations* (pp. 333-376). San Francisco: Jossey-Bass.

London, M., & Moses, J.L. (1990). The changing roles of the industrial/organizational psychologist: from analyst/technician to change agent/strategist. *The Industrial-Organizational Psychologist, 27*, 17-26.

Longenecker, C. O., Sims, H. P., Jr., & Gioia, D. A. (1987). Behind the mask: The politics of employee appraisal. *The Academy of Management Executive, 1*, 183-193.

Lopez, J. A. (1991, December 2). A wake-up call for Bell Atlantic. *Business Week*, pp. 133-135.

Lord, F. M. (1980). *Applications of item response theory to practical testing problems*. Hillsdale, NJ: L. Erlbaum.

Lord, R. G. (1985). An information processing approach to social perceptions, leadership, and behavioral measurement. In L. L. Cummings & B. M. Staw (Eds.), *Research in organizational behavior* (Vol. 7, pp. 87-128). Greenwich, CT: JAI Press.

Lord, R. G., Binning, J., Rush, M. C., & Thomas, J. C. (1978). Effect of performance and leader behavior on questionnaire ratings of leader behavior. *Organizational Behavior and Human Performance, 21*, 27-39.

Lord, R. G., De Vader, C. L., & Alliger, G. M. (1986). A meta-analysis of the relation between personality traits and leadership: An application of validity generalization procedures. *Journal of Applied Psychology, 71*, 402-410.

Lord, R. G., Foti, R. J., & De Vader, C. L. (1984). A test of leadership categorization theory: Internal structure, information processing, and leadership perceptions. *Organizational Behavior and Human Performance, 34*, 343-378.

Lord, R. G., Foti, R. J., & Phillips, J. S. (1982). A theory of leadership categorization. In J. G. Hunt, U. Sekaran, & C. Schriesheim (Eds.), *Leadership: Beyond establishment views* (pp. 104-121). Carbondale, IL: Southern Illinois University Press.

Lord, R. G., & Maher, K. J. (1990). Alternate information-processing models and their implications for theory, research, and practice. *Academy of Management Review, 15,* 9-28.

Lott, A. J., & Lott, B. E. (1965). Group cohesiveness as interpersonal attraction: A review of relationships with antecedent and consequent variables. *Psychological Bulletin, 64*, 259-309.

Lowe, G. S. (1987). *Women in the administrative revolution: The feminization of clerical work*. Oxford, England: Polity Press.

Lublin, J. S. (1991a, December 2). Sexual harassment is topping agenda in many executive education programs. *The Wall Street Journal*, pp. B1, B4.

Lublin, J. S. (1991b, December 12). Companies form teams to expedite decisions. *The Wall Street Journal*, p. B1.

Lublin, J. S. (1991c, December 30). Rights law to spur shifts in promotion. *The Wall Street Journal*, p. B1.

Lublin, J. S. (1992a, February 13). Trying to increase worker productivity, more employers alter management style. *The Wall Street Journal*, pp. B1, B7.

Lublin, J. S. (1992b, August 4). Companies use cross-cultural training to help their employees adjust abroad. *The Wall Street Journal*, p. B1.

Ludeman, K. (1989, November). From work ethic to worth ethic. *Executive Excellence, 6*, 7-8.

Lunneborg, P. W. (1990). *Women changing work*. New York: Greenwood Press.

Luthans, F., Paul, R., & Baker, D. (1981). An experimental analysis of the impact of contingent reinforcement on sales persons' performance behavior. *Journal of Applied Psychology, 66*, 314-323.

Mager, R. F. (1972). *Preparing instructional objectives*. Belmont, CA: Fearon.

Mager, R. F. (1973). *Measuring instructional intent*. Belmont, CA: Fearon.

Mager, R. F., & Pipe, P. (1970). *Analyzing performance problems*. Belmont, CA: Fearon.

Maier, N. R. F. (1958). *The appraisal interview*. New York: Wiley.

Main, J. (1989, November 6). How 21 men got global in 35 days. *Fortune*, pp. 71-76.

Main, J. (1992, October 19). How to steal the best ideas around. *Fortune*, pp. 102 - 106.

Mann, R. D. (1959). A review of the relationships between personality and performance in small groups. *Psychological Bulletin, 56*, 241-270.

Mannes, S. M., & Kintsch, W. (1987). Knowledge organization and text organization. *Cognition and Instruction, 4*, 91-115.

March, J. G., & Simon, H. A. (1958). *Organizations*. New York: Wiley.

Margolis, B. L., Kroes, W. H., & Quinn, R. P. (1974). Job stress: An unlisted occupational hazard. *Journal of Occupational Medicine, 16*, 659-661.

Mark, L., Warm, J., & Huston, R. (Eds.). (1987). *Ergonomics and human factors: Recent research*. New York: Springer-Verlag.

Marquardt, L. D., & McCormick, E. J. (1973). *Component analyses of attribute data based on the Position Analysis Questionnaire* (Report No. 2). Lafayette, IN: Occupational Research Center, Purdue University.

Marrow, A. J., Bowers, D. G., & Seashore, S. E. (1967). *Management by participation*. New York: Harper & Row.

Martocchio, J. J., & O'Leary, A. M. (1989). Sex differences in occupational stress: A meta-analytic review. *Journal of Applied Psychology, 74*, 495-501.

Marx, R. D. (1982). Relapse prevention of managerial training: A model for maintenance of behavior change. *Academy of Management Review, 7*, 433-441.

Maslach, C., & Jackson, S. E. (1981). The measurement of experienced burnout. *Journal of Occupational Behaviour, 2*, 99-113.

Maslow, A. (1943). A theory of motivation. *Psychological Review, 50*, 370-396.

Maslow, A. (1954). *Motivation and personality*. New York: Harper & Row.

Mason, J. W. (1975). A historical view of the stress field. *Journal of Human Stress, 1*, 22-36.

Masuch, M. (1985). Vicious circles in organizations. *Administrative Science Quarterly, 30*, 14-33.

Mathieu, J. E. (1991). A cross-level nonrecursive model of the antecedents of organizational commitment and job satisfaction. *Journal of Applied Psychology, 76*, 607-618.

Mathieu, J. E., & Farr, J. L. (1991). Further evidence for the discriminant validity of measures of organizational commitment, job involvement, and satisfaction. *Journal of Applied Psychology, 76*, 127-133.

Mathieu, J. E., & Kohler, S. S. (1990). A cross-level examination of group absence influences on individual absence. *Journal of Applied Psychology, 75*, 217-220.

Matsui, T., & Ikeda, H. (1976). Effectiveness of self-generation outcomes improving prediction in expectancy theory research. *Organizational Behavior and Human Performance, 17*, 289-298.

Matsui, T., Kakuyama, T., & Onglatco, L. U. (1987). Effects of goals and feedback on performance in groups. *Journal of Applied Psychology, 72*, 407-415.

Matsui, T., Okada, A., & Mizuguchi, R. (1981). Expectancy theory prediction of the goal theory postulate, "The harder the goals, the higher the performance." *Journal of Applied Psychology, 66*, 54-58.

Matthews, K. A. (1982). Psychological perspectives on the Type A behavior pattern. *Psychological Bulletin, 91*, 293-323.

McClelland, D. (1962). Business drive and national achievement. *Harvard Business Review, 40*, 99-112.

McClelland, D. (1965). Achievement motivation can be developed. *Harvard Business Review, 43*, 6-24.

McClelland, D. (1970). The two faces of power. *Journal of International Affairs, 24*, 29-47.

McClelland, D. (1985). *Human motivation.* Glenview, IL: Scott, Foresman.

McClelland, D., & Boyatzis, R. (1982). Leadership motive pattern and long-term success in management. *Journal of Applied Psychology, 67*, 737-743.

McClelland, D., & Burnham, D. H. (1976). Power is the great motivation. *Harvard Business Review, 54*, 100-110.

McConkie, M. (1979). A clarification of the goal setting and appraisal processes in MBO. *Academy of Management Review, 4*, 29-40.

McCormick, E. J. (1976). Job and task analyses. In M. D. Dunnette (Ed.), *Handbook of industrial and organizational psychology* (pp. 651-696). Chicago: Rand McNally.

McCormick, E. J., & Ilgen, D. (1980). *Industrial psychology* (7th ed.). Englewood Cliffs, NJ: Prentice-Hall.

McCormick, E. J., & Ilgen, D. (1985). *Industrial and organizational psychology* (8th ed.). Englewood Cliffs, NJ: Prentice-Hall.

McCormick, E. J., Jeanneret, P. R., & Mecham, R. C. (1972). A study of job characteristics and job dimensions as based on the Position Analysis Questionnaire (PAQ). *Journal of Applied Psychology, 56*, 347-368.

McEnery, J., & McEnery, J. M. (1987). Self-rating in management training needs assessment: A neglected opportunity? *Journal of Occupational Psychology, 60*, 49-60.

McEvoy, G. M., & Cascio, W. F. (1985). Strategies for reducing employee turnover: A meta-analysis. *Journal of Applied Psychology, 70*, 342-353.

McFarland, R. (1946). *Human factors in air transport design.* New York: McGraw-Hill.

McGee, G. W., & Ford, R. C. (1987). Two (or more?) dimensions of organizational commitment: Reexamination of the affective and continuance commitment scales. *Journal of Applied Psychology, 72*, 638-642.

McGehee, W., & Thayer, P. W. (1961). *Training in business and industry.* New York: John Wiley.

McGehee, W., & Tullar, W. L. (1978). A note on evaluating behavior modification and behavior modeling as industrial training techniques. *Personnel Psychology, 31*, 477-484.

McGrath, J. E. (1976). Stress and behavior in organizations. In M. D. Dunnette (Ed.), *Handbook of industrial and organizational psychology* (pp. 1351-1396). Chicago: Rand McNally.

McGregor, D. (1957). An uneasy look at performance appraisal. *Harvard Business Review*, *35*, 89-94.

McGregor, D. (1960). *The human side of enterprise*. New York: McGraw-Hill.

McKeithan, K. B., Reitman, J. S., Rueter, H. H., & Hirtle, S. C. (1981). Knowledge organization and skill differences in computer programmers. *Cognitive Psychology*, *13*, 307-325.

McKenna, J. F. (1992, January 20). Apprenticeships: Something old, something new, something needed. *Industry Week*, pp. 14-22.

McNeil, L. M. (1988). The politics of Texas school reform. In W. Boyd & C. Kerchner (Eds.), *Politics of Education Association Yearbook* (pp. 199-216). Washington, DC: The Falmer Press.

Mecham, R. C., & McCormick, E. J. (1969a, January). *The rated attribute requirements of job elements in the Position Analysis Questionnaire* (Report No. 1). Lafayette, IN: Occupational Research Center, Purdue University.

Mecham, R. C., & McCormick, E. J. (1969b, June). *The use in job evaluation of job elements and job dimensions based on the Position Analysis Questionnaire* (Report No. 3). Lafayette, IN: Occupational Research Center, Purdue University.

Mechanic, D. (1962). *Students under stress*. Glencoe, IL: The Free Press.

Meese, G. B., Lewis, M. I., Wyon, D. P., & Kok, R. (1984). A laboratory study of the effects of moderate thermal stress on the performance of factory workers. *Ergonomics, 27*, 19-43.

Meglino, B.M., & DeNisi, A.S. (1987). Realistic job previews: some thoughts on their more effective use in managing the flow of human resources. *Human Resources Planning*, *10*, 157-167.

Meindl, J. R., Ehrlich, S. B., & Dukerich, J. M. (1985). The romance of leadership. *Administrative Science Quarterly*, *30*, 78-102.

Meister, D. (1985). *Behavioral analysis and measurement methods*. New York: Wiley.

Mento, A., Cartledge, N., & Locke, E. (1980). Maryland vs. Michigan vs. Minnesota: Another look at the relationship of expectancy and goal difficulty to task performance. *Organizational Behavior and Human Performance*, *25*, 419-440.

Mento, A., Steel, R., & Karren, R. (1987). A meta-analytic study of the effects of goal setting on task performance: 1966-1984. *Organizational Behavior and Human Decision Processes*, *39*, 52-83.

Meyer, H., Kay, E., & French, J. (1965). Split roles in performance appraisal. *Harvard Business Review*, *35*, 89-94.

Meyer, J. P., Paunonen, S. V., Gellatly, I. R., Goffin, R. D., & Jackson, D. N. (1989). Organizational commitment and job performance: It's the nature of the commitment that counts. *Journal of Applied Psychology*, *74*, 152-156.

Michael, J., & Meyerson, L. (1962). A behavioral approach to counseling and guidance. *Harvard Educational Review*, *32*, 382-402.

Milbank, D. (1991, November 7). Changes at Alcoa point up challenges and benefits of decentralized authority. *The Wall Street Journal*, p. B1.

Miles, R. H. (1980). *Macro organizational behavior*. Santa Monica, CA: Goodyear.

Milkovich, G. T., & Newman, J. M. (1984). *Compensation*. Plano, TX: Business Publications.

Miller, G. (1956). The magical number seven, plus or minus two. *Psychological Review, 63*, 81-97.

Miller, J. G. (1960). Information input, overload, and psychopathology. *American Journal of Psychiatry, 116*, 695-704.

Miller, L. E., & Grush, J. E. (1988). Improving predictions in expectancy theory research: Effects of personality, expectancies, and norms. *Academy of Management Journal, 31*, 107-122.

Miller, L. K., & Hamblin, R. L. (1963). Interdependence, differential rewarding and productivity. *American Sociological Review, 28*, 768-778.

Miner, J. B. (1978). Twenty years of research on role motivation theory of managerial effectiveness. *Personnel Psychology, 31*, 739-760.

Minors, D. S., & Waterhouse, J. M. (1985). Introduction to circadian rhythms. In S. Folkard & T. Monk (Eds.), *Hours of work: Temporal factors on work-scheduling*. Chichester, England: John Wiley & Sons.

Minstrell, J. (1989). Teaching science for understanding. In L. B. Resnick & L. E. Kopfer (Eds.), *Toward the thinking curriculum: Current cognitive research*. Alexandria, VA: The Association for Supervision and Curriculum Development.

Mintzberg, H. (1973). *The nature of managerial work*. New York: Harper & Row.

Misumi, J., & Peterson, M. F. (1985). The performance-maintenance (PM) theory of leadership: Review of a Japanese research program. *Administrative Science Quarterly, 30*, 198-223.

Mitchell, T. R. (1974). Expectancy models of job satisfaction, occupational preference and effort: A theoretical, methodological, and empirical appraisal. *Psychological Bulletin, 81*, 1053-1077.

Mitchell, T. R., & Kalb, L. (1982). Effects of job experience on supervisor attributions for a subordinate's poor performance. *Journal of Applied Psychology, 67*, 181-188.

Mitchell, T. R., Larson, J. R., & Green, S. G. (1977). Leader behavior, situational moderators, and group performance: An attributional analysis. *Organizational Behavior and Human Performance, 18*, 254-268.

Mitchell, T. R., & Silver, W. (1990). Individual and group goals when workers are interdependent: Effects on task strategies and performance. *Journal of Applied Psychology, 75*, 185-193.

Mitler, M., Carskaden, M., Czeisler, C., Dement, W., Dinges, D., & Graeber, C. (1988). Catastrophes, sleep, and public policy: Consensus report. *Sleep, 11*, 100-109.

Mobley, W. H. (1977). Intermediate linkages in the relationship between job satisfaction and employee turnover. *Journal of Applied Psychology, 62*, 237-240.

Mobley, W. H., Horner, S. O., & Hollingsworth, A. T. (1978). An evaluation of precursors of hospital employee turnover. *Journal of Applied Psychology, 63*, 408-414.

Mobley, W. H., & Locke, E. A. (1970). The relationship of value importance to satisfaction. *Organizational Behavior and Human Performance, 5*, 463-483.

Moch, M. K. (1980). Racial differences in job satisfaction: Testing four common explanations. *Journal of Applied Psychology, 65*, 299-306.

Mohr, D. L., & Clemmer, D. I. (1988). The "accident prone" worker: An example from heavy industry. *Accident Analysis and Prevention, 20*, 123-127.

Monat, A., & Lazarus, R. (1985). *Stress and coping: An anthology* (2nd ed.). New York: Columbia University Press.

Monk, T. H. (1988). Coping with the stress of shiftwork. *Work & Stress, 2*, 169-172.

Monk, T. H. (1989). Human factors implications of shiftwork. *International Review of Ergonomics, 2*, 111-128.

Monk, T. H., & Embrey, D. E. (1981). A field study of circadian rhythms in actual and interpolated task performance. In A. Reinberg, N. Vieux, & P. Andlauer (Eds.), *Night and shift work: Biological and social aspects* (pp. 367-374). Oxford, England: Pergamon Press.

Monk, T. H., & Folkard, S. (1985). Shiftwork and performance. In S. Folkard & T. Monk (Eds.), *Hours of work: Temporal factors in work-scheduling* (pp. 239-252). Chichester, England: John Wiley & Sons.

Moore, M. L., & Dutton, P. (1978). Training needs analysis: Review and critique. *Academy of Management Review, 3*, 532-545.

Morrison, A., & Von Glinow, M. A. (1990). Women and minorities in management. *American Psychologist, 45*, 200-208.

Morrow, P. C., & Goetz, J. F., Jr. (1988). Professionalism as a form of work commitment. *Journal of Vocational Behavior, 32*, 92-111.

Morrow, P. C., & McElroy, J. C. (1987). Work commitment and job satisfaction over three career stages. *Journal of Vocational Behavior, 30*, 330-346.

Morrow, P. C., & Wirth, R. E. (1989). Work commitment among salaried professionals. *Journal of Vocational Behavior, 34*, 40-56.

Moses, S. (1990). Diversity of workers challenges I/O field. *APA Monitor, 21*, pp. 7, 25.

Mossholder, K., & Arvey, R. D. (1984). Synthetic validity: a conceptual and comparative review. *Journal of Applied Psychology, 69*, 322-333.

Motowidlo, S. J., Packard, J. S., & Manning, M. R. (1986). Occupational stress: Its causes and consequences for job performance. *Journal of Applied Psychology, 71*, 618-629.

Mount, M. K. (1984). Psychometric properties of subordinate ratings of managerial performance. *Personnel Psychology, 37*, 687-702.

Moussa-Hamouda, E., & Mourant, R. (1981). Vehicle fingertip reach controls: Human factors recommendations. *Ergonomics, 12*, 66-70.

Mowday, R. T. (1991). Equity theory predictions of behavior. In R. Steers & L. Porter (Eds.), *Motivation and work behavior* (pp. 111-130). New York: McGraw-Hill.

Mowday, R. T., Porter, L. W., & Steers, R. M. (1982). *Employee-organization linkages: The psychology of commitment, absenteeism, and turnover.* New York: Academic Press.

Mowday, R. T., Steers, R. M., & Porter, L. W. (1979). The measurement of organizational commitment. *Journal of Vocational Behavior, 14*, 224-247.

Mudrack, P. E. (1989). Defining group cohesiveness: A legacy of confusion? *Small Group Behavior, 20*, 37-49.

Mulder, G., & Mulder L. J. (1981). Information processing and cardiovascular control. *Psychophysiology, 18*, 392-401.

Mumford, M. D., & Owens, W. A. (1987). Methodology review: Principle, procedures, and findings in the application of background data measures. *Applied Psychological Measurement, 11*, 1-31.

Mumford, M. D., Weeks, J. L., Harding, F. D., & Fleishman, E. A. (1988). Relations between student characteristics, course content, and training outcomes: An integrative modeling effort. *Journal of Applied Psychology, 73,* 443-456.

Munger, S. (1962). *An index of electronic equipment operability: Evaluation booklet.* Washington, DC: American Institutes for Research.

Munger, S., Smith, R., & Payne, D. (1962). *An index of electronic equipment operability: Data store.* Pittsburgh: American Institute for Research.

Munsterberg, H. (1913). *Psychology and industrial efficiency.* New York: Houghton Mifflin.

Murphy, K. R. (1983). Fooling yourself with cross-validation: single sample designs. *Personnel Psychology, 36,* 111-118.

Murphy, K. R., & Balzer, W. K. (1986). Systematic distortions in memory-based behavior ratings and performance evaluations: Consequences for rating accuracy. *Journal of Applied Psychology, 71,* 39-44.

Murphy, K. R., & Davidshofer, C. O. (1991). *Psychological testing* (2nd ed.). Englewood Cliffs, NJ: Prentice-Hall.

Murphy, K. R., Gannett, B. A., Herr, B. M., & Chen, J. A. (1986). Effects of subsequent performance on evaluations of previous performance. *Journal of Applied Psychology, 71,* 427-431.

Murphy, K. R., Garcia, M., Kerkar, S., Martin, C., & Balzer, W. K. (1982). Relationship between observational accuracy and accuracy in evaluating performance. *Journal of Applied Psychology, 67,* 320-325.

Murphy, K. R., Herr, B. M., Lockhart, M. C., & Maguire, E. (1986). Evaluating the performance of paper people. *Journal of Applied Psychology, 71,* 654-661. (Cited on p. 72.)

Murray, H. J. (1938). *Explorations in personality.* New York: Oxford University Press.

Nadler, D. A. (1979). The effects of feedback on task group behavior: A review of the experimental research. *Organizational Behavior and Human Performance, 23,* 309-338.

Naisbitt, J. (1982). *Megatrends.* New York: Warner Books.

Naismith, D. (1975). *Stress among managers as a function of organizational change.* Unpublished doctoral dissertation, George Washington University, Washington, DC.

Nash, A. N., Muczyk, J. P., & Vettori, F. L. (1971). The relative practical effectiveness of programmed instruction. *Personnel Psychology, 24,* 397-418.

National Commission on Excellence in Education. (1983). *A Nation at Risk.* Washington, DC: U.S. Government Printing Office.

National Safety Council (1989). *Accident facts.* Chicago: Author.

Naylor, J. C., Pritchard, R., & Ilgen, D. (1980). *A theory of behavior in organizations.* New York: Academic Press.

Naylor, J.C., & Shine, L.C. (1965). A table for determining the increase in mean criterion score obtained using a selection device. *Journal of Industrial Psychology, 3,* 33-42.

Near, J. P., Smith, C. A., Rice, R. W., & Hunt, R. G. (1984). A comparison of work and nonwork predictors of life satisfaction. *Academy of Management Journal, 27,* 184-190.

Neilson, E. H. (1972). Understanding and managing intergroup conflict. In J. W. Lorsch and P. R. Lawrence (Eds.), *Managing group and intergroup relations* (pp. 329-343). Homewood, IL: Irwin and Dorsey.

Nelson-Horchler, J. (1991, May 6). The myth of the shiftless U.S. worker. *Industry Week*, pp. 42-44.

Netemeyer, R., Johnston, M., & Burton, S. (1990). Analysis of role conflict and role ambiguity in a structural equations framework. *Journal of Applied Psychology*, *75*, 148-157.

Neuman, G. A., Edwards, J. E., & Raju, N. S. (1989). Organizational development interventions: A meta-analysis of their effects on satisfaction and other attitudes. *Personnel Psychology*, *42*, 461-489.

Newbold, E. (1926). *A contribution to the study of the human factor in the causation of accidents* (Report No. 34). London: Industrial Health Research Board.

Nichols, R. G. (1962). Listening is good business. *Management of Personnel Quarterly*, *1*, 2-10.

Nicholson, N., Brown, C. A., & Chadwick-Jones, J. K. (1976). Absence from work and job satisfaction. *Journal of Applied Psychology*, *61*, 728-737.

Noe, R. A. (1986). Trainees' attributes and attitudes: Neglected influences on training effectiveness. *Academy of Management Review*, *11*, 736-749.

Noe, R. A. (1988). Women and mentoring: A review and research agenda. *Academy of Management Review*, *13*, 65-78.

Noe, R. A., & Schmitt, N. (1986). The influence of trainee attitudes on training effectiveness: Test of a model. *Personnel Psychology*, *39*, 497-523.

Noe, R. A., & Steffy, B. D. (1987). The influence of individual characteristics and assessment center evaluation on career exploration behavior and job involvement. *Journal of Vocational Behavior*, *30*, 187-202.

Nord, W. R. (1980). Toward an organizational psychology for organizational psychology. *Professional Psychology*, *11*, 531-542.

Nord, W. R., & Costigan, R. (1973). Worker adjustment to the four-day week: A longitudinal study. *Journal of Applied Psychology*, *58*, 60-66.

Norman, C. A., & Zawacki, R. A. (1991, December). Team appraisals—Team approach. *Quality Digest*, *11*, 68-75.

Norman, D. A. (1984). Stages and levels in human-machine interaction. *International Journal of Man Machine Studies*, *21*, 365-375.

Norman, D. A. (1988). *The psychology of everyday things*. New York: Basic Books.

Nunnally, J. C. (1978). *Psychometric theory*. New York: McGraw-Hill.

Nystrom, P. C. (1978). Managers and the hi-hi leader myth. *Academy of Management Journal*, *21*, 325-331.

Oborne, D. J. (1987). *Ergonomics at work* (2nd ed.). New York: John Wiley & Sons.

O'Brien, G. E., Fiedler, F. E., & Hewett, T. (1971). The effects of programmed culture training upon the performance of volunteer medical teams in Central America. *Human Relations*, *24*, 209-231.

Offerman, L. R., & Gowing, M. K. (1990). Organizations of the future. *American Psychologist, 45*, 95-108.

Offerman, L. R., & Gowing, M. K. (1992). Personnel selection in the future: The impact of changing demographics and the nature of work. In N. Schmitt & W. C. Borman (Eds.), *Personnel selection in organizations* (pp. 385-417). San Francisco: Jossey-Bass.

Office of Technology Assessment, U.S. Congress. (1991, September). *Biological rhythms: Implications for the worker* (OTA-BA-463). Washington, DC: U.S. Government Printing Office.

Ogden, G., Levine, J., & Eisner, E. (1979). Measurement of workload by secondary tasks. *Human Factors, 21*, 529-548.

O'Keefe, J. (1993). Disability, discrimination and the Americans with Disabilities Act. *Consulting Psychology Journal: Practice and Research.*

Ondrack, D. A. (1974). Defense mechanisms and the Herzberg theory. *Academy of Management Journal, 17*, 79-89.

Ones, D., Viswesvaran, C., & Schmidt, F. L. (in press). Comprehensive meta-analysis of integrity test validities: Findings and implications. *Journal of Applied Psychology, 78*, 679-703.

O'Reilly, C. A., III, & Puffer, S. (1989). The impact of rewards and punishments in a social context: A laboratory and field experiment. *Journal of Occupational Psychology, 62*, 41-53.

O'Reilly, C. A., III, & Roberts, K. (1974). Information filtration in organizations: Three experiments. *Organizational Behavior and Human Performance, 11*, 253-265.

O'Reilly, C. A., III, & Roberts, K. H. (1977). Task group structure, communication, and effectiveness in three organizations. *Journal of Applied Psychology, 62*, 674-681.

Organ, D. W. (1988). A restatement of the satisfaction-performance hypothesis. *Journal of Management, 14*, 547-557.

Orpen, C. (1978). Work and nonwork satisfaction: A causal correlational analysis. *Journal of Applied Psychology, 63*, 530-532.

Ostroff, C., & Ford, J. K. (1989). Assessing training needs: Critical levels of analysis. In I. L. Goldstein (Ed.), *Training and development in organizations* (pp. 25-62). San Francisco: Jossey-Bass.

Ouchi, W. (1981). *Theory Z.* Reading, MA: Addison-Wesley.

Ouchi, W., & Maguire, M. A. (1975). Organizational control: Two functions. *Administrative Science Quarterly, 20*, 559-570.

Ouchi, W., & Wilkins, A. L. (1985). Organizational culture. *Annual Review of Sociology, 11*, 457-483.

Parkes, K. R. (1990). Coping, negative affectivity, and the work environment: Additive and interactive predictors of mental health. *Journal of Applied Psychology, 75*, 399-409.

Pasmore, W., Francis, C., Halderman, J., & Shani, A. (1982). Sociotechnical systems: A North American reflection on empirical studies of the 70s. *Human Relations, 35*, 1179-1204.

Patten, T. H., Jr., & Stermer, E. P. (1969). Training foremen in work standards. *Training and Development Journal, 23*, 25-37.

Pavlov, I. (1902). *The work of the digestive glands* (W. H. Thompson, Trans.). London: Charles Griffin.

Payne, R. (1970). Factor analysis of a Maslow-type need satisfaction questionnaire. *Personnel Psychology, 23,* 251-268.

Pearlman, K. (1980). Job families: A review and discussion of their implications for personnel selection. *Psychological Bulletin, 87,* 1-27.

Penley, L. E., & Hawkins, B. (1985). Studying interpersonal communication in organizations: A leadership application. *Academy of Management Journal, 28,* 309-326.

Perrow, C. (1973). The short and glorious history of organizational theory. *Organizational Dynamics, 2,* 2-15.

Perrow, C. (1986). *Complex organizations: A critical essay.* Glenview, IL: Scott, Foresman.

Pervin, L. A. (1985). Personality: Current controversies, issues, and directions. *Annual Review of Psychology, 36,* 83-114.

Peters, L. H., Hartke, D. D., & Pohlmann, J. T. (1985). Fiedler's contingency theory of leadership: An application of the meta-analysis procedures of Schmidt and Hunter. *Psychological Bulletin, 97,* 274-285.

Peters, T. J., & Waterman, R. H. (1982). *In search of excellence: Lessons from America's best run companies.* New York: Harper & Row.

Pfeffer, J. (1977). The ambiguity of leadership. *Academy of Management Review, 2,* 104-112.

Pinder, C. (1984). *Work motivation.* Glenview, IL: Scott, Foresman.

Pinder, C. (1991). Valence-instrumentality-expectancy theory. In R. Steers & L. Porter (Eds.), *Motivation and work behavior* (pp. 144-163). New York: McGraw-Hill.

Pinder, C., & Walter, G. A. (1984). Personnel transfers and employee development. In K. M. Rowland & G. R. Ferris (Eds.), *Research in Personnel and Human Resources Management* (Vol. 2, pp. 186-218). Greenwich, CT: JAI.

Podsakoff, P. M., & Farh, J. (1989). Effects of feedback sign and credibility on goal setting and task performance. *Organizational Behavior and Human Decision Processes, 44,* 45-67.

Podsakoff, P. M., MacKenzie, S. B., Moorman, R. H., & Fetter, R. (1990). Transformation leader behaviors and their effects on followers' trust in leader, satisfaction, and organizational citizenship behaviors. *Leadership Quarterly, 1,* 107-142.

Podsakoff, P. M., & Schriesheim, C. A. (1985). Field studies of French and Raven's bases of power: Critique, reanalysis, and suggestions for future research. *Psychological Bulletin, 97,* 387-411.

Podsakoff, P. M., Todor, W. D., Grover, R. A., & Huber, V. L. (1984). Situational moderators of leader reward and punishment behaviors: Fact or fiction? *Organizational Behavior and Human Performance, 34,* 21-63.

Point counterpoint on I.B.M. (1992, April 2). *The New York Times,* p. F16.

Pokorney, J., Gilmore, D., & Beehr, T. (1980). Job Diagnostics Survey dimensions: Moderating effect of growth needs and correspondence with dimensions of job rating form. *Organizational Behavior and Human Performance, 26,* 222-237.

Pond, S. B., III, & Geyer, P. D. (1987). Employee age as a moderator of the relation between perceived work alternatives and job satisfaction. *Journal of Applied Psychology, 72,* 552-557.

Pond, S. B., III, & Green, S. B. (1983). The relationship between job and marriage satisfaction within and between spouses. *Journal of Occupational Behaviour, 4*, 145-155.

Porter, L. W. (1962). Job attitudes in management: I. Perceived deficiencies in need fulfillment as a function of job level. *Journal of Applied Psychology, 46*, 375-384.

Porter, L. W., & Lawler, E. E., III. (1968). *Managerial attitudes and performance*. Homewood, IL: Dorsey.

Porter, L. W., Lawler, E. E., III, & Hackman, J. R. (1975). *Behavior in organizations*. New York: McGraw-Hill.

Potter, E. E. (1989). Employer's burden of proof may be reduced in testing cases. *The Industrial-Organizational Psychologist, 26*, 43-47.

Power, W., & Siconolfi, M. (1991, December 4). Wall street firms turn up heat on their marginal stockbrokers. *The Wall Street Journal*, pp. C1, C16.

Premack, S. L., & Wanous, J. P. (1985). A meta-analysis of realistic job preview experiences. *Journal of Applied Psychology, 70*, 706-719.

Pressey, S. L. (1950). Development and appraisal of devices providing immediate automatic scoring of objective tests and concomitant self-instruction. *Journal of Applied Psychology, 29*, 417-447.

Preston, R. (1991). *American Steel*. New York: Prentice Hall.

Prien, E. P., & Hughes, G. L. (1987). The effect of quality control revisions on mixed standard scale rating errors. *Personnel Psychology, 40*, 815-823.

Prince, J. B., & Lawler, E. E. (1986). Does salary discussion hurt the developmental performance appraisal? *Organizational Behavior and Human Decision Processes, 37*, 357-375.

Pritchard, R., Campbell, K., & Campbell, D. (1977). The effects of extrinsic financial rewards on intrinsic motivation. *Journal of Applied Psychology, 62*, 9-15.

Pritchard, R., Dunnette, M., & Jorgenson, D. (1972). Effects of perceptions of equity on worker performance and satisfaction. *Journal of Applied Psychology, 56*, 75-94.

Pritchard, R., Hollenbeck, J., & DeLeo, P. (1980). The effects of continuous and partial schedules of reinforcement on effort, performance, and satisfaction. *Organizational Behavior and Human Performance, 25*, 336-353.

Pritchard, R., Jones, S. D., Roth, P. L., Stuebing, K. K., & Ekeberg, S. E. (1988). Effects of group feedback, goal setting, and incentives on organizational productivity. *Journal of Applied Psychology, 73*, 337-358.

Pritchard, R., Leonard, D., VonBergen, C., & Kirk, R. (1976). The effects of varying schedules of reinforcement on human task performance. *Organizational Behavior and Human Performance, 16*, 205-230.

Puffer, S. M. (1987). Prosocial behavior, noncompliant behavior, and work performance among commission salespeople. *Journal of Applied Psychology, 72*, 615-621.

Pulakos, E., White, L. A., Oppler, S. H., & Borman, W. C. (1989). Examination of race and sex effects on performance ratings. *Journal of Applied Psychology, 74*, 770-780.

Putka, G. (1991, June 5). Forceful educator gets teachers and children to be more productive. *The Wall Street Journal*, p. A1.

Quick, J. C., & Quick, J. D. (1984). *Organizational stress and preventive management*. New York: McGraw-Hill.

Quinn, J. B., & Gagnon, C. E. (1986). Will services follow manufacturing into decline? *Harvard Business Review*, *64*, 95-103.

Quinn, R. P., & Shepard, L. J. (1974). *The 1972-73 quality of employment survey.* Ann Arbor, MI: Survey Research Center, Institute for Social Research, University of Michigan.

Rabinowitz, S., & Hall, D. T. (1977). Organizational research on job involvement. *Psychological Bulletin*, *84*, 265-288.

Rafaeli, A. (1986). Employee attitudes toward working with computers. *Journal of Occupational Behaviour*, *7*, 89-106.

Ragins, B. R., & Cotton, J. L. (1991). Easier said than done: Gender differences in perceived barriers to gaining a mentor. *The Academy of Management Journal*, *34*, 939-952.

Ragins, B. R., & Sundstrom, E. (1989). Gender and power in organizations: A longitudinal perspective. *Psychological Bulletin*, *105*, 51-88.

Rahim, M. A. (1983) A measure of styles of handling interpersonal conflict. *Academy of Management Journal*, *26*, 368-376.

Ralston, D., Anthony, W., & Gustafson, D. (1985). Employees may love flextime, but what does it do to the organization's productivity? *Journal of Applied Psychology*, *70*, 272-279.

Rambo, W. W. (1982). *Work and organizational behavior*. New York: Holt, Rinehart and Winston.

Ramos, A. A. (1975). The relationship of sex and ethnic background to job related stress of research and development professionals. *Dissertation Abstracts International*, *9*, 1862A.

Ramsey, J. (1978, May). *Ergonomic support of consumer product safety*. Paper presented at the American Industrial Hygiene Association Conference, Los Angeles.

Randall, D. M. (1987). Commitment and the organization: The organization man revisited. *Academy of Management Journal*, *12*, 460-471.

Randolph, W. A., & Posner, B. Z. (1979). Designing meaningful learning situations: A contingency decision-tree approach. *Academy of Management Review*, *4*, 459-467.

Rauschenberger, J., Schmitt, N., & Hunter, J. (1980). A test of the need hierarchy concept by a Markov model of change in need strength. *Administrative Science Quarterly*, *25*, 654-670.

Read, W. (1962). Upward communication in industrial hierarchies. *Human Relations*, *15*, 3-16.

Reason, J. (1974). *Man in motion: The psychology of travel*. London: Weidenfeld and Nicholson.

Rebello, K., & Schwartz, E. I. (1992, February 24). Microsoft: Bill Gate's baby is on top of the world. Can it stay there? *Business Week,* pp. 60-64.

Reichers, A. E. (1985). A review and reconceptualization of organizational commitment. *Academy of Management Review*, *10*, 465-476.

Reilly, R. R., Brown, B., Blood, M. R., & Malatesta, C. Z. (1981). The effects of realistic previews: A study and discussion of the literature. *Personnel Psychology*, *34*, 823-834.

Reilly, R. R., & Israelski, E. W. (1988). Development and validation of minicourses in the telecommunication industry. *Journal of Applied Psychology, 73*, 721-726.

Reilly, R. R., & Manese, W. R. (1979). The validation of a minicourse for telephone company switching technicians. *Personnel Psychology, 32*, 83-90.

Reilly, R. R., Tenopyr, M. L., & Sperling, S. M. (1979). Effects of job previews on job acceptance and survival of telephone operator candidates. *Journal of Applied Psychology, 64*, 218-220.

Rentsch, J. R. (1990). Climate and culture: Interaction and qualitative differences in organizational meanings. *Journal of Applied Psychology, 75*, 668-681.

Reynolds, R., White, R., & Hilgendorf, R. (1972). Detection and recognition of colored signal lights. *Human Factors, 14*, 227-236.

Rhodes, S. R. (1983). Age-related differences in work attitudes and behavior: A review and conceptual analysis. *Psychological Bulletin, 93*, 328-367.

Rice, F. (1991, June 3). Champions of communication. *Fortune*, pp. 111-120.

Rice, R. W., Gentile, D. A., & McFarlin, D. B. (1991). Facet importance and job satisfaction. *Journal of Applied Psychology, 76*, 31-39.

Rice, R. W., McFarlin, D. B., & Bennett, D. E. (1989). Standards of comparison and job satisfaction. *Journal of Applied Psychology, 74*, 591-598.

Rice, R. W., Near, J. P., & Hunt, R. G. (1980). The job satisfaction/life satisfaction relationship: A review of empirical research. *Basic and Applied Social Psychology, 1*, 37-64.

Rigdon, J. E. (1990, December 5). More firms try to reward good service, but incentives may backfire in long run. *The Wall Street Journal*, pp. B1, B4.

Riley, M. W., & Cochran, D. J. (1984). Dexterity performance and reduced ambient temperature. *Human Factors, 26*, 207-214.

Rizzo, J.R., House, R., & Lirtzman, S. (1970). Role conflict and role ambiguity in complex organizations. *Administrative Science Quarterly, 15,* 150-163,

Robbins, S. P. (1974). *Managing organizational conflict: A nontraditional approach.* Englewood Cliffs, NJ: Prentice-Hall.

Robbins, S. P. (1990). *Organization theory: The structure and design of organizations.* Englewood Cliffs, NJ: Prentice-Hall.

Roberts, K., & Glick, W. (1981). The job characteristics approach to task design: A critical review. *Journal of Applied Psychology, 66*, 193-217.

Robertson, I. T., & Kandola, R. S. (1982). Work sample tests: Validity, adverse impact and applicant reaction. *Journal of Occupational Psychology, 55*, 171-183.

Robinson, D. D., Wahlstrom, O. W., & Mecham, R. C. (1974). Comparison of job evaluation methods: A "policy capturing" approach using the Position Analysis Questionnaire. *Journal of Applied Psychology, 58*, 633-637.

Rodgers, R., & Hunter, J. E. (1991). Impact of management by objectives on organizational productivity. *Journal of Applied Psychology, 76*, 322-336.

Roethlisberger, F. J., & Dickson, W. J. (1939). *Management and the worker*. Cambridge, MA: Harvard University Press.

Rogelberg, S. G., Barnes-Farrell, J. L., & Lowe, C. A. (1992). The stepladder technique: An alternative group structure facilitating effective group decision making. *Journal of Applied Psychology, 77*, 571-587.

Rogers, C., & Skinner, B. (1956). Some issues concerning the control of human behavior: A symposium. *Science, 124*, 1057-1066.

Rohan, T. M. (1991, January 21). Maverick remakes old-line steel. *Industry Week*, pp. 26-36.

Romzek, B. S. (1989). Personal consequences of employee commitment. *Academy of Management Journal, 32*, 649-661.

Ronen, S. (1981). *Flexible working hours: An innovation in the quality of work life*. New York: McGraw-Hill.

Roscoe, S. N. (1968). Airborne displays for flight and navigation. *Human Factors, 10*, 321-332.

Rosen, B., & Jerdee, T. H. (1976). The influence of age stereotypes on managerial decisions. *Journal of Applied Psychology, 61*, 428-432.

Rosen, N. A. (1969). *Leadership change and work group dynamics*. Ithaca, NY: Cornell University Press.

Rosenfeld, M., Shimberg, B., & Thornton, R. F. (1983). *Job analysis of licensed psychologists in the United States and Canada*. Princeton, NJ: Center for Occupational and Professional Assessment, Educational Testing Service.

Roskies, E., & Louis-Guerin, C. (1990). Job insecurity in managers: Antecedents and consequences. *Journal of Organizational Behavior, 11*, 345-359.

Ross, L. D. (1977). The intuitive psychologist and his shortcomings. In L. Berkowitz (Ed.), *Advances in experimental social psychology* (Vol. 10, pp. 173-220). New York: Academic Press.

Rothe, H. F. (1978). Output rates among industrial workers. *Journal of Applied Psychology, 63*, 40-46.

Rotter, J. B. (1966). Generalized expectancies for internal versus external control of reinforcement. *Psychological Monographs, 80*, 1-28.

Rowland, M. (1992, February 9). Pay for quality, by the group. *The New York Times*, p. F17.

Roy, D. F. (1952). Quota restriction and goldbricking in a machine shop. *American Journal of Sociology, 57*, 427-442.

Roy, D. F. (1960). Banana time: Job satisfaction and informal interaction. *Human Organizations, 18*, 158-168.

Rush, M., Phillips, J. S., & Lord, R. G. (1981). Effects of temporal delay in rating on leader behavior descriptions: A laboratory investigation. *Journal of Applied Psychology, 66*, 442-450.

Rush, M. C., Thomas, J. C., & Lord, R. G. (1977). Implicit leadership theory: A potential threat to the internal validity of leader behavior questionnaires. *Organizational Behavior and Human Performance, 20*, 93-110.

Russek, H. I., & Zohman, B. L. (1958). Relative significance of heredity, diet, and occupational stress in coronary heart disease of young adults. *American Journal of Medical Science, 235*, 266-275.

Russell, D. W., Altmaier, E., & VanVelzen, D. (1987). Job-related stress, social support, and burnout among classroom teachers. *Journal of Applied Psychology, 72,* 269-274.

Russell, J. S., Terborg, J. R., & Powers, M. L. (1985). Organizational performance and organizational level training and support. *Personnel Psychology, 38,* 849-863.

Rutenfranz, J., Knauth, P., & Angersbach, D. (1981). Shift work research issues. In L. C. Johnson, D. I. Tepas, W. P. Colquhoun, & M. J. Colligan (Eds.), *Biological rhythms, sleep and shift work* (pp. 165-196). New York: Plenum Press.

Ryan, T. (1970). *Intentional behavior.* New York: Ronald Press.

Saal, F. E. (1979). Mixed standard rating scale: A consistent system for numerically coding inconsistent response combinations. *Journal of Applied Psychology, 64,* 422-428.

Saal, F. E., & Landy, F. J. (1977). The mixed standard rating scale: An evaluation. *Organizational Behavior and Human Performance, 18,* 19-35.

Saari, L. M., Johnson, T. R., McLaughlin, S.D., & Zimmerle, D. M. (1988). A survey of management training and education practices in U.S. companies. *Personnel Psychology, 41,* 731-743.

Saari, L. M., & Latham, G. (1982). Employee reactions to continuous and variable ratio reinforcement schedules involving a monetary reward. *Journal of Applied Psychology, 67,* 506-508.

Sackett, P. R., Cornelius, E. T., III, & Carron, T. J. (1981). A comparison of global judgment vs. task oriented approaches to job classification. *Personnel Psychology, 34,* 791-804.

Sackett, P. R., & DuBois, C. L. Z. (1991). Rater-ratee race effects on performance evaluation: Challenging meta-analytic conclusions. *Journal of Applied Psychology, 76,* 873-877.

Salancik, G. R., & Meindl, J. R. (1984). Corporate attributions as strategic illusions of management control. *Administrative Science Quarterly, 29,* 238-254.

Salancik, G. R., & Pfeffer, J. (1977). An examination of need satisfaction models of job satisfaction. *Administrative Science Quarterly, 22,* 427-456. (Cited on p. 151.)

Salancik, G. R., & Pfeffer, J. (1977). Who gets power—and how they hold on to it: A strategic-contingency model of power. *Organizational Dynamics, 5,* 2-21.

Salancik, G. R., & Pfeffer, J. (1978). A social information processing approach to job attitudes and task design. *Administrative Science Quarterly, 23,* 224-254.

Sales, S. M. (1969). Organizational role as a risk factor in coronary heart disease. *Administrative Science Quarterly, 14,* 325-336.

*San Antonio Light.* (1990, May 24). Bailout could cost $325 billion. *San Antonio Light,* pp. C1, C8.

Sanders, M. S., & McCormick, E. J. (1987). *Human factors in engineering and design* (6th ed.). New York: McGraw-Hill.

Sanders, M. S., & McCormick, E. J. (1993). *Human factors in engineering and design* (7th ed.). New York: McGraw-Hill.

Sauser, W. I., & Pond, S. B. (1981). Effects of rater training and participation on cognitive complexity: An exploration of Schneier's cognitive reinterpretation. *Personnel Psychology, 34,* 563-577.

Sauter, S. L., Hurrell, J. J., Jr., Cooper, C. L. (1989). *Job control and worker health.* New York: John Wiley & Sons.

Schachter, S., & Singer, J. E. (1962). Cognitive, social and physiological determinants of emotional state. *Psychological Review, 69*, 379-399.

Schein, E. H. (1969). *Process consultation: Its role in organizational development.* Reading, MA: Addison-Wesley.

Schein, E. H. (1990). Organizational culture. *American Psychologist, 45*, 109-119.

Schein, V., Maurer, E., & Novak, J. (1977). Impact of flexible working hours on productivity. *Journal of Applied Psychology, 62*, 463-465.

Schendel, J. D., & Hagman, J. D. (1982). On sustaining procedural skills over a prolonged retention interval. *Journal of Applied Psychology, 67*, 605-610.

Scherf, G. (1974). Consumer dissatisfaction as a function of dissatisfaction with interpersonal relationships. *Journal of Applied Psychology, 59*, 465-471.

Schlenker, B. R., & Miller, R. S. (1977). Group cohesiveness as a determinant of egocentric perceptions in cooperative groups. *Human Relations, 30*, 1039-1055.

Schmidt, F. L., Greenthal, A., Hunter, J. E., Berner, J., & Seaton, F. (1977). Job sample versus paper-and-pencil trades and technical tests: Adverse impact and examinee attitudes. *Personnel Psychology, 30,* 187-197.

Schmidt, F. L., & Hunter, J.E. (1977). Development of a general solution to the problem of validity generalization. *Journal of Applied Psychology, 62*, 529-540.

Schmidt, F. L., & Hunter, J.E. (1981). Employment testing: old theories and new research findings. *American Psychologist, 36*, 1128-1137.

Schmied, L. A., & Lawler, K. A. (1986). Hardiness, Type A behavior, and the stress-illness relation in working women. *Journal of Personality and Social Psychology, 51*, 1218-1223.

Schmitt, N., & Bedeian, A. G. (1982). A comparison of Lisrel and two-stage least squares analysis of a hypothesized life-job satisfaction reciprocal relationship. *Journal of Applied Psychology, 67*, 806-817.

Schmitt, N., & Cohen, S. A. (1989). Internal analyses of task ratings by job incumbents. *Journal of Applied Psychology, 74*, 96-104.

Schmitt, N., Coyle, B. W., & Rauschenberger, J. A. (1977). A Monte Carlo evaluation of three formula estimates of cross-validated multiple correlation. *Psychological Bulletin, 84*, 751-758.

Schmitt, N., & Klimoski, R. J. (1991). *Research methods in human resources management.* Cincinnati: South-Western.

Schmitt, N., & Landy, F. J. (1993). The concept of validity. In N. Schmitt & W. C. Borman (Eds.), *Personnel selection in organizations* (pp. 275-309). San Francisco: Jossey-Bass.

Schmitt, N., & Mellon, P. M. (1980). Life and job satisfaction: Is the job central? *Journal of Vocational Behavior, 16*, 51-58.

Schmitt, N., & Robertson, I. (1990). Personnel selection. *Annual Review of Psychology, 41*, 289-319.

Schmitt, N., & Son, L. (1981). An evaluation of valence models of motivation to pursue various post high school alternatives. *Organizational Behavior and Human Performance, 27*, 135-150.

Schneider, B. (1987). The people make the place. *Personnel Psychology, 40*, 437-453.

Schneider, B., & Schmitt, N. (1986). *Staffing organizations* (2nd ed.). Glenview, IL: Scott, Foresman.

Schneier, C. E. (1977). Operational utility and psychometric characteristics of behavioral expectation scales: A cognitive reinterpretation. *Journal of Applied Psychology, 62,* 541-548.

Schor, J. B. (1991). *The overworked American.* New York: Basic Books.

Schover, L. R. (1980). Clinical practice and scientific psychology: Can this marriage be saved? *Professional Psychology, 11,* 268-275.

Schriesheim, C. A., & DeNisi, A. S. (1981). Task dimensions as moderators of the effects of instrumental leadership: A two-sample replicated test of path-goal leadership theory. *Journal of Applied Psychology, 66,* 589-597.

Schriesheim, C. A., House, R., & Kerr, S. (1976). Leader initiation of structure: A reconciliation of discrepant research results and some empirical tests. *Organizational Behavior and Human Performance, 15,* 297-321.

Schriesheim, C. A., & Kerr, S. (1974). Psychometric properties of Ohio State leadership scales. *Psychological Bulletin, 81,* 756-765.

Schuler, R. S. (1976). Participation with supervisor and subordinate authoritarianism: A path-goal theory reconciliation. *Administrative Science Quarterly, 21,* 320-325.

Schuler, R. S. (1982). Definition and conceptualization of stress in organizations. *Organizational Behavior and Human Performance, 24,* 115-130.

Schuler, R. S. (1985). Integrative transactional process model of coping with stress in organizations. In T. A. Beehr & R. S. Bhagat (Eds.), *Human stress and cognition in organizations* (pp. 347-374). New York: John Wiley & Sons.

Schwab, D., & Cummings, L. (1976). A theoretical analysis of the impact of task scope on employee performance. *Academy of Management Review, 1,* 23-35.

Schwab, D. P., & Grams, R. (1985). Sex-related errors in job evaluation: A "real-world" test. *Journal of Applied Psychology, 70,* 533-539.

Schweiger, D. M., Sandberg, W. R., & Ragan, J. W. (1986). Group approaches for improving strategic decision making: A comparative analysis of dialectical inquiry, devil's advocacy, and consensus. *Academy of Management Journal, 29,* 51-71.

Schwenk, C. R. (1990). Effects of devil's advocacy and dialectical inquiry on decision making: A meta-analysis. *Organizational Behavior and Human Decision Processes, 47,* 161-176.

*Science Agenda.* (1991). APA task force releases final report on integrity testing. *Science Agenda, 4,* 1-6.

Scott, K. D., & Taylor, G. S. (1985). An examination of conflicting findings on the relationship between job satisfaction and absenteeism: A meta-analysis. *Academy of Management Journal, 28,* 599-612.

Scott, W. D. (1908). *The psychology of advertising.* New York: Arno.

Scott, W. R. (1987). *Organizations: rational, natural, and open systems* (2nd ed.). Englewood Cliffs, NJ: Prentice-Hall.

Scriven, M. (1967). The methodology of evaluation. In R. W. Tyler, R. M. Gagne, & M. Scriven (Eds.), *Perspectives of curriculum evaluation* (American Educational Research Association Monograph, No. 1, pp. 39-831). Chicago: Rand McNally.

Sears, D. O. (1986). College sophomores in the laboratory: Influences of a narrow data base on social psychology's view of human nature. *Journal of Personality and Social Psychology, 51,* 515-530.

Seashore, S. E. (1954). *Group cohesiveness in the industrial work group.* Ann Arbor, MI: University of Michigan Press.

Segal, T., & Kelly, K. (1992, November 9). Getting serious about sexual harassment. *Business Week,* pp. 78-82.

Sekaran, U. (1986). Self-esteem and sense of competence as moderators of the job satisfaction of professionals in dual career families. *Journal of Occupational Behaviour, 7,* 341-344.

Selltiz, C., Wrightsman, L. S., & Cook, S. W. (1976). *Research methods in social relations.* New York: Holt, Rinehart and Winston.

Selye, H. (1952). *The story of the adaptation syndrome.* Montreal: Acta.

Selye, H. (1956). *The stress of life.* New York: McGraw-Hill.

Selye, H. (1974). *Stress without distress.* Philadelphia: Lippincott.

Seminara, J., Gonzalez, W., & Parsons, S. (1977, March). *Human factors review of nuclear power plant control room design* (Report NP-309). Palo Alto, CA: Electric Power Research Institute.

Sengoku, T. 1985. *Willing workers: The work ethics in Japan, England, and the United States.* Westport, CT: Quorum Books.

Shanker, A. (1992, June 21). Getting rid of algebra. *The New York Times,* p. E7.

Shannon, C., & Weaver, W. (1949). *The mathematical theory of communication.* Urbana, IL: University of Illinois Press.

Shapira, Z. (1989). Task choice and assigned goals as determinants of task motivation and performance. *Organizational Behavior and Human Decision Processes, 44,* 141-165.

Sharon, A. T., & Bartlett, C. J. (1969). Effect of instructional conditions in producing leniency on two types of rating scales. *Personnel Psychology, 22,* 251-263.

Shaw, J. B. (1990). A cognitive categorization model for the study of intercultural management. *Academy of Management Review, 15,* 626-646.

Shaw, J. B., & Riskind, J. H. (1983). Predicting job stress using data from the Position Analysis Questionnaire. *Journal of Applied Psychology, 68,* 253-262.

Shaw, M. E. (1964). Communication networks. In L. Berkowitz (Ed.), *Advances in experimental social psychology* (Vol. 11, pp. 11-147). New York: Academic Press.

Shaw, M. E. (1976). *Group dynamics: The psychology of small-group behavior.* New York: McGraw-Hill.

Shea, G. P., & Guzzo, R. A. (1987). Groups as human resources. In K. M. Rowland & G. R. Ferris (Eds.), *Research in Personnel and Human Resources Management* (Vol. 5, pp. 289-322). Greenwich, CT: JAI Press.

Shechtman, M. R. (1991, November 17). Teaching young workers to grow up. *The New York Times,* Sec. 3, p. 13.

Sheehy, J. W. 1990. New work ethic is frightening. *Personnel Journal, 69,* 28-36.

Shellenbarger, S. (1991, November 15). Workplace: More job seekers put family needs first. *The Wall Street Journal*, p. B1.

Sheridan, J. E., Vredenburgh, D. J., & Abelson, M. A. (1984). Contextual model of leadership influence in hospital units. *Academy of Management Journal, 27*, 57-78.

Sherif, M., Harvey, O. J., White, B., Hood, W., & Sherif, C. (1961). *Intergroup conflict and cooperation: the Robbers' Cave experiments.* Norman, OK: Institute of Group Relations, University of Oklahoma.

Sherman, S. (1993, January 25). A brave new Darwinian workplace. *Fortune,* pp. 50-56.

Shinar, D. (1978). Control-display relationships on the four-burner range: Population stereotypes versus standards. *Human Factors, 20*, 13-17.

Shireman, J. (1991, February 4). Unwillingness to relocate stifles careers. *The Wall Street Journal,* p. A10.

Shirom, A. (1976). On some correlates of combat performance. *Administrative Science Quarterly, 21,* 419-432.

Shockley-Zalabak, P. (1988). Assessing the Hall conflict management survey. *Management Communications Quarterly, 1,* 302-320.

Shore, E., & Sechrest, L. (1961). Concept attainment as a function of positive instances presented. *Journal of Educational Psychology, 52,* 303-307.

Siegel, J., Dubrovsky, V., Kiesler, S., & McGuire, T. W. (1986). Group processes in computer-mediated communication. *Organizational Behavior and Human Decision Processes, 37,* 157-187.

Simon, H. (1990). Fetal protection policies after Johnson Controls: No easy answers. *Employee Relations Law Journal, 15,* 499-514.

Simon, H. A. (1957). *Models of man, social and rational.* New York: John Wiley & Sons.

Simonton, D. K. (1986). Presidential personality: Biographical use of the Gough Adjective Checklist. *Journal of Personality and Social Psychology, 51,* 149-160.

Sinclair, M. A. (1986). Ergonomics aspects of the automated factory. *Ergonomics, 29,* 1507-1523.

Skinner, B. F. (1954). Science of learning and the art of teaching. *Harvard Educational Review, 24,* 86-97.

Skinner, B. F. (1969). *Contingencies of reinforcement: A theoretical analysis.* New York: Appleton-Century-Crofts.

Skrycki, C. (1989, August 20). The drive to downsize. *The Washington Post,* p. B1.

Slavin, R. E. (1983). When does cooperative learning increase student achievement? *Psychological Bulletin, 94,* 429-445.

Slocum, J. W., & Strawser, R. H. (1982). Racial differences in job attitudes. *Journal of Applied Psychology, 62,* 16-19.

Slovic, P., Fischoff, B., & Lichtenstein, S. (1977). Behavioral decision theory. *Annual Review of Psychology, 28,* 1-39.

Smith, C. S. (1989). *Circadian influence on worker affect and performance: A neglected perspective.* Paper presented at the meeting of the Society for Industrial & Organizational Psychology, Boston.

Smith, C. S. (1990). Measurement issues in human factors research: An industrial-organizational psychologist's view of a neglected perspective [Summary]. *Proceedings of the Human Factors Society 34th Annual Meeting, 2,* 865.

Smith, C. S., Olsen, H., & Falgout, K. (1991, April). *A career path investigation of job-related attitudes and behaviors.* Poster presented at the Sixth Annual Conference of the Society for Industrial and Organizational Psychology, St. Louis.

Smith, C. S., Reilly, C., & Midkiff, K. (1989). Evaluation of three circadian rhythm questionnaires with suggestions for an improved measure of morningness. *Journal of Applied Psychology, 74,* 728-738.

Smith, C. S., Reilly, C., Moore-Hirschl, S., Olsen, H., & Schmieder, R. (1989). *The shiftworker's guide to a good night's sleep.* Bowling Green, OH: Bowling Green State University Press.

Smith, C. S., & Sulsky, L. M. (1992). *An investigation of coping with organizational stress across multiple stressors and samples.* Paper presented at the American Psychological Association/National Institute for Occupational Safety and Health (APA/NIOSH) Conference, Washington, DC.

Smith, D. E. (1986). Training programs for performance appraisal: A review. *Academy of Management Review, 11,* 22-40.

Smith, F., J., Scott, K. D., & Hulin, C. L. (1977). Trends of job-related attitudes of managerial and professional employees. *Academy of Management Journal, 20,* 454-460.

Smith, J. E., Carson, K. P., & Alexander, R. A. (1984). Leadership: It can make a difference. *Academy of Management Journal, 27,* 765-776.

Smith, J. E., & Hakel, M. D. (1979). Convergence among data sources, response bias, and reliability and validity of a structured job analysis questionnaire. *Personnel Psychology, 32,* 677-692.

Smith, K. G., Locke, E. A., & Barry, D. (1990). Goal setting, planning, and organizational performance: An experimental simulation. *Organizational Behavior and Human Decision Processes, 46,* 118-134.

Smith, M. J. (1985). Machine-paced work and stress. In C. L. Cooper & M. J. Smith (Eds.), *Job stress and blue collar work* (pp. 51-64). Chichester, England: Wiley.

Smith, M. J., Colligan, M., Frockt, I., & Tasto, D. (1979). Occupational injury rates among nurses as a function of shift schedule. *Journal of Safety Research, 11,* 181-187.

Smith, P. C. (1976). Behaviors, results and organizational effectiveness: The problem of criteria. In M. D. Dunnette (Ed.), *Handbook of industrial and organizational psychology* (pp. 745-776). Chicago: Rand McNally.

Smith, P. C., & Kendall, L. M. (1963). Retranslation of expectations: An approach to the construction of unambiguous anchors for rating scales. *Journal of Applied Psychology, 47,* 149-155.

Smith, P. C., Kendall, L. M., & Hulin, C. L. (1969). *The measurement of satisfaction in work and retirement: A strategy for the study of attitudes.* Chicago: Rand McNally.

Smith, R. W. (1989, October). The Bell Atlantic way: Values and vision. *Executive Speeches, 4,* 6-9.

Smith, S., & Thomas, D. (1964). Colour versus shape coding in information displays. *Journal of Applied Psychology, 48,* 137-146.

Society for Industrial and Organizational Psychology. (1987). *Principles for the validation and use of personnel selection procedures.* College Park, MD: Society for Industrial and Organizational Psychology.

Solem, A. R. (1960). Human relations training: Comparison of case study and role playing. *Personnel Administration, 23,* 29-37.

Spangler, W. (1989). Single-source response bias in the Job Diagnostic Survey. *Psychological Reports, 65,* 531-546.

Spangler, W. (1992). Validity of questionnaire and TAT measures of need for achievement: Two meta-analyses. *Psychological Bulletin, 112,* 140-154.

Sparks, C. P. (1983). Paper and pencil measures of potential. In G. Dreher & P. Sackett (Eds.), *Perspectives on employee staffing and selection* (pp. 349-368). Homewood, IL: Richard D. Irwin.

Spool, M. D. (1978). Training programs for observers of behavior: A review. *Personnel Psychology, 31,* 853-888.

Stagner, R. (1962). Personality variables in union-management relations. *Journal of Applied Psychology, 46,* 350-357.

Stagner, R. (1982). Past and future of industrial/organizational psychology. *Professional Psychology, 13,* 892-903.

Stahl, M., & Harrell, A. (1981). Modeling effort decisions with behavioral decision theory: Toward an individual differences model of expectancy theory. *Organizational Behavior and Human Performance, 27,* 303-325.

Stahl, M. J. (1986). *Managerial and technical motivation: Assessing needs for achievement, power, and affiliation.* New York: Praeger.

Staines, G.L., & Pleck, J. (1984). Nonstandard work schedules and family life. *Journal of Applied Psychology, 69,* 515-523.

Staines, G. L., Pottick, K. J., & Fudge, D. A. (1986). Wives' employment and husbands' attitudes toward work and life. *Journal of Applied Psychology, 71,* 118-128.

Staw, B. M. (1975). Attribution of the "causes" of performance: A general alternative interpretation of cross-sectional research on organizations. *Organizational Behavior and Human Performance, 13,* 414-432.

Staw, B. M. (1977). Motivation in organizations: Synthesis and redirection. In B. M. Staw & G. R. Salancik (Eds.), *New directions in organizational behavior* (pp. 55-96). Chicago: St. Clair Press.

Staw, B. M., McKeachnie, P. I., & Puffer, S. M. (1983). The justification of organizational performance. *Administrative Science Quarterly, 28,* 582-600.

Staw, B. M., & Ross, J. (1985). Stability in the midst of change: A dispositional approach to job attitudes. *Journal of Applied Psychology, 70,* 469-480.

Steelcase. (1978). *The Steelcase national study of office environments: Do they work?* Grand Rapids, MI. Steelcase, Inc.

Steers, R. M., & Porter, L. W. (1991). *Motivation and Work Behavior* (5th ed.). New York: McGraw-Hill.

Steers, R. M., & Rhodes, S. R. (1978). Major influences on employee attendance: A process model. *Journal of Applied Psychology, 63,* 391-407.

Steffy, B. D., & Jones, J. W. (1988). Workplace stress and indicators of coronary-disease risk. *Academy of Management Journal, 31,* 686-698.

Steiner, D. D. (1990). Clarification and correction of Steiner & Truxillo's (1989) improved test of the disaggregation hypothesis. *Journal of Occupational Psychology, 63,* 263-264.

Steiner, D. D., & Truxillo, D. M. (1989). An improved test of the disaggregation hypothesis of job and life satisfaction. *Journal of Occupational Psychology, 62,* 33-39.

Steiner, I. D. (1972). *Group process and productivity.* New York: Academic Press.

Stern, G., Carroll, P. B., & McQueen, M. (1991, December 13). In a weak economy, some top-level aides are bound to topple. *The Wall Street Journal,* pp. A1, A4.

Sternberg, R.J. (1977). *Intelligence, information processing, and analogical reasoning: The componential analysis of human abilities.* Hillsdale, NJ: L. Erlbaum.

Sterns, H. L., & Doverspike, D. (1989). Aging and the training and learning process. In I. Goldstein (Ed.), *Training and development in organizations* (pp. 299-333). San Francisco: Jossey-Bass.

Stevenson, M. K., Busemeyer, J. R., & Naylor, J. C. (1990). Judgment and decision-making theory. In M. D. Dunnette & L. M. Hough (Eds.), *Handbook of industrial and organizational psychology* (Vol. 1, pp. 283-374). Palo Alto, CA: Consulting Psychologists Press.

Stewart, A. J., & Winter, D. G. (1976). Arousal of the power motive in women. *Journal of Consulting and Clinical Psychology, 44,* 495-496.

Stewart, R. (1976). *Contrasts in management.* Maidenhead, England: McGraw-Hill.

Stewart, T. A. (1991a, June 3). Brainpower. *Fortune,* pp. 44-60.

Stewart, T. A. (1991b, August 12). GE keeps those ideas coming. *Fortune,* pp. 41-48.

Sticht, T. G., Armstrong, W. B., Hickey, D. T., & Caylor, J. S. (1987). *Cast off youth.* New York: Praeger.

Stogdill, R. M. (1948). Personal factors associated with leadership: A survey of the literature. *Journal of Psychology, 25,* 35-71.

Stogdill, R. M. (1972). Group productivity, drive, and cohesiveness. *Organizational Behavior and Human Performance, 8,* 26-43.

Stogdill, R. M. (1974). *Handbook of leadership: A survey of theory and research.* New York: The Free Press.

Stogdill, R. M., & Coons, A. E. (1957). *Leader behavior: Its description and measurement.* Columbus, OH: Ohio State University, Bureau of Business Research.

Stone, D. L., Gueutal, H. G., & McIntosh, B. (1984). The effects of feedback sequence and expertise of the rater on perceived feedback accuracy. *Personnel Psychology, 37,* 487-506.

Stone, E. F., Stone, D. L., & Dipboye, R. L. (1992). Stigmas in organizations: Race, handicaps, and physical unattractiveness. In K. Kelley (Ed.), *Issues, theory, and research in industrial and organizational psychology* (pp. 385-457). Amsterdam: Elsevier Science.

Strauss, G. (1967). Related instruction: Basic problems and issues. In *Research in apprenticeship training.* Madison, WI: University of Wisconsin, Center for Vocational and Technical Education.

Stricker, G. (1975). On professional schools and professional degrees. *American Psychologist. 30,* 1062-1066.

Strube, M. J., & Garcia, J. E. (1981). A meta-analytic investigation of Fiedler's contingency model of leadership effectiveness. *Psychological Bulletin, 90,* 307-321.

Sundstrom, E. (1986). *Work places: The psychology of the physical environment in offices and factories.* London: Cambridge University Press.

Swain, A., & Guttman, H. (1983, October). *Handbook of human reliability analysis with emphasis on nuclear power pl  t applications* (Technical Report NUREG/CR-1278). Washington, DC: U.S. Nuclear Regulatory Commission.

Swasy, A. (1991, December 5). What free commodity yields riches? Raw creativity. *The Wall Street Journal,* p. B2.

Tait, M., Padgett, M. Y., & Baldwin, T. T. (1989). Job and life satisfaction: A reevaluation of the strength of the relationship and gender effects as a function of the date of the study. *Journal of Applied Psychology, 74,* 502-507.

Tannenbaum, S. I., Mathieu, J. E., Sales, E., & Cannon-Bowers, J. A. (1991). Meeting trainees' expectations: The influence of training fulfillment on the development of commitment, self-efficacy, and motivation. *Journal of Applied Psychology, 76,* 759-769.

Tarrants, W. (1980). *The measurement of safety performance.* New York: Garland STPM Press.

Tasto, D. L., Colligan, M. J., Skjei, E. W., & Polly, S. J. (1978). *Health consequences of shift work* (DHEW (NIOSH) Publication No. 78-154). Washington, DC: U.S. Government Printing Office.

Taylor, A. (1990, November 19). Why Toyota keeps getting better and better and better. *Fortune,* pp. 66-79.

Taylor, E. K., & Wherry, R. J. (1951). A study of leniency in two rating systems. *Personnel Psychology, 4,* 39-47.

Taylor, F. W. (1911). *The principles of scientific management.* New York: Harper & Row.

Taylor, H. C., & Russell, J. T. (1939). From the relationship of validity coefficients to the practical effectiveness of tests in selection: Discussion and tables. *Journal of Applied Psychology, 23,* 565-578.

Taylor, M. S. (1988). Effects of college internships on individual participants. *Journal of Applied Psychology, 73,* 393-401.

Tepas, D. I., Armstrong, D. R., Carlson, M. L., Duchon, J. C., Gersten, A., & Lezotte, D. V. (1985). Changing industry to continuous operations: Different strokes for different plants. *Behavior Research Methods, Instruments, and Computers, 17,* 670-676.

Terborg, J. R. (1985). Working women and stress. In T. A. Beehr & R. S. Bhagat (Eds.), *Human stress and cognition in organizations* (pp. 245-286). New York: John Wiley.

Terkel, S. (1974). *Working: People talk about what they do all day and how they feel about what they do.* New York: Pantheon Press.

Tesser, A., & Rosen, S. (1975). The reluctance to transmit bad news. In L. Berkowitz (Ed.), *Advances in experimental social psychology* (Vol. 8, pp. 194-229). New York: Academic Press.

Tetlock, P. E. (1985). Accountability: The neglected social context of judgment and choice. In L. L. Cummings & B. M. Staw (Eds.), *Research in organizational behavior* (Vol. 7, pp. 297-333). Greenwich, CT: JAI Press.

Tett, R. P., Jackson, D. N., & Rothstein, M. (1991). Personality measures as predictors of job performance: A meta-analytic review. *Personnel Psychology, 44,* 703-742.

Texas Education Agency (1986/87). *Teacher appraisal system: Teacher orientation manual.* Austin, TX: Texas Education Agency.

Therrien, L. (1989, November 13). The rival Japan respects. *Business Week,* pp. 108-121.

Thomas, K. W., & Kilmann, R. H. (1974). *The Thomas-Kilmann conflict mode instrument.* Tuxedo, NY: Xicom.

Thorndike, E. L., & Woodworth, R. S. (1901). The influence of improvement in one mental function upon the efficiency of other functions. *Psychological Review, 8,* 247-261.

Thurstone, L. L. (1938). *The nature of human intelligence.* New York: McGraw-Hill.

Tjosvold, D. (1986). *Working together to get things done.* Lexington, MA: D. C. Heath.

Tolchinsky, P., & King, D. (1980). Do goals mediate the effects of incentives on performance? *Academy of Management Review, 5,* 455-467.

Treiman, D. J., & Hartmann, H. J. (Eds.) (1981). *Women, work, and wages: Equal pay for jobs of equal value.* Washington, DC: National Academy Press.

Triandis, H. (1959). Cognitive similarity and interpersonal communication in industry. *Journal of Applied Psychology, 43,* 321-326.

Trice, H. M., & Beyer, J. M. (1986). Charisma and its routinization in two social movement organizations. *Research in Organizational Behavior, 8,* 113-164.

Trist, E., & Bamforth, K. (1951). Some social and psychological consequences of the long-wall method of coal-getting. *Human Relations, 4,* 1-8.

Tubbs, M. (1986). Goal setting: A meta-analytic examination of the empirical evidence. *Journal of Applied Psychology, 71,* 474-483.

Tuckman, B. W. (1965). Developmental sequence in small groups. *Psychological Bulletin, 63,* 384-399.

Tullis, T. (1983). The formatting of alphanumeric displays: A review and analysis. *Human Factors, 25,* 657-682.

Tupes, E. C., & Christal, R. E. (1961). Recurrent personality factors based on trait ratings. *USAF ASD Technical Report,* pp. 61-97.

Turnage, J. J. (1990).The challenge of new workplace technology for psychology. *American Psychologist, 45,* 171-178.

Turner, A., & Lawrence, P. (1965). *Industrial jobs and the worker: An investigation of response to task attributes.* Boston: Division of Research, Graduate School of Business Administration, Harvard University.

Umstot, D., Mitchell, T., & Bell, C., Jr. (1978). Goal setting and job enrichment: An integrated approach to job design. *Academy of Management Review, 3,* 867-879.

U.S. Department of Labor. (1972). *Handbook for analyzing jobs.* Washington, DC: U.S. Government Printing Office.

U.S. Department of Labor. (1974). *Women's Bureau Bulletin: The myth and the reality*. Washington, DC: U.S. Government Printing Office.

U.S. Department of Labor. (1977). *Dictionary of occupational titles* (4th ed.) Washington, DC: U.S. Government Printing Office.

U.S. Department of Labor. (1978). *Women in traditionally male jobs: The experiences of ten public utilities companies*. Washington, DC: U.S. Government Printing Office.

U.S. Department of Labor, Bureau of Labor Statistics. (1987). *Workforce 2000*. Washington, DC: U.S. Government Printing Office.

U.S. Department of Labor, Bureau of Labor Statistics. (1988). *Projections 2000* (BLS Bulletin 2302). Washington, DC: U.S. Government Printing Office.

Valenzi, E., & Andrews, I. (1971). Effect of hourly overpay and underpay inequity when tested with a new induction procedure. *Journal of Applied Psychology, 55*, 22-27.

Vance, R., & Colella, A. (1990). Effects of two types of feedback on goal acceptance and personal goals. *Journal of Applied Psychology, 75*, 68-76.

Van Cott, H., & Kinkade, R. (Eds.) (1972). *Human engineering guide to equipment design*. Washington, DC: U.S. Superintendent of Documents.

Van de Vliert, E., & Kabanoff, B. (1990). Toward theory-based measures of conflict management. *Academy of Management Journal, 33*, 199-209.

Vecchio, R. (1981). An individual-differences interpretation of the conflicting predictions generated by equity theory and expectancy theory. *Journal of Applied Psychology, 66*, 470-481.

Vecchio, R. P. (1983). Assessing the validity of Fiedler's contingency model of leadership effectiveness: A closer look at Strube and Garcia. *Psychological Bulletin, 93*, 404-408.

Vecchio, R. P. (1987). Situational leadership theory: An examination of a prescriptive theory. *Journal of Applied Psychology, 72*, 444-451.

Vecchio, R. P. (1990). Theoretical and empirical examination of cognitive resource theory. *Journal of Applied Psychology, 75*, 141-147.

Vecchio, R. P. (1992). Cognitive resource theory: Issues for specifying a test of the theory. *Journal of Applied Psychology, 77*, 375-376.

Verhaegen, P., Vanhalst, B., Derycke, H., & VanHoecke, M. (1976). The value of some psychological theories of industrial accidents. *Journal of Occupational Psychology, 1*, 39-45.

Verity, J., Peterson, T., Depke, D., & Schwartz, E. (1991, December 16). The new IBM. *Business Week*, pp. 112-114.

The Vincennes incident: Congress hears psychologists. (1988). *Science Agenda, 1*, 4-5.

Vincente, K., Thornton, D. C., & Moray, N. (1987). Spectral analysis of sinus arrhythmia: A measure of mental effort. *Human Factors, 29*, 171-182.

von Winterfeldt, D., & Edwards, W. (1986). *Decision analysis and behavioral research*. New York: Cambridge University Press.

Vroom, V. H. (1964). *Work and motivation*. New York: John Wiley & Sons.

Vroom, V. H., & Jago, A. G. (1978). On the validity of the Vroom-Yetton model. *Journal of Applied Psychology, 63,* 151-162.

Vroom, V. H., & Jago, A. G. (1988). *The new leadership: Managing participation in organizations.* Englewood Cliffs, NJ: Prentice-Hall.

Vroom, V. H., & Yetton, P. W. (1973). *Leadership and decision-making*. Pittsburgh: University of Pittsburgh Press.

Wahba, M., & Bridwell, L. (1976). Maslow reconsidered: A review of research on the need hierarchy theory. *Organizational Behavior and Human Performance, 15,* 212-240.

Waldman, D. A., & Avolio, B. J. (1986). A meta-analysis of age differences in job performance. *Journal of Applied Psychology, 71,* 33-38.

Waldman, D. A., & Avolio, B. J. (1991). Race effects in performance evaluations: Controlling for ability, education, and experience. *Journal of Applied Psychology, 76,* 897-901.

Walker, J. (1985). Social problems of shift work. In S. Folkard & T. Monk (Eds.), *Hours of work: Temporal factors in work scheduling* (pp. 211-225). Chichester, England: John Wiley & Sons.

Wall, T. D., Clegg, C. W., & Jackson, P. R. (1978). An evaluation of the job characteristics model. *Journal of Occupational Psychology, 51,* 183-196.

Wall, T. D., Kemp, N. J., Jackson, P. R., & Clegg, C. W. (1986). Outcomes of autonomous workgroups: A long-term field experiment. *Academy of Management Journal, 29,* 280-304.

Wall, T. D., & Payne, R. L. (1973). Are deficiency scores deficient? *Journal of Applied Psychology, 58,* 322-326.

Walsh, W. B. (1989). *Tests and measurements*. Englewood Cliffs, NJ: Prentice-Hall.

Walton, R. E., & Dutton, J. M. (1969). The management of interdepartmental conflict: A model and review. *Administrative Science Quarterly, 14,* 73-84.

Wanous, J. P. (1973). Effects of realistic job preview on job acceptance, job attitudes, and job survival. *Journal of Applied Psychology, 58,* 327-332.

Wanous, J. P. (1976). Organizational entry: From naive expectations to realistic beliefs. *Journal of Applied Psychology, 61,* 22-29.

Wanous, J., & Zwany, A. (1977). A cross-sectional test of need hierarchy theory. *Organizational Behavior and Human Performance, 18,* 78-97.

Wartzman, R. (1992, January 2). Pentagon budget cuts, past ethical lapses, haunt Northrop Corp. *The Wall Street Journal*, pp. A1, A4.

Watson, C. J. (1981). An evaluation of some aspects of the Steers and Rhodes model of employee attendance. *Journal of Applied Psychology, 66,* 385-389.

Watson, D., Pennebaker, J. W., & Folger, R. (1987). Beyond negative affectivity: Measuring stress and satisfaction in the workplace. In J. M. Ivancevich & D. C. Ganster (Eds.), *Job stress: From theory to suggestions* (pp. 141-157). New York: The Hawthorne Press.

Weaver, C. N. (1977). Relationships among pay, race, sex occupational prestige, supervision, work autonomy, and job satisfaction in a national sample. *Personnel Psychology, 30,* 437-445.

Weaver, C. N. (1978). Black-white correlates of job satisfaction. *Journal of Applied Psychology, 63,* 255-258.

Weaver, C. N. (1980). Job satisfaction in the United States in the 1970s. *Journal of Applied Psychology, 65,* 364-367.

Weber, M. (1946). Bureaucracy. In H. H. Gerth & C. W. Mills (Eds.), *From Max Weber: Essays in sociology.* New York: Oxford University Press.

Weber, M. (1924/1947). *The theory of social and economic organization* (A. M. Henderson & T. Parsons, Trans.; T. Parsons, Ed.). New York: The Free Press. (Original work published 1924)

Wedderburn, A. (1975). *Studies of shift work in the steel industry.* Edinburgh, Scotland: Department of Business Organization, Heriot-Watt University.

Wedderburn, A. (1981). Is there a pattern in the value of time off work? In A. Reinberg, N. Vieux, & P. Andlauer (Eds.), *Night and shift work: Biological and social aspects* (pp. 495-504). Oxford, England: Pergamon Press.

Weick, K. E. (1979). *The social psychology of organizing.* Reading, MA: Addison-Wesley.

Weick, K. E. (1987). Organizational culture as a source of high reliability. *California Management Review,* Winter, 112-127.

Weiner, N., & Mahoney, A. (1981). A model of corporate performances as a function of environmental, organizational, and leadership influences. *Academy of Management Journal, 24,* 453-470.

Weiner, Y. (1970). The effects of task-and-ego-oriented performance on two kinds of over-compensation inequity. *Organizational Behavior and Human Performance, 5,* 191-208.

Weiss, D. J., Dawis, R. V., England, G. W., & Lofquist, L. H. (1967). *Manual for the Minnesota Satisfaction Questionnaire: Minnesota studies in vocational rehabilitation* (Vol. 22). Minneapolis: Vocational Psychology Research, University of Minnesota.

Weissenberg, P., & Kavanagh, M. (1972). The independence of initiating structure and consideration: A review of the literature. *Personnel Psychology, 25,* 119-130.

Weitz, J. (1952). A neglected concept in the study of job satisfaction. *Journal of Applied Psychology, 52,* 129-148.

Wexley, K. N., Alexander, R. A., Greenawalt, J. P., & Couch, M. A. (1980). Attitudinal congruence and similarity as related to interpersonal evaluations in manager-subordinate dyads. *Academy of Management Journal, 23,* 320-330.

Wexley, K. N., & Baldwin, T. T. (1986). Posttraining strategies for facilitating positive transfer: An empirical exploration. *Academy of Management Journal, 29,* 503-520.

Wexley, K. N., & Latham, G. P. (1981). *Developing and training human resources in organizations.* Glenview, IL: Scott, Foresman.

Wexley, K. N., & Silverman, S. B. (1978). An examination of differences between managerial effectiveness and response patterns on a structured job analysis questionnaire. *Journal of Applied Psychology, 63,* 646-649.

White, J. B. (1991, August 16). How Detroit Diesel, out from under GM, turned around fast. *The Wall Street Journal,* p. A1.

White, J. B., Patterson, G. A., & Ingrassia, P. (1992, January 10). American auto makers need major overhaul to match the Japanese. *The Wall Street Journal,* p. A1.

White, M. C., DeSanctis, G., & Crino, M. D. (1981). Achievement, self-confidence, personality traits, and leadership ability: A review of the literature on sex differences. *Psychological Reports, 48,* 547-569.

White, S. E., Dittrich, J. E., & Lang, J. R. (1980). The effects of group decision-making process and problem-solving complexity on implementation attempts. *Administrative Science Quarterly, 25,* 428-440.

White, S. E., & Mitchell, T. R. (1979). Job enrichment versus social cues: A comparison and competitive test. *Journal of Applied Psychology, 64,* 1-9.

Whitehurst, H. O. (1982). Screening designs used to estimate the relative effects of display factors on dial reading. *Human Factors, 24,* 301-310.

Whitely, W., Dougherty, T. W., & Dreher, G. F. (1991). Relationship of career mentoring and socioeconomic origin to managers' and professionals' early career progress. *Academy of Management Journal, 34,* 331-351.

Whyte, W. F. (1949). The social structure of the restaurant. *American Journal of Sociology, 54,* 302-308.

Whyte, W. F. (1972, April). Skinnerian theory in organizations. *Psychology Today.*

Whyte, W. H. (1956). *The organization man.* New York: Simon & Schuster.

Wickens, C. (1984). *Engineering psychology and human performance.* Columbus, OH: Merrill.

Wickens, C. (1992). *Engineering psychology and human performance* (2nd ed.). New York: Harper-Collins.

Wiesner, W. H., & Cronshaw, S. F. (1988). The moderating impact of interview format and degree of structure on interview validity. *Journal of Occupational Psychology, 61,* 275-290.

Williams, L. J., & Hazer, J. T. (1986). Antecedents and consequences of satisfaction and commitment in turnover models: A reanalysis using latent variable structural equation methods. *Journal of Applied Psychology, 71,* 219-231.

Wojtczak-Jaroszowa, J., & Jarosz, D. (1987). Time-related distribution of occupational accidents. *Journal of Safety Research, 18,* 33-41.

Wolcott, J., McKeenan, R., Burgin, R., & Yanowitch, R. (1977). Correlation of general aviation accidents with biorhythm theory. *Human Factors, 19,* 283-294.

Wood, R., Mento, A., & Locke, E. (1987). Task complexity as a moderator of goal effects: A meta-analysis. *Journal of Applied Psychology, 72,* 416-425.

Woodman, R. W., & Sherwood, J. J. (1980). The role of team development in organizational effectiveness: A critical review. *Psychological Bulletin, 88,* 166-186.

Worchell, S., & Mitchell, T. (1972). An evaluation on the culture assimilator in Thailand and Greece. *Journal of Applied Psychology, 56,* 472-479.

Wright, P. (1990). Operationalization of goal difficulty as a moderator of the goal difficulty-performance relationship. *Journal of Applied Psychology, 75,* 227-234.

Yates, J. F. (1990). *Judgment and decision making.* Englewood Cliffs, NJ: Prentice-Hall.

Yeh, Y., & Wickens, C. (1988). Dissociation of performance and subjective measures of workload. *Human Factors, 30,* 111-120.

Yerkes, R. M., & Dodson, J. D. (1908). The relation of strength of stimulus to rapidity of habit-formation. *Journal of Comparative Neurology and Psychology, 18,* 459-482.

Yukl, G. (1981). *Leadership in Organizations.* Englewood Cliffs, NJ: Prentice-Hall.

Yukl, G., & Falbe, C. M. (1990). Influence tactics and objectives in upward, downward, and lateral influence attempts. *Journal of Applied Psychology, 75,* 132-140.

Yukl, G., & Latham, G. (1975). Consequences of reinforcement schedules and incentive magnitudes for employee performance: Problems encountered in an industrial setting. *Journal of Applied Psychology, 60,* 294-298.

Yukl, G., Latham, G., & Pursell, E. (1976). The effectiveness of performance incentives under continuous and variable ratio schedules of reinforcement. *Personnel Psychology, 29,* 221-232.

Yukl, G., & Tracey, J. B. (1992). Consequences of influence tactics used with subordinates, peers, and the boss. *Journal of Applied Psychology, 77,* 525-535.

Zaccaro, S. J., Craig, B., & Quinn, J. (1991). Prior absenteeism, supervisory style, job satisfaction, and personal characteristics: An investigation of some mediated and moderated linkages to work absenteeism. *Organizational Behavior and Human Decision Processes, 50,* 24-44.

Zaccaro, S. J., Foti, R. J., & Kenny, D. A. (1991). Self-monitoring and trait-based variance in leadership: An investigation of leader flexibility across multiple group situations. *Journal of Applied Psychology, 76,* 308-315.

Zalesny, M. D., & Farace, R. (1987). Traditional versus open offices: A comparison of sociotechnical, social relations, and symbolic meaning perspectives. *Academy of Management Journal, 30,* 240-259.

Zalesny, M. D., & Ford, J. K. (1990). Extending the social information processing perspective: New links to attitudes, behaviors, and perceptions. *Organizational Behavior and Human Decision Processes, 47,* 205-246.

Zaleznik, A. (1977). Managers and leaders: Are they different? *Harvard Business Review, 55,* 67-80.

Zammuto, R. F., London, M., & Rowland, K. M. (1982). Organization and rater differences in performance appraisals. *Organizational Behavior and Human Decision Processes, 35,* 643-658.

Zanna, M., & Rempel, J. (1988). Attitudes: A new look at an old concept. In D. Bar-Tal & A. Kruglanski (Eds.), *The social psychology of knowledge.* New York: Cambridge University Press.

Zedeck, S., & Cascio, W. F. (1982). Performance appraisal decisions as a function of rater training and purpose of the appraisal. *Journal of Applied Psychology, 67,* 752-758.

Zedeck, S., & Cascio, W.F. (1984). Psychological issues in personnel decisions. *Annual Review of Psychology, 35,* 461-518.

Zedeck, S., Imparto, N., Krausz, M., & Oleno, T. (1974). Development of behaviorally anchored rating scales as a function of organizational level. *Journal of Applied Psychology, 59,* 249-252.

Zedeck, S., & Mosier, K. L. (1990). Work in the family and employing organization. *American Psychologist, 45,* 240-251.

Zedeck, S., Tziner, A., & Middlestadt, S.E. (1983). Interviewer validity and reliability: An individual analysis approach. *Personnel Psychology, 36,* 355-370.

Zollitsch, H. G., & Langsner, A. (1970). *Wage and salary administration.* Cincinnati: South-Western.

Zuboff, S. (1988). *In the age of the smart machine: The future of work and power.* New York: Basic Books.

# Photo Credits

# Table and Figure Credits

## Chapter 1

**Table 1.1:** From *Membership Directory* (1991). Arlington Heights, IL: The Society for Industrial and Organizational Psychology, Inc.

**Table 1.2:** From Education and training committee. The Society for Industrial and Organizational Psychology (1982). *Guidelines for Educational and Training at the Doctoral Level in Industrial/Organizational Psychology*. College Park: MD.

**Table 1.3:** From "Ethical principles of psychologists and code of conduct" by American Psychological Association, 1992, *American Psychologist, 47,* 1597–1611. Copyright (1992) by the American Psychological Association. Reprinted by permission.

**Table 1.4:** From *Organizations: Rational, natural, and open systems* (2nd ed.) by W.R. Scott, 1987, Englewood Cliffs, NJ: Prentice Hall. Adapted from *Environments and organizations: Theoretical and empirical perspectives,* by Marshall W. Meyer and associates (Ed.). Table 1, p. 22. Copyright (1978) by Jossey-Bass Inc., Publishers. Reprinted by permission of the publisher and the author.

**Figure 1.1:** From *Organization theory: Structure, design and applications* (3rd ed.) by Stephen P. Robbins, 1990, Englewood Cliffs, NJ: Prentice Hall, p. 14. Adapted with permission of Prentice Hall, Inc. and the author.

## Chapter 2

**Figures 2.4 and 2.5:** From "Research in the 'real-world' - a conceptual model" by V.R. Boehm, 1980, *Personnel Psychology, 33,* 495–504. Reprinted with permission of the author and publisher.

## Chapter 3

**Table 3.1:** From *Personnel Management* by D.J. Cherrington, 1983, Dubuque, IA: Wm. C. Brown Company Publishers, p. 255. Adapted with permission of Allyn & Bacon.

**Figure 3.1:** From "An Experimental Analysis of the Impact of Contingent Reinforcement on Sales Persons' Performance Behavior" by F. Luthans, R. Paul, and D. Baker, 1981, *Journal of Applied Psychology, 66,* Figure 1, p. 319. Copyright (1981) by the American Psychological Association. Reprinted by permission of the author and publisher.

**Table 3.2:** From "Equity theory predictions of behavior in organizations" by R.T. Mowday, Table 1, p. 115, in R.M. Steers and L.W. Porter (Eds.) *Motivation and Work Motivation.* New York: McGraw-Hill. Adapted by permission of the author and the publisher.

**Figure 3.2:** From "Equity Theory and Interpersonal Attraction" by R. Griffeth, R. Vecchio and J. Logan, Jr., 1989, *Journal of Applied Psychology, 74,* Figure 4, p. 400. Copyright (1989) by the American Psychological Association. Reprinted by permission of the authors and publisher.

**Figure 3.3:** From "An Individual-Differences Interpretation of the Conflicting Predictions Generated by Equity Theory and Expectancy Theory" by R. Vecchio, 1981, *Journal of Applied Psychology, 66,* Figure 1, p. 478. Copyright (1981) by the American Psychological Association. Adapted by permission of the author and publisher.

**Table 3.3:** From "Effects of Goal Difficulty, Self-set Goals, and Monetary Rewards on Dual Task Performance" by M. Erez, D. Gopher and N. Arzi, 1990, *Organizational Behavior and Human Decision Processes, 47,* Table 1, p. 257. Reprinted by permission of the author and the publisher.

**Figure 3.4:** From "An Empirical Examination of the Antecedents of Commitment to Difficult Goals" by J. Hollenbeck, C. Williams and H. Klein, 1989, *Journal of Applied Psychology, 74,* Figure 1, p. 22. Copyright (1989) by the American Psychological Association. Reprinted by permission of the author and publisher.

**Figure 3.5:** From "Goals, Strategy Development, and Task Performance: Some Limits on the Efficacy of Goal Setting" by P.C. Earley, T. Connolly and G. Ekegren, 1989, *Journal of Applied Psychology, 74,* Figure 3, p. 31. Copyright (1989) by the American Psychological Association. Adapted by permission of the author and publisher.

**Figure 3.6:** From *Managerial Attitudes and Performance* by L. Porter and E. Lawler, 1968, Homewood, IL: Dorsey, Exhibit A, p. 17. By permission of the author and publisher.

**Table 3.5:** From "Expectancy Theory Prediction of the Goal Theory Postulate "The Harder the Goals, the Higher the Performance" by T. Matsui, A. Okada and R. Mizuguchi, 1981, *Journal of Applied Psychology, 66,* Table 1, p. 57. Copyright (1981) by the American Psychological Association. Adapted by permission of the author and publisher.

**Table 3.6:** From "Task Choice and Assigned Goals as Determinants of Task Motivation and Performance" by Z. Shapira, 1989, *Organizational Behavior and Human Decision Processes, 44,* Table 3, p. 153. By permission of the author and the publisher.

**Figure 3.7:** From "Motivation Through the Design of Work: Test of a Theory" by J. Hackman and G. Oldham, 1976, *Organizational Behavior and Human Performance, 16,* Figure 1, p. 256. Reprinted by permission of author and publisher.

**Table 3.7:** From *Work Redesign* (Appendix A: The Job Diagnostic Survey. Section Two, Items 1, 4, 8, 11, 13, pp. 280–281) by R.J. Hackman and G.R. Oldham, 1980, Reading, MA: Addison-Wesley Publishing Company, Inc. Reprinted by permission of author and Addison-Wesley Publishing Co., Inc.

**Figure 3.8:** From "An Integrative Model of Work Attitudes, Motivation, and Performance" by R.A. Katzell and D.E. Thompson, 1990, *Human Performance, 3,* Figure 1, p. 71. Reprinted by permission of the author and the publisher.

# Chapter 4

**Table 4.1 (part 1):** From *Job Satisfaction* by R. Hoppock, 1935, New York: Harper, p. 255. Adapted by permission of author.

**Table 4.1 (part 2):** From *Work and Health* by R.L. Kahn, 1981, New York: John Wiley & Sons, Inc. Original data from *The 1972–1973 Quality of Employment Survey* by R.P. Quinn and L.J. Shepard, 1974, Ann Arbor, MI: Survey Research Center, University of Michigan, Table 2.4, p. 29. Adapted by permission of the authors and John Wiley & Sons, Inc.

**Figure 4.1:** From *Motivation in Work Organizations* by E.E. Lawler, 1973, Monterey, CA: Brook/Cole Publishing, Figure 4.3, p. 75.

**Table 4.2:** From "Task Perceptions and Job Satisfaction: A Question of Causality" by D.F. Caldwell and C.A. O'Reilly, 1982, *Journal of Applied Psychology, 67,* Table 1, p. 363. Copyright (1982) by the American Psychological Association. Adapted by permission of the author and publisher.

**Figure 4.2:** From "Work Motivation and Satisfaction: Light at the End of the Tunnel" by E. Locke and G.P. Latham, 1990, *Psychological Science, 1,* Figure 3, p. 244. Reprinted by permission of the author and the publisher.

**Figure 4.3:** From *The Measurement of Satisfaction in Work and Retirement* by P.C. Smith, L.M. Kendall and C.L. Hulin, 1969, Rand McNally & Company. Adapted from "The Construction of a New Type of Attitude Measure" by T. Kunin, 1955, *Personnel Psychology, 8,* Figure 1, p. 75. Copyright 1955 by Personnel Psychology, Inc. Reprinted by permission of Personnel Psychology and Department of Psychology, Bowling Green State University, Bowling Green, OH 43403.

**Table 4.3:** From *Manual of Minnesota Satisfaction Questionnaire: Minnesota Studies in Vocational Rehabilitation* (Items 13, 15, 17, 20) by D.J. Weiss, R.V. Dawis, G.W. England and L.H. Lofquist, 1967, University of Minnesota: Vocational Psychology Research. Copyright 1967. Reproduced by permission.

**Table 4.4:** From *User's Manual for the Job Descriptive Index (JDI) and the Job in General (JIG) Scales* by W.K. Balzer, P.C. Smith, D.E. Kravitz, S.E. Lovell, K.B. Paul, B.A. Reilly and C.E. Reilly, 1986, Bowling Green, OH: Bowling Green State University. Copyright 1985, BGSU, Department of Psychology, Bowling Green, OH 43403.

**Table 4.5:** From "Effects of Contingent and Noncontingent Reward on the Relationship between Satisfaction and Task Performance" by D.J. Cherrington, H.J. Reitz and W.E. Scott, Jr., 1971, *Journal of Applied Psychology, 55,* Table 4, p. 535. Copyright (1971) by the American Psychological Association. Reprinted by permission of the author and publisher.

**Figure 4.4:** From "Major Influences on Employee Attendance: A Process Model" by R.M. Steers and S.R. Rhodes, 1978, *Journal of Applied Psychology, 63,* Figure 1, p. 393. Copyright (1978) by the American Psychological Association. Reprinted by permission of the author and publisher.

**Figure 4.5:** From "An Evaluation of Precursors of Hospital Employee Turnover" by W.H. Mobley, S.O. Horner and A.T. Hollingsworth, 1978, *Journal of Applied Psychology, 63,* Figure 1, p. 410. Copyright (1978) by the American Psychological Association. Reprinted by permission of the author and publisher.

**Table 4.6:** From "The Definition and Measurement of Job Involvement" by T.M. Lodahl and M. Kejner, 1965, *Journal of Applied Psychology, 49,* pp. 24–33, Items 3, 6, 9, 20. Copyright (1965) by the American Psychological Association. Reprinted by permission of publisher.

**Table 4.7:** From "The Measurement of Organizational Commitment" by R.T. Mowday, R.M. Steers and L.W. Porter, 1979, *Journal of Vocational Behavior, 14,* Table 1, p. 228, Items 1, 6, 8, 13.

## Chapter 5

**Table 5.1:** Adapted from "Consequences of Influence Tactics Used with Subordinates, Peers, and the Boss," by G. Yukl and J. Bruce

Tracey, 1992, *Journal of Applied Psychology, 77,* Table 1, p. 526.

**Figure 5.5:** From *The Social Psychology of Organizations* by D. Katz and R.L. Kahn, 1978, New York: John Wiley, Figure 7.1 (a theoretical model of factors involved in the taking of organizational roles), p. 196. By permission of the publisher.

**Figure 5.6:** From "Integrating work environment perceptions: Explorations in the measurement of meaning" by L.A. James and L.B. James, 1989, *Journal of Applied Psychology, 74,* p. 741, Figure 1. Reprinted by permission of the author.

**Figure 5.7:** From "The effects of group longevity on project communication and performance" by Ralph Katz, 1982 (March), *Administrative Science Quarterly, 27,* #1, p. 96, Figure 3. Copyright 1982 by Cornell University. Reprinted by permission of the publisher.

**Figure 5.8:** From "Group tasks, group interaction process, and group performance effectiveness: A review and proposed integration" by J.R. Hackman and C.G. Morris in *Advances in Experimental Social Psychology* by L. Berkowitz (Ed.), 1975, *8,* New York: Academic Press, Figure 5, p. 88. By permission of the author and the publisher.

**Figure 5.9:** From "Effects of group feedback, goal setting, and incentives on organizational productivity" by R.D. Pritchard, S.D. Jones, P.L. Roth, K.K. Stuebing, and S.E. Ekeberg, 1988, *Journal of Applied Psychology, 73,* p. 346, Figure 2. Copyright (1988) by the American Psychological Association. Reprinted by permission of the author and publisher.

## Chapter 6

**Table 6.1:** From "Development and application of new scales to measure the French and Raven (1959) basis of social power" by T.R. Hinkin and C.A. Schriesheim, 1989, *Journal of Applied Psychology, 74,* 561–567. Copyright (1989) by the American Psychological Association. Reprinted by permission of the author and publisher.

**Figure 6.2:** From *Interpersonal communication in organizations* by R. Klauss and B. Bass, 1982, New York: Academic Press, p. 69, Figure 3.1. Reprinted by permission of the authors and publisher.

**Figure 6.3:** From *Pygmalion in management: Productivity as a self-fulfilling prophecy* by Dov Eden, 1990, Lexington, MA: Lexington Books, p. 70, Figure 3-1 (A model of self-fulfilling prophecy at work). Reprinted with the permission of Lexington Books, an imprint of Macmillan, Inc. Copyright © 1990 by Lexington Books.

**Table 6.2:** From "Fiedler's contingency theory of leadership: An application of the meta-analysis procedures of Schmidt and Hunter" by L.H. Peters, D.D. Hartke, and J.T. Pohlmann, 1985. *Psychological Bulletin, 97,* Table 4, p. 281. Copyright (1985) by the American Psychological Association. Adapted by permission of the author and publisher.

**Table 6.3:** From *Leadership and decision-making* by Victor H. Vroom and Philip W. Yetton, 1973, Pittsburgh: University of Pittsburgh Press. © 1973 by University of Pittsburgh Press. Reprinted by permission of the University of Pittsburgh Press.

**Table 6.4, Table 6.5, Figure 6.5:** Reprinted from *The new leadership: Managing participation in organizations* by Victor H. Vroom and Arthur G. Jago, 1988, Englewood Cliffs, NJ: Prentice-Hall. Copyright 1987 V.H. Vroom and A.G. Jago. Used with permission of the authors.

## Chapter 7

**Figure 7.2:** From "Stress and Behavior in Organizations" by J.E. McGrath in *Handbook of Industrial and Organizational Psychology* (Figure 1, p. 1356) by M.D. Dunnette (Ed.), 1976, Chicago: Rand McNally. Permission granted by author and Marvin D. Dunnette (Ed.).

**Figure 7.3:** From "Integrative Transactional Process Model of Coping with Stress in Organizations" by R.S. Schuler in *Human Stress and Cognition in Organizations: An Integrated Perspective* by T.A. Beehr and R.S. Bhagat (Eds.),

1985, New York: John Wiley & Sons, Inc., Figure 13.1, p. 349. Reprinted by permission of Randall S. Schuler and Allyn & Bacon, Inc.

**Table 7.1:** From *Organizational Stress and Preventive Management* by J.C. Quick and J.D. Quick, 1984, New York: McGraw-Hill, Table 6.4, p. 127. Reproduced with permission of McGraw-Hill.

**Figure 7.4:** From THE BLADE, Toledo, OH, November 1991.

**Table 7.2:** From "Role Conflict and Role Ambiguity in Complex Organizations" by J.R. Rizzo, R.J. House and S.I. Lirtzman, 1970, *Administrative Science Quarterly, 15,* Items 4, 5, 21, 26, p. 156. Reproduced by permission of author and *Administrative Science Quarterly.*

**Table 7.3:** From "The Social Readjustment Rating Scale" by T.H. Holmes and R.H. Rahe, 1967, *Journal of Psychosomatic Research, 11,* Table 3, p. 216. Reprinted with permission from Pergamon Press Ltd., Oxford, England.

**Table 7.4:** From *The Activity Survey for Health Prediction,* Form N (Items 29, 30) by C.D. Jenkins, S.J. Zyranski and R.H. Rosenman, 1979, New York: Psychological Corporation. Copyright C. David Jenkins, 1965, 1975.

**Figure 7.6:** From "A Path Analytic Study of the Consequences of Role Conflict and Ambiguity" by A.G. Bedeian and A.A. Armenakis, 1981, *Academy of Management Journal, 24,* Figure 1, p. 419.

**Table 7.5:** Modified and reproduced by special permission of the publisher, Consulting Psychologists Press, Inc., Palo Alto, CA 94303 from ***Maslach Burnout Inventory-Educators Survey*** by Christina Maslach, Susan E. Jackson, and Richard L. Schwab. Copyright 1986 by Consulting Psychologists Press, Inc. All rights reserved. Further reproduction is prohibited without the publisher's written consent.

**Table 7.6:** From "Moderating Effect of Social Support on the Stress-Burnout Relationship" by D. Etzion, 1984, *Journal of Applied Psychology, 69,* Table 1, p. 617. Copyright (1984) by the American Psychological Association. Reprinted by permission of the author and publisher.

**Table 7.7:** From "Coping with Job Stress: Measures and Future Directions for Scale Development" by J.C. Latack, 1986, *Journal of Applied Psychology, 71,* Tables 1 & 2, pp. 380–381. Copyright (1986) by the American Psychological Association. Reprinted by permission of the author and publisher.

## Chapter 8

**Figure 8.1:** From "Job families: A review and discussion of their implications for personnel selection" by K. Pearlman, 1980, *Psychological Bulletin, 87,* Figure 1, p. 5. Copyright (1984) by the American Psychological Association. Reprinted by permission of the author and publisher.

**Figure 8.2:** From "Job-task inventory analysis" by R.E. Christal and J.J. Weissmuller in *The job analysis handbook for business, industry, and government* by S. Gael (Ed.), 1988, *2,* pp. 1036–1050, New York: John Wiley & Sons, Inc. Copyright © 1988 by John Wiley & Sons, Inc. Reprinted by permission of John Wiley & Sons, Inc.

**Figure 8.3:** Adapted from *Dictionary of Occupational Titles* by U.S. Department of Labor. Washington, DC: U.S. Government Printing Office, 1977, pp. 1369–1371.

**Figure 8.4:** From *Dictionary of Occupational Titles* by U.S. Department of Labor, Washington, DC: U.S. Government Printing Office, 1977.

**Table 8.1:** From "Position analysis questionnaire (PAQ)" by E.J. McCormick and P.R. Jeanneret. In *The job analysis handbook for business, industry, and government* by S. Gael (Ed.), 1988, *2,* p. 829. New York: John Wiley & Sons, Inc. Copyright © 1988 by John Wiley & Sons, Inc. Reprinted permission of John Wiley & Sons, Inc. (Adapted from McCormick, E.J., Jeanneret, P.R., and Mecham, R.C., 1972, "A study of job characteristics and job dimensions as based on the Position Analysis Questionnaire (PAQ)" in *Journal of Applied Psychology, 56*(4), 347–368.)

**Table 8.2:** From "The critical incident technique" by J.C. Flanagan, 1954, in *Psychological Bulletin,*

*51,* Figure 3, p. 342. Copyright (1954) by the American Psychological Association. Reprinted by permission of the author and publisher.

**Table 8.3:** From "Evaluating classifications of job behavior: A construct validation of the ability requirements scales" by E.A. Fleishman and M.D. Mumford, 1991, in *Personnel Psychology, 44,* Table 1, p. 535. Reprinted by permission of the publisher.

**Figure 8.5:** From "Evaluating classifications of job behavior: A construct validation of the ability requirement scales" by E.A. Fleishman and M.D. Mumford, 1991, in *Personnel Psychology, 44,* Figure 2, p. 530. Reprinted by permission of the publisher.

**Table 8.4:** From *Wage and salary administration* (2nd ed), (p. 234) by H.G. Zollitsch and A. Langsner, 1970, Cincinnati: South-Western Publishing Co., Table 9.2, p. 234. Reproduced with the permission of South-Western Publishing Co. Copyright 1970 by South-Western Publishing Co. All rights reserved.

**Figure 8.6:** From *Wage and salary administration* (2nd ed), (p. 340) by H.G. Zollitsch and A. Langsner, 1970, Cincinnati: South-Western Publishing Co., Figure 13.6, p. 340. Reproduced with the permission of South-Western Publishing Co. Copyright 1970 by South-Western Publishing Co. All rights reserved.

## Chapter 9

**Figure 9.1:** From *Research methods in human resources management* by N. Schmitt and R.J. Klimoski, 1991, Cincinnati: South-Western Publishing Co., Figure 1, p. 161. Reproduced with the permission of South-Western Publishing Co. Copyright 1991 by South-Western Publishing Co. All rights reserved.

**Figure 9.3:** From "Supermarket cashier" by Lawrence Fogli in *The job analysis handbook for business, industry, and government,* by S. Gael (Ed.), 1988, *2,* p. 1225. New York: John Wiley & Sons, Inc. Copyright © 1988 by John Wiley & Sons, Inc. Reprinted by permission of John Wiley & Sons, Inc.

**Figure 9.5:** From *Increasing productivity through performance appraisal* by G.P. Latham and K.N. Wexley, 1981, Reading, MA: Addison-Wesley, Appendix A, pp. 214–215. © 1981 by Addison-Wesley, Inc. Reprinted by permission of the publisher.

**Figure 9.6:** From "A fallacy in the use of median scale values in employee checklists" by C.E. Jurgenson, 1949, *Journal of Applied Psychology, 33,* Figure 1, p. 57. Reprinted by permission of the author.

**Figure 9.7:** From "Forced-choice performance rating: A methodological study" by J.R. Berkshire and R.W. Highland, 1953, *Personnel Psychology, 6,* pp. 355–378. Reprinted by permission of the publisher.

**Figure 9.8:** From "A cognitive view of the performance appraisal process: A model and research propositions" by A.S. DeNisi, T.P. Cafferty and B.M. Meglino, 1984, *Organizational Behavior and Human Performance, 33,* Figure 1, p. 396. Reprinted by permission of the author and publisher.

**Figure 9.9:** From "Consequences of individual feedback on behavior in organizations" by D.I. Ilgen, C.D. Fisher and M.S. Taylor, 1979, *Journal of Applied Psychology, 64,* Figure 1, p. 352. Copyright (1979) by the American Psychological Association. Reprinted by permission of the author and publisher.

## Chapter 10

**Figure 10.2:** From "Paper and pencil measures of potential" by C.P. Sparks in *Perspectives on employee staffing and selection* by G. Dreher and P. Sackett (Eds.), 1983, Homewood, IL: Richard D. Irwin, Table 2, p. 357. Adapted by permission of the author and publisher.

**Figure 10.4:** From the *Bennett Mechanical Comprehension Test.* Copyright 1942, 1967–1970, 1980 by The Psychological Corporation. Reproduced by permission. All rights reserved.

**Figure 10.5:** From *Personnel Selection and Placement* by M.D. Dunnette, 1966, Monterey,

CA: Brooks/Cole, pp. 47–49. Reprinted by permission of the author and publisher.

**Figure 10.6:** From the *California Psychological Inventory.* Modified and reproduced by special permission of the Publisher, Consulting Psychologists Press, Inc., Palo Alto, CA 94303 from California Psychological Inventory—Form 462 by Harrison G. Gough. Copyright 1986 by Consulting Psychologists Press, Inc. All rights reserved. Further reproduction is prohibited without the Publisher's written consent.

**Figure 10.7:** From the *Strong Interest Inventory of the Strong Vocational Interest Blanks*[R]. Reproduced by special permission from the Strong Interest Inventory of the Strong Vocational Interest Blanks[R], Form T325. Copyright 1933, 1938, 1945, 1946, 1966, 1968, 1974, 1985 by The Board of Trustees of the Leland Stanford Junior University. All rights reserved. Printed under license from Stanford University Press, Stanford, CA 94305. Reproduced by special permission of the Publisher, Consulting Psychologists Press, Inc., Palo Alto, CA 94303. Further reproduction is prohibited without the Publisher's consent.

## Chapter 11

**Figure 11.1:** From *Training in Organizations: Needs Assessment, Development, and Evaluation* by I.L. Goldstein, 1993, Monterey, CA: Brooks/Cole, Figure 2.1, page 21. Copyright by Brooks/Cole. Adapted by permission of the author and the publisher.

**Table 11.1:** From "Self-rating in management training needs assessment: A neglected opportunity?" by J. McEnery and J.M. McEnery, 1987, *Journal of Occupational Psychology, 60,* Table 3, p. 54. Reprinted by permission of the author and the publisher.

**Figure 11.2:** From "Transfer of training: A review and directions for future research" by T.T. Baldwin and J.K. Ford, 1988, *Personnel Psychology, 41,* Figure 2, p. 97. Reprinted by permission of the author and publisher.

**Table 11.2:** From *Training in Organizations: Needs Assessment, Development, and Evaluation*

by I.L. Goldstein, 1993, Monterey, CA: Brooks/Cole, Figure 4.4, p. 125. Reprinted by permission of the publisher and author. (Adapted from D.H. Holding, 1965, *Principles of Training,* London: Pergamon Press.)

## Chapter 12

**Figure 12.1:** From "Human Factors in the Workplace" by W. Howell in *Handbook of Industrial and Organizational Psychology* (2nd ed.) by M.D. Dunnette and L. Hough (Eds.), 1990, Palo Alto, CA: Consulting Psychologists Press.

**Table 12.1:** From *An Index of Electronic Equipment Operability: Evaluation Booklet* from S.J. Munger, 1962, Washington, DC: American Institutes for Research. AIR-C43-1/62-RP(2).

**Figure 12.3:** From *Engineering Psychology and Human Performance* (Figure 1.1, p. 12) by C.D. Wickens, 1984, Columbus, OH: Charles E. Merrill Publishing Co. Copyright 1984 by Scott, Foresman and Company. Reprinted by permission of HarperCollins Publishers.

**Figure 12.4:** From "An Analysis of the Processing Requirements of a Complex Perceptual-Motor Task" by A. Kramer, C.D. Wickens and E. Donchin, 1983, *Human Factors, 25,* Figure 3, p. 605. Adapted with permission from *Human Factors, 25,* No. 6, 1983. Copyright 1983 by the Human Factors & Ergonomics Society, Inc. All rights reserved.

**Figure 12.5 a & b:** From *Human Factors: Understanding People-System Relationships* (a-Figure 10.10, b-Figure 10.11, p. 329) by B. Kantowitz and R. Sorkin, 1983, New York: John Wiley & Sons, Inc. Copyright 1983. Reprinted by permission of John Wiley & Sons, Inc.

**Figure 12.6:** From Applied Ergonomics. (1974). *Applied Ergonomics Handbook.* Surrey, England: IPC Science and Technology Press, p. 10. Reprinted by permission of Butterworth & Company Publishers Ltd. for *Applied Ergonomics Handbook* by Ian Galer (Ed.), 1987, 2nd ed.

**Table 12.2:** From *Anthropometric Source Book, Volume 1: Anthropometry for Designers* (pp. III-30), July 1978, NASA Reference Publication 1024, Washington, DC: National Aeronautics and Space Administration Science and Technical Information Office.

**Figure 12.7:** From "Introduction to Circadian Rhythms" (Figure 1.1, p. 3) by D.S. Minors and J.M. Waterhouse in *Hours of work: Temporal factors in work scheduling* by S. Folkard and T. Monk (Eds.), 1985, Chichester, England: John Wiley & Sons, Inc. Copyright 1985. Reprinted by permission of John Wiley & Sons, Inc.

**Figure 12.8:** From "A Field Study of Circadian Rhythms in Actual and Interpolated Task Performance" by T.H. Monk and D.E. Embery in *Night and Shift Work: Biological and Social Aspects* by A.A. Reinberg, N. Vieux and P. Andlauer (Eds.), 1981, Oxford, England: Pergamon Press. Reprinted with permission from Pergamon Press, Ltd., Headington Hill Hall, Oxford, England OX3 0BW, UK.

**Table 12.3:** From "A Behavioral Approach to Occupational Safety: Pinpointing and Reinforcing Safe Performance in a Food Manufacturing Plant" by J. Komaki, K.D. Barwick and L.R. Scott, 1978, *Journal of Applied Psychology, 63,* Table 1, p. 438. Copyright (1978) by the American Psychological Association. Reprinted by permission of the author and publisher.

**Figure 12.9:** From "A Behavioral Approach to Occupational Safety: Pinpointing and Reinforcing Safe Performance in a Food Manufacturing Plant" by J. Komaki, K.D. Barwick and L.R. Scott, 1978, *Journal of Applied Psychology, 63,* Figure 1, p. 439. Copyright (1978) by the American Psychological Association. Reprinted by permission of the author and publisher.

**Figure 12.10:** From "Ergonomic Support of Consumer Product Safety" by J. Ramsey, 1978. Paper presented at the American Industrial Association Conference.

## Chapter 13

**Table 13.1:** From "New directions for human resources practice" by A. Howard in *Working with organizations and their people*, 1991, Figure 10.2, p. 227, New York: Guilford Press. Reprinted by permission of the author and Guilford Press.

# Name Index

Miner, J., 243, 630, 635
Minors, D., 564, 611
Minstrell, J., 513, 635
Mintzberg, H., 189, 253, 308, 635
Minuto, A., 553, 557, 615
Misumi, J., 248, 635
Mitchell, T. R., 107, 111, 117,
   128, 151, 192, 230, 264, 270,
   409, 523, 524, 607, 610, 615,
   620, 628, 635, 654, 658
Mitler, M., 573, 635
Mitz, L., 319, 623
Mizuguchi, R., 119, 130, 633
Moberg, D., 253, 607
Mobley, W., 151, 166, 167, 635
Moch, M., 159-160, 601, 635
Moeller, N., 127, 128, 630
Mohr, D., 572, 635
Mohr, J., 522, 612
Monat, A., 288, 635
Monk, T., 559-562, 564-565, 573,
   611, 636
Moore, M., 484, 636
Moore-Ede, M., 565, 605
Moore-Hirschl, S., 565, 650
Moorman, R., 279, 640
Moray, N., 544, 655
Morgan, C., 21, 622
Morris, C., 220-221, 616
Morrison, A., 245, 320, 636
Morrow, P., 171, 174, 175, 636
Morse, N., 247, 625
Moses, J., 10, 41, 590
Moses, S., 31, 39, 630, 636
Mosier, K., 590, 660
Mossholder, K., 448, 636
Motowidlo, S., 202, 303, 312,
   600, 636
Mount, M., 242, 405, 470, 596,
   636
Mourant, R., 549, 636
Moussa-Hamouda, E., 549, 636
Mouton, J., 248, 249, 255, 598
Mowday, R., 102, 104, 172-173,
   636
Muchinsky, P., 162-163, 621
Muczyk, J., 511, 637
Mudrack, P., 211, 636
Mueller, C., 173, 605

Mulder, G., 544, 636
Mulder, L., 544, 636
Mumford, M., 363, 462, 520, 636-
   637
Munger, S., 536-537, 637
Munsterberg, H., 15, 637
Murphy, John, 246
Murphy, K., 72, 380, 391, 392,
   411, 419, 440, 447, 467, 468,
   470, 603, 627, 637
Murphy, L., 623
Murphy, S., 245, 610
Murray, H., 87, 133, 637
Murray, M., 160, 625

**N**

Nader, Ralph, 532
Nadler, D., 230, 637
Naisbitt, J., 590, 637
Naismith, D., 310, 637
Nash, A., 511, 637
Naylor, J., 130, 450, 452, 493,
   599, 637, 652
Near, J., 168-169, 637, 643
Neilson, E., 202, 638
Nelson, D., 197, 232, 623
Nelson-Horchler, J., 137, 638
Netemeyer, R., 314, 315, 638
Neuman, G., 224, 638
Newbold, E., 571, 638
Newman, J., 267, 634
Nibler, R., 573, 603
Nichols, R., 186, 638
Nicholson, N., 164, 166, 603,
   638
Nilan, K., 127, 617
Nixon, Richard, 244, 286
Noe, R., 127-128, 171, 486, 501,
   503, 630, 638
Nord, W., 31, 614, 638
Norman, C., 405, 638
Norman, D., 53, 558, 638
Nougaim, K., 88, 93, 617
Novak, J., 566, 646
Nunnally, J., 59, 638
Nystrom, P., 248, 638

**O**

Oborne, D., 568, 638
O'Boyle, T., 214, 621
O'Brien, G., 168, 524, 624, 638
O'Connor, J., 258, 630
Offerman, L., 31, 38, 588, 592,
   639
Ogden, G., 350, 544, 619, 639
Okada, A., 119, 130, 633
O'Keefe, J., 430, 639
Okonek, K., 563, 612
Oldham, G., 124, 125, 127, 128,
   134, 220, 344, 347, 616
O'Leary, A., 319, 320, 632
Oleno, T., 404, 659
Oler, J., 573, 629
Olsen, H., 159, 390, 565, 650
Olsen, K., 532, 546
Ondrack, D., 148, 639
Ones, D., 470, 639
Onglatco, L., 230, 633
Oppler, S., 391, 641
O'Reilly, C., 98, 151, 152, 186,
   602, 639
Organ, D., 202, 639
Orpen, C., 169, 639
Orris, J., 268, 615
Orth-Gomer, K., 563, 564, 626
Osborn, R., 248, 628
Osburn, H., 394, 610
Oskamp, S., 9, 620
Ostroff, C., 484, 639
Ouchi, W., 172, 233, 384, 639
Owens, W., 462, 636

**P**

Packard, J., 303, 312, 636
Packer, A., 589, 590, 592, 623
Padgett, M., 168, 653
Paine, F., 515, 602
Palincsar, A., 513, 600
Panian, S., 258, 594
Paradise, C., 522, 612
Parasuraman, S., 309, 615

# Topic Index

Contingency theories of leadership
    Fiedler's contingency theory, 266-268
    Hershey and Blanchard's Situational Model, 276-277
    House's Path-goal theory of leadership, 268-270
    Vroom/Yetton/Jago's Decision model of leadership, 270-276
Continuance commitment, 172
Contrast effects in performance rating, 388
Control, as means of coping with stress, 323
Control display design, in human factors psychology, 549-551
Control group, 70, 519
Cooperation (see also conflict), 323
Cooperative learning, 496
Coping strategies,
    in shiftwork, 564
    in workstress, 323-324
Coping in stress, 323-330
Coronary heart disease (CHD), 312
Correction for attenuation, 447
Correlation, 52-55
    bivariate coefficient, 52-54
    canonical, 55
    and causality, 63-64, 66
    multiple, 54-55
    statistical tests of significance, 56
Correlational study, 66
Costing personnel decisions, 454
Criteria,
    alternative methods of measuring, 390-406
    criterion development in job analysis, 344
    defined, 380
    ideal (ultimate) criteria, 381
    in training evaluation, 517-518
    in training needs analysis, 483-491
    in the validation of measures, 58-59, 62, 443-446
Criterion-related validity, 58-59, 62, 441, 443-447
Critical incident technique, 148, 360-361, 392, 485
Cross-functional project teams, 200, 374
Cross-validation, 448
Crystallization of norms (see also return potential model), 209
Crystallized intelligence, 467
Culture, organizational, 212, 411-412
Culture assimilator, 523-524
Customer appraisal of performance, 405-406

D

Daily hassles, as a stressor, 310
Data function scale in functional job analysis, 354
Decentralized communication network, 204
Decision model of leadership (Vroom/Yetton/Jago), 270-276
Decision theory, 27, 251-259, 451-456
Declarative knowledge, as a learning outcome, 488
Decoding in communication, 188
Deductive approach to scientific research, 48
Deficiency, in performance appraisals, 381-382
Democratic leadership, 247-248
Demographic change, 590
Demographic effects on performance ratings, 390-391
Dependent variable, 65
Descriptive statistics, 49-55
Dictionary of Occupational Titles, 354, 364, 374
Differential validity, 455
Discriminability in performance appraisals, 381
Discriminant validity, of job attitude scales, 174
Disparate impact in selection (see also adverse impact), 456-458
Disparate treatment in selection, 456-458
Distortion in communication, 185-186
Distributed practice, 492-493
Divided attention, 544
Downsizing, 2, 10, 178-179, 331, 401, 590
Dual career couples, 309

E

EEOC Uniform Guidelines (1978), 457
Elements of a job, 341
Encoding as a cognitive process, 184, 407-408, 541-543
Engineering anthropometry, 555
Engineering psychology, 16
Entropy, 584
Envisioning in leadership, 279
Equal Employment Opportunity Commission (EEOC), 37, 468
Equifinality, 30
Equipment design, 546

# S

## IMPORTANT EVENTS & TRENDS IN I/O

| 1860 | 1900 | 1910 | 1920 | 193 |
|------|------|------|------|-----|

First Studies of Individual Differences Conducted by Galton

Hugo Munsterberg Publishes First Textbook in Industrial Psychology

Develop Assessm for Use i Appraisa

Psychology First Applied to Problems of Advertising, Selection, and Training

Large Scale Use of Intelligence Tests in World War I

Taylor Advocates Scientific Management to Maximize Efficiency and Avoid Labor Strife

Attitude Measu Techniques De Likert, Thurstor

First Laboratory Devoted to Psychological Research

Applied Psychology Emerges as a Recognized Discipline

Hawthorr Attention Job Satisf Leadershi

## DOMINANT PSYCHOLOGICAL THEORY

STRUCTURALISM        FUNC

## DOMINANT ORGANIZATION THEORY

SCIENTIFIC MANAGEMENT / CLASSICAL THEORY

## SOCIETAL CONTEXT

INDUSTRIAL REVOLUTION / WAVES OF IMMIGRATION / RISE OF LARGE CORPORATIONS